SUBSTANCE ABUSE

Fifth Edition

SUBSTANCE ABUSE

INFORMATION FOR SCHOOL COUNSELORS, SOCIAL WORKERS, THERAPISTS, AND COUNSELORS

Gary L. Fisher

University of Nevada, Reno

Thomas C. Harrison

University of Nevada, Reno

PEARSON

Boston Columbus Indianapolis New York San Francisco Upper Saddle River
Amsterdam Cape Town Dubai London Madrid Milan Munich Paris Montreal Toronto
Delhi Mexico City Sao Paulo Sydney Hong Kong Seoul Singapore Taipei Tokyo

Vice President and Editorial Director: Jeffery W. Johnston
Senior Acquisitions Editor: Meredith D. Fossel
Associate Editor: Anne Whittaker
Editorial Assistant: Andrea Hall
Vice President, Director of Marketing: Margaret Waples
Senior Marketing Manager: Christopher Barry
Senior Managing Editor: Pamela D. Bennett
Production Project Manager: Kerry Rubadue
Senior Operations Supervisor: Matt Ottenweller

Senior Art Director: Jayne Conte
Cover Designer: Jayne Conte
Cover Photo: © Tyler Olson/Fotolia
Full-Service Project Management: S4Carlisle
   Publishing Services
Composition: S4Carlisle Publishing Services
Printer/Binder: STP Courier
Cover Printer: STP Courier
Text Font: Times LT Std

Credits and acknowledgments borrowed from other sources and reproduced, with permission, in this textbook appear on the appropriate page within text.

Every effort has been made to provide accurate and current Internet information in this book. However, the Internet and information posted on it are constantly changing, so it is inevitable that some of the Internet addresses listed in this textbook will change.

Library of Congress Cataloging-in-Publication Data
Fisher, Gary L.
   Substance abuse : information for school counselors, social workers, therapists, and counselors/Gary L. Fisher,
Thomas C. Harrison.—5th ed.
     p. cm.
   Includes bibliographical references and index.
     ISBN-13: 978-0-13-261324-8—ISBN-10: 0-13-261324-7   1. Social work with drug addicts—United States.   2. Social work with alcoholics—United States.   3. Drug addicts—Counseling of—United States.   4. Alcoholics—Counseling of—United States. 5. Drug addiction—United States—Prevention.   6. Alcoholism—United States—Prevention.   I. Harrison, Thomas C.   II. Title.
   HV5825.F566 2013
   362.29—dc23   2012000767

10 9 8 7 6 5 4 3 2 1

ISBN 10:   0-13-261324-7
ISBN 13: 978-0-13-261324-8

To our beautiful and loving wives,
Carole and Terianne,
and our children,
Colin, Jacob, Brooke, and Aaron,
and Iain, Ryan, Becky, and Jordan

ABOUT THE AUTHORS

Gary L. Fisher is professor in the College of Health Sciences at the University of Nevada, Reno. He was the founder and first director of the Center for the Application of Substance Abuse Technologies, where he developed undergraduate, graduate, and continuing education activities for addiction counselors, prevention specialists, and allied professionals. Dr. Fisher's career has spanned 38 years and includes work as a private practice clinician and a public school psychologist. In addition to this textbook, he is the author of *Rethinking Our War on Drugs: Candid Talk about Controversial Issues* (2006), the senior editor of the *Encyclopedia of Substance Abuse Prevention, Treatment, and Recovery* (2009), and the author of *Understanding Why Addicts Are Not All Alike: Recognizing the Types and How Their Differences Affect Intervention and Treatment* (2011).

Thomas Harrison is associate dean in the College of Education and professor of Counseling and Educational Psychology at the University of Nevada, Reno. He developed the initial drug testing program for the University of Florida Athletic Department and has been a consultant for the State of Nevada Bureau of Alcohol and Drug Abuse. Dr. Harrison's career has spanned 35 years in the field, including private counseling, sports psychology, and consulting practice. He is the author of *Consultation for Contemporary Helping Professionals* (2004) and several articles in professional journals.

PREFACE

We teach in a counseling department that offers training in school counseling, marriage and family therapy, and school psychology. Our department requires that all students take a course entitled *Models of Prevention, Treatment, and Recovery in Addictions*. The goal of the course is to familiarize students with the Alcohol and Other Drugs (AOD) field, including basic pharmacology, conceptualizations of AOD, assessment, models of prevention, family issues, and the like.

In teaching this course, we reviewed many textbooks. Many were focused primarily on the pharmacology of alcohol and other drugs. Others were directed toward the person who wanted to work in AOD treatment. Some espoused a narrow orientation to understanding addiction. We never found a book designed for the mental health professional in generalist settings that included all the information we believe to be necessary, and that presented a balanced view of addictions. So we wrote one.

That this book is now in its fifth edition is gratifying; but more importantly, it confirms the need for a generalist text in this area. In Chapter 1, we provide our rationale, explaining why we think mental health professionals (school counselors, social workers, marriage and family therapists, mental health counselors, rehabilitation counselors) need this information. We also offer an overview of the topics covered in this book. Both of us have done most of our clinical work in generalist settings (schools, private practice, community mental health centers, universities), and we have used our experiences to select these topics. Our clients have ranged from those with no alcohol or drug problems to those who have been in numerous treatment programs—and everything in between. We hope that this approach results in a balanced presentation of some controversial areas.

While writing and revising this book, we have tried to minimize the common complaints that students express about textbooks: We have illustrated the application of concepts with many examples from our own clinical experiences; we have tried to personalize the writing and avoid the more stilted language of traditional academia. Let us know if this has worked to make the book more interesting and accessible.

NEW TO THIS EDITION

With each revision, we update the content throughout. This fifth edition includes:

- New sections on recovery-oriented systems of care, recovery support services, and recovery and spirituality in Chapters 8 and 9. This increased emphasis on recovery reflects the growing awareness that addiction is a chronic condition that requires attention throughout life.
- New sections on the neurobiology of addiction (Chapter 2), confidentiality and school counseling (Chapter 5), screening (Chapter 6), and prevention specialists (Chapter 15) provide information on the most current issues in addiction prevention, treatment, and recovery.
- In Chapter 7, we increased our coverage of motivational interviewing and included this in the chapter title, bringing increased attention to this evidence-based intervention and treatment approach.

- New and revised information on prenatal exposure to drugs, diverse sexual orientations, persons with disabilities, older adults, and adoptees reflects current research and focus on underserved groups.
- Information on fetal spectrum disorders (Chapter 11) has been revised and expanded, as well as the coverage of brief interventions in Chapter 7.
- The section in Chapter 10 on support groups other than AA has been revised with the addition of Smart Recovery, which is a reflection of the current status of these support groups.
- Revised and expanded sections on evidence-based treatment and prevention, support groups other than Alcoholics Anonymous, and more discussion of the National Registry of Evidence-Based Programs and Practices provides focus on current trends in the field.
- Along with the usual updating of survey data and research, we have tried to bridge the gap between theory and practice by including case examples at the beginning of each chapter and then applying chapter concepts to these cases.
- New "At a Glance" summaries highlight important topics of certain chapter sections and new charts, figures, and tables help enhance student understanding and focus on essential concepts.
- Survey data on prevalence of tobacco, alcohol, and other drug use among youth and diverse populations; treatment admissions; emergency room admissions; and prevalence of addiction have been updated to reflect the most current statistics.
- New information on treating "Other Addictions" has been added.

MyCounselingLab™

Help your students bridge the gap between theory and practice with MyCounselingLab™. MyCounselingLab™ connects your course content to video- and case-based real world scenarios, and provides:

- *Assignments & Activities* assess students' understanding of key concepts and skill development. Hints and feedback provide scaffolding and reinforce key concepts.
- *Building Counseling Skills* exercises offer opportunities for students to develop and practice skills critical to their success as professional helpers. Suggested responses are available to instructors, making grading easy.
- *Multiple-Choice Quizzes* help students gauge their understanding of important topics and prepare for success on licensure examinations.

Access to MyCounselingLab™ can be packaged with this textbook or purchased standalone. To find out how to package student access to this website and gain access as an Instructor, go to www.MyCounselingLab.com <http://www.mycounselinglab.com/>, email us at counseling@pearson.com, or contact your Pearson sales representative.

ACKNOWLEDGMENTS

As with any effort such as this, many people have contributed to the final product. We want to thank Gary Pregal, Katie Swanson, Susan Malby-Meade, Frank Tirado, Priscilla Wu, and the late Cheri Dunning for their efforts on the first edition of this text. Julie Hogan, co-director of CSAP's Center for the Application of Prevention Technologies, and Nancy Roget, director of the Center for the Application of Substance Abuse Technologies at the University of Nevada,

Reno, provided valuable insights in the development of the second edition. In preparing the third edition, we relied on the work of the Addiction Technology Transfer Centers (funded by the Center for Substance Abuse Treatment) and the Centers for the Application of Prevention Technologies (funded by the Center for Substance Abuse Prevention). These outstanding networks helped us identify relevant issues and concepts. We are also grateful to the late John Chappel, emeritus professor of psychiatry and behavioral sciences at the University of Nevada, Reno for reviewing Chapter 2 material in earlier editions.

In preparing the fourth edition, we thank Sabina Mutisya, doctoral student at the University of Nevada, Reno, for her invaluable assistance with research.

For this fifth edition, special thanks is given to Dr. Susan Doctor. She is an expert in fetal alcohol spectrum and shared her incisive knowledge of it in Chapter 11. We also thank Melissa Huelsman, a promising doctoral student in counselor education, who completed library searches and combined the references. Finally, we wish to thank the reviewers of the fifth edition: Susan R. Adams, University of Central Arkansas; Valerie Scarborough-Gebhardt, University of Illinois, Springfield; Gerald A. Juhnke, University of Texas at San Antonio; and Mark S. Parrish, University of West Georgia.

Gary L. Fisher

Thomas C. Harrison

BRIEF CONTENTS

CONTENTS

Chapter 1

The Role of the Mental Health Professional in Prevention and Treatment

It has become almost trite to recite the problems related to the use of alcohol and other drugs (AOD)[1] in our society. Various statistics are frequently reported in newspaper articles, surveys, and research studies. The array of graphs, percentages, and dollar amounts in the billions numb the mind. It is not our purpose to contribute to this data avalanche in an effort to convince you that the abuse of AOD causes a variety of serious problems in our country. If you are reading this book, you are probably in a training program to prepare for a career in one of the helping professions and, one hopes, you have some awareness of the severity of this problem. On the other hand, our experience in training mental health professionals has taught us that there is a need for a framework to understand the extent to which AOD issues affect not only the lives of those individuals you will be working with, but your own lives as well and the society in which we live. Therefore, allow us to provide this framework with a few facts.

---

[1]As is the case with many areas in the helping professions, terminology can be confusing. In this book, we will use the term *alcohol and other drugs* (AOD) to clearly indicate that alcohol is a drug and to avoid having the reader omit alcohol from any discussion about drugs. If tobacco is relevant to a discussion, we will generally refer to "alcohol, tobacco, and other drugs." The term *illegal drugs* will be used to refer to substances such as marijuana, heroin, cocaine, methamphetamine, and ecstasy, which are illegal under most or all circumstances. *Illicit drugs* are illegal drugs as well as legal drugs used inappropriately, such as prescription pain medications.

The use of terms such as alcoholism, drug addiction, chemical dependency, and substance abuse can also be problematic. In Chapter 2, we will give some definitions of terms used in the field, and, in Chapter 6, we provide the criteria to diagnose certain AOD conditions. However, since these terms are used in this chapter, you should think of alcoholism as an addiction to the drug alcohol. Drug addiction refers to the addiction to drugs other than alcohol. Chemical dependency includes addiction to AOD. Substance abuse means that there have been individual or societal problems as a result of AOD use. After reading Chapters 2 and 6, you should have a more useful understanding of these terms.

According to annual survey data, in 2009, 23.5 million Americans age 12 and over needed treatment for an alcohol or illicit drug problem (Substance Abuse and Mental Health Services Administration, 2010). The Substance Abuse and Mental Health Services Administration conducts a yearly survey on the use of all drugs, legal and illegal in the United States (Substance Abuse and Mental Health Services Administration, 2010). In 2009, 8.7% of all individuals age 12 and above reported using an illicit drug in the past month. In the 12 to 17 age group, 14.7% had used alcohol in the past month and 8.8% had engaged in binge drinking. In the same age group, 11.6% smoked cigarettes. According to the Centers for Disease Control and Prevention (2010a), approximately 79,000 annual deaths in the United States are attributable to alcohol, the third leading cause of lifestyle-related deaths in our country. In contrast, almost 38,000 annual deaths are attributable to illicit drugs (Minino, Xu, & Kochanek, 2010). The Centers for Disease Control and Prevention (2010b) reported 443,000 annual deaths in this country as a result of tobacco use.

The relationship between AOD, crime, and violence has also been clearly established. The National Center on Addiction and Substance Abuse at Columbia University published an extensive study of this relationship. Of the 2.3 million Americans in jails and prisons, 1.5 million met the criteria for a substance use disorder (see Chapter 6) and another 458,000 had a history of AOD problems, were under the influence of AOD at the time crimes were committed, committed crimes to buy AOD, were incarcerated for an AOD violation, or some combination of these factors. AOD were a factor in 78% of violent crimes; 83% of property crimes; and 77% of crimes involving public order, immigration or weapon offenses, and probation/parole violations (Center on Addiction and Substance Abuse, 2010). In reviewing literature on the relationship between child abuse and substance abuse, Lee, Esaki, and Greene (2009) indicated that between one-half and two-thirds of abuse cases involved caretaker substance abuse and 80% of cases resulting in foster care were linked to substance abuse. In studying the relationship between substance abuse and domestic violence, Fals-Stewart and Kennedy (2005) found that 50% of partnered men in substance abuse treatment had battered their partner in the past year. Fals-Stewart (2003) reported that these patients were eight times more likely to batter on a day in which they had been drinking.

The monetary costs of AOD abuse also provide tangible evidence of the significance of these problems. In a study for the National Institute on Drug Abuse and the National Institute on Alcohol Abuse and Alcoholism (Harwood, 2000), the 1998 costs of alcohol abuse were estimated at $185 billion and other drug abuse costs at $143 billion. Nearly 50% of the costs of alcohol abuse were due to illness, over 20% were attributable to premature death, and the remaining costs were due to health care, crime, and other factors. For other drug abuse, nearly 60% of the costs were related to crime, with illness, premature death, and health care accounting for nearly all of the remaining costs. Ironically, for every dollar that states spend on substance abuse and addiction, about 96 cents is spent on shoveling up the wreckage caused by AOD use and only about 2 cents is spent on prevention and treatment. (The rest is spent on research, regulation, and interdiction) (National Center on Addiction and Substance Abuse at Columbia University, 2009).

We risk contributing to the data avalanche to illustrate that the abuse of AOD is like a tree with many branches. The trunk is AOD abuse but the branches are the multitude of other problems caused by or related to AOD. To avoid totally clogging your mind with statistics and/or completely depressing you before you read the rest of this book, we neglected to describe other branches of the tree such as the decreased work productivity, excessive school truancy and work absenteeism, and detrimental effects on partners, children, and fetuses resulting from AOD abuse. However, these and other branches exist and are the concern of all helping professionals.

THE NEED FOR GENERALIST TRAINING

Some years ago, one of your authors was asked by a local school district to conduct an independent psychological evaluation of a 14-year-old student who was a freshman in high school. The young man's parents were dissatisfied with the school district's evaluation of their son and had asked for another opinion. The youngster was failing most of his classes and was skipping school frequently. The parents were quite sure that their son had a learning disability that would explain his difficulties. The district's school psychologist had tested the student and not found a learning disability. The school counselor had suggested that there may be an emotional problem and recommended family counseling. In addition, a weekly progress check was initiated at school so the parents could be kept informed of assignments and homework that their son needed to complete. They had also hired a tutor. However, none of these interventions seemed to be helping, so the independent evaluation was requested.

In reviewing the test information, no indications of a learning disability were found. An AOD assessment (which will be discussed in Chapter 6) was conducted and there was evidence that the young man was using AOD on a daily basis. The parents said that they allowed their son and his friends to drink in their home because they believed that this would prevent them from using "drugs" and from drinking and driving. The parents were defensive about their own AOD use and rejected suggestions that the cause of their son's problems could be related to his AOD use. A couple of months later, there was a request for the young man's records from an AOD treatment program. He was referred to the program following an arrest for stealing alcohol from a convenience store.

One of us was supervising a master's student who was in a marriage and family therapy internship. The intern had been seeing a family of four (mom, dad, and two children, aged 3 and 9) who were referred to our university counseling clinic by Children's Protective Services. A child abuse report had been filed at the 9-year-old's elementary school because of bruises on the youngster's face. The father explained that he had slapped his son because of his frustration with the boy's behavior and "back-talking." The parents complained of frequent conflicts related to parenting techniques and family finances. The intern had developed an intervention plan that included referring the parents to a parent education program and working with the family on "communication skills" including "I-messages" and conflict resolution procedures. The intern was frustrated because the parents had failed to follow through on the parent education classes and had not made much progress in improving their communication patterns. It was suggested that the intern assess the AOD use of the parents and she did so at the next session. The mother and father had a heated argument about the father's drinking behavior. They did not show up for their next appointment and, when the intern called, the mother said that they were discontinuing counseling because the father said it was a waste of time.

We regularly consult with a social worker in private practice. One of the social worker's clients is a woman in her early 30s who sought counseling for "depression." The woman had been married twice, and described a series of failed relationships. Her first husband was an alcoholic and the second was a polydrug abuser. For two years she had been living with a man who was in recovery from cocaine addiction. However, she found out that he had been having numerous affairs during their relationship. The woman, who has a master's degree, could not understand why she continued to become involved with this kind of man. She felt that there must be something wrong with her because the men in her life needed alcohol, other drugs, or other women. Her father was an alcoholic and verbally abusive, and she had also been sexually molested by her paternal grandfather.

In the three situations described, the "helping professionals" (school psychologist, school counselor, marriage and family therapy intern, social worker) were not involved in providing substance abuse treatment, but they needed information and skills in the AOD field to perform their job functions in a competent manner. Your two authors have worked in schools as teacher and school psychologist, in a mental health clinic, in a university athletic department, and in private practice. We currently train school counselors and marriage and family therapists, as well as substance abuse counselors. We have found that the frequency of AOD-related problems is so pervasive in the helping field that the lack of training in this area would result in inadequate preparation for mental health professionals. When you read the statistics on the relationship between domestic violence, child abuse, other crime, and AOD, it should be clear that this relationship also applies to criminal justice personnel.

It would be unreasonable to expect all helping professionals to have the same set of skills as substance abuse counselors. We don't expect substance abuse counselors to be able to plan educational interventions or to do family therapy. Similarly, school and mental health counselors, social workers, and marriage and family therapists do not need to be able to monitor detoxification or to develop treatment plans. However, all mental health professionals will encounter individuals who need assessment and treatment for AOD problems and clients who are having problems as a result of relationships with individuals with AOD problems. Included in the related problems that mental health professionals (school counselors, mental health counselors, rehabilitation counselors, psychologists, social workers, and marriage and family therapists) will encounter are children who have been fetally affected by parental AOD use, the psychological impact on children and adults who live or have lived with caretakers who abuse AOD, and the intrapersonal and interpersonal problems of individuals who are in relationships with people who abuse AOD. Many of you have read about fetal alcohol syndrome, adult children of alcoholics, and codependency, which are included in these "related" problems. All of these issues will be discussed in this text.

We hope that you are convinced that mental health professionals need training in the AOD field, not only to identify those clients who need further assessment and treatment but for the multitude of related problems that all mental health professionals will encounter on a regular basis. As with many areas in the mental health field, there are differing views on the causes and treatment of alcoholism and drug addiction based on the variety of disciplines concerned with these problems and the philosophical orientation of different individuals.

PHILOSOPHICAL ORIENTATION

Jerome is a 47-year-old African American man who had been arrested for a DUI (driving under the influence). It was his third DUI, and he had previously been in an alcohol treatment program. He had been arrested previously for writing bad checks and spousal abuse. He is unemployed and dropped out of school in the 10th grade. An assessment revealed a long history of AOD use beginning at age 12. Jerome's mother was an alcoholic, and he was raised by his grandmother. He does not know his biological father.

Jerome's problem may be viewed in different ways by different professionals, depending on their training and experiences. A sociologist may focus on the environmental and cultural factors that modeled and encouraged AOD use. Some psychologists might attend to the fact that Jerome experienced rejection by his biological parents that led to feelings of inadequacy. The use of AOD might be seen as a coping mechanism. A physician might be impressed by the family history of alcoholism and hypothesize that Jerome had a genetic predisposition for chemical dependency. A social worker may think that Jerome's unemployment and lack of education resulted in discouragement and consequent AOD use. A criminal justice worker may see his behavior as willful misconduct and believe that punishment is necessary.

These differing views of the causes and treatment of Jerome's problem are not unusual in the mental health field. However, what is unique in the AOD field is that many drug and alcohol counselors, others involved in the treatment of chemically dependent people, and many people who are recovering from AOD problems believe that Jerome has a disease that has affected him mentally, physically, socially, emotionally, and *spiritually.* This spiritual component separates AOD problems from other mental health problems and has had implications for the understanding and treatment of AOD problems. (We will discuss spirituality in AOD recovery in Chapter 9.) One implication is that methods to attend to the spiritual aspect of treatment (e.g., Alcoholics Anonymous) are a common component of treatment. Another implication is that there are many individuals involved in the treatment of AOD problems who do not have formal training as counselors but who are "in recovery" and hold a fervent belief in a particular orientation to treatment. This belief may be based not on scientific evidence but instead on their own experience and the experience of other recovering individuals. This phenomenon is similar to an individual's religious beliefs that cannot (and should not) be disputed by research since the beliefs are valid for that individual. Clearly, the potential for disagreement and controversy exists when scientific and spiritual viewpoints are applied to the same problem, which has certainly been the case in this field.

In Chapter 3, we will discuss the different models of addiction and will thoroughly discuss the "disease concept" of chemical dependency. Our point here is that we believe that the AOD field requires an openness on the part of the mental health professional to consider a wide variety of possible causes of AOD problems and to employ a multitude of methods by which people recover from these problems. We have worked with people who discontinued their use of AOD without any treatment, individuals who stopped after walking into a church and "finding Jesus," clients and students who swear by AA, and people who have needed a formal treatment program.

If you work in a treatment program, you tend to see people who have experienced many life problems related to AOD use. It is easy to develop a viewpoint about substance abuse based on these clients' experiences. It is important to remember that treatment providers do not see those people who modify or discontinue their AOD use through methods other than formal treatment.

This book is written from the perspective of the mental health professional working in a generalist setting rather than from the perspective of a substance abuse counselor in a treatment setting. Therefore, we will provide the type of information we believe all mental health professionals need in the AOD field to work effectively in schools, community agencies, and private practice, rather than providing all the information needed to work as a substance abuse counselor in a treatment setting. We want to provide a balance in the types of viewpoints that exist in this field so that you can understand these perspectives. We will describe the popular literature in certain areas (e.g., adult children of alcoholics) and contrast this with research in the area so that you can understand that clinical impressions and research do not always match. Finally, we want to communicate our belief that it is not advisable to adopt universal concepts of cause and treatment in this field. In other areas of mental health treatment, we encourage practitioners to assess a client and to develop treatment strategies based on the individual and group characteristics of the client. The same rules should apply in the AOD field.

PROFESSIONAL ORIENTATION

Over the years, this text has been used in undergraduate and graduate courses for students preparing for careers in criminal justice, social work, marriage and family therapy, mental health counseling, rehabilitation counseling, school counseling, school psychology, and substance abuse counseling. As a student, the manner in which you use the information in this book in your career will be dependent on factors such as your personal experiences with the topics, the philosophical orientation of your program, when you take this course in your studies, and your eventual job placement. For example, a social worker who is employed by a hospice may not have as much regular contact with substance abuse issues compared to a social worker involved with investigating child abuse cases. An elementary school counselor will encounter plenty of family issues related to AOD but less abuse by students compared to a high school counselor. The point is that, while you may have a clear vocational goal, it is not possible for you to know in what job setting you will find yourself in 5 or 10 years. Your program of study may have an orientation to understanding human behavior that is not consistent with what you read in some chapters. That is to be expected and is part of the learning process for students preparing for careers in the helping professions. Regardless, we want to encourage you to avoid filtering what you learn through a lens of "I don't need to know that because I won't be dealing with that in my career" or "I don't believe that. It doesn't fit with my view of human behavior." Challenge anything you read here but keep an open mind.

ATTITUDES AND BELIEFS

Close your eyes for a minute and visualize an alcoholic. What did your alcoholic look like? For most people, the alcoholic is a white male, middle aged, who looks pretty seedy. In other words, the stereotypical skid row bum. Did you visualize somebody who looks like former President Bush? Did you visualize one of your professors? Did you visualize a professional athlete?

Attitudes and beliefs about alcoholics and drug addicts have an effect on the mental health professional's work. Imagine that you are a mental health counselor and a well-dressed middle-aged woman comes to see you complaining of symptoms of depression. If you hold false beliefs about alcoholics, such as that they must be dirty and drunk all the time, you might fail to diagnose those clients who do not fit your stereotype.

To help students understand their own attitudes about alcoholics and drug addicts, we have our students attend an Alcoholics Anonymous (AA) or Narcotics Anonymous (NA) meeting as a class assignment. We encourage you to do this as well (if you do go to a meeting, make sure you attend an "open" meeting [see Chapter 10]). In addition to acquiring a cognitive understanding of this type of support for alcoholics and addicts, students report interesting affective reactions that provide information about their attitudes. For example, many students report that they want to tell others at the meeting that they are there for a class assignment and that they are not alcoholics. Our response is that unless you believe that alcoholism or drug addiction is simply a condition that some people develop and has nothing to do with morals or a weak will, you would not care if you were mistakenly identified as alcoholic or drug addicted. If you do care, you must believe that alcoholics and drug addicts have some type of character flaw. This realization helps many potential mental health professionals modify their attitudes and beliefs about alcoholism and drug addiction.

A second type of affective reaction that students report is being surprised with the heterogeneity of the group. At most meetings, they see well-dressed businessmen and women, young people, blue-collar workers, unkempt people, articulate individuals, and people obviously impaired from their years of using AOD. Seeing such a variety of people tends to destroy any stereotypes the students may have.

Although we believe that potential mental health professionals may hold any belief system they want, the belief that alcoholism or drug addiction is due to a moral weakness or a character flaw may have a detrimental effect on providing or finding appropriate help for those with AOD problems. For example, imagine that you are a marriage and family therapist and that you are seeing a couple in which one partner is drinking excessively. You believe that changing heavy drinking to moderate drinking is largely a matter of willpower and desire, and you communicate this to the drinking partner. If this individual is addicted to alcohol, your belief system will be incompatible with this client's reality. Your client may experience shame, because he or she is not strong enough, or anger at your lack of understanding. Resistance and termination are frequent outcomes, and the client fails to get the proper help. Therefore, if you do believe that excessive AOD use is largely due to moral weakness or character flaws, you would be well advised to refer these cases to others.

DENIAL, MINIMIZATION, PROJECTION, AND RATIONALIZATION

Imagine (or maybe you don't have to imagine) that you are in love with someone you believe to be the most wonderful person in the world. You cannot imagine living without this person and firmly believe that you need this person to survive. Your mother sits you down one day and tells you that you must no longer associate with this person. She tells you that this person is destroying your life, that you have changed since becoming involved with this person, and that all your family and friends believe that you need to break off the relationship before something terrible happens to you. How would you react? You might tell your mother that she is crazy and that all her complaints about this person are untrue (denial). Perhaps you acknowledge that your person does have some little quirks, but they really don't bother you (minimization). You tell your mother that she and the rest of your family and friends are really jealous because they do not have someone as wonderful as you (projection) and that you may have changed but these changes are for the better and long overdue (rationalization).

We use this analogy so you can develop an empathic understanding of what many AOD-addicted individuals experience. Obviously, the "love object" in this case is the individual's drug of choice. The addicted individual may be seen as having an intimate and monogamous relationship with alcohol or other drugs and believe that he or she needs the drug to function and survive. In the same way that people deny that a relationship has become destructive, the addicted individual may deny that alcohol or other drugs have become destructive in spite of objective evidence to the contrary. The defense mechanisms of denial, minimization, projection, and rationalization are used so that the person does not have to face a reality that may be terrifying: a life without alcohol or other drugs.

While we know that it may be easy for you to intellectually understand these concepts as applied to alcoholic and other drug-addicted people, we have found it useful for our students to have a more direct experience with their own use of defense mechanisms. At the first class session of our substance abuse class, we ask the students to choose a substance or activity and abstain from this substance or activity for the semester, and that the first thing that popped into their heads and was rejected because it would be too hard to give up is the thing they should choose. Students usually choose substances such as alcohol, coffee, chocolate, or sugar, or activities such as gambling (we live in Nevada where gambling is legal) or watching television. Some choose tobacco and an occasional courageous student will choose an illegal drug. The students record their use of the defense mechanisms through journal entries and write a paper about the experience at the end of the semester.

If you are wondering whether some students "blow off" the assignment and just make up the material in their journals and papers, the answer is "of course." When the assignment is given, this issue is discussed. The students are told that they can do anything they want to; the instructor will never know the difference. However, there is some reason for potential mental health professionals to take a close look at themselves if they are unwilling to abstain from a substance or activity for 15 weeks, particularly when mental health professionals will be encouraging clients to abstain from alcohol or other drugs for a lifetime.

We encourage you, our reader, to examine your own use of denial, minimization, projection, and rationalization, particularly in regard to your own use of AOD. Mental health professionals are not immune to AOD problems and are just as likely to use these defense mechanisms as anyone else is. As you read the rest of this book, take some time to examine your own substance-using behavior. If there is a problem, this would be the ideal time to get some help. This would certainly be preferable to becoming one of the many impaired professionals who may cause harm to their clients and themselves.

HELPING ATTITUDES AND BEHAVIORS

Although we have encountered many mental health professionals with AOD problems, we have found that a more pervasive problem may be the potential mental health professionals who gravitate to the helping professions because of unresolved issues in their lives. Although there may be a sincere desire to help others, these potential mental health professionals may actually be unhelpful to clients. For example, in our counselor education program, we find that many of our students are adult children of alcoholics. Now, that is no problem in and of itself. In fact, as we will discuss in Chapter 12, many adult children of alcoholics have the same or fewer problems than other adults. However, being raised by one or more alcoholic caretakers may lead to certain characteristic ways of behaving that could have implications for a mental health professional's effectiveness. For example, a graduate student in marriage and family therapy whom we will call Debbie (we are changing all of the names of students and clients we are using in this book to protect anonymity) decided to pursue a career in the helping professions because everyone told her that she was easy to talk to and was a good listener. Debbie said that she was one of those people to whom total strangers immediately told their life stories.

Debbie was raised by her biological parents, both of whom were alcoholics. Within her family, she had developed a method of behaving that would minimize the probability of conflict developing. She did most of the cooking and cleaning at home, took care of her younger siblings, and worked very hard at school. Debbie reported being in a constant state of anxiety due to her worry that she had "missed" something that would send one of her parents into a rage.

In hindsight, it is easy to see that Debbie developed a false belief that she could control her parents' moods and behavior by making sure that everything was perfect at home and by her achievements at school. It is not unusual for children raised by alcoholic caretakers to develop a role designed to divert attention away from the real problem in the family. (Again, this will be discussed in detail in Chapter 12.) However, the development of this childhood role had implications for Debbie's work as a marriage and family therapist. We noticed that she was quite hesitant to confront clients and that she seemed very uncomfortable with conflict. Debbie had more than the usual anxiety for a student when counseling and brooded excessively when her clients did not immediately feel better. Clearly, the characteristic ways Debbie had learned to behave as a child were having a detrimental effect on her development as a marriage and family therapist in spite of the fact that people found her easy to talk to.

Another of our graduate students in counseling, Patricia, was taking our substance abuse counseling course. She failed her midterm examination. Patricia came to see the instructor and explained that the content of the course generated a great deal of emotion for her since her parents were alcoholics, and she had been married to a drug addict. Because of these emotions, she said that she had difficulty concentrating on the lectures and the reading material and in following through on class assignments (students were required to attend an Alcoholics Anonymous and an Alanon [for family members of alcoholics] meeting). The instructor communicated his understanding that the course could have that impact on people with history and experiences in the substance abuse area and suggested that Patricia drop the course (he offered a passing withdrawal) and pursue counseling for herself. Patricia chose to avoid working on these issues, she stayed in the course, and failed.

Since most of you who are reading this text are graduate students, this may strike you as rather harsh. However, consider the alternative. Let's say that the instructor had offered his understanding and allowed Patricia to remain in the course without dealing with these issues and passed her. Would Patricia be able to work effectively with individuals and families in which there were alcohol or other drug problems, with adult clients who were raised by substance abusing caretakers, or with clients living with alcohol or other drug-abusing partners? In an attempt to avoid these problems, she might do a poor job of assessment, or she might ignore the signs and symptoms of alcohol or other drug problems. Or she might ignore or fail to inquire about substance abuse in the family of origin or in the current family of her clients. In short, we believe that her unwillingness to face these problems would result in her being a less effective counselor.

What about Debbie? Her excessive anxiety and concern with her performance prevented her from objectively looking at her clients and her own counseling behaviors. Debbie's fear of conflict resulted in an unwillingness to confront her clients, which limited her effectiveness. Fortunately, Debbie was receptive to feedback and suggestions. She did some work on her own issues, and she has become a fine marriage and family therapist.

This discussion is not meant to discourage those of you who are adult children of alcoholics, are in recovery from an alcohol or other drug problem, or have lived or are living with an addicted person from pursuing your careers. It is our experience that most people who want to become helping professionals have a need or desire to help people that is based on family of origin issues that may adversely affect their work. This is certainly the case with both of us. It is not a problem if you enter a training program in one of the helping professions because of your own need to be needed. It is a problem if you avoid examining your own issues and fail to take steps to resolve these issues in order to avoid ineffective (or in some cases, harmful) work with clients.

In this particular field, we find helping professionals who cannot work effectively with clients because of their own AOD use or their experiences with AOD use in their families of origin and/or with partners. In the rest of this book, we will attempt to provide you with information that will enable you to deal effectively with the direct and indirect problems resulting from AOD use that social workers, school counselors, mental health counselors, marriage and family therapists, and other helping professionals will encounter. However, all of this information will be useless if your own use patterns or issues are unresolved and if they impact your work. Since denial is so pervasive, we encourage you to seek objective feedback regarding the necessity to work on your own use of alcohol or other drugs or on other issues and, if necessary, to choose a course of action with professional assistance. But please, for your own benefit and for the benefit of your future clients, don't choose to avoid.

OVERVIEW OF THE BOOK

In our choice of chapter topics and the orientation of each chapter, we have tried to maintain a primary goal of providing useful information in the AOD field to general mental health professionals. Therefore, Chapter 2 (Classification of Drugs), Chapter 3 (Models of Addiction), Chapter 8 (Treatment of AOD Problems), and Chapter 10 (Twelve-Step and Other Types of Support Groups) are overviews of these topics. We have attempted to provide enough detail about treatment and twelve-step groups to reduce any myths about these activities and to allow mental health professionals to make informed referrals. Issues that usually provoke some controversy among generalists (e.g., the disease concept, relative dangers of different drugs, etc.) are also discussed.

In several chapters, we have attempted to integrate the role of the mental health professional in working with clients with AOD problems with the specialist in the field. In Chapter 6 (Screening Assessment and Diagnosis), Chapter 7 (Motivational Interviewing and Brief Interventions), and Chapter 9 (Relapse Prevention and Recovery), our goal is that you will understand the types of AOD services that mental health professionals in generalist settings provide.

Chapter 11 (Children and Families), Chapter 12 (Adult Children and Codependency), and Chapter 14 (Gambling and Other Addictions) involve issues related to AOD problems. In many instances, mental health professionals may work with clients having these problems. In each of these chapters, we have attempted to provide sufficient depth of coverage so that you will have a conceptual framework to understand the relationship of these topics to AOD and to understand the implications for treatment.

Chapter 4 is an in-depth discussion of multicultural issues in the AOD field. As with all mental and other health-related topics, it is essential to understand both individual and group characteristics of clients. The cultural context of AOD use is of crucial importance in both prevention and treatment. We have chosen to highlight its importance by devoting a chapter to the topic rather than integrating multiculturalism into each chapter. Therefore, we encourage you to maintain an awareness of diversity issues as you read the remaining chapters.

Chapter 5 concerns confidentiality and ethics. In teaching a substance abuse counseling class to mental health generalists, we have found nearly universal ignorance of the fact that almost all mental health professionals are bound by federal confidentiality regulations. Students often perceive this topic as "dry." However, we have seen the consequences of lack of awareness of confidentiality regulations. So, please have the stamina to wade through this chapter.

The relationship between HIV/AIDS and substance abuse is discussed in Chapter 13. Our inclusion of a chapter on this topic reflects the increasing need for awareness among all mental and other health professionals regarding transmission and prevention of this and other communicable diseases.

Having only one chapter on prevention (Chapter 15) does not imply that the subject is unimportant. Indeed, if prevention efforts were more successful, there would be less need for the rest of this book. Clearly, school counselors and school social workers must be well informed about effective prevention approaches. However, successful prevention involves all aspects of a community, and all helping professionals must be involved. We are particularly interested in increasing your awareness of our public policy regarding the marketing of legal drugs (alcohol and tobacco) and its effect on prevention efforts.

In each chapter after this introductory chapter, there will be case examples at the beginning of the chapter. We have based these case examples on our own clinical experiences but have obviously changed anything that would personally identify a person. The case examples will be used to illustrate points and concepts.

At the ends of chapters, major points are bulleted in a Summary section. We have added Internet resources for those of you who want more information on subjects in the chapters. Finally, there are some discussion questions designed to provoke your thinking about issues.

We need to mention an aspect of writing style so you understand what we are trying to do in this book. The tone of our writing may be less scholarly than you are accustomed to. We have taught many university courses and have used a lot of textbooks. We also were students for a *long* time. From these experiences, we found that many textbooks were marvelous, non-pharmaceutical methods to induce sleep. Although accurate and scholarly, the stilted style was often a barrier to acquiring information. It has been our intention to make this book accurate and informative but with a lower probability of causing drowsiness. Let us know if it worked.

MyCounselingLab™

Go to Topic 1: *Introduction to Substance Abuse Counseling* in the MyCounselingLab™ site (www.MyCounselingLab.com) for *Substance Abuse: Information for School Counselors, Social Workers, Therapists, and Counselors*, Fifth Edition, where you can:

- Find learning outcomes for *Introduction to Substance Abuse Counseling* along with the national standards that connect to these outcomes.
- Complete Assignments and Activities that can help you more deeply understand the chapter content.
- Apply and practice your understanding of the core skills identified in the chapter with the Building Counseling Skills unit.
- Prepare yourself for professional certification with a Practice for Certification quiz.
- Connect to videos through the Video and Resource Library.

Chapter 2

Classification of Drugs

CASE EXAMPLES

❶ Casey is a 48-year-old male who visits his primary care physician. He complains of insomnia, anxiety, frequent acid indigestion, and fatigue. On his blood panel, he shows some impairment in his liver functioning. He is borderline diabetic and has hypertension.

❷ Matilda is a 33-year-old female who comes in to an emergency room complaining of severe lower back pain. An x-ray is negative. She is restless and agitated, has a runny nose, and complains of an upset stomach. Her vital signs are normal.

❸ Chris and his wife are seeing you for marriage and family therapy. Chris works in the financial industry in a high-paced, stressful environment. His wife says Chris hardly sleeps and does not eat regularly. His moods are erratic. The couple has some financial problems, which Chris attributes to bad investments. The couple was court-ordered to counseling following a domestic violence incident.

As we noted in Chapter 1, this textbook is designed for the mental health professional (e.g., school counselor, mental health counselor, rehabilitation counselor, social worker, marriage and family therapist) who will encounter AOD problems with clientele but who, generally, will not provide treatment for these problems. Therefore, the goal of this chapter is to provide an overview of the drugs (including alcohol and tobacco) that are most often abused and drugs that are used in the treatment of some mental disorders. However, a thorough understanding of the pharmacology of drugs and related issues (e.g., medical management of overdose, use of psychotropic medications in the treatment of mental disorders) would require far more attention than one chapter can offer. Also, information in this area changes rapidly as a result of research. For example, there is no medication that has been found to be effective in significantly reducing cocaine craving. However, there is considerable research in this area. By the time you read this book, there may be pharmacological management of cocaine withdrawal that does not currently exist. We are including an additional reading list at the end of this chapter if you want to acquire more comprehensive information on the topics discussed. In addition, we encourage you to develop contacts with AOD treatment providers who are likely to remain current with regard to research in this area. This will reduce the probability that you will pass along misinformation or outdated information to your clients.

Different methods exist that are used to classify drugs. We will use the method that classifies drugs by their pharmacological similarity. Drugs exist that do not fit nicely into one classification, and these will be noted. For each drug classification, we will mention the common drugs contained in the classification and some common street names, the routes of administration, major acute and chronic effects, signs of intoxication, signs of overdose, tolerance, and withdrawal. First however, we will present information on the federal schedule of drugs, a discussion of the concept of "dangerousness," some simple definitions of terms that will be helpful in understanding the rest of the chapter, and a brief overview of the neurobiology of drugs.

COMPREHENSIVE DRUG ABUSE PREVENTION AND CONTROL ACT

In 1970, the Comprehensive Drug Abuse Prevention and Control Act (often referred to as the Controlled Substances Act) was passed by the U.S. Congress. As part of this law, drugs are placed in one of five "schedules," with regulatory requirements associated with each schedule. Schedule I drugs have a high potential for abuse, no currently accepted medical use in treatment in the United States, and a lack of a safe level of use under medical supervision. Drugs on Schedule I include heroin, methaqualone (Quaalude), LSD, and marijuana. Schedule II drugs also have a high abuse potential and can lead to psychological or physical dependence. However, these drugs have an accepted medical use in treatment. These drugs include morphine, PCP, cocaine, and methamphetamine. As you can probably surmise, the criteria for the other schedules involve less abuse potential, increased medical uses, and less likelihood of psychological and physical dependence.

As you will see from our discussion of the classification of drugs, the way some drugs are classified is clearly illogical. For example, benzodiazepines such as Valium and Xanax are Schedule IV drugs, with part of the criteria for inclusion being that the drugs have a lower abuse potential than drugs on Schedules I, II, and III. In reality, these drugs have at least the same if not greater abuse potential than marijuana, a Schedule I drug. However, the inclusion of a drug on a certain schedule is related to public policy, which will be discussed in Chapter 15. For example, the reclassification downward of a drug such as marijuana would be politically unpopular, and the reclassification of benzodiazepines upward would be resisted by the manufacturers of these drugs.

THE CONCEPT OF DANGEROUSNESS

Related to the preceding discussion of schedules of drugs is the concept of the inherent dangers of certain drugs. Tobacco, alcohol, and other drugs are not safe to use. There are acute and chronic dangers, and these dangers vary by drug. For example, there is little acute danger from the ingestion of a glass of wine by an adult. The acute danger of shooting cocaine is far greater. Chronic use of any drug (including alcohol) has an increased risk, but the danger of smoking one pack of cigarettes a day for 40 years is greater than the dangers from drinking one beer a day for 40 years. Danger is also related to the method used to administer a drug. Smoking a drug or injecting it produces the most rapid and intense reaction, while ingesting a drug generally produces effects with longer duration, although less intensity. Snorting drugs is in between but has more similarities to smoking and injecting than ingesting. Although any method of administration may be dangerous both acutely and chronically, smoking or injecting drugs tends to result in the most acute problems since these routes of administration rapidly introduce the drug to the bloodstream and, subsequently, to the brain. Also, smoking drugs causes damage to the respiratory system, and the intravenous use of drugs may cause serious problems including abscesses, blood clots, allergic reactions to the substances used to "cut" the drug, and communicable diseases such as hepatitis and HIV.

It is certainly important that you understand the acute and chronic effects of different drugs and the addictive potential of tobacco, alcohol, and other drugs. However, it is essential that you understand that any of the psychoactive drugs we discuss in this chapter can be used in an addictive manner. You will learn that hallucinogens are not physically addicting in the sense that body tissues require these drugs for normal functioning. However, this does not imply that people are immune from serious problems resulting from the use of hallucinogens. Alcohol is clearly an extremely dangerous drug in spite of the fact that many people use the drug without problems. Marijuana is not as acutely or chronically dangerous as cocaine, but that does not mean it can be used safely. We have worked with clients who have serious life problems from marijuana use. This is not a sermon to "Just Say No." It is a caution to avoid concluding that you can direct clients away from some drugs to other drugs, and a caution to avoid using your own experience with AOD as a basis for determining which drugs are safe and which are dangerous.

DEFINITIONS

Terminology in the AOD field can be confusing. One author may have a very specific meaning for a particular term while another may use the same term in a more general sense. An analogy might be the use of the term *neurotic* in the mental health field. While one professional may use this term when referring to some very specific disorders, another may use it to describe a wide variety of mental health problems. However, there is no universal agreement about how some of these terms should be used. Therefore, the following definitions should assist you in understanding this chapter and the rest of the book, but you may find differences in definitions as you read professional and popular literature in the AOD field.

Addiction: Compulsion to use alcohol or other drugs regardless of negative or adverse consequences. Addiction is characterized by psychological dependence (*see below*) and, often (depending on the drug or drugs) physical dependence (*see below*). As we will discuss in Chapter 14, the term *addiction* is sometimes applied to behaviors other than AOD (e.g., eating, gambling).

Alcoholism: Addiction to a specific drug: alcohol.

Chemical dependency: A term used to describe addiction to alcohol and/or other drugs and to differentiate this type of addiction from nonchemical addictions (e.g., gambling).

Dependence: A recurrent or ongoing need to use alcohol or other drugs. Psychological dependence is the need to use alcohol or other drugs to think, feel, or function normally.

Physical dependence exists when tissues of the body require the presence of alcohol or other drugs to function normally. All psychoactive drugs can produce psychological dependence and many can produce physical dependence. Dependence will also be defined in Chapter 6, based on the criteria in the *Diagnostic and Statistical Manual of Mental Disorders, Fourth Edition, Text Revision (DSM-IV-TR)* (American Psychiatric Association, 2000), to diagnose AOD dependency disorders.

Intoxication: State of being under the influence of alcohol or other drugs so that thinking, feeling, and/or behavior are affected.

Psychoactive drugs: Natural or synthetic chemicals that affect thinking, feeling, and behavior.

Psychotropic drugs: Chemicals used to treat mental disorders.

Substance abuse: The continued use of alcohol and/or other drugs in spite of adverse consequences in one or more areas of an individual's life (e.g., family, job, legal, financial). Abuse will also be defined in Chapter 6 according to the criteria in the *DSM-IV-TR.*

Tolerance: Requirement for increasing doses or quantities of alcohol or other drugs in order to create the same effect as was obtained from the original dose. Tolerance results from the physical or psychological adaptations of the individual.

Cross-tolerance: Refers to accompanying tolerance to other drugs from the same pharmacological group. For example, tolerance to alcohol results in tolerance to minor tranquilizers such as Xanax, even when the individual has never used Xanax.

Reverse tolerance: Refers to a condition in which smaller quantities of a drug produce the same effects as did previous larger doses.

Withdrawal: Physical and psychological effects that occur when a drug-dependent individual discontinues alcohol or other drug use.

THE NEUROBIOLOGY OF DRUGS[1]

Drugs affect the brain by impacting the way nerve cells send, receive, and process information. Drugs such as heroin and marijuana activate neurons by mimicking natural neurotransmitters. Other drugs like methamphetamine and cocaine cause nerve cells to release extremely large amounts of neurotransmitters or prevent the normal reuptake of neurotransmitters into the nerve cells (see Figure 2.1).

Most drugs of abuse directly or indirectly target the brain's reward system by releasing or blocking the re-uptake of the neurotransmitter dopamine. Dopamine is present in regions of the brain that regulate movement, emotion, cognition, motivation, and feelings of pleasure. When dopamine floods the neuron system in the brain's reward center, euphoria results. Natural human behaviors (e.g., eating, sex) also release dopamine and the person experiences pleasure. Since our brains are designed for the survival of the species, we want to repeat these natural, pleasurable activities. However, when drugs stimulate the brain's reward center, our brain is in effect "fooled" into believing that drug taking is also a survival behavior that should be repeated.

---

[1]This information comes from the National Institute on Drug Abuse (NIDA) *Drugs, Brains, and Behavior—The Science of Addiction* (2010). Available at http://www.nida.nih.gov/scienceofaddiction/index.html. All material, including illustrations, is in the public sector.

FIGURE 2.1   Effect of drugs on neurotransmitters.

Many naturally pleasurable activities are not habitually repeated like drug taking can be. The neurobiological explanation is that 2 to 10 times more dopamine is released by drugs than by natural activities. Furthermore, depending on the method that drugs are administered, this dopamine release is almost immediate and is very intense. Therefore, the euphoric properties of drug taking can be very powerful and highly reinforcing.

Unfortunately, the brain adjusts to high levels of dopamine by producing less or reducing the number of dopamine receptors. When this occurs, the drug user has more difficulty experiencing pleasure and must increase the amount of drugs consumed to feel normal. This is referred to as "tolerance." In Figure 2.2, the gray areas in the white ovals areas are dopamine transporters from PET scans of a normal brain and the brain of a methamphetamine abuser. You can clearly see the reduction of these gray areas in the methamphetamine abuser. When a drug abuser abstains from drugs for a period of time, the brain usually returns to normal. However, the length of time it takes depends on the type of drugs abused and the number of years that drugs were abused.

The neurobiology of addiction is a very complex subject and this brief section is intended to give you only a conceptualized understanding of the topic. (See Table 2.1 for an overview of drug classifications.) There are additional readings at the end of the chapter for those who want to pursue this area in more detail.

CENTRAL NERVOUS SYSTEM DEPRESSANTS

Central nervous system (CNS) depressants (also referred to as *sedative-hypnotics*) depress the overall functioning of the central nervous system to induce sedation, drowsiness, and coma. The drugs in this classification include the most commonly used and abused psychoactive drug, alcohol; prescription drugs used for anxiety, sleep disturbance, and seizure control; and over-the-counter medications for sleep disturbance, colds and allergies, and coughs. In general, CNS depressants are extremely dangerous. There are approximately 79,000 deaths annually caused by excessive alcohol use in the United States, the third leading lifestyle cause of death (Centers for Disease Control and Prevention, 2010a). Alcohol alone or in combination with other drugs accounted for nearly 36% of drug abuse-related emergency room episodes in 2007 (Substance Abuse and Mental Health Services Administration, 2010).

FIGURE 2.2 Effect of methamphetamine on the brain. *Source:* Am J Psychiatry 158:377–382, 2001.

Drugs in This Classification

Alcohol is the most well-known CNS depressant because of its widespread use and legality. The alcohol content of common beverages is beer, 3% to 6%; wine, 11% to 20%; liqueurs, 25% to 35%; and liquor (whiskey, gin, vodka, etc.), 40% to 50%. The "proof" on alcohol beverages is computed by doubling the alcohol content. Therefore, a bourbon that is described as "90 proof" is 45% alcohol. It is important to remember that the amount of alcohol in one 12-ounce beer is the same as the amount of alcohol in 6 ounces of wine or in 1.5 ounces of liquor (all standard drinks). The alcohol in beer is simply contained in a larger amount of liquid.

Barbiturates are prescription drugs used to aid sleep for insomniacs and for the control of seizures. These drugs include Seconal (reds, red devils), Nembutal (yellows, yellow jackets), Tuinal (rainbows), Amytal (blues, blue heaven), and Phenobarbital. There are also nonbarbiturate sedative-hypnotics with similar effects but with different pharmacological properties. These include Doriden (goofballs), Quaalude (ludes), Miltown, and Equinil. Being a Schedule I drug, Quaalude cannot be legally prescribed in the United States.

The development of benzodiazepines or minor tranquilizers reduced the number of prescriptions for barbiturates written by physicians. These drugs were initially seen as safe and having little abuse potential. Although the minor tranquilizers cannot be easily used in suicide as can barbiturates, the potential for abuse is significant. The benzodiazepines are among the most widely prescribed drugs and include Valium, Librium, Dalmane, Halcion, Xanax, and Ativan. In addition, non-benzodiazepine hypnotics are being heavily marketed as sleep aids. These include Ambien, Lunesta, and Sonata. These drugs can be abused and do have addictive potential.

TABLE 2.1 Summary Table of Drug Classifications

	Common Drugs	Main Routes of Administration	Major Acute Effects	Major Chronic Effects	Overdose	Tolerance	Withdrawal
CNS Depressants	Alcohol, barbiturates, benzodiazepines, sleep aids	Drinking, ingesting pills	Relaxation, disinhibition, reduction of anxiety, impaired motor coordination	Alcohol: Damage to every organ system	Common with alcohol, can be dangerous, synergistic effect	Develops rapidly, cross-tolerance occurs	Can be medically dangerous
CNS Stimulants	Cocaine, methamphetamine, caffeine, nicotine	Snorting, smoking, injecting, drinking	Alertness, mood elevation, increased heart rate and blood pressure	Health damage from tobacco products, addiction, depression, suicidal ideation	Tremors, sweating, tachycardia, anxiety, insomnia	Rapid tolerance to pleasurable and stimulating effects	Unpleasant and long-lasting but not medically dangerous
Opioids	Heroin, morphine, methadone, pain pills	Injecting, snorting, swallowing pills	Sedation, pain relief	Addiction, complications from lifestyle and method of administration	Depressed central nervous system functioning, death can occur	Rapid tolerance to pleasurable effects with repeated administration	Very unpleasant but not usually medically dangerous
Hallucinogens	LSD, magic mushrooms, PCP	Ingesting or smoking	Alters perception of sensory stimuli, panic attacks in some users	Flashbacks	Except for PCP, overdose does not occur with PCP, agitation, confusion, aggression	Tolerance to hallucinogenic properties does occur	No physical dependence

Category	Examples	Method	Effects	Adverse Effects	Overdose	Tolerance	Withdrawal
Cannabinols	Marijuana	Smoking or ingestion	Enhanced taste, touch, and smell; relaxation; increased appetite; impaired immediate recall	Adverse effect on lung function, decrease in testosterone, suppression of immune system; impact is controversial	Overdose does not occur; adverse reactions are panic attacks	Tolerance to normal effects occurs but it is probably not physiological	Irritability, insomnia, restlessness
Inhalants and Volatile Hydrocarbons	Solvents, aerosol sprays, amyl nitrate, isobutyl, nitrous oxide	Inhaling (huffing)	Reduced inhibition, dizziness, slurred speech, impaired motor coordination; unconsciousness and death can occur.	Damage to liver, kidneys, brain, and lungs	Hallucinations, muscle spasms, coma	Tolerance to nitrous oxide	No known withdrawal syndrome
Anabolic Steroids	Depo-Testosterone, Danocrine, Halotestin	Ingested or injected	Increased muscle strength, body mass, and aggressiveness	Jaundice, liver tumors, mood swings	Increased doses result in chronic problems	No tolerance	Depression, fatigue, restlessness, insomnia

Rozerem, another widely marketed sleep aid, is not pharmacologically similar to the other non-benzodiazepine hypnotics and is not addictive. It is like the herbal remedy melatonin.

Finally, certain over-the-counter medications contain depressant drugs. Sleep aids such as Nytol and Sominex, cold and allergy products, and cough medicines may contain scopolamine, antihistamines, or alcohol to produce the desired effects.

Routes of Administration

Obviously, alcohol is administered by drinking. Some over-the-counter medications are also in liquid form. The barbiturates, nonbarbiturate sedative-hypnotics, minor tranquilizers, and non-benzodiazepine hypnotics come in pill form. As with many psychoactive drugs, liquid forms of the drugs are produced and administered by injection.

Major Acute and Chronic Effects

The effects of CNS depressants are related to the dose, method of administration, and tolerance of the individual, factors that should be kept in mind as the effects are discussed. At low doses, these drugs produce a feeling of relaxation and calmness. They induce muscle relaxation, disinhibition, and a reduction in anxiety. Judgment and motor coordination are impaired, and there is a decrease in reflexes, pulse rate, and blood pressure. At high doses, the person demonstrates slurred speech, staggering, and, eventually, sleep. Phenobarbital and Valium have anticonvulsant properties and are used to control seizures. The benzodiazepines are also used to clinically control the effects from alcohol withdrawal.

In terms of damage to the human body and to society, alcohol is the most dangerous psychoactive drug (tobacco causes far more health damage). Alcohol has a damaging effect on every organ system. Chronic effects include permanent loss of memory, gastritis, esophagitis, ulcers, pancreatitis, cirrhosis of the liver, high blood pressure, weakened heart muscles, and damage to a fetus including fetal alcohol syndrome and fetal alcohol effect (see Chapter 12). Other chronic effects include family, social, occupational, and financial problems. Acutely, alcohol is the cause of many traffic and other accidents and is involved in many acts of violence and crime. Certainly, the other CNS depressants can cause the same acute problems that are the result of injury and accident and chronic effects on the individual and family due to addiction.

Overdose

Alcohol overdose is common. We refer to this syndrome as being "drunk." The symptoms include staggering, slurred speech, extreme disinhibition, and blackouts (an inability to recall events that occurred when the individual was intoxicated). Generally, the stomach goes into spasm and the person will vomit, helping to eliminate alcohol from the body. However, the rapid ingestion of alcohol, particularly in a nontolerant individual, may result in coma and death. This happens most frequently with young people who participate in drinking contests.

As these drugs depress the central nervous system, overdose is extremely dangerous and can be fatal. Since the fatal dosage is only 10 to 15 times the therapeutic dosage, barbiturates are often used in suicides, which is one reason they are not frequently prescribed. It is far more difficult to overdose on the minor tranquilizers. However, CNS depressants have a synergistic or potentiation effect, meaning that the effect of a drug is enhanced as a result of the presence of another drug. For example, if a person has been drinking and then takes a minor tranquilizer such as Xanax, the effect of the Xanax may be dramatically enhanced. This combination has been the cause of many accidental deaths and emergency room visits.

Tolerance

There is a rapid development of tolerance to all CNS depressant drugs. Cross-tolerance also develops. This is one reason why overdose is such a problem. For example, Bob, a very heavy drinker, is quite anxious and is having difficulty sleeping. He goes to his physician with these symptoms. The physician does not ask about his alcohol use and gives him a prescription of Xanax. Bob follows the directions and takes one pill. However, because he is tolerant to alcohol, he is also cross-tolerant to Xanax and the pill has no effect. He can't sleep so he takes three more pills and has a glass of brandy. The synergistic effect of these drugs results in a coma.

The tolerance that develops to the CNS depressants is also one reason that the use of the minor tranquilizers has become problematic. People are given prescriptions to alleviate symptoms such as anxiety and sleep disturbance that are the result of other problems such as marital discord. The minor tranquilizers temporarily relieve the symptoms but the real problem is never addressed. The person continues to use the drug to alleviate the symptoms, but tolerance develops and increasing dosages must be used to achieve the desired effect. This is a classic paradigm for the development of addiction and/or overdose.

Withdrawal

The withdrawal syndrome from CNS depressants can be medically dangerous. These symptoms may include anxiety, irritability, loss of appetite, tremors, insomnia, and seizures. In the severe form of alcohol withdrawal called delirium tremens (DTs), additional symptoms are fever, rapid heartbeat, and hallucinations. People can and do die from the withdrawal from these drugs. Therefore, the detoxification process for CNS depressants should include close supervision and the availability of medical personnel. Chronic, high-dosage users of these drugs should be discouraged from detoxifying without support and supervision. For detoxification in a medical setting, minor tranquilizers can be used, in decreasing dosages, to reduce the severity of the withdrawal symptoms.

The dangerousness of withdrawal from CNS depressants is one reason why supervised detoxification is needed. In addition, supervision and support are usually required because the withdrawal symptoms are unpleasant and rapidly alleviated by using CNS depressants. For example, a 47-year-old man decides that he has been drinking too much and wants to quit. He doesn't tell anyone and is going to "tough it out." Although he doesn't have any medically dangerous symptoms, he is anxious, irritable, and has trouble sleeping. His family, friends, and co-workers remark about how unpleasant he is, and he is quite uncomfortable. He has a few drinks and finds that the symptoms are gone. Very rapidly, he is drinking heavily again.

CENTRAL NERVOUS SYSTEM STIMULANTS

CNS stimulants affect the body in the opposite manner as do the CNS depressants. These drugs increase respiration, heart rate, motor activity, and alertness. This classification includes highly dangerous, illegal substances such as crack cocaine, medically useful stimulants such as Ritalin, drugs with relatively minor psychoactive effects such as caffeine, and the most deadly drug used, nicotine. The drugs in this classification were mentioned in 34% of the drug abuse-related emergency room episodes in 2007 (Substance Abuse and Mental Health Services Administration, 2010).

Drugs in This Classification

Cocaine (coke, blow, toot, snow) and the freebase or smokeable forms of cocaine (crack, rock, base) are the most infamous of the CNS stimulants. Cocaine is found in the leaves of the coca shrub that grows in South America. The leaves are processed and produce coca paste. The paste is, in turn, processed to form the white hydrochloride salt powder most of you know as cocaine. Of course, before it is sold on the street, it is adulterated or "cut" with substances such as powdered sugar, talc, arsenic, lidocaine, strychnine, or methamphetamine. Crack is produced by mixing the cocaine powder with baking soda and water and heating the solution. The paste that forms is hardened and cut into hard pieces, or rocks. The mixing and heating process removes most of the impurities from the cocaine. The vaporization point is lowered so the cocaine can be smoked, reaching the brain in one heartbeat less than if it is injected. Therefore, crack is a more pure form of cocaine than is cocaine hydrochloride salt powder.

Amphetamines are also CNS stimulants, and one form in particular, methamphetamine, is a major drug of addiction. The amphetamines include Benzedrine (crosstops, black beauties), Methedrine or methamphetamine (crank, meth, crystal), and Dexedrine (dexies). There are also nonamphetamine stimulants with similar properties such as Ritalin and Cylert (used in the treatment of attention deficit-hyperactivity disorder) and Preludin (used in the treatment of obesity). These drugs are synthetics (not naturally occurring), and the amphetamines were widely prescribed in the 1950s and 1960s for weight control.

Some forms of CNS stimulants are available without a prescription and are contained in many substances we use on a regular basis. Caffeine is found in coffee, teas, colas, and chocolate as well as in some over-the-counter products designed to help people stay awake (e.g., No Doz, Alert, Vivarin). Phenylpropanolamine is a stimulant found in diet-control products sold over-the-counter (e.g., Dexatrim). These products are abused by individuals who chronically diet (e.g., anorexics). Pseudoephedrine is a substance in many nasal decongestants. Since it is used in the manufacture of methamphetamine, federal and state laws have been passed to restrict the quantities of these over-the-counter medications that can be purchased.

Although it has mild euphoric properties, nicotine is the highly addictive stimulant drug found in tobacco products. According to the Centers for Disease Control and Prevention (2010b), an estimated 440,000 Americans die each year from smoking-related illnesses. This is more than five times as many deaths as result from alcohol. By a wide margin, nicotine is the most deadly drug we will discuss. Ironically, it is not only legal, it is marketed. We will mention this contradiction in public policy in Chapter 15.

Routes of Administration

With CNS stimulants, every method of administration is possible and utilized. Caffeine is consumed in beverage form, but it is also eaten (e.g., chocolate) or taken in pill form (e.g., No Doz). Nicotine is obviously smoked but can be chewed (chewing tobacco, nicotine gum) or administered through a skin patch. Cocaine and amphetamines can be snorted, smoked, injected, and ingested.

Major Acute and Chronic Effects

As with most of the psychoactive drugs, some of the CNS stimulants (cocaine and methamphetamine) have a recreational use. The purpose is to "get high," or to experience a sense of euphoria. Methamphetamine and cocaine users report a feeling of self-confidence and self-assurance. There is a "rush" that is experienced, particularly when cocaine is smoked and when cocaine and methamphetamine are injected. The high from methamphetamine is generally less intense but longer acting than cocaine.

CNS stimulants result in psychomotor stimulation, alertness, and elevation of mood. There is an increase in heart rate and blood pressure. Performance may be enhanced with increased activity level, one reason why athletes use CNS stimulants. These drugs also suppress appetite and combat fatigue. That's why people who want to lose weight and people who want to stay awake for long periods of time (e.g., truck drivers) will use amphetamines.

The acute effects of CNS stimulants can be dramatic and fatal. These include heart attacks, strokes, seizures, and respiratory depression. However, the results of chronic use cause the most problems. The addictive properties of these drugs are extremely high. Individuals with addictions to cocaine and methamphetamine spend a tremendous amount of money to obtain drugs, and they encounter serious life problems related to their addiction. Also, there is an increased risk of strokes and cardiovascular problems, depression, and suicide in chronic users. Symptoms of paranoid schizophrenia can occur. If cocaine or methamphetamine is snorted, perforation of the nasal septum can occur. Injection of CNS stimulants has the same risks as injecting other drugs (e.g., hepatitis, HIV). Since these drugs suppress appetite, chronic users are frequently malnourished.

If you are smugly saying to yourself that the only CNS stimulant you use is caffeine, see the caffeine-induced disorders that are described in the *DSM-IV-TR* (see Chapter 6). Also, caffeine may precipitate panic attacks in individuals predisposed to panic disorders, and the drug may be detrimental to some heart patients. A woman who is considering having a baby should reduce caffeine intake, and pregnant and breastfeeding women are advised to abstain.

Clearly, the chronic effects of nicotine addiction are damaging to health. The number of health-related problems, deaths, and days of work missed due to the chronic use of tobacco products is astounding.

Overdose

CNS stimulants stimulate the reward center of the brain. The most powerful of these drugs result in the body's not experiencing hunger, thirst, or fatigue. There is no built-in satiation point, so humans can continue using cocaine and methamphetamine until there is no more or they die. Therefore, the compulsion to use, the desire to maintain the high, and the unpleasantness of withdrawal make overdose fairly common. There may be tremors, sweating and flushing, rapid heartbeat (tachycardia), anxiety, insomnia, paranoia, convulsions, heart attack, or stroke. Death from overdose has been widely publicized because it has occurred with some famous movie stars and athletes. However, far more people experience chronic problems from CNS stimulant addictions than from overdose reactions.

Tolerance

There is a rapid tolerance to the pleasurable effects of cocaine and methamphetamine and the stimulating effects of tobacco and caffeine. If you drink five or six cups a day of combinations of coffee, tea, and colas, you probably know this with regard to caffeine. You will find that if you stop using caffeine for a couple of weeks and then start again, the initial doses of caffeine produce a minor "buzz," alertness, and/or restlessness.

The rapid tolerance to the euphoric effects of cocaine and methamphetamine leads to major problems with these drugs. The pleasurable effects are so rewarding, particularly when the drugs are smoked or injected, that the user is prone to compulsively use in an effort to recapture the euphoric effects. When injected or smoked, the effects are enhanced but of relatively short duration. Continual use to achieve the high leads to rapid tolerance. The user is then unable to feel the pleasure but must continue to use the drug to reduce the pain of withdrawal.

A sensitization or reverse tolerance can occur, particularly with cocaine. In this instance, a chronic user with a high tolerance has an adverse reaction (i.e., seizure) to a low dose.

Withdrawal

Unlike the withdrawal from CNS depressants, the withdrawal from these drugs is not medically dangerous. However, it is extremely unpleasant. If you have an addiction to caffeine and want to get a small taste of the withdrawal from CNS stimulants, discontinue your use of caffeine. The symptoms you can expect include a chronic headache, irritability, restlessness, and anxiety. You may have trouble sleeping and concentrating.

The withdrawal from cocaine and methamphetamine is called "crashing." The severe symptoms usually last two to three days and include intense drug craving, irritability, depression, anxiety, and lethargy. However, the depression, drug craving, and an inability to experience pleasure may last for several months as the body chemistry returns to normal. Suicidal ideation and attempts are frequent during this time, as are relapses. Recovering cocaine and methamphetamine addicts can become very discouraged with the slow rate of the lifting of depression, and, therefore, support is very important during this time.

If you have been or are addicted to nicotine, you probably have experienced the unpleasant withdrawal symptoms during attempts to quit (we are assuming that nearly everyone addicted to nicotine has tried to quit or has succeeded). Enhance the severity of your experience dramatically, and you may be able to achieve an empathic understanding of the withdrawal syndrome for cocaine and methamphetamine addicts.

OPIOIDS

The opioids[2] are naturally occurring (opium poppy extracts) and synthetic drugs that are commonly used for their analgesic (pain relief) and cough-suppressing properties. Opium was used by early Egyptian, Greek, and Arabic cultures for the treatment of diarrhea since there is a constipating effect to this drug. Greek and Roman writers such as Homer and Virgil wrote of the sleep-inducing properties of opium, and recreational use of the drug in these cultures did occur. Morphine was isolated from opium in the early 1800s and was widely available without prescription until the early 1900s when the nonmedical use of opioids was banned. Heroin accounted for 10% of drug abuse–related emergency room episodes for illicit drugs in 2007 while other opioids were involved in nearly half of emergency room visits for nonmedical pharmaceuticals (Substance Abuse and Mental Health Services Administration, 2010). The large number of emergency room visits resulting from nonmedical pharmaceuticals reflects the increasing abuse of prescription pain medications such as oxycodone (i.e., OxyContin) and hydrocodone (i.e., Loratab, Vicodin).

Drugs in This Classification

The opioids include opium, codeine, morphine, heroin (smack, horse), and buprenorphine, as well as familiar brand names such as Dilaudid (hydromorphone), OxyContin and Percocet (oxycodone), Loratab and Vicodin (hydrocodone), Darvocet (propoxyphene), Dolophine (methadone) and Demerol (meperidine). Propoxyphene will no longer be available due to adverse side effects.

Routes of Administration

We are familiar with many of these drugs in the pill or liquid form when used for pain relief or cough suppression. When used illicitly, the opioids are often used intravenously, but this is also

---

[2]We will use the term *opioid* to refer to any natural or synthetic drug that has an analgesic (pain relieving) effect similar to that of morphine. The terms *opiate, narcotic,* and *analgesic* are also used to describe this classification of drugs.

a route of administration when these drugs are used medically for pain relief. Heroin, which is used only illicitly in the United States, can be snorted or smoked in addition to the common intravenous method. As the danger of disease from dirty needles has been widely publicized, alternative routes of administration for heroin have become more popular. Opium has been smoked for centuries.

Major Acute and Chronic Effects

Opioids have medically useful effects including pain and cough suppression and constipation. Obviously, there is also a euphoric effect that accounts for the recreational use of these drugs. They can produce nausea and vomiting and itching. A sedating effect occurs, and the pupils of the eyes become constricted.

Methadone or Dolophine is a synthetic opioid that does not have the dramatic euphoric effects of heroin, has a longer duration of action (12 to 24 hours compared with 3 to 6 hours for heroin), and blocks the symptoms of withdrawal when heroin is discontinued. This is the reason for the use of methadone in the treatment of opioid addiction. In the last few years, methadone in pill form is being frequently prescribed for pain relief. Buprenorphine (usually sold under the brand name Suboxone) is now being prescribed in an office setting to treat opioid dependence.

There is an acute danger of death from overdose from injecting opioids, particularly heroin. Also, the euphoric effects of opioids rapidly decrease as tolerance increases, and, as this tolerance occurs, the opioid use is primarily to ward off the withdrawal symptoms.

Compared with the chronic use of CNS depressants, chronic use of the drugs themselves is less dangerous to the body. However, the route of administration and the lifestyle associated with chronic opioid use clearly has serious consequences. Obviously, there is the risk of communicable disease from the intravenous use of opioids and sharing needles. The lifestyle of heroin addicts often includes criminal activity to secure enough money to purchase heroin. Women may participate in prostitution, which adds the associated risks of diseases and violence. Nutrition is frequently neglected. However, those individuals who have been involved in methadone maintenance programs for long periods of time do not experience negative health consequences from the use of methadone (which is taken orally).

Overdose

Death from overdose of injectable opioids (usually heroin) can occur from the direct action of the drug on the brain, resulting in respiratory depression. Death can also occur from an allergic reaction to the drug or to substances used to cut it, possibly resulting in cardiac arrest.

Overdose of other drugs in this classification may include symptoms such as slow breathing rate, decreased blood pressure, pulse rate, temperature, and reflexes. The person may become extremely drowsy and lose consciousness. There may be flushing and itching skin, abdominal pain, and nausea and vomiting.

As abuse of prescription pain medications has skyrocketed, so have overdoses from these drugs. Oxycodone is sold in time-release form, which is crushed and snorted to get a more intense effect. This has resulted in unintentional overdose. In addition, methadone in pill form has been increasingly prescribed for pain relief. However, methadone dissipates from the body very slowly. Therefore, an individual may increase the dosage beyond the recommended level or time between doses and overdose because of the residual methadone in the body from prior doses.

Tolerance

Frequency of administration and dosage of opioids is related to the development of tolerance. Tolerance develops rapidly when the drugs are repeatedly administered but does not develop when there are prolonged periods of abstinence. The tolerance that does develop is to the euphoric, sedative, analgesic, and respiratory effects of the drugs. This tolerance results in the individual's using doses that would kill a nontolerant person. The tolerant individual becomes accustomed to using high doses, which accounts for death due to overdose in long-time opioid users who have been detoxified and then go back to using.

Cross-tolerance to natural and synthetic opioids does occur. However, there is no cross-tolerance to CNS depressants. This fact is important, because the combination of moderate to high doses of opioids and alcohol or other CNS depressants can (and often does) result in respiratory depression and death.

Withdrawal

When these drugs are used on a continuous basis, there is a rapid development of physical dependence. Withdrawal symptoms are unpleasant and uncomfortable but are rarely dangerous. The symptoms are analogous to a severe case of the flu, with running eyes and nose, restlessness, goose bumps, sweating, muscle cramps or aching, nausea, vomiting, and diarrhea. There is significant drug craving. These symptoms rapidly dissipate when opioids are taken, which accounts for relapse when a person abruptly quits on his or her own ("cold turkey"). When the drugs are not available to the dependent individual, the unpleasant withdrawal symptoms also result in participation in criminal activities in order to purchase the drugs.

HALLUCINOGENS

Many of the hallucinogens are naturally occurring and have been used for thousands of years. Some have been (and are currently) used as sacraments in religious rites and have been ascribed with mystical and magical properties. Today, many types of hallucinogens are synthetically produced in laboratories. Some of the hallucinogens became very popular in the 1960s and 1970s, with a drop in use in the 1980s. While there was a resurgence of use from 1992 to 2001 among youth, recent surveys have shown relatively low and stable levels of use (Johnston, O'Malley, Bachman, & Schulenberg, 2010).

Drugs in This Classification

This classification comprises a group of heterogeneous compounds. Although there may be some commonality in terms of effect, the chemical structures are quite different. The hallucinogens we will discuss include LSD (acid, fry), psilocybin (magic mushrooms, shrooms), morning glory seeds (heavenly blue), mescaline (mesc, big chief, peyote), STP (serenity, tranquility, peace), and PCP (angel dust, hog). PCP is used as a veterinary anesthetic, primarily for primates.

Routes of Administration

Hallucinogens are usually swallowed. For example, LSD may be put on a sticker, stamp, or sugar cube. Psilocybin is eaten. However, hallucinogens can also be snorted, smoked, or injected. PCP is often sprinkled on a marijuana joint and smoked.

Major Acute and Chronic Effects

These drugs produce an altered state of consciousness, including altered perceptions of visual, auditory, olfactory, and/or tactile senses and an increased awareness of inner thoughts and impulses. Sensory experiences may cross into one another (e.g., "hearing color"). Common sights and sounds may be perceived as exceptionally intricate and astounding. In the case of PCP, there may be increased suggestibility, delusions, and depersonalization and dissociation. Physiologically, hallucinogens produce a rise in pulse and blood pressure.

A fairly common and well-publicized adverse effect of hallucinogens is the experience of flashbacks. Flashbacks are the recurrence of the effects of hallucinogens long after the drug has been taken. Reports of flashbacks more than five years after taking a hallucinogen have been reported although abatement after several months is more common.

With regard to LSD, there are acute physical effects including a rise in heart rate and blood pressure, higher body temperature, dizziness, and dilated pupils. Mental effects include sensory distortions, dreaminess, depersonalization, altered mood, and impaired concentration. "Bad trips" involve acute anxiety, paranoia, fear of loss of control, and delusions. Individuals with preexisting mental disorders may experience more severe symptoms. With regard to chronic effects, we have already mentioned the rare but frightening experience of flashbacks.

On the other hand, PCP does result in significant adverse effects. Chronic use may result in psychiatric problems including depression, anxiety, and paranoid psychosis. Accidents, injuries, and violence occur frequently.

Overdose

With the exception of PCP, the concept of "overdose" is not applicable to the hallucinogens. "Bad trips" or panic reactions do occur and may include paranoid ideation, depression, undesirable hallucinations, and/or confusion. These are usually managed by providing a calm and supportive environment. An overdose of PCP may result in acute intoxication, acute psychosis, or coma. In the acute intoxication or psychosis, the person may be agitated, confused, and excited, and may exhibit a blank stare and violent behavior. Analgesia (insensibility to pain) occurs that may result in self-inflicted injuries and injuries to others when attempts are made to restrain the individual.

Tolerance

Tolerance to the hallucinogenic properties of these drugs occurs, as well as cross-tolerance between LSD and other hallucinogens. No cross-tolerance to cannabis has been demonstrated. Tolerance to PCP has not been demonstrated in humans (American Psychiatric Association, 2000).

Withdrawal

There is no physical dependence that occurs from the use of hallucinogens, although psychological dependence, including drug craving, does occur.

CANNABINOLS

Marijuana is the most widely used illegal drug. Over 18% of adults in the 18- to 25-year range reported using marijuana in the previous month (Office of Applied Studies, 2010). The earliest references to the drug date back to 2700 B.C. In the 1700s, the hemp plant (*Cannabis sativa*) was grown in the colonies for its fiber, which was used in rope. Beginning in 1926, states began to outlaw the use of marijuana since it was claimed to cause criminal behavior and violence. Marijuana use became popular with mainstream young people in the 1960s. Some states have basically decriminalized possession of small amounts of marijuana although, according to the federal government, it remains a Schedule I drug. Emergency room episodes in which marijuana was mentioned comprised 16% of the total drug abuse-related emergency room visits in 2007 (Substance Abuse and Mental Health Services Administration, 2010).

Drugs in This Classification

The various cannabinols include marijuana (grass, pot, weed, joint, reefer, dube), hashish, charas, bhang, ganja, and sinsemilla. The active ingredient is delta-9-tetrahydrocannabinol (THC). Hashish and charas have a THC content of 7% to 14%; ganja and sinsemilla, 4% to 7%; and bhang and marijuana, 2% to 5%. For simplicity, we will refer to the various forms of cannabinols as "marijuana."

Routes of Administration

Marijuana is usually smoked in cigarette form or pipes. It can also be ingested, normally by baking it in brownies or cookies.

Major Acute and Chronic Effects

Marijuana users experience euphoria; enhancement of taste, touch, and smell; relaxation; increased appetite; altered time sense; and impaired immediate recall. An enhanced perception of the humor of situations or events may occur. The physiological effects of marijuana include increase in pulse rate and blood pressure, dilation of blood vessels in the cornea (which produces bloodshot eyes), and dry mouth. Motor skills and reaction time are slowed.

As you are all aware, marijuana has been and continues to be controversial. Ballot measures in several states have involved marijuana laws. This controversy is related to the facts and myths regarding marijuana's acute and chronic effects. However, the professional community has as many views of the "facts" regarding marijuana as does the general public. While our interpretation of the research may be different than others, we are confident in saying that this issue is not "black and white." Marijuana should clearly not be a Schedule I drug. However, no psychoactive drug is safe. Marijuana can and does result in significant life problems for many people.

Marijuana is certainly not acutely or chronically dangerous when death is the measure of dangerousness. However, the effect on motor skills and reaction time certainly impairs the user's ability to drive a car, boat, plane, or other vehicle.

Chronic use of marijuana does seem to have an adverse effect on lung function, although there is no direct evidence that it causes lung cancer. Although an increase in heart rate occurs, there does not seem to be an adverse effect on the heart. As is the case with CNS depressants, marijuana suppresses the immune system. Chronic marijuana use decreases the male hormone testosterone (as does alcohol) and adversely affects sperm formation. However, no effect on male fertility or sexual potency has been noted. Female hormones are also reduced, and impairment in ovulation has been reported.

Marijuana may be medically useful in reducing nausea and vomiting from chemotherapy, stimulating appetite in AIDS and other wasting-syndrome patients, treating spasticity and nocturnal spasms complicating multiple sclerosis and spinal cord injury, controlling seizures, and managing neuropathic pain. However, further clinical studies are necessary to reach conclusions on the value of marijuana in medical treatment.

For an objective review of the literature on all aspects of marijuana, we recommend *Cannabis Use and Dependence: Public Health and Public Policy* by Hall and Pacula (2003).

Overdose

Overdose is unusual because the normal effects of marijuana are not enhanced by large doses. Intensification of emotional responses and mild hallucinations can occur, and the user may feel "out of control." As with hallucinogens, many reports of overdose are panic reactions to the normal effects of the drug. In individuals with preexisting mental disorders (e.g., schizophrenia), high doses of marijuana may exacerbate symptoms such as delusions, hallucinations, disorientation, and depersonalization.

Tolerance

Tolerance is a controversial area with regard to marijuana. Tolerance does rapidly occur in animals but only with frequent use of high doses in humans (Hanson, Venturelli, & Fleckenstein, 2006). At the least, chronic users probably become accustomed to the effects of the drug and are experienced in administering the proper dosage to produce the desired effects.

Withdrawal

A withdrawal syndrome can be observed in chronic, high-dosage users who abruptly discontinue their use. The symptoms include irritability, restlessness, decreased appetite, insomnia, tremor, chills, and increased body temperature. The symptoms usually last three to five days.

INHALANTS AND VOLATILE HYDROCARBONS

Inhalants and volatile hydrocarbons consist largely of chemicals that can be legally purchased and that are normally used for non-recreational purposes. In addition, this classification includes some drugs that are used legally for medical purposes. As psychoactive drugs, most of these substances are used mainly by young people, particularly in low socioeconomic areas. Since most of these chemicals are accessible in homes and are readily available for purchase, they are easily used as psychoactive drugs by young people who are beginning drug experimentation and by individuals who are unable to purchase other mind-altering substances due to finances or availability.

Drugs in This Classification

The industrial solvents and aerosol sprays that are used for psychoactive purposes include gasoline, kerosene, chloroform, airplane glue, lacquer thinner, acetone, nail polish remover, model cement, lighter fluid, carbon tetrachloride, fluoride-based sprays, and metallic paints. Volatile nitrites are amyl nitrite (poppers), butyl and isobutyl (locker room, rush, bolt, quick silver, zoom). Amyl nitrite has typically been used in the gay community. In addition, nitrous oxide (laughing gas), a substance used by dentists, is also included in this classification.

Route of Administration

As the name of this classification implies, these drugs are inhaled, a method of administration referred to as "huffing" or sniffing. The industrial solvents and aerosol sprays are often poured or sprayed on a rag and put in a plastic bag. The individual then places his or her head in the plastic bag and inhales rapidly and deeply.

Major Acute and Chronic Effects

The solvents and sprays reduce inhibition and produce euphoria, dizziness, slurred speech, an unsteady gait, and drowsiness. Nystagmus (constant involuntary movements of the eyes) may be noted. The nitrites alter consciousness and enhance sexual pleasure. The user may experience giddiness, headaches, and dizziness. Nitrous oxide produces giddiness, a buzzing or ringing in the ears, and a sense that the user is about to pass out.

The most critical acute effect of inhalants is a result of the method of administration, which can result in loss of consciousness, coma, or death from lack of oxygen. Respiratory arrest, cardiac arrhythmia, or asphyxiation may occur. Many of these substances are highly toxic, and chronic use may cause damage to the liver, kidneys, brain, and lungs.

Overdose

Overdose of these substances may produce hallucinations, muscle spasms, headaches, dizziness, loss of balance, irregular heartbeat, and coma from lack of oxygen.

Tolerance

Tolerance does develop to nitrous oxide but does not seem to develop to the other inhalants.

Withdrawal

There does not appear to be a withdrawal syndrome associated with these substances.

ANABOLIC STEROIDS

Anabolic steroids are synthetic drugs that are illicitly used to improve athletic performance and increase muscle mass. These drugs resemble the male sex hormone, testosterone. Although some anabolic steroids are approved for use in the United States for medical purposes, the abuse of these drugs led Congress to pass the Anabolic Steroids Act of 1990. This law regulated the distribution and sale of anabolic steroids and added these drugs to Schedule III of the Controlled Substances Act. In 2010, 1.5% of high school seniors reported steroid use in the previous year (Johnston et al., 2010).

Drugs in This Classification

Anabolic steroids approved in the United States include Depo-Testosterone, Durabolin, Danocrine, and Halotestin. Some veterinary anabolic steroids are illicitly sold for human use and include Finiject 30, Equipoise, and Winstrol. Delatestryl, Testex, and Maxibolan are sold legally only outside of the United States.

Routes of Administration

Anabolic steroids are taken orally or injected. "Stacking" refers to combining oral and injectable steroids.

Major Acute and Chronic Effects

Anabolic steroids are used medically for testosterone replacement and treatment of muscle loss, blood anemia, and endometriosis. However, the abuse of these drugs by athletes and by those who wish to improve their physical appearance is prompted by the effects of anabolic steroids on muscle strength, body mass, and personality. These drugs increase muscle strength, reduce body mass, and increase aggressiveness, competitiveness, and combativeness.

For males, atrophy of testicles, impaired production of sperm, infertility, early baldness, acne, and enlargement of the breasts occurs. In females, there are masculinizing effects including increased facial and body hair, lowered voice, and irregularity or cessation of menses. There is an increased risk of coronary artery disease due to reduced "good" cholesterol (HDL) and increased "bad" cholesterol (LDL). An association has also been established between oral anabolic steroids and jaundice and liver tumors. Mood swings, with periods of unreasonable and uncontrolled anger and violence, have been noted.

Overdose

When used illicitly to improve athletic performance or physical appearance, the dosage is well beyond the therapeutic dose. Although there is no immediate danger of death or serious medical problems from high dosage levels of anabolic steroids, there are serious complications from long-term use (see Major Acute and Chronic Effects).

Tolerance

No evidence of tolerance to anabolic steroids exists.

Withdrawal

Physical and psychological dependence on anabolic steroids does occur, and there is a withdrawal syndrome. The symptoms of withdrawal include depression, fatigue, restlessness, insomnia, loss of appetite, and decreased interest in sex.

CLUB DRUGS

Rather than sharing pharmacological similarities, the drugs that will be discussed in this section are grouped together because of the environment in which they are commonly used. The use of these drugs is primarily by youth and young adults associated with dance clubs, bars, and all-night dance parties ("raves").

It would not make sense to discuss the common characteristics of overdose, tolerance, withdrawal, and acute and chronic effects since the drugs are not related pharmacologically. However, we felt that it was important to reference these drugs as a separate class because of the wide media coverage of club drugs. We will refer to the most appropriate pharmacological classification for each drug, and you can refer to the characteristics in the designated section.

Rohypnol (roofies) is a benzodiazepine (CNS depressant) that is illegal in the United States, but widely prescribed in Europe as a sleeping pill. When used in combination with alcohol, Rohypnol produces disinhibition and amnesia. Rohypnol has become known as the "date rape" drug because of reported instances in which women have been unknowingly given the drug while drinking. When women are sexually assaulted, they cannot easily remember the events surrounding the incident.

MDMA (ecstasy) has the properties of the CNS stimulants and hallucinogens. It is taken in tablet form primarily, but can also be found in powder and liquid forms. It is relatively inexpensive ($10 to $20 per pill) and long lasting. Ecstasy is primarily used by youth and college-age adults. The euphoric effects include rushes of exhilaration and the sensation of understanding and accepting others. Some people experience nausea, and depression may be experienced following use. Deaths have been reported from ecstasy use primarily as a result of severe dehydration from dancing for long periods of time without drinking water. Ecstasy can be used compulsively and become psychologically addictive.

Ketamine (K or special K) is generally considered to be a hallucinogen. It is used as a veterinary anesthetic and is usually cooked into a white powder from its liquid form and snorted. The euphoric effect of ketamine involves dissociative anesthetics or separating perception from sensation. Users report feeling "floaty" or outside their body. Higher doses expand this experience. They may have some numbness in extremities. Ketamine is very dangerous in combination with depressants, since higher doses depress respiration and breathing. Frequent use may lead to mental disorders due to the hallucinogenic properties of the drug. Psychological dependence also occurs in frequent users.

GHB (gamma hydroxybutyrate) is actually a synthetic steroid originally sold over the counter in health food stores as a body-building aid. GHB is usually sold as an odorless liquid that has a slight salty taste. The effects are similar to CNS depressants, with low doses resulting in euphoria, relaxation, and happiness. However, higher doses can cause dizziness, drowsiness, vomiting, muscle spasms, and loss of consciousness. Overdoses can result in coma or death, as can mixing GHB with other CNS depressants such as alcohol. Physical dependence can occur.

Other drugs, such as LSD, PCP, mescaline, and marijuana are sometimes classified as club drugs. However, since these drugs have a wider use, we have discussed them in other drug classifications.

DRUGS USED IN THE TREATMENT OF MENTAL DISORDERS

Mental health professionals will work with clients who are taking a variety of legally prescribed drugs to treat many mental disorders. These drugs generally have little or no euphoric effects and, therefore, are not used for recreational purposes. However, it is certainly important for helping professionals to have some familiarity with the uses and effects of these drugs.

Drugs Used in the Treatment of Psychotic Disorders

Antipsychotic or neuroleptic drugs are used in the treatment of schizophrenia and other psychotic disorders. These major tranquilizers produce psychomotor slowing, emotional quieting, and an indifference to external stimuli. Although these drugs are called "tranquilizers," the effects are not euphoric or pleasant. Therefore, they are not drugs of abuse. The phenothiazines (Thorazine, Stelazine, Prolixin, Mellaril) and nonphenothiazines (Navane, Haldol) control agitation and hallucinations. Disturbed thinking and behavior is reduced. These effects have allowed many schizophrenic individuals to live in noninstitutional settings and to function more effectively. However, if the drugs are discontinued, the psychotic symptoms reappear. The drugs do not produce tolerance or physical or psychological dependence. Acute side effects include a dry mouth and Parkinson-like symptoms such as disordered motor movements, slow motor movements, and underactivity. Chronic effects include repetitive, involuntary movements of the mouth and tongue, trunk, and extremities. Massive overdoses are usually not lethal.

A new generation of antipsychotics is now on the market. These drugs include Risperdal, Zyprexa, Clozaril, Seroquel, and Zeldox. They have fewer side effects than the earlier drugs.

Drugs Used in the Treatment of Affective Disorders

Antidepressant drugs elevate mood, increase physical activity, improve appetite, reduce insomnia, and reduce suicidal ideation in most depressed clients. They are used for the treatment of acute and chronic depression. There are three types of antidepressant drugs. The MAO (monoamine oxidase) inhibitors (Nardil, Parnate) are used infrequently today because these drugs can raise blood pressure if foods with tyramine (cheeses, herring, Chianti wine) are consumed. The tricyclics (Tofranil, Elavil, Sinequan) were widely used as antidepressants until the development of the "second generation" antidepressants (Prozac, Luvox, Paxil, Zoloft). These drugs, although no more effective than the tricyclics, have a more rapid onset of effect and fewer adverse side effects. The tricyclics may take two to three weeks to produce the desired effects, while the newer drugs take about one week. This time difference can be critical with depressed clients. The tricyclics can produce cardiac problems and potentiate the effects of alcohol. Lethal overdoses are also possible. The media has widely publicized claims that Prozac has caused homicidal or suicidal behavior, but no cause-and-effect relationship has been scientifically established. However, these drugs have warnings for adolescents as there has been an established relationship between the use of antidepressants and the risk of suicidality in youth (Hammad, Laughren, & Racoosin, 2006). Second-generation antidepressants have also been used in the treatment of obsessive-compulsive disorder and panic disorders.

Lithium is used in the treatment of bipolar disorder. It is an antimanic, rather than an antidepressant, drug. Clients who take lithium must be closely monitored, since high concentrations can cause muscle rigidity, coma, and death.

The treatment of panic attacks has included antianxiety agents (benzodiazepines) that were discussed in the Central Nervous System Depressants section of this chapter (Librium, Valium, Xanax, Ativan). However, these drugs are dependence producing and are abused. Nonbenzodiazepines that are used to treat panic disorders but are noneuphoric include Atarax, Buspar, and many antidepressants.

Drugs Used in the Treatment of Attention Deficit Disorder

There has been a great deal of attention directed toward children and adults who have attention deficit disorder. This condition may exist with or without hyperactivity and is characterized by distractibility, inability to concentrate, short attention span, and impulsivity. It has been found that Ritalin, Cylert, and amphetamines (e.g., Adderall) reduce many of these symptoms. Ritalin and amphetamines have a rapid onset of effect and a short duration, although these drugs now can be purchased in time-release form so they can be taken once a day. Cylert is longer acting but also takes longer to work. These drugs are CNS stimulants and can be abused. The use of stimulants to control the symptoms of attention deficit disorder has always seemed paradoxical. However, it may be that this disorder is due to unfocused electrical activity in the brain, and the stimulant drugs may improve the ability of the individual to concentrate and focus. Rather than calming the person down, the affected client is simply better able to focus his or her energy, concentrate, and reduce attention to extraneous stimuli. This may also reduce the anxiety that often accompanies attention deficit disorder.

Since these drugs are CNS stimulants, there are the associated side effects of appetite suppression, sleep disruption, and growth disturbance when these drugs are continuously used by preadolescents. A small number of individuals experience lethargy and emotional blunting. If these symptoms occur, the physician should immediately be contacted to adjust the dose or to prescribe a different drug.

A newer drug to treat attention deficit disorder is atomoxetine, marketed as Strattera. This is a nonstimulant drug that does not seem to have abuse potential. This makes the drug desirable for adolescents who may abuse drugs like Ritalin, Cylert, or Adderall. Strattera takes longer to work than drugs such as Ritalin, where the effect is very rapid.

It should also be mentioned that these drugs should not be prescribed to control unruly behavior in children. Attention deficit disorder should be diagnosed only after a careful multidisciplinary assessment. The best protocol to evaluate the efficacy of medication is a double-blind procedure in which neither the school nor parent is aware when a placebo or active drug has been taken. Behavior should be observed at school and at home, and the case manager can then determine whether medication will be helpful.

There has been speculation that children with attention deficit-hyperactivity disorder (ADHD) who are treated with stimulant drugs would be more likely to develop problems with alcohol or other drugs later in life. However, in a meta-analysis of studies, Wilens, Faraone, Biederman, and Gunawardene (2003) found that ADHD children treated with stimulant drugs are *less* likely to develop substance abuse problems later in life than ADHD children who do not take medication.

MyCounselingLab™

Go to Topic 2: *The Major Substances of Abuse and the Body* in the MyCounselingLab™ site (www.MyCounselingLab.com) for *Substance Abuse: Information for School Counselors, Social Workers, Therapists, and Counselors,* Fifth Edition, where you can:

- Find learning outcomes for *The Major Substances of Abuse and the Body* along with the national standards that connect to these outcomes.
- Complete Assignments and Activities that can help you more deeply understand the chapter content.
- Apply and practice your understanding of the core skills identified in the chapter with the Building Counseling Skills unit.
- Prepare yourself for professional certification with a Practice for Certification quiz.
- Connect to videos through the Video and Resource Library.

Summary

- The federal Controlled Substances Act classifies drugs into five schedules based on the addictive potential and medical uses of the drug.
- Psychoactive drugs mimic natural, pleasurable behaviors by stimulating neurotransmitters in the reward center of the brain.
- The classifications of drugs include central nervous system depressants (alcohol, minor tranquilizers), central nervous system stimulants (cocaine, methamphetamine), opioids (heroin, pain pills), hallucinogens (LSD, magic mushrooms), cannabinols (marijuana), inhalants and volatile hydrocarbons, anabolic steroids, and club drugs (ecstasy).
- Drugs are used to treat various mental disorders such as psychotic disorders, affective disorders (depression, anxiety), and attention deficit-hyperactivity disorder.

Additional Reading

Abadinsky, H. (2008). *Drug abuse: An introduction* (7th ed.). Chicago: Nelson-Hall.

Hanson, G., Venturelli, P. J., & Fleckenstein, A. E. (2008). *Drugs and society* (10th ed.). Boston: Jones and Bartlett.

Inaba, D. S., & Cohen, W. E. (2007). *Uppers, downers, all arounders: Physical and mental effects of psychoactive drugs* (6th ed.). Ashland, OR: Cinemed.

Inciardi, J. A., & McElrath, K. (eds.) (2007). *The American drug scene: An anthology* (5th ed.). Los Angeles: Roxbury.

Julien, R. M., Advokat, C. D., & Comaty, J. E. (2011). *A primer of drug action: A comprehensive guide to the actions, uses, and side effects of psychoactive drugs* (11th ed.). New York: Worth.

Maisto, S. A., Galizio, M., & Connors, G. J. (2008). *Drug use and abuse* (6th ed.). Belmont, CA: Wadsworth.

Internet Resources

Comprehensive Drug Abuse Prevention and Control Act
usdoj.gov/dea/pubs/csa.html

Facts about specific drugs
nida.nih.gov/drugpages.html

Science of addiction
drugabuse.gov/scienceofaddiction/

Drug use surveys

National Household Survey on Drug Use and Health
oas.samhsa.gov/nsduh.htm

Monitoring the Future
monitoringthefuture.org/index.html

Further Discussion

1. Review the three case examples at the beginning of the chapter. From the information provided, what drugs or drug classifications do you think each person is struggling with?

2. Do you agree with the classification of marijuana as a Schedule I drug? Why or why not?

3. Compare the monthly rate of use of alcohol for minors to the monthly rate of use of illicit drugs for 8th, 10th, and 12th graders (from the Monitoring the Future website). What conclusions do you reach and what are the implications?

4. Which classification of drugs is the most dangerous in your opinion? What are the public policy implications of your view?

Chapter 3

Models of Addiction

CASE EXAMPLES

❶ Bill, a bartender, was diagnosed as alcoholic at the age of 50. He was drinking over a fifth of whiskey a day. Of his own volition, he went to a treatment program that used aversive conditioning techniques (see Chapter 8). At the time he entered treatment, his liver functioning was at about 20% of normal. In other words, if he had continued to drink much longer, he would have died. After completing the program, Bill returned to his job as a bartender. He never attended an AA meeting or returned to the treatment program for follow-up. Bill once said, "I'll drink myself to death rather than go back to that (treatment center) place." In 19 years, he never had a slip or relapse. Bill finally died of lung cancer, because he could not quit smoking.

❷ Loretta, a 30-year-old woman, was on probation for possession and distribution of methamphetamine. She lived with a man who used drugs and who was physically abusive to her and to her daughter. Another daughter had been removed from her custody. She lost her license to work in her profession due to her felony conviction. After her "boyfriend" was sent to prison, she found a job and a new place to live and was on the road to regaining custody of her other daughter. However, a random urinalysis by her probation officer came up dirty, and she was placed in an in-patient treatment program as an alternative to prison. Loretta lost her job, home, and custody of her children. Before this relapse, she had been sober for six months and was attending NA meetings.

❸ Marvin, a 63-year-old man, had been a heavy drinker for 40 years. He was retired and relatively healthy. He developed a respiratory illness that required prolonged use of a medication that affected liver functioning. Marvin was told that he could not drink alcohol while taking the medication and that he was to take the medication for one year. His doctor suggested that his withdrawal from alcohol be medically supervised due to his prolonged and heavy use. Marvin rejected this suggestion, discontinued his alcohol use, and has been clean and sober with no slips for 10 years. He has never attended an AA meeting or any other form of treatment.

❹ Hector, a 30-year-old man, began using alcohol and other drugs at the age of 13. He was in street gangs, involved in crimes, and incarcerated as a juvenile. Hector was placed in a drug treatment program at the age of 16 and attended NA meetings after treatment. He remained sober for about six months, at which time he again began to use cocaine, marijuana, and alcohol. At age 23, he married, had a child, and discontinued his heavy use. He continues to use alcohol and marijuana on an irregular basis. Hector is a successful officer in a small company, although he cannot read or write at a functional level.

❺ Rebecca is currently 43 years old and has been sober for seven years. She reported that her husband expressed concern about her level of alcohol use prior to their marriage and that she "just decided to stop." Rebecca did not go through any treatment program, nor has she attended any AA meetings. She says that she has problems doing anything on a moderate basis, and, as a result, she has to monitor her eating behavior and work habits. Rebecca says, "I can't eat just a couple of M&Ms. If I start, I'll keep eating until they are all gone." She likes to drink nonalcoholic beer and wine, saying "It makes me feel like a grown-up."

❻ Salvador is in his mid-60s. When he was in his 20s, he was addicted to heroin. Salvador was arrested for distribution and possession of drugs and spent some time in federal prison. After being released, he entered a faith-based, residential treatment program and has never used heroin again. Salvador drinks alcohol moderately.

In January of 2011, a man named Jared Lee Loughner went to a public event held by Congressional Representative Gabrielle Giffords in Tucson, Arizona. Mr. Loughner opened fire with a semi-automatic gun, seriously wounding Representative Giffords and killing six people, including a federal judge and a 9-year-old girl. In the days and weeks following this horrible event, speculation regarding Mr. Loughner and the reason why he committed this act ran rampant. Mental health professionals thought he was suffering from paranoid schizophrenia. Law enforcement described him as a cold-blooded killer. Others believed that he was driven by political motivations. Some pundits focused on his parents and wondered if they were to blame. There were even some religious leaders who thought he was possessed by the devil. Whatever explanation makes the most sense probably depends on a person's values and beliefs, formal and informal training, and experience. However, it is important to critically examine the explanations of the behavior of someone such as Jared Lee Loughner, since different explanations have different implications for the proper method to deal with him. For example, if you believe that he is possessed by evil spirits, there may be a spiritual method to treat him (i.e., exorcism). If you accept the explanation that he is a cold-blooded killer (i.e., a sociopath), then the appropriate method may be firm punishment for his actions. If his behavior is due to a traumatic childhood, he may deserve our sympathy and be in need of therapeutic interventions. Finally, if Loughner's behavior is due to a serious mental illness caused by a chemical imbalance, then he is not responsible for his behavior and may need medication to manage his condition.

You can see that values and beliefs play a role in whichever explanation you accept. If you believe in evil spirits, this explanation may appeal to you. Formal and informal training will have an effect, since you may have taken some courses in sociology or social psychology and been taught that traumatic childhood experiences are related to violent behavior in adulthood. Maybe you work in law enforcement and have directly seen the victims of brutality, and, from these experiences, have come to believe that the perpetrators must be lacking in conscience to commit such crimes.

However, all of these explanations for the abnormal behavior of Jared Lee Loughner may have some validity. He may have a spiritual deficit, lack a conscience in the manner in which most of us understand this concept, be influenced by his childhood experiences, and have some form of physiological abnormality. The "amount" of explanation of his behavior may not be equally divided among these factors (they may not have equal weight in explaining Loughner's behavior), and determining the most appropriate course of action might depend on many different variables. For example, the brutality of the crime, Loughner's lack of remorse, and his potential for future violence may lead to a decision to incarcerate a person such as Loughner, no matter what the "true" explanations are for his behavior.

The AOD field has also been characterized by a variety of explanations for the same behavior. This is certainly not unusual in the mental health or medical field. However, the fervor and inflexibility with which some proponents of certain models of addiction adhere to their models has produced controversy in this field. Furthermore, the use of AOD interests and elicits extensive involvement from the legal system, business, government, the religious community, as well as from the medical and mental health fields. The differing goals and orientations of these disciplines have resulted in sharp differences regarding the explanation of problematic use of AOD. Consequently, the manner in which those people with AOD problems are dealt has also been a controversial issue. We will discuss some of the various "models" or explanations of addiction, giving particular attention to the popular "disease concept." Also, we will discuss some cases that illustrate that one explanation alone for addictive behavior may be insufficient.

AT A GLANCE

Moral Model: AOD use is a choice; addiction is a symptom of moral deficiency and/or lack of willpower.

Sociocultural Models: Cultural, ethnic, religious and environmental conditions are causal factors in addiction.

Psychological Models: Addiction is a secondary symptom of underlying psychological disorders; AOD use is learned and reinforced behavior.

Disease Model: Addiction is a primary, chronic, and progressive disease, probably caused by a genetic predisposition.

Biopsychosocial Model: Addiction is the result of multiple, interacting variables, the strength of which vary between individuals.

THE MORAL MODEL

The moral model explains addiction as a consequence of personal choice. Individuals are viewed as making decisions to use AOD in a problematic manner and as being capable of making other choices. This model has been adopted by certain religious groups as well as by the legal system. Drunkenness is viewed as sinful behavior by some religious groups and the use of alcohol is prohibited by certain religions (e.g., the Mormon Church). From this perspective, religious or spiritual intervention would be necessary to change behavior. Years ago, we conducted an AOD workshop for clergy, and the moral model was strongly advocated by many of the members who were present. Many saw acceptance of a particular religious persuasion as the necessary step to overcome AOD problems.

A 1988 Supreme Court decision found that crimes committed by an alcoholic were willful misconduct and not the result of a disease (Miller & Hester, 2003). Certainly, the manner in which states deal with drunk driving violations may relate to the moral model. In states where violators are not assessed for AOD problems and are not diverted to treatment, the moral model guides policy. If excessive alcohol use is the result of personal choice, then violators should be punished.

The moral model is a common way that the general public has of conceptualizing alcoholics and addicts. For example, when you see a homeless person who is obviously affected by alcohol or other drugs, do you experience disgust, laugh at him or her, or express a moral judgment? Furthermore, as William White (2001), a well-known recovery advocate, notes, the language in the field is related to the moral model:

> Of all the words that have entered the addiction/treatment vocabulary, "abuse" is one of the most ill-chosen and . . . pernicious. . . . to suggest that the addict mistreats the object of his or her deepest affection is a ridiculous notion. Alcoholics do not "abuse" alcohol . . . nor do addicts "abuse" drugs.
>
> Addicts, more than anyone, treat these potions with the greatest of devotion and respect. . . . references to alcohol/drug/substance "abuse" drip with centuries of religious and moral censure. (p. 5)

As White and other recovery advocates have noted, the moral model of addiction has contributed to creating a stigma about addiction and addicts. This stigma may cause barriers to getting help. For example, if you are having problems with alcohol or other drugs and if those around you believe that alcoholics and addicts are weak-willed and/or immoral, then you are more likely to try to solve the problem yourself or hide it than you would be to seek outside help.

SOCIOCULTURAL MODELS OF ADDICTION

While the moral model explains addiction as a matter of personal choice caused by spiritual or character deficiencies, other explanations of addiction focus on factors that are external to the individual, such as cultural, religious, family, and peer variables or psychological factors. With regard to sociocultural factors, Westermeyer (1999) conducted a thorough meta-analysis of the literature in this area. He defined populations at risk for addiction in special sociocultural settings such as youth in industrial societies, immigrants and refugees, poverty and affluence, and child rearing and culture.

According to Westermeyer (1999), adolescence in the mid-1990s developed as a period of self-doubt and social anxiety as a result of an industrialized society where adolescents had little to contribute. In comparison, adolescence in an agrarian society did not exist as it does today. Children worked when they were physically able. For the adolescent in an industrial society, AOD helped alleviate self-doubt and anxiety while enhancing social interaction. Obviously, not all adolescents in our industrial society became addicts but this could help explain the initiation of heavy AOD use among some members of this group.

Contrary to what might be expected, immigrants and refugees have low rates of substance abuse following relocation but rates begin to rise after several years (Westermeyer, 1999). In some instances, substances abused in the country of origin are introduced to the United States. For example, opium smoking was virtually nonexistent in the country until it was introduced by Southeast Asian immigrants. In other cases, younger immigrants begin to use and abuse substances that were not common in the country of origin to fit in and because they and their families may not be knowledgeable about the dangers of these unfamiliar substances.

Westermeyer (1999) noted that both poverty and affluence can impact substance use and abuse. It is quite understandable how poverty can lead to substance abuse as a way of coping with the stress of everyday life. In addition, participation in illicit drug dealing may be one of the most readily available methods to make money without education or training. However, rising disposable income is also associated with increasing AOD use. The reasons are not clear, although one would expect that people who are deterred from purchasing AOD when money is tight feel greater freedom to indulge when money is sufficient to cover basic needs.

People who are involved in cultural and religious groups that discourage or prohibit AOD use experience a low rate of addiction as long as they remain in the group. A low rate of addiction is also the case among groups that have culturally sanctioned moderate AOD use that begins in childhood or early adolescence. Obviously, cultures and families who model and support heavy AOD use are much more likely to have children who develop AOD problems.

PSYCHOLOGICAL MODELS OF ADDICTION

While sociocultural or external factors have been used to explain addiction, psychological explanations of addiction also exist. It is beyond the goals of this text to discuss each of these theories, but we will spend some time on the most widely held psychological explanations of addiction. Perhaps the most accepted view, particularly by those outside the addiction field, is that the problematic use of alcohol and other drugs is secondary to some other psychological problem or condition. The primary psychological problem causes emotional pain, and alcohol and other drugs serve to temporarily relieve this pain. For example, a woman was sexually molested as a child by a relative. She does not tell anyone, or her story is not believed, and she does not receive any assistance. The woman experiences anger, guilt, embarrassment, and anxiety as a result of the experience and gravitates toward alcohol and other drugs to relieve these uncomfortable feelings. Another example is the person who suffers from endogenous depression and self-medicates with stimulants to relieve the constant symptoms of depression.

Related to the view that AOD problems are secondary to other psychological problems is the question about whether an alcoholic or addictive personality exists. Clearly, alcoholics and drug addicts who seem to be free of any identified psychological problems prior to their problematic use patterns do exist. Proponents of psychological explanations of addiction believe that there may be an "addictive personality" that could be identified and that would explain why individuals with AOD addictions often have problems with nondrug addictive behavior (e.g., gambling, food, work, sex) following successful recovery from their drug of choice. However, this effort to identify the "addictive personality" has largely been unsuccessful. As Miller (2003) noted, ". . . people with alcohol dependence appear to be about as variable in personality as the general population" (p. 133).

Social learning theory is another psychological theory that has been used to explain addictive behavior. As a leading proponent of this theory, Alan Marlatt, has stated, "From a social-learning perspective, addictive behaviors represent a category of 'bad habits' including such behaviors as problem drinking, smoking, substance abuse, overeating, compulsive gambling, and so forth." (Marlatt, 1985, p. 9). In this conceptualization, drug use is initiated by environmental stressors or modeling by others and is reinforced by the immediate effects of the drug on the feelings generated by the stressor(s) or by acknowledgment or recognition from role models with perceived status. One example would be the case of the sexually molested woman we discussed earlier. From a social learning viewpoint, this woman used alcohol and other drugs to avoid the unpleasant emotions generated by her molestation (environmental stressor). Since alcohol or other drug use provides immediate (although temporary) relief from these negative feelings, its use is reinforced. Another typical example is the individual who uses alcohol to "unwind" after a stressful day at work. Since tolerance to alcohol develops, over time this person must use an increasing amount of alcohol to experience the reinforcing effects of alcohol on tension. A "bad habit" is developed.

The first author has a vivid recollection of his initial experience with alcohol and how modeling contributed to this experience and subsequent alcohol use. A wide variety of alcohol was available in his house, and he saw it used daily with few observed negative consequences. One night when he was 12, he was alone at home and began experimenting with a variety of alcoholic beverages. He became quite ill. Although his parents were upset, they also talked and laughed somewhat about their first experiences with becoming sick from alcohol. He also received a lot of attention from his friends when he told them about the incident. Therefore, in spite of some negative consequences (nausea and parental anger), he received sufficient positive reinforcement to increase the probability of repeated use.

In a social learning model, the sociocultural factors we discussed play a role in determining what type of drug is used, when it is used, and how it is used. For example, social use of alcohol may be acceptable, but drinking alone may be perceived as deviant. Snorting or smoking drugs may be within the behavior parameters of a social group, but intravenous use of drugs may result in ostracism. Furthermore, the psychological state of the person is also important. For example, if a child sees the parents using alcohol excessively in social situations, the child may be more likely to see drug use as acceptable in a social situation as a means of creating social comfort and fun. In contrast, imagine that the father in a family isolates himself and drinks in response to negative emotions. The child may see drug use as the appropriate reaction to negative emotions. The psychological state of the individual would be important, since social discomfort might elicit the desire for alcohol or other drugs in the first example, while negative emotions would elicit this desire in the second example.

Eventually, as the individual uses more and more, a physiological state of dependence occurs, and, consequently, he or she experiences withdrawal symptoms if the drug is removed. The use of the drug to relieve withdrawal symptoms is highly reinforcing, since an immediate and effective reduction or elimination of symptoms occurs. The social learning model of addiction has been widely used in the development of relapse prevention strategies, a topic that will be discussed in detail in Chapter 9.

Disease Concept of Addiction

This popular and controversial model of addiction is credited to E. M. Jellinek, who presented a comprehensive disease model of alcoholism (Jellinek, 1960) (see Figure 3.1 depicting Jellinek's Curve). This model has become an implicit component of the Alcoholics Anonymous and Narcotics Anonymous programs, as well as a guiding model for many treatment programs. The World Health Organization acknowledged alcoholism as a medical problem in 1951, and the American Medical Association declared that alcoholism was a treatable illness in 1956. Following Jellinek's work, the American Psychiatric Association began to use the term *disease* to describe alcoholism in 1965, and the American Medical Association followed in 1966. As with many concepts and theoretical models in the addiction field, the disease concept was originally applied to alcoholism and has been generalized to addiction to other drugs.

The disease of addiction is viewed as a primary disease. That is, it exists in and of itself and is not secondary to some other condition. This is in contrast to the psychological models discussed earlier in which addictive behavior is seen as secondary to some psychological condition. In Jellinek's (1952) own words:

> The aggressions, feelings of guilt, remorse, resentments, withdrawal, etc., which develop in the phases of alcohol addiction, are largely consequences of the excessive drinking . . . these reactions to excessive drinking—which have quite a neurotic appearance—give

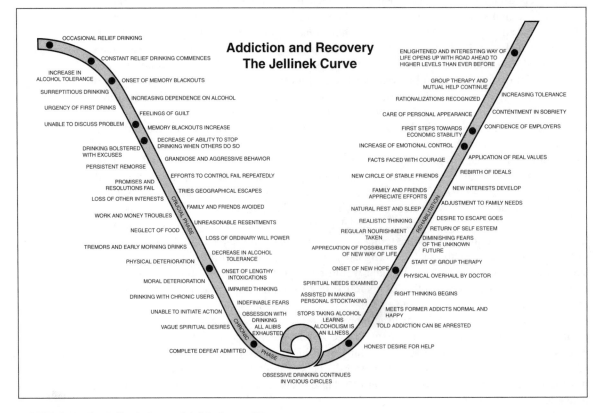

FIGURE 3.1 The Jellinek Curve of Addiction and Recovery.

the impression of an "alcoholic personality," although they are secondary behaviors superimposed over a large variety of personality types. . . . (p. 682)

Jellinek (1952) also described the progressive stages of the disease of alcoholism and the symptoms that characterize each stage. The early stage, or prodromal phase, is characterized by an increasing tolerance to alcohol, blackouts, sneaking and gulping drinks, and guilt feelings about drinking and related behaviors. The next stage, the middle or crucial phase, is defined by a loss of control over drinking, personality changes, a loss of friends and jobs, and a preoccupation with protecting the supply of alcohol. The issue of "loss of control" has come to be a central defining characteristic of alcoholism and one of the more controversial aspects of the disease concept. We will examine this issue when discussing criticisms of the disease concept. The late stage, or chronic phase, is characterized by morning drinking, violations of ethical standards, tremors, and hallucinations.

It is important to conceptualize these stages as progressive. In other words, the stages proceed in sequence and, in the disease model of addiction, are not reversible. Therefore, an individual does not go from the middle stage back to the early stage of alcoholism. The rate at which this progression occurs depends upon factors such as age, drug of choice, gender, and physiological predisposition (Royce, 1989). For example, adolescents progress more rapidly than adults, females faster than males, and users of stimulants more quickly than alcohol users (Royce, 1989). Proponents of the disease concept also do not believe that the progression of addiction disease is affected by a period of sobriety, no matter how long the period of sobriety lasts. As David Ohlms (1995), a physician, has stated:

> Let's say that Jack or Jane stops drinking. Maybe because of some formal treatment: maybe he or she just goes on the wagon, and there is a prolonged period of sobriety for, say, 10 or 15 or even 25 years. . . . then for some reason, . . . Jack or Jane decides that they can drink again, and tries to return to the normal, social, controlled type of drinking that any nonalcoholic can get away with. But poor alcoholic Jack or Jane can't. Within a short period of time, usually within 30 days, the symptoms that the alcoholic will show are the same symptoms showed when drinking was stopped 25 years before. And usually worse. It's as if the alcoholic hadn't had that 25 years of sobriety, as if they meant nothing. An alcoholic cannot stay sober for awhile and then start over and have early symptoms of alcoholism. (p. 5)

Consistent with this concept (that the individual with addictive disease does not reverse the progression of the disease even with a prolonged period of sobriety) is the notion that addictive disease is chronic and incurable. That is, if an individual has this disease, it never goes away, and no drug or other treatment method will allow the alcoholic or addict to use again without the danger of a return to problematic use. One implication of this notion is that the only justifiable goal for the alcoholic or addict is abstinence, which is the stance of Alcoholics Anonymous. Furthermore, the idea that addiction is chronic and incurable is the underlying rationale for alcoholics and addicts who are maintaining sobriety for referring to themselves as "recovering" as opposed to "recovered" or "cured" (Royce, 1989).

In addition to the idea that abstinence must be the goal for those with addictive disease, other implications of the disease concept also exist. First, if addictive disease is progressive, chronic, and incurable, then it is logical to assume that a person with this condition who does not enter "recovery" will eventually die. Death occurs as a result of accidents or the physical effects of alcohol and other drugs over time. For example, consider the individual who, after many years of heavy drinking, develops a liver disease. Eventually, he dies of liver failure. Is the cause of death liver failure or alcoholism? In the disease concept of addiction, these deaths are the result of untreated addiction.

A further implication of the disease concept of addiction is that, if a person has this disease and, for example, the drug of choice of the person is alcohol, the person will continue to exhibit all the symptoms of the disease if he or she discontinues the use of alcohol and begins to use some other drug. This is true no matter what the drug of choice is. As Royce (1989) stated, "We mentioned the recovered alcoholics who relapse when given a painkiller by the dentist and have seen long-recovered alcoholics whose doctor prescribed tranquilizers after a mild heart attack relapse into alcoholic drinking within three weeks and death in six months" (p. 132). This phenomenon is not restricted to alcohol. "Based on extensive clinical experience, use of any psychoactive drug will usually lead back to use of the primary drug or addiction to the secondary drug (drug switching). I believe the only safe path to follow is complete abstinence from all psychoactive drugs" (McCarthy, 1988, p. 29).

Evidence to Support the Disease Concept

The evidence to support the disease concept is based on the similarity of alcoholism and drug addiction to other chronic diseases and on research on the brain chemistry and brain changes in addicts. McLellan, Lewis, O'Brien, and Kleber (2000) reviewed the literature on chronic illnesses, such as diabetes, asthma, and hypertension, and compared the characteristics of these diseases to addiction. They found that the genetic heritability, established by examining rates of diseases in identical versus fraternal twins, was very similar for alcoholism and drug addiction compared to the other chronic illnesses. In addition, response to treatment is similar. Left untreated, the condition of most alcoholics and drug addicts becomes worse. Remission is unusual. This also occurs with diabetes, asthma, and hypertension. McLellan et al. (2000) also showed that the percentages of clients who comply with treatment and the relapse rates of addiction and other chronic illnesses are the same. Addiction, diabetes, asthma, and hypertension are all conditions in which there is no "cure." However, all these problems can be managed through proper treatment, and this treatment must be followed for life.

McLellan et al. (2000) also discuss the issue of the "voluntary" nature of alcohol and other drug use. Again, they compare the choice to use alcohol and other drugs to other chronic illnesses. For example, diet, physical activity, and stress level are all factors affecting hypertension. These factors are all within voluntary control. However, what is not in voluntary control is the person's physiological response to these factors, and the physiological response is strongly influenced by genetic factors. Therefore, addiction is similar to other chronic diseases in that the management of the condition requires voluntary treatment compliance. However, the development of the disease is not due to choice, but to factors beyond voluntary control.

In addition, the National Institute on Drug Abuse (NIDA) has funded a great deal of research on the neuroscience of addiction. For example, Alan Leshner (2000), former director of NIDA, stated:

Researchers have already identified some of the changes involved in two of the key phenomena associated with addiction: drug tolerance and drug craving. . . . we now know that drugs significantly increase the availability of dopamine, a neurotransmitter that activates the brain's pleasure circuits. When cells are exposed to repeated surges of dopamine due to chronic drug abuse, they may eventually become less responsive to dopamine signals. . . . As for drug craving . . . researchers have shown that it is related to widespread alterations in brain activity, especially to changes in the nucleus accumbens area of the forebrain. (p. 1)

Critics of the Disease Concept

As we said earlier, the disease concept is controversial and not without critics. For example, "because the majority of the treatment programs are based on the disease concept of alcoholism, their lobbying, public relations, and advertising efforts inevitably propagate the disease theme" (Fingarette, 1988, p. 23). Probably, the two most famous critics are Stanton Peele and Herbert Fingarette, both of whom have written books (Fingarette, 1988; Peele, 1989) as well as articles disputing the disease concept of addiction. Some of their arguments will be summarized here.

Since the disease concept is widely attributed to Jellinek, much criticism has been directed at his research, which was the basis for his conclusions about the disease concept. Jellinek's data were gathered from questionnaires distributed to AA members through its newsletter, *The Grapevine*. Of 158 questionnaires returned, 60 were discarded because members had pooled and averaged their responses. Also, the study used no questionnaires from women. Jellinek himself acknowledged that his data were limited. Therefore, one might wonder why Jellinek's concept of the disease of alcoholism received such widespread acceptance. One reason is that the disease concept is consistent with the philosophy of AA, which is by far the largest organized group dedicated to help for alcoholics.

Furthermore, Fingarette (1988) accuses the alcohol industry itself of contributing to the public perception of alcoholism as a disease:

> By acknowledging that a small minority of the drinking population is susceptible to the disease of alcoholism, the industry can implicitly assure consumers that the vast majority of people who drink are *not* at risk. This compromise is far preferable to both the old temperance commitment to prohibition, which criminalized the entire liquor industry, and to newer approaches that look beyond the small group diagnosable as alcoholics to focus on the much larger group of heavy drinkers who develop serious physical, emotional, and social problems. (p. 27, italics in original)

The progressive nature of addiction has also been criticized. George Vaillant (1983), a proponent of the disease concept, has suggested that the stages of alcoholism proposed by Jellinek do not follow an inevitable progression:

> The first stage is heavy "social" drinking. . . . This stage can continue asymptomatically for a lifetime; or because of a change of circumstances or peer group it can reverse to a more moderate pattern of drinking; or it can "progress" into a pattern of alcohol abuse. . . . At some point in their lives, perhaps 10–15 percent of American men reach this second stage. Perhaps half of such alcohol abusers either return to asymptomatic (controlled) drinking or achieve stable abstinence. In a small number of such cases . . . such alcohol abuse can persist intermittently for decades with minor morbidity and even become milder with time. (p. 309)

Similarly, Royce (1989), in describing the patterns and symptoms of alcoholism, stated, "Even when progression occurs, it does not follow a uniform pattern. The steps may be reversed in order, or some steps may be omitted. Symptoms progress, too; something that was minor in an early stage may appear later in a different form or to a greater degree. . . . Rate of progression varies also" (p. 89). As does Vaillant, Royce takes a favorable position toward the concept of addiction as a disease.

As we have seen, some of those with sympathetic views toward the disease model of addiction have recognized that the concept of a rigid and inevitable progression of stages is not consistent with reality in working with individuals with AOD problems. However, the issue of "loss of control" has been a more contentious one. As Fingarette (1988) stated, loss of control may be "the central premise of the classic disease concept of alcoholism" (p. 31). Certainly, the first step of the Twelve Steps of Alcoholics Anonymous implies this loss of control: "We admitted that we were powerless over alcohol—that our lives had become unmanageable" (Alcoholics Anonymous World Services, 2009, p. 5).

Several arguments have been advanced to dispute the notion of loss of control. Fingarette (1988) pointed out that if alcoholics lack control only after first consuming alcohol, then they should have no difficulty abstaining. Obviously, however, alcoholics do have difficulty abstaining. If loss of control exists before the first drink (which would explain the difficulty in abstaining), it implies a difficulty in exercising self-control or willpower, which is a much different model of addiction. Furthermore, experimental studies have demonstrated that alcoholics do exert control over their drinking and that variables such as the amount of effort to get alcohol, the environment in which drinking occurs, the belief about what is being consumed, rewards, and the like influence how much is consumed by an alcoholic (Fingarette, 1988; Peele, 1989). In one classic study, Marlatt, Demming, and Reid (1973) divided alcoholics into four groups. One group believed that they were taste-testing three brands of a vodka-tonic beverage when they were actually drinking tonic water only. A second group believed that they were taste-testing tonic water only, when they were actually drinking vodka and tonic. The third group was correctly told they were drinking a vodka-tonic beverage, and the fourth group was correctly told they were drinking tonic water only. The results showed that it was the alcoholic's belief about what they were drinking that determined the amount they drank and not the actual alcohol content of the beverage they consumed. The alcoholics who expected tonic and got alcohol drank an almost identical amount to those alcoholics who expected and got tonic. Both of these groups drank considerably less than the groups who expected alcohol, and the alcoholics who received and expected alcohol drank nearly the same amount as those alcoholics who expected alcohol but got tonic.

Defenders of the disease concept point out that "experimenters took too literally the idea that one drink always means getting drunk," and "Many research projects set out to disprove the 'one drink' hypothesis in laboratory or hospital settings so artificial and with criteria so wooden that nobody with real experience in alcoholism could take the results seriously" (Royce, 1989, p. 135). Loss of control has been modified to mean that the alcoholic or addict cannot predict the situations in which he or she will exercise control and the situations in which he or she will lose control. Therefore, this loss of predictability is thought to define the alcoholic or addict. Fingarette's (1988) response is that "This new approach to loss of control so emasculates the concept that it becomes useless in explaining or predicting drinking behavior" (p. 44).

Advantages of the Disease Concept

Perhaps the greatest advantage to the articulation that addiction is a disease has been to remove the moral stigma attached to addiction and to replace it with an emphasis on treatment of an illness. We do not punish a person for having a disease; we provide assistance. In a more functional sense, defining addiction as a disease has also resulted in treatment coverage by insurance companies. Using medical terminology to describe addiction has also led to greater interest in scientific research. Few medical scientists would be interested in investigating the physiological correlates of a lack of willpower or to a moral deficiency. For the individual who has problems with alcohol or other drugs (and for the family as well), the concept of a disease removes much of the stigma and associated embarrassment, blame, and guilt. You would not feel guilty if you were diagnosed with diabetes and, therefore, a person with addictive disease need not feel guilty for having this disease. As we have said, people who believe that addiction is due to a lack of willpower or to a moral deficiency may avoid treatment, since the admission of the need for help is an admission that some character flaw exists. Therefore, an acceptance of the disease concept may make it easier for some people to enter treatment. Another advantage of the disease concept is that it is clearly understandable to people and provides an explanatory construct for the differences in their alcohol and other drug-taking behavior compared with others. To reuse the analogy with diabetes, people with diabetes clearly understand that they cannot use certain foods in the same manner as those who do not have diabetes. If they do, there will be certain predictable consequences. Knowledge about the disease allows the alcoholic or addict to understand that he or she is physiologically different from others. In the same way that it may be unwise for the diabetic to eat a hot fudge sundae (in spite of the fact that friends may do so without consequences), the alcoholic learns that it would be unwise to drink (in spite of the fact that friends may do so without consequences). Finally, the disease concept has a logical treatment objective that follows from its precepts: abstinence. If you have a physiological condition that results in severe consequences when alcohol or other drugs are used, you can avoid these consequences by abstaining from alcohol or other drugs. If you attempt to use moderately, you will eventually lose control, progress through predictable stages, and suffer the consequences. Since most individuals who seek treatment for alcohol or other drug problems have experienced some negative consequences already, this argument can be compelling.

Disadvantages of the Disease Concept

As the critics of the disease concept have pointed out, the orthodox precepts of the disease concept may not be accurate. The symptoms and stages are not inevitable and completely predictable, nor do they consistently result in loss of control. Therefore, individuals with alcohol or other drug problems who may need some form of intervention or treatment may avoid help since they do not fit the "disease model." For example, we were told by a substance abuse program counselor about an inquiry from a man whose girlfriend thought he had a drinking problem. Although he drank on a daily basis, his use of alcohol had not progressed in the last few years. When asked if he was having any financial, occupational, legal, or family problems, he said that he was not. Now certainly, denial may be at work here, but the point is that the intake counselor did not encourage the man to seek help since he did not fit the classic "disease" characteristics, while the program in which the counselor works is based on this model.

The notion that the disease concept removes responsibility from the alcoholic or addict for his or her behavior is frequently cited as a disadvantage of this model. Since the alcoholic or addict is "powerless" over the disease, inappropriate or even criminal behavior may be attributed to the "disease." Relapse may also be blamed on the disease: "If alcoholics come to view their drinking as the result of a disease or physiological addiction, they may be more likely to assume the passive role of victim whenever they engage in drinking behavior if they see it as a symptom of their disease. . . . " (Marlatt & Gordon, 1985, p. 7). In other words, if an alcoholic believes the disease concept and the AA slogan "one drink away from a drunk," then a slip (return to use) may result in the alcoholic's giving up responsibility for maintaining sobriety and returning to a previous level of use, since the slip is symptomatic of the loss of control. Proponents of the disease concept counter this argument by saying that the addict is not responsible for the disease but is completely responsible for recovery. In addition, court rulings have rarely allowed a defense of addiction for criminal behavior (Miller & Hester, 2003).

BIOPSYCHOSOCIAL MODEL OF ADDICTION

At the beginning of the chapter, we described six people we have known or worked with. Each has a history of heavy alcohol or other drug use.

Although we have changed the names of people, these cases are all real. We are not implying that they are typical or atypical, and we did not include those individuals who completed traditional treatment programs or use AA as a primary method of maintaining sobriety, although we know plenty of people who do so. These cases are meant to illustrate the concept that is well articulated by Pattison and Kaufman (1982):

> Most scientific authorities in the field of alcoholism now concur that the construct of alcoholism is most accurately construed as a multivariate syndrome. That is, there are multiple patterns of dysfunctional alcohol use that occur in multiple types of personalities, with multiple combinations of adverse consequences, with multiple prognoses, that may require different types of treatment interventions. (p. 13)

Bill and Loretta had patterns of use that could well fit within the disease model of addiction. Bill's progression was very similar to that described by Jellinek (1952), but he responded to a treatment that was quite unlike the traditional models based on the disease concept. Loretta also continued to use in spite of having every reason to stop, which certainly seems like a loss of control.

In contrast, Marvin's drinking remained at a heavy but nonproblematic stage of use for many years with no apparent progression. In opposition to what might be expected, he had no physical or psychological problems discontinuing his use when faced with a strong motivation to stop. Hector, who seemed to have serious problems with alcohol and other drugs, reverted to moderate use when he matured and acquired responsibilities for others. His behavior could be explained from a social learning perspective. Rebecca seemed to demonstrate an "addictive personality." She constantly had to be aware of her characteristic of going overboard. Her use of nonalcoholic beer and wine is contrary to what is recommended by most treatment programs, but it works for her. Salvador might be seen as being a disease concept addict whose recovery program was faith-based. However, his moderate use of alcohol would conflict with the disease concept. In Salvador's early social and cultural environment, heroin use was common. Perhaps these social and cultural variables help explain Salvador's heroin use in his early adulthood.

It's quite natural for treatment providers to develop a concept of addiction based on the clients they come in contact with. Helping professionals who work in substance abuse treatment programs see individuals who have had some pretty serious life problems as a result of their alcohol and other drug use. They are not likely to see individuals who have successfully discontinued their use on their own or through a nontraditional method, or to work with clients who interrupt their use patterns before they experience serious life problems. Finally, alcohol and other drug treatment providers do not usually see clients who are heavy users but who do not have life problems as a result of their use. Therefore, it is logical that those professionals who work in the substance abuse treatment field may develop a concept of addiction that is based on a biased sample. This is not to say that the disease concept does not fit many alcoholics and addicts or that traditional treatment approaches and twelve-step recovery programs are not useful. Certainly, as we illustrated with Bill and Loretta, many alcoholics and addicts fit the characteristics of the disease concept, and many, many people have been helped by traditional treatment programs based on the disease concept and utilizing AA and NA. We are arguing that readers should also consider other explanations for problematic alcohol and other drug use and a variety of treatment options. Interestingly, Jellinek (1960), who is credited with developing the disease concept, identified five different types of problem drinking patterns, only two of which were thought to demonstrate the characteristics of the disease. This seems to be ignored by many disease concept proponents.

People begin AOD use on an experimental basis for lots of different reasons. They continue using because such outcomes as reduction of pain, experience of euphoria, social recognition acceptance, and/or success reinforce their use. Some people progress to abuse and addiction. Why?

It is certainly possible that progression in some people is due to a genetic predisposition and that this genetic predisposition may be understood through physiological differences. It is also plausible that personality characteristics may explain some progression, or that physical or emotional pain may explain some problematic use, or environmental circumstances may provide answers. Any combination of these factors may also be possible. With a certain client, we may find that the reduction of chronic back pain leads to a reduction in alcohol use. Another client (as with Hector) may have a change in environmental factors that leads to a change in use. Through therapy, another client may come to a greater self-awareness with regard to personality characteristics, and thus modify his or her use. With other clients, reduction of pain, change of environment, and self-knowledge does not affect their use at all.

In an effort to reflect the multivariate nature of addiction, many authors now refer to the "biopsychosocial" model of addiction (e.g., Donovan, 2005). In the biopsychosocial model of addiction, the interactions of biological, psychological, cognitive, social, developmental, and environmental variables are considered to "explain" addiction. This model is a reasonable conceptualization because it incorporates the other models into a single model. Therefore, important factors in the treatment of a particular client are not ignored when all variables are considered. For example, the parents of Loretta (our methamphetamine user) were alcoholics. She was sexually and physically abused as a child. Her parents introduced her to alcohol at the age of 9. She consistently became involved with men who abused alcohol and other drugs. As you can imagine, all of these factors would be crucial in understanding Loretta's addiction and in designing a treatment program for her.

We suggest that mental health professionals, whether or not they work with substance abuse problems, thoroughly assess clients (see Chapter 6), develop multiple hypotheses to explain the client's AOD problem based on the assessment, avoid forcing the client to fit a rigid or preconceived notion of addiction, and utilize a variety of treatment methods and interventions (see Chapter 8) evolving from the assessment, hypotheses, and most important, the needs of the client.

MyCounselingLab™

Go to Topic 3: *Etiological Theories of Substance Abuse*, in the **MyCounselingLab™** site (www.MyCounselingLab.com) for *Substance Abuse: Information for School Counselors, Social Workers, Therapists and Counselors*, Fifth Edition, where you can:

- Find learning outcomes for *Etiological Theories of Substance Abuse* along with the national standards that connect to these outcomes.
- Complete Assignments and Activities that can help you more deeply understand the chapter content.
- Apply and practice your understanding of the core skills identified in the chapter with the Building Counseling Skills unit.
- Prepare yourself for professional certification with a Practice for Certification quiz.
- Connect to videos through the Video and Resource Library.

Summary

- The moral model is not widely accepted and discourages people from seeking treatment.
- Sociocultural and psychological models explain addiction as a result of environmental or personality factors.
- The disease model is widely accepted because of its medical orientation and because abstinence is logically related to the model.
- The disease model has helped to reduce the stigma of addiction and has enlisted the support of the medical community in treatment.

- A disadvantage of the disease model is that some addicts blame their behavior on the "disease."
- The biopsychosocial model incorporates all the relevant variables in the etiology and treatment of addiction.

Internet Resources

Disease concept of addiction
bhrm.org/papers/Counselor1.pdf

Addiction as a brain disease
drugabuse.gov/scienceofaddiction

Criticism of the disease concept
peele.net/index.html

Further Discussion

1. Think about some celebrity you have heard about who has an AOD problem. Given what you know about this person, use different models of addiction to explain the celebrity's condition.
2. Which model of addiction appeals to you the most? Why?

3. Using each of the case examples at the beginning of the chapter, apply a model of addiction to "explain" each case.

Chapter 4

Culturally and Ethnically Diverse Populations

MyCounselingLab™

Visit the MyCounselingLab™ site (www.MyCounselingLab.com) for *Substance Abuse: Information for School Counselors, Social Workers, Therapists and Counselors,* Fifth Edition to enhance your understanding of chapter concepts. You'll have the opportunity to practice your skills through video- and case-based Assignments and Activities as well as Building Counseling Skills units and to prepare for your certification exam with Practice for Certification quizzes.

CASE EXAMPLES

❶ Dawne is a 23-year-old Native American who lives on a reservation 37 miles from the nearest city in the western United States. She lost a brother in a DUI car accident when she was 12 years old. As a result, Dawne has been diagnosed with depression and anxiety. While she does her best to refrain, her friends smoke marijuana and engage in binge drinking on the weekends. She was engaged to her boyfriend, John, until he began drinking and physically abusing her.

❷ Rumi is an international student from Japan who came to the United States to study for her undergraduate degree in chemistry. Rumi considers her three Euro-Caucasian roommates her best friends. She even spends most holidays at one of her roommate's families. As a result, she has not gone home to visit her parents for three years. Her English speaking is nearly flawless, and she says that she really has no deep desire to return home to her families' "old, out-of-date ways." Recently, she began drinking more so that she could decompress from the pressures of school.

❸ Rolando is a 64-year-old Hispanic gay man who was adopted at birth. He retired from his job as a computer technician after he fell off a ladder while painting his brother's home, and seriously injured his back. His daughter recently found him motionless on the floor of his apartment and called an ambulance. Upon his arrival at the city hospital emergency room, doctors determined that Rolando's condition was due to long-standing addiction to pain medication and alcohol. After stabilizing him, they referred Rolando to a treatment center in the next county, where he was placed on a waiting list.

As mentioned in Chapter 3, it is quite natural for treatment providers to develop a concept of addiction based on the clients with whom they come in contact. An important ingredient in this tentative formulation is the treatment provider's possession of a sound theoretical basis of the general nature of addictions. The same holds true when working with individuals and groups of different cultural and ethnic backgrounds. One needs to be well grounded in the understanding of the cultural values of that individual or group so that the formation of tentative hypotheses about alcohol and other drug use, abuse, and addiction are more likely to be accurate. This is especially true now because, by the time you read this, more than one-third of all Americans will be persons of color, and Delva, Wallace, O'Malley, Bachman, Johnston, and Schulenberg (2005) assert that the Hispanic population alone will make up 25% of the total U.S. population. Areas of growth are not relegated only to people of color. As the U.S. population grows, so will the number of persons with disabilities (PWDs), who currently number about 50 million (U.S. Census Bureau, 2010).

Without sensitivity to cultural differences and cultural competency, providers will likely be ineffective from the outset, because attempts to assess alcohol and other drug involvement will be met with both cultural and therapeutic resistance. This double whammy will undoubtedly preclude an accurate assessment of any type, let alone that of drug involvement.

Room (2005) maintains that ethnic and cultural identity in a diverse society is partly assigned and partly constructed. Ethnic and cultural assignment are particularly amenable for "visible minorities" who are identifiable by skin color, language differences, age, physical disability, or some other such external sign(s). However, ethnic and cultural assignment is also made for the more "invisible minorities" as well, such as those with learning disorders/differences and those differing in sexual orientation. Although little is known about adolescents with disabilities and their AOD use, the few studies published consistently show significantly higher substance use rates for youth with disabilities (Grafsky, Letcher, Slesnick, & Serovich, 2011).

When assigned (and thus, stereotyped), individuals and groups will often act out or perform the identity. This can serve to delineate and maintain sharper differences and separation between groups of people. Some of the acting out includes AOD use and abuse. For example, Lurie (1971) believes that the heavy drinking by Native Americans can be likened to the world's oldest ongoing protest demonstration, which serves to demark and maintain the Indian–Euro-American boundary. Some recent research suggests support for this idea. For example, Native Americans and Alaska Natives account for 1% of the United States population (U.S. Census Bureau, 2010). Yet, while the rate of alcohol use may be lower than the national average (43.9% versus 55.2%), the rates of binge alcohol use and illicit drug use continue to be higher among Native Americans and Alaskan Natives than the national average (30.6% versus 24.5%; 11.2% versus 7.9%, respectively) (U.S. Department of Health and Human Services, 2010). In addition, the percentage of Native American or Alaska Native adults who need treatment for AOD use is about twice the national average (18.0% versus 9.6%). Stivers (2000) found that drinking in Ireland in the 1800s eventually led to the British stereotyping of the Irish as heavy drinkers, and when the Irish came to America in the mid-19th century, they acted out that stereotype in the United States so that drinking made the Irish "more Irish."

Based on the need for cultural awareness, sensitivity, and competency, this chapter will present information on Native Americans and Alaska Natives, Asian and Pacific Islanders, African Americans, and Latino and Hispanic populations. We will also examine persons with disabilities and the elderly. Concerns for helping professionals when working with members of these populations will conclude the chapter.

NATIVE AMERICANS AND ALASKA NATIVES

Native Americans (which include American Indians, Alaska Natives, and Aleuts) have been separated by the U.S. government into three categories: (1) federally recognized tribes and bands, (2) nonfederally recognized tribes and bands, and (3) urban Native Americans. More than 562 tribes/nations are federally recognized, who speak 253 different languages. According to the U.S. Census Bureau (2011), there are about 5 million people who identify themselves as American Indian/Alaska Native (AI/AN) alone or in combination with one or more other races, and 27% are under 18. As a group, AI/AN make up 1.6% of the total U.S. population. As of 2010, the Native American, Alaskan Native, and Aleut populations residing in the United States tended to live in one of 10 major cultural areas: Northeast, Southeast, Plains, Arctic, Subarctic, Northwest Coast, Plateau, Great Basin, California, and the Southwest (U.S. Census Bureau, 2010). These cultural areas are further subdivided into urban or reservation lifestyles. About 2 million of Native Americans/Alaskan Natives live on reservations or trust lands, and 60% live in metropolitan areas—the lowest percentage of any racial group (U.S. Department of Health and Human Services, 2008). If you were to spend a moment reflecting upon the differences between the Euro-Americans living in the northeastern United States and the South, or between the Southwest and the Midwest, or between California and the rest of the United States, you would begin to see that there are now and always have been vast differences in the ways that people speak, eat, dress, and approach life in general. The Native American populations are no different. Alaska Natives, for example, differ along geographic lines that reflect a difference in cultures (Attneave, 1982). Alaskan Eskimos inhabit the coastal areas to the north while the Aleuts occupy settlements along the Aleutian Islands. Fairbanks is the cultural hub for the Athabascan-speaking tribes who reside in the surrounding mountains and valleys. Yet very different are the coastal tribes who reside on the islands close to Juneau and Ketchikan and along the coast of the Alaskan panhandle. An example that underscores the geographic distribution and variety of Native American cultures is that most Native Americans who live outside of the Southwest would consider the silver and turquoise jewelry of the Southwest Pueblo Indians an exotic art form, much as would non–Native Americans—regardless of whether they lived in urban centers, on reservations, or in rural settings (Attneave, 1982).

Background

According to Attneave (1982), no Native American or Alaskan Native person today categorically lives out a traditional lifestyle. All are involved in the non–Native American U.S. culture to some degree. For example, more than half of the Native American and Alaskan Native populations do not use the reservation as their principal residence. Since urban centers offer different opportunities for work, education, and other endeavors, thousands of Native Americans can be found residing in these urban areas for varying lengths of time.

In the late 1700s, trappers, traders, and frontiersmen introduced alcohol as a social beverage to Native Americans on a widespread scale. Prior to that, little or no use of alcohol existed among Native Americans north of Mexico, with the exception of use for certain ceremonial purposes. Woodland and plains tribes especially used the methods of dancing, fasting, drumming, sleep deprivation, and isolation to obtain altered states of consciousness as a means to communicate with the Great Spirit and the spirits of nature (Westermeyer & Baker, 1986).

As the concept of Manifest Destiny became the accepted orientation fueling the exploration of the lands to the West, so did alcohol become the most important item exchanged for furs (Chittenden, 1935). With little history to guide alcohol consumption, Native Americans as a group were uncertain about how to view it. Many tribes came to believe that alcohol had magical powers associated with curing disease. Other tribes simply viewed drunken people as unaccountable for their behaviors. It has been stated that perhaps Native Americans first learned to drink in a binge pattern at the trade fairs where drinking parties often lasted several days, accompanied by games, acts of bravado, and fighting (Westermeyer & Baker, 1986). Still others saw drinking as more social and economic. Although leaders cautioned them to abstain, alcohol was accepted by many Native Americans as a gesture of friendship from the white-skinned traders. Thus, alcohol took on an economic value. Accepting alcohol, even drinking with the whites, was believed to cement good trade relations.

Many Native American leaders became so disturbed by the spate of drinking among their people that they appealed to government officials for help. Federal intervention finally came in 1832 with the Indian Prohibition Act, which prohibited the selling or providing of liquor to American Indians. However, the act was deemed largely unsuccessful: Alcohol was deeply infused into the trading economy and social practices of many tribes by the 1830s, creating a demand for the drug. As a result, many Native Americans as well as whites turned to smuggling alcohol, and they made good profits. Moreover, by the 1830s, Native Americans had learned to ferment alcohol from their plethora of carbohydrate sources. Although the Indian Prohibition Act was ineffective, the U.S. government did not revoke the law until 1953. In its absence, many Native American leaders remained vigilant about the potentially destructive nature of alcohol, so that currently 69% of all U.S. reservations are under a self-imposed system of prohibition (Young, 1992).

The Native American relationship with alcohol has also been mitigated by the historical events of forced relocation of tribes, the break-up of Native American families, and the constant harassment from settlers and soldiers. In an attempt to assess the influence of these historical events upon Native American drinking behaviors, as many as 42 theories have been promulgated—the most notable of which is the sociocultural explanation (Young, 1992). This theory maintains that, as a culture, Native Americans are continuing to mourn the loss of their heritage and culture and are reacting to the stresses of acculturation and the demands to integrate into the mainstream of Euro-American society. In this theory, alcohol is seen as salubrious, anesthetizing the pain associated with the multiple losses incurred by Native Americans. Aside from whatever biophysiological proclivities that exist among Native Americans (and the jury is still out on this issue), the current state of anomie or normlessness is seen as acting to maintain the abuse of alcohol.

It becomes important, then, to examine the values that are purported to be at the heart of this grieving process. Sadly, it will become apparent that Native American values were functional prior to the introduction of alcohol but may have now become seriously compromised in the development of current Indian drinking patterns. The grieving process for the Native Americans and Alaskan Natives thus includes not only mourning the loss of a culture, but mourning the deleterious effects of alcohol on their peoples.

Values

In spite of the enormous diversity among Native American populations, some basic values are thematic for Native Americans and Native Alaskans. These values focus upon orientation to time, the relationship between humans and the natural world, social relationships, and the concept of "noninterference." Many Native American and Euro-American cultures hold these values, but they usually vary in philosophy or in the emphasis placed on them.

TIME   Attneave (1982) and Ivey, D'Andrea, Bradford-Ivey, and Simek-Morgan (2007) explain that Euro-American culture is concerned with present time in terms of minute-by-minute awareness: What time is it? How much time do I have left? How long will it take me to drive to Long Island? Native Americans and Native Alaskan peoples also view time in the present. However, for them, present time is cyclical or universal rather than linear. Native Americans view present time as it relates to personal rhythms (not unlike the popular notion of biorhythms) and seasonal rhythms that encompass days, months, and even years. Native American life is thus organized in broad context around these various rhythms and not organized by traditional calendars and watches—both of which are seen as external.

Attneave (1982) and Ivey et al. (2007) point out that the Native American concept of past time has little or nothing to recommend its revival to the Native American population. The immediate past is measured in one or two generations, and this timeline is filled with a grim and depressing past. The future, no longer anchored to the seasonal variations, remains unknown and unpredictable. In spite of it all, though, it is important to note that today Native Americans will likely have preserved some of their original concept of time and, because of the clash of cultures, some distortions of it as well.

HUMANS, THE NATURAL WORLD, AND SOCIAL RELATIONSHIPS   Since the Industrial Revolution, the prevailing view of nature in Euro-American culture is that it is wild and capricious. Therefore, nature is seen as needing to be controlled, and increasing or improving technology is viewed as increasing control over nature. For Native Americans and Native Alaskans, nature cannot be controlled. They advocate the need to understand and to harmonize with the natural forces of nature rather than to attempt to control or dominate them. Thus, Native American populations aim to surrender control. Surrendering with regard to alcohol means that if one is going to drink, so be it. But surrendering to the forces of nature is not the same as being passive. Moreover, becoming drunk might be met with temporary ostracism.

Native Americans believe that the group takes precedence over the individual, which may go a long way in explaining the rapid spread of alcohol among earlier Native American peoples. In the past, the ability to preserve perishables from season to season was very limited. Sharing of food, clothing, and transportation was the norm as well as the necessity, so it is not unreasonable that in the Native American culture, alcohol would have been passed around until it was gone. For this reason, some consider this idea the underlying explanation for "binge drinking" (Attneave, 1982).

NONINTERFERENCE   Another source of grieving, and a source of explanation for early Native American alcohol use patterns, revolves around a concept called "noninterference." Although the Native American peoples respected the idea of the group, there was an underlying principle explaining the proper place of the individual. Just as there was respect for the natural forces of nature, there was also respect for the natural unfolding of the potential in each person. "Noninterference" is an academic term used to describe this approach to human behavior (Attneave, 1982). This philosophy allows Native American parents to nurture their children while allowing them to learn from their mistakes. In this process, much more emphasis is placed upon having children learn by doing, so they can learn from their own mistakes. Noninterference is also practiced with the elderly. For example, no matter how senile or ill the elders in the tribe may be, they still retain the right to determine their own courses of action. This notion of allowing one to learn from mistakes may have had a significant impact upon the development of alcohol abuse and alcoholism among Native Americans throughout generations.

Risk Factors for Alcohol and Other Drug Abuse Psychosocial Factors

Psychosocial risk factors are usually divided into personal and social dimensions. Personal risk factors include such things as stress, financial problems, relational victimization, and physical victimization. Social risk factors can involve peer groups, families, and communities. For example, drugs may be easier to obtain in some communities than in others. Some communities may have low neighborhood attachment, a population that is transient, and one that is in poverty. These communities present heightened risk factors. Families can be another source of risk for substance abuse, and this is especially true if persistent family conflict and/or favorable parental attitudes and involvement in the problem behavior occur. It is very important to remember that a risk factor for one person may not be for another. Moreover, risk factors are related to age so that what is a risk factor at one age may or may not be a risk factor at another age or developmental phase. For most folks, life transitions are the period when the risk for substance abuse is the highest.

According to the National Survey on Drug Use and Health (U.S. Department of Health and Human Services, 2010), binge drinking and illicit drug use was higher for this population than the national average. Not surprisingly, the percentage of American Indian or Alaska Natives who needed treatment for AOD problems was also higher than the national average. Native American youth start using alcohol, tobacco, and other drugs at an earlier age than does the general population (Napoli, Marsiglia, & Kullis, 2003). In a review of literature, Marlatt and VandenBos (1997) suggest that modeling variables, peer pressure, and experimental substance use as an expression of stage-related rebelliousness are correlates of substance abuse in the Native American youth population. In addition, other related variables include the use of substances for tension coping, as well as general feelings of alienation.

Andre (1979) found that 75% of all Native American deaths are related to alcohol in some way. Aside from the sociocultural theories pointing to mourning as a significant risk factor, Westermeyer advances another risk factor. In citing studies that examine drinking patterns among various subgroups of Native Americans, Westermeyer (1991) found differences between Native Americans living in the West and those residing in other geographic locations. Motor vehicle crashes and injuries, usually associated with intoxication, are elevated among Western mountain tribes. Given that the Western states are significantly larger than other states and the fact that most reservations prohibit the sale of alcohol, those Native Americans living in the West and desiring alcohol have greater distances to travel in order to purchase it. Therefore, Westermeyer (1991) believes that the sheer number of miles involved in procuring alcohol may contribute significantly to the higher incidence of alcohol-related accidents. To an extent, the results of this early study may be indirectly corroborated by the fact that motor vehicle crashes are the leading cause of unintentional injury for the 1–44 age population of Native Americans and Alaska Natives and the leading cause of injury-related death among the 19-year-olds and younger (Centers for Disease Control and Prevention, 2010c). Related to the geographical dimensions of risk, Kidney, Alvarez, Jason, Ferrari, and Minich (2011) believe that socioeconomic inequities as well as the lack of treatment facilities in proximity to reservations also contribute to the likelihood of abusing substances.

Ross (2004) states that female Native American adolescents are more likely to have significant depression and/or anxiety disorders, and Walters and Simoni (2002) assert that these co-occurring disorders are associated with increased AOD use and abuse in Native communities. In addition, these women are disproportionately affected by violence, and the resulting posttraumatic stress is also associated with elevated AOD use. Dawne, the Native American female described in Case Example 1 at the beginning of the chapter reflects a host of risk factors that are present for Native American females. She lost a brother to a DUI accident as he traveled the 37 miles home to the reservation from a party in town. She was diagnosed with anxiety and depression, had friends who misused substances, and was a victim of physical abuse.

Paltrow (2004) maintains that another factor that influences the maintenance of AOD problems is the criminal justice system. This includes racial profiling as well as judges who believe in the myth that using drugs is a choice for Native Americans and Alaska Natives rather than seeing female AOD use associated with oppression and socioeconomic injustices. Both Paltrow (2004) and Owen (2004) claim that drug laws along with subsequent incarceration destroy the lives of women. This makes it almost impossible for female Native Americans to recover from such punishing policies. Current laws and morality related to homosexuality also influence AOD use and recovery from it for Native Americans. For example, Gilley and Co-Cké (2005) see that Native American gay males often feel alienated from their tribal, ceremonial, and social communities because of homophobia. As with the gay population in general, the gay bar scene makes healthy living difficult for Native American gay males.

BEHAVIORAL RISK FACTORS   Behavioral risk factors relate to such things as school engagement, academic achievement, healthy lifestyle, internalizing/externalizing issues of control, and drug involvement. For Native Americans or Alaska Natives, binge drinking and smoking are risk factors for multiple adverse outcomes (Centers for Disease Control and Prevention, 2010d). Binge drinking is noteworthy because of the distances that many Native Americans have to drive in order to get alcohol, as mentioned earlier. In a review of the literature, Gordon summarized that neither one cause of heavy drinking nor one recognizable, common response to alcohol ingestion exists. Alcohol-related behaviors vary. It appears as though the outcomes vary according to tribal background, acculturation level, and individual inclination (Coyhis, 2000; Gordon, 1994).

Marlatt and VandenBos (1997) developed 16 substance abuse risk categories for Native American youth that heighten risk factors, and these continue to be risk factors today. These categories include: (1) smoking tobacco, (2) use of smokeless tobacco, (3) family smoking, (4) peer smoking, (5) family smokeless tobacco use, (6) peer smokeless tobacco use, (7) experimentation, (8) intentions to use, (9) peer use of alcohol, (10) inhalants, marijuana, and crack/cocaine, (11) quality of family relationships, (12) school adjustment, (13) orientation, (14) non–substance-related deviant behaviors, (15) perceived deviance in school environment, and (16) cultural identification and religiosity. According to Marlatt and VandenBos, the category with the highest positive correlation to overall risk is reported lifetime smokeless tobacco use. Native Americans' use of smokeless tobacco (8.6%) is higher than that for other ethnic minorities as well as being higher than the national average (3.3%) (Centers for Disease Control and Prevention, 2010b). The next highest correlation is reported lifetime tobacco use, which is an alarming 32% of adult Native Americans. This is not only higher than the national average (20.9%); it is higher than other minorities. The next risk factor is lifetime alcohol use. Remember that these are correlations and therefore cannot be interpreted as causative. Nonetheless, the rates are alarming and underscore the risk for Native Americans' health.

AT A GLANCE

NATIVE AMERICANS AND ALASKA NATIVES

Population

4.9 million American Indian/Alaska Natives make up 1.6% of U.S. total population.

1.9 million live on reservations in 36 states.

60% live in metropolitan areas.

562 tribes/nations are federally recognized.

253 different languages are spoken.

Education

76% 25 and older have high school diploma.

14% have bachelor's degree.

Income

25% live at poverty level.

$33,627 is the median family income.

Children and Parenting

Practice of noninterference reflects parents allowing children to make mistakes and learn rather than directly controlling children's growth.

Spiritual Beliefs and Practices

Time is viewed as seasonal and chromatic (versus digital), and the immediate past is measured in one or two generations.

People believe that Nature cannot be controlled.

Some Native cultures believe language and thought shape reality and control events.

Family Organization and Communication

Group takes precedence over the individual.

Families are patriarchal and structured with well-defined role expectations.

ASIAN AMERICANS AND PACIFIC ISLANDERS

From your reading of the section on Native Americans, you would accurately anticipate that the Asian population is also diverse. Asians include Asian Indians (India), Pakistanis, Thais, Filipinos, Vietnamese, Laotians, Cambodians, and the Hmong peoples (Highland Laotian). The peoples of East Asia include Chinese, Japanese, and Koreans. Pacific Islanders include Hawaiians, Samoans, and people from Guam.

Typical Western observers tend to view all East Asians as being very similar—if not the same. Nothing could be further from the truth. Asian Americans/Pacific Islanders comprise more than 60 discrete racial/ethnic groups and subgroups, and these groups are heterogeneous with vast variation within. Language is the most apparent difference. Yet, the histories of China, Japan, and Korea reveal vastly differing social and economic development. Moreover, once living in the United States, all Asian groups demonstrate significant within-group differences that will become more pronounced in future years.

Virtually all of the world's great religions are represented in this culturally and ethnically diverse group of Asian and Pacific Islander Americans, including Animism, Hinduism, Buddhism, Judaism, Christianity, and Islam. The culturally and ethnically diverse populations presented in this chapter all have conflict as part of their history, and Asian Americans are no different. However, the Asian population is distinctive in that its members also have a history of fighting among themselves. This single variable may distinguish Southeast Asians in another significant way: Although Asian Americans (including Southeast Asians) tend to group themselves ethnically, Southeast Asian Americans, especially those living in urban centers, have demonstrated a lack of pulling together due to their history of internal fighting (Burns & D'Avanzo, 1993). The transitions involving acculturation and accommodation will only exacerbate this cultural tension and can increase the risk factor for alcohol and other drug abuse.

Background

Although Islamic laws eschew alcohol, and most Muslim, Hindu, and Buddhist groups avoid alcohol, many Asian and Pacific cultures do use alcohol in rituals (Shon & Ja, 1982). An example of this is found in the "tribal binge" drinking of Pacific Islanders and in ceremonial and traditional events in Japan. Drinking in Japan is reported to start as early as age 11, and alcohol use is organized and institutionalized (Tani, Haga, & Kato, 1975). Japanese Americans consume more alcohol than Asian Americans of other national origins (Galvan & Caetano, 2003). Yet, research consistently shows that Asian Americans' drinking behavior is the lowest among minority groups (Centers for Disease Control and Prevention, 2010d; Collins & McNair, 2002).

Working men of all ages have their favorite drinking establishments. The more exclusive establishments have a host of taxis and private automobiles to transport their regular customers home. In less prestigious places, friends and companions transport those who drink too much. Oashi and Nishimura (1978) have categorized four types of Japanese drinking: (1) drinking at dinner done mainly by the man to relax after work; (2) drinking to celebrate annual events; (3) drinking with one's friends after work; and (4) drinking at a roundtable after meetings and conventions—usually to lessen communication barriers. Oashi and Nishimura state that using drinking to lessen communication barriers is important in Japan and that it is acceptable for a subordinate to be very frank with one's boss when either one or both are drunk.

The Chinese not only allow the use of alcohol at social functions, but virtually push it on guests as a display of hospitality. However, they discourage drunkenness. Traditionally, Hong Kong has few drinking-centered establishments, generally restricts the use of alcohol to males, and values drinking alcohol at meals. In Chinese culture, alcohol is often viewed in a somewhat similar fashion to that of the abolitionist in the temperance movement in America's 19th century (see section on African Americans). That is, alcohol is associated with lack of restraint, but it is not generally feared that drunkenness will lead to violence. In a significant yet early study, Chafetz (1964) noted that Taiwanese have well-defined ways of behaving, have strong social sanctions against excessive drinking, and encourage drinking only at meals or at special events.

He also found that the Taiwanese have little official concern about alcohol treatment programs due to the overall lack of psychiatric resources and the low level of alcoholism in the dominant Chinese population.

Polynesians do not employ guilt as a means to regulate drinking and drunkenness. However, Tongans and Samoans, many of whom are Christian, do seem to use guilt to control the amount of drinking. Drinking to excess is seen as potentially threatening in the Samoan culture. Studies report that a large number of Samoan wives left their marriages because of the heavy drinking of their physically abusing husbands (Lemert, 1964; Room & Mäkelä, 2000).

Values

When attempting to describe the values held by Asians or Pacific Islanders, the vast within-group differences prohibit any attempt at brevity. What follows are some general descriptions that would more likely apply to recent Asian immigrants and are less likely to describe earlier generations of Asian Americans. Such discrepancies are mostly due to the effects of acculturation. According to Lee and Mock (2005), traditional Asian families see the symbol of the samurai as the epitome of Japanese valor. They view *bushido* as the way of the warrior that combines stoicism, bravery, and self-sacrifice. *Gaman* is the "down-to-earth" version of bushido. This reflects the gritting of one's teeth and getting on with life. It is also associated with the traditional awareness of humankind's powerlessness over an omnipotent nature. If you saw the videos of the great tsunami that hit Japan on March 11, 2011, you saw clearly how the Japanese people responded with all of these values.

FAMILY ROLES   Most Asian societies are structured with well-defined role expectations. This includes a patriarchal family structure consisting of elders or extended family members and a structure in which children are seen as subordinates. According to Fukuyama and Inoue-Cox (1992), Ivey et al. (2007), and others, a strong sense of "filial piety" and respect for authority reinforces obedience and protection of the family name. The father's decisions are beyond reproach and are categorically accepted. The mother nurtures both her husband and her children. Whereas at one time it was socially desirable for the father to be the disciplinarian, the contemporary Asian father is not home as much, so the discipline is essentially left to the mother.

The male is expected to provide for the economic welfare of his family and in so doing is the one on whose shoulders rests the responsibility for the family's successes or failures. Because the physical appearance of Asians differs significantly from Euro-Americans concomitant with the presence of racial and cultural discrimination toward Asian Americans (Lee & Mock, 2005; Shon & Ja, 1982), Asian men can face extraordinary pressures when attempting to provide financially for their families. Research suggests that it usually takes about 10 or more years for them to find economic security (Burns & D'Avanzo, 1993). This length of time and the pressures to succeed increase their risk for AOD abuse. Risk for substance abuse also seems to increase with the level of educational attainment for these men—especially for Chinese, Korean, and Japanese men. Chi, Lubben, and Kitano (1989) found consumption rates of alcohol increased with educational attainment.

Shame, especially the idea of "saving face," controls behaviors in the Asian family and is learned early in life. The concept of shame and loss of face involves not only the exposing of one's actions for all to see, but also family, community, or social withdrawal of confidence and support (Ivey et al., 2007; Shon & Ja, 1982). Inextricably woven into the value of shame is obligation. Obligation in the Asian/Pacific Islander community contains spoken and unspoken elements of reciprocity, and the greatest obligation is toward one's parents. This is an obligation that cannot ever truly be repaid (Fukuyama & Inoue-Cox, 1992; Lee & Mock, 2005). Regardless of what the parents may do to the child, the child is still obligated to give respect and obedience to them. The more Asian children are exposed to Euro-American schools, the more this sense of obligation can come into question and become a source of confusion. The transition will produce a period of anomie for the Asian offspring, and it is during this period of normlessness that they may be at an increased risk for AOD abuse.

COMMUNICATION   Roles also play an interesting and important part in communication for the Asian/Pacific Islander population. Communication between individuals is governed by such characteristics as age, gender, education, occupation, social status, family background, marital status, and parenthood (Lee & Mock, 2005; Shon & Ja, 1982). These variables influence behavior in terms of who will bow the lowest, who will initiate and change topics in a conversation, which person will speak more loudly, who will break eye contact first, and who will be most accommodating or tolerant. Most of the newly immigrated Asian Americans/Pacific Islanders are likely to want to avoid confrontation, keeping conversations on a harmonious level, and often maintain self-control over their facial expressions while avoiding direct eye contact. This information is important when assessing for AOD problems, because it can work in reverse. If responses from Asian clients appear to upset the professional conducting the assessment, answers may not be given accurately so as to avoid confrontation.

RELIGION   Beliefs about health and responses to offerings of health care are influenced by religious beliefs in the Asian/Pacific Islander population. For example, Buddhism holds that life is suffering, and suffering emanates from desire. Pain or other suffering is seen as punishment for transgressions in this or previous lives. Alcohol and other drug problems may fall into this context. The notion of pain and suffering may so strongly influence one's beliefs that the likelihood of seeking help for AOD problems may be severely diminished (Shon & Ja, 1982). Animism is the idea that evil spirits, demons, or gods have control over one's life. Because of this, the "shaman" may be the primary caregiver or helper in situations involving alcohol or other drug abuse. However, Western helpers may be invited to aid in the process. Confucianism is prevalent among older Vietnamese and is a moral and ethical code that includes the worshipping of ancestors. Because Confucianism stresses a hierarchical order in both family and social systems, it will be the family elder who would have the final say in decisions involving treatment for AOD abuse. As a helping professional, you need to be very careful to demonstrate respect for this individual.

Taoism, which stresses harmony, is also quite prevalent among the Asian population. Harmony also plays a significant role in one's intention to seek help. A passive posture toward treatment may be assumed by an individual of Asian or Pacific Islander descent because anything else would disrupt harmony and perfection.

The Hawaiian term *nā 'Ohana* reflects the family " . . . as a collective that gives life, nourishment, and support for the growth and prosperity of blood relatives as well as extended family, those joined in marriage, adopted children or adults, and ancestors living and deceased" (Kanuha, 2005, p. 66). Children are the foundation of nā 'Ohana and their relationship to elders, their ancestors, and the material, physical, and spiritual surroundings. Clinicians need to understand the key historical events as well as being familiar with the concept of nā 'Ohana and the traditional values of unity, connection, love and affinity, and generosity (Kanuha, 2005).

Risk Factors for Alcohol and Other Drug Abuse

At one time, the Japanese culture seemed to excuse drinking behavior as an opportunity to let repressed workers tell the bosses what they think. However, that is changing. While alcohol consumption is declining in most of the developed world, Japan remains an exception because the number of heavy drinkers has more than doubled since the 1980s. For Asian Americans, this is not the case. Current research shows that the Asian American population, in general, has the lowest rates of substance abuse problems (Hong, Huang, Sabir, & Kim, 2011). Although at least 32 different national and ethnic groups of Asian Americans and Pacific Islanders exist, research on subgroups has been limited. The existing research reflects that subgroups of this population do not always show the same trend. Ebberhart, Luczak, Avanecy, and Wall (2003) studied family history of two Asian American subgroups, Chinese and Koreans. The study aimed to explore the relationship of a positive history of alcoholism among Chinese and Koreans and the later development of alcohol dependence. Results supported the notion of the variability among subgroups in that Korean Americans reported higher rates of first-generation history of alcohol dependence. Another example is seen with Native Hawaiians.

Austin (2004) maintains that alcohol, tobacco, and other drug use and associated violent behavior have become alarming to the community since the late 1990s. Austin found that individuals who identified strongly with being Hawaiian reported being happier and had fewer instances of witnessing, perpetrating, or being a victim of violence. At the time, ethnic pride was seen as an important protective factor against AOD problems. However, a study across two large-scale samples found that while Chinese respondents reported the lowest rate of use, Pacific Islanders and Native Hawaiians reported the highest rates (Wong, Klingle, & Price, 2004). These same researchers reported that Japanese and Filipinos fell in the middle. The findings are significant because when the results are aggregated they do seem to run counter to the Asian American/Pacific Islander "model minority" stereotype. The authors suggest that ethnic pride may no longer be as strong a protective factor as it once was. Another study (Saint-Jean, Martinez, & Crandall, 2008) refutes that. The researchers examined 63,000 self-report data from middle and high school students and found that language used at home was a significant predictor in the level of acculturation and that acculturation is a strong predictor of adolescent substance abuse among minority populations.

The traditional values and ethnic pride mentioned will be mediated by the adjustment patterns of Asian Americans/Pacific Islanders once they enter the United States. The sheer number of immigrants concomitant with the age distribution of this group suggests that these families are in a constant state of transition once they arrive. The process of acculturation will impact all family members and will differentially affect their risk for AOD abuse. For example, a newly arrived Asian American homemaker will be confronted with Euro-American values of female independence, assertiveness, achievement, and work. As a result, elder Asian Americans, expecting to be cared for by family members, can experience great shock and loneliness when faced with nursing home care. Such conflicts between newly acquired values and traditional values can place these individuals at risk for AOD abuse.

While the family hierarchy may provide a stabilizing force to deal with the pressures of financial adjustment, youths who are exposed to the parental pressures for high achievement and financial success may fall victim to feelings of isolation and self-blame. To help brace against fear of long-term insecurity, many Asian Americans also work hard to send their children to schools in hopes that they will become high-paid professionals. This value is reflected in the sheer numbers of Asian American youth attending prestigious universities in the United States.

However, attempts to further the education of their children can be met with resistance, in that the younger children are likely to be attending English-speaking schools while their older siblings and parents may still prefer or use their native language. This would suggest that there might be a bicultural splitting within this population in terms of language. Language differences within families can lead to increased levels of stress, thereby increasing individual family members' risk factors for AOD abuse.

Moreover, language difficulties in school may preclude the Asian Americans/Pacific Islanders' abilities to fulfill their parents' wishes to excel. This would be especially true for first-generation immigrants who came to the United States involuntarily or because of economic hardships faced in their homelands. The sum total of language difficulties and perceived inabilities to meet parental wishes can lead to alienation inside the family (Ivey et al., 2007; Shon & Ja, 1982). For example, the father's insistence upon obedience may be called into question and, when the father's beliefs are called into question, it may significantly contribute to a breakdown of traditional family structure. Thai, Connell, and Tebes (2010) studied the relative influence of acculturation, peer substance use, and academic achievement on adolescent substance use. In their study of 1,248 Asian American youth, they found that peer use is a risk factor. Support for Wong, Klingle, and Price's contention related to the stereotypical "model minority," Thai and Connell also found that academic achievement was not a very strong protective factor against substance use. Perhaps, more importantly, these same authors state that, similar to ethnicity, level of acculturation does not seem to be as strong a predictor of substance use as it once was.

AT A GLANCE

ASIAN AMERICANS AND PACIFIC ISLANDERS

Population

15.5 million live mainly in California, New York, Hawaii, Texas, New Jersey, and Illinois.

Comprise 5% of U.S. total population.

1.1 million Native Hawaiians/Other Pacific Islanders (30% under 18) live mainly in Hawaii, California, Washington, Texas, New York, Florida, and Utah.

Asian Americans/Pacific Islanders make up less than 1% of U.S. total population.

Education

86% 25 and older have a high school diploma.

50% have a bachelor's degree.

Income

10% live at poverty level.

Median family income is $15,600 higher than national median for all households.

$50,992 is median family income.

(continued)

AT A GLANCE (Continued)

Children and Parenting

Children are seen as subordinates.

Behavior controlled by "saving face" and through shame.

Children's greatest obligation is toward their parents.

Family Organization and Communication

Respect for authority and "filial piety" reinforce obedience and protection of the family name.

Communication is usually governed by age, gender, education, occupation, social status, family background, marital status, and parenthood.

Spiritual Beliefs and Practices

Taoists believe that man is a microcosm for the universe and that the body is tied directly into the five elements of fire, earth, air, water, and ether as well as to the five organs and the seasons.

Traditional Hawaiian religion is polytheistic and animistic, which is based on a belief that spirits are found in non–human being objects and object such as animals, the ocean waves, and the sky.

AFRICAN AMERICANS

The role of alcohol in the contemporary African American community varies from that of many other groups. African Americans have culturally acceptable means for achieving spontaneity, sociability, and relaxation. Alcohol, then, is not seen as a requisite for a feeling of celebration. In addition, specific drinking patterns of African Americans are found to be somewhat different from those of Euro-Americans. Early ethnographic studies suggest that taverns appear to be social centers for a majority of African Americans who drink (Sterne & Pittman, 1972). As would be true with any group regardless of ethnicity, African Americans who frequent taverns and bars are a group unto themselves and, as you would expect, are regarded as candidates for the underclass in African American culture rather than as responsible participants in community life. The exception would be a man who is a weekend tavern drinker and is otherwise a capable wage earner and family man. Women who frequent taverns and bars, however, would likely be socially compromised in the wider African American community.

In general, alcohol is often perceived to be a "party food" and is associated with being palliative, while the potential harmful effects are often overlooked or not understood. Alcohol consumption at parties or other social gatherings has a minor role in terms of setting the mood of gaiety and spontaneity. Therefore, a person abstaining from alcohol is not perceived as being staid or a "party pooper."

Many African Americans drink almost exclusively on the weekends, traditionally a time of relaxation, visitation, and celebration. Brand names and the quantity of alcohol drunk reflect status in many African American communities. While earlier studies (e.g., Bourne, 1973; Harper, 1976) reported that African Americans either abstained or drank heavily, began to drink at an earlier age, purchased larger containers of alcohol than their Euro-American counterparts, and concentrated their drinking on the weekends, more recent studies have found that African Americans have later onset drinking problems than their Euro-American counterparts (Chartier, Hesselbrock, & Hesselbrock, 2011).

The history of the relationship between African Americans and alcohol is engaging. Since the institutionalization of slavery in the early 1600s, a broad social and intellectual climate, known as Enlightenment thinking, has prevailed in American thought and has had a significant impact upon views of alcohol and its relationship to African Americans. So, to understand the history of African Americans and alcohol is to trace the institutionalization of slavery up through the prohibition period in the 20th century.

Background

Early stereotyping of Africans (who became "African Americans" after the Emancipation Proclamation) and the institutionalization of slavery in the United States led to subsequent fears of slave insurrection and fueled numerous social measures aimed at controlling this population. In addition to legislation rigidly restricting their ability to trade, Africans were also prohibited from using alcoholic beverages. A West Jersey (New Jersey) law of 1685, for example, stated: "Any person convicted of selling or giving of rum, or any manner of strong liquor, either to a negro or Indian, except the stimulant be given in relief of real physical distress is liable to a penalty of five pounds" (Herd, 1991, p. 355). Similar laws were in effect in most of the colonial governments including Maryland, North Carolina, Georgia, Delaware, Pennsylvania, and New England (Larkin, 1965). Rather than being fueled by the fear that drunkenness would lessen their work ethic, the assumptive premise of these laws was based on the fear that intoxicated slaves would foment rebellion. While the relationship with alcohol and insurrection was presumptive, the manner in which the early African slaves were treated certainly did little to quell the fear of insurrection.

The American Revolution witnessed the abolition of slavery in most of the northern states, but not in the newly formed states of the South. And for southern slaveholders, the discrepancy between the "free north" and the "slave south" exacerbated fears of insurrection. Many new laws were instituted that further restricted the use of alcohol by slaves. However, in spite of laws, the popular views held by slave owners varied on the use of alcohol as a means of controlling Africans. As stated earlier, some believed that prohibiting slaves' use of alcohol would help guard against rebellion. This view was based on the southern planters' widely held view that alcohol was an important cause of every insurrectionary movement in the United States (Freehling, 1968). Another popular view stood in direct opposition. This view was equally concerned with controlling Africans, but held that the sober, thinking slave was the one who was dangerous and needed the constant vigilance of the owner (Douglass, 1855). Herd (1991) summarized these two views:

> One [view of alcohol] inspired images of force and rebellion, whereas the other suggested images of passivity and victimization. From the former perspective liquor was believed to be a powerful agent of disinhibition capable of unleashing violent and irrational behavior in otherwise civilized people. Hence, alcohol was regarded as a cause of crime and violence, a substance that made people commit barbaric and cruel acts. In the latter view alcohol was believed to be a powerfully addicting substance that forced men to drink and left them weak, slothful, and in a thoroughly degraded condition. (p. 357)

What were the views of alcohol held by the Africans themselves? They varied, of course. But interestingly enough, Africans were essentially split on the issue as well. Many regarded drinking as a natural reaction to being held against their will. For example, Stampp (1956) maintains that the consumption of alcohol by slaves was internally motivated as the "only satisfactory escape from the indignities, the frustrations, the emptiness, [and] the oppressive boredom of slavery" (p. 368). According to this view, there was a demand for alcohol by slaves, and Stampp offers a quote from a former slave to corroborate this assertion: To be sober during the holidays "was disgraceful; and he was esteemed a lazy and improvident man, who could not afford to drink whiskey during Christmas" (p. 370). However, during the same period, black and white abolitionists alike maintained that holidays were perhaps the paragon of travesty. To these abolitionists, when slave owners offered libations to slaves during times of celebration, their intent was anything but to celebrate. They believed that holidays instilled more docile and passive resistance among slaves (Herd, 1991).

The views of alcohol as the enslaver and the disinhibitor, coupled with the Enlightenment philosophy of the time, inspired a spontaneous practice of temperance in the middle 19th century. Temperance ideology was focused on Enlightenment thinking and the role of self-control, since it was this ability to control one's irresistible desires that would free humans to be rational and productive. The temperance movement did not stop there, however. Temperance was seen in a broader scope as a vehicle for freeing the will as well as having significant social implications for freeing slaves. Freedom and self-control meant freedom for all and freedom from all. This included freedom from slavery as well as freedom from alcohol. It is not surprising, then, to see that the northern abolitionists embraced a view of alcohol as the enslaver, and therefore, the enemy. Those southern slave owners who believed in temperance adopted the view that alcohol was the disinhibitor and could unleash dangerous impulses in slaves. In describing the abolitionist view, Fredrickson (1971) writes:

> What made slavery such a detestable condition was not simply that it created a bad environment; it was a severely limiting condition that was incompatible with the fundamental abolitionist belief that every man was morally responsible for his actions. (p. 37)

For many Africans, intemperance was seen as analogous to promoting slavery. The popularity of abstinence was reflected in the spate of temperance societies and in the periodicals promulgated by Africans at the time. The pledge of the American Temperance Union adopted at a New England temperance convention in 1836 demonstrates the rigid adherence to the value of abstinence:

> Being mercifully redeemed from human slavery, we do pledge ourselves never to be brought into the slavery of the bottle, therefore we will not drink the drunkard's drink: whiskey, gin, beer, nor rum, nor anything that makes drunk come. (n.d., p. 4)

Curiously, the temperance movement among Africans was less a movement toward curtailing high alcohol consumption among their own than it was part of a larger movement of social reform that marked the era. In fact, estimates of the quantity of consumption by Africans during this period are conflicting. So, it cannot be said that alcohol was the primary motivator for African interest in temperance (Sterne, 1967). Herd (1991) believes the lure of temperance was more a reflection of African abolitionist views on slavery and the lure of Enlightenment thinking that valued the social betterment of all.

At the beginning of the 20th century, stereotyping and the perceived problems with the African American population had become central to the issue of alcohol reform for southern prohibitionists. Influenced by the Victorian Age and the preoccupation with sexual mores, women and children were now seen as needing protection from the disinhibited African Americans who were being portrayed as sexual perpetrators in the sensationalistic periodicals of the time (Sterne, 1967). The hackneyed views of African Americans spilled over into the disenfranchisement campaigns aimed at controlling both the poor white and African American vote (Herd, 1991). "Whiskey-sodden, irresponsible" African American voters "needed" to be controlled. So, many politicians urged restrictive voting rights. The temperance movement, which had advocated freedom, was thus thwarted by restrictions on voting rights, and there was a decline in the movement's popularity among many African American reformists who now saw alcohol regulation as antithetical to the true tenets of the temperance movement (Du Bois, 1928). However, Herd (1991) claims that it was at the popular level where the most profound changes in views of alcohol among African Americans of the time took place. A new fascination with a sensual lifestyle overshadowed the now anachronistic temperance movement.

Accompanying this fascination were significant demographic and socioeconomic changes in the African American population. Escaping intense oppression in the South, thousands migrated to the northern "wet" cities, only to find many northern industrialists, especially those resisting the union movement, offering only low-paying jobs—primarily recruiting African Americans as strikebreakers. Many took these jobs, while many others found bootlegging much more profitable than farm and other unskilled labor. Speakeasies and cabarets, emphasizing excitement and sensual pleasure, became the arenas for this new lifestyle. As a result, the views of alcohol among African Americans shifted 180 degrees: Whereas many African Americans had embraced the temperance movement of one hundred years earlier as a means to demonstrate defiance, intemperance in early 20th century America was the means to demonstrate defiance against an oppressive and restrictive legal system.

Values

While there is no such thing as "The African American Family," studies on the African American family structure can be used to guide a general understanding of this diverse population. According to Black and Jackson (2005), families of African origin present themselves in diverse ways. They can vary in their geographic origin, level of acculturation, skin color, socioeconomic status, and religious backgrounds. For example, when studying African American families, you might study African immigrants, families of British West Indies descent, Haitians, and African Muslim families.

FAMILY ROLES As you would expect, the roles of males and females in the African American family vary. Historically, the displacement of African Americans from agriculture into service and industrial employment, with little adjustment in the amount of racism, left this group as the "last hired, first fired." Unemployment was always high outside of southern agriculture, and out of necessity African American women worked outside the home. Perhaps as a result, African American women are seen as the "strength of the family" (Hines & Boyd-Franklin, 2005). Nonetheless, the male/female relationships are influenced by the larger social grand narrative of differential power.

The abilities of African American men to engage in relationships is clearly diminished by incarceration, mental and physical disabilities, death due to hazardous jobs, and drug and alcohol abuse. Thus, you can see how Franklin's (2004) term, "invisibility syndrome" influenced views of African American males as being irresponsible. A more accurate view of the role of fathers reflects the pressures of providing for the family in a society where job ceilings exist and oppression abounds (Hines & Boyd-Franklin, 1982; 2005). These same authors also indicate that the African American father may have to spend an inordinate amount of time and energy trying to provide for the family's basic survival needs, a preoccupation that drains the psychic energy that would otherwise be infused into the family. Faced both with pressures to provide and with barriers thwarting their efforts, underemployed and unemployed African American fathers may be at risk for turning to alcohol and other drugs as a means of relieving the pain.

KINSHIP AND EXTENDED FAMILY BONDS   The flexibility of roles in African American culture is also influenced by an atavistic value emphasizing strong kinship bonds. While slavery certainly reinforced this value, its origins can be traced to Africa where Africanian thinking had produced the syllogism "We are, therefore I am" (Hines & Boyd-Franklin, 1982). Prevalent among many African American families and tied to the value of kinship is a phenomenon known as "child-keeping." Child-keeping occurs when a child is informally "adopted" or reared by other family members who have more resources than the biological parents. Rather than seeing child-keeping as the disruption of the family system, Hines and Boyd-Franklin (1982; 2005) believe that this occurrence actually elevates the importance of the child. Yet African American children may be subjected to ridicule and ostracism by a mainstream Euro-American culture that fails to recognize and/or appreciate this value—believing instead that the child who is raised by grandparents reflects a broken home. As a result of these misperceptions and other factors, African American children may experience stress at school and can turn to alcohol and other drugs.

RELIGION   The crucial role of the church in the emancipation of slaves in America is reflected in current views of the importance of a strong religious orientation among many African Americans. In times of slavery, cryptic messages about times and places for escape often came from the pulpit during the church service (Hines & Boyd-Franklin, 1982; 2005). Interestingly, these same authors point out that songs sung today in many African American churches, such as "Steal Away" and "Wade in the Water," often carry the remains of those messages. The power of those messages, hidden in church protocol, and their relationship to emancipation issues should leave no one surprised that some of the most notable contemporary leaders in the African American culture are or were preachers: the Reverend Martin Luther King, Jr., the Reverend Jesse Jackson, Malcolm X, and others. Although these individuals are of international stature, the local church is an important vehicle allowing for the emergence of leaders in local African American communities. Free from the oppression that exists in mainstream Euro-American culture, the church allows outlets for creative talents that otherwise might be thwarted. The racism and oppression experienced by low-paying jobs during the week may be offset somewhat by becoming a deacon or trustee on Sunday. Hines and Boyd-Franklin remind us that numerous church activities, such as dinners, trips, singing in the choir, and participation in Sunday school, provide an intricate social life for many African Americans and promote their mental health and a sense of connectedness. A recent study by Sunshine and Starks (2010) found that religiosity does play a role as a protective factor for African Americans.

Risk Factors for Alcohol and Other Drug Abuse

The results of research on the relationship between African Americans and alcohol and other drugs are complicated and mixed. Yet, some interesting trends indicating use are notable. For example, studies have found that risk for substance abuse problems in the African American population is linked to an interrelationship of individual attributes and characteristics, environmental characteristics, historical experiences, cultural factors, poverty, stress, unemployment, and racism and discrimination (Gordon, 1994; Kingree & Sullivan, 2002). A study of African American youth (Burlew et al., 2009) brings this point home. These authors examined neighborhood risk factors and found that both exposure to negative neighborhood activities and low parental supervision increase the onset of substance use by the eighth grade. To a degree, parental supervision can mediate these risk factors and act to protect African American adolescents. At the same time, another study of 8,879 12th-grade students suggests that individuals with high levels of risk behaviors benefit less from the protective factor of a positive family or neighborhood context (Cleveland, Collins, Lanza, Greenberg, & Feinberg, 2010). High-risk youth (11–18 years) who do poorly in school and who hang with peers who use drugs seem to be the most vulnerable African American population for marijuana and alcohol use (Clark, Belgrave, & Nasim, 2008).

Another factor increasing risk is availability. For instance, in 1978, Los Angeles had approximately three liquor stores per block in addition to those neighborhood stores offering beer and wine. Gordon (1994) found that, 25 years later (1993), 10 times more liquor stores were in the African American communities than in predominantly Euro-American communities. In 2000, LaVeist and Wallace (2000) researched and found evidence that alcohol continued to be more available in African American communities than in white communities. One factor is that advertising in urban areas entices drinking. Naa and Meyer (2009) found that African American women's exposure to inner-city outdoor advertising was associated with current problem drinking among the 139 females they studied.

The scope of problems that affects the African American community, especially the younger population, is still poorly understood. Some of the problem comes from the fact that most studies of African American youth come from impoverished urban areas, which are organized differently than other settings, such as rural (Vazsonyi, Trejos-Castillo, & Young, 2008). Yet, it is not only the inner cities that reflect AOD problems. These authors found that levels of drug use and delinquency were higher in rural youth in comparison to nonrural ones. In addition, Boyd, Mackey, Phillips, and Travakoli (2006) found that African American women who live in rural areas experience a disproportionate number of negative health and social consequences as a result of their AOD use when compared to the AOD use of white women.

DEVELOPMENTAL ISSUES Evidence related to African American youth's drug use is contradictory. On the one hand, and contrary to myth, Johnston, O'Malley, Bachman, and Schulenberg (2011) found that African American eighth, ninth, and 12th graders reported lower rates of illicit drug use than did their non-Hispanic white and Hispanic counterparts. However, another study demonstrated that this group reported higher rates for marijuana use than did all other ethnic groups except those who indicated two or more races (Centers for Disease Control and Prevention, 2006d). The Centers for Disease Control and Prevention (CDC) (2010b) reported that tobacco use during adolescence is associated with AOD use, and African Americans' rates in the use of tobacco in middle school are higher than most other groups. Yet, it is the lowest among high school students.

Studies that show that adolescent substance use is correlated to neighborhood risk and low parental supervision only drive home the risk for Hurricane Katrina survivors (Burlew et al., 2009). A 2010 study by Rowe, La Greca, and Alexandersson (2010) looked at family and individual factors associated with the effects of Hurricane Katrina. They were particularly interested in adolescents and the effects of posttraumatic stress disorder (PTSD) and substance involvement. Adolescents who reported posttraumatic stress and substance involvement were found to have low family cohesion, low parental monitoring, and more adolescent delinquency. A large number of African American families were displaced as a result of Hurricane Katrina, and the effects of this catastrophe will be felt for years to come as they transition back to a sense of normalcy.

There has been a history of studies that reflect the AOD problems that African Americans face during life transitions. In an early study, Levinson (1978) had theorized that the years from 30 to 40 may be especially difficult for an African American male who is attempting to match aspirations with achievement. Failing to achieve one's goals can be expressed in depression and dependency, and this is exactly what Steer, Shaw, Beck, and Fine (1977) found in their study of African American alcoholics. These authors believe that, having failed to achieve their dreams, many African American men may turn to alcohol in their early 30s to offset feelings of inadequacy and depression. King (1982) asked a rather intriguing question regarding African American drinking patterns: "Why is the consumption of alcohol (3+ drinks per day) most prevalent in the age decades 40 to 49 and 50 to 59 among African Americans?" He conducted a search of the literature published between 1977 and 1980 and found that most American men (regardless of ethnicity) go through a transition in the middle years. He postulated that the increase of heavy drinking in African American men during the middle years may be due to frustrated attempts at attaining satisfactory love and work aspirations. Adding support to this view is Williams (1986), who points out that unemployment can have a deleterious effect on drinking behavior in that it is correlated with increased risk of alcohol problems. Martin, Tuch, and Roman (2003) believe that "escapist drinking" is found among this population during the middle years. "Escapist" drinking is based upon the idea that the utility of drinking is a means of reducing stress. Finally, the Centers for Disease Control and Prevention (2010d) report statistics that confirm studies showing that African American males tend to drink more in their middle years.

AT A GLANCE

AFRICAN AMERICANS

Population

41 million African Americans live mainly in New York, Florida, Texas, Georgia, California, and North Carolina.

African Americans make up 13.2% of U.S. total population.

Education

80% age 25 and older have a high school diploma.

30% have a bachelor's degree.

Income

24.5% live at poverty level.

$33,916 is the median family income.

Children and Parenting

Many childrearing concerns such as caretaking, discipline, financial responsibility, companionship, emotional support, and problem-solving are shared.

Children occupy a central role in the marriage and essentially tie the marriage together.

Family Organization and Communication

Children can be informally "adopted" or reared by other family members who have more resources than the biological parents (child-keeping).

Spiritual Beliefs and Practices

Religion is important, and the church is seen as potentially providing an intricate social life while promoting mental health and a sense of connectedness.

Involvement with the church allows outlets for creative talents that otherwise might be thwarted.

LATINO AND HISPANIC POPULATIONS

The term *Latino American* is used to describe those persons living in the United States who share a common cultural background. The term *Hispanic* refers to Spaniards and Portuguese, while *Latino* includes those known as Chicanos, Cubanos, Puerto Ricans, Latin Americans, and Mexican Americans. The Latino population comprises three major groups: Mexican Americans, Puerto Ricans, and Cuban Americans. The following section will present information on these groups as well as some information on Central and South Americans. In general, differences between these three groups of people are influenced largely by educational level, socioeconomic status, immigration status, age/generation, rural versus urban residence, country of origin, and degree of acculturation (Torres, 1993).

Background

The immigration patterns among Cuban Americans, Puerto Rican Americans, Central and South Americans, and Mexican Americans are varied. Joining the 50,000 Cubans already living in the states were large numbers of Cubans who emigrated during the political unrest of the 1950s. The majority of those leaving were the highly educated, professional and business upper-class people (Garcia-Preto, 2005). About 3,000 wealthy Cubans left when Fidel Castro came into power in 1959, and these were joined by another wave of middle-class immigrants who came to the United States in 1960. Finally, in 1980, came a wave of working-class Cubans, some 125,000 strong, who were mostly African American Cubans. Puerto Rican Americans have immigrated to the United States mainly for economic reasons in slow but steady rates. Central and South Americans represent the most recent Latino/Hispanic immigrants to the United States. Most of these individuals came because of political upheaval in their respective countries. Exact figures of immigrants are unavailable, mostly due to their being illegal aliens, but it is known that a majority come from Guatemala, El Salvador, and Nicaragua (Burns & D'Avanzo, 1993; Garcia-Preto, 2005). These same authors note that this group experiences a high incidence of posttraumatic stress disorder (PTSD). The authors attribute the PTSD to the violence experienced by these individuals in their homelands as well as to the trauma, such as beatings and rape, experienced while traveling to the United States through Mexico. With the exception of those living in the southwestern United States, the majority of Mexican families living in the United States are immigrants.

The presence of Latinos/Hispanics in the southwest region of the United States dates back to the early 1500s. The outcome of the Mexican War (1846–1848), caused by conflict over Texas, witnessed the annexation of Arizona, California, Colorado, New Mexico, Texas, and portions of Utah and Nevada. Along with this annexation came over 75,000 Mexican people who were granted U.S. citizenship (Burns & D'Avanzo, 1993). The Mexican Revolution of 1910 was the cause of another influx of Latino/Hispanic immigrants to the United States. In addition, Burns and D'Avanzo point out that, between World War II and the 1960s, the Braceros Programs allowed for seasonal laborers to enter the country to work in the fields of California, Arizona, Washington, Texas, and the Midwest.

Values

Hispanic and *Latino* are adjectives used to describe people in this country in a way that would not be used in their country of origin (Garcia-Preto, 2005). The term *Hispanic* was initiated in the 1970s and was used by the U.S. Department of Education to track population. It refers to the Spanish culture and language, whereas the term *Latino* refers to Spain's former colonies in South America, Central Mexico, and Mexico. As with the other culturally and ethnically diverse populations discussed in this chapter, values indigenous to the Latino/Hispanic culture come into frequent conflict with the Euro-American value system, which can cause distress for the Latino/Hispanic individual and family. Feelings of guilt, self-doubt, and even betrayal can create disharmony within and among Latino/Hispanic families. Similar disruptions can occur when individual family members take advantage of economic or educational opportunities not taken by other family members.

FAMILY AND CARING   Traditional Latino/Hispanic families value the family above almost everything else. However, Mexican American families do not necessarily place as much emphasis on this value. The traditional Latino/Hispanic family is private, and this is especially true with problems such as AOD abuse. The family protects the individual and demands loyalty while stressing the importance of family proximity, cohesiveness, and respect (*respeto*) for parental authority. *Orgullo* (pride), *verguenza* (shame), *confianza* (confidence), *dignidad* (dignity), and *pobre pero honesto* (poor but honest) are typical values in traditional Latino/Hispanic families (Falicov, 1982; 2002). However, as Latinos/Hispanics become more acculturated into mainstream Euro-American society, these values become a source of conflict. Joining gangs, where these values operate strongly, becomes one way Latino/Hispanic youths cope with the conflict of values. Similar to, yet different from, many African American families, Latino/Hispanic families usually live in a nuclear arrangement but do have extended families living nearby. The large size of the family, usually consisting of parents and four or five children, influences the family structure in many ways. Depending on the degree of acculturation, Latino/Hispanic families value affiliation and cooperation while placing much less value upon confrontation and competition

(Falicov, 1982; 2002). Moreover, many childrearing concerns such as caretaking, discipline, financial responsibility, companionship, emotional support, and problem solving are shared. In traditional Latino/Hispanic families, for example, the role of godparents is very pronounced. The emphasis on intergenerational and lateral interdependence, however, does not diminish the value of *cariño,* or deep caring for the family, nor does it eliminate the need for strong adherence to a high degree of hierarchical organization in which rules are clearly organized around age and gender. Even though, traditionally, older male children are given the greatest authority and power, Latino/Hispanic families place emphasis on equality and on unconditional acceptance of family members. Parents often provide much nurturance and protection for children and do not push them into achievement when it involves unhealthy competition between family members (Falicov, 1982; 2002).

Children also occupy a central role in the marriage. Because *el amor de madre* (motherly love) is seen as a much greater love than romantic love, it is the existence of the children that essentially ties the marriage together. Even though children enjoy a central role in the family, their status is lower than that of their parents. It is *respeto* (respect) that maintains the child's status while allowing parents to reinforce a dependence and dutiful posture among their children (Garcia-Preto, 2005).

GENDER ROLES   Almost everyone is familiar with the hackneyed version of Latino/Hispanic *machismo* or *muy hombre.* According to Falicov, this value dictates the need for males to be strong, brave, protective of their women (mothers, sisters, wives), aggressive, sexually experienced, courageous, and authoritarian. The implication is for women to be humble, submissive, virtuous, and devoted to their home and children. This value for females is known as *hembrismo* or *marianismo* and underscores the importance of the self-sacrificing mother. *Marianismo* and *hembrismo* (discussed below) also serve to counterbalance the male value of *machismo* (Stevens, 1973).

In actuality, many Latino/Hispanic men are dependent and submissive, and it is the women who are dominant and controlling (Falicov, 1982; Garcia-Preto, 2005). In public, the "self-denial" of the mother is reinforced by the father's insistence that the children obey and help her. Often, however, he is much less involved with the children other than to discipline them, and, on more than one occasion, the mother may find herself in covert disagreement with him. When this occurs, she may act as a mediator between the children and the father, thus adding more to her central position in the family (Stevens, 1973).

Hembrismo is the female counterpart to the male machismo and reflects "femaleness" through strength, perseverance, flexibility, and the ability to survive. The conflict of values arising between the male need to demonstrate *machismo* and the female values of *marianismo* and *hembrismo* can create stress for Latino/Hispanic males. Alcohol, the most commonly abused drug among contemporary Latino/Hispanics, did at one time help to build a social structure into their societies. It now appears that drinking alcohol is an accepted way of dealing with stresses of acculturation and the problems related to social, environmental, and political structures (Gallardo & Curry, 2009).

Risk Factors for Alcohol and Other Drug Abuse

SOCIOLOGICAL RISK FACTORS   As with other culturally and ethnically diverse populations, the resulting tensions involved in acculturation raise the level of risk for alcohol and other drug abuse among the Latino/Hispanic population. Patterns of risk vary across male and female populations and between adults and youth and appear to be influenced by both cultural acceptance of alcohol as well as by role-modeling of drinking behaviors. In general, Latino youth are less likely to drink than their non-Hispanic white counterparts. Yet, a significant share of youth do drink, and some drink heavily (Wahl & Eitle, 2010).

Lipsky and Caetano (2009) showed that the prevalence of males' illicit drug use, abuse, and dependence is nearly twice that of females in nearly all minority subgroups. In general, studies on Latino/a substance abuse suggest an increase in substance abuse in this population (Vasquez, 2009). This is truer for adult immigrants who began living in the United States as children or during early adolescence and for those second and third generation Latinos born in the United States (Vega, Canino, Cao, & Alegria, 2009). Vasquez said, " . . . acculturation is basically bad for your health. Being born outside of the United States had a protective effect; in the same group, someone born in the United States was significantly more likely to have a behavioral disorder than an immigrant" (p. 303).

Studies on African American adolescents have shown the relationship between perceived discrimination and substance use, and similar studies focusing on these same factors for Hispanic youth demonstrate mixed findings. For example, Kam and Cleveland (2011) found that while perceived discrimination did seem to have a direct effect on AOD use, they found that neither parental nor peer influences were significant factors. Yet, other studies looking at parental monitoring underscore the importance of parental influence—especially as it relates to the role that parents play in the lives of their children—report different results. For instance, Parsai, Marsiglia, and Kulis (2010) and Parsai, Voisine, Marsiglia, Kulis, and Nieri (2009) found that youth do benefit from parental influences such as having clear rules and consequences regarding substance use.

Other sociological risk factors for substance abuse by Latino/Hispanic youth reflect the problems confronted in the schools. Varying degrees of language proficiency are excessive and can pose serious problems both in seeking and maintaining employment or when children attend English-speaking schools. Limited language proficiency can lead to decreases in self-esteem, thus elevating the risk for abusing substances (Valencia & Johnson, 2008).

Researchers have found that Latino adolescents increase drug use with gang affiliation and, after leaving the gang, use more drugs (De La Rosa, Rice, & Rugh, 2007). These authors found that risk factors for Latino youth were associated with family attitude toward deviance, friends' use, school truancy, and living in neighborhoods with high crime rates. According to a U.S. Department of Health and Human Services report (2003), Mexican American men and women were somewhat more likely to have drinking problems and to drink more heavily than their Cuban, Puerto Rican, or Central and South American counterparts. For the female population, this heavy use could be a result of the breakdown of traditional Hispanic culture and the concomitant loss of social supports and ensuing lack of socialization into the Euro-American culture.

In the Puerto Rican community, heavy drinking takes place most often in public and in full view of children. As long as family and social obligations are fulfilled, heavy drinking is widely tolerated (Hispanic Health Council, 1987). In general, the Puerto Rican population views alcohol as a socially approved reward for hard work or achievement and sees alcohol as a means to escape undesirable circumstances. Some of these circumstances include escape from racism and discrimination (Todorova, Falcon, Lincoln, & Price, 2010). While Puerto Rican men who had more education and had been working longer had higher reports of discrimination, it was Puerto Rican women who seem to report more substance use problems than men. Puerto Rican youth between 10 and 13 years of age who reported PTSD symptoms and trauma were more likely to initiate drinking alcohol within two years of their trauma (Wu et al., 2010).

AT A GLANCE

LATINO AND HISPANIC POPULATIONS

Population

46.9 million Hispanics live mainly in California, Texas, New York, Florida, and Illinois.

Latinos and Hispanics make up 15.2% of U.S. total population.

Education

61% 25 and older have a high school diploma.

12.5% have a bachelor's degree.

Income

21.5% live at poverty level.

55% earn $55,000 or more.

Children and Parenting

Group takes precedence over individual ("We are, therefore I am").

Latinos and Hispanics have strong kinship bonds.

"Family" includes extended family.

Family Organization and Communication

Family protects the individual, demands loyalty, and stresses the importance of family proximity, cohesiveness, and respect (*respeto*) for parental authority.

Family organization is hierarchical.

Traditionally, older male children are given the greatest authority and power, but there is also unconditional acceptance of family members and an emphasis upon equality.

Communication rules are clearly organized around age and gender.

Spiritual Beliefs and Practices

Over two-thirds of Hispanics are Catholic and half of those practice charismatic Catholicism, speaking in tongues, miraculous healings, and prophesying.

THE ELDERLY, DISABLED, AND SEXUAL MINORITY POPULATIONS

Anyone—anytime and anywhere—can become disabled. Some disabilities appear at birth while others can be detected before birth. Other disabilities can be experienced during the course of one's life. The significance of this statement is punctuated by the fact that between 2010 and 2030, the U.S. population of adults aged 65 and older will practically double. This population of "baby boomers" will also live longer. The 65-plus age group will grow from 37 million to more than 70 million, or almost 20%, of the U.S. population (Duncan, Nicholson, White,

Bradley, & Bonaguro, 2010). Along with growth, this is a group characterized by greater eth-nic and racial diversity, higher divorce rates, fewer children, higher levels of education, lower poverty levels, and a greater openness to sexual diversity than previous generations. The swell-ing baby-boomer population also includes Persons With Disabilities (PWDs), who number 49.7 million. Two-thirds of this population has a severe disability (U.S. Department of Labor, Office of Disability Employment Policy, 2011).

The rapidly expanding elder population also includes a larger number of lesbian, gay, bisexual, transgender, queer, and questioning individuals (LGBTQQI). While the rates of sub-stance abuse for gay men and lesbians are high, they are leveling off. However, the youth in this sexual minority population are increasing their use of alcohol and other drugs (Rowan & Faul, 2011). The number of LGBTQQI persons living in the United States is difficult to estimate. The reason is because the earlier versions of individual census forms did not provide space to identify transgender, single, separated, widowed lesbians, gay men, or bisexuals. Hence, Cook-Daniels (2008) says that the 600,000 individuals identifying themselves as LGBTQQI in 2000 probably reflected about 1.2 million individuals. A rather large study (N = 1000) provided more infor-mation about this group of baby boomer LGBTQQIs (Metlife Mature Market Institute, 2010). The profile reflected an LGBTQQI as being a well-educated, middle-income employed adult who was living in a committed relationship. One in five was a parent to one or more children. One in 10 of these couples included at least one person 65 or older. Eighty-four percent self-identified as white, 3.5% identified as Hispanic, 3.5% as African American, 2.5% as Asian, and 2% as "other." The LGBTQQI population of baby boomers will represent the first cohort to have experienced the visibility that accompanied the modern gay rights movement. This group will bring very different issues than the LGBTQQI that preceded them into retirement. They will also bring both similar and different issues from other minority groups. For instance, within the LGBTQQI community, Social Security benefits are not available to same-sex couples regardless of how long they have been together or structured their financial lives. This holds true regard-less of whether they live in a gay marriage, license-granting state. A more subtle and profound issue relates to family bonds. While the LGBTQQI population lifestyle and values separate it as a group from traditional American values, these differences may also be driving apart LGBTQQI elders from other minority elder groups who value traditional views of the family (Cook-Daniels, 2008).

The potential family implosion further dividing LGBTQQI families is not relegated solely to the elderly population. Asian American/Pacific Islander sexual minority youth struggle to integrate their ethnic identities within the North American culture while also trying to establish an authentic sexual identity. This identity may be incongruent with the norms of both main-stream culture as well as with their parents' culture of origin (Hahm & Adkins, 2009). For South Koreans, that original culture sees homosexuality as a deviant behavior that shames and dishon-ors the family and brings into question the importance of personal sacrifice for family tranquility (Hahm & Adkins, 2009). African American gay men encounter daily racism and homophobia within multiple contexts within communities. Gresham (2009) maintains that the lived experi-ence of African American gay men reflects marginal disclosure, negative self-referent beliefs, and minimal social engagement. The same author states that scholars have consistently found that the African American community exhibits homophobia because it is seen as a threat to the existence of the African American family structure (Gresham, 2009). Hence, the group of elderly African Americans who are gay or lesbian can face even more stress and isolation. The ensuing isolation from family is among the Asian/Pacific Islander group where sexual minorities were found to be less likely to engage their families for important decisions or emotional support

(Rowan & Faul, 2011). The exception is the Native American LGBTQQI individual. Sutton and Broken Nose (2005) say that traditionally, many Native American tribes consider these individuals to be Two Spirits. This is a contemporary name associated with Native American LGBTQQIs that was first adopted in 1990. Two Spirits refer to the male/female spirit, and these individuals are often seen as holding sacred and ceremonial roles.

In addition to the age-related disabilities that will likely accompany all individuals regardless of sexual orientation or cultural background, this larger elderly population of baby boomers will also bring with them drug problems. For example, the elderly already have a high prevalence of drug-averse reactions. These reactions are simply to legal drugs. This aside, this population will also bring with them problems with illicit drugs at higher rates than their predecessors (Rowan & Faul, 2011). Support for this assertion is reflected by Duncan et al. (2010). They say that there has been a significant increase in the number of hospital admissions by the older addicts whose primary substance abuse problem is other than alcohol. Furthermore, the health care system is largely unprepared for the incoming wave of baby boomers and their diverse health needs and especially unprepared for substance abuse treatment. This is significant. The research strongly suggest that elderly persons using drugs will only increase between 2010 and 2030 (Colliver, Compton, Gfroerer, & Condon, 2006). The issue is punctuated by Andrews (2008), who estimates that those Latinos who need AOD treatment will triple from 1999 to 2020.

Adoptees comprise another group that is unique. The 2000 census was the first time that data on adoption were collected, and current estimates suggest that more than 6 million adoptees reside in the United States (U.S. Census Bureau, 2011). Although research suggests that adoptees may experience a higher level of psychosocial advantages, they also experience problems in identity development, perceived lack of control, learning disabilities, feelings of shame, loss, guilt, and disruptions in the connections with family. They also experience high rates of AOD issues (Westermeyer, Bennett, Thuras, & Yoon, 2007). In their study of 608 adoptee patients, these researchers found that adoptees had substance use disorders 14 times higher than was expected. They conclude that adoptees and their families should remain alert to issues of substance abuse.

The *homeless* constitute an ever-growing population with AOD issues. In any given year, 3.5 million people will experience homelessness. Seven hundred thirty thousand (730,000) people are homeless on any given night (National Coalition for the Homeless, 2011). Substance abuse is often a cause of homelessness. Although it is difficult to obtain an accurate number of homeless people who are abusing substances, the National Coalition for the Homeless estimates that 38% of homeless people are dependent on alcohol and 26% abuse other drugs. Some homeless people may view drug and alcohol use as necessary to be accepted among the homeless community (Didenko & Pankratz, 2007).

Addictive disorders disrupt relationships with family and friends and often cause people to lose their jobs. For people who are already struggling to pay their bills, the onset or exacerbation of an addiction may cause them to lose their housing.

Risk Factors for Alcohol and Other Drug Abuse

Clearly, sexual minority groups, the elderly, PWDs, adoptees, and the homeless face at least the same risks as other minority groups. In fact, they face greater risks. For example, recall Rolando's case, presented at the outset of this chapter. Rolando is Hispanic. Andrews (2008) found that older Latino men have a history of AOD practices and problems and is convinced that these issues will persist for years to come. This risk of being an older Hispanic male is heightened if he is adopted. In addition, Rolando also has a number of "deviant" labels: baby boomer, gay, and disabled. Li and Moore (2001) believe that deviant labels alone can push individuals into further deviant actions such as AOD abuse. Along the same lines, Taggart, McLaughlin, Quinn, and McFarlane (2007) found reasons that people with disabilities misused alcohol and other drugs centered on "self-medicating against life's negative experiences" (p. 362). Psychological trauma and social distance from the community were cited as specific reasons. It is easy to see that AOD misuse is at least influenced by perceived (and real) trauma which, in turn, leads to physiological, psychological, financial, and relational problems. This creates more trauma. The vicious cycle that ensues raises the risk of AOD abuse.

More specifically, PWDs face challenges that can include increased likelihood of obtaining a secondary disabling condition, increased likelihood of being a victim of crime, of being unemployed, and of having overall family dysfunction. These risks run 10% to greater than 50% compared to the general U.S. population (West, Graham, & Cifu, 2009). Among the LGBTQQI population, gay males and lesbians are at high risk (Rowan & Faul, 2011). Even without a disability, elderly individuals are at risk for substance abuse. With advanced technology and medicine, individuals are able to live longer with better quality lives. This is both good news and bad news. According to Lay, King, and Rangel (2008), elderly who have substance abuse issues will be able to enhance their abilities to adapt ways that allow them to continue AOD misuse and abuse as they age. Brucker (2008) is concerned that these same medical advances can also increase the likelihood of prescription drug abuse among the elderly and disabled populations. As with many, if not all of these special populations, that type of cycle clearly heightens the risks for substance abuse.

HELPING CULTURALLY AND ETHNICALLY DIVERSE POPULATIONS

Issues for the Helping Professionals

Mental health professionals are taught to empathize with their client or clients. Moreover, helping professionals are taught to avoid power struggles and coercive relationships with their clients. Power struggles can come in many forms, and stereotyping is a subtle form of power that can be used to coerce clients of varying cultural and ethnic backgrounds. Another form can be labeling and grouping individuals. By understanding a given group as having certain characteristics and certain drinking or other drug use patterns, a professional can make some gross assumptions about what he or she might be working with. At the same time, we hope you can see that as many differences as commonalities exist among individuals and subgroups.

You, as a mental health professional, should take care to undertake an examination of your own worldview regarding culturally and ethnically diverse groups. You should develop the mindfulness and skills necessary to interact with minority clients in a culturally sensitive and responsive manner. Cornish, Schreier, Nadkarni, and Metzger (2010) argue that worldviews allow for making sense or meaning of the world. It is critical that you develop an awareness of how race/ethnicity, culture, and gender impact your view of the world. In describing "cultural intentionality," Ivey et al. suggest that mental health professionals (1) need to develop an ability and a willingness to generate additional thoughts, words, and behaviors in an effort to communicate with self and others within a given culture; (2) need to develop an ability to develop alternative thoughts, words, and behaviors in an effort to communicate with a variety of diverse groups across cultures; and (3) need to develop enhanced abilities to formulate plans, act on a variety of possibilities that may exist in a given culture, and reflect on these actions. Vasquez (2009) believes that cultural mutuality is an important value for therapists who wish to be competent in working with people of color and those who have historically been disenfranchised. The author reminds us of the importance of relating to women, to clients of color, and to other oppressed groups in a respectful, connecting manner based on our knowledge of the clients' culture while being able to "tune in" to those areas of the clients' needs. Vasquez also says we need to distance our minority clients from socially created labels, especially those that carry negative connotations (LGBTQQI, for example). Others see the importance of helping our clients to both reflect upon their concerns while learning how to reframe and integrate these into a cultural context (Gallardo & Curry, 2009).

A critical issue for counselors relates to the understanding of a racial/ethnic client's story. On one level, counselors are trained to listen carefully. At the same time, when the racial/ethnic minority client with AOD problems brings such issues as power, powerlessness, oppression, and addiction into the counseling dialogue, Euro-American counselors will likely feel threatened on other levels. Meaningful ways of dealing with this issue have been proposed by many authors. Cornish et al. (2010), Cartwright and D'Andrea (2005), and Pedersen (2002) all support the idea that multiculturalism is not a complication as much as it is a complexity. Pedersen favors the term "culture-centered" counseling over the concept of multicultural counseling in order to emphasize the centrality of culture in the counseling process. Pedersen sees culture-centered counseling as essentially

helping with the accuracy of assessment

providing common ground for conflict management

increasing identity

increasing health through biodiversity

protection from culture encapsulation

helping the future global village survive

increasing social justice right thinking that is both linear and nonlinear

helping people to learn about culture shock, spirituality, political pluralism, and good psychology (Cartwright & D'Andrea, 2005, p. 218)

Harper (2006), Tucker (2006), and other researchers (e.g., Cornish et al., 2010) extend the work on treating diverse populations and emphasize the necessity for counselors to be *culturally competent* (as opposed to culturally sensitive). In discussing ethical multiculturalism, Harper sees ethical treatment of a diverse clientele as including moral reasoning, cultural competence, beneficence/nonmaleficence, and respect for persons and communities. This includes the need for counselors to have cultural knowledge, awareness, sensitivity, skills, and an understanding of ethical principles. Given the stigma associated with alcoholism and being a minority, one can clearly see how important it is to embrace the level of professionalism inherent in cultural competence and culture-centered approaches. Recent research into cultural competency reflects a shift from skills of counselors to the overall management, organizational policy, and processes of care (Guerrero, 2010). An interesting study of processes of care was conducted by Bamatter et al. (2010). Studying the transcripts of 23 counselors, they found that 83% used informal discussions of topics unrelated to treatment with their Hispanic clients, and this was seen as a negative. This was especially true for non-Latino counselors. Results showed that counselors should endeavor to maintain more formal relationships with Hispanic clients in early treatment sessions in order to enhance treatment.

Assessment and Treatment Issues

Remember, this book is written for the generalist in the helping field, rather than for a specialist in the field of addictive behaviors. You will likely assess your client for the extent of involvement with alcohol and other drugs, then refer him or her to a specialist if needed. In order to make an assessment, mental health professionals must understand how the client's culture views alcohol and other drug use. What may be defined as problematic drug use in a predominantly Euro-American culture may be viewed as normal in a nonwhite culture. For example, an Asian American's frank confrontation with his or her boss when both are drunk is sometimes considered appropriate. Therefore, sharing with clients that you suspect a problem with their use of alcohol or another drug without an understanding of acceptable use in their culture may be incorrect. It may also be inappropriate. Your lack of knowledge may discourage the client from seeking further assistance from you or others in the helping services. If a problem does exist, you may have missed an opportunity to help. If there is a serious problem, it may become more serious.

When assessing for treatment needs of minority populations, Cochran, Peavy, and Cauce (2007) and Cunningham, Foster, and Warner (2010) discuss the issues faced by practitioners. These researchers are in agreement that little is known about the challenges faced by sexual minorities. It is important to identify the psychotherapeutic process that has favorable contributions to client outcomes for these populations, and this is especially important within family-focused, evidenced-based treatments for youth.

Treatment does work. Yet, Henderson, Dakof, Greenbaum, and Liddle (2010) say that little is known about why treatments work and which treatments work best for different types of clients. In general, motivation to change or client readiness is considered critical for successful treatment, and enhancing motivation to change substance use is a significant component of many intervention programs. However, Austin, Hospital, Wagner, and Morris (2010) maintain that specific factors predicting the motivation to change are poorly understood, and this is especially true among racial/ethnic minority youth. In their study of 310 substance-abusing minority youth, they found that parental factors may have a strong influence on motivation to change. The involvement of families in treatment is critical (Henderson et al., 2010). The reason for this is because family relationship issues have been found to be significant risk factors for the initiation and maintenance of substance abuse problems, and it stands to reason that involving family members to enhance relationships should be able to counter the risk factors.

WORKING WITH NATIVE AMERICANS   When working with Native Americans, remember that "Direct confrontation is limited to making sure the individual is aware of the consequences of behavior. Then, it is left to the innate forces within the individual to operate" (Attneave, 1982, p. 70). In terms of treatment, Coyhis and Simonelli (2008) state that the Wellbriety Movement, and the rallying cry of "Our culture is prevention" is good for Native American peoples because it uses their own cultural and ethnic strengths to foster recovery. Wellbriety means achieving sobriety and abstinence from substance abuse while going beyond "clean and sober." It suggests that Native Americans should recover culturally by entering a journey of healing and balance mentally, emotionally, physically, and spiritually. This dimension addresses sociopolitical causes without diminishing the individual's need to do the hard work required for recovery. This also signifies the deep desire for Native Americans to live through the best attributes of traditional Native cultures while living in today's world. This view is echoed by Chong, Fortier, and Morris (2009), who say that cultural traditional practices should include a treatment approach that matches Native Americans' worldview, life experiences, and attitudes. This approach is important because many Natives do not have the cultural history of their ancestors, and to promote healing, this connection is critical. Coyhis and White (2002a) proclaim that "the most efficacious and enduring solutions to Native American drinking problems are the ones that emerge from the very heart of tribal cultures" (p. 163). Another treatment program is based upon The Red Road (White Bison Inc., 2002) in which Native Americans in treatment are encouraged to focus on a positive journey of life that embodies the relational world of Native spirituality and values (Chong et al., 2009).

WORKING WITH ASIAN AMERICANS/PACIFIC ISLANDERS   Research suggests that Asian Americans, while exhibiting lower rates of alcohol problems than other minority groups, continue to underutilize substance abuse treatment facilities (Yu, Clark, Chandra, Dias, & Lai, 2009). This is likely due to language and cultural barriers. However, once the language and cultural barriers are addressed through culturally sensitive treatment modalities, this group tends to be more committed to achieve their treatment goals (Yu et al., 2009). If, when assessing Asian Americans/Pacific Islanders, you determine that an individual might benefit from treatment, remember that your suggestions for treatment need to be addressed through the father or elder, who will be making the decision for himself or for other family members. An element of cultural sensitivity and bilingualism needs to be intrinsic to whatever intervention is agreed upon. For example, DUI classes are offered for Asian Americans/Pacific Islanders, and AA groups exist for Japanese-speaking individuals. It is important to remember that when culturally competent services are combined with effective case management and motivational interviewing, Asian clients tend to increase their accomplishment of goals (Yu et al., 2009).

WORKING WITH AFRICAN AMERICANS   Pope, Wallhagen, and Davis (2010) maintain that even though prevalence studies are difficult to obtain for the African American substance abuser population, it is estimated that by 2020, this older group of substance-abusing African American adults will reach almost half a million people. Assessing African Americans for alcohol and other drug abuse varies from that of other culturally and ethnically diverse populations. For instance, African American youth who report substance abuse problems receive less specialty and informal care than Hispanic youth (Alegria, Carson, Goncalves, & Keefe, 2011). For a middle-aged African American male who reports drinking heavily at the local tavern with friends on Saturday, a mental health professional might be well advised to suggest that a friend drive him home rather than refer him for assessment and potential treatment. Another example of difference relates to African American youth because, once in treatment, African American youth are more than twice as likely as their Hispanic counterparts to leave treatment prematurely (Austin & Wagner, 2010).

Multidimensional Family Therapy (MDFT) (Liddle, 2010) is an effective treatment for substance abusing adolescents. MDFT integrates an assessment and treatment among a) the adolescent as an individual and as a member of a family and peer network; b) the parents as individuals and in their respective roles as parents; c) the family environment and family relationships, focusing on transactional patterns; and d) extrafamilial sources of influence such as peers, schools, and juvenile justice. Different versions are used for varying age groups so that it is not a "one size fits all" treatment. MDFT has been shown to be effective with African Americans (Henderson et al., 2010). Specifically, results indicate that it is quite effective with those adolescents who exhibit more severe drug use.

According to Sanders (2002), the 1980s and 1990s reflected attempts to adopt traditional recovery support networks. Networks such as Alcoholics Anonymous and Narcotics Anonymous were seen as more culturally relevant and attractive to African Americans, and treatment centers that were being developed were aimed at being more culturally sensitive. Currently, taking from Chief Andy Chelsea's proclamation that the Native American community is the treatment center, indigenous addiction treatment for African Americans is also strongly emphasized. The Glide Memorial Methodist Church in San Francisco is an example of such a community-oriented treatment approach. Initiated in 1989, approximately 80% of today's community-based congregation is working on recovery. In this treatment approach, the overt expression of rage and anger is encouraged, because the expression of it is seen as an important component of recovery. Another example is the One Church–One Addict project, founded in 1993 by Father George Clements. More than 900 churches are involved with the project as of 2002. The goal of this project is to recruit faith-based communities such as churches, temples, and synagogues to provide post-release aftercare for addicts leaving prisons. Another indigenous approach is the Free-N-One recovery program. Sanders (2002) describes this as a Christian-centered recovery program that provides various support groups for addicts and their families. Spread throughout the country, Illinois alone has more than 50 such programs (Sanders, 2002, p. 170). A fourth type of indigenous program is the Nation of Islam program. This program has been in existence since the 1950s and is aimed at helping African American male substance abusers in the criminal justice system. A fifth community-based approach is called the African American Survivors Organization. The purpose of this organization is to provide African American men a safe place to talk about issues. Often, these issues are the very ones that would not be talked about in recovery meetings if a racial mix of members attended. The format of the African American Survivors Organization is somewhat similar to the traditional twelve-step meetings that we will discuss in Chapter 10. However, the opening of these African American meetings is focused on teaching group members some of the principles of African culture. The Seven Principles of Nguza Saba are read and discussed in the meetings. These principles are unity, self-determination, collective works and responsibility, cooperative economics, purpose, creativity, and faith. According to Sanders, the group meetings offer both support and challenges to group members. It is important for mental health counselors to remember that virtually every church in the African American community is involved in helping addicts, regardless of which specific type of treatment program or project exists.

WORKING WITH LATINOS AND HISPANICS   Traditional values may influence efforts to assess alcohol and other drug use in the Latino/Hispanic population. The traditional value of *machismo* implies that Latina/ Hispanic women are not to drink. Yet they do, and younger Latina/Hispanic women are experimenting with alcohol in greater numbers. Many older women may be reluctant to report substance abuse because of the shame associated not only with their loss of control but also with their violation of tradition. So, when assessing for substance abuse in Latino/Hispanic individuals it is important, if not crucial, to determine the extent of the client's acculturation. Because of the strong value placed on children, an assessment of AOD abuse in the Latino/Hispanic population should include referral to a facility where child care is available or where frequent visits by children are allowed. Without such a consideration, the Latina/Hispanic woman's fear of losing her children may pose significant barriers to treatment. Initial assessment of drug use by Latina/Hispanic women might focus on the impact of use on the family system, and especially the impact on the children.

Ironically, approaching men through the *machismo* value may prove effective in assessing use. While *machismo* allows for heavy drinking, being a strong family provider is also valued and often stands in direct opposition to excessive drinking behavior. By focusing on the man's need to be a strong provider and a good role model for his sons especially, the helping professional may be able to help the Latino/Hispanic father determine whether a problem exists. Nevertheless, hembrismo, the female version of machismo, reminds us that while approaching Hispanic males through machismo might be helpful, it should not be at the expense of the Hispanic females.

The Latino/Hispanic population generally is a religious one and includes traditional and nontraditional religious practices with many Cuban Americans and Puerto Ricans following nontraditional practices. Assessment and referrals should include attention paid to services offered by churches and facilities that allow for a variety of religious practices. Helpers also need to keep this in mind because some Mexican families often consult with *curanderos* (folk healers) for help in dealing with stress-related symptoms (Falicov, 2005). In general, the significance of the location of the treatment facility for Hispanics echoes that of African Americans. Flaskerud (2008) believes that the location of the treatment facility for Hispanics must be such that the clients feel safe and familiar in their surroundings.

In determining possible courses of action for treatment for Latinos, it is important to keep several things in mind. Delgado (2002) as well as Gallardo and Curry (2009) maintain that substance abuse specialists need to reflect upon how helpers treat, intervene, and prevent the manifestation of future psychological concerns for this population. It is also important to work toward reducing the perceived stigma that is often attached to alcohol-related problems in order to help this population to become more amenable to treatment (Keyes et al., 2010). Finally, it is important for helpers to understand that Hispanic families might have a norm whereby they would first speak to trusted members of the family, then a pastoral counselor or folk healer, rather than to a health professional about a problem (Conner, LeFauve, & Wallace, 2009).

WORKING WITH ELDERLY POPULATIONS   Elderly populations are at risk due to amount of medications prescribed, discrimination, and increasing age-related disabilities. Proehl (2007) believes that we often deny that the elderly population has mental illness and addictions, and when we do acknowledge them, we configure them as anomalies. Substance abuse treatment designed and focused on the elderly is rare in the United States. When one adds elderly homelessness into the equation, the problem only escalates. Proehl believes that the problem escalates because the elderly homeless population is confronted with losses of hearing and vision, which creates hypervigilance and a lack of trust and faith in treatment. Moreover, because the elderly homeless are often targets in homeless shelters, they may prefer to remain on the street rather than face the fear of becoming institutionalized.

WORKING WITH LGBTQQI POPULATIONS   Treatment for the LGBTQQI has not been well-researched (Senreich, 2011). Chaney, Filmore, and Goodrich (2011) find that counselors need to understand the nature of discrimination, hostility, and oppression in order to work effectively with this population. Sexual stigma needs to be addressed, and counselors need to be in an "affirming position that normalizes and validates their identities" (p. 34).

SENSITIVITY TO MULTICULTURAL ISSUES   A review of the research suggests that for minority clients, treatment centers should be close to the client's family, residence, and/or social network. Moreover, since the fear of discrimination, stigma, and other forms of oppression is very real in the lives of racial/ethnic minorities, it is critical that this client population be allowed to "be themselves" in treatment. Hence, mental health counselors need to be aware of the extent to which the treatment facility or program promotes the use of the client's language and cultural traditions. It is also important that the facility or program employ people at all levels of staff who reflect the makeup of its clients. With outpatient facilities specifically, the days and hours of operation are important considerations. When referring to a local center, be aware that clients may be working swing-shifts or nights and will need services that are congruent with their work schedules and family-care situations. Subgroups within these larger diverse populations experience risk factors for developing AOD problems, and this includes adolescents, the elderly, persons with disabilities, LGBTQQI, and adoptees. Substance abuse counselors and service providers need to remain culturally responsive and focus on building alliances, using culturally appropriate instruments, becoming aware of sociopolitical issues, and dealing effectively with stigma.

MyCounselingLab™

Go to Topic 11: *Working with Diverse Cultures,* in the MyCounselingLab™ site (www.MyCounselingLab.com) for *Substance Abuse: Information for School Counselors, Social Workers, Therapists and Counselors,* Fifth Edition, where you can:

- Find learning outcomes for *Working with Diverse Cultures* along with the national standards that connect to these outcomes.
- Complete Assignments and Activities that can help you more deeply understand the chapter content.
- Apply and practice your understanding of the core skills identified in the chapter with the Building Counseling Skills unit.
- Prepare yourself for professional certification with a Practice for Certification quiz.
- Connect to videos through the Video and Resource Library.

Summary

- Today's minority populations will increase in numbers and make up approximately one-third of the general U.S. population in the next two decades.
- Diverse populations traditionally are at heightened levels of risk for substance abuse.
- Diverse populations generally mistrust the treatment system.
- Treatment for adolescence of diverse groups should include family involvement such as multidimensional family therapy (MDFT) because it is viewed as more culturally relevant for many minority groups.
- "Multicultural counseling" should be replaced with "culture-centered counseling," and

counselors need to demonstrate "cultural intentionality" in order to be competent in their understanding and appreciation of differences when engaged in treating these groups.
- Culture-centered approaches include counselor competencies in knowledge, attitudes, and skills and understanding of social justice, spirituality, political pluralism, and common ground for conflict resolution.
- It is best to use culturally appropriate assessments in order to enhance the treatment possibilities.
- Treatment centers that are close to the clients' homes should be utilized as much as possible to preserve the sense of community.

Internet Resources

Native Americans and AOD
whitebison.org/wellbriety_movement/index.html

African Americans quitting AOD
thehealingministries.net/donaldson.html

Hispanics and AOD
chestnut.org/li/apss/Common/Multicultural/
Hispanic_Resources.pdf

Asian Americans and AOD
napafasa.org/

Culture-centered approaches
apa.org/

Further Discussion

1. What role does discrimination play in perpetuating the assessment of AOD problems among diverse populations?
2. How does the issue of social justice influence the treatment of diverse groups with AOD abuse problems?
3. Given the view that Native Americans are engaged in the longest ongoing protest by drinking, what are your thoughts regarding the issue of responsibility?

Chapter 5

Confidentiality and Ethical Issues

CASE EXAMPLES

❶ A high school counselor has been working with a student with multiple problems. After being caught with marijuana, the student had been referred to an AOD treatment center for an assessment. The treatment program specialist determined that the student was not in need of formal treatment but did recommend that the school counselor work with the student on some social skills and minor family issues. During a discussion, the student tells the school counselor that he is selling pot at school. What should the counselor do?

❷ A licensed clinical social worker works in a nonprofit mental health agency. The agency does not provide AOD treatment but does provide aftercare services for recovering clients. This social worker has been working with a recovering intravenous drug user on life skills, such as hygiene, appearance, work behaviors, and leisure-time activities. The client tells the social worker that he is HIV positive and has been having unprotected sex with a number of partners. What should the social worker do?

❸ A marriage and family therapist is in private practice. She has been seeing a woman for depression. The woman works in a management position for a large company. The company has a self-funded insurance plan that pays for the woman's treatment. The personnel manager of the company contacts the therapist, reports that evidence has surfaced that the woman is using cocaine, and tells the therapist that the company is considering termination. She asks the therapist for guidance. What should the therapist do?

❹ A very large corporation has an employee assistance program counselor on staff. Any employee can see the counselor for three sessions, after which the counselor must develop a plan that, depending on the employee's problem, usually involves a referral to a private therapist or treatment program. This counselor has been contacted by the CEO of the corporation and told to see one of the vice presidents who the CEO believes is alcoholic. After talking to the vice president, the counselor believes that a referral to an alcohol treatment program is appropriate. However, the vice president refuses to follow the recommendation and tells the counselor that she will sue the counselor if he reveals any information to the CEO. The vice president claims that the discussions they have had are confidential. What should the counselor do?

❺ A middle school counselor has met several times with a 13-year-old student regarding his problems at home. The student has told the counselor that his mother is addicted to prescription pain pills and he admits to taking a few himself. One day, the principal calls the counselor to her office where the student's mother demands to know what her son has been talking to the counselor about. What should the counselor say?

I n these five situations, we have illustrated some confidentiality issues in the AOD area for mental health professionals. In the remainder of the chapter, we will discuss confidentiality laws that can assist mental health professionals in deciding on the appropriate course of action in such situations, provide guidance for helping professionals in documenting their work with clients, and bring up some of the ethical issues for helping professionals related to the AOD field.

CONFIDENTIALITY: 42 CODE OF FEDERAL REGULATIONS, PART 2 (42 CFR)

Confidentiality for mental health professionals is always problematic, since many federal and state laws are often complex and confusing, as are the ethical guidelines developed by professional organizations. As a future mental health professional, you may become familiar with confidentiality guidelines in your training program and then, once in the field, be faced with specific situations that do not fit the general guidelines and legal parameters presented in courses and workshops.

In the AOD area, federal regulations exist to govern confidentiality. We will discuss these regulations in some detail, because even if mental health professionals are not providing AOD treatment services in their work setting, the regulations usually still apply. However, these regulations can be complex, and an infinite number of situations related to confidentiality can develop. We suggest the following in situations in which you might be unsure of the appropriate action to take:

1. Consult your supervisor and/or legal counsel.
2. Contact your state attorney general's office regarding state laws on privileged communication and mandatory reporting.
3. Contact the Legal Action Center[1], an organization that specializes in legal and policy issues in the AOD area.

---

[1] The Legal Action Center provides direct legal services to individuals, and publications, training, technical assistance, and education to agencies. The Legal Action Center can be reached at 225 Varick Street, New York, NY 10014, (1-800-223-4044).

AT A GLANCE

42 CFR requires that patient confidentiality be maintained with regard to AOD assessment, diagnosis, and treatment except:

- With the written consent of the patient
- In internal discussions with program staff who need the information
- To third-party payers
- To a central registry for patients treated with addictive drugs
- If treatment is a condition of criminal proceedings
- In a medical emergency
- In response to a valid court order
- To qualified service organizations
- If there is a commission of a crime on the organization's premises or against program staff
- For research, audit, or evaluation purposes
- In cases of actual or suspected child abuse or neglect

Does 42 CFR Apply to You?

Issued in 1975 and amended in 1987, 42 CFR contains the regulations issued by the Department of Health and Human Services related to the confidentiality of AOD abuse patient records (terminology used in the regulations). These regulations supersede any local or state laws that are less restrictive than the regulations. Federal regulations in this area were seen as necessary because individuals with AOD problems might be hesitant to seek treatment if their confidentiality could not be guaranteed. This was particularly true when treatment for illegal drug abuse was separate from alcohol treatment and, therefore, simply contacting a drug treatment program became an admission of illegal activity.

Before you conclude that these regulations are irrelevant because you will not be providing AOD treatment, please read further. 42 CFR defines a *program* as any person or organization that, in whole or in part, provides alcohol/drug abuse diagnosis, treatment, or referral for treatment and receives federal assistance. Federal assistance is defined as receiving federal funds in *any* form, even if the funds do not directly pay for AOD services. This includes tax-exempt status by the IRS, authorization to conduct business by the federal government (e.g., Medicaid provider), or conducting services for the federal government or for branches of state government that receive federal funds. This means that, if you work in a school district that has a free lunch program and also has a program that refers students to treatment, 42 CFR applies. If you work for a mental health agency that accepts Medicaid or CHAMPUS (Civilian Health and Medical Program for Uniformed Services) and diagnoses substance use disorders, 42 CFR applies. If you are an employee assistance program (EAP) counselor who works for or has a contract with a company that does business with state or federal government, 42 CFR applies. In fact, the only scenario we can imagine in which 42 CFR would not apply to readers of this text would be a counselor or therapist in private practice who does not accept Medicaid or CHAMPUS or any other state or federal insurance reimbursement and does not refer, diagnose, or treat clients with AOD problems. This scenario is unlikely.

The General Rule

The general rule in 42 CFR regarding disclosure of records or other information on AOD clients (42 CFR uses the term *patients*) is *don't*. Except under the conditions we will describe later, you are prohibited from disclosing *any* identifying information regarding clients who receive any service from a program as defined in the regulations. Clients who never enter treatment but inquire about services or are assessed to determine whether they need services are also included, as is information that would identify someone as a client. Finally, this includes information that a person (other than the patient) may already have or may be able to obtain elsewhere, even if the person is authorized by state law to get the information, has a subpoena, or is a law enforcement official.

Let's make this general rule more concrete. You work in a community mental health center that accepts Medicaid and provides a variety of mental health services, including group counseling for AOD abusers. You do an intake on a self-referred client (Frank) and recommend that he join the group. Frank says, "No thanks" and leaves. A week later, you receive a visit from a detective from another state. He is looking for Frank and has reason to believe that you have seen him. He has a subpoena for any records on Frank. You must say, "Federal confidentiality regulations require that I neither confirm nor deny my contact with clients." You must not provide any records to the detective. If you fail to maintain Frank's confidentiality, you are subject to a fine of up to $500 for the first offense and up to $5,000 for subsequent offenses. Ironically, if you had not met Frank, you could legally tell the detective that Frank had never come to the mental health center, since this would mean that Frank had never been a client (had not applied for, requested, or received services) and, therefore, you are not bound by 42 CFR.

As with any good rule, exceptions to the general rule against disclosure exist, which we will discuss. However, we want to caution you that it is best to seek advice if you are unsure about disclosure, because these exceptions can be complex and difficult to interpret in practical situations.

Written Consent

The first exception to the confidentiality rule is that disclosure can be made if the client gives written consent for the disclosure. 42 CFR specifies that the written consent must include the name of the program making the disclosure; the name of the individual or organization receiving the disclosure; the name of the client; the purpose or need for the disclosure; how much and what kind of information will be disclosed; a statement that the client may revoke the disclosure at any time; the date, event, or condition upon which the disclosure expires; the signature of the client and/or authorized person; and the date the consent is signed. A separate consent form must be signed for each individual or organization receiving information on the client. The consent form must also include a written prohibition against the redisclosure of the information to any other party.

In the case of a minor client, a parent or guardian signature is necessary only if state law requires parental consent for treatment. If parental consent is required, the parent or legal guardian and the minor client must both sign the consent. If a minor contacts a treatment program in a state in which parental consent for treatment is required, the program cannot disclose the contact to the parent(s) unless the program director believes the minor lacks the capacity to make a rational choice or represents a substantial threat to his or her life or well-being. Clearly, these decisions can be subjective.

The regulations regarding written consent for disclosure allow treatment providers to release information to third-party payers (e.g., managed care organizations) and employers.

However, the release of this information also provides an opportunity for the misuse of such information. Third-party payers and employers are prohibited from redisclosing this information. Equally important is the stipulation regarding how much and what kind of information will be disclosed. Treatment providers must be careful to limit disclosure to information necessary to accomplish the disclosure's purpose. In the case of a third-party payer, this might be limited to the diagnosis, estimated duration of treatment, and services needed. Employers may need only a general statement regarding participation in treatment and progress.

Clients who enroll in treatment programs that use addictive drugs (e.g., methadone) as part of the treatment program are required to consent to disclosure to a central registry. The purpose of this disclosure is to prevent a client from enrolling in multiple programs that use such drugs. Thus, programs may confer about the client if multiple enrollment is detected. The consent remains in force as long as the client is in a treatment program that utilizes addictive drugs.

The only situation in which an irrevocable consent is allowed would be in the case of criminal justice referrals. If treatment is a condition of any disposition of criminal proceedings (e.g., dismissal of charges, parole or probation, sentence), the disclosure can be made irrevocable until the client's legal status changes. For example, if a probationary status has been completed, the client may then revoke consent.

It should be noted that written consent does not mandate the program to disclose. There may be situations in which the program staff members believe that disclosure is not in the best interests of the client. This may present an ethical dilemma for the program, which we will discuss later in this chapter. We advise you to seek legal counsel in any situation in which you believe that disclosure in accordance with a valid written consent would be contrary to the client's welfare.

Other Exceptions to the General Rule

In addition to clients' written consent for disclosure, another exception to the prohibition would be communication among staff within an organization, if such communication is necessary to provide services. For example, staffings occur in which clients are discussed among staff members who have either direct or indirect contact with the client. Also, in a multiservice agency (e.g., a hospital), information on clients can be provided to central accounting departments for billing purposes.

This exception can be delicate in public schools. Can or should disclosure of information on a student be made to the student's teachers? The regulations state that the recipient must need the information in connection with duties that are related to providing alcohol or drug-abuse diagnosis, treatment, or referral. Let's say that a student assistance program refers a student to a treatment program and the student is admitted for inpatient treatment. The student is in a special education program, and the teacher is asked to provide some assignments for the student during the time he or she is not in school. Does the teacher need to know where the student is to fulfill this responsibility? Probably not. After treatment, the student returns to school and the teacher is asked to report weekly on the student's behavior and academic performance. Again, the teacher probably does not need to know the reasons for this request. However, the teacher may be better able to help if he or she knows the purpose of monitoring the student. In such cases, the best practice is to request a written consent to disclose to teachers or other school personnel. Having such knowledge will also prevent teachers from innocently asking students where they have been. The problem in schools, as well as other large organizations, is that information is often disclosed to individuals who should not receive it. Therefore, confidentiality education for staff is often needed.

Program staff may discuss clients with people outside of the program as long as the communication does not identify the person as an AOD abuser and does not verify that the client receives AOD treatment services. For example, case histories may be discussed as long as the client cannot be identified from the history. A treatment program may tell a newspaper reporter that 37% of its clients are cocaine users. A hospital that provides a variety of services and has an AOD treatment program can say that John Smith is a patient in the hospital, as long as John is not identified as receiving AOD treatment.

A medical emergency is another exception to the prohibition on disclosure. A medical emergency is defined as a situation that poses an immediate threat to the health of an individual and requires immediate medical intervention. The disclosure must be made only to medical personnel and only to the extent necessary to meet the medical emergency. The name and affiliation of the recipient of the information must be documented, along with the name of the individual making the disclosure, the date and time of the disclosure, and the nature of the emergency. Such an emergency might arise in social detoxification programs, when clients are withdrawing from central nervous system depressants without medication or medical supervision. If a client begins to have a seizure and requires medical attention, emergency medical personnel clearly need to know where the client is and why the seizures are occurring. Other situations considered medical emergencies include drug overdoses and suicide threats or attempts.

Earlier in the chapter, we gave the example of a detective with a subpoena for records on a client of a mental health center. As we discussed, the program must not provide records, since a subpoena alone is not sufficient for disclosure according to 42 CFR. However, a subpoena *and* a court order *are* sufficient. Usually, the court notifies the program and client regarding the application for a court order and provides an opportunity for a response from the program and/or client, but this is not the case when a subpoena is issued. Since these issues involve legal proceedings, we suggest you seek legal counsel if you are served with a subpoena or if a court order is issued for client information.

Another exception involves disclosure to an organization with a contract to provide services to programs. These contracts are called Qualified Service Organization Agreements (QSOA). For example, in contracting for drug testing or accounting services, a program must disclose identifying information. This disclosure is allowed as long as the QSOA documents comply with the confidentiality regulations.

Another exception to disclosure includes the commission of a crime by a client on the premises of the program or against program personnel. In such an instance, the crime can be reported to the appropriate law enforcement agency, and identifying information on the client can be provided.

Identifying information regarding clients can also be disclosed for research, audit, or evaluation purposes. Although the research exception does allow programs to disclose confidential client information to individuals with a proper research protocol, the researcher is prohibited from redisclosing the information. Similarly, regulatory agencies, third-party payers, and peer review organizations may have access to client information for audit and/or evaluation of the program, but the information can be used only for these purposes.

Finally, an exception to disclosure occurs in cases of actual or suspected child abuse or neglect. Confidentiality does not apply to initial reports of child abuse or neglect, as when a client is suspected of, or admits to, child abuse or neglect or when a minor client is the victim. After the initial report, any follow-up reports or contacts do require consent. For example, an adolescent female in an inpatient program reports that she has been sexually molested by her stepfather. The program must make an initial report to the appropriate county or state office of children's protective services. However, any follow-up visits by law enforcement officials or child welfare workers require the client's written consent.

One caution regarding the report of child abuse or neglect: A client with children will not be charged with abuse or neglect simply because he or she has abused alcohol or other drugs. A danger to the child must exist before authorities will take action. Child abuse and neglect frequently occur but are not inevitable or always readily apparent when parents abuse AOD.

Other Confidentiality Issues

Mental health professionals often ask about reporting past crimes of clients or clients' threats to commit future crimes. 42 CFR is clear regarding the exception to disclosure when a crime is committed on program premises or against program personnel. If a proper court order is issued, disclosure can also be made without client consent. Crimes may be reported as well if the report can be worded in such a way that the client is not identified as a client in an AOD program (remember the broad definition of program). However, state laws regarding privileged communication vary by state and by profession. Psychologists may have one set of guidelines, social workers another, and licensed professional counselors another. It is essential that you become familiar with the state laws regarding privileged communication in your profession. However, remember that, unless the state laws regarding disclosure of clients in AOD programs are more restrictive, they are superseded by the federal regulations.

Does a mental health professional have the duty to warn a potential victim if an AOD client threatens to harm the person? In *Tarasoff* v. *Regents of the University of California* [17 Cal. 3d 425 (1976)], a case often used as a precedent, the court found a counselor negligent for failing to warn a person whom the client had threatened and did harm. However, this case applies only in California (Brooks, 1992). Because a conflict may occur between the duty to warn and 42 CFR, Brooks suggests that mental health professionals warn potential victims in such a way that the client is not identified as an AOD program client.

Finally, the question of disclosure of communicable diseases, particularly HIV, has become a sticky confidentiality issue. All states mandate health care providers to report cases of communicable diseases to local public health authorities (Lopez, 1994). Lopez suggests several strategies that would allow compliance with such mandates as well as with 42 CFR. Clearly, the simplest strategy is to secure the client's written consent for the mandated report and for follow-up by public health authorities. If the client provides consent, public health officials would have no problem locating the client for examination (that is extremely important in the case of diseases such as tuberculosis [TB] and hepatitis), interviewing to identify partners and contacts, counseling, and monitoring compliance.

If the client does not provide written consent, program personnel could make an anonymous report. However, the client's location could not be provided if this information identified the client as an AOD client, as would be the case in inpatient settings. Also, most states require the person making the report to identify him- or herself, which could also violate 42 CFR. An alternative suggestion (Lopez, 1994) is for the program to enter a QSOA with the local public health authority, who would screen clients for communicable diseases and could then legitimately follow up with clients.

According to Lopez (1994), the "medical emergency" exception to 42 CFR would not apply in cases of sexually transmitted diseases and HIV/AIDS. In both instances, no immediate threat to life is apparent, and, in the case of HIV/AIDS, emergency medical intervention would not impact the condition. However, TB is transmitted by casual contact, is difficult to confirm, and is potentially deadly. Therefore, suspected or confirmed TB may constitute a medical emergency and, therefore, be an exception to disclosure. Although Lopez does not mention hepatitis, the same situation would probably apply.

Program personnel may feel a duty to warn sexual partners of, and those who have shared needles with, an HIV/AIDS client. Again, the best practice is to attempt to convince the client to provide written consent to disclose, but, failing this, anonymous reporting can be considered. The wording in 42 CFR would probably not justify using the medical emergency exception to disclosure.

CONFIDENTIALITY AND SCHOOL COUNSELING

School counselors can face some very tricky confidentiality issues. They are generally working with minors, which may complicate confidentiality. In addition, school districts are covered by the Family Educational Rights and Privacy Act, which gives parents of minor students the right to inspect any educational records kept by the school. Unless you have a state law that provides guidance in this area, school counseling notes may be considered educational records.

The American School Counselor Association has ethical standards that deal with confidentiality (the link to these standards is included in the Internet Resources at the end of the chapter). However, these standards will not provide you much clarity in difficult situations. For example, these are statements from the standards on confidentiality: "Keep information confidential unless legal requirements demand that confidential information be revealed or a breach is required to prevent serious and foreseeable harm to the student" and "Recognize their (school counselors') primary obligation for confidentiality is to the students but balance that obligation with an understanding of parents'/guardians' legal and inherent rights to be the guiding voices in their children's lives. . . ." You can see that students telling a school counselor about AOD use can be a very difficult area to determine if it fits in these guidelines for confidentiality.

Based on the discussion of 42 CFR, you may think you should keep all information about student drug use confidential. This may be a valid legal argument in a state that does not require parental approval for treatment of a minor child. However, if you are pressured by a parent, principal, and other school administrators, 42 CFR may not be much comfort. We strongly urge school counselors to consult with more experienced peers and/or with school administrators whenever they are uncertain about the ethics and legality of maintaining student confidentiality, whether it involves AOD or another issue. Also, keep in mind that any record about a student that is shared with other personnel is considered an educational record. Therefore, parents can compel the disclosure of notes a school counselor makes if these notes are shared with administrators, teachers, or other school personnel such as a school psychologist. School counselors should keep records about a conversation with a student brief and should not share these records with other school personnel if they are concerned about the future disclosure to parents or guardians. School counselor notes that are kept private are not considered to be part of the student's educational record.

HEALTH INSURANCE PORTABILITY AND ACCOUNTABILITY ACT (HIPAA)

HIPAA was passed by Congress in 1996 and requires standardization of electronic patient health, administrative, and financial data; unique health identifiers for individuals, health plans, and health care providers; and security standards to protect the confidentiality and integrity of individually identifiable health information. HIPAA affects health care providers, health plans, employers, public health authorities, life insurers, clearinghouses, billing agencies, information system vendors, service organizations, and universities. All these organizations were required to comply with the privacy provisions of HIPAA by April 14, 2003.

For most of us, the privacy and confidentiality standards in HIPAA are the most relevant part of the law. Generally, HIPAA and 42 CFR are in agreement on these standards. However, HIPAA involves general health care, while 42 CFR is specific to AOD. Therefore, in the areas in which the two laws overlap, providers should follow the *most restrictive* law. HIPAA's privacy and confidentiality standards involve the rights of patients to control the release of their medical information, the use of their medical information, and security of patient records. If you work for any of the applicable agencies or organizations, you should be provided with training on HIPAA. Mental health professionals should ask the agency officials responsible for HIPAA compliance about the integration of 42 CFR with HIPAA.

DRUG TESTING

Drug testing in the workplace and school raises serious privacy issues. The Substance Abuse and Mental Health Services administration has developed guidelines for drug-free workplaces that include drug testing, and the Office of National Drug Control Policy has a publication called *What You Need to Know About Drug Testing in Schools* (see Internet Resources at the end of the chapter). However, we should note that the current federal stance on drug testing is weighted toward "do it," while organizations such as the American Civil Liberties Union oppose many of the ways drug testing is implemented. There have been many court rulings on the topic, but it is beyond the scope of this chapter to review all the complex issues involved. The following general information is based on the court decisions up to this time.

PREEMPLOYMENT TESTING   Employers can conduct preemployment drug tests and make offers of employment contingent on a negative drug test. A prospective employee cannot be singled out for preemployment drug testing. In other words, preemployment drug testing must be part of the hiring policy of the organization and applied uniformly.

RANDOM TESTING   Employees occupying positions of safety or security sensitivity can be randomly tested without cause. For example, the Nuclear Regulatory Commission, Department of Transportation, and Department of Defense conduct random testing of individuals in designated positions. The issue of who should be considered in a designated position has been the subject of legal actions.

REASONABLE SUSPICION TESTING   Clearly, this is a very subjective area and has also been the subject of legal actions. However, employers with drug testing policies can require a drug test of an employee if evidence exists such as direct observation of use or possession, physical symptoms of being under the influence, erratic or abnormal behavior, or an arrest for a drug-related offense. Evidence is the critical part of this type of testing and has precipitated many of the legal challenges.

POSTACCIDENT TESTING   Employers who intend to do drug testing following job-related accidents must have a clearly stated policy to that effect. In such cases, employees can be required to submit to a drug test directly after an accident. In many cases, insurance carriers require a drug test as part of the claim process.

TREATMENT FOLLOW-UP TESTING   This is another ambiguous privacy area. An employer may have a policy of random testing of employees who return to work following drug treatment. However, in the absence of any symptoms of drug use, it is easy to see how this type of testing may be construed as an intrusion of privacy. Furthermore, it is certainly stigmatizing for the individual. Generally, this type of testing has only been upheld for individuals in positions of public safety or high security.

DRUG TESTING IN SCHOOLS   In June 2002, the U.S. Supreme Court upheld the use of random drug testing for secondary students participating in competitive extracurricular activities. Schools can conduct random testing for cause (evidence of drug use or possession). It should be noted that a study by Yamaguchi, Johnston, & O'Malley (2003) found that drug testing had no impact on the rate of drug use in schools that conduct such testing compared to schools that do not do drug testing.

DOCUMENTATION

All mental health professionals must be particularly attentive to the issue of written documentation. As Marino (1995) reported:

> By keeping good records, counselors can ensure that their clients and their own best interests are served. . . . Without proper records there is no way another counselor can intervene when the assigned counselor is not available, no way to defend themselves in a lawsuit and no way to verify a payable service. (p. 8)

In the AOD treatment field, accrediting bodies and state agencies often have regulations that specify the form and content of treatment plans and progress notes and the frequency with which written documentation must be made. For the mental health professional working in an agency or institutional setting, there may also be a structure to guide written documentation. However, many school counselors and private therapists must depend on their own experiences and judgment. For those mental health professionals who are uncertain about the form and content of their progress notes on clients, the guidelines developed by Roget and Johnson (1995) for AOD counselors may be helpful. These authors recommend that progress notes should be written with the idea that they could potentially be used in a legal proceeding. Therefore, the entries should be brief and largely factual. Opinion and conclusions should be clearly labeled as such. Terms not commonly recognized in the professional vernacular (e.g., toxic codependency, wounded inner child) should be avoided. Any reports of child abuse and neglect should be clearly documented, including the name and title of the person who received the report. The person making case notes should be especially careful to document any incidents in which the health, safety, or security of the client is an issue. For example, any threat or attempt at suicide should be documented, along with the actions taken by the mental health professional.

ETHICS

Professional organizations, such as the American Psychological Association, American Counseling Association, American Association of School Counselors, National Association of Social Workers, and the American Association of Marriage and Family Therapists, have ethical standards for their members. Many AOD counselors belong to the Association for Addiction

Professionals, which also has published ethical standards. You are obligated to become familiar with both the ethical standards of your profession and the state laws relating to ethical practice for licensed or certified professionals in your field. While most ethical issues are common to all mental health professionals and you will probably receive information about these ethical standards in your training program, we want to mention several areas that present particular problems in the AOD field.

Scope of Practice

Most mental health professionals recognize that their training and expertise is insufficient for an actively psychotic client and would refer such a client to an appropriate treatment setting, which would include medical personnel. The perception that any licensed or certified mental health professional is competent to treat AOD clients is, unfortunately, not uncommon. For example, in our state (Nevada), licensed psychologists can diagnose and treat AOD problems, but the state has no training requirement in this area for licensure. In most cases, it is up to the professional to determine his or her own areas of competence, and an ethical professional will refer clients who fall outside these areas of expertise to the appropriate person and/or agency. We hope that the information in this book will help you make the determination regarding whom to refer. As you will see in Chapter 6, you should have specific training in the diagnosis of Substance Use Disorders before making a diagnosis in this area. Furthermore, it is our belief that a client with a Substance Dependence Disorder diagnosis (see Chapter 6) should be referred to an AOD treatment program rather than being seen by a mental health generalist. We strongly recommend consultation with a specialist in the field regarding appropriate treatment settings and planning if a client is diagnosed with a Substance Abuse Disorder.

Scope of practice is also an issue for AOD counselors who do not have other counselor training. Although training in the field is changing, many AOD counselors have minimal formal training, and their training may be specific to AOD treatment. Therefore, the counselor may be unprepared to treat clients with co-occurring disorders (see Chapter 8) or may be unable to differentiate substance use disorders from other disorders. The ethical practice would be to consult with licensed mental health professionals and refer when there is any question regarding the client's diagnosis.

Client Welfare

The mental health professional has a primary responsibility to the welfare of the client. Therefore, if a counselor, social worker, or marriage and family therapist is seeing a client who is not benefiting from treatment, the mental health professional is obligated to terminate treatment and refer the client. This may mean that a client with an escalating pattern of AOD use may need a referral to a treatment program in spite of the rapport you have established, the client's great insurance benefits, or your own conceptualization of AOD problems. For example, if most of the programs in your area operate on the basis of the disease concept (see Chapter 3) and your point of view differs, you are not relieved of your responsibility to refer clients who need treatment. Conversely, you should not refer all clients to the same type of treatment program because you have a professional or personal relationship with a specific treatment program.

Earlier in this chapter, we discussed the fact that written consent for disclosure does not mandate that a program disclose information. Instances may occur in which the client would be harmed by disclosure. Of course, clients can revoke consent at any time (in all instances except criminal justice situations), but they may be reluctant to do so. For example, imagine you are a licensed professional counselor working at a mental health center where you are providing relapse prevention services for a recovering polydrug abuser. The client has provided a written consent to disclose treatment compliance and relapses to the client's company. One day, the client admits to a slip that you believe is an isolated event. In your opinion, the client has actually learned a great deal from the slip. On one hand, the client does not want to revoke consent because it is a condition for continued employment, while, on the other hand, you believe that reporting the slip would cause harm to the client, since termination would result. Ethically, you should not disclose the slip even though you have written consent to do so. But, we should add that it would be unethical to lie to the employer. Your best course of action would be to refuse to provide information about slips.

If a client insists that you disclose information that you believe would result in harm to the client, you should seek legal advice. However, instances may occur in which legal advice and ethical practice are in conflict. Remember, your primary responsibility is the welfare of your client.

Managed Care

Many mental health professionals are either employed by managed care companies (e.g., health maintenance organizations) or are under contract with them. Certain ethical issues have arisen as a result of managed care. While these issues involve scope of practice and client welfare, we want to specifically mention them in this section because they seem to be increasing in frequency as the managed care movement spreads.

Imagine that you are a licensed mental health professional who also has the appropriate certification for addiction counseling. You work for an agency that has contracts with a number of managed care companies. You conduct an assessment on a client and believe that the client has a cocaine and alcohol problem. However, the client's behavioral health care coverage does not include AOD treatment. The only way the client can get any service is if you make another mental disorder diagnosis. Another client is clearly alcohol dependent. You think an inpatient program would be the most appropriate. However, this client is in a managed care program that covers only outpatient treatment. A third client is referred to you after receiving a DUI. After a careful assessment, you determine that this was an isolated mistake and the client only needs some education. However, your agency runs an outpatient AOD program and the census has been low. Your client has coverage for outpatient treatment and your agency director is pressuring you to recommend the program to your client. A fourth client clearly needs outpatient treatment. This client's managed care company has a preferred provider arrangement with a local treatment agency. You know that this agency employs "counselors" who are not properly certified to provide AOD treatment services.

In a perfect world, mental health professionals would not be faced with these ethical dilemmas. Your diagnostic decisions and treatment recommendations would be based solely on client welfare, professional judgment, and appropriate practices. However, other issues (i.e., money) have intruded. While you are in a training program, it is very easy for others to tell you how to behave ethically. When you are employed and your boss is pressuring you, when you have clients who need help, or when your livelihood is dependent on paying clients, you may find yourself tempted to cross ethical boundaries. We won't patronize you by lecturing about the need to maintain the ethical standards of any mental health profession. However, we do believe that the frequency of these dilemmas would be reduced if all citizens had access to appropriate AOD treatment services. This might stimulate you to be proactive with policy makers in advocating for this.

APPLICATION OF CONFIDENTIALITY REGULATIONS

Now that you are familiar with the confidentiality regulations, let's see how they apply to the situations presented at the beginning of the chapter. In the first case, a high school counselor is working with a student who was referred through the school's student assistance program, and the student disclosed that he had been selling marijuana on campus. The counselor is covered under 42 CFR because the school district receives federal support and the student assistance program does refer students to treatment. However, this situation would be an exception to confidentiality since it concerns a crime that is committed on the premises. In some states, the discussion between the counselor and the student may be protected as privileged communication, in which case the counselor would not have the option of reporting the crime. In such a state, the state law is actually more restrictive than 42 CFR and therefore takes precedence. If the state has no privileged communication law, the counselor is not obligated to report the crime but could legally report it under the provisions of 42 CFR. In this case, the counselor must decide the course of action that is in the best interests of the client.

In the second case, a social worker is providing aftercare services in a mental health agency. The client is a recovering IV drug user who reports being HIV positive and admits to having unprotected sex with a variety of partners. Again, the social worker must comply with 42 CFR. The social worker is providing treatment services and the agency is nonprofit and, therefore, federally supported. If the client is aware of being HIV positive, he or she has probably already been reported to public health officials. However, the social worker can probably make a report without violating 42 CFR. Since the agency provides a variety of services and the social worker does not provide AOD services exclusively, the report can be made without identifying the client as an alcohol or other drug treatment client. Of course, the social worker should attempt to get written consent for disclosure from the client. However, if the client lives in a halfway house for recovering addicts, the social worker cannot give the client's address to the public health authority because to do so would identify the client as an alcohol or other drug client.

Since the social worker is able to make a report to the public health authority without violating 42 CFR, the issue of warning sexual partners of the client's condition would best be left to public health officials. If the social worker has the names of sexual partners but the client would not give written consent for disclosure, the social worker can make anonymous reports to the partners. However, the social worker would probably not have names. Of course, we would hope that the social worker would counsel the client regarding his or her sexual behavior.

In the third situation, whether a marriage and family therapist in private practice falls under 42 CFR is questionable. Marriage and family therapists are generally not eligible for Medicaid or CHAMPUS payments, but the therapist may be a preferred provider for a state-funded insurance plan, and in such an instance would have to comply with 42 CFR. When the personnel manager contacts the therapist to inquire about the employee who is seeing her, the first issue to address is consent. If the client has not given written consent for the therapist to disclose information to the personnel manager, she should neither confirm nor deny that the woman is in therapy. If written consent has been provided, the therapist has several options for handling the suspicion of cocaine use. Since depression has been the focus of treatment, we would hope that AOD use has been assessed and ruled out as a problem. However, the therapist may feel that this issue exceeds her scope of practice, and so she refers the client for a more thorough assessment. Drug testing may also be needed. Clearly, if a therapeutic relationship has been developed, the therapist should discuss the issue of cocaine use with the client.

The EAP counselor for the large corporation will have to comply with 42 CFR if the company does any business with state or federal government. In the situation described, the counselor would have a problem if he or she did not obtain a written consent for disclosure from the vice president *before* providing services. Once the counselor interviews the vice president, the vice president becomes a client and the information discussed is confidential. The CEO has no right to be informed, regardless of who is paying the bill or the fact that the counselor is an employee of the company. However, if the company does not meet the criteria in 42 CFR for federal support, then the counselor has an ethical dilemma. The EAP counselor first needs to clearly establish the parameters of reporting before providing any services and, ethically, must then ensure that anyone who sees the counselor understands these parameters.

When an employer insists that an employee see the EAP counselor as a condition of avoiding an adverse action, such as suspension or termination, the employee must give written consent to disclose before any services are provided. However, the disclosure is limited to a report of the EAP counselor's recommendation(s) and a report about whether the employee followed the recommendation(s). Clearly, a less restrictive disclosure would inhibit most employees from being open with the counselor. However, EAP counselors should warn clients that, if employees sue employers or file Workers' Compensation claims, all records of contacts with EAP counselors and other mental health professionals may be disclosed during legal proceedings (Schultz, 1994).

In the final situation, the middle school counselor should follow the confidentiality sections in the American Association of School Counselor's ethical standards. As the case is presented, it does not appear that the student's drug use exceeded experimentation. Obviously, the school counselor would want to be very confident that this is the case but, if it was, there would be no reason to violate the student's confidentiality with regard to pill use. Hopefully, the school counselor would have had a discussion with the student regarding what, if any, information the student would be comfortable sharing with the parent. Regardless, the school counselor can keep the conversation general (e.g., "We talk about how he can get along better at school and at home") and use the opportunity to suggest that the parent and student may want to talk to the school counselor together or meet with an outside mental health professional. As we noted in the section on confidentiality and school counselors, the counselor's notes are part of the educational record if they are shared with other school personnel and, therefore, would be available to the parent upon request.

MyCounselingLab™

Go to Topic 13: *Ethical and Legal Issues in Substance Abuse Counseling*, in the MyCounselingLab™ site (www.MyCounselingLab.com) for *Substance Abuse: Information for School Counselors, Social Workers, Therapists and Counselors*, Fifth Edition, where you can:

- Find learning outcomes for *Ethical and Legal Issues in Substance Abuse Counseling* along with the national standards that connect to these outcomes.
- Complete Assignments and Activities that can help you more deeply understand the chapter content.
- Apply and practice your understanding of the core skills identified in the chapter with the Building Counseling Skills unit.
- Prepare yourself for professional certification with a Practice for Certification quiz.
- Connect to videos through the Video and Resource Library.

Summary

- 42 CFR ensures that people who seek AOD treatment are in no more legal jeopardy than those who do not seek treatment.
- Almost all mental health professionals will have to comply with 42 CFR.
- The best advice to handle complexity in the law is to keep all identifying information confidential, including confirmation or denial regarding whether someone is a client.

- Any exceptions to confidentiality should be discussed with legal counsel.
- Mental health professionals should conform to ethical standards of professional associations and licensing boards.
- Mental health professionals should be very familiar with ethical standards regarding scope of practice and child welfare issues.

Internet Resources

42 CFR Part 2
lac.org/pubs/gratis.html

Drug testing
drugtestingnews.com

HIPAA
hhs.gov/ocr/hipaa

Ethics
naadac.org/documents/index.php?CategoryID=23
(addiction counselors)
schoolcounselor.org/files/EthicalStandards2010.pdf
(school counselors)

txca.org/Images/tca/Documents/ACA%20Code%20 of%20Ethics.pdf (counselors)
naswdc.org/pubs/code/default.asp (social workers)
aamft.org/imis15/content/legal_ethics/code_of_ ethics.aspx (marriage and family therapists)

Legal Action Center
lac.org

Workplace drug testing
dwp.samhsa.gov/DrugTesting/DTesting.aspx

School drug testing
whitehousedrugpolicy.gov/pdf/drug_testing.pdf

Further Discussion

1. Discuss any laws or administrative regulations in your state regarding confidentiality for AOD counselors, social workers, school counselors, licensed professional counselors, and/ or psychologists.
2. What do you see as the advantages and disadvantages of random drug testing in schools and the workplace?

3. If a housecleaner was seeing you for counseling, what would be the ethical concerns with trading your services for your client's housecleaning service?

Chapter 6

Screening, Assessment, and Diagnosis

MyCounselingLab™

Visit the MyCounselingLab™ site (www.MyCounselingLab.com) for *Substance Abuse: Information for School Counselors, Social Workers, Therapists and Counselors,* Fifth Edition to enhance your understanding of chapter concepts. You'll have the opportunity to practice your skills through video- and case-based Assignments and Activities as well as Building Counseling Skills units and to prepare for your certification exam with Practice for Certification quizzes.

CASE EXAMPLES

❶ Sheldon is a 53-year-old man who is visiting his primary care physician for his annual physical. Sheldon is overweight, has high blood pressure, and is borderline for diabetes. He complains of stress at work and problems at home. Sheldon says he is having difficulty sleeping. The doctor recommends a diet and exercise and prescribes Ativan to help Sheldon sleep.

❷ Theresa is a 16-year-old high school sophomore. She is referred to the school counselor by her English teacher after an angry confrontation between the two over Theresa's frequent tardiness. Theresa was a "B/C" student in middle school but her grades and attendance have deteriorated since the last half of her freshman year.

❸ A marriage and family therapist works in a community mental health center. A couple are referred for counseling by the court following an incident of domestic violence (no one was seriously hurt). When the therapist asks the couple why they have come to counseling, they begin to vigorously argue with each other. They accuse each other of being lazy, irresponsible, unreasonable, and poor parents.

A few years ago, we were supervising a marriage and family therapy intern in our clinic at the university. The intern had just seen her first client and was eager to show the videotape of her session during supervision. The client was a middle-aged woman whose presenting problem was management of her 7-year-old son. The intern was excited about working with the woman because the intern had experience with a structured program for parenting skills and, therefore, thought that she knew exactly what to do to help. The intern asked a few questions about the discipline techniques the client used and gathered a little information on the family constellation. She then described the type of parenting strategies that they could work on in counseling. In watching the tape of the session, we noticed how anxious the client appeared to be, and it seemed that she was not really absorbing the information the counselor was presenting. We asked the intern whether she was sure that she had identified the correct problem. The intern seemed surprised because the client had clearly stated that she needed help with the discipline of her child and had given many examples that illustrated her difficulties with parenting. As the third session began, the client immediately began to cry and told the intern that she thought she was alcoholic.

If you know anything about the counseling process, you probably can identify several problems with this description of counseling. You might attribute the intern's actions to inexperience and a desire to demonstrate success. However, imagine yourself working as a school counselor or in a community mental health agency. You have an extremely heavy caseload and see people for a variety of problems, so you feel pressured to make a rapid determination of the problem and to quickly come up with interventions. When a client comes in with a clear statement of the issue and you are familiar with a course of action, it may not occur to you that there is an unstated problem. You are thinking, "Great. I know how to handle this in only a few sessions. Then I can go on to the next person."

Many clients attribute their problems to something other than alcohol or other drugs or, if concerned about their use, the client may be hesitant to discuss these concerns until he or she feels comfortable with the mental health professional. For example, a client comes to a mental health center complaining of depression. A recent relationship has ended, and the therapist works with the client on grief and loss. The therapist never finds out that the client is a frequent cocaine user. Or, a high school student makes an appointment with the school counselor supposedly to discuss his schedule, when in reality he wants to talk about his increasing use of marijuana but wants to "check out" the counselor first.

In any counseling or helping situation, the best methods to identify the "real" problem are to establish a trusting relationship with clients and to conduct a thorough assessment. In your counseling skills classes, you learn about the facilitative conditions that are necessary to build a trusting relationship (i.e., warmth, respect, positive regard, empathic understanding). Hopefully, you have also learned about the assessment process. In this chapter, we will focus on the assessment that any helping professional can (and should) perform, with an emphasis on the signs and symptoms that would indicate the possible existence of an alcohol or other drug problem. In keeping with the goals of this text, the purpose of this discussion of assessment is to ensure that school counselors, social workers, mental health counselors, marriage and family therapists, rehabilitation counselors, and other helping professionals will *always* consider the possibility of AOD problems in the normal assessment process. We believe that the prevalence of AOD problems in our society necessitates their consideration as a causal or contributing factor with nearly every client. We are not presenting an assessment protocol specific to AOD problems, because this type of assessment would be conducted by those involved in the treatment of AOD problems. However, we will describe some of the instruments that are used in the assessment process so you will be aware of the advantages and disadvantages of these tools.

We also want to discuss the diagnosis of AOD problems. Helping professionals need to be aware of the criteria that are used to determine whether someone is or is not chemically dependent. However, awareness does not imply competence in reaching diagnostic decisions. Assessment is the process of gathering information, and diagnosis is the conclusion that is reached on the basis of the assessment. Therefore, we strongly recommend that you refrain from diagnosis unless you have had thorough training specific·to assessment and diagnosis of substance use disorders.

DEFINITIONS OF USE, MISUSE, ABUSE, AND DEPENDENCE OR ADDICTION

For most helping professionals who do not have extensive training in the AOD field, it is somewhat difficult to determine whether a client's substance use is or is not problematic. They may rely on personal experience and information (or misinformation) they pick up. For example, a high school counselor gets a call from a parent of one of the students. The young man is 17 years old, came home from a party on Saturday night smelling of alcohol, and admitted to drinking at the party. His parents belong to a religious group that prohibits the use of alcohol, so neither one has any experience with alcohol or other drug use. They want to know whether their son has a problem. The high school counselor did her share of experimentation in adolescence but is a moderate user as an adult. She assures the parents that nearly all adolescents experiment and they have nothing to worry about. Is she right?

A simple conceptualization of the distinction between different levels of use can be helpful to the mental health professional in determining the type of intervention that is appropriate for a client. However, these definitions are not appropriate for diagnosis. They simply are a guide for the mental health professional in recommending the course of action for a client.

Nearly everyone uses alcohol or other drugs (including caffeine and tobacco) at some point in his or her life. We define *use* as the ingestion of alcohol or other drugs without the experience of any negative consequences. If our high school student had drunk a beer at the party and his parents had not found out, we could say that he had used alcohol. Any drug can be *used* according to this definition. However, the type of drug taken and the characteristics of the individual contribute to the probability of experiencing negative consequences. For example, it is illegal for minors to drink alcohol. Therefore, the probability that our high school student will experience negative consequences from drinking alcohol may be far greater than that probability is for an adult. The chances that an adult will experience negative consequences from shooting heroin are greater than experiencing negative consequences from drinking alcohol.

When a person experiences negative consequences from the use of AOD, it is defined as *misuse*. Again, a large percentage of the population misuses alcohol or other drugs at some point. Our high school student misused alcohol because his parents found out he had been drinking at a party and because it is illegal for him to drink. Many people overuse alcohol at some point, become ill, and experience the symptoms of a hangover. This is misuse. However, misuse does not imply that the negative consequences are minor. Let's say that an adult woman uses alcohol on an infrequent basis. It is her 30th birthday, and her friends throw a surprise party. She drinks more than usual and, on the way home, is arrested for a DUI. She really doesn't have any problems with alcohol, but, in this instance, the consequence is not minor.

You may be wondering about the heavy user of alcohol or other drugs who does not *appear* to experience negative consequences. First, remember that these definitions are meant to provide the helping professional with a simple conceptualization as a guide. Second, the probability of experiencing negative consequences is directly related to the frequency and level of use. If a person uses alcohol or other drugs on an occasional basis, the probability of negative consequences is far less than if one uses on a daily basis. However, since we are talking about probability, it is possible that a person could be a daily, heavy user and not experience negative consequences that are obvious to others. We say "obvious" because a person may be damaging his or her health without anyone being aware of this for a long period of time.

We define *abuse* as the continued use of alcohol or other drugs in spite of negative consequences. Our high school student is grounded for two weeks by his parents. Right after his grounding is completed, he goes to a party and drinks again. He continues to drink in spite of the consequences he experienced. Now, he might become sneakier and escape detection. However, as we discussed previously, the probability of detection increases the more he uses and, if he does have a problem with alcohol, it is likely that his use will be discovered. As another example, let's go back to the woman who was arrested for a DUI after her birthday party. For people who do not have an alcohol or other drug problem, getting a DUI would be so disturbing that they would avoid alcohol altogether or drink only at home. If, a month after the DUI, the woman was at another party or a bar drinking when she would be driving, this is considered abuse.

Addiction or dependence is the *compulsive* use of alcohol or other drugs regardless of the consequences. We worked with a man who had received three DUIs in one year. He was on probation and would be sentenced to one year in prison if he were caught using alcohol. But, he continued to drink. The man was clearly addicted to alcohol, because the negative consequences did not impact his use.

The relationship between the level of intervention and these definitions can be illustrated with our high school student. If the assessment (which will be described in this chapter) indicates that the student misused alcohol, he may need to suffer a significant consequence to impress upon him the fact that drinking by minors is illegal and unacceptable. He may also need education about the effects and consequences of alcohol use. Furthermore, the student may also need counseling or social skills training if his use is related to peer pressure or to a desire to fit in. If the assessment indicates that he has been abusing alcohol, a referral to a treatment program or helping professional who specializes in alcohol and other drug problems may be the appropriate intervention. Obviously, if he has been using alcohol in a compulsive manner, referral to a treatment program is appropriate.

Although the definitions of use, misuse, abuse, and dependence or addiction provide a rough conceptual framework for the helping professional, it would be erroneous to perceive these categories as discrete. Substance use can more logically be viewed as a continuum. However, as we discussed in Chapter 3, an assumption that there is an inevitable progression along the continuum would be inappropriate. The mental health professional must conduct a thorough assessment to determine a client's placement on the continuum and then decide on the appropriate intervention given the level of use, life problems, and relevant client characteristics.

SCREENING

In today's world of health care (including mental health), screening often precedes a thorough assessment because of time and cost constraints. Screening is usually a brief procedure used to identify individuals with possible problems or who are at risk for developing a problem. Assessment is a more thorough process that should involve multiple procedures and is designed to result in diagnostic, placement, and treatment decisions.

In situations where only a proportion of the population may have an AOD problem, screening can be an effective first step in determining who needs a more thorough assessment for a possible substance use disorder. For example, in primary health care settings, screening through self-report inventories (these inventories are discussed later in the chapter) can be completed by patients before they see health care providers. This is similar to all the other health-related questions patients complete in the waiting room. The patient's responses are used by the health care professionals to focus their limited time on possible areas of concern.

The federal government became convinced that screening in primary health care, emergency rooms, and mental health settings was so effective that initiatives called Screening, Brief Interventions, and Referral to Treatment, or SBIRT, were created. We will focus on the screening and referral part of SBIRT in this chapter and on the brief interventions portion in the following chapter.

While screening can be very useful in identifying those who may be at risk for substance use disorders, you should be aware of certain cautions. For example, you probably have heard of or participated in some type of cancer screening. If you have a positive result on a cancer screening, you are referred for a thorough evaluation. A proportion of people who are positive on a cancer screening do not have cancer. These are called "false positives." Some people who are negative on a cancer screening actually have cancer. These are called "false negatives." The relative "cost" of false positives and false negatives determines how useful the screening is. In cancer, it is worse to have a false negative, so tolerance for false positives is higher. But, false positives cause a lot of unnecessary anxiety and costly tests.

In AOD screening, we have many more false negatives than false positives. As you will see later in the chapter, screening is normally done through self-report inventories, so you must rely on the honesty of the respondent. If someone self-reports that his or her AOD use is heavy and that he or she has had consequences as a result of use, he or she probably has a problem. However, if someone does not report honestly, the screening will be negative in spite of the fact that the respondent has an AOD problem. The point is that screening can be a useful process but it is far from infallible.

The potential advantages to screening can be seen in the first case example of Sheldon. All of Sheldon's conditions may be related to heavy alcohol use. If that were the case, the physician's prescription of Ativan would be counterproductive and potentially dangerous. Furthermore, if Sheldon's alcohol use is not addressed, other medical problems (hypertension, obesity, diabetes) will become worse, necessitating more expensive medical treatment. In this case, a very quick alcohol use screening might save time, money, and Sheldon's health.

PSYCHOSOCIAL HISTORY

We assume that you have taken (or will take) a course in assessment as part of your training program and have learned (or will learn) that a psychosocial history is a critical part of the assessment process, regardless of the client's presenting problem. We want to focus on the information that you would gather on the psychosocial history that may relate to alcohol and other drug use problems. However, a couple of remarks related to assessment in general and the psychosocial history in particular are necessary first.

Assessment is a process that should be ongoing during counseling, and a helping professional should be continually gathering information that will assist the client. The psychosocial history is a structured method of gathering information in areas that may relate to the client's difficulties. This method ensures that a helping professional rules out possible causal factors. However, a psychosocial history is not an interrogation. A helping professional must use the same facilitative skills in a structured interview as would be used in any counseling situation.

Certainly, the nature of a psychosocial history necessitates that the interviewer ask questions. However, if the helping professional asks a series of questions without sensitivity to the client, the relationship may be damaged, and the interviewer may elicit resistance from the client that would hinder the assessment process. The helping professional should tell a client that the purpose of a psychosocial history is to learn as much about him or her as possible so that the best service can be provided. Often, the analogy of a physician gathering a complete health history before seeing a patient makes sense to clients. Also, it is best to begin a psychosocial history with areas that are the *least likely* to be threatening to a client.

Every assessment should consider individual characteristics and group differences of clients and, in Chapter 4, we discussed AOD issues specific to various ethnically diverse groups. Although it would be erroneous to make *a priori* assumptions about clients from ethnically diverse groups, the interviewer must be aware of group differences and must account for these differences during the assessment. The notion of cultural relativism discussed in Chapter 4 may be helpful in this regard.

Finally, we know that taking a complete psychosocial history is not always practical. For example, a school counselor is rarely in a position to gather such a history due to time constraints, lack of access to the information, or to the restraints of confidentiality. Parents may not be willing to see the school counselor, or a student may ask that the counselor refrain from contacting parents or teachers. In such cases, the helping professional should gather as much information as possible but should exercise caution in reaching conclusions with incomplete information. While real-world barriers are not excuses for poor practice, these barriers do exist and must be acknowledged. However, helping professionals should make every effort to gather a complete psychosocial history to avoid missing the real problem.

With these parameters in mind, we will discuss the areas to be assessed in a psychosocial history and the signs and symptoms of alcohol and other drug use issues related to these areas. As we stated earlier, the prevalence of AOD problems necessitates consideration of these problems as a causal or contributing factor in most client difficulties. However, believing that all client problems are caused by or related to AOD would certainly be in error. If you want to do a competent job of assessment, you should be open to a variety of possible explanations.

AOD Use History

We suggest beginning the psychosocial history with an area that is least likely to elicit client resistance, and an AOD use history would generally not fit this criterion. Therefore, you probably should not begin the interview with this history. However, it certainly is the most direct manner to assess AOD problems. Clearly, assessment of substance use problems through direct questions about client use requires honesty and accuracy from the client, but this is true with regard to all areas of the psychosocial history. Certainly, some clients minimize their use, particularly if they perceive a problem. However, it is surprising how often clients report heavy use and do not perceive it as a problem, or minimize their actual use when it is still excessive compared to others.

Clients should be asked "How much (alcohol, marijuana, cocaine, etc.) do you use?" rather than "Do you use (alcohol, marijuana, cocaine, etc.)?" While the latter question elicits a "yes" or "no," the former question is more open ended. For example, when one client was asked how much alcohol he used, he said, "Not much. About as much as most guys." Follow-up revealed that this was two to three cases of beer a week.

The interviewer should ask about use in each of the psychoactive drug classifications mentioned in Chapter 2. Don't assume—based on gender, ethnicity, appearance, or other characteristics—that a client is involved only with certain drugs. Also, don't forget to ask about tobacco use. Clients should be questioned regarding quantity of use, frequency, setting (alone, at home, with friends), the methods used to procure their supply (e.g., from friends, purchased, stolen, or in exchange for sex), and the route of administration (e.g., ingestion, snorting, smoking, intravenously). With adolescents, it is helpful to ask what drugs their friends use, particularly if they deny their own use, since having friends who use is predictive of adolescent drug problems (Hawkins, Catalano, & Miller, 1992).

The alcohol and drug use history of a client is helpful to determine progression (or lack thereof) on the continuum of use and because age of first use (prior to age 15) is also predictive of later problems (DeWit, Adlaf, Offord, & Ogborne, 2000). With regard to progression, clients who report little or no use should be asked whether there were times when their use was heavy. If so, what occurred to change this pattern—treatment, maturity, life changes, or some other event? If their use is currently heavy, how long has it been at this level? Has there been a gradual or sudden increase in use?

The information in this and other chapters of this book should be helpful to you in determining whether the client's reported use is problematic. However, one simple rule may be helpful. Ask yourself this question: "Does a normal drinker (user) drink (use) as this client does?" To answer this question, you must have some knowledge of "normal" and consider the client's *age, gender, ethnicity,* and other characteristics. For example, you are interviewing a 47-year-old man who suffered a back injury in his construction job and is applying for vocational rehabilitation. He reports drinking a six-pack of beer each night and two cases on the weekend. He has a stable marriage, has never been arrested, and had stable employment until his injury. Does he have a problem? Or, a 20-year-old college junior was found in possession of a quarter-ounce of marijuana in his dorm room. He and his friends smoke on the weekend. He does not drink alcohol, and he began his marijuana use last year. You are a college counselor, and you must determine the type of intervention or discipline required. Does he have a problem? Maybe you are a probation officer. One of your clients is a 27-year-old African American man who lives in an urban area. He was involved in a fight in a bar and was arrested. He drinks alcohol on Friday and Saturday nights and usually drinks to the point of intoxication. His drinking started at age 18 and he does not use other drugs, except tobacco. Does he have a problem?

Does a normal drinker (user) do what these individuals do? Our 47-year-old beer drinker is a heavy drinker with no reported problems. Based on what you have learned about alcohol in Chapter 2, you should know that this level of alcohol use on a daily basis is not normal. If the man has no other problems at this time (which would be surprising but possible), he will probably have physical problems from his alcohol use in the future. The situation with the college student and probation client are less clear. They have both experienced problems related to their use of alcohol and other drugs. However, we also must consider the social and cultural context of their use. The probation client may have an alcohol problem or he may have a problem with his social group, expectations for male behavior in his culture, or the like. The college student may be using marijuana in a manner that is quite consistent with his social group and does not result in any difficulties, with the exception of the illegality of the drug. The rest of their psychosocial histories may help clarify the extent of their problems.

Family History

A psychosocial interview will always have some focus on the client's current family constellation and family of origin. With regard to AOD problems, it is well known that a history of alcoholism or other drug addiction in the family of origin is a risk factor for substance abuse (e.g., Hawkins, Lishner, & Catalano, 1985). However, it is best to ask the client if there were any problems in the family with regard to alcohol or other drugs rather than asking if the parents were (are) alcoholic or drug addicted. The client may be unable to make such a diagnosis, and may be hesitant to apply these labels due to the stigma associated with them.

A variety of problems in families may be related to AOD problems (as well as other problems). These include physical and sexual abuse. Since studies have found that a high percentage of women in AOD treatment programs have been sexually abused (e.g., Bartholomew, Courtney, Rowan-Szal, & Simpson, 2005), this is particularly important to assess with women clients. Other types of family problems including financial difficulties, communication problems, and excessive conflict may be caused by or related to alcohol and other drug use, so these issues also should be assessed.

Often clients will report a divorce in the family of origin or current family or the death of a parent or caretaker. The psychosocial interviewer should investigate such events further. For example, a client may say that her parents divorced when she was young because her father was "irresponsible." The interviewer should attempt to determine whether alcohol or other drugs contributed to this "irresponsibility." A parent's death in an automobile accident may have been caused by substance abuse, as well.

The importance of assessing alcohol and other drug use in the family of origin and current family is not restricted to the client's own use. As we will discuss in Chapters 11 and 12, children who live in substance-abusing homes and adult children who were raised by alcoholic or other drug-addicted caretakers may have a variety of problems as a result. The issue of codependency is significant, which will also be discussed in Chapter 12. Although codependency is a controversial issue in the field, it is certainly the case that some individuals are attracted to people with AOD problems and tend to repeatedly choose such people as partners. Therefore, a positive family history of alcohol or other drug abuse may help explain the current problems of some clients, even if the clients have no alcohol or other drug use problems of their own.

Social History

Individuals who have progressed in their alcohol or other drug abuse may go through a gradual change in social activities and relationships. There may be a shift to friends who use in the same manner as the client, while nonusing friends are dropped. Parents of adolescents will frequently notice this, although the reason for the change in social groups may not be identified by the parents. Eventually, more and more isolation may occur if the social group does not "keep up." Clients (or significant others) may report that previously enjoyed activities have been discontinued, which may be attributed to depression in adults and rebellion in adolescents. We worked with an adult who had been an avid snorkler but had greatly reduced his involvement as his alcohol and tobacco use progressed. An adolescent client had been involved in the school band but had dropped out and was spending his spare time playing his guitar in his room as a result of heavy marijuana use.

It is also important to assess the client's relationship history for involvement with partners who have alcohol or other drug problems. This may provide some evidence for codependency (see Chapter 12). One of our clients was a woman in her mid-30s who was referred by a state agency for depression following a disabling injury that prevented her from working. She was involved in a 10-year relationship with a polydrug abuser and had previously lived with an addict who had been murdered. Her father was alcoholic. In discussing relationships with this client, we found that she had absolutely no idea that it was possible to have a relationship with a man who did not abuse alcohol or other drugs. In treating this client, the social history was important since a good deal of her depression was related to the fact that she could no longer support herself, and she thought that she would be forever dependent on alcoholic and drug-addicted men.

Legal History

A client's report of DUIs or arrests for public intoxication or possession or distribution of drugs are clearly related to AOD. However, as we discussed in Chapter 1, a relationship exists between all types of criminal behavior and AOD use. Therefore, a client's report of a history of shoplifting, assault, robbery, burglary, and other crimes may indicate alcohol or other drug problems. With adolescents, status offenses such as running away, truancy, curfew violations, and incorrigibility may be symptoms of substance abuse problems. Although this area seems very straightforward in a psychosocial assessment, we find it is the most frequently neglected. This may be due to the interviewer's own hesitancy to ask such questions.

The case study at the beginning of the chapter involved a couple referred by the court for counseling following an incident of domestic violence. The relationship between intimate partner violence and AOD problems is very strong (Stuart, O'Farrell, & Temple, 2009). Therefore, given the offense (and the couple's behavior during counseling), the marriage and family therapist should strongly suspect AOD issues. In fact, both of these individuals were heavy methamphetamine users.

Educational History

Educational history is a particularly important area to assess with adolescents. Hawkins et al. (1985) found that academic failure and lack of commitment to school were risk factors for adolescent substance abuse. In addition, Karacostas and Fisher (1993) found that a higher proportion of students identified as learning disabled were classified as chemically dependent compared with non–learning disabled students. Finally, Archambault (1992) includes the following signs of adolescent substance abuse: truancy, absenteeism, incomplete assignments, sudden drop in grades, verbal abuse toward teachers or classmates, and vandalism.

With adolescents, it is particularly important to determine whether there has been a change in behavior or academic performance over time. In particular, a change that occurs from the elementary grades to middle or high school may suggest alcohol or other drug involvement. Because school counselors may be gathering information in this area from cumulative files, teachers, and parents, they should be particularly attentive to this issue of change. In addition to the signs noted by Archambault (1992), there may be an increase in suspensions or expulsions, fights, or stealing. Teachers may indicate problems with the student's falling asleep in class, belligerence, or increasing withdrawal.

A retrospective report from adults of these kinds of school problems may indicate past or current AOD problems. In addition to inquiring about behavioral and academic issues, the mental health professional should ask whether the client has a history of dropping out of educational programs, including postsecondary institutions.

Educational history can be particularly helpful with a young adult (18 to 25) who is being seen for presenting problems unrelated to AOD abuse. For example, we assessed a 24-year-old man who had been hit by a car while riding his bike. Some brain damage had resulted, and the man had requested vocational rehabilitation services. The purpose of the assessment was to determine his cognitive and academic capabilities. During the psychosocial history, the man reported increasing academic problems in high school, although he had graduated. Subsequently, he started and dropped out of college three times. He admitted to being under the influence of LSD when the accident occurred (no one had ever asked him if he was using). He had also begun heavy AOD use in his junior year in high school and continued to be a heavy user of alcohol and hallucinogens.

Occupational History

With many adults, work history may indicate more current problems with AOD than an educational history that occurred long ago. However, the same types of issues (poor performance and behavioral and attitudinal problems) that we discussed regarding school may occur in the work setting. For example, frequent job changes, terminations, and reports of unsatisfactory performance may be noted. For a person who maintained a job for an extended period of time, there may be a report of a gradual progression of deteriorating performance. There may also be frequent absenteeism, moodiness and irritability, uncharacteristic displays of anger, and deteriorating relationships with supervisors and colleagues. A good indication that an employee may have a substance abuse problem is frequent absence from work on Mondays (perhaps the employee has been involved in heavy use on the weekend and is too hungover or too tired to come to work).

Underemployment may be reported by a client whose alcohol or other drug use has progressed to a problematic level. Clients may gradually seek jobs that require less responsibility, skills, or time as their substance use impairs their ability to perform at work, and their AOD use becomes the primary preoccupation.

Military history should also be addressed. Alcohol, marijuana, and heroin were frequently abused in Vietnam, and many veterans from this era returned to the United States with AOD problems. Furthermore, stressful military experiences and the subsequent development of emotional problems may put a veteran at risk for difficulties with AOD. However, according to a prevalence study, the percentage of veterans with substance use disorders is very similar to the general population (Wagner et al., 2007).

Medical History

Not only do alcohol and other drugs cause some specific ailments, but people who abuse substances get sick more often. For example, alcohol abuse results in lowered immunity to infection. Also, substance abusers may not be as attentive to nutrition and exercise as those who abstain or use in a nonabusive manner (refer to the case example of Sheldon). Furthermore, a relationship between substance abuse and injuries caused by accidents that result from impaired judgment, perception, coordination, reaction time, and by violence needs to be recognized. Therefore, a medical history that includes frequent illnesses and/or accidents may indicate substance abuse problems.

In Chapter 2, we discussed some of the medical problems associated with the abuse of different drugs. For example, if a client reports a medical history that includes gastritis, peptic ulcers, or a fatty liver, the mental health professional should certainly suspect alcohol abuse. You should also keep in mind that the long-term use of legal drugs (alcohol and tobacco) may result in medical problems in clients who show no other symptoms of substance abuse.

Psychological and Behavioral Problems

When people see a mental health professional, either of their own volition or through some form of coercion, they may not recognize a causal relationship between their presenting problem and substance abuse. For example, a woman came to see us at the insistence of her husband. She had symptoms of depression, and the husband had threatened to leave her if she did not get help. The woman's physician had prescribed an antidepressant, but this had not helped. During the psychosocial assessment, we learned that the woman used alcohol and Valium on a daily basis.

The common problems cited by people seeking assistance from mental health professionals may be due to or exacerbated by alcohol or other drug use. Depression, anxiety, panic attacks, mood swings, irritability, outbursts of anger, problems in sleeping and eating, sexual dysfunction, and the like may be related to substance abuse. However, we are not implying that all psychological and behavioral problems are due to substance abuse. Certainly, a client could present with any of the problems we have listed and have no substance abuse problem at all. Nor are we saying that the existence of alcohol or other drug abuse is always the cause of the client's problems. A client may be highly anxious for some reason and begin to use alcohol or other drugs to relieve the symptoms of anxiety. Even if the client stopped using, he or she would still be anxious if the cause of the anxiety still existed. However, the client's use can become a *contributing factor* to the anxiety and must, therefore, be a focus of treatment.

You should also be aware that substance use disorders and other mental disorders frequently occur concurrently in clients. In Chapter 8, we will discuss the issue of "co-occurring disorders."

If your reaction to reading this section is, "You seem to be saying that every problem I might see as a mental health professional could be related to AOD use," you get an *A*. That's why we are stressing the assessment of AOD use and are providing information on the signs of substance abuse that you may find on taking a psychosocial history. Ruling out substance abuse as a contributing or causal factor can save you and your clients time, frustration, and (often) money. Furthermore, given the frequency of these problems, we believe it is simply an element of good practice.

SIGNS OF ADOLESCENT SUBSTANCE ABUSE

Although many of the areas of the psychosocial history may be useful with adults and adolescents in determining the probability of an alcohol or other drug problem, additional signs of adolescent substance abuse may be apparent or discernible. Since adolescents may not have experienced the variety or the severity of life problems as adults have, the typical psychosocial history may not assess some of these signs. However, a careful assessment of adolescents who are experiencing school or home problems is important in order to intervene in the adolescent's use pattern before more serious problems occur.

Fisher and Harrison (1992) described a protocol for the assessment of AOD abuse with adolescents who are referred in a school setting. Those of you preparing for careers as school counselors or school social workers might find these procedures useful. As part of this protocol, the authors recommend that assessment procedures involve a careful examination of changes in the adolescent's behavior in a variety of areas. As we discussed in the educational history section of the psychosocial history, these changes may involve a deterioration in academic performance, increased absenteeism and truancy, fighting, verbal abuse, defiance, or withdrawal. This is illustrated in the case example of Theresa. In addition, it is important to look at the adolescent's social relationships. There may be less and less involvement with friends who do not use and more involvement with peers who use. The adolescent may identify with a particular school group that typically uses (e.g., "I'm a stoner"). There may be a decreasing involvement and interest in previously enjoyed activities such as athletics or social groups. Furthermore, adolescents may gravitate toward music and dress that depict AOD use in a positive manner or are associated with substance-using adolescents. Adolescents may need money to support their use and turn to stealing, selling possessions, or dealing drugs. In the latter instance, parents and teachers may become aware that the adolescent has a large amount of cash at various times that cannot be adequately explained. Finally, it should go without saying that if an adolescent is in possession or under the influence, a problem exists. It is the severity of the problem that must be assessed.

It is often difficult to differentiate adolescent behavior that may indicate alcohol or other drug problems from normal adolescent behavior. If you tell a group of parents that defiance and changes in friends can be signs of adolescent substance abuse, they may all send their children for drug testing. It is important for a mental health professional who works with adolescents to have a thorough understanding of adolescent development to differentiate "normal" adolescent behavior from unusual behavior and to examine all areas of a psychosocial history as well as the additional signs of adolescent substance abuse. It would be an error to isolate one or two signs and attach undue importance to them. For example, if a lot of kids at school are wearing T-shirts with the insignias of beer companies and a child buys one, this does not mean that he or she is using or abusing alcohol. (However, we do encourage everyone to express their disapproval of this type of drug advertising.) As with the assessment of any individual, you should consider all the information you gather before making a judgment.

SELF-REPORT INVENTORIES

Many screening and assessment devices and protocols have been developed to help a clinician determine if a client has a substance abuse problem. Many of these devices and protocols have been designed for use in substance abuse treatment programs to determine whether a client is appropriate for treatment and the type of treatment setting and services that would be the most appropriate. Discussing these various devices and protocols goes beyond the objectives of this text, but the interested reader will find reviews of the most frequently used screening and assessment devices and procedures in the Center for Substance Abuse Treatment (1999a) and Donovan and Marlatt (2008). Generally, we will discuss self-report inventories that are used in both substance abuse treatment and generalist settings. Since these instruments may be used for diagnostic purposes, they should be used only by professionals who have formal training in assessment and diagnosis and who have specific training in the diagnosis of substance use disorders.

Also, we want to caution you about self-report inventories in general. Certainly, as a part of a comprehensive assessment, self-report inventories can be useful. However, they are not meant to be used in isolation from other assessment data. Second, all tests have validity issues, and self-report inventories are no exception. Since a self-report inventory is a test in which the client "self-reports," you cannot be sure that the client has responded in a truthful manner. Also, the assumption is often made that the inventory is measuring what it is supposed to be measuring, and this may not always be the case.

Michigan Alcohol Screening Test (MAST)

The Michigan Alcohol Screening Test (MAST) (Selzer, 1971) is a 25-item inventory of drinking habits that is simple to administer and score. It takes about 10 minutes when self-administered but can also be read to a client. Each item is scored 0 for a nondrinking response or, depending on the item, 1, 2, or 5 for a drinking response. The total possible score is 53. A score of 0 to 4 is considered to be nonalcoholic, 5 to 6 suggests an alcohol problem, 7 to 9 is alcoholism, 10 to 20 is moderate alcoholism, and above 20 is severe alcoholism. Examples of questions on the MAST are "Does your wife, husband, a parent or other near relative ever worry or complain about your drinking?" (No = 0, Yes = 1), "Are you able to stop drinking when you want to?" (Yes = 0, No = 2), and "Have you ever attended a meeting of Alcoholics Anonymous?" (No = 0, Yes = 5).

Based on this sample of questions, you can see that the MAST would be easy to fake. The content of the questions is obvious and this results in many false negatives (client scores in the nonalcoholic category when an alcohol problem does, in fact, exist). Obviously, the test only measures alcohol problems. However, as Vanable, King, and deWit (2000) have noted, the MAST is designed to determine the likelihood that an alcohol dependence disorder rather than an alcohol abuse disorder may be present (the difference between the two disorders will be discussed later in the chapter). In addition, the MAST questions do not differentiate between past and current problems so those who have abstained for a period of time may still appear to have a problem. The MAST can be given to other family members (who are asked to respond about their perceptions of the client), and the results can be compared with the client's responses.

A similar instrument to measure other drug use was developed by Skinner (1982). The Drug Abuse Screening Test was derived from the MAST and contains 20 items. It is designed for use with adult clients. Also, Westermeyer, Yargic, and Thuras (2004) adapted the MAST for alcohol and other drugs (MAST-AD).

CAGE

This extremely short and simple screening instrument for alcohol problems was first reported by Ewing (1984). The CAGE consists of four questions, each question associated with a letter in the name of the test: Have you ever felt the need to *C*ut down on your drinking? Have you ever felt *A*nnoyed by someone criticizing your drinking? Have you ever felt bad or *G*uilty about your drinking? Have you ever had a drink first thing in the morning to steady your nerves and get rid of a hangover (*E*ye-opener)? Responding "yes" to two or more questions indicates an alcohol problem.

As might be expected from such a brief test with such obvious content, the CAGE should not be expected to result in precision in identifying those with alcohol use disorders. Many of the criticisms of the MAST occur with the CAGE too. Therefore, the CAGE should be viewed as a very rough screening and should be followed by further questioning when a respondent gives an affirmative answer to any item (Cooney, Kadden, & Steinberg, 2005).

Alcohol Use Disorders Identification Test (AUDIT)

This 10-item questionnaire was designed for use in primary health care settings (Babor, de la Fuente, Saunders, & Grant, 1992). The Alcohol Use Disorders Identification Test (AUDIT) can be used as a self-report survey or as part of a structured interview and then incorporated into a general health interview, lifestyle questionnaire, or medical history. The content of the questions is obvious and involves the consumption of alcohol, symptoms of alcohol dependence, and problems caused by alcohol. The respondent indicates the frequency at which the event or activity in the question occurs. For example, "How often during the last year have you failed to do what was normally expected from you because of drinking?" (never, less than monthly, monthly, weekly, daily, or almost daily). Each frequency has a point value (i.e., 0 for never and 4 for daily or almost daily). A score of 8 in men and 7 in women is considered indicative of a strong likelihood of hazardous or harmful alcohol consumption, and scores of 13 or more suggest alcohol-related harm. As the authors acknowledge, the questions may not be answered accurately because some clients may be hesitant to admit the extent of their alcohol use or the problems it is causing.

The AUDIT has demonstrated excellent detection of alcohol use disorders in a variety of clinical settings and with various populations (e.g., Babor, Higgins-Briddle, Saunders, & Monterio, 2001; Bradley et al., 2003). It can be administered and scored via computer and, because it was developed by the World Health Organization, it is available at no cost. Of course, like the other self-report inventories, the AUDIT is vulnerable to false negatives and does not assess drugs other than alcohol.

Problem-Oriented Screening Instrument for Teenagers (POSIT)

The Problem-Oriented Screening Instrument for Teenagers (POSIT) is a 139-item screening instrument developed by a panel of experts for the National Institute on Alcohol Abuse and Alcoholism to identify potential problems in a variety of areas, including substance abuse, mental and physical health, family and peer relations, and vocational functioning. The items are responded to with "yes" or "no," and the test can be administered by school personnel, juvenile and family court workers, medical and mental health care providers, or staff in treatment programs. It is designed for 12- to 19-year-old clients and is available in English and Spanish. The reading level is advertised as being at the fifth grade level. The POSIT can be scored using templates or through computerized scoring and interpretation services. Two empirically based cutoff scores indicate low, medium, or high risk in each of 10 problem areas. Because the POSIT was developed by a federal agency, it is available at no cost (see Internet Resources at the end of the chapter).

Addiction Severity Index (ASI)

At the beginning of this section, we said that we wanted to focus on instruments that could be used in generalist and substance abuse treatment settings. The Addiction Severity Index (ASI) is an exception. This instrument should only be used by trained professionals in substance abuse treatment settings. We are mentioning it because it has arguably become the most widely used assessment system in substance abuse treatment programs. Even if you will not be working in substance abuse treatment, you should at least have a basic understanding of the ASI.

The ASI was developed by Tom McLellan and his colleagues (McLellan, Luborsky, O'Brien, & Woody, 1980) and is now in its fifth edition. It is a semistructured interview designed to assess seven potential problem areas for clients referred for substance abuse treatment: medical status, employment and support, drug use, alcohol use, legal status, family and social status, and psychiatric status. It is designed for adults (although an adolescent version has been developed) and takes about an hour to administer. It consists of seven subscales and about 200 items, and it can be scored by hand or through computerized scoring and interpretation. The ASI provides two scores: subjective severity ratings of the client's need for treatment (interviewer generated) and composite scores of problem severity during the prior 30 days (computer generated). The ASI has been normed on a variety of treatment groups and subject groups and has been extensively used as a basis to establish the most appropriate type of treatment setting and the intensity of treatment services needed (see Chapter 8). The ASI is available at no cost (see Internet Resources at the end of the chapter).

REFERRAL

In one of the case examples at the beginning of the chapter, we described Theresa, a high school sophomore who had a confrontation with her English teacher. Imagine you are the school counselor. You interview Theresa, contact her other teachers to find out about her academic performance and behavior, review the cumulative file, and administer a self-report inventory. Based on the assessment, you have some reasons for concern about an AOD issue. You talk to Theresa's parent who expresses her concern about Theresa's behavior and has seen some evidence of alcohol, marijuana, and pill use. You really didn't know Theresa before you interviewed her and she was not particularly forthcoming. You have some doubts about Theresa's truthfulness on the self-report inventory. What should you do?

You are unsure about Theresa's placement on the continuum of use, and you do not have the time to work with her individually. So, you want to refer Theresa and her mother to someone or someplace outside the school. Certainly, asking colleagues for referral sources is great. However, we want to discuss a few guidelines in making referrals.

If you are unsure about the results of your assessment and want another opinion, you may refer clients to any AOD treatment program that conducts assessments. Often, these assessments are free of charge. However, you should be aware that assessments are a marketing tool of for-profit treatment programs. There may be a tendency for programs to find problems and refer to themselves. Therefore, you have a professional obligation to make sure that you are referring to a program that conducts objective assessments.

First, be sure that your referral source has the training and experience to work with AOD-related problems, as it is erroneous to assume that all credentialed mental health professionals have this capability. In some states, licensure as a psychologist, marriage and family therapist, or other mental health professional does not require training in AOD. Therefore, simply having a license in one of the helping professions does not guarantee expertise in this field.

Each state has an agency (called the "Single State Authority") to coordinate AOD treatment and prevention services. This agency will have a listing of all treatment programs and the services they offer. Generally, the state will have some sort of accrediting process for programs. Most, but not all, states also have a certification or licensing process for AOD treatment providers. There should also be a record of complaints and/or sanctions imposed on credentialed counselors or programs. Not all licensed or certified professionals or accredited programs are competent, and sometimes uncredentialed helpers and programs do a good job. However, you are always safest in referring to an accredited program or certified or licensed individual to ensure that some minimum standards have been met and that there is some method of monitoring competence and ethical practice.

In many work and school settings, programs exist to provide screening, assessment, and referral services for employees and students. Although these programs provide services for a number of life problems, AOD issues are almost always included. In most instances, employees or students can initiate a contact with the program or work supervisors, teachers, or school administrators may refer someone whom they are concerned about. At work, the programs are usually called the *employee assistance program;* and in schools the terms *student assistance program, student intervention team,* or *student identification and referral program* are used. In the workplace, the company or organization may have its own employee assistance program personnel or it may contract with a group that specializes in providing program services. While the type of services may vary, employee assistance programs normally provide brief (one to three) sessions with a professional in order to determine a course of action for the employee's problem. In the case of alcohol or other drug problem, the employee would be referred to a treatment program. Schools vary widely in the services provided because of differing school district policies and state laws. In many cases, a team consisting of school personnel (e.g., counselors, teachers, and administrators) is trained to recognize the symptoms of many common (but serious) problems of adolescents. When a student is referred, the team may gather information from the student's teachers and one or more of the team members may meet with the student and/or the parents. After gathering information, the team meets and decides on a course of action. If an alcohol or other drug problem were suspected, the parents would normally be referred to an outside professional or a treatment program for an assessment.

DIAGNOSIS

After all our cautions to avoid diagnosis, it might seem contradictory to include a section on this topic. The cautions involve two issues. First, diagnosing a condition not only implies that you understand the criteria for making that particular diagnosis but that you can differentiate that condition from others. For example, if you diagnose a person as alcohol dependent, were you able to rule out dysthymia, posttraumatic stress disorder, and generalized anxiety disorder? Do any of these conditions exist concurrently? Second, there can be a scope of practice and associated liability issues involved in making a diagnosis. If your training and license or certification do not allow you to diagnose, you are exceeding your scope of practice if you do.

However, many mental health practitioners work in settings that require a diagnosis and either are qualified or are supervised by qualified professionals. Even if you do not diagnose as part of your job, knowing the criteria to diagnose substance abuse or substance dependence is important in your conceptual framework of what constitutes an alcohol or other drug problem. We will provide such a conceptual framework and then discuss the specific criteria for diagnosing "Substance Dependence" and "Substance Abuse" as defined in the *Diagnostic and Statistical Manual of Mental Disorders, Fourth Edition, Text Revised (DSM-IV-TR)*.

The easiest conceptual framework to diagnose an alcohol or other drug problem is "trouble." Someone who has medical, social, psychological, family, occupational, educational, legal, or financial trouble as a result of alcohol or other drug use usually has a problem. However, the easiest framework is not necessarily the most accurate. In the section on "AOD Use History" on the psychosocial interview, we gave an example of a 47-year-old man who drinks large quantities of beer. No *trouble* was reported but he has a problem. We worked with a couple in which the husband drank three or four beers a week. The wife thought he was alcoholic because she was raised in a home in which no alcohol was used and she had no framework to understand moderate use. This man had family trouble related to his alcohol use, but he was not an abuser or dependent. You can see that there can be exceptions, but, usually, *trouble* equals a problem. In some cases, a mental health professional must assist clients in identifying trouble. We recently listened to a woman tell of her family and relationship history. Her grandfather, father, husband, brothers, and so on drank to excess on the weekends, were verbally and physically abusive when intoxicated, and spent a great deal of money on alcohol. She did not know that this behavior was abnormal because it was what she grew up with and observed in her community. Her awareness was stimulated by observations made by a nurse in an emergency room after her husband broke her nose while drunk.

At this point, review the case examples described at the beginning of the chapter. Identify the "trouble" in each case. As you read the diagnostic criteria for substance use disorders in the next section, see how the criteria fit (or do not fit) for the brief descriptions of the cases and what additional information you would need to gather.

The Diagnostic and Statistical Manual of Mental Disorders (DSM-IV-TR)

The *Diagnostic and Statistical Manual of Mental Disorders* published its fourth edition with text revisions in 2000 (American Psychiatric Association, 2000). For those of you unfamiliar with the *DSM-IV-TR,* the manual contains a list of diagnostic criteria for mental disorders that are the focus of treatment for psychiatrists, psychologists, social workers, mental health counselors, marriage and family therapists, and the like. For each disorder, the manual specifies features of the condition, the diagnostic criteria, associated features and disorders, specific culture, age, and gender features, prevalence, course, familial pattern, and differential diagnosis. Mental health professionals who work in agency or private settings use the *DSM-IV-TR* for diagnosis. All insurance companies that we are aware of require a *DSM-IV-TR* diagnosis for payment. Many publicly funded agencies also require a *DSM-IV-TR* diagnosis of clients. Therefore, regardless of your feelings about labeling clients, the use of the *DSM-IV-TR* is a reality in the mental health field.

For our purposes, the most important part of the *DSM-IV-TR* (American Psychiatric Association, 2000) involves the chapter on "Substance-Related Disorders." Included in this chapter are the "Substance Use Disorders" ("Substance Dependence" and "Substance Abuse") and "Substance Induced Disorders" ("Substance Intoxication," "Substance Withdrawal," and a variety of other disorders). We will focus most of this discussion on the Substance-Related Disorders since mental health professionals would generally be involved with diagnoses in this classification.

In the *DSM-IV-TR,* substance dependence is defined as "a cluster of cognitive, behavioral, and physiological symptoms indicating that the individual continues use of the substance despite significant substance-related problems" (p. 192). You may recall that, earlier in the chapter, we gave a working definition of addiction/dependence that specified use of alcohol or other drugs regardless of the consequences. Although more technical language is used, the *DSM-IV-TR* definition is similar. The diagnostic criteria for substance dependence are as follows:

A maladaptive pattern of substance use, leading to clinically significant impairment or distress, as manifested by three (or more) of the following, occurring at any time in the same 12-month period:

(1) tolerance, as defined by either of the following:
  (a) a need for markedly increased amounts of the substance to achieve intoxication or desired effect
  (b) markedly diminished effect with continued use of the same amount of the substance
(2) withdrawal, as manifested by either of the following:
  (a) the characteristic withdrawal syndrome for the substance (refer to Criteria A and B of the criteria sets for Withdrawal from the specific substances)
  (b) the same (or a closely related) substance is taken to relieve or avoid withdrawal symptoms
(3) the substance is often taken in larger amounts or over a longer period than was intended
(4) there is a persistent desire or unsuccessful efforts to cut down or control substance use
(5) a great deal of time is spent in activities necessary to obtain the substance (e.g., visiting multiple doctors or driving long distances), use the substance (e.g., chain-smoking), or recover from its effects
(6) important social, occupational, or recreational activities are given up or reduced because of substance use

(7) the substance use is continued despite knowledge of having a persistent or recurrent physical or psychological problem that is likely to have been caused or exacerbated by the substance (e.g., current cocaine use despite recognition of cocaine-induced depression, or continued drinking despite recognition that an ulcer was made worse by alcohol consumption).

Specify If:

With Physiological Dependence: evidence of tolerance or withdrawal (i.e., either Item 1 or 2 is present)

Without Physiological Dependence: no evidence of tolerance or withdrawal (i.e., neither Item 1 or 2 is present)

Course Specifiers

Early Full Remission

Early Partial Remission

Sustained Full Remission

Sustained Partial Remission

On Agonist Therapy

In a Controlled Environment

Notice that the first two criteria, tolerance and withdrawal, are not necessary for a diagnosis of dependence. Remember from Chapter 2 that tolerance is the need for increasing amounts of the substance to achieve the desired effect. This may be difficult to determine in some individuals, and individuals vary considerably in initial sensitivity to AOD. Also, with some drugs (e.g., PCP) tolerance has not been demonstrated. Similarly, withdrawal signs and symptoms are not observed with hallucinogen use. Therefore, tolerance and withdrawal are not necessary or sufficient for a diagnosis of dependence. Criteria 3 through 7 are self-explanatory and involve the compulsivity and *trouble* we have previously discussed in substance dependence.

The diagnosis of substance dependence can be specified as being with or without physiological dependence so that it is clear whether tolerance and withdrawal are present. Also, a description of the status of recovery can be given after none of the criteria for dependence (or abuse) have been observed for at least one month. If the client has been in recovery for 1 to 12 months and none of the criteria for dependence or abuse are met, "Early Full Remission" is specified. If one or more criteria are met but the client cannot be diagnosed as "Substance Dependence" (i.e., does not meet three or more of the criteria), "Early Partial Remission" is specified. "Sustained Full Remission" and "Sustained Partial Remission" are the specifiers when the period of recovery is 12 months or longer. The "partial remission" specifiers are generally used to indicate recovering clients who have had one or more "slips" or returns to use but have not had full-blown relapses (see Chapter 9).

"On Agonist Therapy" and "In a Controlled Environment" are specified so that clients who have a low probability of use due to external circumstances can be identified. For example, if a recovering alcoholic is taking Antabuse (see Chapter 8), the diagnosis would specify "On Agonist Therapy." A recovering opioid addict who is incarcerated for two years has a low probability of use because he or she is in prison. Thus, "In a Controlled Environment" would be specified.

The *DSM-IV-TR* defines substance abuse as "a maladaptive pattern of substance use manifested by recurrent and significant adverse consequences related to the repeated use of substances"

(p. 198). Again, this is consistent with the earlier definition of abuse in this chapter as continued use of alcohol and other drugs in spite of negative consequences. The criteria are as follows:

    A. A maladaptive pattern of substance use leading to clinically significant impairment or distress, as manifested by one (or more) of the following, occurring within a 12- month period:

        (1) recurrent substance use resulting in a failure to fulfill major role obligations at work, school, or home (e.g., repeated absences or poor work performance related to substance use; substance-related absences, suspensions, or expulsions from school; neglect of children or household)

        (2) recurrent substance use in situations in which it is physically hazardous (e.g., driving an automobile or operating a machine when impaired by substance use)

        (3) recurrent substance-related legal problems (e.g., arrests for substance-related disorderly conduct)

        (4) continued substance use despite having persistent or recurrent social or interpersonal problems caused or exacerbated by the effects of the substance (e.g., arguments with spouse about consequences of intoxication, physical fights)

    B. The symptoms have never met the criteria for Substance Dependence for this class of substance.

You may notice that tolerance and withdrawal are not mentioned in the criteria for abuse and that a pattern of compulsive use is also restricted to "dependence." The criteria for "abuse" emphasize harmful consequences from repeated substance use. Clearly, if an individual meets the criteria for Substance Dependence, the person could also be diagnosed with Substance Abuse. However, "A diagnosis of Substance Abuse is preempted by the diagnosis of Substance Dependence" (p. 198).

Descriptions for dependence and abuse for a variety of substances follow the general criteria for Substance Dependence and Substance Abuse. Those substances include alcohol, amphetamines, cannabis, cocaine, hallucinogens, inhalants, opioids, phencyclidine (PCP), sedative, hypnotic, or anxiolytics, and other or unknown substances (e.g., anabolic steroids, nitrite inhalants [poppers], nitrous oxide [laughing gas]). A short discussion is included on the unique characteristics of the particular drug in relationship to the criteria for dependence or abuse. In addition, the *DSM-IV-TR* discusses dependence for nicotine (but not abuse) and polysubstance dependency, defined as dependence on three or more groups of drugs. Caffeine is included for Caffeine-Induced Disorders (e.g., Caffeine Intoxication, Caffeine-Induced Anxiety Disorder, Caffeine-Induced Sleep Disorder), but classifications do not include dependence and abuse.

The *DSM-IV-TR* contains a variety of Substance-Induced Disorders. As the name implies, these are mental disorders caused by the use of AOD. They may be associated with abuse or dependence. For example, Substance Intoxication "is the development of a reversible substance-specific syndrome due to the recent ingestion of [or exposure to] a substance . . . [with] clinically significant maladaptive behavioral or psychological changes associated with intoxication [e.g., belligerence, mood lability, cognitive impairment, impaired judgment, impaired social or occupational functioning]" (p. 199). Substance Withdrawal "is the development of a substance-specific maladaptive behavioral change, with physiological and cognitive concomitants, that is due to the cessation of, or reduction in, heavy and prolonged substance use" (p. 201). Substance-Induced Disorders other than intoxication and withdrawal are included elsewhere in the *DSM-IV-TR* and are referenced under the appropriate substance. These include Substance-Induced Delirium, Substance-Induced Persisting Dementia, Substance-Induced Persisting Amnestic Disorder, Substance-Induced Psychotic Disorder, Substance-Induced Mood Disorder, Substance-Induced Anxiety Disorder, Substance-Induced Sexual Dysfunction, and Substance-Induced Sleep Disorder. For example, nine Alcohol-Induced Disorders are listed in the *DSM-IV-TR*.

AT A GLANCE

Screening

- Brief, general
- May involve self-report inventories
- Many false negatives

Assessment

- Thorough, leads to diagnosis
- Multiple procedures including psychosocial history, self-report inventories

Diagnosis

- Substance abuse disorders
  - One or more criteria in last 12 months
  - Problems in personal, social, family, legal, vocational/educational, or physical areas
- Substance dependence disorders
  - Three or more criteria in last 12 months
  - May include tolerance and withdrawal
  - Considered more serious than substance abuse disorders

MyCounselingLab™

Go to Topic 4: *Assessment and Diagnosis*, in the MyCounselingLab™ site (www .MyCounselingLab.com) for *Substance Abuse: Information for School Counselors, Social Workers, Therapists and Counselors*, Fifth Edition, where you can:

- Find learning outcomes for *Assessment and Diagnosis* along with the national standards that connect to these outcomes.
- Complete Assignments and Activities that can help you more deeply understand the chapter content.
- Apply and practice your understanding of the core skills identified in the chapter with the Building Counseling Skills unit.
- Prepare yourself for professional certification with a Practice for Certification quiz.
- Connect to videos through the Video and Resource Library.

Summary

- Identification of the signs and symptoms of AOD problems is important for all mental health professionals to avoid misdiagnosing client problems.
- Mental health professionals must be able to differentiate AOD use, misuse, abuse, and dependence.
- Psychosocial histories, with or without self-report inventories, are the best method to identify AOD problems.
- When referring clients for treatment, mental health professionals must be sure providers have the proper license or certification to provide AOD treatment services.
- The criteria in the *DSM-IV-TR* should be utilized in making substance use disorder diagnoses but the proper training, experience, and supervision is needed before mental health professionals make these diagnoses.

Internet Resources

Screening and assessment instruments
lib.adai.washington.edu/instruments

Alcohol Use Disorders Identification Test (AUDIT)
whqlibdoc.who.int/hq/2001/WHO_MSD_MSB_01.6a.pdf

Problem-Oriented Screening Instrument for Teenagers (POSIT)
nhtsa.gov/people/injury/alcohol/juvenile/posit.pdf

Workplace drug testing
dol.gov/asp/programs/drugs/workingpartners/dfworkplace/dt.asp

School drug testing
whitehousedrugpolicy.gov/dfc/files/random_student.pdf

Psychosocial history example
ssw.umich.edu/public/currentProjects/icwtp/substanceAbuse/Sub_Abuse_Assess_Form.pdf

Addiction Severity Index (ASI)
tresearch.org/resources/instruments/ASI_5th_Ed.pdf

DSM-IV-TR (Note: URL provides excerpts only. Full access requires a fee)
psychiatryonline.com/resourceTOC.aspx?resourceID=1

Further Discussion

1. For each of the case examples at the beginning of the chapter, describe the assessment process you would conduct. What additional information would you need to form a tentative diagnosis?

2. Discuss the importance of utilizing screening instruments in conjunction with clinical interviews when making diagnostic decisions. What potential diagnostic, treatment, and ethical problems can occur if a diagnosis is based solely on the results of screening and assessment instruments?

3. Since the *DSM-IV-TR* has specific criteria for diagnosing substance use disorders, what is the problem with having any AOD counselor or mental health professional making diagnoses?

4. Discuss the advantages and disadvantages of computerized psychosocial histories as a way of saving time and money.

Chapter 7

Motivational Interviewing and Brief Interventions

MyCounselingLab™

Visit the MyCounselingLab™ site (www.MyCounselingLab.com) for *Substance Abuse: Information for School Counselors, Social Workers, Therapists and Counselors,* Fifth Edition to enhance your understanding of chapter concepts. You'll have the opportunity to practice your skills through video- and case-based Assignments and Activities as well as Building Counseling Skills units and to prepare for your certification exam with Practice for Certification quizzes.

CASE EXAMPLES

❶ Frank is a 37-year-old man who was arrested for his second DUI and court-ordered to outpatient treatment. He has been using cocaine and drinking on a regular basis for over 15 years. Frank is divorced and works sporadically in the construction industry.

❷ Angelica is a social worker who works in an employee assistance program with a large corporation. One of the vice presidents comes to her to discuss his concerns about the deteriorating job performance of Drew, one of the managers. Drew's behavior has become unpredictable. He seems to function well one day and the next day is irritable and even explosive. Drew was rude to an important client and yelled at one of the secretaries in front of other employees. One of his friends has told the vice president that Drew is a frequent cocaine user. Angelica meets with Drew, who tells her that he has been under a great deal of stress in his job and that the rumors of his drug use were started by jealous colleagues.

❸ Sara is a high school counselor. One day, two students come to see her to discuss their concerns about their friend Marlow. The students describe a progression of marijuana and prescription pain pill use. Marlow is frequently under the influence at school and is selling methamphetamine to support his drug use. Sara contacts Marlow's teachers, who describe absenteeism, failure to complete assignments, and sleeping in class. She calls Marlow's home and talks to his mother. The mother is a single parent who says that Marlow's father is an alcoholic who rarely has contact with the family. She tells Sara that she is also concerned about Marlow's drug use but feels completely helpless to do anything about it. In the past, she has tried to get Marlow to go to a treatment program for an assessment but he refuses.

❹ Miguel is a marriage and family counselor who works for a community mental health center. He sees a family who was referred by a child protection case worker after an incident of physical abuse of the 10-year-old son was reported by the school. After one session, the father does not return to counseling. The mother describes an increasing pattern of alcohol use and verbal and physical abuse by the father. He has had a DUI in the last month and she is concerned that he will be fired from his job. When the mother tries to talk to the father about his alcohol use, he becomes angry and leaves the house.

It would be convenient if mental health professionals could learn to identify potential AOD problems in their clients, present the client with this information, refer the client to treatment, and move on to something else. Unfortunately, in most cases, this does not reflect reality. To help you understand the reasons for this reality, you must have an empathic understanding of the importance of AOD to the alcoholic or addict. Therefore, we will restate a metaphor from Chapter 1. Think about the most important person in your life. Imagine that one day, a friend comes up to you and says, "(the person you care most about) is no good for you. You need to get rid of him/her right now and never see him/her again." We don't think that your response would be, "You're right. I've been thinking the very same thing. I'll go home right now and tell him/her that it's over." It is much more likely that you would defend this person and your relationship, tell your friend to mind his own business, and leave.

Many alcoholics or addicts have developed a relationship with their drugs of choice that they believe to be critical to their functioning and of primary importance to their lives. Just as you may have difficulty imagining yourself being happy without this most important person, alcoholics or addicts may not be able to imagine functioning without their drugs of choice. Of course, problems do develop in relationships, and there may come a time when the problems outweigh the perceived importance of the relationship. Similarly, alcohol or other drug users may start to have problems as a result of their use and might not experience the euphoria that was once a part of the relationship with their drug(s). In the situations that are described at the beginning of the chapter, you might question the relationship metaphor. After all, the people described in these situations are having significant problems in their lives as a result of their AOD use. Surely, you think, they can see the harm that AOD are having on them and those around them. If this occurs to you, we would ask whether you have ever been in love with someone and, when the relationship ended, you looked back and wondered what you ever saw in the person. If anyone criticized your lover or your relationship while you were in love, you probably responded that no one could possibly understand the depth of your feelings and the intensity of the relationship. Although in hindsight, you may now believe that the relationship was unhealthy, at the time any objective data to support this perception were ignored. Think about the alcoholic or addict as being "in love" with the drugs of choice.

The reality is that people often do not acknowledge the harm that a relationship is having in their lives, or, if the harm is acknowledged, the person may be reluctant to abandon the relationship. The old saying "Love is blind and lovers cannot see" applies to human relationships as well as the relationship people can have with AOD. Many authorities in the field attribute this "blindness" to the psychological defense mechanism of denial. An alternative explanation is that people are fearful of abandoning a relationship that, while harmful, is familiar. For example, the fact that women who leave abusive relationships frequently return to them generates considerable interest (Griffing et al., 2002). One explanation is that the women have no other concept of relationships, and, although the abuse is unpleasant, they are at least familiar with the "rules" and are afraid of the alternatives. The alcoholic or addict may be aware of the undesirable consequences of addiction but be immobilized by the fear of living without alcohol or drugs.

Whatever the explanation, the mental health professional still faces a problem: a client with alcohol or other drug problems and an unwillingness to change. What can be done? In the rest of this chapter, we will describe a model of motivating an alcohol or other drug-affected person to get help called "motivational interviewing" (Miller & Rollnick, 2002). Finally, we will discuss some strategies to assist clients who have not reached the stage of substance use dependence (see Chapter 6). These strategies are called *brief interventions.*

CLIENT ENGAGEMENT

Client engagement is a term used to describe the process of motivating a person to actively engage in treatment or less intensive methods of reducing the harm caused by AOD. These "less intensive methods" can range from a school-based educational program for students caught smoking to the brief interventions described later in this chapter. Some methods of client engagement are confrontational and/or coercive, while others use counseling strategies designed to elicit active participation from clients on their own volition.

In the AOD field, the term *intervention* was historically used to describe the process of moving clients from problem identification to treatment. However, intervention implies that something is being done to the client. For example, for many years the main process to motivate addicts and alcoholics to enter treatment was an "intervention" process described by Johnson (1973). The process involved a planned confrontation of the alcoholic or addict by significant people in his or her life (e.g., spouse, children, friends, employer). This emotionally charged event was designed to break through the denial system of the alcoholic or addict. There are reality television shows today that depict these "Johnson-model interventions." In contrast, client engagement emphasizes the freedom for clients to make a choice to either genuinely participate in treatment or to resist it. For example, the court system can force a person to enter treatment (intervention), but cannot force the person to honestly involve himself or herself in the treatment process. Therefore, we prefer the term *client engagement.*

MOTIVATIONAL INTERVIEWING

An alternative to the Johnson method of client engagement has been developed by William Miller and Stephen Rollnick in 1991 and is described in their second edition book *Motivational Interviewing: Preparing People for Change* (Miller & Rollnick, 2002). Motivational interviewing (MI) is included in the National Registry of Evidence-based Programs and Practices developed by the federal government's Substance Abuse and Mental Health Services Administration. Only programs that have been able to demonstrate significant outcomes through peer-reviewed research can be included in this registry.

According to Miller and Rollnick (2002), "We define motivational interviewing as *a client-centered, directive method for enhancing intrinsic motivation to change by exploring and resolving ambivalence* (p. 25, italics in original). By "client-centered," they are referring to the counseling theory of Carl Rogers, which you are probably familiar with from your counseling theory class. MI relies on Roger's person-centered therapy with its focus on current behavior, thoughts, and feelings (as opposed to the past or the future) and its emphasis on counselor characteristics such as empathy, respect, genuineness, unconditional positive regard, and congruence. However, unlike Roger's description of the counseling process, MI is consciously directive in that the counselor attempts to resolve client ambivalence (the mixed feelings a client has about changing) and points the client to a particular direction of change.

Miller and Rollnick emphasize that MI is a method of communication rather than a series of strategies or techniques. It does not impose change through extrinsic motivators such as money, fear of punishment, or social pressure but through the internal motivation of the client. The counselor's role is to elicit a client's ambivalence about changing, thoroughly explore this ambivalence, and facilitate the resolution of the ambivalence.

Four General Principles of MI

The four general principles of MI are express empathy, develop discrepancy, roll with resistance, and support self-efficacy. The first principle, express empathy, is a basic concept in person-centered counseling and does not require much explanation. Carl Rogers emphasized that accurate reflective listening was a demonstration of counselor empathy: communicating understanding, comprehension, and validation to the client.

In Miller and Rollnick's words, "A goal of motivational interviewing is to develop discrepancy—to make use of it, increase it, and amplify it until it overrides the inertia of the status quo" (p. 39). A skilled MI counselor helps clients see the discrepancy between their current behavior and their values and goals without feeling pressured or coerced. This is where MI differs from person-centered counseling by actively directing clients to examine their discrepancies.

When clients examine the discrepancies between their behavior and their values and goals, it is natural for resistance to occur. No one enjoys facing such discrepancies, which is why a client demonstrates resistance. An MI counselor must demonstrate skill by avoiding arguing for change with the client, not directly opposing the resistance, relying on the client for answers and solutions, and recognizing that resistance signals that a different counselor response is needed.

Finally, the first three principles are necessary for the client to believe that he or she can change. Self-efficacy is the belief a person has in his or her own capabilities. The MI counselor strives to communicate that the client is responsible for choosing the type of change and for carrying out this change. "A general goal of motivational interviewing is to enhance the client's confidence in his or her capability to cope with obstacles and to succeed in change" (p. 41).

Ambivalence

As Miller and Rollnick (2002) point out, ambivalence is a predictable and normal part of the change process:

> People who are struggling with problem drinking, drug addiction, bulimia, or pathological gambling often recognize the risks, costs, and harm involved in their behavior. Yet for a variety of reasons they are also quite attached and attracted to the addictive behavior. They want to drink (or smoke, or purge, or gamble), and they don't want to. They want to change, and at the same time they don't want to change. (p.14)

Although this ambivalence is normal, a goal of motivational interviewing is to resolve this ambivalence (hopefully, by choosing change). Certainly, the facilitative conditions for counseling (e.g., empathy, respect, warmth, concreteness, immediacy, congruence, genuineness, and authenticity) are necessary conditions for change in any counseling situation. In addition, MI counselors are trained to avoid certain traps that may be barriers in resolving client ambivalence.

Perhaps the most common trap that would interfere with client resolution of ambivalence is called the *confrontational trap.* In an earlier section of this chapter, we described the type of confrontational intervention that was commonly used to "motivate" people to get treatment. Interventions of this type are still portrayed in reality shows on television. Treatment providers used to hold a common perception that most addicts were in denial about their condition and that harsh confrontation was necessary to break through this denial system. In MI, where ambivalence is seen as a normal part of the change process, confrontation is counterproductive. If the counselor is arguing for one part of the ambivalence (e.g.,"Just admit you are an addict"), the client will take the opposite end of the ambivalence (e.g., "I am not. You are crazy"). If the client is ambivalent and the practitioner argues for the "there is a problem" side of the ambivalence, the client will argue for the "there isn't a problem" side of the ambivalence.

Additional traps are the question–answer trap, in which the client answers a series of closed questions by the mental health professional. Hopefully, you have been taught to avoid this type of interviewing in a basic counseling skills course. Also keep in mind the expert trap, in which a "professional" attempts to fix the problem by exerting expertise. Clients may elicit this from a helping professional in order to remain passive and thus minimize their responsibility for change. The labeling trap involves the attempt to attach a diagnostic label (e.g., alcoholic) to a client. As Miller and Rollnick point out, no research evidence suggests that the acceptance of such a label predicts favorable treatment outcome, and, clearly, many people resist such labels. Finally, stay alert for the premature focus trap and the blaming trap. In the former, the mental health professional focuses the client on the AOD issue before the client is ready, and, in the latter, the client perceives that blame is being assessed for his or her behavior.

The strategies that Miller and Rollnick suggest for resolving the client's ambivalence use many of the basic counseling interventions of Carl Rogers's person-centered therapy. For example, the use of open-ended questions, reflective listening, affirming and supportive statements, and summarization are all recommended. However, the elicitation of "change talk" is the guiding strategy for resolving ambivalence:

> . . . motivational interviewing is the opposite of a confrontational approach, in which the counselor advocates for the "problem-change" position and the client defends against it. We believe that such a confrontational dialogue is often detrimental, precisely because it causes the person to defend a no-change position. The idea in motivational interviewing is to have the client give voice to exactly the opposite kinds of statements, to present the arguments for change. It is the counselor's task to facilitate the client's expression of such change talk, referred to in our earlier writings as self-motivational statements. (p. 76)

Eliciting Change Talk

Miller and Rollnick categorize change statements as cognitive (problem recognition), affective (statements of concern), and behavioral (intentions to act). Evocative questions can be used to elicit change statements in any of the categories. For example, "In what ways has your marijuana use been a problem for you?" (problem recognition), "What worries you about your cocaine use?" (statement of concern), and "What would be the advantages of changing your drinking habits?" (intention to act) are examples of evocative questions designed to elicit change statements.

Another method to evoke change talk is to have clients rate the importance (e.g., on a 1–10 scale) of a behavior and then ask what would it take for her to get to the more favorable rating. For example, the client ranks the severity of his cocaine a "10" (most severe). The counselor says, "What would it take to get you to a 5?" Clients can be asked for both the positive and negative aspects of their AOD use as a method to elicit change statements. Expressions of concern are often elicited when the client lists the negative aspects of use. The client can then be asked to elaborate on these concerns. Related to this technique is asking clients to describe the aspect of their use that concerns them the most, comparing the times that they experienced problems to the present, and imagining what life would be like if they changed their use pattern. The clients can also be asked to examine their goals in life and then to describe how their current use pattern facilitates or hinders their ability to achieve their goals

Client Resistance and Counselor's Behavior

The avoidance of traps and the use of techniques to elicit change statements should be helpful in reducing ambivalence. However, a mental health professional can expect clients to remain ambivalent in spite of these efforts and can also expect that this ambivalence will be demonstrated through client resistance.

A working assumption of MI is "persistent resistance is not a client problem, but a counselor skill problem . . . It is how you *respond* to client resistance that makes the difference and that distinguishes motivational interviewing from other approaches. If resistance is increasing during counseling, it is very likely in response to something that you are doing" (p. 99, italics in original). In addition, the reduction of client resistance is seen as a favorable outcome of motivational interviewing. The logical extension of this point of view is that helping professionals must change their behavior to reduce client resistance: " . . . [C]ounselors can change their style in ways that will decrease (or increase) client resistance, and it is desirable to decrease client resistance because this pattern is associated with long-term change . . ." (p. 99). Miller and Rollnick (2002) describe four categories of resistance: arguing (challenging, discounting, hostility), interrupting (talking over, cutting off), denying (blaming, disagreeing, excusing, claiming impunity, minimizing, pessimism, reluctance, unwillingness to change), and ignoring (inattention, nonanswer, no response, sidetracking). Although it is not important for the helping professional to categorize the type of resistance, it is important to recognize resistance in order to handle it appropriately.

To illustrate the use of the techniques to minimize resistance, let's look at a client statement and the helping professional's possible responses. The first case example at the beginning of the chapter will be used for illustration and we encourage you and your colleagues to role play with the other case examples. To review, the case involves Frank, a 37-year-old, and his drugs of choice were cocaine and alcohol. After Frank's second DUI, he was ordered by the court to attend NA and individual counseling. Based on an assessment, Frank was easily diagnosed as Psychoactive Substance Dependent (see Chapter 6). He recognized that the problems he had were the result of alcohol and cocaine use and was afraid of going to prison, but he resisted the label "alcoholic/addict" and complained about the NA meetings. During the third session with his counselor, Frank said:

> I hate going to those (profanity) NA meetings. Man, you should see those people, bikers with tattoos, old needle pushers, bums. And all that God (profanity). I'm an atheist, man. I'm not like those people. I know I can't drink or do coke any more. If I do, they'll put me away. But I'm no junkie or wino.

Frank's statements are certainly reflective of the denying category of resistance. MI utilizes reflective responses and other beyond-reflective responses. Reflective responses include simple reflection, a skill that you have probably practiced many times in a basic counseling skills course. A simple reflecting response to Frank would be, "You really feel out of place at NA meetings." This avoids the confrontation trap and provides a sense of empathic understanding to the client that may be helpful in moving the client away from resistance and toward further exploration of the problem.

Amplified and double-sided reflections can also be used to focus on the other side of the client's ambivalence as well. An amplified reflection exaggerates the client's perception of the situation, which may result in the client's talking about the other side when he or she hears how extreme his or her position sounds. In Frank's case, an amplified reflection might be, "You feel like NA is completely wrong for you. You can't see any similarity between NA members and yourself, and the philosophy is totally wrong for you." The double-sided reflection presents both parts of the client's ambivalence. Such a response to Frank would be, "You don't feel comfortable at NA meetings, but you know you need to stay away from coke and booze."

Responses that go beyond reflections include shifting the focus so that the client does not continue to use the issue as a barrier to movement. In Frank's case, the "God" issue in NA was consistently raised. A "shifting focus" response would be, "You know Frank, I really hear how the 'God' stuff in NA turns you off. You also mentioned that the topic of the meeting last night was gratitude. What did you think about that?" In using "shifting," it is important that the helping professional clearly reflect an understanding of the client's thoughts and feelings prior to shifting. Again, the helping professional would use this technique when the issue presented is seen as a barrier to the client's moving ahead.

Another approach to working with an issue that causes resistance is to agree with the client but with a twist. In other words, the helping professional concurs with the content of the client's concern but takes the discussion in a slightly different direction. For example, with regard to the God issue, Frank's counselor might say, "You are right. There is a heavy emphasis on spirituality in NA and 'God' is mentioned a lot. In fact, I know some people who go to AA and NA regularly but don't believe in 'God'." The twist in this counselor statement is to motivate Frank to ask about this apparent contradiction, possibly leading to clarification of his resistance to attending NA.

Miller and Rollnick (2002) also suggest that the helping professional emphasize the personal choice and control of the client as a method of reducing resistance. Although Frank may dislike NA because of a genuine philosophical difference, the fear of being labeled, or discomfort, his resistance may also be related to the fact that he was ordered by the court to attend. In this case, you might think that Frank actually does not have personal choice or control. Although, theoretically, he could choose not to attend, the consequence of such a choice would be imprisonment; therefore, it would be not be constructive to point out that he has personal choice. However, the counselor could say, "Well, you are court-ordered to go to NA and maybe that is upsetting to you. But, no one can make you believe what you hear at the meetings, and no one can make you listen. That's up to you."

A helping professional can also reduce resistance by focusing on the content of the client's statements but interpreting them in a different manner. This is called *reframing*. Reframing may result in the client's acknowledging a different point of view, especially if the counselor has developed the client's trust by clearly hearing the client's perspective. In Frank's case, a reframing response might be, "When you say 'junkie' and 'wino,' I know what you mean. But, think about (name some famous athletes or movie stars who are in recovery). They go to AA or NA, and I think you'd agree that they aren't 'junkies' or 'winos.' I wonder if you just focus on the people at the meeting who fit your stereotype and ignore the others. What do you think?"

Finally, MI utilizes "coming alongside," a special case of amplified reflection. The counselor adopts the same side of the ambivalence argument as the client. Miller and Rollnick (2002) are cautious about calling this a *therapeutic* paradox because of the concern that a paradox is a way to "trick" clients. "Coming alongside" is not used because the counselor has given up or as a last resort. Rather, it may be a helpful way to change client resistance. In Frank's case, the counselor might say, "You know, Frank, maybe you shouldn't go to NA. You aren't finding anything useful there and you don't see any similarity between you and the other members." A statement by the counselor may elicit a more measured response from Frank (e.g. "Well, I didn't mean there isn't anyone like me there"). Notice that this counselor statement is different than the amplified reflection. In "coming alongside," the counselor is taking Frank's position rather than simply reflecting his position.

Transition from Resistance to Change

MI does not end with managing client resistance. When ambivalence is largely resolved and resistance has decreased, the client is ready to take action for change. First, the client's confidence to make change must be enhanced. You may recall that the fourth general principle of MI is to enhance client self-efficacy, and MI includes strategies to elicit and strengthen confidence talk. Even when the client's ambivalence has been resolved, he or she may not feel confident in his or her ability to change. Through the use of evocative questions, reviewing past successes and personal strengths, brainstorming, giving information and advice, reframing, considering hypothetical change, and responding appropriately to confident statements by the client, the MI counselor helps increase client self-efficacy. Finally, the MI counselor works with the client on a change plan that includes setting goals, considering the options to achieve the goals, deciding on a plan, and eliciting commitment to the plan.

If MI sounds appealing to you, we suggest you read Miller and Rollnick's book and take one of the many MI training workshops offered around the country. Like any counseling approach, it is essential that mental health professionals implement the processes and strategies with fidelity. That means that it is important to have supervised practice and feedback.

AT A GLANCE

- MI is an evidence-based process utilizing person-centered but directive methods to motivate client change.
- The four principles of MI are empathy, develop discrepancies, roll with resistance, and support self-efficacy.
- Ambivalence is normal; the counselor's role is to evoke change talk.
- Client resistance is a counselor skill problem; reflective responses and beyond reflective responses are used to deal with resistance.
- MI can enhance client self-efficacy to transition from resistance to change.

MI and Stages of Change

The transtheoretical model of intentional behavior change developed by Prochaska and DiClemente (1982) has been closely identified and intertwined with motivational interviewing. The stages of change are (1) Precontemplation, (2) Contemplation, (3) Determination, (4) Action, (5) Maintenance, and (6) Relapse.

At the precontemplation stage, the individual may not be aware that a problem exists and would generally be surprised to learn that others perceive a problem. A client may need information and feedback at this stage to raise awareness. However, Miller and Rollnick believe that coercion or aggressive confrontation would be counterproductive at this stage. Let's use our case example of Drew, our manager with a possible cocaine problem whom we described at beginning of the chapter. When Drew was 26 and just starting in his career, his social group consisted of people who used cocaine recreationally. He starts to date a woman who doesn't use drugs and she expresses concern about his cocaine use. Drew is genuinely surprised that his girlfriend perceives a problem. Everyone he works and plays with snorts cocaine and he has never experienced any negative consequences from his use.

At the contemplation stage, the individual is ambivalent about the problem. He or she has become aware that others perceive a problem and vacillates between considering change and rejecting it. For example, let's say that Drew's girlfriend convinces him to talk to a marriage and family therapist she knows to "get a professional opinion." Drew is interested in pleasing his girlfriend, so he agrees. In the course of the conversation, Drew says things such as, "I know a couple of guys who have gotten pretty strung out on coke and I don't want to end up like that but I know when to stop" and "I guess I should think about not doing so much partying, but everyone would laugh at me." According to Miller and Rollnick, the techniques of motivational interviewing can be helpful at this stage to tip the balance toward change. However, if the therapist moves to the action stage before the client is ready, resistance may develop. At the determination stage, the helping professional is presented with a window of opportunity to facilitate client movement toward action. If the opportunity is missed, the client moves back to contemplation. At this stage, the techniques of motivational interviewing may help the client find a change strategy that is acceptable, accessible, appropriate, and effective. If Drew seems to be at the determination stage and talks about "slowing down," the counselor might suggest a short-term "experiment" in which he limits his cocaine use to once a month and then comes back and discusses the experience.

The action stage is when people intentionally act, with or without assistance, to bring about change. After trying the experiment for a couple of months, Drew goes on a binge with his friends and stays out all night for three nights in a row. His girlfriend finds evidence that he and his friends spent a lot of time in a strip club, and she tells him that she doesn't want to see him anymore. Drew is too embarrassed to go back to the therapist and admit his failure so he "goes on the wagon" on his own.

In the maintenance stage, the person tries to maintain the change that resulted from his or her actions without relapsing. However, people may need specific skills to maintain a behavior change. Drew does well for a while. He doesn't go out at all, and his girlfriend agrees to start seeing him again. They spend their evenings at home watching TV. One Friday, his girlfriend is going to spend the evening with her friends and Drew feels that he is ready to go out with the guys. The guys want to do a few lines and go out stripping. Drew says "no." His friends start teasing him. At the maintenance stage, Drew needs some skills to deal with this social pressure.

Since Drew does not have these skills, he relapses.[1] (In Chapter 9, we will discuss the strategies of maintaining a behavior change related to AOD use and relapse-prevention techniques.) With regard to motivational interviewing, an important issue in the maintenance and relapse stages is for the mental health professional to create an environment in the counseling

---

[1] The differences between slips and relapses will be discussed in Chapter 9.

relationship so that the client feels safe in discussing difficulties in maintaining the behavior change and to report relapses that often occur during the change process. Since Drew's therapist was not aggressively confrontational and did not impose a label on him, Drew felt comfortable returning after his relapse. He will again go through the stages of change but, hopefully, Drew will begin at the determination stage and avoid the relapse stage. However, the mental health professional who uses motivational interviewing strategies would recognize that clients often cycle through the stages of change several times.

A client in the determination or action stage may be amenable to a confrontational intervention. However, if the confrontation is too aggressive in the determination stage, it may alienate the client, and the client may return to the contemplation stage. We would like to motivate a client to change who is at the contemplation stage, where he or she may not have yet experienced serious consequences of AOD use, and we do not want to alienate clients at the determination stage through aggressive confrontation. Motivational interviewing is designed to accomplish these goals.

MI APPLICATIONS TO CASE EXAMPLES

Review the case examples at the beginning of the chapter. We used the first case of Frank to illustrate some MI counselor responses. In the second case (Drew), we illustrated how he might progress through the stages of change. In the scenario described in the case example, we can assume Drew has resumed his cocaine use and is progressing to the point where other significant people in his life are concerned about him. When Angelica (the social worker) meets with Drew, she may not have any information about his drug use history. While Drew is very likely at the contemplation stage of change (again), Angelica must be very skilled in her use of MI. Unless Drew is confident that his confidentiality will be maintained (review the material in Chapter 5), he will probably not reveal anything about his cocaine use. Assuming he does believe that whatever he says will be kept confidential, Angelica will spend time ensuring that Drew feels that she understands what he is saying. If you role play this case with your colleagues, focus on the reflective MI statements.

In the case of the school counselor Sara and the student Marlow, Sara must determine Marlow's stage of change. Since his mother has talked to him, and his friends are concerned, it is very likely that he is at least at the contemplation stage and maybe at the determination stage. Assuming that Marlow's drug use is as bad as it is depicted in the case, Sara's goal is to get Marlow to agree to an assessment. Therefore, the goal is not abstinence from drugs but just a step toward determining the extent of the problem. When you role play this example, assume that Marlow's ambivalence is about whether he should agree to an assessment. Sara should try to evoke change statements and work to enhance Marlow's self-efficacy.

Miguel (the marriage and family therapist) is going to call the father to encourage him to return to counseling. As with the other examples, he does need to determine the father's stage of change. For this example, we will assume he is in the contemplation stage. Miguel must try to engage the father so he is willing to return. He wants to evoke change statements. In role playing, Miguel should practice both reflective statements and statements that go beyond reflection.

Research Outcome Studies

As we said at the beginning of the section on MI, the fact that it is included in the federal registry of effective, evidence-based practices means that research results support MI. A chapter in Miller and Rollnick's book (Burke, Arkowitz, & Dunn, 2002) reviews the research on the efficacy of MI, particularly adaptations of MI. They concluded that adaptations of MI of one to four sessions produced moderate to large effects and good maintenance over time in alcohol and other drug problems. Although MI was more efficacious than no treatment, it was not significantly different from other evidence-based treatment.

Since that time, there have been numerous studies of MI and various adaptations of MI with a variety of problems, in numerous settings, and with diverse populations. A meta-analytic review of brief interventions using MI for excessive drinking did conclude that MI was effective (Vasilaki, Hosier, & Cox, 2006). Another meta-analysis examined 72 clinical trials of MI on a range of clinical problems and found positive effects of MI between groups, which decreased over time. The effect sizes were larger with ethnic minority populations and when MI was not manual guided. The authors noted the highly variable effectiveness of MI across providers, populations, target problems, and settings (Hettema, Stelle, & Miller, 2005). Finally, a 2010 meta-analysis examined 119 studies on various problems. MI did produce small but significant results that were durable over time. However, MI was not significantly different than other types of treatment. The authors noted that MI was robust across many moderators but that variables such as feedback, delivery time, manualization, delivery mode (group vs. individual), and ethnicity impacted results (Lundahl, Kunz, Brownell, Tollefson, & Burke, 2010).

BRIEF INTERVENTIONS

Individuals with moderate or risky levels of AOD use may not be diagnosed with a substance use disorder but still be in need of assistance. This group is responsible for a disproportionate percentage of motor vehicle accidents and other injuries, deaths from AOD, poor workplace performance, medical illnesses, marital problems, and family dysfunction (Wilk, Jensen, & Havighurst, 1997). The techniques to engage these clients to change their AOD behaviors are called *brief interventions:*

> Brief interventions for excessive drinking should not be referred to as a (*sic*) homogenous entity, but as a family of interventions varying in length, structure, targets of intervention, personnel responsible for their delivery, media of communication, and several other ways, including their underpinning theory and intervention philosophy. (Heather, 1995)

Since brief interventions frequently are conducted in general health care settings, schools, or social service agencies, mental health professionals should be familiar with them. The procedures can range from a five-minute explanation of the harm of AOD by a health care provider, to a mental health counselor encouraging a client to see if he or she can stop drinking on his or her own, to more structured programs.

The Center for Substance Abuse Treatment (CSAT) has published a manual titled *Brief Interventions and Brief Therapies for Substance Abuse* (Center for Substance Abuse Treatment, 1999a) (see Internet Resources at the end of the chapter). We will summarize the chapter on brief interventions.

The goal for a client is to reduce the risk of harm from AOD. The stages-of-change model and techniques of motivational interviewing are the basis of the brief intervention techniques described in this manual. The type of intervention is generally related to the level of AOD use. Light or moderate users may need education about guidelines for low-risk use and the problems that may occur from increased use. If the light or moderate alcohol user occasionally has five or more drinks (defined as "binge drinking"), he or she can be encouraged to stay within the guidelines of no more than four drinks at any one time and no more than 14 drinks per week. Pregnant women or women contemplating pregnancy can be advised to abstain from AOD. At-risk drinkers are those who frequently exceed recommended guidelines but do not meet criteria for a substance abuse disorder (see Chapter 6). At-risk drug users are determined by the frequency and level of use and the drug(s) used. For this group, brief interventions are designed to encourage moderation or abstinence. Education about the consequences of continued high-risk use may also be offered.

The flow chart in Figure 7.1 is from a National Institute on Alcohol Abuse and Alcoholism publication called *Helping Patients Who Drink Too Much: A Clinician's Guide* (National Institute on Alcohol Abuse and Alcoholism, 2005). It is designed for use by health care professionals in working with at-risk drinkers. As you can see, it is quite simple and prescriptive.

There are also brief interventions for the client with a substance abuse disorder or substance dependence disorder. However, these clients would normally be seen in a treatment setting, and this will be discussed in Chapter 8.

The CSAT manual (1999a) describes six elements for effective brief interventions and five basic steps in the brief intervention process. The six elements utilize the acronym FRAMES for ease of understanding: 1. **F**eedback (The client[2] is given information about his or her use of AOD and the risks of his or her use pattern, 2. **R**esponsibility (the responsibility for change lies with the client), 3. **A**dvice (the clinician gives the client advice), 4. **M**enu (a variety of options are offered to the client) 5. **E**mpathy (the clinician demonstrates this core condition), and 6. **S**elf-efficacy (the clinician helps the client feel empowered). As you can see, the fifth and sixth elements are consistent with MI principles.

In the first step of the brief intervention process, the clinician introduces the issue in the context of the client's health. This includes building rapport with them, defining the purpose of the discussion, obtaining the client's permission to proceed, and helping the client to understand the reason for the brief intervention.

The next step is screening, evaluating, and assessing. You already have an understanding of this step from Chapter 6. This is obviously important to determine whether the person is a light or moderate user or at-risk.

Providing feedback follows screening, evaluating, and assessing. Using information from the preceding step, an interactive discussion of the findings is conducted. A specific piece of information should be given, followed by a request for client response. In this step, it is important for the helping professional to assess the client stage of change in order to determine what to do in the next step.

After giving feedback and assessing the client's stage of change, the possibility of changing behavior and setting goals is discussed. You can see how important the stage of change is. For example, you would meet high resistance if you suggested abstinence to an at-risk drinker in the precontemplation stage. The helping professional can suggest a course of action and then negotiate with the client. For example, we worked with a young woman who was an at-risk drinker in the contemplation stage of change. We suggested she limit her drinking to no more than two drinks and no more than two days a week. She resisted this, and we finally agreed to three drinks one day a week and two drinks no more than two days a week.

The final step is summarizing and reaching closure. This is important so that both the helping professional and the client have a clear understanding of the changes that were agreed on. Scheduled follow-up is an important part of this step. Depending on the type of brief intervention and the client's level of use, this follow-up may involve another face-to-face meeting or a telephone call.

The CSAT manual also contains a brief intervention workbook. The workbook is based on the summarized steps and contains useful tools like substance use contracts.

---

[2] The term "client" is used interchangeably with "patient" since brief interventions are often implemented in health care settings.

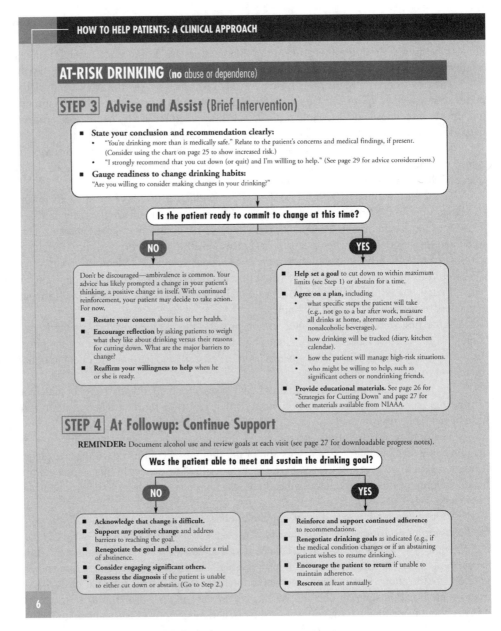

HOW TO HELP PATIENTS: A CLINICAL APPROACH

AT-RISK DRINKING (**no** abuse or dependence)

STEP 3 Advise and Assist (Brief Intervention)

- **State your conclusion and recommendation clearly:**
  - "You're drinking more than is medically safe." Relate to the patient's concerns and medical findings, if present. (Consider using the chart on page 25 to show increased risk.)
  - "I strongly recommend that you cut down (or quit) and I'm willing to help." (See page 29 for advice considerations.)
- **Gauge readiness to change drinking habits:**
  "Are you willing to consider making changes in your drinking?"

Is the patient ready to commit to change at this time?

NO

Don't be discouraged—ambivalence is common. Your advice has likely prompted a change in your patient's thinking, a positive change in itself. With continued reinforcement, your patient may decide to take action. For now,

- **Restate your concern** about his or her health.
- **Encourage reflection** by asking patients to weigh what they like about drinking versus their reasons for cutting down. What are the major barriers to change?
- **Reaffirm your willingness to help** when he or she is ready.

YES

- **Help set a goal** to cut down to within maximum limits (see Step 1) or abstain for a time.
- **Agree on a plan,** including
  - what specific steps the patient will take (e.g., not go to a bar after work, measure all drinks at home, alternate alcoholic and nonalcoholic beverages).
  - how drinking will be tracked (diary, kitchen calendar).
  - how the patient will manage high-risk situations.
  - who might be willing to help, such as significant others or nondrinking friends.
- **Provide educational materials.** See page 26 for "Strategies for Cutting Down" and page 27 for other materials available from NIAAA.

STEP 4 At Followup: Continue Support

REMINDER: Document alcohol use and review goals at each visit (see page 27 for downloadable progress notes).

Was the patient able to meet and sustain the drinking goal?

NO

- **Acknowledge that change is difficult.**
- **Support any positive change** and address barriers to reaching the goal.
- **Renegotiate the goal and plan;** consider a trial of abstinence.
- **Consider engaging significant others.**
- **Reassess the diagnosis** if the patient is unable to either cut down or abstain. (Go to Step 2.)

YES

- **Reinforce and support continued adherence** to recommendations.
- **Renegotiate drinking goals** as indicated (e.g., if the medical condition changes or if an abstaining patient wishes to resume drinking).
- **Encourage the patient to return** if unable to maintain adherence.
- **Rescreen** at least annually.

6

FIGURE 7.1 Brief intervention flow chart.

In a very comprehensive examination of brief interventions (and brief treatments), Madras et al. (2009) analyzed results from nearly 460,000 patients screened in a variety of health care settings across the country for alcohol and illicit drug use. Nearly 16% were recommended for brief interventions with much smaller percentages recommended for brief treatment or referral for treatment. At six-month follow-up, illicit drug use was nearly 68% lower and heavy alcohol use was nearly 39% lower. The results were comparable across sites, gender, race/ethnicity, and age subgroups.

Summary

- Motivational interviewing is an evidence-based
counseling process utilizing person-centered
concepts and techniques but is directive in trying
to evoke client change
- Brief interventions are generally used with
nondependent clients to reduce the harm that
may result from AOD use.
- Most brief interventions are targeted to the
stage of change of the client and use motivational interviewing techniques.

Internet Resources

Motivational interviewing
motivationalinterview.org

Brief interventions
*ncbi.nlm.nih.gov/books/bv.fcgi?rid=hstat5
.chapter.59192*
*pubs.niaaa.nih.gov/publications/practitioner/
cliniciansguide2005/guide.pdf*

Further Discussion

1. Given that motivational interviewing is directive and
designed to move clients to change, what are the ethical issues involved in this kind of counseling process?
2. In the helping professions, it is often said that for
someone to benefit from treatment, they must have
the desire to change. In light of this, should clients
at the precontemplation stage of change be forced by
schools, the legal system, or employers to seek treatment for AOD problems?
3. Discuss the concept of providing screening for AOD
problems and brief interventions in all primary health
care settings and emergency rooms.

Chapter 8

Treatment of AOD Problems

CASE EXAMPLES

❶ Celest is a 33-year-old white woman. Her drug of choice is methamphetamine and she is on probation for possession and court-ordered to treatment. After completing an inpatient, 28-day program, she attends counseling on a weekly basis. Celest regularly attends NA meetings and seems sincerely interested in living a drug-free life. She lives in a small house with 14 people, including her daughter and an abusive, drug-using boyfriend. Celest tells her boyfriend that she wants to leave the relationship and the house. He threatens to kill both her and her daughter. Celest has lost her license to work in her trained profession (slot machine mechanic) due to her felony conviction. She is unemployed, with no child care, and is diabetic. When she does not manage her diet and insulin, she experiences severe mood swings.

❷ Javier is a 17-year-old Hispanic male. His mother brings him to a treatment program for an assessment. Javier has been smoking marijuana, drinking beer, and taking prescription pain pills on a regular basis for some time. He dropped out of school in his junior year and his mother suspects that he is selling marijuana. Javier's reading is at the third-grade level and his primary language is Spanish.

❸ Devon is a 47-year-old African American male. Over the past 25 years, Devon has spent 10 years in prison for a variety of offenses including drug possession and distribution, burglary, grand larceny, and assault. He has been a heroin user for many years and is HIV positive. Devon has just been paroled and is ordered to get some kind of drug counseling.

❹ Richard is a 67-year-old retired, white, gay male whose long-time partner recently passed away. Richard's family has convinced him to talk to a counselor about his grief and his increasing alcohol use. While he has always been a heavy drinker, recently his alcohol use has resulted in increasing confusion, accidents, and medical issues.

In a textbook for helping professionals who are not planning to work in substance abuse treatment, a thorough discussion of treatment may not seem necessary. However, we have found that helping professionals have an almost mystical conception of substance abuse treatment. Once the social worker, school counselor, mental health counselor, rehabilitation counselor, or marriage and family therapist has referred a client for treatment, there seems to be an expectation that the client will return cured. In fact, alcoholics used to say they were going for "the cure" as a euphemism for treatment. This view may be encouraged by the fact that clients often "disappear" (in the case of inpatient treatment) or discontinue other forms of counseling or therapy at the insistence of the substance abuse treatment program. The helping professional may never see the client again, which reinforces the idea that alcoholics and addicts have been cured as a result of treatment.

The questions we are asked most often in teaching helping professionals about the AOD field are "What happens in treatment?," "What are the specific interventions?," and "Does treatment work?" Answers to these questions are important for mental health professionals, since clients referred for treatment expect that they are being directed toward an appropriate and helpful program. However, treatment programs differ in their orientation, in the specific strategies used, in the settings in which treatment occurs, and in treatment for special populations. We want to acquaint you with these aspects of treatment in order to dispel any mystical views you hold and, most important, so that you are familiar with evidence-based treatment strategies. Also, we will discuss the research on the effectiveness of treatment. Finally, we think that it is important for you to understand some of the controversial issues in the treatment of AOD problems.

RECOVERY-ORIENTED SYSTEMS OF CARE

The conceptualization of working with people with substance use disorders has changed in recent years. The material in the remainder of this chapter is concerned with a fairly well-defined period of acute care that has always been referred to as "treatment." In the next chapter, we discuss relapse prevention and recovery. From this delineation, it would appear that treatment, relapse prevention, and recovery are all separate processes. In fact, if you think of addiction as a chronic condition, treatment, relapse prevention, and recovery (and more) are all part of the same process which is now called recovery-oriented systems of care (ROSC).

The federal government held a number of summits on ROSCs in 2005 and produced a document summarizing the results of these meetings (Substance Abuse and Mental Health Services Administration, 2009a). For our purposes at this point in the book, the principles of ROSCs emphasize continuity of care; the inclusion of the family, community, and peers in the process; individualized and comprehensive services across the lifespan; culturally responsive services; community-anchored services; inclusion of voices and experiences of recovering individuals and their families; and outcomes-driven, research-based services. While the role of ROSCs is far greater than described here, please keep in mind as you read the rest of this chapter that what we refer to as *treatment* is only one part of ROSCs. ROSCs also include screening and assessment (Chapter 6), client engagement and brief interventions (Chapter 7), and relapse prevention and recovery support (Chapter 9).

HOW MANY ARE IN TREATMENT? HOW MANY NEED TREATMENT?

According to the Substance Abuse and Mental Health Services Administration (2009b), in 2007, more than 1.8 million persons were admitted to treatment programs that report data to state government agencies. About 22% were in treatment for alcohol problems and nearly 18% for alcohol with a secondary drug involved. A little more than 17.5% of the admissions involved opioids (e.g., heroin) as the primary drug problem, nearly 13% cocaine, almost 16% marijuana, and nearly 8% stimulants such as methamphetamine. In 2007, of those clients in treatment for services beyond detoxification, over 75% were in outpatient treatment and less than 25% were in residential treatment (Substance Abuse and Mental Health Services Administration, 2009b). Treatment settings will be discussed later in the chapter. Of the treatment facilities in this country in 2007, 58% were private, nonprofit, 29% were private for-profit, 12% were state or local government, and a little over 1% were tribal government facilities. Thirty-seven percent of the facilities offered treatment programs for co-occurring disorders, 31% served adolescents, 14% had programs for pregnant or postpartum women, 32% served other adult women groups, 7% had senior citizen programs, 27% had programs for criminal justice populations, and 6% served gay and lesbian groups. Treatment services in sign language for the hearing impaired were available in 30% of all facilities and 49% used languages other than English (Substance Abuse and Mental Health Services Administration, 2008).

The Substance Abuse and Mental Health Services Administration (2010) reported that, in 2009, an estimated 22.5 million Americans needed treatment for an alcohol or other drug problem (this includes people with both alcohol and drug problems). Of that number, 2.6 million, or about 12%, actually received treatment (the 1.8 million treatment admissions cited in the previous paragraph includes only those admissions reported to state government agencies, whereas treatment agencies or organizations that are not licensed by state government have no reporting requirements, leading to the higher figure. Also, the data on treatment admissions in the earlier paragraph are a couple years older than these data). Of the remaining 88% of people who needed treatment, only about 1 million (5%) *felt* they needed treatment. From that group, about one-third tried to get treatment but were unable to do so (reasons are not reported) and about two-thirds made no effort to get help.

WHAT HAPPENS IN TREATMENT?

Approaches to Treatment

As you might expect after reading Chapter 3 on models of addiction, many different approaches to treatment exist, based on the model of addiction adhered to by the program developer(s). However, a growing trend toward more eclectic approaches to treatment has emerged that combine aspects of different treatment models. While this may be good practice, it may also be driven by financial concerns, particularly in for-profit treatment programs. For example, some insurance companies pay for substance abuse treatment only if there is another mental disorder as well. This consideration has resulted in treatment programs' developing "co-occurring disorders" programs and using components from all of the treatment approaches we will discuss. Co-occurring disorders will be discussed further under "Treatment and Special Populations."

Perhaps the most well-known and widely emulated approach to treatment is the Minnesota Model developed by the Hazelden Foundation in the 1940s and 1950s. As described by Cook (1988), the Minnesota Model:

> is an abstinence orientated, comprehensive, multi-professional approach to the treatment of the addictions, based upon the principles of Alcoholics Anonymous. It espouses a disease concept of drug and alcohol dependency with the promise of recovery, but not cure, for those who adhere to it. The programme is intensive, offering group therapy, lectures, and counselling. (p. 625)

The philosophy of the Minnesota Model can be described by four components (Cook, 1988). The first is the belief that clients can change attitudes, beliefs, and behaviors. Famous persons who have completed the program, such as former First Lady Betty Ford, actress Elizabeth Taylor, comedian Chevy Chase, and actor Robert Downey Jr. are used as models to illustrate this belief. Second, the Minnesota Model adheres to the disease concept of addiction. The term *chemical dependency* is preferred to *addiction* or *alcoholism* and is seen as a physical, psychological, social, and spiritual illness. The major characteristics of the disease concept are taught. That is, the disease model conceptualizes chemical dependency as a primary disease that is chronic, progressive, and potentially fatal. The focus of treatment is on the disease and not on secondary characteristics.

The third philosophical component is illustrated by the long-term treatment goals of the Minnesota Model: abstinence from all mood-altering chemicals and improvement of lifestyle. Clients are not considered cured since the disease is incurable. However, through abstinence and personal growth, a chemically dependent individual can be in the process of recovery, "an ongoing, lifelong, process of increasing insight and commitment to change" (Cook, 1988, p. 627). Finally, the Minnesota Model uses the principles of Alcoholics Anonymous (AA) and Narcotics Anonymous (NA) in treatment. While we will devote a large portion of Chapter 10 to AA and NA, at this point it is sufficient to mention that the utilization of AA and NA principles implies a heavy spiritual component to treatment in the Minnesota Model.

Cook (1988) also describes the elements and structure of the Minnesota Model program. A continuum of care including assessment and diagnosis, detoxification, inpatient, therapeutic communities, halfway houses, outpatient, and aftercare has been developed using the Minnesota Model. Group therapy is used and is concerned with present and future behavior as opposed to past causal factors. Groups are often confrontational. The family also receives therapy. Didactic experiences including lectures and videotapes are used to educate clients about the disease of chemical dependency and the consequences of the disease. While the staff is composed of professionals from a number of disciplines (physicians, social workers, psychologists, nurses, and clergy), recovering addicts and alcoholics also function as counselors. Clients have reading and writing assignments, such as reading the AA Twelve Steps and Twelve Traditions (see Chapter 10) and writing their life histories. Attendance at AA/NA meetings is required, and clients are expected to work through the first three to five steps of AA while in treatment. Work assignments and recreational activities may also be expected, depending on the treatment setting. Aftercare includes attendance at AA or NA.

In contrast to the disease model of treatment exemplified by the Minnesota Model, behavioral models of treatment use techniques of classical and operant conditioning in the treatment of AOD problems. Perhaps the best-known behavioral technique applied to alcohol problems is aversion therapy, which seeks ". . . to develop in the client, via classical Pavlovian conditioning, a conditioned negative response to the sight, smell, taste, and even thought of alcohol" (Miller, Wilbourne, & Hettema, 2003, p. 32). The unpleasant stimuli most widely used are nausea, apnea (paralysis of breathing), electric shock, and various images. Nausea is the oldest and most commonly used of these stimuli, with fairly wide use in the former Soviet Union and in certain hospitals in the United States. The process is to give the client a drug that, when combined with alcohol, produces severe nausea. In a supervised setting, the client is then allowed to drink. In the classical conditioning paradigm, the feeling of severe nausea should quickly become associated with drinking alcohol. Electric shock can also be administered when the client drinks, or a drug can be administered that produces apnea when alcohol is consumed. Since these procedures are painful, stressful, and potentially dangerous, careful screening of clients and medical supervision is necessary. As might be expected, there is also a high dropout rate from programs using these techniques. In Chapter 3, we described Bill, who completed an aversive conditioning program and remained sober for 19 years until his death. Although the treatment was successful, he found the whole experience extremely unpleasant, which was exactly the effect intended. While electric shock can be used in the treatment of addiction to drugs other than alcohol, most references to aversive conditioning are related to the treatment of alcoholism.

Although aversive conditioning is not widely used in the United States now, other behavioral approaches to treatment have strong research evidence to support their effectiveness. The most widely studied of these is contingency management. According to Stitzer (2006), "Contingency management (CM) . . . is an approach in which tangible incentives of various types and magnitudes have been offered to drug abuse treatment clients based on urinalysis evidence of recent and sustained abstinence. A substantial number of high quality efficacy studies have now been published that focus on reinforcing abstinence from specific drugs of abuse, ranging from opiates and cocaine through alcohol, marijuana and smoked tobacco" (p. 1536). Voucher-based reinforcement therapy, in which vouchers that can be exchanged for goods and services are provided for "clean" urine samples, is one of the many variations of CM (Higgins et al., 1995), as is the "fishbowl" procedure in which patients with clean urine samples draw a slip of paper from a bowl containing prizes of various value (Petry & Martin, 2002). This is a type of variable reinforcement. Three different meta-analyses of CM (Griffith, Rowan-Szal, Roark, & Simpson, 2000; Lussier, Heil, Mongeon, Badger, & Higgins, 2006; Prendergast, Podus, Finney, Greenwell, & Roll, 2006) have concluded that CM produces clinically significant effects. Stitzer (2006) noted that these meta-analyses ". . . support the efficacy and effectiveness of contingency management as a clinical technique and underpin its status as an evidence-based clinical practice" (p. 1536).

A comprehensive approach to treatment that incorporates CM is the community reinforcement approach (CRA). According to Roozen, Boulogne, van Tulder, van den Brink, De Jong, and Kerkhof (2004), CRA ". . . is a biopsychosocial multifaceted approach to change a lifestyle of substance abuse. . . . Emphasis is placed on changing environmental contingencies in the aspects of life, such as labor, recreation, family involvement, etc., to promote a lifestyle that is more rewarding than substance abuse. CRA integrates not only cognitive behavioral interventions, but also pharmacological interventions . . . (and) voucher-based incentive programs to promote abstinence" (p. 1).

A treatment approach for stimulant (e.g., methamphetamine) abuse was developed by researchers at UCLA (Rawson et al., 1995). The matrix model includes elements of group and family therapies, education, support groups, and relapse prevention. The relationship between the counselor and the client is emphasized, with the counselor utilizing the relationship to reinforce positive behavior change. The approach is not confrontational and seeks to promote self-esteem, dignity, and self-worth. Detailed manuals have been developed to guide this approach.

Further, the National Institute on Alcohol Abuse and Alcoholism (NIAAA) has developed treatment manuals for three very different approaches to alcohol treatment. The manuals were used in a large-scale study to investigate the effects of matching clients to treatment approaches (see "Treatment Effectiveness"). The first manual, "Twelve- Step Facilitation Therapy," is based on the principles of Alcoholics Anonymous. The treatment protocol familiarizes clients with the AA philosophy and encourages participation in AA. This approach is similar to the Minnesota Model. The second manual, "Cognitive—Behavioral Therapy," is based on a social-learning theory model. Skills to avoid relapse are taught. Many of the specific techniques in this approach will be covered in Chapter 9, when we describe the cognitive–social learning model to relapse prevention. Finally, the third manual, "Motivational Enhancement Therapy," is designed to help clients identify and utilize personal resources to effect change. This approach is based on motivational psychology and is related to motivational interviewing (see Chapter 7).

Pharmacological procedures are also used in treatment. However, these procedures are rarely the only intervention. Rather, they are usually used in conjunction with other treatment methods. The philosophy of treatment and the treatment setting may also determine whether drugs are used to treat AOD problems. One would expect that treatment programs adhering to the disease concept would be adverse to using drugs in treatment. However, Cook (1988) stated that detoxification at Minnesota Model programs may use medication. Treatment programs in nonhospital settings without medical staff obviously should not use drugs in treatment.

Detoxification, the period of time in which a client is withdrawing from AOD, is frequently a time when medication is used. In the past, this process occurred in an inpatient, hospital setting. However, outpatient detoxification is now a common practice due to the high costs of hospitalization. In the detoxification process for alcohol and other CNS depressants, minor tranquilizers such as Valium or Xanax are often used to reduce the danger of seizures and the other uncomfortable and dangerous withdrawal symptoms. Careful medical supervision with a gradually decreasing dosage is necessary, since these minor tranquilizers are in the same drug classification as alcohol (see Chapter 2).

Methadone is widely known for its use in treating opioid addiction. Methadone is a synthetic narcotic with a longer duration of effect than heroin, and ingestion blocks the euphoric effects of opioids. Once a client is stabilized on a particular dose, he or she takes it to reduce or eliminate any withdrawal symptoms from heroin abstinence. The client must visit a methadone clinic to receive the dose. Once a client is stabilized on methadone, he or she can function normally.

A medication that can be administered through outpatient physician offices (as opposed to a specialized clinic) has been approved for use in treating opioid addiction. Buprenorphine is an opioid that has proved to be as effective as methadone. The advantages of buprenorphine are that it is taken in tablet form, daily doses do not appear to be necessary, and it has relatively mild withdrawal symptoms. In the pill form administered to opioid addicts, naloxone is added to buprenorphine. The naloxone decreases the likelihood of abuse, because it blocks the "high" that could be achieved by injecting buprenorphine alone. The approval of buprenorphine by the Federal Drug Administration has greatly increased the access to opioid agonist treatment for heroin addicts, particularly for people who would have to travel a great distance to get to a methadone clinic. Buprenorphine is sold under the brand name Suboxone.

Antabuse (disulfiram) has been used in conjunction with other forms of alcohol treatment. When Antabuse is taken and alcohol is ingested during the following 24- to 48- hour period, the client experiences facial flushing, heart palpitations and rapid heart rate, difficulty in breathing, nausea, and vomiting. Since Antabuse takes 30 minutes to work after ingestion, it has been of limited value in aversive conditioning. The client must take Antabuse on a daily basis, and this raises an issue of the need for such medication. If an individual were motivated to take Antabuse daily, it would seem that he or she would probably be motivated to remain abstinent without Antabuse. However, some alcoholics, when tempted to use alcohol, are comforted by the fact that Antabuse will result in an unpleasant reaction if they drink. This awareness often reduces or eliminates the urge to use. Clients who use Antabuse must be warned against using over-the-counter products that contain alcohol, since the Antabuse will cause a reaction from the use of these products.

Another drug that is used in alcoholism treatment is naltrexone. Naltrexone is an opioid antagonist (i.e., a drug that blocks the effects of other drugs). However, it has also been found to reduce the craving for alcohol. Therefore, naltrexone is recommended as one strategy in a comprehensive treatment program, but not as the *only* strategy. A panel of experts developed a protocol on the use of naltrexone in alcoholism treatment (Center for Substance Abuse Treatment, 1998) and reported:

> Naltrexone therapy improves treatment outcomes when added to other components of alcoholism treatment. For patients who are motivated to take the medication, naltrexone is an important and valuable tool. In many patients, a short regimen of naltrexone will provide a critical period of sobriety, during which the patient learns to stay sober without it. (p. xv)

While some recent studies have shown mixed results on naltrexone, Fuller and Gordis (2001) suggest that individuals with stable support and living situations who have been drinking for 20 years or less appear to be the most likely to benefit from naltrexone.

Acamprosate is another drug used in alcoholism treatment. Although acamprosate does not seem to be very effective with patients who are not abstinent at the beginning of treatment and those patients who abuse other drugs in addition to alcohol, it does have some evidence of effectiveness in reducing craving in those patients who are abstinent and motivated to remain that way (O'Malley & Kosten, 2006).

At this point, no effective pharmacological treatments for stimulant (e.g., cocaine and methamphetamine) or marijuana use disorders have been identified.

TREATMENT STRATEGIES AND TECHNIQUES

In describing the major approaches to treatment, we have already mentioned some of the techniques used in the treatment of alcoholics and addicts. For example, the disease or Minnesota Model uses group therapy, education, twelve-step meetings, and other strategies as well. In this section, we want to describe the most common procedures that are used in treatment. However, understand that not all of these strategies may be used in all treatment programs, or more or less emphasis may be placed on particular interventions depending on the treatment approach and setting. It is a good idea for helping professionals to contact treatment programs in their areas to determine the exact components of the particular program *before* making referrals.

Treatment planning and the treatment plan are the methods by which treatment staff determine what the problems are and what to do about them. Any substance abuse treatment program that is accredited by a state or other accrediting body will have individual treatment plans for all clients. That does not mean that all treatment plans in all treatment programs are comprehensive or useful—just that potential for usefulness exists. Treatment planning involves the assessment and diagnosis of the client (discussed in Chapter 6), the actual written treatment plan, and an aftercare plan. While the form and content of the treatment plan may vary from program to program and state to state depending on accreditation requirements, every treatment plan should include a statement of the problem(s), long-term goals, short-term objectives that are measurable, strategies to achieve goals and objectives, and review and target dates.

To illustrate a problem statement, long-term goal, and short-term objective, we asked to look at some treatment plans at one of our local treatment programs (with names deleted, of course). This example is representative of the treatment plans we reviewed.

Example of Treatment Plan

Problem Statement: (Client's Name) has used alcohol and cocaine on a daily basis for the last 16 months.

Long-Term Goal: (Client's Name) will remain abstinent from all mind-altering drugs.

Short-Term Objective: (Client's Name) will remain abstinent from all mind-altering drugs for one month.

Strategies:

1. Attend one AA or NA meeting per day.
2. Attend all program lectures.
3. Participate in two individual counseling sessions per week.
4. Participate in three group counseling sessions per week.
5. Participate in one family counseling session per week.

Let's examine these strategies more closely, along with some that are not addressed on this treatment plan.

Individual, Group, and Family Counseling

Because you are preparing for a career as a mental health professional, you have had or will have courses in individual, group, and family counseling. Although it is beyond our scope to thoroughly discuss the processes and theoretical approaches to counseling, we believe that an individual who enters a counseling relationship with any client should be trained and credentialed to perform counseling functions. At the very minimum, mental health professionals should possess the facilitative qualities of counseling, such as empathy, respect, warmth, concreteness, immediacy, congruence, and genuineness. While you have undoubtedly learned the need for training, credentialing, and facilitative qualities, making this message seem redundant, these issues are of utmost concern in the substance abuse counseling field. In many states, substance abuse counselors need only a high school diploma or GED and little formal training. A master's degree is rarely required for initial certification.

Royce (1989) described the counseling models he sees as most useful in counseling alcoholics:

Whether group or individual, it seems that the most appropriate psychotherapeutic modes for alcoholics are those that focus on the present and future rather than on the past. Examples are the reality therapy of William Glasser, the existential here-and-now logotherapy of Viktor Frankl, the rational-emotive therapy (RET) of Albert

Ellis, and other such nonanalytic therapies. . . . Psychodrama and role-playing can be very useful under a skilled therapist, because of their appeal to both imagination and emotion. Transactional analysis (TA) . . . can be useful provided one does not get too involved in analyzing the games people play or think of alcoholic addiction as merely learned behavior that can be easily unlearned. (p. 256)

Traditionally, group counseling is often the primary approach of both inpatient and outpatient treatment programs. However, in many treatment programs, group counseling may actually be a confrontation of individuals in the group who are not "working the program" or it may be dissemination of educational information. This is considerably different from the group counseling described by Corey (2008) that is probably part of your training program. It would be more useful for group work to help to develop concrete, usable skills and to rehearse these behaviors in the group. In addition, such group counseling can be used to analyze drinking and drug-taking behaviors and to develop methods of coping, problem solving, and assertiveness, rather than being focused on gaining client compliance to admit to having a disease.

There has been an increasing use of family counseling in treatment programs. As with group counseling, what is sometimes called family counseling is actually education about the disease concept and the family's role in the disease process. However, family counseling is an essential component of treatment as O'Farrell and Fals-Stewart (2003) explain:

Many alcohol abusers have extensive marital and family problems . . . and positive family adjustment is associated with better alcoholism treatment outcomes at follow-up. . . . Marital and family problems may stimulate excessive drinking, and family interactions often help to maintain alcohol problems once they have developed. . . . Finally, even when recovery from the alcohol problem has begun, marital and family conflicts may often precipitate renewed drinking by abstinent alcohol abusers. (p. 188)

Conceptually, Kaufman and Kaufman (1992) suggested the following paradigm in working with families of substance abusers:

Treating the family of a substance abuser is a complicated process. Treatment takes place simultaneously on many levels. In meeting the needs of the family as an entity, the spouse subsystem, the sibling subsystem, and the individual needs of each person in the family must be considered. These three areas must interlock and work in harmony. Teaching and demonstrating effective parenting is an important aspect of treatment. Encouraging families to form positive social networks aids in the total treatment. Part of family therapy is the problem-solving process that occurs. Hopefully, these techniques become internalized so that the family maintains them throughout its lifetime. (p. x)

A treatment approach for adolescents that primarily focuses on the family has been developed by Howard Liddle (Diamond & Liddle, 1996). Multidimensional family therapy is conducted in the treatment setting, in the home, and in community settings. Parents work on their parenting style, learn to distinguish influence from control, and develop a positive and developmentally appropriate influence on their child. Other evidence-based approaches for couples and families include behavioral couples therapy (O'Farrell & Fals-Stewart, 2006), brief strategic family therapy (Szapocznik & Kurtines, 1989), and family behavior therapy (Donohue, Allen, & Lapota, 2009).

Support Groups

We will thoroughly discuss twelve-step and other forms of support groups in Chapter 10. However, twelve-step groups are such a central part of most treatment programs that this type of strategy deserves mention here. In fact, many programs throughout the country utilize an Alcoholics Anonymous (AA) or Narcotics Anonymous (NA) twelve-step approach for both in- and outpatient treatment. Again, we will save a discussion of the components and effectiveness of twelve-step groups for the following chapter. However, the use of twelve-step meetings as a treatment strategy and as a philosophy in treatment programs is consistent with the disease model of addiction and, as we have already discussed, with the orientation of the Minnesota Model of treatment.

While AA and NA are recommended for the alcoholic/addict, family members are encouraged to attend either Al-Anon or Alateen meetings. This is to introduce family members to the potential support available through Al-Anon or Alateen while the client is still in treatment. For those of you unfamiliar with these groups, Al-Anon is a support group for family members of alcoholics/addicts using the twelve-step model, and Alateen is a similar support group specifically for teenagers who have an alcoholic/addicted parent. Clients and family members may also be referred to ACOA (twelve-step support for adult children of alcoholics) or CODA (twelve-step support for codependents).

Many alternative support groups that do not use the twelve-step model exist. However, the acceptance of these alternatives in disease-model treatment programs may be resisted.

Lifestyle Changes

Irrespective of the orientation of the treatment program, treatment strategies designed to bring about changes in the lifestyle of the client are essential. For example, if clients return to the same friends and activities that were a part of their lives prior to treatment, relapse is highly probable. The range of lifestyle changes that must be addressed illustrates the complexity of comprehensive treatment and the need for long-term interventions for alcoholic/addicted individuals. We will discuss some of these strategies for lifestyle change in more detail in Chapter 9, "Relapse Prevention and Recovery," since mental health professionals may be involved in the implementation of many of these strategies. The lifestyle areas that should receive attention for a particular client should be determined during the assessment of the client and should then be included in the treatment plan.

The issue of friends, lovers, family members, and acquaintances is a focus of treatment. If a client has close associations with individuals who use AOD, some difficult and painful decisions must be made. These topics may be discussed in individual, group, and family counseling. In addition, clients may need assistance with social skills in order to enhance their ability to make new friends. Many alcoholic/addicted individuals have relied on the use of AOD to feel comfortable in social situations and/or as a common bond to those with whom they spend time. The difficulty of this particular area can be clearly illustrated with an adolescent who is told during treatment to avoid contact with friends who use. The adolescent returns to school after treatment and perceives his or her options as returning to a previous social group or having no friends at all. If relapse is to be avoided, the adolescent who is treated for an alcohol or other drug problem clearly needs continued support and assistance to help develop a new social group.

Since many individuals with AOD problems have used these substances to avoid negative emotions or to manage stress and pain, alternative methods of dealing with common life problems must also be taught in treatment. Strategies may involve stress management techniques, relaxation procedures, and assertiveness training. The intent of such training is to provide the client with skills to use in situations or in response to situations in which alcohol or other drug use was the only perceived option available. For example, a business executive is treated for alcoholism. He returns to work after treatment and, as happens to everyone, has "one of those days." In the past, he has used alcohol to cope with the stress and tension of work. If the client is not taught alternative methods for managing stress and tension, along with techniques to relax that do not involve drugs, relapse is a predictable response.

Other lifestyle areas that may be a focus of intervention include vocational and educational planning, financial planning, living environment, and nutrition. To illustrate how these factors can influence recovery, review the first case example of Celest.

You can easily see all the areas mentioned required attention, any of which could result in a return to use if ignored. Celest was not able to work in her chosen profession, which resulted in financial stress. Her living environment was clearly horrible for a number of reasons. She had health issues, parenting and child care concerns, and personal safety worries. These practical issues in treatment go beyond the model used and are critical determinants in whether a client is able to maintain a drug-free lifestyle. So you won't be kept in suspense, this particular situation had a fairly happy ending (as far as we know today). Celest's boyfriend was sent to prison for a variety of offenses, and she was able to move in with her brother. A vocational rehabilitation counselor helped her find employment, and a latchkey program through her daughter's school provided child care. Again, the point of this case is to illustrate how vocational guidance, financial planning, living arrangements, and nutritional counseling may all be necessary components of treatment.

Education

Many treatment programs, particularly those using a disease-concept model, use lectures and films to provide clients with information on the disease concept, on family issues in AOD use, and on the social, medical, and psychological consequences of AOD use. Miller and Hester (2003) discuss the rationale for the use of education in the treatment of alcoholism:

> Twentieth-century alcohol treatment programs in the United States often included a series of lectures and films. . . . Implicit in such strategies is the assumption that alcohol problems arise from deficient knowledge, from a lack of accurate information. When armed with correct and up-to-date knowledge, individuals presumably will be less likely to use alcohol (and other drugs) in a hazardous fashion and to suffer the consequences. (p. 5)

Although the teaching of educational information is a commonly used strategy in treatment, no evidence exists that providing information to alcoholics/addicts changes their behavior. However, as we discussed in Chapter 7, education can be helpful for light or moderate users and at-risk users. Furthermore, as part of a comprehensive treatment program, it certainly makes sense to provide information to clients and family members. But education and information dissemination should not be expected to produce miraculous changes and, therefore, these activities should not be conducted at the expense of more useful treatment strategies. As an aside, it has always been fascinating to us that didactic methods are used to present information to clients in treatment with little or no regard for the learning capacity or learning style of the client. For example, since research by Karacostas and Fisher (1993) has found a higher-than-expected proportion of learning-disabled adolescents with probable AOD problems, it would be logical to assess clients to determine the most effective method for imparting information. However, we have found that this is rarely a part of the assessment in treatment programs.

Aftercare

For those individuals who enter AOD treatment, recovery can be conceptualized as a three-stage process. The first stage is formal treatment, the second stage is aftercare, and the third stage is ongoing recovery. *Aftercare* refers to the interventions and strategies that will be implemented after formal treatment is completed. However, it more accurately should be called "continuing care," since aftercare programs are usually continuations of many of the strategies from formal treatment. Our focus is on the issues that require attention following discharge from formal treatment.

The case of Celest described earlier is a good example of how issues that cannot possibly be solved in a month-long treatment program can be carried on in aftercare. Frequently, individual and family therapy will be components of an aftercare program as well as vocational, educational, and financial guidance. Attendance at twelve-step meetings will usually be mentioned in aftercare plans. Aftercare meetings may be a part of the treatment program, or the client may be referred to a mental health professional for management of the aftercare program. Since the aftercare program is an essential element in relapse prevention, we will discuss this in detail in Chapter 9.

TREATMENT SETTINGS

Choice of Treatment Setting

The strategies and interventions described can be implemented in a variety of treatment settings. Klar (1987) discussed the concept of "least restrictive environment" with regard to the appropriate treatment setting. Those of you with a background in special education are familiar with this concept as it relates to placement of students, and the rationale is similar for AOD treatment. Clients should be placed in the treatment setting that offers the least amount of restriction, with the highest probability of success, while all the factors identified in the assessment are considered. What are some of these factors? Nace (1987) identified criteria for determining whether outpatient alcoholism treatment was appropriate. These criteria included client motivation, ability to discontinue use, social support, employment, medical condition, psychiatric status, and treatment history. Clients who are poorly motivated to discontinue use (i.e., court mandated) or who admit to a failure to abstain if AOD are available may fail in outpatient treatment. Also, we have already discussed the importance of social support. Employment may be a double-edged sword. While continued employment may strongly motivate a client to succeed in outpatient treatment, the work environment is often a source of stress for people, or coworkers might encourage the client to use (e.g., going out for drinks after work). An individual who is unemployed (and, ironically, is probably the least able to afford more expensive inpatient treatment), may be a poor candidate for an outpatient program since the client is not occupied for a large segment of time by a job. Obviously, individuals with medical and/or psychiatric conditions may need more restrictive treatment environments. A person with liver damage may need medical supervision and an environment that ensures abstinence. Similarly, a client who is receiving pharmaceutical treatment for a psychiatric condition may (but not always) require inpatient treatment. Finally, if someone has already failed in outpatient treatment, more intensive treatment may be needed.

Unfortunately, all of these factors might not be used in determining the treatment setting for a client. In other words, money, insurance, and the availability of publicly funded treatment programs, rather than client factors, may determine where a person is placed for treatment.

As a result of "nonclient" factors being used to determine treatment setting, many states are adopting "uniform patient placement criteria" to determine the appropriate treatment setting. The most widely used patient placement criteria was developed by the American Society of

Addiction Medicine (ASAM) and is called ASAM PPC 2R to denote the second edition revision of this system. ASAM PPC 2R utilizes a multidimensional assessment that includes acute intoxication and/or withdrawal potential, biomedical conditions and complications, emotional/behavioral/cognitive conditions and complications, readiness to change, relapse/continued use/continued problem potential, and recovery environment (i.e., social, family, vocational support) (Mee-Lee, 2005). The major levels of care (there are many sublevels) are: Level .5, Early Intervention Services; Level I, Outpatient; Level II, Intensive Outpatient/Partial Hospitalization; Level III, Residential; and Level IV, Inpatient. We will briefly describe these settings as well as therapeutic communities.

Therapeutic Communities

The therapeutic community is a residential environment usually associated with treatment for drugs other than alcohol. As the website for Treatment Communities of America (2008) states:

> The primary goal of a Therapeutic Community is to foster individual change and promote positive growth. This is accomplished by changing an individual's lifestyle through a community of concerned people working together to help themselves and each other. Being part of something greater than oneself is an especially important factor in facilitating positive growth. Therapeutic Communities offer a holistic approach in regards to treating the whole person and not just the addiction. Clients in a Therapeutic Community (TC) are members, as in a family setting, they are not patients, as in an institution. These members play a significant role in managing the TC and act as positive role models for others to emulate. (therapeuticcommunitiesofamerica.org)

The duration of treatment in TCs is typically longer than other types of treatment, usually one year or more. Synanon, one of the earliest and most famous therapeutic communities, expected permanent involvement by clients. The characteristics of therapeutic communities include a highly structured daily routine, a system of rewards and punishments for behavior, and frequent group confrontation, self-reflection, and confession of past wrongdoing. Because of the isolation and long-term nature of most therapeutic communities, the drop-out rates tend to be high. This type of treatment setting is often a treatment of last resort. In other words, most therapeutic community residents have failed in one or more other types of treatment setting.

Interestingly, therapeutic communities are increasingly popular as a treatment setting in jails and prisons. Obviously, the length of this type of approach is no barrier in these institutions. The needs of institutional clients are often well suited to this type of program since the primary goal of a therapeutic community is "global life-style change, including abstinence from (alcohol and other drugs), elimination of antisocial behavior, enhanced education, constructive employment, and development of prosocial attitudes and values" (Center for Substance Abuse Treatment, 1995, p. 51).

Religious-based TCs such as Teen Challenge are also available. This specific program has an evangelical Christian orientation and the TC portion of the program lasts for one year (Teen Challenge, 2009).

Inpatient and Residential Treatment

Although this treatment environment is usually associated with hospitals, this is not always the case. Residential treatment may occur in nonhospital settings. The duration of treatment is shorter than in therapeutic communities, and the social isolation is reduced. Most inpatient and residential programs gradually reintroduce the client to a normal environment through community outings and home passes. These programs generally offer supervised detoxification that may involve medication in a hospital setting or social detoxification (i.e., no medication) in a nonhospital setting. The typical 28-day treatment duration has no research base. It has come about as a result of financial constraints, particularly the reluctance of insurance companies to pay for treatment. Inpatient and residential treatment settings have the advantages of 24-hour supervision, the reduced likelihood of clients using AOD while in treatment, highly structured days, and a total immersion in treatment, with removal from the everyday stressors and pressures that may interfere with treatment. The disadvantages of this setting are the expense (a 28-day program in a hospital setting may be well over $10,000) and the artificiality of the environment. In a supervised, structured, and protective setting, a client may have little difficulty maintaining abstinence. In a well-supervised program, there may be no choice. However, the client may have little or no opportunity to practice new behaviors and may develop a false belief in self-efficacy (competence to deal with the environment). The real world may quickly dispel the client's perception of self-efficacy, and relapse results.

Partial Hospitalization and Day Treatment

As you can probably tell from the heading of this section, these types of treatment settings can also occur in hospitals or free-standing treatment centers. The client normally spends all or some of the evenings (and overnight) at home. These programs are less expensive than inpatient or residential programs and allow clients to remain involved with some normal aspects of life while they are in treatment. Since the client's life is less artificial than it would be if he or she were in 24-hour care, the client has greater opportunity to apply the knowledge and skills acquired during treatment. The client also the opportunity to figure out some of the possible barriers in his or her daily life to a changed lifestyle during the time the client has frequent contact with the treatment program. This allows the client to work on solutions to these barriers before the formal treatment program ends. However, some risks are associated with partial hospitalization and day treatment, the most obvious being opportunities for the client to use AOD. Unless the client admits to using, or if drug testing is conducted, a return to use may not be discovered. Also, if the client's friends and family are using or are not supportive of the client's efforts, living in the "normal" environment for even brief periods may be counterproductive.

Intensive Outpatient and Outpatient

These types of treatment programs are usually associated with free-standing treatment programs or clinics, such as mental health centers. Intensive outpatient programs normally are held for three or four evenings in the week for 2 to 4 hours each evening. Outpatient treatment is usually less frequent (one or two evenings a week) and shorter (1 to 2 hours per session). As you might imagine, outpatient clients usually would not be classified as substance dependent (see Chapter 6), although some insurance policies will pay only for outpatient treatment. Outpatient treatment can also be a point in a gradual reduction in treatment intensity (i.e., client starts treatment in a residential setting and transitions to outpatient).

The major advantage (aside from cost) of intensive outpatient and outpatient programs is that clients can continue to work or go to school. It is often the case that a person's only expressed barrier to treatment is the perceived or actual necessity to work or go to school. Whether this barrier is real or used as an excuse, it does not exist in outpatient programs.

> ## *AT A GLANCE*
>
> ### Treatment Approaches
>
> - Minnesota Model
> - Behavioral Approaches
>   - Aversive conditioning
>   - Contingency management
>   - Community reinforcement approach
> - Matrix Model
> - Twelve-Step Facilitation
> - Cognitive–Behavioral Therapy
> - Motivational Enhancement Therapy
> - Pharmacological Procedures
>   - Methadone and buprenorphine
>   - Antabuse (disulfiram)
>   - Naltrexone
>   - Acamprosate
>
> ### Strategies and Techniques
>
> - Treatment plan
>   - Problem statement
>   - Long-term goals
>   - Short-term objectives
>   - Strategies
> - Individual, group, family counseling
> - Support groups
> - Life-style changes
> - Education
> - Aftercare
>
> ### Treatment Setting
>
> - ASAM PPC 2R for standardized determination
> - Therapeutic communities
> - Inpatient and residential
> - Partial hospitalization and day treatment
> - Intensive outpatient and outpatient

PRINCIPLES OF EFFECTIVE TREATMENT

The National Institute on Drug Abuse (NIDA) published a booklet in 2009 called "Principles of Drug Addiction Treatment: A Research-Based Guide," second edition. This short booklet is available online (see Internet Resources at the end of the chapter) and contains evidence-based principles, methods, and programs in treatment. The following 13 principles, which are listed in this booklet, are extremely useful for all mental health professionals.

1. ***Addiction is a complex but treatable disease that affects brain function and behavior***
   Drugs of abuse alter the brain's structure and function, resulting in changes that persist
   long after drug use has ceased. This may explain why drug abusers are at risk for relapse
   even after long periods of abstinence and despite the potentially devastating consequences.
2. ***No single treatment is appropriate for everyone***   Matching treatment settings, interventions, and services to an individual's particular problems and needs is critical to his or
   her ultimate success in returning to productive functioning in the family, workplace, and
   society.
3. ***Treatment needs to be readily available***   Because drug-addicted individuals may be uncertain about entering treatment, taking advantage of available services the moment people
   are ready for treatment is critical. Potential patients can be lost if treatment is not immediately available or readily accessible. As with other chronic diseases, the earlier treatment is
   offered in the disease process, the greater the likelihood of positive outcomes.
4. ***Effective treatment attends to multiple needs of the individual, not just his or her drug
   abuse***   To be effective, treatment must address the individual's drug abuse and any
   associated medical, psychological, social, vocational, and legal problems. It is also important that treatment be appropriate to the individual's age, gender, ethnicity, and culture.
5. ***Remaining in treatment for an adequate period of time is critical***   The appropriate
   duration for an individual depends on the type and degree of his or her problems and
   needs. Research indicates that most addicted individuals need at least three months in
   treatment to significantly reduce or stop their drug use and that the best outcomes occur
   with longer durations of treatment. Recovery from drug addiction is a long-term process
   and frequently requires multiple episodes of treatment. As with other chronic illnesses,
   relapses to drug abuse can occur and should signal a need for treatment to be reinstated or
   adjusted. Because individuals often leave treatment prematurely, programs should include
   strategies to engage and keep patients in treatment.
6. ***Counseling—individual and/or group—and other behavioral therapies are the most
   commonly used forms of drug abuse treatment***   Behavioral therapies vary in their focus
   and may involve addressing a patient's motivation to change, providing incentives for abstinence, building skills to resist drug use, replacing drug-using activities with constructive
   and rewarding activities, improving problem-solving skills, and facilitating better interpersonal relationships. Also, participation in group therapy and other peer support programs
   during and following treatment can help maintain abstinence.
7. ***Medications are an important element of treatment for many patients, especially when
   combined with counseling and other behavioral therapies***   For example, methadone and
   buprenorphine are effective in helping individuals addicted to heroin or other opioids sta-
   bilize their lives and reduce their illicit drug use. Naltrexone is also an effective medication
   for some opioid-addicted individuals and some patients with alcohol dependence. Other
   medications for alcohol dependence include acamprosate, disulfiram, and topiramate. For
   persons addicted to nicotine, a nicotine replacement product (such as patches, gum, or loz-
   enges) or an oral medication (such as bupropion or varenicline) can be an effective component of treatment when part of a comprehensive behavioral treatment program.
8. ***An individual's treatment and services plan must be assessed continually and modified
   as necessary to ensure that it meets his or her changing needs***   A patient may require
   varying combinations of services and treatment components during the course of treatment
   and recovery. In addition to counseling or psychotherapy, a patient may require medication,
   medical services, family therapy, parenting instruction, vocational rehabilitation, and/or

social and legal services. For many patients, a continuing care approach provides the best results, with the treatment intensity varying according to a person's changing needs.

9. *Many drug-addicted individuals also have other mental disorders* Because drug abuse and addiction—both of which are mental disorders—often co-occur with other mental illnesses, patients presenting with one condition should be assessed for the other(s). And when these problems co-occur, treatment should address both (or all), including the use of medications as appropriate.

10. *Medically assisted detoxification is only the first stage of addiction treatment and by itself does little to change long-term drug abuse* Although medically assisted detoxification can safely manage the acute physical symptoms of withdrawal and, for some, can pave the way for effective long-term addiction treatment, detoxification alone is rarely sufficient to help addicted individuals achieve long-term abstinence. Thus, patients should be encouraged to continue drug treatment following detoxification. Motivational enhancement and incentive strategies, begun at initial patient intake, can improve treatment engagement.

11. *Treatment does not need to be voluntary to be effective* Sanctions or enticements from family, employment settings, and/or the criminal justice system can significantly increase treatment entry, retention rates, and the ultimate success of drug treatment interventions.

12. *Drug use during treatment must be monitored continuously, as lapses during treatment do occur* Knowing their drug use is being monitored can be a powerful incentive for patients and can help them withstand urges to use drugs. Monitoring also provides an early indication of a return to drug use, signaling a possible need to adjust an individual's treatment plan to better meet his or her needs.

13. *Treatment programs should assess patients for the presence of HIV/ AIDS, hepatitis B and C, tuberculosis, and other infectious diseases as well as provide targeted risk-reduction counseling to help patients modify or change behaviors that place them at risk of contracting or spreading infectious diseases* Typically, drug abuse treatment addresses some of the drug-related behaviors that put people at risk of infectious diseases. Targeted counseling specifically focused on reducing infectious disease risk can help patients further reduce or avoid substance-related and other high-risk behaviors. Counseling can also help those who are already infected to manage their illness. Moreover, engaging in substance abuse treatment can facilitate adherence to other medical treatments. Patients may be reluctant to accept screening for HIV (and other infectious diseases); therefore, it is incumbent upon treatment providers to encourage and support HIV screening and inform patients that highly active antiretroviral therapy (HAART) has proven effective in combating HIV, including among drug abusing populations.

EVIDENCE-BASED TREATMENT

Federal and state government agencies involved in AOD treatment are increasingly requiring that funding provided to agencies must be used for strategies that research has shown to be effective and that have demonstrated consistent results in multiple studies. "Evidence-based" treatment is the term generally used to describe these methods or strategies but "empirically-based," "science-based," and "research-based" are also used.

In an effort to standardize the process of designating a strategy, program, or technique as evidence-based, the Substance Abuse and Mental Health Services Administration, a federal agency in the Department of Health and Human Services, developed the National Registry of Evidence-Based Programs and Practices (NREPP). NREPP includes mental health promotion and treatment, substance abuse prevention and treatment, and co-occurring disorders.

At the time this edition is published, 50 treatment interventions in NREPP have been iden-tified. Some are comprehensive manuals for treatment (e.g., "Twelve-Step Facilitation Therapy," "Cognitive–Behavioral Therapy," and "Motivational Enhancement Therapy"); some interven-tions are for special populations (e.g., "A Woman's Path to Recovery," "Adolescent Commu-nity Reinforcement Approach," "Friends Care" [for parole and probationers], "Healthy Living Project for People Living with HIV," "Pathways' Housing First Project" [for co-occurring disor-ders]; some are for specific substances (e.g., "Cocaine Specific Coping Skills Training," "Brief Marijuana Dependence Counseling," "Broad Spectrum Treatment [BST]", and "Naltrexone for Alcohol Dependence"); and other programs that target discrete parts of the treatment process (e.g., "Computer-Assisted System for Patient Assessment and Referral," "Contracts, Prompts, and Reinforcement of Substance Use Disorder Continuing Care [CPR]").

In order to be accepted by NREPP, every aspect of the intervention, including outcomes, are evaluated by an independent expert review panel. The intervention is graded on the reliability and validity of the measurement instruments, the fidelity of the intervention (how closely the evaluators make sure that things happen as they are supposed to happen), missing data and attri-tion, potential confounding variables, and the appropriateness of the data analysis. Since it would not do much good to include an intervention in NREPP that others could not adopt, the program or strategy is also graded on its readiness for dissemination, including the availability of imple-mentation materials, training and support, and quality assurance procedures.

With this rigorous procedure, you can have some faith that the programs and strategies included in NREPP are effective. However, evidence-based interventions may be implemented poorly by clinicians, applied in settings or with populations for which the intervention has not been validated, or employed incompletely, thus negating the effectiveness of the process. So, neither assume that simply because a treatment is described as "evidence-based," its success is inevitable, nor that an approach that has not been labeled "evidence-based" cannot possibly be effective.

TREATMENT AND SPECIAL POPULATIONS

As with any aspect of the helping professions, the individual and group differences of clients must be considered in designing treatment. We have previously focused on the need to tailor treatment to the unique characteristics of the client rather than forcing a client to fit a particular model of treatment or addiction. Similarly, group characteristics are important to consider in treatment. This is not to imply that clients should be stereotyped simply because they are mem-bers of a particular age, gender, or ethnic group. However, demographic information may be relevant in understanding the client and in designing appropriate treatment. A comprehensive discussion of the treatment issues for all special populations would be beyond our goals for this book. However, we do want to acquaint you with some of these issues so you will be informed when directing your clients to treatment.

Ethnically Diverse Populations

The issues with regard to ethnically diverse populations were discussed in detail in Chapter 4, with regard not only to treatment but to other AOD issues as well.

At this point, we want to restate several points specifically with regard to treatment. First, diversity in the treatment population and the staff is clearly beneficial for client comfort and understanding. Second, the attitude of an ethnic group toward AOD problems may present a bar-rier for the individual seeking treatment. For example, in some African American communities alcoholism is seen as immoral or sinful behavior, a view that is clearly incompatible with the disease concept of alcoholism. In this view, the person, not alcohol, is responsible for problems, and the use of alcohol could be controlled if the person so desired. This barrier is certainly not unique to African Americans. Any families who hold this view would be less likely to encourage and support family members and friends to seek treatment. This barrier to disease-model programs requires education for the family. Third, the customs, beliefs, and language of the group must be considered in treatment. An obvious example is the barrier presented in treatment for Spanish-speaking clients when the treatment staff are not bilingual. With regard to Native Americans, Coyhis and White (2002b) stated:

> The most viable frameworks of addiction recovery for Native Americans tap the deepest roots of tribal cultures. The job of the conscientious addiction counselor is to become a student of these cultures—their histories, their organization, their values, their ceremonies and folkways, and their systems of healing. The addiction counselor can help forge a bridge between the treatment agency and tribal cultures by encouraging the involvement of family elders, tribal elders and traditional medicine people (herbalists, shamanic healers, spiritual advisors) in the design and delivery of treatment services for Native clients. The goal here is to create a menu of words, ideas, rituals and experiences within the counseling milieu that can be selectively used by Native people who bring enormous diversity in terms of their personal histories, personalities, religious and spiritual beliefs, and degree of acculturation. . . . Such an approach recognizes the multiple sources and patterns of Native alcohol problems as well as the multiple pathways and styles of long-term recovery among Native peoples. (p. 3)

Elderly

According to Patterson and Jeste (1999), "baby boomers" (who are joining the ranks of the elderly) have an increasing risk of substance use disorders because of their relaxed attitudes toward substance use when they were younger. However, diagnosis in this group may be challenging because the *DSM-IV-TR* (see Chapter 6) criteria for substance use disorders may not apply to the elderly, or their difficulties can be caused by other problems. Furthermore, health care providers and family members may hesitate to ask about substance use issues because of embarrassment or a belief that symptoms such as falls or cognitive difficulties are due to age-related issues (Drew et al., 2010).

With regard to alcohol abuse, the National Institute on Alcohol Abuse and Alcoholism's guidelines recommend that those over 65 limit their use to no more than three standards drinks in any one day and no more than seven per week (National Institute on Alcohol Abuse and Alcoholism, 2005). While this is the same for women below the age of 65, it is significantly different than the quantity for men. Therefore, an elderly man may develop problems with alcohol from using the same quantity he was able to drink when he was younger. This is due to the fact that the elderly have slower metabolism and a smaller volume of distribution (Drew et al., 2010).

The problems of the elderly are often different from those of younger clients and may require specific attention in treatment. For example, the elderly client may be experiencing an emotional reaction to retirement, feelings of bereavement from the death of a spouse and/or friends, loneliness, and physical pain from illnesses or age. Drew et al. (2010) cite some evidence that age-specific programs for older alcoholics significantly improve abstinence rates posttreatment. However, as was noted at the beginning of the chapter, only 7% of treatment facilities had specialty programs for the elderly.

The case example of Richard illustrates some of the problems an elderly man can have with alcohol. Although his alcohol intake had not increased, he experienced more consequences from his use. In addition, Richard had the added problems of grief from losing his long-time partner and social isolation.

Adolescents

As was noted earlier in the chapter, nearly 33% of treatment facilities have specialized programs for adolescents. Twelve to 17-year-olds accounted for 7.6% of treatment admissions in 2008 (Substance Abuse and Mental Health Services Administration, 2009c). Marijuana was a primary drug for this age in group in nearly 31% of the cases, hallucinogens in nearly 23%, and stimulants in 58% (more than one primary drug can be indicated) (Substance Abuse and Mental Health Services Administration, 2009c).

We met Javier (the second case example at the beginning of the chapter) some time ago. Javier was in an inpatient treatment program and the senior author conducted a psychological evaluation of him. During the evaluation, Javier reported that he (and others, so he claimed) had learned that if they publicly (defined as being in a group) said that they had a disease and were powerless, they would be released from the program. Javier was quite rebellious (one reason the evaluation had been requested), and he refused to say that he had a disease. In fact, he told everyone that he had every intention to use again when he got out.

Javier's statements are indicative of some of the treatment issues for adolescents. Adolescents have difficulty relating to a concept of a life-long disease. They have rarely experienced the same level of life problems resulting from their AOD use as adults have. When they attend AA or NA meetings, they may hear stories from older adults who have little relationship to the adolescents' lives. If you have worked with adolescents at all, you probably know that they can be skilled at saying what they need to say to get what they want. After working with adolescents with AOD problems for some time, we have little doubt that what Javier said was true. Many of the adolescents told the staff what they wanted to hear. Finally, adolescents may reject the idea that lifestyle change is necessary. Adults who have lost jobs, families, and possessions and have been arrested for DUIs may have little difficulty accepting the need to change their lives. An adolescent who has been busted at school for smoking pot may not feel the same way. Even when the problems have been more significant, it is very difficult to convince an adolescent that he or she needs to change his or her social group.

In a meta-analysis of treatment outcome studies for adolescents, Waldron and Turner (2008) identified functional family therapy, multidimensional family therapy, and group cognitive-behavioral therapy as efficacious treatments for adolescents.

Persons with Disabilities

Individuals with sensory (hearing or visually impaired), motor, mental, and learning handicaps can and do have AOD problems. For example, Karacostas and Fisher (1993) found evidence that adolescents diagnosed as learning disabled had a higher rate of chemical dependency than did nonlearning disabled peers. Javier, the adolescent case we mentioned earlier, had a reading disability (in addition to his language barriers). Many treatment programs require a great deal of reading and writing "homework" and for clients with learning disabilities, this can represent a barrier. Furthermore, clients identified as defensive, resistant, and rebellious may have unidentified learning or intellectual disabilities. Acting out behavior may be a reaction to these disabilities.

The nature of the disability and the age at which the disability occurred may be factors in the development of a substance use disorder and are certainly factors in treatment. For example, a young person who becomes physically disabled as a result of an accident may have problems handling the grief resulting from the loss of mobility and increased dependence on others. Using substances can be a way of coping with these issues but would be an important focus of treatment if a substance use disorder develops.

Irrespective of the model of addiction, persons with disabilities have treatment needs that require attention. We have already mentioned the grief that a person may experience, particularly if the disability was acquired later in life. Problems communicating are intrinsic to sensory handicaps, so in a program with a heavy educational component, the methods of imparting information must be adapted for the sensory-impaired client. It is encouraging that nearly 33% of treatment programs utilized sign language for hearing impaired clients (see earlier section "How Many Are in Treatment? How Many Need Treatment?"). For individuals with learning disabilities, instructional strategies must be modified to accommodate the type of learning disability (Karacostas & Fisher, 1993). Individuals with intellectual handicaps may not be able to grasp abstract concepts and, therefore, may be unable to understand the disease concept. More behavioral interventions may be necessary.

Designing the treatment of persons with disabilities is clearly consistent with the notion of client/treatment matching that we will discuss later in this chapter. Rather than forcing the person to fit a treatment program (which might be impossible with persons with disabilities), the treatment program must meet the client's needs. However, the complexity of treatment for persons with disabilities also indicates the need for greater prevention efforts for this population. While many prevention programs for young people who are not disabled (see Chapter 15), few efforts have been made to design programs for young people with disabilities.

Women

While it seems ironic to talk about half of the population as a special group, most of the older research and concepts about treatment came from studies with predominantly male subjects. Although about half as many women as men have a substance use disorder (Substance Abuse and Mental Health Administration, 2010), women represented only about a third of treatment admissions (Substance Abuse and Mental Health Services Administration, 2009c). Greenfield et al. (2007a) conducted a review of literature on treatment entry, retention, and outcomes for women. Among the barriers to treatment the researchers identified were pregnancy, lack of services for pregnant women, fear of losing custody of the unborn child, fear of prosecution for drug use while pregnant, and lack of child care outside of treatment or as part of the treatment services. As noted in the earlier section of the chapter, only 14% of treatment agencies had specialized services for pregnant or postpartum women. Additional barriers for women included lack of employment or other means to pay for treatment, high rates of co-occurring disorders (a discussion of this topic follows in this section) and the associated lack of appropriate treatment, greater social stigma and discrimination than faced by men, and histories of physical and/or sexual abuse making mixed-gender treatment programs undesirable. With regard to this latter barrier, Najavits, Weiss, and Shaw (1997) reported that between 30% and 59% of women in treatment for substance use disorders suffered from posttraumatic stress disorder, mostly as a result of physical and/or sexual abuse.

Greenfield et al. (2007a) found that gender was not a significant predictor of treatment retention, completion, or outcome. While these researchers did not find that women-only treatment was more effective than mixed-gender treatment, treatment that addressed problems more common to women or that was designed for specific sub-groups of women did show greater effectiveness. A more extensive discussion of women and their treatment is included in Chapter 11.

The case example of Celest contains many of the elements that make treatment and recovery for women challenging. She was economically dependent on an abusive male partner, had a child to consider, and a chronic health condition. Hopefully, you can see how the concept of "recovery-oriented systems of care" makes sense for clients like Celest. Regardless of how successful her episode of acute treatment was, she needed continued support, counseling, and services following treatment.

Lesbian, Gay, Bisexual, and Transgender (LGBT) Individuals

Some research cites evidence to support the fact that lesbian, gay, bisexual, and transgender (LGBT) persons have a greater rate of substance use disorders than strictly heterosexual individuals (e.g., Cochran, Ackerman, Mays, & Ross, 2004; Hughes et al., 2006; Trocki, Drabble, & Midanik, 2009). Senreich (2010) found gay and bisexual men had better outcomes in specialized programs for lesbian, gay, bisexual, and transgender clients, and Rowan and Faul (2011) examined the predictor variables of treatment success within a specialized program for LGBT clients. However, as stated in an earlier section of the chapter, only 6% of treatment facilities have specialized programs for this population.

According to Senreich (2010), lesbian, gay, and bisexual (LGB) clients in nonspecialized treatment often receive heterosexist comments and reactions from other clients. In addition, treatment providers may not have training in the specific issues important to LGB clients. The result for gay and bisexual men (but not women) is that they are less likely to complete treatment and to report that the reason they left treatment early was that their needs were not met (Senreich, 2009).

Additionally, Senreich (2010) pointed out that because LGB clients do not feel safe in the nonspecialized treatment environment they do not explore two significant issues for this population. The first issue involves the relationship between the use of AOD and being LGB. For gay/bisexual men in particular, the association between sexual behavior and AOD use is important to explore. Because of the central role of AOD in many social environments for the LGB population, social isolation is a great concern in initial recovery. As a result, gay and lesbian Alcoholics Anonymous meetings have developed.

The second issue involves internalized heterosexism and the stress of society's attitudes and actions regarding the LGBT community. As Senreich has indicated, an honest discussion of sexual orientation is essential to resolve these problems and would be hindered by a treatment environment perceived as nonsupportive to LGBT clients. This is another argument for specialized programs for LGBT clients.

Criminal Justice Populations

The interest in treatment issues for individuals involved with the criminal justice system is the result of the large numbers of such people with AOD problems. In Chapter 1, we noted that 65% of adult inmates could be diagnosed with a substance use disorder (see Chapter 6). Nearly a half million of adults in jails and prisons had a history of AOD problems, were under the influence of AOD at the time crimes were committed, committed crimes to buy AOD, were incarcerated for an AOD violation, or some combination of these factors. AOD was a factor in over three-quarters of all violent crimes and property crimes. In 2004, nearly one-quarter of federal arrests were for drug offenses. Almost 14% of these arrests were for drug possession and nearly 29% for distribution (Center on Addiction and Substance Abuse, 2010).

Since so many arrests for drug possession and selling are made, many states have implemented "drug courts." Although drug courts vary widely in scope and organization, all have an underlying premise that drug use is not simply a criminal justice problem but a public health problem. Criminal justice agencies collaborate with substance abuse treatment centers and other community resources to design and implement drug court programs. The success of these programs is based on the fact that the post-arrest period can provide a good opportunity for interventions designed to break the drug–crime cycle. Drug courts may utilize a variety of models including supervised or conditional release (offender is released from pretrial custody), diversion from incarceration (offender pleads guilty but goes to treatment instead of to prison), dismissal of charges if the offender successfully completes treatment, and jail-based treatment for those in custody or who fail other forms of treatment.

Treatment options for offenders may take a variety of forms. The least intensive is education, such as in DUI schools. This type of intervention is normally for persons arrested for DUI but who do not have a substance use disorder. However, it should be noted that many areas do not conduct comprehensive evaluations on DUI offenders. DUI school may simply be mandated for first-time offenders. At the other end of the treatment spectrum are therapeutic communities in prison, a type of treatment discussed earlier in the chapter.

Brown (2010) reviewed the literature on the effectiveness of drug courts. There have been very few randomized effectiveness studies and many studies have limitations due to methodological issues. The observational and quasi-experimental studies do indicate that drug court participants have fewer incidents of criminal behavior and lower rates of AOD use, at least in the short term, than offenders in traditional criminal justice adjudication.

While legal involvement is a good motivator and allows for client control (e.g., random urine screening, threat of incarceration), comprehensive services, community links, and aftercare services for these clients are also needed. As you can imagine, the variety of life problems for criminal justice populations is immense. The treatment strategies and techniques we described earlier in the chapter must be customized to each individual in treating this difficult population.

The third case example at the beginning of the chapter (Devon) illustrates the issues in the treatment of criminal justice clients. Devon did not have the benefit of a drug court diversion program or a treatment program in the prison. Therefore, being ordered to get "some kind of drug counseling" was ineffective. Devon relapsed within three months and his parole was revoked. He died of AIDs while incarcerated. Unfortunately, this sad outcome happens too frequently. Besides the human costs, it is very expensive to have someone like Devon in a revolving door of crime, prison, parole, re-arrest, reincarceration. As the Center on Addiction and Substance Abuse (2010) has shown, treatment of criminal justice populations is very cost-effective.

Clients with Co-Occurring Disorders

Similar to the interest in the treatment of criminal justice populations, clients with a substance use disorder and other mental disorders have become a focus of attention due to large numbers of individuals with "co-occurring" disorders (i.e., having a substance use disorder and another mental disorder). According to the Center for Substance Abuse Treatment (2005) researchers have found that from 50% to 75% of clients in treatment for a substance use disorder have a co-occurring mental disorder, and from 20% to 50% of clients in treatment for a mental health disorder have a co-occurring substance use disorder. Treatment outcomes for clients with co-occurring disorders are less favorable than for other clients (e.g., Crome, 1999; Menezes et al., 1996), and Fisher (2011) has speculated that the presence of co-occurring disorders may be among the best predictors of early treatment termination. Although the variability in the combinations of co-occurring disorders ranges widely, common examples include major depression and cocaine addiction, panic disorders and alcoholism, alcoholism and polydrug addiction and schizophrenia, and borderline personality disorder and episodic polydrug abuse (Center for Substance Abuse Treatment, 2005). The percentage of clients and their types of substance use disorder are broken down according to three major types of mental disorders in Figure 8.1. These data are from a national treatment outcome study (described in the section on Treatment Effectiveness) and reported by the Center for Substance Abuse Treatment (2005). These percentages are quite astonishing when you compare the proportion of the general population who has these conditions (antisocial personality disorder: 3% males, 1% females; major depression: 3% males, 9% females; generalized anxiety: 3%) (American Psychiatric Association, 2000).

The treatment of clients with co-occurring disorders has been problematic. According to Drake, O'Neal, and Wallach (2008):

> ". . . clients with co-occurring disorders . . . were highly unlikely to receive treatments for both mental health and substance use problems under the existing circumstances of parallel and independent service systems. . . . Instead, they would tend to be assigned to one system or the other, which would view them through its own particular lens only. Sometimes each system would try to cede these clients to the other. Even when clients did receive both treatments, the service interventions were often incompatible or inconsistent. Such problems continue in the fragmented U.S. healthcare system. A recent national household survey found that only 12% of people with coexisting mental health and substance use problems received interventions for both. . . . (p. 123)

Traditionally, AOD treatment programs would assume that other mental disorders, such as depression, were secondary to the substance abuse problem or that clients with clear psychiatric problems (e.g., schizophrenia) were inappropriate for AOD treatment programs. It is true that

Drug dependency	Antisocial personality	Major depression	Generalized anxiety
Alcohol only	34.7	17.8	5.5
Heroin only	27	7	2
Heroin and alcohol	46.3	13.2	3.2
Cocaine only	30.4	8.4	2.7
Cocaine and alcohol	47	13.6	4.7
Cocaine and heroin	44	10.8	2.2
Cocaine, heroin, and alcohol	59.8	17.1	6.3
Overall	39.3	11.7	3.7

FIGURE 8.1 Rates of antisocial personality, depression, and anxiety disorder by drug dependency (%). Taken from the Drug Abuse Treatment Outcome Study (DATOS).

Source: Flynn et al. 1996; data are from the NIDA-supported DATOS study.

symptoms of a mental disorder may be secondary to an AOD problem. For example, clients who abuse cocaine clearly become significantly depressed in the early stages of recovery. Individuals who abuse methamphetamine may develop symptoms that are indistinguishable from paranoid schizophrenia. Therefore, the true co-occurring disorder client may be difficult to accurately diagnose until a period of detoxification or until a very accurate history is available. Also, how should these clients be treated? Should the client be treated first for the substance abuse problem or the psychiatric problem? If the client is treated in an AOD treatment program, will the staff be trained to work with the psychiatric problem (and vice versa)?

These issues have resulted in the development of programs that can treat AOD problems along with other mental disorders. As we noted in the beginning of the chapter, 37% of treatment facilities treat clients with co-occurring disorders. In such programs, staff members who are trained to work with both AOD problems and mental disorders are clearly needed. Therefore, these programs need to have staff members from a variety of mental health professions (e.g., psychiatrists, psychologists, clinical social workers, licensed professional counselors) as well as certified and licensed addiction counselors. In some states, professionals can get dual certification or licensure in addiction counseling and mental health counseling.

In a review of literature of interventions for clients with severe mental health and substance use disorders, Drake et al. (2008) found that group counseling, contingency management, and residential dual diagnosis treatment showed consistent positive effects on substance use disorders.

CASE EXAMPLE APPLICATIONS

This is an appropriate point in the chapter to take a look at the case examples presented in the beginning. After reading about treatment approaches, treatment strategies and techniques, treatment settings, principles of effective treatment, evidence-based treatment, and treatment for special populations, you can probably see that designing treatment for each of the cases has to be individualized and is complex. Obviously, we can't provide you with all of the information you would need to make decisions about each aspect of treatment for each case. However, each example has some applications from the section on special populations. Celest is a woman with a history of abuse; Javier is an adolescent who is Hispanic and has a learning disability; Devon is African American, in the criminal justice system, and HIV positive; Richard is a senior citizen and gay. These cases are not atypical in the current public sector treatment system. What kind of treatment setting would be most appropriate? Should any or all of these persons have specialized treatment? Of all the treatment strategies mentioned, which ones are the most critical for each case? Which of the treatment approaches and evidence-based practices do you think are most appropriate?

You know that no completely correct answer exists in every case, and we hope you won't be overly frustrated about this. We suggest discussing these questions in your class. The point we want to emphasize is that treatment planning is complicated, and all the questions we have raised have to be addressed based on a comprehensive assessment of the client.

TREATMENT EFFECTIVENESS

Does treatment work? This issue is complex but extremely important, given the time and expense of AOD treatment and the costs to society if people continue abusing AOD following treatment. While numerous studies have examined treatment effectiveness, making sense of the results is difficult because of several underlying problems. Before discussing some of these studies, let's look at some of these problems.

Treatment programs (for the most part) are not designed to scientifically evaluate the aspects of treatment that are most effective. This makes research immediately problematic, since control over the many variables that may affect results is virtually nonexistent. The numerous client variables that may impact treatment effectiveness include age, gender, duration of use, type of substances used, life problems experienced, voluntary or involuntary admission to treatment, prior treatment, client health, psychological problems, criminal activity, level of education, and income. The type of treatment environment (e.g., private, for profit; public, nonprofit; hospital inpatient; free-standing outpatient; therapeutic community) may impact effectiveness. To adequately research the effectiveness of a treatment program or treatment approach, a control group is necessary. Ethical (and practical) issues in the random assignment of clients to treatment must be considered when the researcher hypothesizes that one form of treatment is superior to another.

Equally as important to the issues that create barriers to well-designed research are the types of outcomes in effectiveness studies. Is client success defined by program completion, abstinence, length of sobriety, and/or reduction in life problems? What if a client completes a program, relapses, goes to a different program, and then remains abstinent? Was the first program a failure or did it contribute to the client's sobriety later on?

Fortunately, three major long-term studies have been completed to help answer the question "Does treatment work?" The Center for Substance Abuse Treatment sponsored a congressionally mandated study of treatment outcomes for clients in public sector treatment programs. The National Treatment Improvement Evaluation Study (NTIES) (Gerstein, 1997) followed 4,411 clients in 78 treatment sites across the country for five years. Clients were from vulnerable and underserved populations such as minorities, pregnant women, youth, public housing residents, welfare recipients, and those involved in the criminal justice system. Many of the persons studied did not complete treatment, which would tend to depress any positive results. In spite of these factors, there were significant reductions in AOD use 1 year after treatment regardless of the amount of time spent in treatment or the amount of treatment received. In addition, positive outcomes were found in employment income, mental and physical health, criminal activity, homelessness, and high-risk behaviors for HIV infection. This study also demonstrated that the average savings per client in the year after treatment was $9,177, which is more than three times the average cost of one treatment episode (Center for Substance Abuse Treatment, 1999b). The savings occurred in reduced health care and crime-related costs and increased earnings by clients. Outpatient and long-term residential treatment showed the largest cost savings, but short-term residential treatment and outpatient methadone also were cost-effective.

The National Institute on Drug Abuse followed more than 10,000 clients in nearly 100 treatment programs for two years. The Drug Abuse Treatment Outcome Study (DATOS) (Mueller & Wyman, 1997) involved four types of treatment programs: outpatient methadone, outpatient drug-free, long-term residential, and short-term inpatient. In all treatment modalities, significant reductions occurred in the use of heroin, cocaine, marijuana, and alcohol one year following treatment. Positive outcomes were noted in criminal activity, depression, and employment. The outcomes were most pronounced for clients in long-term treatment but were significant for short-term clients as well.

Five-year follow-up data are available on 708 subjects from 45 programs in eight cities who met DSM criteria for cocaine dependence (Simpson, Joe, & Broome, 2002). Large decreases in cocaine use occurred in the first year after treatment discharge, which were maintained at five years. Similarly, improvements in heavy alcohol use and criminal activity continued. The level of severity of drug use and psychosocial problems at treatment entry were predictive of long-term outcomes. However, outcomes improved in direct relationship to the level of treatment exposure (i.e., those who were in treatment longer did better).

Furthermore, data on 1,167 adolescents from the DATOS sample were also analyzed (Hser et al., 2001). At one year posttreatment, significant reductions in marijuana use, heavy drinking, use of illicit drugs, and criminal involvement were noted. The clients also reported better psychological adjustment and school performance.

The third study was conducted by the National Institute on Alcohol Abuse and Alcoholism and was called "Project MATCH" (Project MATCH Research Group, 1997). This study was designed to determine if different types of alcoholics respond differently to specific treatment approaches. More than 1,700 alcoholics in outpatient treatment or aftercare were studied. The clients were matched with one of three treatment approaches based on client characteristics, including severity of alcohol involvement, cognitive impairment, psychiatric severity, conceptual level, gender, meaning-seeking, motivational readiness to change, social support for drinking versus abstinence, sociopathy, and typology of alcoholism. The three treatment approaches (twelve-step facilitation, cognitive–behavioral, motivational enhancement) were described earlier in this chapter. Overall, the clients in this study demonstrated significant improvement in increased percentage of abstinent days and decreased number of drinks per drinking days. Few differences among the treatment approaches emerged. In spite of many efforts, researchers have been unable to identify the reasons why one approach was superior to another in the rare instances where differences were noted (Longabaugh, 2001). Positive outcomes were also noted in the use of other drugs, depression, and alcohol-related problems.

Finally, outcome studies on the use of pharmacological approaches to treatment have been conducted. For example, naltrexone has been shown to reduce the percentage of days a client spends drinking, the amount of alcohol consumed on a drinking occasion, and the relapse to excessive and destructive drinking (Center for Substance Abuse Treatment, 1998). Methadone has been shown to be an extremely effective treatment for opioid addiction. For example, Ball, Corty, Petroski, and Bond (1987) found that over 92% of methadone maintenance clients were abstinent from other opioids after 4½ years on methadone. Improved social functioning, reduced mortality and morbidity, and decreased criminal activity have also been demonstrated (e.g., Ball & Ross, 1991; Hubbard & French, 1991). Methadone treatment is also extremely cost-effective, with $4 in economic benefits for every $1 spent for treatment (Parrino, 2002).

Although it is not possible to comprehensively review all treatment effectiveness research, several conclusions can be reached. Treatment does appear to have a beneficial, long-term effect on a variety of client behaviors, including AOD use. Treatment length may be related to improved outcomes, but even short-term treatment is helpful. A variety of treatment approaches and treatment settings have proven effective, and even the most vulnerable clients benefit from treatment.

SPECIAL PROBLEMS IN TREATMENT

Recovering Individuals as Counselors

Royce (1989) said, "Since the first Yale Plan Clinic in 1944, recovered alcoholics have been a part of most treatment teams, whether or not they belonged to a profession or had a college degree. . . . The understanding and empathy those workers gained from their own experience as alcoholics has long been recognized as a valuable contribution to the recovery process" (p. 341). We agree.

The question is not whether recovering individuals should be AOD counselors but whether all counselors receive the appropriate type and amount of training. An assumption has been made in the field that the attribute of being in recovery is sufficient for effectiveness as an AOD counselor. However, we would be hard-pressed to find support for the notion that if one has attempted suicide, he or she would be an effective crisis intervention counselor. We have trained many master's level counselors who are in recovery, and we believe that the combination of personal experience and professional training can be dynamic. By the same token, an individual who is well trained and has good interpersonal skills can be an effective AOD counselor regardless of whether that person is in recovery. A person with little or no training and poor interpersonal skills will be ineffective, whether he or she is in recovery or not. What about the individual in recovery who has little training and good interpersonal skills? This person might be a natural counselor and can undoubtedly be helpful. Lack of training is simply a factor limiting the type of client issues this counselor should work with. The outstanding natural counselors we have worked with who are in recovery and have returned for formal training have been able to recognize this limitation and have sought assistance to increase their effectiveness.

Confrontation as a Treatment Strategy

The association of confrontation with substance abuse treatment came about from the use of high levels of confrontation in therapeutic communities such as Synanon. Confrontation is seen as the therapeutic technique to break through the alcoholic/addict's denial. However, a hostile, confrontational counseling style has been found to be associated with poor long-term results (Miller, 2003).

The controversy regarding confrontation probably results from the association of this technique with hostility and aggression. In fact, some AOD counselors may use confrontation in this manner because that is what they have seen and heard. However, confrontation is simply a matter of pointing out to a client that a discrepancy exists between what he or she says and he or she means, or between what is said and what is done (Ivey, Bradford-Ivey, & Simek-Morgan, 1996). In this context, confrontation is a valuable technique in AOD treatment just as it is in other counseling situations. The inappropriate use of confrontation by counselors is a result of poor training and/or poor judgment. For the best results, a counselor will determine the proper type of confrontation for a particular client and will not assume that all alcoholics/addicts must be confronted in a hostile and aggressive manner.

The Use of Medication

In the section of this chapter on treatment approaches, we discussed the use of medications in the management of detoxification, and the treatment of AOD addiction. Minor tranquilizers are used to prevent the medically dangerous withdrawal symptoms suffered in the detoxification from CNS depressants. Drugs such as naltrexone and methadone are used to treat alcoholism and opioid addiction, and various nondependence-producing psychoactive drugs are used to treat disorders such as depression and bipolar disorder. The controversy in this area is probably related to a misinterpretation of AA's position on the use of drugs by alcoholics. Royce (1989) explains this misinterpretation:

> AA rightly takes a strong stand against substituting one addictive drug for another. Overenthusiasm has trapped some AA members into incautious statements about pills that are not substitute addictions and may be medically necessary for a recovering

alcoholic. Thus one sometimes hears horror stories about advice to a heart patient not to take digitalis, a diabetic not to take oral insulin, an epileptic not to take Dilantin, or a psychotic not to take lithium. . . . AA has never approved that kind of advice and in fact strongly disapproves. (p. 352)

It is certainly important for a physician to be made aware of the recovering status of a patient before prescribing pain medication with addictive potential, and alternatives to the use of pain medications are recommended (Royce, 1989). However, recovering persons should not be discouraged from taking medically necessary drugs.

Controlled Use

The question of whether alcoholics can learn to use alcohol in a moderate or nonproblematic manner has been a controversial issue in treatment for some time. In the early 1970s, the Sobells (Sobell & Sobell, 1973) were able to demonstrate that chronic alcoholics could successfully be taught controlled drinking in an experimental setting. Also, reports of the Rand study (Armor, Polich, & Stambul, 1978; Polich, Armor, & Braiker, 1981) indicated that many previously treated alcoholics had been drinking in a nonproblematic manner over a four-year period. The Sobell and Sobell study has been criticized since few of the alcoholic subjects maintained controlled drinking over an extended period of time. As Royce (1989) noted, "The Rand report and other studies have been criticized . . . for using too short a time period, taking inadequate care in followup, subjective reporting, small number, sampling fallacies, lack of control group, and employing absurdly artificial settings" (p. 134). However, Sobell, Cunningham, and Sobell (1996) reported that large numbers of persons with previous mild to moderate alcohol problems were able to drink in moderation without ongoing problems related to alcohol. Similarly, Hester (2003) provided evidence that behavioral self-control training (a behavioral treatment approach) is effective in maintaining moderate drinking with clients with a shorter duration of problem drinking.

While the debate about controlled use makes for some fascinating reading in the field, largely because it evokes emotional as well as scholarly arguments and because it pits disease concept proponents against others, the practical issues seem more clear-cut. It makes very little sense to teach a person to use alcohol in a controlled manner when the person has had numerous, serious life problems and has consistently demonstrated an inability to control alcohol use. If an individual can be diagnosed as having a substance dependence disorder based on the *DSM-IV-TR* (see Chapter 6), controlled use is not a reasonable goal. Even proponents of controlled use recognize that this is not a productive goal for everyone (e.g., Hester, 2003). Therefore, treatment programs, particularly if they use a disease model, would oppose controlled use because their clients would usually be classified as alcoholics/addicts.

Who would be a candidate for learning to use in a controlled manner? These types of clients would more often be seen by generalist mental health professionals or AOD counselors in private practice or working in mental health clinics. Generally, the best candidates would be young, healthy drinkers, with few life problems related to alcohol, whose problems with alcohol are of recent duration and who resist abstaining. These drinkers would usually be considered at-risk drinkers and may benefit from brief interventions (see Chapter 7).

If a client can be diagnosed with an alcohol abuse disorder (see Chapter 6), the decision as to whether or not controlled drinking is a wise option is very difficult. Therefore, we would advise any AOD counselor or mental health professional to be very cautious in working with a client on controlled use. An abstinent client has no risk of problems from use; a client who uses at any level is at risk. However, some clients will resist treatment or drop out of treatment if abstinence is demanded. If such a client fits the criteria previously described, controlled use might be a treatment goal. Also, there are times when working with a resistant client on controlled use demonstrates to the client that he or she is unable to use in a nonproblematic manner. We worked with a young woman in individual counseling who had experienced a few minor problems as a result of her alcohol, marijuana, and cocaine use and would not agree to abstain. We asked her to set goals regarding her intake for two weeks and then to keep track of her actual use. It became very clear to her that her use was out of control since she almost always exceeded her goal. This resulted in her referral to an outpatient program and successful abstinence for at least one year (the last time we saw her).

Again, we suggest that controlled use be a treatment goal only when other alternatives have been explored and when it is probable that the client will experience more serious problems from an insistence on abstinence.

Natural Recovery

The fact that some persons discontinue their problematic use of AOD without treatment has been documented by researchers (e.g., Sobell, Sobell, & Toneatto, 1991; Tuchfield, 1981) and is certainly something we have seen in our own experience. The question that is raised is whether the person who becomes abstinent without treatment is recovering or is a *dry drunk.* A dry drunk is defined as a person who "may exhibit any or all the feelings and behavior associated with intoxication although no alcohol is consumed" (Royce, 1989, p. 299). This is not to imply that euphoria is experienced, as can be seen in Royce's (1989) description of the symptoms of the dry drunk: "Shakes, insomnia, stiffness, headaches, and other flu-like symptoms may accompany the irritability, fatigue, depression, hunger, egocentrism, over-reaction, unexplained sadness, aimless puttering or wandering, and a host of negative emotions" (p. 299).

There has been a sense from the treatment community and twelve-step adherents that persons who try to quit drinking or using on their own end up in the dry drunk syndrome. This sense probably arises from the same dynamics that cause treatment providers to view all alcoholics/addicts as having a disease. In other words, if you are a treatment provider or an AA member, when would you see someone who is trying to abstain on his or her own? You would see this person when he or she was having problems (such as the dry drunk symptoms) and was referred, by self or by others, to a treatment program or to an AA meeting. It would be logical to conclude that discontinuing use without treatment or twelve-step support is difficult, if not impossible. However, those who discontinue problematic use without experiencing the dry drunk syndrome do not show up in treatment or at meetings. Sobell et al. (1991) suggested that natural recovery is much more frequent than has been suspected. In fact, Cunningham, Sobell, Sobell, and Kapur (1995) and Sobell et al. (1996) have identified significant numbers of people with previous alcohol problems who reported recovering without formal treatment or support groups. These researchers believe that an in-depth investigation of these "natural recovering" individuals may help identify important interventions for treatment providers.

Some research of this type has been conducted. Researchers Granfield and Cloud (2001) interviewed 46 formerly substance-dependent men and women who recovered without treatment. They discovered that the subjects in this research had what they termed *recovery capital.* This was defined as *social capital,* or the presence of a social network or social support of family, friends, or colleagues who were available to provide help and motivation. *Physical capital* included tangible resources that provided flexibility and options for courses of recovery that did not involve formal treatment. Finally, recovery capital included *human capital,* such as knowledge, skills, and personal attributes. The researchers noted that most of their subjects had college degrees or vocational skills and that recovery capital may not be equitably available to everyone.

MyCounselingLab™

Go to Topic 5: *Treatment Setting and Treatment Planning,* in the MyCounselingLab™ site (www.MyCounselingLab.com) for *Substance Abuse: Information for School Counselors, Social Workers, Therapists, and Counselors,* Fifth Edition, where you can:

- Find learning outcomes for *Treatment Setting and Treatment Planning* along with the national standards that connect to these outcomes.
- Complete Assignments and Activities that can help you more deeply understand the chapter content.
- Apply and practice your understanding of the core skills identified in the chapter with the Building Counseling Skills unit.
- Prepare yourself for professional certification with a Practice for Certification quiz.
- Connect to videos through the Video and Resource Library.

Summary

- Recovery-oriented systems of care encompass continuity of care; the inclusion of the family, community, and peers in the process; individualized and comprehensive services across the lifespan; culturally responsive services; community-anchored services; inclusion of voices and experiences of recovering individuals and their families; and outcomes-driven, research-based services.
- Only about 12% of those with substance use disorders receive formal treatment.
- Approaches to treatment include the Minnesota Model, behavioral models (aversive conditioning, contingency management), matrix model, and pharmacological procedures.
- Treatment strategies and techniques include individual, group, and family counseling; support groups; lifestyle changes; education; and aftercare.

- Treatment occurs in therapeutic communities, inpatient and residential settings, partial hospitalization and day treatment settings, and intensive outpatient and outpatient settings.
- The National Institute on Drug Abuse has established 13 principles of effective treatment.
- Evidence-based practices can be found in the National Registry of Evidence-based Programs and Practices.
- Treatment must be designed individually and must consider diversity issues including gender, ethnicity, age, sexual orientation, criminal justice involvement, and co-occurring mental disorders.
- A variety of studies on treatment effectiveness have found all forms of treatment to be effective in reducing alcohol and other drug use, criminal justice involvement, and healthcare utilization and in improving employment.

Internet Resources

Treatment facility locator
dasis3.samhsa.gov/

Treatment statistics
drugabuse.gov/infofacts/treatmenttrends.html

Evidence-based treatment
nrepp.samhsa.gov/

Principles of Effective Treatment
drugabuse.gov/PODAT/PODATIndex.html

Further Discussion

1. For each of the case examples in the beginning of the chapter, discuss the most appropriate treatment setting, treatment approach, and treatment strategies.
2. How could treatment for AOD problems be improved? Design your ideal treatment program.

3. Why do you think the Principles of Effective Treatment are not utilized in every treatment program and setting across the country?

Chapter 9

Relapse Prevention and Recovery

MyCounselingLab™

Visit the **MyCounselingLab**™ site (www.MyCounselingLab.com) for *Substance Abuse: Information for School Counselors, Social Workers, Therapists, and Counselors,* Fifth Edition to enhance your understanding of chapter concepts. You'll have the opportunity to practice your skills through video- and case-based Assignments and Activities as well as Building Counseling Skills units and to prepare for your certification exam with Practice for Certification quizzes.

CASE EXAMPLES

❶ Anna, a 16-year-old, was in an intensive outpatient treatment program for polydrug use problems, with her drugs of choice including tobacco, alcohol, marijuana, LSD, and methamphetamine. She was court-ordered to treatment and a psychological assessment following a variety of status offenses and crimes. On the basis of the assessment, Anna was diagnosed with Alcohol Abuse, Amphetamine Abuse (see Chapter 6), and posttraumatic stress disorder (PTSD). The diagnosis of PTSD was related to a history of sexual molestation by Anna's stepfather that began when she was 8 and ended when she was 13, when her biological mother discovered the molestation and divorced the perpetrator. The crime had been reported, but Anna had never been in therapy. Shortly after the molestation began, Anna began to demonstrate a series of problems in school, including deteriorating academic performance, fighting, and noncompliance with teachers. These problems continued until she entered treatment. Anna's biological father left the family when Anna was 2, and was an active alcoholic who had been in two treatment programs. He maintained sporadic contact with his daughter. Anna was slightly obese and had an acne problem. On an IQ test, she scored 88 (low average), and her academic skills were at the sixth to seventh grade level (she was a sophomore). Anna's mother was 33-years-old, did not complete high school, and worked in a service position at a hotel/casino. She used alcohol and marijuana on an infrequent basis. She and Anna had a volatile relationship with a great deal of conflict. The mother noted a strong similarity between Anna and her biological father. She also expressed guilt over not discovering the sexual molestation sooner. Anna completed her treatment program in three months. She was initially resistant and defiant. However, she bonded with a female counselor in the program and, for the first time, found support and consistency from both adults and peers. She maintained abstinence for the last two months of her program. Her mother participated in the program and began to learn about the disease of chemical dependency (which was the orientation of the program) and about her own enabling. Anna and her mother had four family counseling sessions and made a little progress. There was still a lot to do, so they were referred to a marriage and family therapist. The school counselor was invited to the discharge conference and encouraged to assist Anna in readjusting to school. She had earned just two credits in high school (that means she had passed only two classes). Anna began attending AA meetings and was encouraged to go to four to five meetings a week. She was scheduled to attend a weekly two-hour aftercare meeting at the treatment program.

NEED FOR GENERALIST TRAINING IN RELAPSE PREVENTION

Imagine that you are the marriage and family therapist whom Anna and her mother contact, or the school counselor at Anna's high school. We hope that you can identify some of the issues that might lead Anna to return to AOD use and would require attention in family therapy or at school. The first issue is the history of sexual molestation, which we have discussed as a frequent issue for women in substance abuse treatment programs. Some of the other issues include academic problems at school, conflict with Mom, contact with an actively drinking father, and physical appearance. (We are not making a judgment here. Just remember what it was like when you were in high school for a kid who was overweight and had acne.) Other problems, although not explicitly stated, might be logically assumed to exist. For example, we would expect that Anna's social group involved kids who use AOD. If she returns to the same school, how will she handle her peer group? She may have some deep-seated emotional issues involving abandonment by her father and anger at her mother for not protecting her from her stepfather. Finally, given her intellectual ability and academic achievement, school may be challenging.

In Chapter 1, we gave examples of how social workers, school counselors, and marriage and family therapists work with clients with AOD problems whether or not these helping professionals work in treatment programs. The area of relapse prevention is a clear illustration of this. In Anna's case, the marriage and family therapist and school counselor would probably have more intensive and a longer duration of contact with Anna than the staff at the treatment program. Therefore, the therapist and counselor are critically important to Anna's success in recovery. She could also have a probation officer and contact with social service professionals (e.g., through vocational training programs). Their work could also impact Anna's abstinence.

Although a formal discharge staffing that included all relevant parties and a formal relapse prevention plan would be nice, our experience is that these are not the norm. The mental health professional usually has sketchy information from the client and/or treatment program and is left to develop his or her own relapse prevention plan. That is why we will spend considerable time in this chapter acquainting you with the specifics of relapse prevention.

DEFINITION OF SLIP AND RELAPSE

As we shall see, a need exists to differentiate a *slip* from a *relapse*. A slip is an episode of AOD use following a period of abstinence, while relapse is the return to uncontrolled AOD use following a period of abstinence. Usually, a slip or slips precede relapse, and there is some evidence (e.g., Laudet & White, 2004) that slipping is the rule rather than the exception for those clients who receive AOD treatment.

The disease model of addiction and AA slogans (an alcoholic is always "one drink from a drunk") can promote the idea that a slip inevitably leads to relapse. The depiction of addiction as a progressive, chronic disease that can be managed only through abstinence may create a sense that a slip means complete deterioration to pretreatment levels of functioning. The result of clients' adopting this point of view is that, when a slip occurs (as it is likely to), the client may experience guilt, anxiety, or hopelessness. These negative emotions may lead to further, heavier use. The cognitive process of the client may go something like this: "Well, I used again. Since that means I'm back to square one, I might as well do it up right."

Regardless of the model of addiction or orientation to treatment, AOD treatment providers will tell you that a return to some level of use is a frequent occurrence. (Shortly, we will examine data on how frequent.) Although we believe that abstinence is the safest and healthiest "level" of use, we also believe that it is foolish to ignore the reality of slips, and it is poor practice to leave clients unprepared to prevent a slip from escalating to a relapse. As we discussed in Chapter 3, there is no evidence that addiction proceeds in an inevitable progression. Therefore, there is no reason to treat a slip as a catastrophe, and every reason to view a slip as a signal to the client, treatment providers, and other mental health professionals to reexamine the aftercare plan (see Chapter 8) in order to prevent slips from occurring in the future and to prevent the current slip from escalating.

FREQUENCY OF SLIPS AND RELAPSES

Regardless of the researcher, drug or drugs of choice, and population studied, a consistent finding from studies is that many people who receive treatment for AOD problems use again after leaving treatment. McLellan, Lewis, O'Brien, and Kleber (2000), in reviewing literature on relapse, noted that 40% to 60% of patients in treatment relapsed within one year and another 15% to 30% had resumed using AOD but not at dependent levels. Laudet and White (2004) reported that 71% of addicts returned to using AOD and 50% of this group had four or more abstinent periods of at least one month before returning to AOD use. Dennis, Foss, and Scott (2007) found the risk of relapse particularly high in the first three years following treatment.

We are not presenting these data to generate an argument (which is important from a research point of view) regarding the many factors that influence these research results. Certainly, the length of time following treatment, the type of treatment setting and methods, the method of defining *relapse,* the drug or drugs of choice, the client and the environmental characteristics, and other variables influence the data. Our point is that many, if not most, clients return to use at some point following treatment. Therefore, the issue of return to use must be a focus of treatment and aftercare.

IS RELAPSE IN ADDICTION SIMILAR TO OTHER CHRONIC CONDITIONS?

McLellan et al. (2000) have written a historic paper, "Drug Dependence, a Chronic Medical Illness." Their extensive review of the literature, as noted earlier, revealed that about 40% of patients treated for alcohol, opioid, or cocaine dependence were continually abstinent for one year. An additional 15% returned to a nondependent level of use. In comparison, at least 30% of adult-onset, insulin-dependent diabetic patients and 40% of adult, medication-dependent hypertensive and asthmatic patients annually require restabilization of medication and/or hospitalization because of reoccurrence of symptoms. Furthermore, these researchers found the rates of compliance with prescribed medications (40% to 60%) and with behavioral change regimens (30% to 50%) to be similar between addiction disorders and other chronic illnesses such as diabetes, hypertension, and asthma. Therefore, while the relapse rate of substance disorders is certainly a focus of attention and intervention, it really is no different than the relapse and noncompliance rates for other chronic conditions.

MODELS OF RELAPSE PREVENTION

The Cenaps Model

The Cenaps Model was developed by Terence Gorski (president of the Cenaps Corporation) and articulated in a variety of articles and books (e.g., Gorski, 1988, 1989, 1990, 1992, 1993; Gorski & Miller, 1986). The disease concept is the underlying philosophy of the model, although the methods used are eclectic. In Gorski's words, the Cenaps Model "integrates the fundamental principles of AA and the Minnesota Model Treatment [see Chapter 8] to meet the needs of relapse-prone patients" (Gorski, 1990, p. 126). The model is proposed as a formal program within AOD treatment programs.

With the disease concept as a guiding philosophy, chemical dependency is viewed as a biopsychosocial disease. This means that the disease affects biological, or physical, psychological, and social functioning. Although there is a complex interaction among these areas, Gorski (1990) states that "The physical consequence of chemical dependence is brain dysfunction . . . [that] disorganizes the preaddictive personality and causes social and occupational problems" (p. 126). Since the disease is chronic and affects the brain (causing psychological and social problems), total abstinence is necessary. However, this is not the exclusive goal of the model. Personality, lifestyle, and family functioning are also areas that require change for biopsychosocial health. For example,

> Being raised in a dysfunctional family can result in self-defeating personality traits or disorders. These traits and disorders do not cause chemical dependence; however, they can cause a more rapid progression of the chemical dependence, making it difficult to recognize and to seek treatment. . . . Self-defeating personality traits and disorders also increase the risk of relapse. As a result, family-of-origin problems need to be appropriately addressed in treatment. (Gorski, 1990, pp. 126–127)

Gorski (1990) differentiates clients who have completed the "primary goals" of treatment from those who have not completed these goals. These primary goals are:

> (1) the recognition that chemical dependency is a biopsychosocial disease, (2) the recognition of the need for lifelong abstinence from all mind-altering drugs, (3) the development and use of an ongoing recovery program to maintain abstinence, and (4) the diagnosis and treatment of other problems or conditions that can interfere with recovery. (p. 127)

If a client has not completed the primary goals, then, in Gorski's view, a relapse prevention program is inappropriate. The relapse prevention program outlined in the Cenaps Model is for clients "who believe that they have the disease, require abstinence, and need to use recovery tools, but are unable to maintain abstinence" (Gorski, 1990, p. 127). As can be seen from the primary goals of treatment, this would limit the number of clients who would be seen as appropriate for a relapse prevention program.

According to Gorski (1990), recovery and relapse are related processes. Recovery follows a sequence of six steps:

(1) abstaining from alcohol and other drugs; (2) separating from people, places, and things that promote chemical use and establishing a social network that supports recovery; (3) stopping compulsive self-defeating behaviors that suppress awareness of painful feelings and irrational thoughts; (4) learning how to manage feelings and emotions responsibly without resorting to compulsive behaviors or the use of chemicals; (5) learning to change addictive-thinking patterns that create painful feelings and self-defeating behaviors; and (6) identifying and changing the mistaken core beliefs about self, others, and the world that promote the use of irrational thinking. (p. 128)

The relapse process begins at step 6 and proceeds upward. For example, let's take a look at Anna's situation and see how a relapse might occur based on Gorski's model. Remember that she was sexually molested by her stepfather. Anna starts thinking about the molestation and how unfair it is that this happened to her. She believes that she must have encouraged this behavior to get attention and affection from her stepfather and blames herself for the molestation (mistaken core belief about herself, step 6). She ponders this and feels guilty, embarrassed, and victimized (painful feelings, step 5). Anna becomes sexually involved with a 22-year-old who is initially kind and attentive. When she is with this man, she feels worthwhile and does not experience the feelings of guilt, embarrassment, and victimization (managing feelings in an irresponsible manner, step 4). However, the man becomes verbally abusive and openly sees other women. Anna's painful feelings return, but she tries desperately to hang on to the relationship (self-defeating behavior, step 3). The man uses AOD, as do his friends (people, places, and things that promote chemical use, step 2). In an effort to impress the man and cope with her feelings, she returns to use (step 1).

The Cenaps Model uses a variety of procedures in relapse prevention, including client self-assessment of problems that might result in relapse, education about relapse, identification of the signs of the relapse progression, strategies to manage or modify the signs, and the involvement of others, such as family members. Techniques from cognitive, affective, and behavioral therapies are used (Gorski, 1993). Therefore, while the Cenaps Model is based on the disease concept of addiction, eclectic treatment strategies are utilized. Furthermore, techniques have been developed for involving the family and the employee-assistance counselor, and procedures have been adapted for adolescents (Bell, 1990).

A Cognitive–Social Learning Model

In contrast to the Cenaps Model, cognitive–social learning approaches to relapse prevention do not have a prerequisite requirement that the client achieve "primary goals" of treatment. Therefore, the strategies of relapse prevention in this model could be used with any client who wants to maintain a behavior change. This change may involve abstinence from AODs or a moderation in use.

The cognitive–social learning model of relapse prevention has been presented by Alan Marlatt (e.g., Marlatt & Gordon, 1985) and Helen Annis (e.g., Annis, 1986, 1990). Marlatt

(1985) views addictive behaviors as "overlearned *habits* that can be analyzed and modified in the same manner as other habits" (p. 9, italics in original). This model of addiction was discussed in Chapter 3. With regard to relapse prevention, Marlatt (1985) states that those who believe in this model

> are particularly interested in studying the *determinants* of addictive habits, including situational and environmental antecedents, beliefs and expectations, and the individual's family history and prior learning experiences with the substance or activity. In addition, there is an equal interest in discovering the *consequences* of these behaviors, so as to better understand both the reinforcing effects that may contribute to increased use and the negative consequences that may serve to inhibit the behavior. . . . [A]ttention is paid to the social and interpersonal reactions experienced by the individual before, during, and after engaging in an addictive behavior. Social factors are involved both in the initial learning of an addictive habit and in the subsequent performance of the activity once the habit has become firmly established. (pp. 9–10, italics in original)

Although the language is different from that used by Gorski, the steps of recovery and relapse delineated by Gorski are similar to Marlatt's determinants and consequences of addictive behaviors. Both emphasize the need to attend to behavior, thoughts, and feelings (Marlatt uses the terms "social and interpersonal reactions" for feelings, and "beliefs and expectations" for thoughts). As we will see later in the chapter, the similarities are probably the reason for the overlap in relapse prevention techniques between the two models.

Annis (1990) criticizes traditional solutions to relapse that emphasize:

> "[b]ooster" sessions of the same treatment . . . added over time to reinforce the initial effects of treatment . . . intensify and broaden the number of treatment components offered . . . [or] adoption of a model of lifelong treatment, such as that embodied in Alcoholics Anonymous (AA) and other self-help groups. (p. 117)

Rather than focus on a model of addiction, Annis argues that the principles that guide the maintenance of a behavior change may be different from the principles that determine the initiation of a change. In other words, a person may enter treatment under coercion, be exposed to and accept the disease concept of addiction, and discontinue his or her use of AOD as a result. However, this same individual may be unable to maintain abstinence. This is the population who Gorski believed was appropriate for the Cenaps Model. However, Annis (and Marlatt) conceptualize this inability to maintain the "habit" change through self-efficacy theory:

> when a client enters a high risk situation for drinking, a process of cognitive appraisal of past experiences is set in motion which culminates in a judgment, or efficacy expectation, on the part of the client of his or her ability to cope with the situation. The judgment of personal efficacy determines whether or not drinking takes place. . . . (Annis & Davis, 1989, p. 170)

For example, let's say Anna returns to school after treatment. One day after school, she sees a group of students with whom she previously used. They invite her to "party." She says no and the kids make fun of her. In this model, Anna makes a judgment about her ability to cope with the peer pressure. If she decides that she can handle the situation and does so (i.e., asserts herself appropriately and has a social support system), her self-efficacy is enhanced. If she does not believe she can handle the situation or does not have the skills, her self-efficacy is threatened. Annis (1990) reported a high correlation between a client's situation-specific self-efficacy ratings and relapse episodes. Using self-efficacy theory, Marlatt developed a model of relapse that involves the coping strategies that an individual utilizes in high-risk situations. A high-risk situation is defined as "any situation that poses a threat to the individual's sense of control and increases the risk of potential relapse" (Marlatt, 1985, p. 37). These high-risk situations may be either unexpected or covertly planned.

Unexpected high-risk situations are similar to the situation in which Anna runs into her former using friends. She did not plan to encounter this situation; it just happened. In Marlatt's conceptualization, if Anna does not possess an appropriate coping response to the high-risk situation, she will experience decreased self-efficacy that may result in a slip. The slip may have associated thoughts and feelings such as conflict, guilt, and blame, which Marlatt termed the "abstinence violation effect (AVE)." The probability of a slip progressing to a relapse is related to the intensity of the AVE, which, in turn, is related to factors such as the length of sobriety, the commitment to abstinence, and the knowledge of the slip by significant others.

Anna does not have an effective coping mechanism to apply. To stop the teasing, she goes with the group and smokes a little pot. Unfortunately, at aftercare the next night, she has a random urinalysis. Anna's counselor calls her to discuss her positive drug test. Anna has an intense AVE. She is disappointed in herself for not resisting her friends and embarrassed that her counselor found out. Due to these painful feelings, Anna begins a relapse.

If Anna did have an effective coping response to the high-risk situation, Marlatt's model predicts that she will experience increased self-efficacy and a resulting decreased probability of slipping. Let's say that Anna asserts herself appropriately with her friends and goes to aftercare that night and reports the incident to her group. She is praised and supported by her peers and her counselor. Anna feels proud of herself and her renewed confidence in her ability to remain abstinent.

High-risk situations can also be encountered due to the covert planning of the individual. This occurs when the person has a "lifestyle imbalance." Marlatt defines this as having "shoulds" that are greater than "wants." Let's use Anna again to illustrate. She is trying to make up lost credits at school, attending four to five AA meetings a week, going to aftercare, trying to get along with her mother, going to counseling, and meeting with her probation officer. She is a busy young woman. Anna is 16 years old and has the same goals as most 16-year-olds—have friends and have fun. But her "shoulds" eat up all her time. Anna starts to feel resentful and victimized. When she has felt this way before, she has used alcohol and other drugs because using helps her forget (at least temporarily) her painful feelings. Also, she starts thinking that she deserves a little fun and relaxation. Although she thinks about using, Anna also has pangs of guilt when she imagines herself doing so. So, instead of simply getting alcohol or another drug and using it, she covertly makes decisions that will place her in a high-risk situation. For example, Anna decides to go to Dorothy's house on Friday to get back some video games that she loaned Dorothy before going to treatment. Dorothy is a former using friend, and Anna knows that there are usually kids there on Friday after school getting high. Anna gets there, sees everyone loaded, and joins in. Marlatt calls Anna's decision to go to Dorothy's house an "apparently irrelevant decision (AID)." An AID is covertly planned to result in a high-risk situation. In isolation, it seems unrelated to alcohol or other drug use.

Annis and Marlatt describe a variety of interventions to prevent slips and also to prevent slips from escalating into relapse. Some of the interventions are designed to teach coping strategies in high-risk situations, and others are directed toward global lifestyle changes. Consistent with the model, the strategies are cognitive and behavioral. Many of these will be described in the following section. For those who are interested in school counseling, Fisher and Harrison (1993a) have applied Marlatt's model and strategies to adolescents in the school setting.

AT A GLANCE

Cenaps Model of Relapse Prevention (Gorski)

- Chemical dependency is a biopsychosocial disease.
- Model is appropriate for clients who complete "primary goals" of treatment.
- Recovery and relapse follow a sequence of six steps.

Cognitive–Social Model of Relapse Prevention (Marlatt, Anis)

- Maintaining a behavior and initiating a behavior change may be guided by different principles.
- Belief in self-efficacy determines probability of relapse.
- Ability to cope with high-risk situations is critical.
- Apparently irrelevant decisions (AIDs) result from lifestyle imbalances and lead to relapse.
- Abstinence violation effect (AVE) results in escalation of slips to relapse.

ESSENTIAL COMPONENTS OF RELAPSE PREVENTION

As we have seen from the discussion of models of relapse prevention, differences exist between the two models with regard to the definition of client readiness for relapse prevention programming. In the Cenaps Model, a client must have completed the primary goals of treatment (which involve acceptance of the disease model of addiction) to be appropriate for relapse prevention. Annis and Marlatt do not discuss prerequisite conditions for relapse prevention. However, regardless of whether the Cenaps or a cognitive–social learning model of relapse prevention is the choice, the strategies employed to prevent relapse are quite similar. Therefore, we want to describe the strategies of relapse prevention that seem to be necessary in either model. Certainly, some strategies are associated to a larger extent with a particular model, which will be highlighted. However, our goal is to emphasize the techniques that a mental health professional may have to utilize in helping clients with AOD problems to remain abstinent or avoid relapse. Keep in mind that these strategies often must be developed by generalists in schools, agencies, and private practice settings, since mental health professionals in these settings usually have the most contact with clients after formal AOD treatment has ended.

Assessment of High-Risk Situations

The first step in a relapse prevention program must be to determine the specific situations for each client that may lead to a slip. Calling these situations *high risk* denotes a high probability of use based on past experience. The type of situations that are risky varies from client to client, although Cummings, Gordon, and Marlatt (1980) found that 75% of the relapses by alcoholics, smokers, and heroin users were due to negative emotions, interpersonal conflict, and social pressure.

In Gorski's (1990) model, the first step in determining high-risk situations is a client self-assessment that "involves a detailed reconstruction of the presenting problems, the alcohol and other drug use history as well as the recovery and relapse history to identify the past causes of relapse" (p. 129). Next, an examination of the client's life history helps identify any lifestyle issues that are associated with relapse. Finally, the client's recovery and relapse history is analyzed, with the goal being to "examine each period of abstinence to identify the recovery tasks that were completed or ignored, and to find the sequence of warning signs that led back to chemical use" (p. 130).

The cognitive–social learning model incorporates a "highly individualized analysis of a client's drinking behavior over the previous year to determine the high-risk situations for heavy drinking experienced by that particular client" (Annis, 1990, p. 118). For this purpose, Annis (1982) developed a 100-item self-report questionnaire called the Inventory of Drinking Situations. Obviously, the same type of assessment would occur for clients who use drugs other than alcohol. Anna, our 16-year-old with polydrug problems, has a number of high-risk situations. Negative emotions, such as guilt, shame, and embarrassment related to her history of sexual molestation, have resulted in AOD use in the past. She also feels unattractive and unintelligent. Interpersonal conflicts with her mother and with teachers have also been identified as high-risk situations. Finally, in the past, Anna used when she experienced social pressure from her peers. Anna's current lifestyle involves a lot of time alone, because she has not established a nonusing social group. She watches a lot of TV and plays video games, and she has been using food as a substitute for AOD.

Coping with High-Risk Situations

Once the high-risk situations have been identified, it is necessary for the client to have strategies to deal with these situations effectively. Education and information sharing may be useful to clients. "Relapsers need accurate information about what causes relapse and what can be done to prevent it. This is typically provided in structured relapse education sessions and reading assignments that provide specific information about the recovery and relapse process as well as relapse prevention planning methods" (Gorski, 1990, p. 130).

Daley and Marlatt (2005) recommend that clients be taught that relapse is a process and an event by reviewing the common relapse warning signs identified by recovering clients. Following a relapse, clients should review their experiences in detail in order to learn the connections among thoughts, feelings, events, or situations, and subsequent relapse.

As we saw in the Chapter 8 discussion on methods of treatment, education is rarely sufficient for long-lasting change. Individualized strategies for high-risk situations are usually needed. Gorski (1990) recommends managing high-risk situations on situational–behavioral, cognitive–affective, and core issue levels. On the situational–behavioral level, the client often must avoid the people, places, and things that are high risk and learn to modify his or her behavioral response if a high-risk situation were to occur. For example, Anna identified peer pressure as a high-risk situation. She should avoid her friends with whom she previously used. She might attend a different school following treatment, but, because this is not always possible, she may not be able to avoid these peers. Anna may need assertiveness skills training to learn how to respond to the peer pressure she encounters.

Since Annis (1990) focuses on self-efficacy as the critical component of relapse prevention, a situational–behavioral intervention from this orientation "focuses on having the client engage in homework assignments involving the performance of alternative coping responses in high-risk situations" (p. 119). A hierarchy of progressively riskier situations is developed, and coping behaviors in these situations are planned, imagined, and used when needed. The underlying rationale is that the most powerful way to change thinking about self-efficacy is behavioral performance. For Anna, this hierarchy might begin with a chance meeting with one of her using friends in the hall at school, then progress to having a group of these friends sit down with her at lunch, and finally to encountering the group on Friday afternoon on their way to "party."

On the cognitive–affective level, the irrational thoughts and intense feelings that emerge in high-risk situations may need to be challenged. For those clients in twelve-step recovery programs, the acronym HALT is used to advise recovering people to avoid getting too hungry, angry, lonely, or tired. The term "stinking thinking" is used to challenge irrational thoughts, and members are told to get off the "pity pot" when they are immobilized by their feelings. Daley and Marlatt (2005) recommend a worksheet that lists the relapse-related thought, a statement or statements that dispute the thought, and a new, rational thought. As an example, Anna forgets to do her homework in math one day. Her teacher points this out in front of the class and tells her that she will fail unless she "gets with the program." Anna becomes angry and tells the teacher to "shut up." She is told to leave class. On the way to the office, Anna is consumed with her anger and has an inner dialog with statements such as "Mr. C. (the teacher) hates me. He's always picking on me." "I should just get loaded. No one cares anyway." Fortunately, Anna goes to see her school counselor, who listens to her, lets her emotions reduce in intensity, and then confronts her about her responsibility in completing her homework and also the fact that she is allowing Mr. C. to control her recovery program. While not condoning the public reproof by a teacher, the counselor points out the irrationality of Anna's thinking: "I should have done my homework. It embarrassed me to have it pointed out in front of the class. I conclude that the teacher hates me, nobody cares about me, and therefore, I have an excuse to use." A more rational sequence of thoughts would be: "I need to remember to do my homework and ask for help if I'm stuck. I don't like to be embarrassed and would prefer that Mr. C. handle the situation differently. None of this has anything to do with people caring about me or using."

The school counselor might also conceptualize that Anna's decision not to complete her homework was part of a covert relapse plan and constitutes the "apparently irrelevant decision" we discussed in the cognitive–social learning model. In other words, Anna covertly planned a relapse by deciding not to complete her homework in a class in which the teacher often reacts with a public reprimand. Since interpersonal conflict with teachers is a high-risk situation that Anna has identified, she has an excuse to create a conflict, thus giving her an excuse to use. In this case, it would be useful to determine how much of Anna's thoughts and feelings involve her "shoulds" being greater than her "wants" and, if this is the case, to help her to modify this disparity. In addition, the AID needs to be confronted.

On the core issue level, the psychological issues that lead to high-risk situations need to be identified. Anna has identified guilt, shame, and embarrassment as negative emotions that are high risk for her. As these feelings originate from her history of sexual molestation, her need for therapeutic attention to this issue is obvious. Low self-esteem, depressive and anxiety disorders, and codependency are examples of other psychological issues that can result in high-risk situations.

An additional issue in coping with high-risk situations involves urges and cravings. Marlatt (1985) defines a craving as the degree of desire for the positive effects a person expects as a result of use and an urge as the intention to engage in use to satisfy the craving. As Anna leaves her math class and is experiencing intense anger, she has an urge to smoke pot to satisfy a craving for the calming effect and the dissipation of her anger. In a high-risk situation, clients often report that the cravings and urges are so powerful that they lose focus on other aspects of relapse prevention. Therefore, strategies specific to coping with urges and cravings are necessary.

Daley and Marlatt (2005) suggest a variety of strategies to cope with urges and cravings. For example, intentional cognitive strategies such as changing thoughts or self-talking through the cravings can be used. Let's say you are mulling over a conflict you had at work and are having trouble falling asleep. You say to yourself, "I'm going to stop thinking about that and think about something more pleasant." Self-talking through the craving might involve an internal dialogue such as, "OK, I know what is happening. I'm upset and I'm thinking that a drink will make me feel better. It's happened before and it will probably happen again. I can get through it." It is often helpful for the client to combine this self-talk with an inner dialogue about the negative consequences of use and the positive benefits of not using (e.g., "If I drink, I'll blow nine months of sobriety and feel terrible about myself. If I don't, I'll feel really strong and proud of myself."). For some clients, calling their AA or NA sponsor or attending a meeting is helpful, while others find that getting involved in a strenuous or pleasant activity takes their thinking away from the urges and cravings.

AT A GLANCE

COPING WITH HIGH-RISK SITUATIONS

- Situational–behavioral: Managing people, places, and things that are high risk (e.g. hierarchy of high-risk situations and strategies to avoid or cope)
- Cognitive–affective: Coping with irrational thoughts and intense feelings (e.g., confront irrational thoughts or AIDs)
- Core issues: Psychological issues that lead to relapse (e.g., counseling)
- Urges and cravings (e.g., self-talk)

Support Systems

As Gorski (1990) has stated, "Relapse-prone patients cannot recover alone. It is the therapist's responsibility to involve significant others in the structured process of relapse prevention planning. Family members, Twelve-Step sponsors, and employee-assistance program counselors are significant resources who need to be involved" (p. 132). We would expand on Gorski's statement in several ways. First, the "therapist" may be you—school counselor, marriage and family therapist, social worker, mental health counselor, or rehabilitation counselor. Many treatment programs do not have a formal, structured relapse-prevention program that coordinates the necessary services and people for successful relapse prevention (one reason we want you to be familiar with relapse-prevention strategies). Second, Gorski says "therapist" as if the assumption is that all clients will have such a person. If you have been attending to the discussion in this chapter, you can see that it is essential that recovering individuals be involved with a mental health professional, preferably one with AOD training and experience. The behavioral, cognitive, and affective strategies we have mentioned require the expertise of trained "helpers."

Although twelve-step meetings are a wonderful form of support in recovery, they are not designed to individually address the needs of recovering individuals. The "core psychological issues" that may lead to relapse require the involvement of mental health professionals. Finally, for adolescents, support involves more than just family members and twelve-step meetings and sponsors. Imagine that Anna returns to school after treatment. As a 16-year-old, her primary goals in life are to have friends and have fun. She also sincerely wants to remain abstinent. If she does not have a school-based support group of nonusing peers and no organized activities are available that are AOD-free, it is highly probable that she will relapse, in spite of her good intentions. We believe school personnel have an obligation and a challenge to help recovering adolescents such as Anna develop school-based support.

The involvement of the family in relapse prevention is certainly critical. Laudet, Savage, and Mahmood (2002) found that family was tied with spirituality/faith as the number one source of support for long-term recovery. Furthermore, as Daley and Marlatt (2005) have noted, the families of addicts are more likely to support rather than sabotage recovery if they are involved in the recovery process and have an opportunity to heal from any emotional pain the family members experienced. This is not as simple a process as it may seem. As we will see in Chapter 11, although family therapy may be necessary in many cases, constellations and dynamics of families are very complex. For example, Anna and her mother are in family therapy. But, what about her actively alcoholic biological father? He's not involved and may have some investment in Anna's returning to use in order to justify his own use pattern. In a family in which the child with an alcohol or other drug problem plays the "scapegoat" role, the family "hero" may subtly sabotage recovery to maintain the family roles (see Chapter 11).

Lifestyle Changes

At the risk of beleaguering poor Anna, let's look at other aspects of her life that require some attention. We have already mentioned the history of sexual molestation that needs therapeutic attention. In addition to the negative emotions that have been generated, implications arise with regard to her sexual behavior, choice of partners in relationships, and more. She is obese and has problems with acne, indicating a need for nutritional and hygiene advice. Her IQ is low average and her academic skills are below grade level, so she needs remediation and vocational guidance. She also needs to work on her social skills, her conflict with her mother, her relationship with her father, developing support systems at school, and more.

Does this seem like a lot of "stuff" to work on? It certainly is, and each area can lead to relapse. Now imagine a 47-year-old man who has been abusing alcohol for 25 years. Due to his use, he has physical, legal, financial, family, and vocational problems, all of which cause stress and conflict—high-risk situations for relapse.

As you can see, successful relapse prevention does not simply involve a client's ability to cope with high-risk situations. Many high-risk situations result from the lifestyle of the client and the client's inability to modify this lifestyle. Many such modifications are difficult and require significant investments of time and resources. Let's examine some of these lifestyle areas and the modifications necessary for relapse prevention.

LEISURE TIME What do you do in your spare time? (We know. You are a student and you don't have spare time. Just pretend.) Do you read, exercise, have a hobby? Many people with AOD problems have had only one leisure time activity—using. When you remove AOD, these people don't know what to do with themselves. They become bored, but are avoiding their only known method to relieve boredom. We have had clients become intense workaholics after treatment to alleviate the fear of having any free time. We also find clients attending one AA meeting after another because they don't know what else to do. We worked with a middle-aged man who had completed an alcohol treatment program at the Salvation Army. Each day, he would work at the Salvation Army, attend an AA meeting, and then wander around the casinos in town. Not surprisingly, it wasn't long before he started to use again.

SUPPORT SYSTEMS   We have already mentioned the importance of support systems. This is certainly related to leisure time. If a recovering person has a circle of friends, he or she has something to do with his or her free time and will become involved with the interests and activities of friends. However, many recovering people have not had contact for years, if at all, with people who are nonusers. Furthermore, recovering clients are often advised during treatment to discontinue contact with friends who use but, as we will discuss, may not have developed the social and communication skills needed to develop new friendships. If the recovering person does not develop an alternative social support system, the options may be isolation or the resumption of the old relationships that involved AOD use. Certainly, twelve-step meetings provide a structure to meet nonusing people. However, it is essential to assist in the development of healthy support systems and to not rely solely on twelve-step meetings, particularly with adolescents.

SOCIAL AND COMMUNICATION SKILLS   If a client does not have appropriate social and communication skills, he or she can attend all the twelve-step meetings available and still not be able to develop a social network. Many people with AOD problems have not had to rely on social or communication skills to have "friends." Simply having money and alcohol or other drugs probably created a social network. They may have never been in a social situation without being under the influence. Clients might need training in listening skills, asking people questions about themselves, or practice in "small talk." We have found the lack of social skills to be a particular problem with adolescents, who normally feel awkward in new social situations. But many adult clients feel like adolescents too, because their social skill development has been truncated by their AOD use. In addition, assertiveness training and stress and anger management may be needed. Clients may have simply used AOD in situations in which stress was encountered. In the absence of using AOD, these clients may demonstrate passive or aggressive responses to conflict.

SELF-CARE   Anna needs advice on nutrition and hygiene in a caring and supportive way. If her self-esteem improves, she might pay more attention to this area, but she simply may not know how to eat, dress, or even wash to make herself look better. She may need an adult's help in making the best of what nature has given her. Self-care is a relapse issue because people tend to tease or reject those who are inattentive to their appearance and hygiene. Teasing and rejection can certainly elicit negative emotional states, which we discussed earlier as a significant cause of relapse. While self-care is a sensitive area and may be embarrassing to discuss, the following case illustrates the importance of this area in relapse prevention. We worked with a man who was recovering and trying to find employment. He was quite obese, sloppily dressed, and had halitosis and body odor. Needless to say, he was not having much luck in interviews. We would not have been doing a good job if we had not been honest with him about his self-care issues, especially since his discouragement over his lack of a job created a high-risk situation.

Advice on nutrition, dress, and hygiene are not the only self-care issues with which clients may need assistance. Exercise might have been neglected during the time the clients were using, and they may need guidance with the development of an exercise program. Clients may also need assistance with the discontinuation of other unhealthy addictions such as tobacco use. In addition to the health hazards of tobacco use, smoking has an effect on energy level, and the growing intolerance of smoking can have social ramifications.

EDUCATIONAL AND VOCATIONAL GUIDANCE   It is common for school and jobs to be affected by AOD problems. Also, these areas can be high-risk situations for many different reasons. As we saw with Anna, her scholastic aptitude and poor academic achievement contributed to making school an unpleasant experience. An unsatisfying or unpleasant job can also elicit negative emotions. Frequently, a client may be reluctant to return to the same school or to the job he or she had before treatment because the people and/or the situation there may be associated with use. With adult clients, community colleges and vocational rehabilitation can be resources for educational and vocational guidance. For school-aged clients, high schools generally have vocational counselors and school psychologists who may be of assistance with low-achieving or low-scholastic-aptitude youngsters.

FINANCIAL PLANNING   Clients may need financial guidance for two reasons. The first is that they may have financial problems because of their AOD use. Second, the client may have little experience with budgeting, since the priority for money was to secure the drug(s) of choice. Financial issues may require attention because they can be a source of stress, negative emotions, and interpersonal conflict. For example, a client goes through treatment and is working on remaining abstinent. For the first time in a long time, the client is taking his responsibilities seriously. Whereas creditors were ignored when the client was using, now he is making an attempt to clear up his debts, but he has no idea how to negotiate with creditors and budget his current income. Creditors are making harassing phone calls, he can't get his car fixed, and he has no money for recreation. Does this sound like a setup for relapse?

RELATIONSHIPS   A few years ago, we worked with a 37-year-old client named Gene who had been sober for 18 months. Gene had been using AOD since he was 14. The longest relationship he had ever been in had lasted 6 months. Due to the length of time he had been using, emotional attachment, commitment, and interdependence were all unfamiliar to Gene. He sought therapy when he slipped after the end of a short relationship with a woman he met in AA. After a couple of dates and sex, he had proposed to the woman and she had dumped him. Clearly, Gene needed some help with many aspects of relationship development and management.

Although Gene may seem to be an extreme case, relationship problems are a cause of many relapses. Recovering adults may have virtually no experience in relationships while drug free. They may not be able to make logical decisions in the face of the intense emotions that romantic relationships can generate. They may not have a basis for making decisions about potential partners. In many ways, working with adult recovering clients can be like counseling an infatuated adolescent who is "in lust" for the first time. The emotional roller coaster of relationships can be high risk for many clients.

BALANCE   In reading this section, you may have experienced some sense of being overwhelmed with all the areas that may need attention. Clients can have this experience as well. As a mental health professional, you might contribute to a client's frustrations if you list all the lifestyle changes a client must make to prevent relapse. Presenting a recovering client with all of these lifestyle changes at once would probably result in an immediate relapse. Certainly, these areas must be prioritized and then be worked on in increments. As we discussed in the section on covert relapse planning, if a client perceives a great imbalance between "shoulds" and "wants," this perception alone can lead to relapse. It is usually easy for clients and mental health professionals to develop long lists of "shoulds." But it is also important to help clients achieve a balance in their lives so they can have some fun and pleasure. It takes most people a number of years to mess up their lives with AOD. So in spite of a client's desire to repair everything quickly, it will probably take a number of years to clear up their lives as well.

PREVENTING SLIPS FROM ESCALATING

Earlier in the chapter, we discussed the frequency of slips and relapses. Given the fact that it is more common than not for a client to return to use following treatment, it makes sense to develop strategies to reduce the likelihood of a slip's progressing to a relapse. However, this is a sticky issue in the treatment field. Since most treatment programs are abstinence based, you might feel a hesitancy to introduce such strategies, since doing so may provide an excuse to a client to use again. The alternative to withholding these techniques is not attractive either because, if a client does slip, he or she has no "weapons" to use to prevent the slip from escalating. In fact, without the knowledge that slips are common, the client's feeling of failure might contribute to further use. As we stated earlier, the conflict, guilt, and shame a client may experience after a slip has been termed the *abstinence violation effect* (AVE) by Marlatt (1985). Annis (1990) says, "The AVE involves perceived loss of control that undermines self-efficacy and increases expectations of continued failure" (p. 121). In our own experience, we have found it useful to discuss slips, AVE, and strategies to limit slips in the context of an expectation that the client will remain abstinent. We believe that it is important to attempt to limit a client's guilt and blame if a slip occurs, so that the client will be more likely to discuss the slip with a mental health professional.

Marlatt (1985) describes strategies to limit slips. One such strategy is a relapse contract. "The purpose of this procedure is to establish a working agreement or therapeutic contract to limit the extent of use should a lapse occur" (p. 59). The contract includes an agreement to "time out" if a slip occurs. In other words, the client agrees to leave the situation when this happens. Clients can also carry reminder cards that contain specific steps, including people to call if a slip occurs. The cards also have cognitive and behavioral reminders such as "Remember, you are in control," "This slip is not a catastrophe. You can stop now if you choose," and "Imagine yourself in control." Clients may also carry a decision matrix they have developed with a counselor. The decision matrix contains the immediate and delayed consequences of use and, hopefully, would be reviewed after a slip, reminding the client of the consequences of continuing to use. Clearly, these strategies rely on preplanning that would convince a client to use the techniques immediately following a slip. If the slip continues, the cognitive impairment resulting from use would impact the effectiveness of these strategies.

RECOVERY

Recovery from addiction can be conceptualized as a continuous, lifelong process. It begins with an intentional action on the part of a person to discontinue the harmful use of AOD. For many people, this intentional act involves entering a treatment program (voluntarily or involuntarily) and continues with a formal aftercare and relapse-prevention program. For many others, the intentional act involves going to a twelve-step meeting. For others, it may involve starting a methadone maintenance program. Some people discontinue their harmful AOD use through support from a religious institution. Some people stop on their own with or without various support systems.

In other words, people start the recovery process in many different ways. There is no one right way. For those of us in the helping professions, most of the recovering people we encounter have been through formal treatment programs and/or are involved in twelve-step groups. These clients are the most likely to define themselves as being "in recovery." However, that does not mean that other methods of beginning the recovery process are less useful. (Although we have never encountered this situation, we might have some disagreement with the person who has moderated his or her use of AOD and defines himself or herself as being "in recovery.")

The concept of a continuous, lifelong process may be difficult for you. It may help if we personalize this a bit. As was said in Chapter 1, the first author of this textbook (Gary) is a recovering alcoholic and drug addict. Speaking for myself, I (Gary) see the recovery process as similar to many other therapeutic, religious, or spiritual philosophies. Personal development involves qualities and actions such as introspection, honesty, forgiveness, gratitude, humility, responsibility, and service to others. So, whether I attend twelve-step groups, participate in a religious program, practice yoga, read self-help books, or attend a therapy group, I will probably be encouraged to do much the same things. In other words, whether you are in recovery or not, you hear a fairly consistent message from a variety of sources about what qualities and actions are likely to produce contentment and serenity. For me, when I am actively engaged in my personal recovery program, I have that sense of contentment and serenity (most of the time). When I get distracted or lazy, I start to feel dissatisfied, restless, angry, and resentful, and I get urges and cravings. Since I don't want to go back to AOD use, I have to keep moving forward for the rest of my life. It doesn't feel like a burden. It is just my reality. I just accept it and am grateful that some wise people showed me how to have a great life without AOD.

It's a little weird to write about my personal recovery in a textbook (and I didn't include it in the first two editions). The reasons for this personal disclosure are very well expressed by William White, a leader of the recovery advocacy movement:

> The stigma of addiction—the price that even those in long-term recovery can pay in disclosing this aspect of their personal history—leads many recovering people to "pass" as a "normal," scrupulously hiding their recovery journey from members of the larger community. Some recovering people live a socially cloistered existence, interacting almost exclusively with others in recovery. Does such isolation constitute a failure at re-entry, a missed opportunity for reconciliation, and an abdication of the responsibility to teach and serve the community?
>
> The answers to these questions are not easy to answer because recovering people and their styles of recovery and the styles of living are extremely diverse. . . .
>
> If recovering people have not fully returned to their communities, it is as much a cultural failure as a personal one. It is the cultural stigma—the very real price that can be exacted for disclosure of recovery status—that is a primary culprit here. It is time for a new recovery advocacy movement that, by removing the cultural stigma that continues to be attached to addiction/recovery, can open the doors for recovering people to return to their communities. It is time recovering people shared the boon of their recovery, not just with others seeking recovery, but with the whole community. (White, undated, pp. 1–2)

People in recovery are joining together in groups and organizations to advocate for treatment, to combat stigma, and to share the miracle of recovery with those who are still suffering from addiction, their family members, policy makers, and the entire community. Faces and Voices of Recovery is a national recovery movement, and you can find information about recovery organizations in your area. In addition, you can find out about National Alcohol and Drug Addiction Recovery Month (held each September) at the Center for Substance Abuse Treatment website listed in the Internet Resources section at the end of the chapter.

Recovery Support Services

In Chapter 8, we discussed recovery-oriented systems of care (ROSC). Recovery support services are an essential part of ROSC. As Kaplan (2008) defined these services in a white paper for the federal government:

> Recovery support services (RSSs) are nonclinical services that assist individuals and families to recover from alcohol or drug problems. They include social support, linkage to and coordination among allied service providers, and a full range of human services that facilitate recovery and wellness contributing to an improved quality of life. These services can be flexibly staged and may be provided prior to, during, and after treatment. RRSs [*sic*] may be provided in conjunction with treatment, and as separate and distinct services, to individuals and families who desire and need them. Professionals, faith-based and community-based groups, and other RSS providers are key components of ROSCs. (pp. 7–8)

RSSs can be provided by recovery community organizations (i.e., non-profit, community-based organizations created by recovery individuals, their loved ones and allies), treatment agencies, and faith-based organizations. The services may include employment services and job training, case management, service coordination, linkages to other services, outreach, housing assistance, child care, transportation, peer recovery services (e.g., mentoring and coaching), support groups, life skills, and parent education. From the previous discussion on relapse prevention, you can see how valuable RSSs can be in this process.

Recovery and Spirituality

In the next chapter, we will discuss twelve-step groups such as Alcoholics Anonymous. As you probably know, twelve-step groups involve spirituality. This represents a unique aspect of the AOD field compared to other mental health areas since a very prevalent method of managing addiction involves spirituality. While faith and/or spirituality are certainly a part of many counseling approaches, they are incomparably integrated in the addiction field. According to Ringwald (2003):

> Spirituality, that connection with some transcendent reality, truth, or meaning, can exist outside religion—and religion may contain a range of spiritual methods. Spirituality does not require belief in a God, but beliefs alone do not constitute spirituality. What is necessary is for those beliefs to lead to values through personal verification . . . (p. 32)

If the spiritual component of recovery makes you uncomfortable, Ringwald (2003) has this advice:

> . . . take heart and be bold; spiritual interventions are quintessentially evidence-based. Second, these also appeal to many members of disadvantaged or minority

groups, which satisfies the demand for cultural competence and diversity. Third, spiritual interventions are low-cost during treatment, and self-sustaining and community-based after treatment. It's the perfect aftercare. Finally, recovery offers the oldest and most established form of a faith-based solution, one that should be studied for lessons by proponents of faith-based services. (p. 32)

As Ringwald mentions research results support the protective nature of spirituality and religion and of spiritual/religious interventions (e.g., Miller, 1998). Also, as we will discuss in the next chapter, secular support groups are available for those clients who are not comfortable with references to God in twelve-step groups.

MyCounselingLab™

Go to Topic 9: *Retaining Sobriety: Relapse Prevention Strategies*, in the MyCounselingLab™ site (www.MyCounselingLab.com) for *Substance Abuse: Information for School Counselors, Social Workers, Therapists, and Counselors,* Fifth Edition, where you can:

- Find learning outcomes for *Retaining Sobriety: Relapse Prevention Strategies* along with the national standards that connect to these outcomes.
- Complete Assignments and Activities that can help you more deeply understand the chapter content.
- Apply and practice your understanding of the core skills identified in the chapter with the Building Counseling Skills unit.
- Prepare yourself for professional certification with a Practice for Certification quiz.
- Connect to videos through the Video and Resource Library.

Summary

- Relapse prevention often involves mental health professionals in addition to AOD treatment providers.
- Relapse prevention strategies common across models or approaches include assessment of high-risk situations, strategies for coping with high-risk situations, lifestyle changes, and strategies for preventing slips from escalating to relapse.
- Mental health professionals must be cautious to avoid overwhelming clients with relapse prevention activities.

- Recovery is a lifelong process that can start in many different ways, including support groups, religious or spiritual experiences, and independent efforts.
- Recovering people who choose to do so can help combat stigma, advocate for treatment services, and encourage those still suffering from AOD addiction to seek treatment by sharing their recovery experiences.
- Recovery support services may be offered in the community and include many of the essential elements for relapse prevention.

Internet Resources

General Guidelines on Relapse Prevention
kap.samhsa.gov/products/manuals/taps/11j.htm

Cenaps Model
*tgorski.com/gorski_articles/developing_a_relapse_
prevention_plan.htm*

Faces and Voices of Recovery
facesandvoicesofrecovery.org

National Recovery Month
recoverymonth.gov

Further Discussion

1. You may have been asked to participate in an abstinence experience for the class you are taking. If not, you have probably tried to cut down or stop doing something before (smoking, drinking, caffeine, sugar, shopping, video games). When you have tried to cut down or stop a behavior you felt was nonproductive, what high-risk situations did you encounter? How did you handle these situations?

2. When you read about all the areas that recovering individuals have to attend to in order to avoid relapse, what occurs to you about the nature and duration of posttreatment services and support that recovering people need?

Chapter 10

Twelve-Step and Other Types of Support Groups

MyCounselingLab™

Visit the **MyCounselingLab**™ site (www.MyCounselingLab.com) for *Substance Abuse: Information for School Counselors, Social Workers, Therapists, and Counselors,* Fifth Edition to enhance your understanding of chapter concepts. You'll have the opportunity to practice your skills through video- and case-based Assignments and Activities as well as Building Counseling Skills units and to prepare for your certification exam with Practice for Certification quizzes.

CASE EXAMPLES

❶ Meredith is a 43-year-old woman who has just completed a court-mandated, intensive outpatient treatment program for alcohol and polydrug addiction. She has a history of sexual and physical abuse in her family of origin and was working in the sex industry to support her addiction. Meredith was physically and sexually assaulted by her pimp and customers. After completing treatment, she was required to attend twelve-step support groups three times per week. In a meeting with her probation officer, Meredith says that she cannot tolerate twelve-step meetings because every time she hears the first step about "powerlessness," she has flashbacks about her sexual and physical abuse. She says she never wants to feel powerless again.

❷ Terrance, a 57-year-old man, has been ordered by a judge to attend twelve-step meetings after receiving a second DUI. If he fails to attend meetings twice a week for the next six months, he will be diverted to jail for 30 days. He is employed and will lose his job if he goes to jail. Terrance is gay and was sexually abused by a priest when he was 10. Since that experience and because he believes that religious groups discriminate against gays and lesbians, he completely rejects religion and any concept of God. Terrance is a committed atheist. He is totally opposed to attending twelve-step groups because they mention God.

If we were to specify one characteristic of the AOD field that differentiates it from other areas in mental health, it would be the role of support groups in treatment. One would be hard-pressed to find another area in which the most common method of intervention is through groups that are organized and led by nonprofessionals. The unique contribution of support groups in the recovery of individuals with AOD problems warrants a chapter in this text for several reasons. The first and most obvious reason is that, if you work in the helping professions, you will have clients who have attended, are attending, or have been encouraged to attend some type of support group. Therefore, you need to know about such groups. Second, some inevitable conflict seems to exist between mental health professionals and those who are advocates of support groups, and this conflict requires discussion. Finally, the proliferation of support groups based on the Twelve Steps of Alcoholics Anonymous has led to considerable confusion with regard to the methods and purposes of these groups.

In Chapter 8, we discussed support groups as a component of AOD treatment programs. As we noted, twelve-step groups such as Alcoholics Anonymous (AA) and Narcotics Anonymous (NA) are an essential part of many, if not most, treatment programs. In particular, treatment programs that are disease-model-based will almost always require (or strongly recommend) attendance at AA or NA as part of the treatment program and aftercare plan. Family members may be encouraged to attend Al-Anon and teenagers to attend Alateen. CODA meetings for codependents and ACOA meetings for adult children of alcoholics are also available. A variety of other twelve-step groups have developed for group support for other issues: Emotions Anonymous, Overeaters Anonymous, Sexaholics Anonymous, Spenders Anonymous, and Gamblers Anonymous.

Since twelve-step support groups predominate in the support group area and have generated the most confusion and controversy, we want to thoroughly discuss the origin and elements of this type of group. Because twelve-step support groups originated with AA, and AA meetings are the most common type of twelve-step group, we will spend the most time discussing the history, elements, and effectiveness of AA. We will also discuss the advantages and disadvantages of twelve-step groups. Finally, we want you to be aware of other types of support groups that have developed as alternatives to twelve-step groups.

The topic of twelve-step groups can generate emotions in those people who have been or who are still actively involved in these groups. A person who actively attends a group such as AA and maintains sobriety may be a fervent advocate for twelve-step groups. An individual who had an unfavorable reaction to this type of group may be a vocal critic. Many of you may have had some personal experience with twelve-step groups and have strong feelings one way or another. Therefore, before discussing AA, we would like you to keep two points in mind. First, twelve-step groups were not designed as treatment. As you will see from the following discussion, AA groups were developed to support alcoholics who were trying to remain sober. Formal treatment and AA do not conflict. Some people do both, some one or the other, and some neither. The fact that many people remain abstinent with support from AA meetings has resulted in some AA members' preaching a philosophy of "AA is the only way." This point of view is not an official stance of AA and is, in fact, contrary to the AA philosophy.

Second, it is common knowledge that twelve-step meetings contain references to "God" and "Higher Power." In the previous chapter, we discussed the topic of recovery and spirituality and we will discuss spirituality in twelve-step groups later in this chapter as well. In our experience, people tend to have an emotional, as opposed to a logical, reaction to anything that appears to be religious. If you have preconceptions about twelve-step groups because of the spiritual nature of these groups, we ask that you try to put them aside as you read this chapter. We want you, as a mental health professional, to completely understand a very prevalent type of support group and to know when such groups (or others) may be useful for clients. If you have not attended a twelve-step meeting before, we strongly encourage you to do so. (Make sure you go to an open meeting.) If twelve-step meetings have benefited you personally, remember that each client is an individual, and what has worked for you may not work for someone else. The spiritual nature of Twelve-Step groups present some interesting and challenging issues for mental health professionals. However, your primary concern should be to objectively assess the needs of your clients and recommend the interventions that best address those needs. To do so, you must put aside any personal preferences for or against Twelve-Step groups and objectively determine whether such groups would benefit your clients.

ALCOHOLICS ANONYMOUS

The oldest and largest twelve-step support group consists of about 61,500 groups and nearly 1.4 million members in the United States and Canada. Almost 116,000 groups and more than 2 million members exist worldwide (Alcoholics Anonymous General Services Office, 2010). According to the most recent survey of members (Alcoholics Anonymous World Services, 2008), the average age of members is 47, two-thirds are males, and 85% are white.

History of AA

An excellent history of AA is presented in a book by William White (1998), a leading recovery advocate. June 10, 1935, is considered the birth date of AA, since that is the date that Bill Wilson, a stockbroker, and Bob Smith, a surgeon, met, and "Dr. Bob" had his last drink.

The sequence of events that brought Bill W. and Dr. Bob, the co-founders of AA, together began with the famous psychiatrist, Carl Jung, and his treatment of Roland H., an alcoholic and an American businessman. Jung had told Roland H. that he had done all that medicine and psychiatry could do. Jung suggested that he needed a spiritual awakening if he were to recover from his alcoholism. Roland H. joined the Oxford Group, a popular nondenominational religious group that sought to recapture the essence of first-century Christianity. Roland H. was able to abstain from alcohol after associating with the Oxford Group, and he convinced a friend, Ebby T., to do the same. Ebby T. was a friend of Bill W. When Bill offered Ebby a drink, Ebby replied, "I don't need it anymore. I've got religion" (Kurtz, 1979, p. 7). Bill W., an agnostic, did not immediately see the implication of Ebby's statement. However, after being admitted to a hospital for detoxification, Bill W. had a spiritual experience. Following his release, he read a book by William James, *The Varieties of Religious Experiences,* which became the foundation of the Twelve Steps. Bill W. was able to stop drinking and his life improved dramatically. During a business trip to Akron, Ohio, Bill W. had a strong desire to drink after a business deal fell through. He wanted to talk to another alcoholic, so he called an Oxford Group minister and was referred to Dr. Bob, an active alcoholic. Dr. Bob reluctantly agreed to talk to Bill W. They ended up talking for hours. Bill W. had made this contact because he needed to talk to another alcoholic to avoid drinking himself. Through this contact, Bill W. avoided relapsing and Dr. Bob stopped drinking. This was the start of the AA method of alcoholics talking to other alcoholics in order to remain sober. Bill W. had no plan or desire to change Dr. Bob. He only wanted to maintain his own sobriety.

What AA Is About

The AA preamble, which is usually read at meetings, is a good description of the purpose of AA:

> Alcoholics Anonymous is a fellowship of men and women who share their experience, strength, and hope with each other that they may solve their common problem and help others to recover from alcoholism.
>
> The only requirement for membership is a desire to stop drinking. There are no dues or fees for AA membership; we are self-supporting through our own contributions. AA is not allied with any sect, denomination, politics, organization, or institution; does not wish to engage in any controversy, neither endorses nor proposes any causes. Our primary purpose is to stay sober and help other alcoholics to achieve sobriety. (*AA Grapevine,* 1985, p. 1)

AA meetings may be closed (for AA members only) or open. Closed meetings are usually "step" meetings in which members can choose which of the twelve steps to focus on. Open meetings may be "speaker" meetings in which people voluntarily tell their stories (their histories of drinking and recovery) or discussion meetings where a topic is suggested by the meeting chair or a participant. The topics relate to some aspect of recovery or a barrier to recovery, such as "forgiveness," "anger," "humility," or "serenity."

As the AA preamble indicates, the only requirement for membership is a *desire* to stop drinking. Those who relapse are not banned but are offered support in their struggle for sobriety. The bible for AA is the book *Alcoholics Anonymous* (Alcoholics Anonymous World Services, 2001), commonly referred to as "The Big Book." Anonymity, a central concept in AA, protects the identities of members and ensures that no one person or persons become spokespeople for AA. To further the ideal of equality among members, meetings chairs rotate and there are no elected directors. Special committees and service boards are created as needed from AA members.

At AA meetings, you will hear many slogans that are amusing, catchy, or clever and are easily remembered. For example, the famous "One day at a time" is meant to reinforce the concept that sobriety is a day-to-day (sometimes minute-to-minute) process to keep the alcoholic focused on the present as opposed to the future. Other examples include "Keep it simple" (sobriety is a simple process: don't drink), "Let go and let God," and "Get off the pity pot."

When a person speaks at an AA meeting, he or she usually starts by saying, "Hi. My name is (first name of speaker) and I'm an alcoholic." The rest of the participants respond by saying, "Hi, _____." The statement of the speaker acknowledges his or her alcoholism, and the response of the participants indicates acceptance and support. At some meetings, a person may be called upon to speak. One can always say, "Hi, my name is _____, and I pass."

In the introduction to this book, we told you that we require our students to attend an AA or an NA meeting, and the students generally are impressed with the friendliness and encouragement they encounter at the meetings. However, some of the students are concerned with another aspect of AA meetings, which is the "no cross talk" rule. When someone speaks at an AA meeting, subsequent speakers do not address previous speakers. For example, one of our students was very concerned about a woman at a meeting who was emotionally distraught and disoriented in her speech. The next speaker did not react to the woman at all. As we explained, AA meetings are for support in maintaining sobriety. They are not designed to provide therapy. If cross talk were allowed, there would be a tendency for nonprofessionals to provide therapy. Also, as

Bill W. discovered, he was able to avoid drinking simply by talking about himself to another alcoholic. Input and feedback from Dr. Bob was not necessary and, therefore, is not necessary at meetings.

As a helping professional, you might wonder about the advisability of eliminating feedback from members, since this can be a valuable method of growth. Although feedback does not occur in meetings, members are encouraged to seek a "sponsor." McCrady, Horvath, and Delaney (2003) describe sponsors as follows:

> A very important part of the AA experience is sponsorship. The process of sponsorship involves two alcoholics, one of whom has made more progress in recovery and who shares that experience in an ongoing manner with another who is trying to achieve or maintain sobriety. Some groups offer temporary sponsors, matching a newcomer with someone until they are able to meet enough members to select their own sponsor. A sponsor should be the same gender as the person being sponsored, and is contacted as often as needed. . . . Sponsors help with an assortment of problems, ranging from how to stay away from the first drink to what to do if a relapse occurs to how to work the 12 steps of the program. (p. 171)

The Twelve Steps and the Twelve Traditions

> A.A.'s Twelve Steps are a group of principles, spiritual in their nature, which, if practiced as a way of life, can expel the obsession to drink and enable the sufferer to become happily and usefully whole. A.A.'s Twelve Traditions apply to the life of the Fellowship itself. They outline the means by which A.A. maintains its unity and relates itself to the world about it, the way it lives and grows. (Alcoholics Anonymous World Services, 2009, p. 15)

The core of the AA program and the basis of similar groups developed on the AA model are the Twelve Steps. As a statement in the Big Book indicates, "Rarely have we seen a person fail who has thoroughly followed our path" (p. 58). It is truly astounding that these twelve statements, written over 70 years ago, have generated so great a number of adherents, groups, and critics. We will present the Twelve Steps and comment briefly on them. If desired, you can find a thorough discussion in *Twelve Steps and Twelve Traditions* by Alcoholics Anonymous World Services. Professional analysis of the twelve steps can be found in articles such as Peteet (1993).

The Twelve Steps[1]

1. We admitted we were powerless over alcohol—that our lives had become unmanageable.
2. Came to believe that a Power greater than ourselves could restore us to sanity.
3. Made a decision to turn our will and our lives over to the care of God *as we understood Him.*

---

[1] The Twelve Steps and Twelve Traditions are reprinted with permission of Alcoholics Anonymous World Services, Inc. ("AAWS"). Permission to reprint the Twelve Steps and Twelve Traditions does not mean that AAWS has reviewed or approved the contents of this publication, nor that AA necessarily agrees with the views expressed herein. AA is a program of recovery from alcoholism *only*—use of the Twelve Steps and Twelve Traditions in connection with programs and activities that are patterned after AA, but which address other problems, or in any other non-AA context, does not imply otherwise.

4. Made a searching and fearless moral inventory of ourselves.
5. Admitted to God, to ourselves, and to another human being the exact nature of our wrongs.
6. Were entirely ready to have God remove all these defects of character.
7. Humbly asked Him to remove our shortcomings.
8. Made a list of all persons we had harmed, and became willing to make amends to them all.
9. Made direct amends to such people wherever possible, except when to do so would injure them or others.
10. Continued to take personal inventory and when we were wrong promptly admitted it.
11. Sought through prayer and meditation to improve our conscious contact with God *as we understood Him,* praying only for knowledge of His will for us and the power to carry that out.
12. Having had a spiritual awakening as the result of these steps, we tried to carry this message to alcoholics, and to practice these principles in all our affairs.

Let us point out a couple of things about the twelve steps. First, alcohol is mentioned only in step 1. Steps 2 through 11 are the ways to improve a person's life. You can see how these might be applied to many issues other than alcohol. The focus is on surrender, forgiveness, humility, limitations, and service to others. The influence of the Oxford Group on Bill W. also is clear from these aspects of the twelve steps. As Miller and Kurtz (1994) stated in a fascinating article contrasting AA and models of addiction, "Practice of the 12 Steps brings a recovery characterized by growth in character traits such as honesty, humility and patience" (p. 161). In this light, the twelve steps can be conceptualized as a way of living.

The Twelve Traditions[2]

The Twelve Traditions govern the operation of AA. They are as follows:

1. Our common welfare should come first; personal recovery depends upon AA unity.
2. For our group purpose there is but one ultimate authority—a loving God as He may express himself in our group conscience. Our leaders are but trusted servants; they do not govern.
3. The only requirement for AA membership is a desire to stop drinking.
4. Each group should be autonomous except in matters affecting other groups or AA as a whole.
5. Each group has but one primary purpose—to carry its message to the alcoholic who still suffers.
6. An AA group ought never endorse, finance, or lend the AA name to any related facility or outside enterprise, lest problems of money, property, and prestige divert us from our primary purpose.
7. Every AA group ought to be fully self-supporting, declining outside contributions.
8. Alcoholics Anonymous should remain forever nonprofessional, but our service centers may employ special workers.
9. AA, as such, ought never be organized; but we may create service boards or committees directly responsible to those they serve.
10. Alcoholics Anonymous has no opinion on outside issues; hence the AA name ought never be drawn into public controversy.

---

[2]Ibid.

11. Our public relations policy is based on attraction rather than promotion; we need always maintain personal anonymity at the level of press, radio, and films.
12. Anonymity is the spiritual foundation of all our Traditions, ever reminding us to place principles before personalities.

The emphasis of the Twelve Traditions is on maintaining anonymity and avoiding controversy, thereby reducing the likelihood that AA will be diverted from its mission. You will not find AA endorsing or criticizing any model of addiction or approach to treatment. There is no AA lobbyist to help pass legislation. AA has no "spokesperson" and does not solicit or accept contributions. No matter what your opinion is of AA, you have to be impressed with the singular focus of AA and its ability to maintain this focus for nearly 80 years.

Elements of AA Meetings

Although there may be some variability in what you will hear and see at AA meetings, most open meetings have common elements. By describing these, we are not trying to provide a substitute for actual attendance at meetings. However, your experience when you first go to an AA meeting might be similar to attending a religious service of an unfamiliar denomination. You are not quite sure when to do what, and you don't want to call attention to yourself.

Generally, people socialize for a short time before the meeting starts. Coffee and other beverages are usually available. If the meeting is not advertised as nonsmoking, be prepared for cigarette smoke. People who regularly attend the meeting may introduce themselves to those who are obviously new and offer to sit with a newcomer. Remember, last names are not used.

The meeting chair or secretary will introduce the meeting by saying something like, "Welcome to the Gemini meeting of Alcoholics Anonymous. May we have a moment of silence for those alcoholics who are still suffering." The Serenity Prayer will then be recited: "God grant me the serenity to accept the things I cannot change, the courage to change the things I can, and the wisdom to know the difference." The AA preamble is read and newcomers (those with fewer than 30 days of sobriety) and out-of-towners are given an opportunity to introduce themselves. Members participate in reading part of Chapter 3 of the Big Book, titled "More about Alcoholism" or Chapter 5, "How It Works," the Twelve Steps, and the Twelve Traditions. The chair then speaks, usually telling his or her story. If the meeting is a discussion meeting, the chair either suggests a topic of discussion, asks for suggestions, or has a member read something from AA literature. The reading selection then becomes the basis for the meeting discussion. If it is a speakers' meeting, the chair asks for volunteers or calls on people to speak. Remember, if you are called upon to speak and do not wish to, you can always say "Pass." It is nice if you say, "Hi, my name is _____ and I pass," but you don't have to. Also, don't be confused by the title "discussion meeting." It really isn't an exchange—rather, a series of speakers talk about the meaning of the topic of discussion in their sobriety. As we stated previously, cross talk is not permitted. After the discussion or speakers, AA-related announcements are made and a basket for contributions is passed around. The chair may sign attendance records for those who are court ordered to attend. "Chips" may be given to those in attendance who have achieved sobriety milestones (i.e., 30, 60, and 90 days; 6 months; 9 months) and those who have "birthdays" (anniversary of sobriety). "A Vision for You" from the Big Book is read, and participants stand in a circle, join hands, and recite the Lord's Prayer. They then say "Keep coming back. It works if you work it, so work it 'cause you're worth it," and the meeting is over. Participants usually socialize for a brief period following the meeting.

Research on AA

A professional work group was formed by the Substance Abuse and Mental Health Services Administration and the Department of Veterans Affairs (2003) to examine self-help organizations. This work group reviewed the literature on the effectiveness of AA and other twelve-step groups and concluded the following:

> **1.** Longitudinal studies associate 12-step self-help group involvement with reduced substance use and improved psychosocial functioning, (2) Twelve step self-help groups significantly reduce health care utilization and costs, (3) Self-help groups are best viewed as a form of continuing care rather than as a substitute for acute treatment services, (4) Randomized trials with coerced populations suggest that Alcoholic [*sic*] Anonymous (AA) combined with professional treatment is superior to AA alone.

A more recent meta-analysis of studies of AA (Kaskutas, 2009) found that:

> Rates of abstinence are about twice as high among those who attend AA . . . levels of attendance are related to higher rates of abstinence . . . these relationships are found for different samples and follow-up periods . . . prior AA attendance is predictive of subsequent abstinence . . . and mechanisms of action predicted by theories of behavior change are present in AA. (p. 145)

However, this analysis found mixed results on the specificity of an effect for AA or for Twelve Step Facilitation (a manualized treatment based on the Twelve Steps and described in Chapter 8).

AA and Spirituality

The effectiveness of AA has been related to elements in the group process, ego function development, empathic understanding, disintegration of pathologic narcissism, and so forth (Nace, 2005). However, as Miller and Kurtz (1994) point out, "It would be helpful for treatment and research professionals to . . . understand the essential nature of AA as a spiritual program of living" (p. 165). As Nace states, "Spirituality is rarely part of the lexicon of the mental health professional . . ." (p. 595). Therefore, the well-intentioned efforts to conceptualize the effects of AA in terms of psychological theories or processes and to research AA through traditional scientific methods may be misguided. As we mentioned at the beginning of the chapter, the broad utilization of a spiritual support program is unique in the helping professions. The mental health professional may need to be flexible in order to gain some understanding of the impact of AA on many recovering alcoholics.

Nace (2005) discusses the spiritual themes of AA: release, gratitude, humility, and tolerance. Release is clearly experienced when the alcoholic no longer feels the compulsion to drink. Gratitude results from the release from compulsion. The alcoholic's powerlessness over alcohol elicits humility, since it is a humbling experience to acknowledge one's inability to handle this drug. The theme of tolerance of differences among people and of one's own shortcomings helps the recovering individual to achieve serenity. If you now reread the Twelve Steps and Twelve Traditions, you can see the themes of release, gratitude, humility, and tolerance in these basic precepts of AA.

Misconceptions Regarding AA

In the minds of many professionals, AA is associated with a particular model of addiction and specific methods of dealing with alcoholics. For example, AA is often associated with the disease concept of addiction (see Chapter 3) and with the need to confront the denial system of alcoholics (see Chapter 8). Miller and Kurtz (1994) compare different models of addiction with AA through AA literature and the writings of Bill W. They conclude that:

> AA writings do not assert that: (1) there is only one form of alcoholism or alcohol problems; (2) moderate drinking is impossible for everyone with alcohol problems; (3) alcoholics should be labeled, confronted aggressively or coerced into treatment; (4) alcoholics are riddled with denial and defense mechanisms; (5) alcoholism is purely a physical disorder; (6) alcoholism is hereditary; (7) there is only one way to recover; or (8) alcoholics are not responsible for their condition or actions. These assertions involve outside economic, political, social, moral, legal, and disciplinary issues on which AA takes no stand. (p. 165)

However, we should note that many AA members may not be familiar with the original writings of Bill W. and therefore may perpetuate some or all of these misconceptions.

OTHER TWELVE-STEP GROUPS

As we mentioned earlier, many other groups have adapted the twelve steps to areas other than alcohol. Narcotics Anonymous (NA) was founded in 1953. AA and NA are not officially affiliated. However, NA uses the same twelve steps as AA, replacing "alcohol" and "alcoholism" with "drugs" and "addiction." From the first NA group, membership expanded to 1,600 groups in 1982 and to more than 20,000 in 1992 (Fiorentine & Hillhouse, 2000). According to the most recent membership survey, more than 58,000 meetings worldwide now exist (NA World Services, 2010). This increase is understandable considering the tremendous rise in illicit drug use in this country since the formation of NA. Since so many people present polydrug problems, the choice of whether to attend AA or NA has become less clear. It is probably best to let clients with polydrug problems (if one of the drugs is alcohol) attend both AA and NA meetings and decide which is most comfortable. Other organizations exist as well, such as Cocaine Anonymous, and Dual Diagnosis Anonymous and Dual Recovery Anonymous, which are twelve-step programs for those with co-occurring mental disorders.

When AA was founded, its members were men. The wives of the members would get together and talk about their problems. Lois W., the wife of Bill W., founded Al-Anon Family Groups in 1954. Royce (1989) describes Al-Anon:

> Al-Anon is a recovery program for people who suffer because someone close to them drinks too much. At Al-Anon meetings members learn . . . that their own recovery is possible whether or not the drinker seeks help or even recognizes that a drinking problem exists. (p. 280)

The twelve steps have been adapted for Al-Anon with step 1 being an admission that the person is powerless to control the drinking of significant others. Essentially, Al-Anon provides support for family members of alcoholics. Al-Anon does not advocate that family members abandon the alcoholic or coerce the alcoholic into treatment. Rather, it is a spiritual program that encourages detachment and self-improvement. At Al-Anon meetings, you will find family members living with recovering alcoholics, those living with active alcoholics, and those who have separated from alcoholic family members. Alateen is a component of Al-Anon that was started by a teenager in 1957 and is designed for young people who are living with an alcoholic family member. Alateen has its own Big Book, structured along the same lines as that of AA (Al-Anon Family Group, 1973). In our area, Alateen meetings are held at schools, providing these young people with a convenient way to attend and experience the support of others with similar issues. At both Al-Anon and Alateen meetings you will find participants who are living with or involved with people who have addictions to drugs other than alcohol. We encourage you to attend some Al-Anon meetings so you will have first-hand experience with this type of support group.

As we mentioned previously, numerous other twelve-step groups have been created that focus on a variety of issues and where the twelve steps are adapted for the particular focus of the group. Twelve-step groups exist for codependency, adult children of alcoholics, eating disorders, sexual behavior, gambling, spending, and other issues.

ADVANTAGES AND DISADVANTAGES OF TWELVE-STEP GROUPS

Twelve-step groups have many obvious advantages. First of all, they are free. In the mental health field, this is certainly unique. Second, meetings such as AA are available at a variety of times and places (of course, this depends on the size of the area and the type of meeting). An AA member who is on either a business or pleasure trip can usually find a meeting. Third, at meetings, twelve-step participants find a group of people who share similar concerns and problems and who can provide group support. This type of support is helpful to many people and would be difficult for them to achieve on their own. Additionally, a social network is often developed through twelve-step meetings. For the recovering person, this is a useful way to make nonusing friends. Fourth, the structure and ritual of twelve-step meetings may be comforting and helpful to people whose lives have been chaotic and unpredictable. Fifth, the spiritual nature of twelve-step groups, with its themes of release, gratitude, humility, and tolerance, can be a productive focus for self-improvement and general contentment with life. For one who has experienced excessive guilt, blame, and embarrassment, the spiritual themes can refocus the person on more positive emotions. Finally, twelve-step groups are consistent with the concepts of recovery-oriented systems of care (see Chapter 9) and with the view of addiction as a chronic condition that requires management throughout a person's life. Through regular attendance at twelve-step meetings, an addict is always focused on recovery.

The disadvantages of twelve-step meetings are usually focused on the differentiation (or lack thereof) between spirituality and religion and the concept of "powerlessness." While twelve-step meetings are supposed to be nondenominational, the recital of the Lord's Prayer implies a Christian orientation. Those who are members of other religious groups may be alienated by this prayer. Atheists can certainly have difficulty with the notion of "Higher Power." Even though steps 3 and 11 refer to "God as we understood Him," the notion of Higher Power in twelve-step meetings is clearly that of the Judeo-Christian God. However, remember that AA was formed in 1935 when diversity was hardly a predominant concept. In the context of the times, it is a tribute to Bill W.'s openness that "God as we understood Him" was included. Regardless, the rituals of twelve-step meetings and the references to God and a Higher Power can be problematic for clients who have negative attitudes and/or experiences with organized religion or those who are not Christian.

As Miller and Kurtz (1994) pointed out, AA does not promulgate the notion that alcoholics are not responsible for their condition or actions. Although the first of the twelve steps contains the word "powerlessness" and the third step involves turning "our will and our lives over to the care of God," steps 4 through 8 involve taking responsibility for past wrongs and shortcomings. However, critics of twelve-step groups and some participants have interpreted steps 1 and 3 to mean that the twelve-step philosophy supports the notion that addicted individuals are not responsible for their actions. Clearly, such a view would be counterproductive for clients.

Additional disadvantages of twelve-step groups arise from the individuals involved in such groups rather than from the ideas themselves. As the membership statistics show, AA is predominately composed of white, middle-aged males. This might alienate women, ethnically diverse individuals, and young people. Groups for different demographic groups have developed in response.

Some participants in twelve-step groups feel so strongly about the benefits of the program that they denigrate other interventions, such as therapy or psychotropic medications. Again, nothing in the AA philosophy opposes other forms of intervention or preaches that AA is the only way to recovery. However, just as some adherents of religious views misinterpret the doctrines based on their personal characteristics and experiences, some twelve-step participants appear dogmatic.

Finally, critics of twelve-step groups claim that many people simply switch addictions from alcohol and other drugs to going to meetings. Certainly, attendance at twelve-step meetings can interfere with social, family, and occupational functioning, and, if a person continued with constant participation in spite of these consequences, this would constitute problematic behavior. Personally, we would rather see someone constantly attending meetings than committing armed robbery to get money for drugs. However, we have no doubt that compulsive twelve-step meeting attendance could be a barrier to mature functioning.

To close this discussion of twelve-step groups, we want to reemphasize our personal view that twelve-step meetings should not be confused with treatment. Twelve-step groups, with the support they offer and the emphasis on spiritual development, can be an important part of a comprehensive treatment program. As we said earlier in the chapter, some people maintain sobriety (or whatever behavior change they are focused on) without any other form of intervention or support. Others maintain these changes without ever going to a twelve-step meeting. As we said in Chapter 6, it is the counselor's responsibility to do a thorough assessment on every client and to design treatment strategies designed to meet the client's needs. You will find that many clients

---

AT A GLANCE

TWELVE-STEP GROUPS

- AA was started in 1935; NA in 1953; Al-Anon in 1954.
- The Twelve Steps are the basic principles for living; the Twelve Traditions govern the operation of twelve-step groups.
- Twelve-step support group meetings are associated with abstinence and other positive outcomes but are not a substitute for treatment.
- AA is singularly focused on helping alcoholics to stop drinking; it has no opinion on therapy or other treatment, models of addiction, medications, or any other issue.
- Twelve-step groups are free, readily available, provide an abstinent social group and activities, can provide a structure for improving the quality of life, and help recovering addicts maintain a focus on recovery.
- The spiritual nature of twelve-step groups may present challenges for some addicts.
- The concepts of powerlessness and responsibility for recovery are sometimes misunderstood by addicts and the public.

can benefit from this type of free, available support group consisting of people with similar problems. Whether the group is a twelve-step group or one of the other groups we will now discuss depends on the needs, background, and experiences of the client. The recommendation for a support group should not depend on your own preconceptions or stereotypes.

OTHER TYPES OF SUPPORT GROUPS

Many Roads, One Journey

In her 1992 book (revised in 2002), *Many Roads, One Journey: Moving beyond the 12 Steps,* Charlotte Davis Kasl argues that issues such as child abuse, sexism, racism, poverty, and homophobia are in opposition to twelve-step concepts such as conformity, humility, personal failings, and powerlessness. For example, an adult woman who was sexually molested as a child or has been in an abusive relationship and has a substance abuse problem may find the first of the twelve steps unacceptable. To admit powerlessness over anything may rekindle the feelings of powerlessness in the abusive situations.

To begin meetings, Kasl suggests an introductory reading of *Many Roads, One Journey.* We have excerpted some of the content to illustrate the philosophy of this approach:

> Our purpose in coming together is to support and encourage each other in our healing from addiction, dependency, or internalized oppression. The only requirement for membership is a desire to maintain sobriety as we each define it. . . . We do not impose our beliefs on others or expect others to tell us the way. . . . Healing is a balance between gentle self-acceptance and a firm commitment to sobriety. We overcome addiction and internalized oppression because we want to honor and enjoy the life we have been given. Healing from addiction and dependency is not about moral worth. We are all sacred children of Creation this moment. . . . We believe that through bonding with others, speaking genuinely from our hearts, forgiving ourselves and others, finding purpose, helping create social change, and accepting the imperfections of life, we will find a sense of fulfillment that we have sought to fill through our addictive and dependent behavior. (pp. 356–357)

Kasl has developed 16 steps for "discovery and empowerment" (p. 337). Some examples of these steps are

1. We affirm we have the power to take charge of our lives and stop being dependent on substances or other people for our self-esteem and security.
2. We come to believe that God/the Goddess/Universe/Great Spirit/Higher Power awakens the healing wisdom within us when we open ourselves to that power.
3. We make a decision to become our authentic Selves and trust in the healing power of truth.
4. We examine our beliefs, addictions, and dependent behavior in the context of living in a hierarchal, patriarchal culture (p. 338).

The spiritual nature of the steps is clear, although acceptance of alternatives to God is more clearly specified than in the Twelve Steps. An emphasis is also placed on power*ful*ness, choice, and the relationship of behavior to culture.

Kasl also provides guidelines for *Many Roads, One Journey* groups. Rather than suggesting a rigid structure and rituals, the groups are more flexible. Kasl does suggest that the purpose of the group be defined, a moderator chosen, and time constraints adhered to. She also suggests a six-week commitment for new members and two-week notice when a member is leaving. Readings of poems, sayings, or other literature are recommended. However, that is the extent of structure suggested, since, as the name *Many Roads, One Journey* implies and as Kasl writes,

> Let's weave together, creating a form and a process that builds a foundation for positive change. Instead of one linear model, we can have many circles with many ways, all working toward growth, empowerment, and an ability to appreciate life. (p. 371)

Women for Sobriety

Jean Kirkpatrick found AA meetings to be rigid, dogmatic, and chauvinistic and felt that the meetings increased her desire to drink. She found hypocrisy in AA members' resistance to taking blood pressure medication or using vitamins to control the effects of alcohol withdrawal, and in the heavy use of caffeine and tobacco at meetings. After 28 years of alcoholism during which Kirkpatrick experienced hospitalization, violence, and depression, she founded Women for Sobriety in 1976. According to Kirkpatrick (1990):

> The Women For Sobriety Program . . . is a product of women's new awareness of self developed through the feminist movement. . . . Through this self-help Program, women take charge of their alcoholism. . . . For women to take full charge of self is a revolutionary concept. For too long, women's health has been governed by persons other than themselves. The Program challenges women to learn their strengths and values, to become aware that they are competent women, that sobriety depends upon the discovery and maintenance of strong feelings of self-value and self-worth which, ultimately, will lead to strong self-esteem. (Preface)

She believes that women begin to drink because of frustration, loneliness, emotional deprivation, and harassment, while men drink for power. In her opinion, treatment programs have not been responsive to the needs of women, and separate self-help groups are necessary to affirm women's autonomy from men.

Kirkpatrick's program emphasizes a holistic approach to recovery. She emphasizes good nutrition, meditation, and cessation of smoking. Consistent with this philosophy, coffee, sugar, and smoking are not permitted at Women for Sobriety meetings.

Kirkpatrick's 13 "statements" reflect her view that self-esteem is the "magic building block" (Kirkpatrick, 1986, p. 131) of recovery. Some examples of these statements are:

1. I have a drinking problem that once had me.
2. Negative emotions destroy only myself.
3. Happiness is a habit I will develop.
4. I am a competent woman and have much to give to others. (p. 251)

In commenting on Kirkpatrick's program, Kasl (2002) writes:

> Kirkpatrick understands the need for women to have groups of their own that stress choices, the positive power of the mind, imaging, broadening one's perspective, the ability to love, and physical healing. Her approach to self-empowerment through monitoring one's thoughts is well documented in psychological research on cognitive therapy with depression. (p. 169)

Secular Organizations for Sobriety/Save Our Selves (SOS)

James Christopher had his last drink on April 24, 1978. He attended AA meetings although "[I] gritted my teeth and said the Lord's prayer; after all, these AA people were *sober*" (Christopher, 1988, p. 96, italics in original). In 1985, Christopher published an article expressing his frustration with "AA's religiosity and my belief that the needs of free thinkers are not being met there" (Christopher, p. 95). In 1986, the first SOS meeting was held, and the program now has more than 20,000 members (Secular Organizations for Sobriety, nd).

While Christopher (1988) is a firm adherent to the disease concept of addiction, he rejects the notion that spirituality is a necessary component for recovery:

> My personal thoughts, feelings, and experiences within Alcoholics Anonymous were suppressed on a number of occasions, and AA was not particularly fulfilling or supportive to me as an alcoholic free thinker. I had to "go it alone" for many years. But through it all, I kept my sobriety through prioritizing it on a day-to-day basis. There is no higher power keeping me sober. I make this choice and reacknowledge it daily. No one can do it for me. (p. 95)

As indicated in Christopher's (1988) statement, the central component of the SOS program is the "sobriety priority":

> As a sober alcoholic I must daily recommit, reaffirm, reaccept, resurrender, and reacknowledge my disease and its antidote: the sobriety priority. My priority frees me up for another day of life with all its pain, sorrow, joy, fear, sickness, achievements, failures, and goals, rather than trapping me in my previous subhuman, coma-like addiction to alcohol. Sobriety is assured *only* by prioritizing it daily on a day-at-a-time basis. This keeps my addiction to alcohol under "house arrest" day to day, hopefully lifelong.
>
> I have the right to fail in any other area of my life. My sobriety priority is the one exception. (p. 51, italics in original)

Christopher suggests five secular guidelines for sobriety. These include an acknowledgement of alcoholism; choosing to remain sober one day at a time; reaching out to those who have been directly or indirectly affected by the person's alcoholism; working toward self-acceptance, change, and growth; and taking responsibility for providing meaning in life. SOS meetings are one-and-a-half hours long with a different person acting as moderator each week. Often soft, classical music is played and a short selection from secular literature related to alcoholism is read. The group may choose a topic to discuss or have an open discussion. Meetings are closed with a short, humanistic reading. Christopher does suggest an opening for an SOS meeting, which stresses sobriety, personal growth, secularism, and humanism. He also emphasizes that his structure and suggestions may be modified as the group wishes.

Moderation Management

This behavioral change program and support group network was developed in 1994 to assist problem drinkers with modifying their use of alcohol. It was not designed for those who have been diagnosed with an Alcohol Dependence Disorder (see Chapter 6) but rather for those people who are concerned about their drinking and want to cut back or quit drinking before serious problems develop. The Moderation Management program is based on the premise that alcohol abuse is a learned behavior rather than a disease. Therefore, people can learn to use alcohol in a moderate manner.

Moderate Management advocates a nine-step program that includes attendance at (free) meetings and abstinence from alcohol for 30 days. The rest of the steps are behavioral in nature and involve tracking drinking behavior, setting drinking goals, and making positive lifestyle changes. The program neither encourages nor discourages abstinence as a goal but does acknowledge that moderation may not be a workable goal for all problem drinkers.

SMART Recovery®

Self-Management And Recovery Training (SMART) was started in 1994 and is an alternative support group system that claims to have a scientific rather than a spiritual orientation. According to its website, SMART Recovery® differs from twelve-step recovery because:

> SMART Recovery® teaches increasing self-reliance, rather than powerlessness. SMART Recovery® meetings are discussion meetings in which individuals talk with one another, rather than to one another. SMART Recovery® encourages attendance for months to years, but probably not a lifetime. There are no sponsors in SMART Recovery®. SMART Recovery® discourages use of labels such as "alcoholic" or "addict." (SMART Recovery, 2011)

The SMART Recovery® program consists of four points: (1) Enhance and maintain motivation to abstain, (2) Cope with urges, (3) Manage thoughts, feelings, and behaviors, and (4) Balance momentary and enduring satisfactions (SMART Recovery, 2011). The strategies involve cognitive–behavioral techniques including a cost-benefit analysis, disputing irrational beliefs about urges and cravings, the ABC analysis from Albert Ellis's rational emotive therapy (i.e., **A**ctivating event or experience; **B**elief about **A**; emotional or behavioral **C**onsequences of **B**). Meetings are free and both online and in person. Meeting facilitators receive training.

CASE EXAMPLE APPLICATIONS

If you go back to the beginning of the chapter and review the case examples, you can see both Meredith and Terrance have alternatives with regard to support groups. Two groups for women that Meredith may find more comfortable are Many Roads, One Journey or Women for Sobriety. Terrance could participate in SOS or SMART Recovery since neither has a spiritual component.

Unfortunately, the alternatives to twelve-step support groups are not as readily available as are twelve-step groups. The alternative groups may be difficult to find where Meredith and Terrance live or at convenient times. As a result, more and more people are choosing to participate in alternative groups online. Online participation is also available for twelve-step groups.

Another consideration in both Meredith's and Terrance's cases and for other clients who are resistant to attending twelve-step groups is that both of them felt that they had very good reasons for feeling uncomfortable and out of place at twelve-step meetings. We could argue about what is meant by "powerlessness" with Meredith and about the meaning of "Higher Power" with Terrance. But, feelings are feelings and both said that they were not willing to attend twelve-step meetings. As a helping professional, you just want to be sure that resistance to attending twelve-step meetings is not the client's way of resisting recovery. Both Meredith and Terrance were willing to participate in alternative support groups. Therefore, they were motivated to work on their recovery. A client who finds faults with all types of support groups may not be.

MyCounselingLab™

Go to Topic 7: *Group Treatment*, in the **MyCounselingLab™** site (www .MyCounselingLab.com) for *Substance Abuse: Information for School Counselors, Social Workers, Therapists, and Counselors,* Fifth Edition, where you can:

- Find learning outcomes for *Group Treatment* along with the national standards that connect to these outcomes.
- Complete Assignments and Activities that can help you more deeply understand the chapter content.
- Apply and practice your understanding of the core skills identified in the chapter with the Building Counseling Skills unit.
- Prepare yourself for professional certification with a Practice for Certification quiz.
- Connect to videos through the Video and Resource Library.

Summary

- Support groups organized around the Twelve Steps of Alcoholics Anonymous have grown to include groups for other drug addicts, family members, and various nondrug problems.
- Twelve-step support groups involve a spiritual approach to recovery and a commitment to the anonymity of members.

- Alternatives to twelve-step groups are available for those who are uncomfortable with the twelve steps or a spiritual approach to recovery.
- Mental health professionals should attempt to match clients with the type of support group that matches their needs and values.

Internet Resources

Alcoholics Anonymous
aa.org/

Narcotics Anonymous
na.org

Al-Anon and Alateen
al-anon.alateen.org

Support groups other than twelve-step
womenforsobriety.org
cfiwest.org/sos/index.htm
moderation.org
smartrecovery.org

Blogs, chatrooms
dryblog.blogspot.com

Further Discussion

1. Should coerced clients (i.e., people mandated to attend treatment by courts, employers, or schools) be required to attend twelve-step meetings? Why or why not?

2. Do you think that recovering people can become too dependent on support group meetings? Why or why not?

Chapter *11*

Children and Families

CASE EXAMPLES

❶ Mary, the wife of an alcoholic, is sharing in her first recovery meeting:

"Well . . . Tony is a very successful businessman. We have three children together. They are good kids, you know? They knew their roles and did what they were supposed to do for the most part . . . None of us ever thought that Tony had a problem; or, that he was an alcoholic; or, that our family had a problem until later when our son, Mark, began having problems. It all seemed so normal to us."

❷ Mr. Aguilar is Hispanic and had been exposed to drinking at an early age in a culture where heavy drinking was more tolerated than in the United States. As a result, he was caught between his culture of origin and the practices of his current cultural environment. He maintained that his drug use situation was inevitable due to the structural oppression he experienced. He saw his drinking as an appropriate way to cope. His wife was in a paradox: She did not want to be disrespectful of her husband and, at the same time, she had a need to help him manage his problematic drinking.

In Chapter 1, we discussed a conceptualization of addiction in which the alcoholic or drug addict is in an intimate and monogamous relationship with the drug of choice. Clearly, if the primary relationship is with alcohol or other drugs, other relationships will be adversely impacted, and the effect on the family is particularly dramatic. Investigators in the field have identified a myriad of problems that occur in children in substance-abusing families as well as in the family system itself. Since the early 1980s, studies have consistently shown that children from these families suffer in a variety of ways (Hussong, Huang, Curran, Chassin, & Zucker, 2010; Usher, Jackson, & O'Brien, 2005; Zucker, Donovan, Masten, Mattson, & Moss, 2009). Other studies describe the impact of AOD use in families in terms of communication and parenting style (Barrett & Turner, 2006; Copello, Velleman, & Templeton, 2005; Patock-Peckham & Morgan-Lopez, 2009; Rangarajan & Kelly, 2006). This is not meant to be a comprehensive review of the vast literature related to children and families in which an alcohol or other drug problem exists. Rather, these examples illustrate the obvious fact that, if a family member has an alcohol or other drug problem, the family will be affected. Individuals living in such families did not need researchers to discover this, as evidenced by the development of Al-Anon in 1954 and Alateen in 1975 (see Chapter 10). Furthermore, comprehensive treatment programs include family education and family therapy as a component of treatment (see Chapter 8). They acknowledge that alcoholism and drug addiction affect each member of the family and that successful recovery necessitates the involvement of the entire family.

As we discussed in Chapter 3, different models of addiction and, predictably, differing conceptualizations, occur in families in relation to AOD problems. Some may argue that the individual with an alcohol or other drug problem is reflecting dysfunction in the family. Others see the alcohol or other drug problem as the primary cause of family dysfunction. As with other controversies in this field, both conceptualizations are probably true. In some families, dysfunction may be acted out through the abuse of AOD. For example, an adolescent female may use drugs to cope with the emotional trauma of sexual abuse. A fairly functional family may become tumultuous as a result of the father's progressive alcoholism. Regardless of the "chicken or the egg" question, we find that the understanding of families and AOD abuse is aided through a family-systems conceptualization. You should be aware that even the definition of *family* varies across cultures. "Family" is a traditional white Anglo-Saxon Protestant definition based on an intact nuclear family, where lineage is of importance when tracing one's ancestry. In contrast, the traditional African American family is focused on a wide, informal network of kin and community that goes beyond blood ties to include close, longtime friends. The traditional Asian American family includes the entire family group and all ancestors and all their descendants. Differences in the life cycle of the family also reflect cultural and ethnic differences. For example, Giordano, and McGoldrick (2005) state that the traditional Euro-American family begins with a psychological being, and growth and development is measured by the human capacity for differentiation. In the traditional Asian American family, each member is a social being (as opposed to a psychological being), and growth and development are measured by the capacity for empathy and connection. A great deal of the research into alcoholic families has focused upon the Euro-American population. However, as we pointed out in Chapter 4, culturally and ethnically diverse families are at risk for AOD abuse. While a growing body of literature focuses on diverse family systems, there continues to be a dearth of information focusing on the effects of AOD on these family systems and structures. Notwithstanding, interesting and provocative ideas addressing this issue are appearing in the emerging professional literature. For example, Cornish, Schreier, Nadkarni, and Metzger (2010) and Krestan (2000) write about the issue of addiction as it relates to power and powerlessness in a multicultural society. In her conceptualizations,

Krestan maintains the importance of the sociocultural impact of power and powerlessness as they are experienced by various racial/ethnic groups. From this perspective, family theorists and therapists can readily see how racial/ethnic family structures might be affected. For instance, African American males often learn to "play the game" to get ahead in a Euro-American domi-nated society. When at home, they may and often do behave very differently. While the strategy of playing the game is successful for many, some individuals may experience distress at having such a marked split between home and work. This split tends to create an additional family struc-ture for some racial/ethnic families. This additional structure and the concomitant stressors can increase risk factors for AOD abuse among this population.

CHILDREN'S EXPOSURE TO ALCOHOL AND OTHER DRUGS

Essentially two types of AOD exposure occur for children: prenatal and interpersonal. Both types of exposure can have dramatic effects on children. Since the 1970s, concern has increased regarding the passage of drugs through the human placenta and through the mother's breast milk. The resulting research indicates that the use of tobacco, alcohol, and other drugs during preg-nancy affects the fetus. Some of these problems may remain even if the mother discontinues her use or if the child is raised in a nonusing environment (Jones, 2007). Jones asserts that the issue of drug use during pregnancy is now considered a critical health concern.

Interpersonal exposure from parental AOD use can affect a child's social and psychologi-cal development through adulthood. However, the effects on children will vary. This is due to individual and environmental differences including age of exposure, progression of use, charac-teristics of the child and of the AOD abuser, family dynamics, and external events. Copello et al. (2005) assert that a growing body of evidence says that not all children will suffer adversely ei-ther in childhood or adulthood. Some children will develop resilience and do not develop signifi-cant problems. Therefore, it would be unwise to assume that all children who experience AOD abuse in their families of origin will exhibit similar behaviors.

Prenatal Exposure to Alcohol and Other Drugs

Perhaps you are wondering why we include a section discussing the possible impairment resulting from prenatal substance use and abuse in a textbook providing comprehensive substance abuse in-formation for school counselors, social workers, therapists, and counselors. The answer will prob-ably become apparent to you as you read through the information. In the meantime, in order to provide a foundation for your understanding of the relationship between what is presented here and your profession(s), let's look at the many facets of prenatal exposure to alcohol and other drugs.

A few of the variables, or "layers," relative to prenatal substance use and abuse are the na-tional attachment to partying; the desire to change how one feels, especially if those feelings are uncomfortable; easy access to and availability of legal and illegal substances regardless of age; the stigma of asking for help with AOD use/abuse, especially for pregnant women; limited long-term residential AOD treatment facilities; few treatment facilities for women; even fewer treatment facili-ties for women and their children; ignorance regarding this issue and ethnic/cultural considerations; the possible loss of custody of the unborn child at birth as permitted by state law; the possibility of maternal prison time; the possible loss of home and family when in treatment and/or prison; and on and on. . . . When seeking to adequately address the complexities of impairment resulting from prenatal AOD exposure, all of these variables need to be taken into consideration and addressed.

Similar to many issues in the AOD field, prenatal exposure to alcohol and other drugs can generate a great deal of public and media attention. As a result, the topic of the pregnant women's use of AOD has become emotionally charged and widely publicized, enhancing the shame already experienced. As suggested previously, what woman wants to admit that her AOD use has impacted her helpless, unborn child? What woman wants to risk the possibility of having her child removed from her, being forced to go to residential treatment to address her AOD issues, or possibly going to prison? The stigma relating to this issue is another detriment to accessing much-needed help. For all of these reasons, estimated prevalence rates vary.

For example, Jones (2007) and data from the Substance Abuse and Mental Health Services Administration (2005) both reflect that among pregnant women, almost 10% report using alcohol, 4% report using at least one illicit drug, and 18% report smoking tobacco. Other data from the National Institute on Drug Abuse (2006) estimate that nearly 20% of infants are exposed to alcohol in utero, 17% to marijuana, 5% to cocaine or heroin, and 40% to tobacco. Further, the NIDA data show that about one-half of the pregnancies are unplanned and that the population of pregnant women report binge drinking as well as chronic drinking, both of which may result in the most severe prenatal impairment. Half of the pregnant women surveyed reported drinking in the three months prior to recognizing the pregnancy. These data indicate that the unborn children could have been exposed to alcohol for at least six weeks.

IMPACT OF FETAL EXPOSURE TO ALCOHOL AND OTHER DRUGS The diagnosis of fetal alcohol syndrome (FAS) was first discovered in 1973 when David Smith and Ken Lyons Jones studied 11 newborns exposed to substantial amounts of alcohol in utero.

Scientific reports confirm that alcohol is a teratogenic drug capable of producing lifelong disabilities after intrauterine exposure. Alcohol is a solvent (i.e., capable of dissolving something, causing a solution [Brown, 1993]) that influences the cells of the developing brain, thus resulting in a spectrum of cognitive deficits. Efforts to provide parameters for understanding this broad range of possible outcomes produced the term *fetal alcohol spectrum disorders* (FASD). FASD is *not* a diagnosis; rather it is an umbrella term under which diagnoses fall. FASD diagnoses include fetal alcohol syndrome (FAS), partial fetal alcohol syndrome (pFAS), alcohol-related birth defects (ARBD), and/or alcohol-related neurodevelopmental disorder (ARND). You also might hear the term *prenatal alcohol exposure* (PAE), although it is not considered an FASD diagnosis; rather, it simply acknowledges in utero alcohol exposure.

May and Gossage (2001, p. 166) estimate a prevalence rate for fetal alcohol syndrome (FAS) between 0.05% and 2.0% per 1,000 births. When combining FAS, partial FAS (pFAS), alcohol-related neurodevelopmental disorder (ARND), and alcohol-related birth defects (ARBD), the estimate is likely to be at least 10 per 1,000. This ratio translates to 1% of all births.

According to Streissguth et al. (1996), FAS is recognized as the leading known cause of mental retardation in the United States, surpassing Down's syndrome and spina bifida. Streissguth (1996) also reports that only 16% of 415 individuals diagnosed with an FASD legally qualify as having mental retardation. In other words, 86% of the 415 have an IQ in the "normal" range and subsequently do not qualify for services for developmental disabilities. Streissguth reports that the average IQ of an individual with FAS is 79 and the average IQ of an individual with pFAS or ARND is 90.

Therefore, no time, no type, and no amount of alcohol is safe to drink when pregnant. Fetal alcohol syndrome does not include all individuals affected by alcohol in utero; rather it represents the severe end of the spectrum of disabilities caused by maternal alcohol abuse during pregnancy (Brown, 1993, p. 1961).

We do not want to minimize the problems that can result from prenatal exposure to AOD. We also do not want you to conclude that all children prenatally exposed will have serious and permanent learning, behavioral, social, and emotional problems.

The cognitive impairment, a diagnostic criterion for the FAS, pFAS, and ARND diagnoses results in the behavioral and learning problems that remain throughout the lifetime of an individual with an FASD. Impairment varies from individual to individual and is potentially influenced by many variables. Risk factors such as polysubstance abuse, socioeconomic status, poor nutrition, lack of prenatal care, homelessness, domestic violence, maternal age and health, fetal health, even placental health may also impact the developing fetus. Sadly, this is far from a complete list.

In 1996, a significant study was conducted at the University of Washington by one of the pioneers in the FASD field, Dr. Ann Streissguth (1996). From a descriptive study of a sample population of 415 subjects with an FASD diagnosis, she sought to provide information regarding the occurrence of disabilities/issues that are *secondary* to the FASDs. The results are as follows:

- 94% had mental health problems (age 6 to 51)
- 43% had disrupted school experience (age 12 and up)
- 60% had legal problems (age 12–51)
- 50% experienced confinement in jail or treatment facilities (age 12–51)
- 45% engaged in inappropriate sexual behavior (age 12–51)
- 30% of adolescents, 47% of adults had AOD problems
- 83% of the adults were living dependently
- 79% of the adults had problems maintaining employment

Although the sample was based on a limited number, the results were significant.

Compared to how much is known about the possible impairments of in utero exposure to alcohol, very little is known about the possible impairments of in utero exposure to other drugs. The following information discusses the outcomes of various longitudinal studies focusing on prenatal use of tobacco, marijuana, cocaine, and heroin.

Established Consequences of Maternal Smoking During Pregnancy

Lester, Andreozzi, and Appiah (2004) maintain that the effects of prenatal tobacco use/abuse can include low birth weight, intrauterine growth restriction, and sudden infant death syndrome (SIDS). Pickett and Wakschlag (2011) report as "established consequences of maternal smoking during pregnancy" health problems at two developmental stages (i.e., infancy and childhood and beyond).

INFANT HEALTH PROBLEMS   In addition to the three effects reported by Lester et al., (2004), infant health problems reported in the Pickett and Wakschlag study include congenital malformations such as cleft palate and cleft lip, limb reductions, and genitourinary malformations. Their 2011 study reports "infants exposed to tobacco *in utero* are 40% more likely to die in the first four weeks after birth than those born to non-smokers. . . ." The risk of infant death is notably increased if tobacco exposure continues after birth. Similarly, most SIDS deaths occur between 2 and 4 months of age, with maternal smoking when pregnant being an established cause. The risk of SIDS doubles when the fetus is exposed to tobacco in utero. The risk continues to increase if the infant is exposed to secondhand smoke after birth.

HEALTH PROBLEMS IN CHILDHOOD AND BEYOND   Health problems primarily include reduced lung function due to impaired development of airways, and respiratory illnesses such as asthma, lower respiratory tract infections (e.g., pneumonia, bronchitis, bronchiolitis, and croup). As with infant mortality and SIDS, the risk of each illness mentioned is compounded by exposure to environmental secondhand smoke.

POSSIBLE EFFECTS OF PRENATAL COCAINE EXPOSURE   Singer and Minnes (2011) report the following information regarding in utero exposure to cocaine beginning at pregnancy/birth and progressing to conditions remaining throughout a lifetime. Fortunately the current research pertaining to the possible effects of prenatal cocaine exposure has increased substantially since the initial media frenzy regarding so-called "cocaine babies."

Birth Outcomes:	Poor fetal growth including lower birth weight, reduced length and head circumference, preterm birth, and intrauterine growth retardation
Physical Development:	Significant early catch-up growth with indicated shorter stature and symmetrical growth retardation at school age
Infant Behavior:	Neurobehavioral abnormalities include jitteriness, attentional problems, and movement and tone
Health:	Early cardiac abnormalities include diastolic alterations and blunted vagal tone in heavily exposed infants; increased incidence of iron deficiency anemia
Language:	Expressive and receptive language delays
Attention:	Impaired visual information processing in infancy; selective and sustained attentional deficits
Behavior:	Increased aggressive behavior, oppositional defiant disorder, and hyperactivity
Cognition:	Impairments in visuospatial information processing and arithmetic deficits in perceptual reasoning and abstract categorical processing
Neuroimaging:	Volumetric reduction in corpus callosum and parietal areas; reduced maturational white matter pathways in the frontal lobes

POSSIBLE EFFECTS OF PRENATAL OPIATE EXPOSURE   Singer and Minnes (2011) provide helpful information regarding the possible effects of prenatal opiate exposure in the table below once again beginning at pregnancy/birth and progressing to conditions remaining throughout a lifetime.

Pregnancy/Birth Outcomes:	Increased rates of stillbirth, premature rupture of membrane, preterm delivery, sudden infant death syndrome (SIDS), decreased birth weight, length, and head circumference
Central Nervous System (CNS):	Seizures (2%–11% of neonates), high muscle tone, high-pitched cry, difficulty being consoled, irritability, excessive and poor sucking. Research outcomes indicate that combined cocaine and opiate exposure results in greater negative CNS effects.
Cognition:	Suggestion of poor cognitive function at 3 years, lower verbal and performance ability, impaired reading and arithmetic achievement
Behavior:	Associated with behavioral problems in children, attention deficit disorder, hyperactivity disruptive behaviors (at 10 years of age)
Neuroimaging:	9- to 11-year-old children exposed to opiates had smaller brain volumes, thinner cortex, and reduced pallidum and putamen size.

POSSIBLE EFFECTS OF PRENATAL METHAMPHETAMINE EXPOSURE   The drug that is readily available and much sought after on our streets today is meth (i.e., methamphetamine). Service providers and caregivers working with children who may be impaired by prenatal meth exposure are clamoring for research results that determine possible effects of the exposure as well as intervention strategies specific to the learning and behavioral special needs presented. However, the idiosyncratic nature of the drug's manufacturing process (i.e., the "ingredients" of the "recipe" most often vary from batch to batch and "manufacturer" to "manufacturer" with ephedrine as the only constant) obstructs researchers' efforts to determine the long-term impact of prenatal meth exposure. Longitudinal research available thus far consists of sample populations studying the impact of prenatal meth exposure on mice that carefully control for variables that may lead to inaccurate conclusions. If the same controls could be applied to human studies about the effects of prenatal exposure to methamphetamines, we are sure that volumes could be written.

Neonatal Abstinence Syndrome

Neonatal abstinence syndrome (NAS) (National Institutes of Health and Prevention, 2011) potentially occurs when a pregnant woman ingests addictive substances, including prescription, drugs during the pregnancy. Drugs pass through the placenta and reach the developing fetus. If the mother becomes chemically dependent on the substance, the fetus does as well. If that mother continues substance use throughout the pregnancy, mother and baby are still chemically dependent on the drug at birth. If the drug dependence is unknown to those caring for mother/baby at delivery, symptoms of withdrawal may be unrecognized and medical treatment delayed.

NAS symptoms depend on the drug used; the quantity of the drug used; the period of time over which the drug was used; whether other substances were used during the pregnancy as well; and the length of time in utero (i.e., premature to full-term birth). NAS symptoms can present within 1 to 3 days after birth, or 5 to 10 days following birth. NAS symptoms are consistent with the symptoms presented by the child's mother. Treatment for the symptoms varies and is determined by medical professionals.

Implications for Interventions

The first recommendation relates to individual interventions, which are "simple but not easy." The truth is that any old intervention won't do the job of assisting the person with cognitive impairment resulting from in utero exposure to alcohol. Perhaps the most difficult step is the acceptance that the area(s) of deficit result in an inability to carry out certain life functions (i.e., it's not about won't, it's about can't)."

Individual interventions build on the person's strengths and include simple strategies such as consistently providing routine, repetition, ritual, predictability, and structure; minimizing transitions and keeping environmental stimuli at a minimum; teaching by role play and multiple sensory modalities, and so on. This is far from a complete list, but it provides an idea of how extensive and pervasive the interventions need to be.

Another concept that is very important for caregivers and service providers to understand is that once supportive interventions result in positive learning and behavioral outcomes, those interventions *must not* be eliminated. In addition, if the intervention(s) does not result in the hoped-for outcome, changes must be made by the caregivers and service providers.

Doctor's second intervention recommendation for the person with an FASD is that dynamic case management (DCM) be used. Briefly stated, DCM expands *intra-agency* case management to *interagency* case management. This model pulls together representatives of each agency providing services to the individual with an FASD so that they collectively collaborate to develop a *single case management plan* accommodating the life circumstances of that individual. If the individual is receiving services from alcohol/drug treatment, probation, drug court, Child Protective Services, and so on, each agency generates a plan that addresses their process with that person. Someone with an FASD usually finds it difficult to be in compliance with one case management plan, let alone three or four. DSM addresses this dilemma and leads to positive outcomes for the one served.

It is imperative to assess the protocols and policies that enhance or obstruct the provision of services for the person with an FASD. This is far easier to say than to do, since in many cases it is the agency's policies/protocols that stand in the way of adequate provision of services and that complicate the life of the individual with an FASD. Rather than being thwarted by a policy issue, the support team is encouraged to consider "plan B," a method of getting the desired results despite interference from a damaging policy. Conversely, it is imperative to evaluate the agency's policies that are an asset to the provision of services for a person with an FASD.

Interpersonal Exposure to Alcohol and Other Drug Abuse

Fraser, McAbee, and the Committee on Medical Liability (2004) maintain that between 11 and 17.5 million children in the United States younger than 18 currently live with a parent with alcoholism. The number of children living in homes where other drugs are abused is relatively unknown. However, multiple studies confirm that many children do experience negative effects as a result of being exposed to the interpersonal and environmental influences of AOD abuse in their homes (Eiden, Molnar, Colder, Edwards, & Leonard, 2009; Coppello et al., 2005; Hussong et al., 2010). Studies demonstrate that children who grow up in homes where AOD are abused may view themselves as worthless, may feel unimportant as a result of being consistently rejected, and may feel responsible for their parents' substance abuse (Towers, 1989). Around the holidays, especially, elementary-school-aged children of alcoholics may become moody and "withdrawn, irritable, and certainly not ready or able to participate with the rest of the class and the teacher in holiday-related lessons and activities" (Towers, 1989, p. 20). Another result may be seen in the young child's expressed defiance toward activities of these kinds. It is thought that reasons for this behavior center on the child's anxiety regarding a family get-together or celebration in which drugs will likely be abused.

In a review of the literature, Kroll (2004) used content analysis to investigate the impact of AOD misuse on children. Findings revealed that children's lives were affected in six overarching areas: denial, distortion and secrecy; attachment—separation and loss; family functioning—conflict and breakdown, violence, abuse, and living with fear; role reversal, role confusion and child as caretaker; and what children would say that they needed. A study by Ohannessian and Kesselbrock (2009) found that children have feelings of hostility and guilt as well.

Apart from the idiosyncratic behaviors demonstrated during or around holidays, general feelings of alienation can lead children into social isolation and reinforce the child's beliefs that they are socially incompetent. A child who comes to school having slept little the night before because of anxiety or because of parental fighting or abuse cannot really be expected to perform well. As a result, the child's self-concept can be diminished by repeated failures at learning. A vicious cycle can be born. The result can be that the child feels hopeless, fearful, and lonely. In some cases, the effects can be fateful. Although the impact on children is not always severe, the possibility exists that parental drug abuse may be a significant factor in adolescent suicide attempts.

More often than not and depending on the child's age when first encountering parental alcohol or other drug abuse, the impact of interpersonal and environmental exposure will be reflected in the school classroom and can affect students' hygiene, cognitive issues such as concentration, achievement, attitudes toward learning, attitudes toward teachers and others in authority, attitudes toward classmates, attendance, completion of homework assignments, and participation in extracurricular activities and sports (Lawson & Lawson, 1998; Towers, 1989; Woolfall & Sumnall, 2010).

IMPLICATIONS FOR INTERVENTION   The Centers for Disease Control and Prevention (CDC) (2010e) suggest that school connectedness is a significant protective factor that can help insulate children from substance abuse and a range of other maladaptive behaviors. These factors include having adult support, belonging to a positive peer group, having a commitment to education, and having positive perceptions of the school environment. Counselors and social workers who work in the schools will be faced not only with student–clients who are children of alcoholics but will, as well, be consulting with teachers who attempt to teach these children. Helping teachers become familiar with the symptoms is important. Teachers need to know basic facts about AOD abuse. With some empathic guidance from school counselors and social workers, teachers can emphasize the need to make their classrooms safe havens where students can learn to overcome their difficulties and experience success. As in dealing with children affected by in utero exposure to AOD, school counselors can help teachers emphasize the need for structure in their classrooms where children can learn or reinforce appropriate social skills. Helping teachers see the need for students' healthy expression of feelings, including anger and frustration, and helping teachers see the need for activities that aim at bonding, autonomy, and problem solving can aid in helping students develop protective factors against drug abuse and can help with students' self-esteem and successes at learning in school.

FAMILY EXPOSURE TO ALCOHOL AND OTHER DRUGS

So far, we have discussed the effects of AOD misuse only on children. Substance misuse can also negatively impact other family members and disrupt a range of family dynamics and processes including family rules and rituals, routines, communication structures, social life, finances, homeostasis, and family roles (Arcidiancono et al, 2010; Copello et al., 2005). Rhodes, Bernays, and Houmoller (2010) reviewed the literature of the impact of drug use on parenting and of the impact of parental drug use on the family functioning. These researchers concluded that drug use is "overwhelmingly damaging." No consistent or accurate figures that estimate the number of family members who are affected by substance misuse are available. However, in taking a global perspective, Copello, Templeton, and Powell (2010) estimate that a minimum of 91 million family members are affected across the world.

Homeostasis

Regardless of ethnicity, families are dynamic systems and are influenced by changes that occur both within and outside of the family context. The larger social, political, and economic forces exert their influence in the family from the outside, while internal changes such as illness, aging, entering and leaving the family, changes occurring in the workplace, changing geographical locations, and changes in stress levels affect families from within.

Jackson (1957) first used the term *family homeostasis* to describe the natural tendency of families to behave in such a manner as to maintain a sense of balance, structure, and stability in the face of change. Significant to the concept of homeostasis is the notion that, as one family member experiences change in his or her life, the entire family will be affected and will adjust in some fashion. Family members can adjust overtly and covertly in an effort to maintain this balance and will exert much effort during times when the balance is threatened. This natural resistance can be both a blessing and a bane: by facing some changes with resistance, families can avoid losing their structures and becoming chaotic systems. However, there will inevitably be times when change requires the family to adjust (Gladding, 2011).

During these times, the family, to varying degrees, will need to reorganize its roles, rules, boundaries, and values to create a new balance that fits. If families are too resistant to change, they can become rigid and unable to adjust adequately, and family dysfunction can follow. For example, Ewing and Fox (1968) describe the alcoholic marriage as a homeostatic mechanism that is "established to resist change over long periods of time. The behavior of each spouse is rigidly controlled by the other. As a result, an effort by one person to alter typical role behavior threatens the family equilibrium and provokes new efforts by the spouse to maintain status quo" (p. 87). Alcohol is seen as playing a key role in attempting to maintain the status quo in alcoholic families.

Wegscheider (1981) believes that, in an alcoholic family, members attempt to maintain balance by compulsively repressing their feelings while developing survival behaviors, as well as emotional walls, to ward off the pain associated with the family member's drinking. If drinking is removed from the family system, the family can be thrown into chaos. For example, an alcoholic father who becomes sober may attempt to reexert his influence as head of the household, thus throwing the marriage out of the balance to which it had become accustomed. The mother is no longer needed as a buffer between the children and their father, so she fades into the background as the children begin to address their father directly. The oldest son is no longer the surrogate father and begins acting out his frustration. The relationship between the mother, who has relied upon this son for support, and her son becomes strained as the father cannot hide his jealousy over this relationship. Unless the family can adjust adequately, drinking may be initiated again to reestablish balance.

Roles

FAMILY ROLES   We pointed out in Chapter 4 the variety of roles assumed by culturally and ethnically diverse families. Roles are an important part of Euro-American families as well. Role is often defined by the individual's behaviors in performing the rights and obligations associated with a certain position, and usually involves a set of complementary expectations concerning one's own actions as well as the actions of others with whom one is involved (Gladding, 2011). Irrespective of the presence of alcohol, one of the basic principles of family homeostasis is predictable family roles. Through these roles, family members can act out the overt and covert family rules in an effort to maintain homeostasis within the family system. According to Satir (1964), because the marital relationship is the "axis around which all other family relationships are formed" (p. 1), it is the interaction of roles in the marital relationship that influences the character of the family homeostasis.

Roles can also be further divided into affective and instrumental areas. Instrumental roles are those aimed at addressing the day-to-day human needs. The latter, affective roles, have particular significance in alcoholic or other drug-abusing families. Often in these families, certain individuals will experience and express particular emotions for the family. For example, the alcoholic who becomes angry and sullen when drunk may be carrying the anger for other family members who have difficulty in expressing this emotion. So, when the alcoholic gets angry, things may finally be said (inappropriately or not) to other family members that might not be discussed otherwise because the sober family members do not overtly express their own hostility. In this example, the anger role is carried by the alcoholic, and the emotions of sadness and helplessness may be carried and expressed by other nonalcoholic family members.

CHILDHOOD ROLES   Children in families carry two essential roles. One role is that of child. The other is the role of family member. Roles exist within roles, and the child may assume any of them. For example, many believe that birth order in the Euro-American family affects the child's role in the family and see the oldest child as taking on a dominant role with the second child taking on a more rebellious role. Youngest children are often used to having things done for them and take on a more passive role. While birth order alone does not determine an individual's perception of relationships, it does have an influence.

These two role structures remain fairly constant across families of varying ethnic and racial origins. However, the manner in which these roles are played out in the family as well as in the larger social contexts is different. For instance, many Latino families who immigrate to the United States may leave some of their children behind temporarily for practical and financial reasons. In these situations, the mother may tend naturally to overcompensate by showering abundant affection upon those with whom she does have contact. As a result, Latino children may appear infantilized or overprotected to Euro-American teachers and counselors when, in fact, the family's transitions and subsequent reorganization may greatly intensify these behaviors (Garcia-Preto, 2005). In more traditional families, children may also have bonded with their mothers, and the centrality of their position allows them to wield great power when it is used against a disengaged, authoritarian father (Giordano & McGoldrick, 2005). For African American youth, significant family difficulties may be brought on by the compounding effects of poverty, racism, and the general vulnerabilities of adolescence. Families in poverty will vary in structure, coping styles, and levels of resilience (Hines & Boyd-Franklin, 2005). Some families may support themselves by exchanging resources within their family support systems. Ho (1992) and other researchers maintain that in many Asian American families, the roles of family members are highly interdependent. The family structure is arranged so that conflicts in the family are minimized in order not to disrupt family peace and harmony. Even when adult children marry, allegiance to their parents—especially among the adult sons—is to remain paramount. Male offspring have especially revered roles in traditional Asian American families. Native American perceptions of family are universal in that the entire universe is thought of as a family in which every member serves a useful and necessary function. The Native American child may live in several different households at various times (Iron Eye Dudley, 1992). In these traditional Native families, grandparents, aunts, uncles, and community members are all responsible for the raising of the children. One can readily see how the roles of the child in Native American families are both stable and quite varied (Sutton & Broken Nose, 2005).

Little data exist on childhood roles among culturally and ethnically diverse populations in alcoholic or other drug abusing families. Most, although not all, of what we know about childhood roles in AOD-abusing families is the result of early clinical impressions of the Euro-American population and the research that has been reported in the popular literature (Vernig, 2011). It is clear that the roles are very difficult to operationalize, and the researchers' attempts to operationalize roles has not produced consistent results.

Nonetheless, while their clinical utility may not be as significant as previously thought, some understanding of the potential roles and dynamics that can occur in families is important.

Black (1981) described the roles adopted by children of alcoholic homes as based upon their perceptions of what they need to do to survive and bring stability to their lives. It was Wegscheider (1981) who first described the dysfunctional family roles of "hero," "scapegoat," "lost child," "mascot," and "enabler." Other researchers have written about these roles since Wegscheider's initial identification.

According to Howard et al. (2010), the hero or heroine child is often a compulsive high achiever who, through accomplishments, defocuses attention from the alcoholism in the family system. Music, sports, and academics are frequent arenas in which the heroes or heroines act out their roles, often at the expense of their own needs. Because they can often excel in one or more undertakings, they create the impression that their family must be quite well adjusted. In our own practice, we have seen many adolescents who are valedictorians, captains of sports teams, cheerleaders, and/or student government officers who come from homes where alcohol is abused.

The scapegoat child is seen as acting out the family problem by demonstrating defiance and irresponsibility. The unconscious or conscious agenda for these children is to create a need for overt parental attention as they attempt to defocus from the problem of alcohol.

Lost children are believed to be shy, withdrawn, and require very little attention so that the family does not have to worry about them These children often cope through avoidance that, unfortunately, leaves them isolated from the joys and richness of life, feeling unloved and unworthy of love.

The family mascot is the funny and often mischievous child who defuses the tension inherent in alcoholic families. In the classroom, this child may act out as the class clown.

The enabler is the person who attempts to protect the alcoholic or drug addict from experiencing the natural and logical consequences of his or her behavior. These roles are seen as survival roles in alcoholic families and are deemed as dysfunctional or maladaptive in that they do not allow children to experience the normal, full range of emotions and behaviors.

Family Rules

All culturally and ethnically diverse families as well as Euro-American families have overt and covert contracts between their members that operate as rules governing family interactions (Gladding, 2011). In general, these rules govern (1) what, when, and how family members can communicate their experiences about what they see, hear, feel, and think; (2) who has permission to speak to whom about what; (3) the extent and manner in which a family member can be different; (4) the manner in which sexuality can be expressed; (5) what it means to be a male or female; and (6) how family members acquire self-worth and how much self-worth a member can experience. In all likelihood, culturally and ethnically diverse families are governed by these same rules. The only differences between these families revolves around what happens if the rules are broken. For example, a Euro-American family may punish the child who has talked back to his or her parents. An Asian American family might use shame to correct aberrant behavior.

CASE EXAMPLE

Tony and His Family

In 1981, Black stated three imperatives or rules that govern alcoholic families: Don't talk; Don't trust; Don't feel. In families where alcohol and other drugs are abused, these rules form the basis for family interactions and for the alliances between individual family members and society at large.

Tony, a very successful businessman, was married to Mary, and they had three children: Loretta, Mark, and Donnie, ages 16, 15, and 9. Tony was an alcoholic, but nobody in the family believed his drinking to be problematic. That was rule 1: Do not believe that your father has a drinking problem.

Every night when he arrived home after 12 hours on the job, the children would come downstairs and greet their father, then allow him to change clothes while their mother would mix their father's usual drink: his favorite Scotch with crushed ice. She would have a glass of red wine. The children would leave their mother and father alone to discuss the day. That was rule 2: Do not disturb your father's ritual.

Even when the children had something exciting to talk about that had occurred during the day, they were not to disrupt the ritual until it was time for dinner. Gathered around the table, with Tony nursing his second or third drink or even a beer, the children would then "report" the day to their father. The children were not allowed to leave the table until everyone, including their Dad, was finished. Sometimes, if Tony was drinking a lot, the dinner could last an entire evening. Frustrations about wasting time at dinner were not to be discussed; however, when they were eventually aired, out of exasperation, Tony would most often respond by becoming argumentative, oppressive, threatening, and upon occasion physically abusive. This was rule 3: Your father is the head of the household and you must do exactly as he wants.

When Tony lost his temper at the table, Mary would jump in to mediate between Tony and the children. Usually, the fighting occurred between Tony and Mark, the oldest son, so Mary usually wound up arbitrating between these two. While they did not like the situation, Loretta and Donnie did appreciate Mark's intervening on their behalf because it allowed dinner to be over. The shouting and threatening behavior created so much chaos that Loretta and Donnie could slip away while Mary, Tony, and Mark were fighting it out. This was rule 4: Mark is the scapegoat.

Two or three times during the week, dinners would proceed in a fashion similar to that just described. Hence, rule 5: Even when things are unpleasant and could be changed, do not change the family.

The weekends were just an extension of the weekdays, except that on the weekends Tony would play tennis in the mornings rather than spend time with the family and would begin drinking at lunchtime. Often, he would come home drunk or noticeably high from alcohol. If he had had a good game of tennis, his mood would be pleasant; if he played poorly, he was easily agitated. The children knew enough to be gone all day Saturday to avoid whatever might occur, while Mary would do household chores until Tony came home. Because Tony and Mary would usually go out on Saturday night, the children would most often find something to do until they were sure that their dad and mom were out of the house before coming home to eat the meal their mother had prepared for them. On Saturday nights, whoever was home would sit watching television with the lights out, prepared to run to their rooms and feigning sleep at the first sign of their parents' arrival home.

It was Loretta who first asked her mother about her dad's drinking. This occurred after the school counselor had done a guidance unit on alcohol and other drugs during Loretta's fifth-period social studies class. Her mother readily confessed to having similar concerns but told Loretta that her dad worked very hard and everyone should be understanding because he was under a great deal of stress. She told Loretta not to worry and to keep this information between the two of them. Rule 6: Do not talk about your feelings about your dad's drinking problem to anyone.

As Tony's drinking progressed over the next two years, Mark became the focus of his dad's displaced hostility. Mark felt as if he could do nothing right in his father's eyes, and, during his later teen years, began to express his own hostility toward his dad. However, when Mark confronted his dad about how unreasonable he was when he drank, his father would respond by yelling, pointing his finger in his son's face, and would eventually become more angry than his son. Mark learned to back down, swallowing his pride, his feelings, and his lowered sense of self-respect. Gradually, his grades began to drop. In spite of his being a very talented golfer, Mark lost his eligibility to participate in athletics due to his grades. Having lost his friends who were busy participating in after-school sports, Mark fell into a crowd who used alcohol and other drugs, and he began drinking alcohol on the weekends and eventually began using marijuana and cocaine. Loretta continued her attempts to soothe her father's nerves by doing whatever he asked but emotionally removed herself from the family and focused her attentions on her boyfriend and her grades. She confided in Mark that she couldn't wait to get out of the house. Donnie was his mother's favorite, and Mary did everything she could to protect Donnie from her husband. Donnie was able to escape the direct wrath of his father by keeping quiet, getting straight A's, and devoting himself to helping his mother.

What was most confusing to Loretta, Mark, and to some extent to Donnie was how their father could be seen as so successful at work, yet be so different at home. When their father was away on business trips and the discussion about his drinking would come up during dinner, Mary would consistently respond by saying that the children's father loved them very much so they need not worry. When pressed by Loretta and Mark, their mother would usually start crying, saying that she did not know what to do, yet she would balk at suggestions to see a counselor and/or confront their dad. Loretta and Mark would comfort their mother by telling her that she was a good mother and that she did not need to cry because her children loved her. Rule 7: Believe that your mother is helpless and that you need to take care of her.

This example shows how rules are developed and maintained by family members. Nobody was supposed to confront the alcohol problem because "there was no alcohol problem." That their father loved the children was supposed to be enough. There was to be no anger. If that rule were broken, Tony would become angrier than anyone, thereby overpowering the family's anger and sending it back into a repressed state. Eventually the children, especially Loretta and Mark, learned to control their emotions—especially anger, hurt, and fear. The rigidity of the rule "don't talk, don't trust, don't feel" led to Loretta's desire to leave the family and to never confront her father, so that her father never knew how she really felt. Mark responded to his feelings of helplessness and frustration by internalizing his shame and coming to believe that he was to blame for his father's drinking since he was usually the one who fought with his dad. As a result of his internalized shame, he began using drugs and acted out his helplessness by becoming irresponsible, thus neglecting his own desires and hopes in life. Donnie eventually became the family "hero" by getting exceptional grades and becoming involved in student government. He posed "no threat and no problem" to the family. Mary worked herself to the bone as a mediator between her children and their father, all the while attempting to become the apple of her husband's eye. Her whole life was her family, and the centrality of her position provided her with a sense of meaning in an otherwise unhappy marital situation. Because these family rules were rigid, the family system functioned to maintain itself as best it could, but there were grave consequences. In spite of the severity of the consequences, the family was unable to adjust until Tony's alcohol problem was addressed and the rules changed.

Underlying Family Themes

Reilly (1992) identifies two underlying themes that serve to fuel the interactive patterns of families experiencing drug abuse: impaired mourning and homeostasis collusion. Impaired mourning refers to the family's preoccupation with "issues of attachment and separation, loss and restoration, and death and rebirth" (p. 109). Because of the strong sense of loss, either through abandonment, death, divorce, rejection, or neglect, concomitant with an inability to transform the experience, children never fully grieve the loss, and the family can become stuck. In the example, Tony's drinking problem precluded his ability to develop a strong attachment to his family. The ensuing abandonment left his children and his wife grieving for a relationship with him. The rules were such that any attempt to work through the grieving process would have been met with severe opposition from Tony. So the children and their mother were left to deal with the problem either indirectly or surreptitiously. As a result, the family was not able to fully grieve the loss of a functional and healthy relationship with their father.

Remember how, in Chapter 4, we discussed the issue of Native American mourning and its impact on the risk factors for AOD abuse among this population? Knowing that impaired mourning seems to be characteristic of alcoholic families in general, you can readily see how the issue of impaired mourning may have an additive effect with regard to the Native American family. That is, mourning for their lost culture has been cited as increasing the risk among Native Americans for substance abuse (Young, 1992), and impaired mourning is seen as fueling the dysfunctional interactive patterns among families once AOD are abused in the family. It would seem that mourning, in some form, can be seen as both partly causing alcoholism and helping to maintain the resulting dysfunctional family patterns in the Native American population.

When the whole family becomes stuck or unable to transform itself due to its following the "don't talk, don't trust, don't feel" rule, as it did in this case example, family collusion can occur (Haley, 1973; Noone & Reddig, 1976). Paul (1967) points out that families who have not grieved the losses in the early cycles of their system develop a family style that reflects a lack of empathy, a lack of respect for individuality, and a tenacious and unconscious attempt to hold back the passage of time, with the concomitant need to keep individual family members in a dependent position.

Paul's (1967) study demonstrates how family collusion results from a break in the grieving process and how it reinforces the interactive patterns characteristic of families with AOD abuse. In the example, Mark turned to using AOD as a means to identify with his father. Eventually, Mark's problem became the focus of attention for the family, thereby diminishing the centrality of Tony's drinking. Mark gained much power in the family because he became a rallying point around which the family could address issues of his drug abuse. Without that rallying point, Mary might have chosen to leave the marriage. She stayed in order to help the family deal with Mark's problems. Also, the family colluded and remained stuck because they covertly reinforced Mark's drug problems. Loretta would occasionally buy marijuana for her brother and often bought him beer until he became of legal age. When she periodically found drug paraphernalia in her son's room, Mary chose to not confront Mark. And Donnie remained distant from his older brother, although he loved him deeply. While these were all conscious decisions, the family members unconsciously knew that, if Mark's problems were addressed and corrected, Tony's alcohol problems would once again become the focal point of concern as well as reminding each of their shame, grief, and helplessness. To avoid the pain, the family unconsciously colluded to keep Mark the scapegoat and the family member with the problem.

Clearly, the character and extent of family collusion in culturally and ethnically diverse families will be influenced by family values, by values regarding AOD, and by the degree of acculturation among family members. The collusion transpiring in Latino/Hispanic, African American, and Asian American families could include extended family members who likely live nearby and who probably share in child rearing, discipline, and problem solving. Gallardo and Curry (2009) found that "escapist drinking" of alcohol is an accepted way of dealing with the stresses of acculturation for Latino/Hispanic males, and that the value of *machismo* tends to strengthen that notion. In this example, should the alcoholic family member be a less acculturated male, then family collusion might include the male members of the immediate and extended family who share a common value of machismo. The resulting collusion might serve to sharpen the differences between male and female family members as well as exacerbate the generic difficulties found in the process of acculturation.

Family Subsystems and Boundaries

All families, regardless of cultural or ethnicity diversity, are made up of subsystems and boundaries. The Euro-American family essentially consists of three family subsystems: marital, parental, and sibling. In Native American, Asian American, African American, and Latino/Hispanic families, the family subsystems would include, to varying degrees, extended family members or other significant individuals. For example, the participation of godparents in the child-rearing practices of many Latino/Hispanic families and its parallel value, known as "child-keeping," seen in many African American families, might reflect an extended parental subsystem.

The primary subsystem is the marital or couple subsystem made up of the wife and husband. This subsystem is closed in that certain duties and primary functions are performed only by the married partners (e.g., earning money, managing the home). With the birth of a child, the marital subsystem extends to that of a parental subsystem. Interactions continue between the marital partners, which are aimed at the marriage itself (e.g., having a romantic dinner after the child is asleep) or are carried out between the spouses with an aim toward their parenting (e.g., juggling schedules to cover child care). A third main subsystem is the sibling subsystem. The number of children, along with their ages, sexes, and interests, will suggest the number of potential sibling subsystems. In addition, African American and Latino/Hispanic families may have sibling subsystems that include cousins.

Rules or boundaries help define these subsystems. Boundaries are like fences surrounding one's home: They define one's property and regulate the nature and type of interactions between neighbors. In essence, boundaries result from cultural and family values and define who can talk to whom, when one can talk, and what one can talk about. Regardless of cultural or ethnic background, both subsystems and boundaries need to be flexible enough to allow for adjustments to changes brought on either within the family or as a result of outside influences. However, in families where AOD are abused, boundaries are often violated (Kelley et al., 2007).

Our example of Tony and Mary reflected a disengaged family in which Tony was rather removed from his spouse and his children. The children were not allowed to talk with their father about his drinking problem and so began to disengage and live their lives emotionally distant from other family members. With the onset of Mark's drug use, the disengaged nature of the family made it very difficult to regroup in order to address the underlying issue that was Tony's alcohol abuse. Nor was the family able to find ways to deal effectively with Mark's drug use. To avoid interacting with her father, Loretta spent all of her available time with her boyfriend. Donnie, despite his strong feelings for his older brother, remained rather aloof from him because he didn't understand or like what his brother was doing. Mary, the mother, was emotionally removed from her husband after years of emotional neglect by him. She tolerated her husband's drinking patterns so that she could avoid conflict and more hurt and pain in their relationship.

The issue of disengagement is clearly culturally biased. In traditional Asian American families, the father is expected to be disengaged. Therefore, the construct of disengagement would not always be an appropriate measure of family unity. An African American male who works two jobs and is not home much in order to help get his family out of poverty may be labeled as disengaged when, in fact, his disengagement is a healthy adaptation to poverty. Likewise, "el amor de madre" (motherly love), a value highly regarded in Latino/Hispanic families, could be described as enmeshment, but this enmeshment is central to Latino/Hispanic culture and is not seen as dysfunctional behavior.

Where AOD abuse exists, all families, regardless of cultural or ethnic background, act as "the fulcrum, the pivot point, the mediator, and the interpreter between its members and their culture" (Reilly, 1992, p. 105). The family thus is seen as having a significant influence upon the socialization of its members. As a social lens, the family screens, filters out, or magnifies social influences from the outside. These influences may be antisocial. Reilly maintains that the disturbed Euro-American family system needs a symptom bearer, and this would be the member who is susceptible to drug abuse. In our example, the symptom bearer was Mark, the eldest son. Reilly also believes that the family will consciously or unconsciously push this individual into antisocial, drug-abusing values as was reflected in our case example.

THE MARITAL OR COUPLE SUBSYSTEM Living with an addicted partner is demanding and difficult. Research suggests that partners affect the long-term drinking patterns of their partners most strongly in the initial phase of their relationship (Otten, van der Zwaluw, van der Vorst, & Engels, 2008). Additionally, some research suggests that heavy drinking does have deleterious effects on the drinkers' health.

McKinney, Caetano, Rodriguez, and Okoro (2010) found that the marital relationship where alcoholism exists reflects communication that is hostile, critical, and disapproving. As alcoholism progresses, the communication between spouses tends to increase in hostility, thereby suggesting a growing cycle of hostility and resentment. The cycle of hostility produces couples who are at greater risk for relationship dissolution, unless couples have similar drinking patterns. This means that couples where one drinks and the other spouse does not are more likely to dissolve the relationship than in those relationships where both drink (Ostermann, Sloan, & Taylor, 2005). Dethier, Counerotte, and Blairy (2011) found that the alcoholic's wife experiences quite a bit of stress, including verbal and physical abuse, and this eventually leads to a lowering of her self-esteem. If the relationship lasts into older adulthood, and the drinker stops drinking, research suggests that the nondrinking spouse can regain a sense of efficacy (Moos, Brennan, Schutte, & Moos, 2010).

THE PARENT–CHILD SUBSYSTEM In a seminal study, Kaufman and Kaufman (1992) identified structural patterns in families affected by AOD abuse, based on the works of Minuchin (1974). Most of their sample was observed for more than six months, and the research design included postgroup discussions of patterns. In addition, verbatim transcripts of all sessions were made and were analyzed to confirm initial clinical impressions. Videotapes were produced and were given to a group of experienced clinicians who rated the structural patterns they observed. The sample consisted of 75 families representing eight different ethnic groups (Latino/Hispanic, 23%; Italian, 19%; Euro-American, 18%; Jewish, 13%; African American, 10%; Irish, 9%; Greek, 1%; and

Mixtures, 6%). Kaufman and Kaufman found that of the 75 families, 88% had enmeshed (undifferentiated boundaries) mother–child relationships and 40% had enmeshed father–child relationships. Forty-two percent of the fathers were considered disengaged while only two mothers were seen as such. The mothers of addicts were seen as enmeshed across all ethnic groups. Seven of 13 Italian fathers were described as enmeshed as were six of 13 Jewish fathers. Puerto Rican, African American, and Euro-American fathers tended to be disengaged. The authors found that, while the sample of African Americans was too small to generalize, "most of the Black families had strong, involved mothers" (p. 39). Categorically, no relationship between the addicted family member and other family members was seen as having clear boundaries. A more recent study of Japanese drinking in relationships found that women's care of their alcoholic husbands was institutionalized and normalized by Japanese views of human relationships that values female dependency (Borovboy, 2009). Hence, a traditional Japanese female spouse would likely be hesitant to confront her drinking husband.

In a study on family dysfunction and alcoholism, Dube, Anda, Felitti, Edwards, and Croft (2002) found interesting results. These researchers agree with the professional literature indicating the relationship between adult alcohol abuse and childhood abuse and family dysfunction. However, Dube et al. were interested in the impact of multiple adverse childhood experiences (ACEs) with parental alcohol abuse and later alcohol abuse by the child. From their data, they categorized eight adverse childhood experiences associated with parental alcohol abuse. The results indicated a strong association between each of the eight adverse childhood experiences and risk for later alcohol abuse. When multiple ACEs were involved, it did not seem to matter whether parental alcohol abuse was involved or not. Compared to persons with no ACEs, those experiencing multiple ACEs were two to four times more likely to self-report adult alcoholism, marry an alcoholic, and be at risk for heavy drinking.

While many studies show that dysfunctional family structure imposes a significant influence on the risk for AOD use patterns among family members (e.g., Barrett & Turner, 2006; Dunn et al., 2002; Ledoux, Miller, Choquet, & Plant, 2002; Meness, 2000), other studies offer hope for families. Results of a systematic review of longitudinal studies on parenting factors associated with adolescent alcohol indicates that families provide strong protective factors against AOD abuse (Ryan, Jorm, & Lubman, 2010). Specifically, these authors identified protective factors that include parental modeling, limiting availability of alcohol to the child, parental monitoring, high quality parent–child relationship, parental communication, and general parental involvement with their children.

THE SIBLING SUBSYSTEM Siblings do appear to have an influence on adolescent drug use in terms of providing the drug and/or modeling drug behaviors (e.g. Friese, Grube, Seninger, Paschall, & Moore, 2011; Slomkowski et al., 2009). In a seminal study, Kaufman & Kaufman (1992) studied the impact of siblings upon sibling drug use. In their study, the researchers identified an *environmental reactive mechanism,* which refers to the ways in which brothers are linked through their environment. That is, when the relationship between brothers is characterized by tension, there appears to be an increase in the intrapsychic distress in the younger brother. As a result of that distress, the younger brother may disengage from the relationship and withdraw from responsibility. In the case study example, Donnie's distancing from his brother exemplified the environmental reactive mechanism.

Not much research on the unique experiences of being a sibling of a "user" has been conducted. However, some general themes emerge: efforts aimed at trying to stand out, trying to step back, feelings of anger, hurt, resentment, guilt, compassion, love, frustration, hope, loss, and numerous others (Howard et al., 2010). Sibling violence is often underreported. However, an important finding is that sibling relationships characterized by violence are associated with substance abuse, delinquency, and aggression (Button & Gealt, 2010).

INTERGENERATIONAL TRANSMISSION OF ALCOHOLISM

When examining the intergenerational processes involved in the transmission of alcoholism, the terms *adult child of alcoholic* and *codependency* immediately rise to the surface. These terms are easily recognized in the AOD field. Yet one aspect often overlooked is the effect that family systems have on the transmission process. Thus, while these terms and concepts are discussed elsewhere in the text, this section focuses on the family system and structures related to the transmission process of alcoholism.

Family therapists will recognize Bowen's (1978) notions of the intergenerational emotional transmission process. This is the mechanism by which family rituals and rules are passed down from one generation to another. In the AOD field, the issue of intergenerational transmission of alcoholism is of keen interest as well, and studies consistently demonstrate that a family history of alcoholism is one of the strongest risk factors (Campbell & Oei, 2010). These same researchers agree with the works of Steinglass, Bennett, Wolin, and Reiss (1987) and Lawson, Lawson, and Rivers (2001), who maintain that the transmission of alcoholism across generations tends to involve the whole family system over time. In other words, the transmission process is both subtle and overt, and it includes the entire system of family interactions, rituals, attitudes, and beliefs that define the family. To refer to the origin of the process is something of a misnomer, as no particular starting pointing, specific ending point, or specific nodal event exists—it is an ongoing process. In general, genetics clearly play a major role in the father–son transmission of alcoholism, while family environment may be a significant factor in the transmission of alcoholism among females (Lawson et al., 2001).

Lawson et al. (2001) describe several other studies aimed at understanding the intergenerational transmission process. For instance, they cite the Bennett, Wolin, and Reiss (1988a) study that identified several behaviors tending to decrease the likelihood that alcoholism would be transmitted downward to other generations. The researchers found that spouse selection and the establishment of new family rituals in which families participate in the community are helpful to reduce risk. Moreover, these researchers found that families who utilized a selective disengagement strategy to distance themselves from the dysfunctional aspects in their families of origin reduced the transmission of alcoholism across generations. Jennison and Johnson (2001) found children modeling their parent's use of alcohol as a means to cope. In addition, these same researchers see alcoholism transmitted through a variety of disturbed family interactions that result from marital distress, health problems, legal problems, vocational/financial instability, and disrupted family rituals such as holidays, birthdays, or other special family occasions.

WOMEN AND ALCOHOLISM

Back, Contini, and Brady (2007) report that there has been a growing awareness of the importance of gender differences in medical treatment and research. Attention to gender differences is very important in light of Cyr and McGarry's (2002) review of the National Household Survey on Drug Abuse (Substance Abuse and Mental Health Services Administration, 2001) which found that women account for one-third of those abusing alcohol or having alcohol dependence. In addition to environmental and biological factors, women's substance use and addictions are mitigated by cultural norms and practices of the ethnic group to which they belong. For instance, Conner, LeFauve, and Wallace (2009) reviewed the literature on addictions among diverse women. They found that African American substance abuse was a way to numb painful feelings of loss, racism, prejudice, rejection, physical abuse, incest, and feelings of shame. Another finding was that educated, employed, and/or acculturated Hispanic women faced higher risks for addiction. These authors go on to say that, in general, the psychological fallout from historical trauma, powerlessness, marginalization, gender socialization, violence, and victimizations contribute significantly to addictions in women.

Tuchman (2010) and others (e. g. Hood, 2003; van der Walde, Urgensen, Weltz, & Hanna, 2002) have noted differences between males and females. These differences include variations in etiology, social factors, biological responses, progressions to dependence, medical consequences, co-occurring psychiatric disorders, and barriers to treatment entry, retention, completion and recovery. Specifically, women are at higher risk for breast cancer (Aronson, 2003), cardiovascular disease, osteoporosis, and hip fractures (Cyr & McGarry, 2002). Women drink most heavily during their midlife, and these women are more likely to be involved with a partner suffering from addiction. They are also more likely than men to present themselves in a more severe state of psychological or physical impairment, such as cardiovascular disease or cancer (Chang, 2002).

Assessment of Problems in Women

Some global initiatives are aimed at improving the primary care of the 2.5 million women meeting the criteria for alcohol use disorder. Nevertheless, many women with serious problems are not seen, are misunderstood, misdiagnosed, or ignored (Vandermause & Wood, 2009). The complicated presentation of symptoms is only one factor that influences the lower rate of diagnosing alcoholism in women. Women need to seek help before a diagnosis can be rendered, and research suggests that women with alcohol problems have a difficult time coming in for help. This difficulty may be due to the stigma of alcoholism and/or the associate feelings of shame. For example, Corrigan, Miller, and Watson (2006) found that the stigma of "drug dependence" was viewed as more negative than the stigma for "other mental disorders." Beckman (1994) found shame associated with drinking and not fulfilling traditional roles to be a factor in women not seeking help.

Even when women present for help at a physician's office, research indicates many more women than men deny that they have a drinking problem or that they identify problems other than drinking (Chang, 2002). The fact that their situations may be more medically complicated when they do seek help increases the likelihood that other conditions will be identified by the patient as problematic. In many cases, a diagnosis of depression will precede substance abuse (Ambrogne, 2007). This makes a diagnosis of alcoholism more difficult. A confounding result can be a diagnosis for one disorder and a misdiagnosis for another. Hence, physicians cans be prescribing medications for one disorder that obscures the symptoms of the other (van der Walde et al., 2002).

However, a more insidious factor may be the stereotyping of the disease of alcoholism itself. Conner et al. (2009) and Cyr and McGarry (2002) maintain that a major reason for not diagnosing women with alcohol problems is that alcoholism is seen as a male disease based on male characteristics. In essence, the cultural discourse has not overtly posited a connection between alcoholism and being female, and the myths that have resulted are hard to dispel. Cho and Crittenden (2006) have identified three major streams of research in the professional literature. Some research suggests that women drink more alcohol because of the multiple roles and conflicting expectations they experience when they enter the workforce. In opposition to this perspective is a second line of research holding that performing multiple roles is gratifying to women, which would preclude an increased need for drinking. A third line of inquiry is that working women simply drink more because they have more opportunity. Cho and Crittendon (2006) attempted to research women and drinking and found that drinking for women is a multidimensional construct in which adult roles "differentially influence a woman's likelihood of being a drinker, if she drinks, how much alcohol she consumes, and how likely she is to become a 'problem' drinker" (p. 27). While Cho and Crittenden's research is revealing as well as promising to spawn further research, their present results further complicate the issue. More studies and more time will be needed to re-narrate the cultural discourse to reflect the relationship between women and alcoholism.

The preceding discussion clearly points to the need for early screening of alcohol problems in women. Conner et al. (2009) believe that it is a categorical imperative that counselors understand the values and cultural expectations of diverse women when assessing for addictions. Counselors must ask themselves such questions as 1) What are the historical contributions to the shaming and destructive behaviors of diverse women? 2) Does the exploration of family histories (ethnic, cultural, familial) help build resilience or heighten risk among these women? and, 3) What are the culturally appropriate guidelines for prevention and treatment of diverse women?

As discussed in Chapter 6, the CAGE is an effective screening instrument that is easy to administer and score. Dhalla and Kopec (2007) maintain that the CAGE is less reliable for white women, prenatal women, and college students. What is important to note is that when used to screen women, the scoring on the CAGE can be adjusted. The CAGE has a cutoff score of 2. This indicates a positive for alcohol disorders in both men and women. In applying this for women, Bradley, Boyd-Wickizer, Powell, and Burman (1998) believe that a cutoff score of 1 point may be indicative of a problem. In addition, Bradley et al. found in their study of brief alcohol screening instruments that the CAGE was relatively insensitive for racial/ethnic minorities. The National Institute on Alcohol Abuse and Alcoholism (2007) recommends that the threshold for a positive AUDIT-C for women be lowered to 4 (from the standard point of 8). In all cases, these various screening instruments should be used along with other measures because their performance as stand-alone assessments is unclear (Burns, Gray, & Smith, 2010).

Treatment Concerns for Women

Clearly, the best treatment for AOD problems is primary prevention. Dethier et al. (2011), Cadiz et al. (2004), and Schuck and Spatz (2003) suggest that efforts to increase women's sense of self-efficacy are also an important protective factor in reducing the risk for alcohol use problems. They assert that this is especially true for women who have been abused or neglected. These same researchers found that high self-efficacy was significantly associated with lower levels of alcohol symptoms among women who were abused or neglected. They suggest that interventions can be aimed at showing the importance of improving educational achievement and increased feelings of self-efficacy. Schuck and Spatz believe that this can potentially be very powerful in enhancing protective factors for these women.

Women are still underrepresented in most substance abuse treatment programs.Multiple research studies have focused on the barriers that women, especially rural women, face (e.g. Greenfield & Grella, 2009; Greenfield, Trucco, McHugh, Lincoln, & Gallop, 2007; Kim, Xiang, Yang, & Lewis, 2010; Small, Curran, & Booth, 2010; Taylor, 2010). Among the barriers are social stigma, denial, fear of losing children, and a reluctance of primary care physicians to refer. Although researchers maintain that once in treatment, males and females receive similar benefits, many women who abuse alcohol have a history of sexual and physical abuse and are hesitant to come in to work through issues for fear that the environment will not be safe and gender sensitive. In addition, women are often very concerned about their children and will not present themselves for treatment because of a lack of child care. Once there, these women may drop out of treatment when a problem arises with their children. In addition, Blume (1997) found that some state laws view alcohol abuse by women as child neglect or endangerment. So, some women have a real fear that they will be considered unfit as a parent and risk losing their children. Pregnancy is also a potential barrier to treatment. Kinney (2012) says that if a woman is pregnant, many treatment programs will not admit out of fear of being liable if something goes awry. Pregnancy and drinking should be addressed early on in the process, and efforts should be focused on helping the pregnant women stop drinking or, at least, curtailing it as much as is possible. In those cases where the prospective father is also alcohol-dependent, it is critical to provide additional support and help for the mother.

In addition, economic concerns are seen as potentially significant barriers to treatment (van der Walde et al., 2002). Men will often divorce their alcoholic wives. This can leave a woman with few financial resources. Women who experience divorce are often left with inadequate insurance coverage, and if the alcoholic and divorced woman is unemployed, she is more likely to be uninsured (Blume, 1997). Even though studies show that insurance status is not a consistent predictor for who seeks treatment (Kim et al., 2010; Mojtabai, 2005), the fear of being left alone and destitute through divorce or legal separation while in treatment can preclude women from wanting to get treatment. Finally, cultural and linguistic gaps in communication, lack of familiarity with the treatment community, and concerns about discrimination and/or stigma can be a significant deterrent for diverse women seeking treatment (Taylor, 2010)

Nonetheless, a growing body of research supports gender-specific treatment for women abusing alcohol in a variety of settings (Greenfield & Grella, 2009; Sideman & Kirschbaum, 2002). In general, helpers who understand, utilize empathy, invoke good communication skills, and are gender sensitive and initially less problem-focused are seen as more helpful. Regarding gender-specific treatment, van der Walde et al. (2002) believe that to understand and appreciate the issues, counselors need to remember several other things in treating women of any racial/ethnic background. First, it is important to know that women are especially sensitive to their peers, significant others, and family members. Second, care for alcoholic women must be ongoing and focused on the individual needs of each woman. Successful treatment requires sensitivity to the plight of minority women. Krejci, Marholin, Rowland, and Wetzell (2008) and others note that substance abuse and trauma co-occur at high rates for women. Hence, the integration of relational modeling, motivational interviewing, emotional regulation, and distress tolerance should be included in the treatment of women.

McCrady (2009) believes that alcohol behavioral couple therapy (ABCT) is more effective than individual therapy in treating women alcoholics. Kinney (2012) strongly advocates for children of all ages to be included in treatment. Even though a child may appear too young to comprehend what is going on, it is important to remember that children can sometimes say what the parents are only hinting at. Leaving children out of treatment can increase their feelings of isolation and vulnerability. Kinney goes on to say the children are asking, "What will become of me?" and "Who will be taking care of me?" Because of this, children should be included in the treatment plan and allowed to ask questions in the process (p. 312). Finally, it is worth repeating that the stigma for women who abuse alcohol is a significant and deleterious factor. Clearly, regardless of whether treatment is gender specific, these issues need to be addressed with all women during treatment.

STEPFAMILIES: SYSTEM AND STRUCTURE

The Centers for Disease Control and Prevention (2009a) reported that the rate of divorces (per 1,000 total U.S. population) has fallen from 8.2 in 2000 to 6.8 in 2009. Nonetheless, this still confirms that since the 1980s, at least 50% of marriages, many with children, end in divorce (Jay, Freisthler, & Svare, 2004).

This means that, statistically speaking, it is almost as normal to come from a traditional two-parent family as it is to come from any number of alternative family structures. Unfortunately, research on the stepfamily system and structure does not usually include alternative forms of family structure. One thing seems to be clear: Children in stepfamilies are at higher risk for AOD abuse (Brown & Rinelli, 2010).

Little research has been conducted on the dynamics of other forms of parenting related to AOD. So, when discussing the research on traditionally defined stepfamilies, it is important to consider those observations in a more general way when applying the findings to racial/ethnic groups and gay and lesbian couples. Some issues may be the same for these groups as for the Euro-Caucasian population, and some issues may be different or more complex. For instance, think of how different and complex it might be for a stepfamily to learn about a previously hidden GLBTQQI lifestyle in one of their new members. This new family would not only be dealing with the adjustments of a new formation, but they would concurrently be dealing with the "coming out" of one (or more) of its members. The stepparent may be drawn into the disciplinarian role if the biological parent has been ineffective in dealing with AOD issues, and this move can result in marital strife if the biological parent steps in to protect the adolescent. Such a situation certainly reinforces the biological parent–child coalition, while continuing to exacerbate the child's feelings of guilt and stress (Jay et al., 2004). This dynamic can also lead to acting out with substance abuse. Still another variation in stepfamilies concerns adoption. Stewart (2010) maintains that adopted stepchildren have significantly more behavior and emotional issues than children with two biological parents, and this is true regardless of the age of the adoptee. The point here is that when you think of stepfamilies, you need to think of the variations and complexities.

Although many of the same problems in stepfamilies also exist in other families, stepfamilies are different in terms of the family developmental tasks. In general, stepfamilies are seen as having psychic and physical boundaries that are more permeable than those in a nuclear family (Anderson, 1992). Emotional bonds or psychic boundaries have to be loose enough to allow for affections to be expressed to both the biological parent as well as to the stepparent. The physical boundaries need to be permeable enough to allow for the revolving door of noncustodial visitation and need to be able to allow for visits of a longer duration, such as coming or leaving for an entire school year. Anderson also identifies the complexities involved in decision making in stepfamilies. Often, a coordinated effort of two households in making plans is required. The stepfamily does not have the history that the nuclear family does, and sometimes children (and their parents) can experience a type of culture shock. Anderson says that this culture shock is "an acute feeling of an unfamiliar, sometimes alien, environment that is very disorienting to their basic sense of what 'my family' is" (p. 174). Because stepfamilies are born out of previous losses due to divorce or death, children (and parents) need to be able to grieve the loss adequately. However, grieving the loss is often painful, and many may be reluctant to do so when it appears that the grieving process may impinge upon the happier times of the current relationship.

While stepfamilies have a host of issues, many factors can produce resilience in these families. For example, Greeff and Du Toit (2009) identified eight factors that can help insulate stepfamilies from problems, including those concerning AOD use and abuse: 1) supportive family relationships; 2) affirming and supportive communication; 3) a sense of control over outcomes in life; 4) activities and routines that help families spend time together; 5) a strong marital relationship; 6) support from family and friends; 7) reframing stressful events; and, 8) spirituality and religion within the family (p. 114).

HELPING FAMILIES

Helping families includes both equipping clinicians with appropriate and effective assessment techniques and providing families with the necessary level and structure of care. Assessing for AOD problems was covered in Chapter 6. Here, among other things, we want to draw your attention to issues of spirituality in families as well as to a particular assessment strategy that can help in working with various racial/ethnic families. With this information, treatment concerns for many racial/ethnic families can be better aimed.

Treating families with substance abuse problems is a complicated process, and treatment takes place on many different levels (Kaufman & Kaufman, 1992). Templeton, Belleman, and Russel (2010) conducted a review of the literature on psychological interventions with families of alcohol misusers. These researchers found that interventions involving family members fell into three essential categories: interventions oriented toward the engagement of the alcohol abusing person into treatment; interventions oriented toward working with the abuser and his or her partner; and interventions that work with family members.

Fischer, Pidcock, Munsch, and Forthun (2005) believe that the concepts of "hero" or "lost child" are easily recognized by families and are effective to use with some families in treatment. However, in discussing the process of differentiation in families, they caution against limiting the child's roles only to those roles. Interventions should expand the choices for children while honoring the role(s) that they have taken on for the family. They go further to state that when enhancing the positive roles, helpers should not do it by exaggerating the differences between siblings on the negative roles. It is critical that as helpers work through roles they do not substitute one sibling for another. In other words, in the process of helping one work through the scapegoat role, helpers should be cautioned against the possibility of another sibling taking on that role. Finally, these researchers say that in identifying positive forms of differentiation, helpers should work through a perspective of difference rather than labeling one role as better or worse than another.

SPIRITUALITY   The treatment of families is usually aimed at enhancing the cognitive, physical, emotional, and social development of individual family members. What is often overlooked is the need to help individuals and families develop spiritually. Pargament (2006) maintains that spirituality involves profound changes across development of individuals and families. Spirituality is different from religiosity in that the former emphasizes a relationship between an individual and a higher power or some other transcendent force, while religiosity refers more to religious practices and beliefs. The spiritual development in families reflects individuals attempting to differentiate themselves within families as they attempt to reconcile the dialectical tension of autonomy and connectedness. This means that individual family members are both autonomous individuals and connected members of a family. The process of differentiation increases autonomy and intimacy potential while decreasing emotional reactivity and enmeshment among family members.

Spirituality helps many families cope and be resilient. For instance, the spirituality for African American families is seen as providing buffers against the effects of structural oppression while promoting the values of compassion and service to others (Neff, 2008). In Chapter 4, we discussed the value of the collective or communalism among African Americans. This interpersonal orientation is a core spiritual value, and it is also a key component in treatment of this group for substance abuse disorders. This means that treatment should involve family, friends, church, and others because it is through others that individuals make meaning of their own existence.

In general, families who share common beliefs and who are intrinsically motivated by religious/spiritual orientation report more relationship satisfaction than those whose partners are divided on the issue. Spirituality in families can be especially helpful during times of crisis or dramatic change because it allows families to ground their stress.

To help address the spiritual issues in families, treatment often involves spiritual aspects of recovery. This orientation is clearly embedded in the twelve-step programs (see Chapter 10). However, various spiritual interventions for substance abuse treatment are available, and these vary across diverse groups. In reviewing the literature, Stoltzfus (2007) found several spiritual interventions that are used in substance abuse treatment. The Native American *sweat lodge ceremonies* use steam and high temperatures in a round, womblike structure. This process is a spiritual one in which people rid themselves of infections and contaminants while helping them contact the sacred substances that include stones, water, and the earth. *Mindfulness meditation* is another spiritual intervention that involves developing an ability to be both focused and detached while being nonjudgmental and self-accepting. *Religious treatment* programs, usually associated with evangelical churches, include such programs as Teen Challenge, Celebrate Recovery, and the Salvation Army Adult Rehabilitation Centers. *Prayer, shamanism, and exorcism* are other spiritual interventions used by diverse groups to treat substance abuse.

Because of the nature of these various spiritual treatments for AOD abuse, it is difficult to study their effectiveness. They do not easily lend themselves to scientific inquiry. A main reason is that spirituality itself is a concept, an awareness, and way of being. It cannot be separated from the rest of an individual's life because it is pervasive and incorporates all aspects of one's being. Nonetheless, its presence and power cannot be disputed, and it is wise for helpers to respect all forms of spiritual perspectives used in treating those with substance abuse issues.

Barón's Integrative Cross-Cultural Model (ICM)

In discussing addiction treatment for Mexican Americans, Barón (2000) builds on the multidimensional perspectives of several researchers and presents a model aimed at helping therapists integrate the complex individual, family, and culturally related variables that underlie and color the various beliefs, cognitions, and adaptive as well as maladaptive behaviors (p. 227). When used in assessment, this model is thought to constitute a comprehensive assessment of the internal and external influences affecting racial/ethnic minorities. The concepts still guide other culturally sensitive models such as multdimensional family therapy (Liddle, 2009).

The integrative cross-cultural model (ICM) draws from the earlier works of Jones (1985), who conducted research on African Americans. Jones's earlier model identifies four sets of interactive factors that need to be considered with minority clients and their families: (1) personal experiences and endowments, (2) influence of native culture, (3) reactions to racial oppression, and (4) influence of the majority culture (Barón, 2000; Jones, 1985). The more recent ICM enhances the earlier approach by expanding these interactive factors and reorienting them as general *domains of inquiry*. These domains of inquiry include (1) individual and systemic variables and dynamics, (2) cultural and ethnically related variables, (3) dominant group influences, and (4) minority group experiences.

Individual and systemic variables and dynamics incorporate neurobiological conditions, developmental issues, family-of-origin dynamics, childhood experiences, education, and the like. Specific to AOD issues, clients and/or their families might be queried about use, frequency, presence, toler-ance and withdrawal symptoms, alcoholic family dynamics, and the centrality of AOD in the client's life. Regarding *culturally and ethnically related variables,* clinicians would likely assess the cultur-ally based beliefs regarding AOD use and the beliefs surrounding being clean and sober. Clinicians would also find it important to assess differences in help-seeking behavior, family organization, fam-ily life cycle, hierarchies, gender roles, parenting styles, subsystems, and other related variables. The *dominant group influences* describe the extent to which the individual or family incorporates beliefs, values, attitudes, and patterns of behavior reflecting the dominant discourse. According to Barón, an assessment aimed at AOD abuse would focus on differences and similarities between the client's views of use, misuse, and abuse and those of the dominant culture. Included in this domain of assess-ment would be the identification and discussion of the client's perspectives on abstinence, sobriety, help-seeking behavior, and the twelve-step programs. Understanding the degree of congruence or incongruence with the dominant culture's view is also needed. Finally, the client's experience with being a member of a minority group (*minority group experience*) should be examined. This is a type of within-minority group variance in which the assessment would become more specific to the minor-ity person's experience as a unique minority member. According to Barón, differential treatment by members of society's dominant group as well as treatment by other minority groups related to person-ality development, beliefs, attitudes, and origin and maintenance of the current problem profoundly influence a minority person's experiences. Because of the differential effects on individuals, it is important to examine the prevalence and impact of these particular beliefs on a case-by-case basis.

The four domains are considered effective in the understanding of the significant contex-tual influences affecting the general experience of racial/ethnic minorities. When working with a racial/ethnic family suspected of having alcohol and other drug problems, a clinician using this ICM approach would first want to construct a profile based on three mediator variables: level of acculturation, stage of ethnic-identity development, and worldview related to locus of control and responsibility. From here, the clinician can advance some hypotheses about the relative con-tribution of each of the four domains of inquiry (individual and systemic variables, cultural and ethnic variables, dominant group influences, and minority group experiences) that were just de-scribed. According to Barón, the ICM can be especially helpful in the early stages of assessment.

CASE EXAMPLE   Imagine a situation in which the ICM was used with a Mexican American couple. The Mexican American couple was referred to a mental health counselor for help with Mr. Aguilar's (husband's) drinking. The *individual and systemic variables* would reveal valu-able information that could help explain why they stated they were experiencing distress over acculturating. It could reflect the fact that the Aguilars are first-generation immigrants without documents. By using the model, the clinician would easily note the Aguilars' preference to speak Spanish to one another while at home and at most places in public. The individual and systemic domain would reflect the fact that Mrs. Aguilar's mother spoke almost exclusively Spanish. As is also common, her mother also lived with her daughter and son-in-law.

The assessment would reveal that the Aguilars' children were bilingual and more ac-culturated than their parents. The model would allow the interview to guide a discussion of Mr. Aguilar's beliefs about the dominant culture being misguided and that he preferred to mingle with other Mexican Americans. His beliefs were seen as both helpful and hurtful by his children.

Questions guided by interest in the individual and systemic variables could also reveal that Mr. Aguilar had been exposed to drinking at an early age. This exposure came in a culture where heavy drinking was more tolerated. As a result, Mr. Aguilar was seen as being caught between his culture of origin and the practices of his current cultural environment with regard to AOD use. He maintained that his situation was inevitable and blamed his condition on the system. To his way of thinking, drinking was an appropriate way to cope.

An assessment of the second domain, *cultural and ethnic variables,* could reveal the family's proclivity to respond to stress through culturally congruent behaviors, which reflected more tolerance. Moreover, this assessment domain would show that the family would not ordinarily go about solving problems through the help of a therapist. In assessing the impact of the Aguilars' *dominant group and minority group experiences,* it was clear that he was resentful and bitter over his adaptation woes. Perhaps the family's most telling difficulty in seeing the problem from a different perspective was the fact that they had identified their 15 year-old son, Enrico, who was having academic problems, as the issue.

In the treatment phase of the ICM, initial efforts were aimed at establishing credibility and an effective psychological and therapeutic contract. Motivational interviewing techniques were employed to help to create dissonance for Mr. Aguilar between his perception of what his role as a father and provider needed to be and the impact that his behavior was having on his family— and on Enrico in particular. Barón (2000) suggests the use of psychoeducational approaches as well. In this case, the psychoeducational component was actually a professional's confirmation about the existence of a problem.

It was also pointed out that Enrico was not trying to be disrespectful of his father. Through family therapy, Mr. Aguilar came to see how Enrico's behaviors were a way to signal to his father that something was wrong. The fact that Mrs. Aguilar often wanted to speak to the clinician in private reflected her own cultural conflicts. She was caught between being seen as disrespectful to her husband and her need to help him to manage his problematic drinking.

In this hypothetical case, the ICM would be able to help the clinician formulate the appropriate cultural context for the Aguilars' problems. By understanding the interplay of acculturation, ethnic identity development, and worldviews related to responsibility and locus of control, the clinician was able to be more effective in the planning of treatment.

As previously mentioned in working with racial/ethnic families in Chapter 4, several authors underscore the importance of narrative approaches to individual and family treatment. Krestan (2000), Harrison (2004), and others suggest the relevancy of postmodern narrative principles in working with diverse populations. In writing about the relationship between addiction and power and powerlessness among diverse populations, Krestan discusses the influence of the dominant social discourse regarding the conceptions of power and powerlessness for racial/ethnic minorities. Krestan notes the particular challenges facing counselors in discussing the culturally powerless client's need to accept the concept of powerlessness in recovery (p. 35).

In general, the narrative approaches underscore the importance of the relationship in the helping process. A fundamental principle of the narrative and dialogic approaches is the ability of individuals to create a sense of power through the helping relationship. According to the theory, this power is then re-created over and over in the relationship so that it becomes a dominant reality for helpees (Abney & Harrison, 2003). In relating narrative principles to racial/ethnic families in need of AOD treatment, the approach itself is not so much effective as the adherence to the importance of the helping relationship developed in the process. Because the relationship between the counselor and the person being counseled is emphasized to such a great degree, it is imperative that the counselor maintain professional standards in keeping the roles of counselor and counselee distinct. Application of the narrative approach to counseling can be very effective and can open the doors to a deepened understanding and appreciation of diversity.

Krestan, Abney, and Harrison, and other researchers attempt to describe how the dominant class narrative or discourse related to power, powerlessness, and difference serves to promote the narrative discourse of risk factors for addiction among racial/ethnic families. Researchers such as Coyhis (2000), who writes about Native Americans, and Chang (2000), who writes about Asian/Pacific American addicts, are not asserting that the dominant discourse is causal. They are describing the manner in which this discourse interacts with racial/ethnic populations and the importance of understanding cultural differences in intervening so as to not promote the deleterious components of the dominant discourse.

In other research, Roberts and McCrady (2003) write about working with alcohol problems in intimate relationships. These researchers identify several modalities of change, such as family-involved treatment, change through referral, and change through self-help groups. These same authors claim that cognitive–behavioral therapy (CBT), motivational enhancement therapy (MET), and twelve-step facilitation (TSF) approaches have been empirically proven to be effective. To their credit, Roberts and McCrady also identify and discuss alternative treatment models and programs, even though these are not empirically tested. Approaches that are designed specifically for certain populations, such as gay and lesbian clients, women, racial/ethnic populations, and those programs designed to use alternative spiritual, medical, or nutritional approaches, do not lend themselves to empiricism. As a result, these treatment modalities will likely not be accepted by insurance and managed-care organizations because they are hard to measure. It would be a mistake to assume that the models themselves are ineffective simply because they cannot be measured or because managed-care does not recognize the treatment. In some cases, individuals and families can benefit from these more idiosyncratic approaches. The important thing to remember is that no one approach holds the magic key to recovery for all people. Appreciating diversity means appreciating the potential benefits of diverse approaches (Chan, 2003).

Kaufman and Kaufman's Family Types

Four types of Euro-American families will likely present themselves for treatment (Kaufman & Kaufman, 1992). In one family type, members might talk openly about drinking or drugging but are more concerned with other important issues. In these families, drinking or drugging may be present but not to the degree that it is a problem, and helping professionals should focus on the presenting problems but should also attempt to emphasize the possible connection between AOD use and other problems in their lives. In the second family type, clues to alcohol and other drug-use problems may be present, but the clues are oblique and difficult to discern. In these families, the symptom bearer will probably be the child who could be involved in drug abuse. Other clues may be found in reports of drinking in the parents' families of origin, in parental role reversals, in children's attempts to protect their parents, in children's fears of talking about the family, or when the parents present themselves as overly concerned about teenage alcohol and drug abuse. The mental health professional should focus on the presenting problem and should attempt to infuse drinking or drugging into the presenting issue. The third family type is the one whose members present themselves for therapy after the alcohol or other drug abuser has completed some type of treatment program and is clean and sober. The issues here will likely be rebalancing the family system to avoid a full-blown relapse. Slips (see Chapter 9) are to be expected, so the work of the mental health professional is to help the family anticipate situations in which a slip might occur and help the family to determine effective ways to keep the slip from becoming a relapse. The fourth family type is the one presenting alcohol or other drug abuse as the major problem. In these families, alcohol or other drug abuse is the focus of the family, and the conflict will be quite open and apparent. Mental health professionals may need to take more control of these sessions if emotional reactivity is running too high.

Regardless of which family type presents itself for counseling, mental health professionals need to attend to the spousal subsystem, the parent–child subsystem, and the sibling subsystem. The reason for this is simple: Families will balance themselves. So, mental health professionals need to take into account how interventions impact these critical subsystems, the individual family members, and the family itself so that the rebalancing that inevitably will take place will be beneficial.

Kaufman and Kaufman (1992) point to situations in which individual counseling may be the preferred mode of treatment for alcoholic families. They see individual work being done in those situations in which family therapy may be misused to deny personal responsibility, psychopathology of one family member can be prevented by individual work, the parents are psychopathological to the point that helping a child cope with the psychopathology is preferred, a family member is deceitful, individual pathology remains after family intervention, and detoxification or getting the client clean and sober is needed prior to family therapy.

Many avenues are open for helping the alcohol or other drug-abusing client or family. The actively drinking or using family member should be directed to a facility where he or she can become clean and sober. Abstinence may be just an ideal for some families. Therefore, if the individual does not want to go into treatment, the family members have a decision to make: They can learn to cope better with the abusing family member, known as maintaining a "wet" system, or they can decide to go further into an intervention (see Chapter 7) and attempt to move their family into a "dry" system. In either case, support groups for family members such as Al-Anon, Alateen, and Codependents Anonymous (see Chapter 10) can be very effective in many, but not all cases.

MyCounselingLab™

Go to Topic 8: *Family Treatment,* in the MyCounselingLab™ site (www .MyCounselingLab.com) for *Substance Abuse: Information for School Counselors, Social Workers, Therapists, and Counselors,* Fifth Edition, where you can:

- Find learning outcomes for *Family Treatment* along with the national standards that connect to these outcomes.
- Complete Assignments and Activities that can help you more deeply understand the chapter content.
- Apply and practice your understanding of the core skills identified in the chapter with the Building Counseling Skills unit.
- Prepare yourself for professional certification with a Practice for Certification quiz.
- Connect to videos through the Video and Resource Library.

Summary

- Children can be exposed to AOD use and abuse while in the uterus as well as interpersonally exposed after birth.
- Prenatal exposure to AOD is a critical health concern, because fetal alcohol syndrome is the leading known cause of mental retardation.

- In general, children interpersonally exposed to AOD abuse can take on survival roles that include hero, mascot, lost child, scapegoat, and/ or enabler.
- Research shows that these children experience a host of problems related to loss, denial,

distortion, and secrecy as well as attachment and separation, and families suffer also in terms of family functioning, violence, abuse, and living with fear.

- Children from AOD abuse families have difficulty in stating what they need or want in the family.
- Families often invoke rules such as "Don't talk, don't trust, and don't feel."
- One reason that families with AOD problems maintain dysfunction is due to underlying family themes related to impaired mourning, which revolves around separation and loss as well as family collusion.
- Stepfamilies and adoptees are at higher risk for AOD misuse and abuse due to a myriad of obvious reasons.
- Women present much later in the course of alcoholism, by which time other medical issues may obscure a diagnosis; however, once in treatment they benefit about the same as males.

- Although women account for one-third of those abusing AOD, alcoholism is still considered a "male" disease, and women alcoholics often go undiagnosed.
- The CAGE and AUDIT are assessment instruments that can be used effectively with the general as well as diverse populations; clinicians can also assess for AOD problems by being aware of Kaufman and Kaufman's four family types.
- Evidence exists that family-based interventions can work.
- Culture plays an important role in determining the type of treatment for alcoholism.
- Spiritual interventions are important for families and individuals.
- Barón's integrative cross-cultural model (ICM) for treating racial/ethnic minority families attends to four domains of inquiry that include individual and systemic variables and dynamics, cultural and ethnically related variables, dominant group influences, and minority group experiences.

Internet Resources

Fetal alcohol syndrome
cdc.gov/ncbddd/fas

Children of alcoholics
coaf.org

Stepfamilies
stepfamilies.info

Women and alcohol
pubs.niaaa.nih.gov/publications/brochurewomen/ women.htm

Family AOD treatment
treatment-centers.net/women's-recovery.html

Further Discussion

1. What, if any, drugs did your mother engage in while you were in the womb?
2. Since FAS is the leading cause of mental retardation, how is it that this is still a public health crisis?
3. Why would you think that stepfamilies and adoptees are at greater risk for AOD problems?

4. Many issues are related to women and AOD. What role does gender play in the identification and treatment concerns for women?
5. What are the reasons that diverse populations mistrust the treatment system, and what would you recommend be done to counter the problem?

Chapter 12

Adult Children
and Codependency

MyCounselingLab™

Visit the MyCounselingLab™ site (www.MyCounselingLab.com) for *Substance Abuse:
Information for School Counselors, Social Workers, Therapists, and Counselors,* Fifth Edition
to enhance your understanding of chapter concepts. You'll have the opportunity to practice your
skills through video- and case-based Assignments and Activities as well as Building Counseling
Skills units and to prepare for your certification exam with Practice for Certification quizzes.

CASE EXAMPLES

❶ At his wife's urging, Tim attended a weekend workshop on codependence. As a result of
his attendance, he began to understand what Becca (his wife) was talking about when she
would say that he was "codependent." Tim bought several books related to codependency,
ACOAs, and shame. He began attending Codependents Anonymous (CoDA) meetings during
his lunchtime. Although he was the only male in a group of seven women, he found many
common themes with what the women were reporting and what he was experiencing.

❷ Charlene is the eldest daughter of an alcoholic mother. She has a younger stepsister with
whom she has a good relationship. Her younger brother was born after Charlene's mother
stopped drinking. She states that she has never had much of a relationship with her mother.
Although a loner throughout her freshman and sophomore years at college, Charlene began
binge drinking with some friends on the weekends at her sorority during the fall semester of
her junior year. She self-identified as an adult child of an alcoholic to her friends and came to
find out that her other binge-drinking friends had no history of family alcohol abuse. However,
almost every one of them had experienced some type of trauma or neglect by their parents.
When her younger sister came to campus for a visit, Charlene was surprised to see that her
younger sister did not drink or use other drugs.

In the last chapter, we discussed the impact that AOD abuse has on children and families. The topic "Children and Families" could not have been written without some reference to adult children. However, we wanted to look at children as children. Thus, we want to focus the discussion in this chapter on the impact that AOD use has on the lives of adults who grew up in homes where substances were abused. Although we could identify and discuss a variety of populations who could present with AOD issues (such as professionals in recovery, grandparents of addicted individuals, adopted parents and alcoholism), we wanted to spend time on this special population because the labels of "Adult Children of Alcoholics" (ACOAs), "Adult Offspring of Families with Alcohol and Other Drug Problems" (AODF) (Harkness, Manhire, Blanchard, & Darling, 2011), and "Codependency" revolutionized the field of substance abuse and substance abuse treatment. In many ways, these populations brought issues that were previously only given passing glances to the forefront of the field.

According to Juliana and Goodman (1997), scholarly writing about the effects of alcohol upon children first appeared in the late 19th century with a study on the possible long-term effects of fetal opioid exposure. The more modern movement appears to have been initiated by interest in Cork's (1969) book *The Forgotten Children,* which examined 115 school-aged children of alcoholics and found them to be suffering from varied problems such as difficulty in expressing anger and resentment, low self-confidence, and difficulty in initiating and maintaining friendships. El-Guebaly and Offord (1977, 1979) reviewed the early empirical literature on children of alcoholics and attempted to identify problems that members of this group had across their life spans.

Intense popular interest then ensued with the publication of such books as Wegscheider's (1981) *Another Chance: Hope and Health for the Alcoholic Family,* Black's (1981) *It Will Never Happen to Me,* and Woititz's (1983) *Adult Children of Alcoholics.* As a result of these publications, a Children of Alcoholics (COA) movement began (Sher, 1991). The surging interest in COAs and adult children of alcoholics (ACOAs) has been prolific enough to have spawned a cottage industry. Essentially, the message promulgated in these books is that one should confront one's chaotic childhood and work through the repressed pain (Blau, 1990).

From time to time, you may have heard people label themselves as being an "adult child of an alcoholic" (ACOA) or, more simply in support groups and amongst likeminded individuals, as an "adult child." You may also be somewhat familiar with the term *codependency* because some adult children may describe themselves as being "codependent." There is much debate regarding the benefits of such labeling. On the one hand, such a label can act as a shortcut in conversations where others are familiar and/or may subscribe to the same sobriquet. A "shortcut" means that others "know what you mean" when you use that label. However, in professional circles, there is concern that labeling can have its own life. For example, George, La Marr, Barrett, and McKinnon (1999) studied the relationship among alcoholic parentage, self-labeling, and endorsing oneself as an ACOA. They found that parents' drinking did affect whether the subjects labeled themselves as an ACOA–codependent. However, the researchers state that it was unclear if a certain number of subjects were simply responding to the fact that "Since my parents drank, I must be an ACOA–codependent." George et al. (1999) also found that when subjects labeled themselves as codependent, they endorsed more pathological statements. In an earlier study, Sher (1991) found "strong negative stereotypes associated with the COA label, both from peer group and from mental health professionals" (p. 169). These negative consequences are supported by the concept of "secondary deviance." This means that individuals can play into the label and justify deviant behaviors (Li & Moore, 2001). Some of these behaviors can include AOD use and misuse.

Aside from the potentially negative consequences of labeling oneself as a COA during school-aged years, there may be some positive aspects to the labeling process for Adult Children of Alcoholics (ACOAs). Burk and Sher (1988) reviewed the literature in an attempt to determine the relevance of labeling theory for research on ACOAs. One of the possible benefits of labeling might be raising one's consciousness about the need for help. In addition, labeling oneself as an ACOA allows access to a variety of self-help support groups such as Codependents Anonymous and Al-Anon (see Chapter 10). Burk and Sher (1988) take a narrative perspective and suggest that labeling oneself as an ACOA allows for an external attribution to be made that can provide a structure for individuals' insight and understanding into their problems. Kaminer (1990) believes that identifying oneself as an adult child begins a recovery process that can lead to a lifestyle of recovery. In the final analysis, the authors of this text believe that, to the extent to which a label allows an individual to grow, subscribing to a label can be beneficial. However, to label oneself as an ACOA in order to avoid personal responsibility is not helpful and can serve to maintain one's self-deprecation and self-defeating behaviors.

ADULT CHILDREN OF ALCOHOLICS (ACOAS)

The labeling controversy aside, millions of adults do identify with the term and relate this to present dissatisfaction in life. Regardless of the extent to which one subscribes to the concepts of adult children, this area is a focal point of current research.

Research on ACOAs has focused on three areas. One branch of research, referred to as risk factors for later substance abuse, includes both qualitative and quantitative studies that examine the variables believed to influence ACOAs' own drug or nondrug use in adulthood. The quantitative research is aimed at identifying the characteristics that predispose ACOAs to alcoholism, other drug dependence, or other substance-related problems. The qualitative writings in this area focus upon identifying the personality characteristics and problematic behaviors that increase an ACOA's risk for choosing a partner with an identifiable substance abuse problem. A second branch of research focuses on identifying the clinical characteristics of ACOAs. This area of research is probably the most well-known among the general population of adults. The third branch of research centers on attempts to empirically validate the clinical characteristics. As you will see, the current state of these three research venues generally reveals mixed results.

It is important to remember that many siblings do share a common family environment while growing up, and some parenting will be the same across siblings throughout the family life cycle. Yet, because other aspects of parenting might vary, this could well be the case with alcohol. Just as in the case example of Charlene, a parent might quit drinking between sibling births. This means that an older sibling might be directly affected by a parent's drinking, while the younger sibling is impacted indirectly. So, when discussing Adult Child of an Alcoholic, it is important to remember that the dynamics can vary between siblings and other family members.

Clinical Characteristics and Empirical Research

Several researchers have identified some of the characteristics distinctive to an adult child of an alcoholic (see Ackerman, 1983, 1987; Beattie, 1987; Black, 1981; Brown, 1988; Cermak, 1986; Goodman, 1987). These characteristics are fundamentally based upon the assumption that children see parental behavior as a reflection of the child's own sense of self-worth (Ackerman, 1983). In general, characteristics of ACOAs are seen as emanating from dysfunctional family systems and include excessive use of denial, all-or-nothing thinking, exaggerated need for control, avoidance of anger and other feelings, avoidance of self-disclosure, lack of trust, and difficulty with intimate relationships and/or emotional regulation (Brown, 1988; McCarty, Zimmerman, DiGuiseppe, & Christakis, 2005; Sher, 1991).

Other research suggests that a central issue for ACOAs relates to boundaries. Recall in the last chapter we discussed boundaries and likened them to a fence between people. Kelley et al., (2007 studied female college students who self-identified as ACOAs. Results reflected a group of participants who reported more *parentification* (a child treated like an adult), instrumental and emotional caregiving, and feelings of past unfairness in their families of origin. It is interesting to note that ACOAs who thought that their mothers had the problem with alcohol reported more parentification and caretaking than did both ACOAs and non-ACOAs who identified their fathers as having the problem. Given the results of this study, ACOAs raised in homes with maternal drinking problems predictably report less positive relationships with their mothers as well as with their peers. At the same time, paternal substance abuse did not predict the quality of parental or peer relationships. In another study, Kelley et al. (2008) also found that those ACOAs who suspected their mothers having alcohol problems reported less support and attachment from their mothers.

In general, empirical studies suggest that ACOAs do often show an increased vulnerability to life stressors and report more symptoms of adjustment difficulties (Hall & Webster, 2002; Hall, Webster, & Powell, 2003). The adjustment difficulties can play out in relationships, where they may regulate their attachments to others by being defensive, self-protective, and mistrusting (e. g. Harter, 2000; Kearns-Bodkin & Leonard, 2008; Kelley, Cash, Grant, Miles, & Santos, 2004).

Perhaps the most controversial assertion made about the clinical characteristics of ACOAs is that their relational difficulties can be described as "codependent." Because of the overwhelming popularity of this observation, we will discuss the notion of codependency in detail later in this chapter. It needs to be noted here that codependency is variously described as boundary problems that often result in enmeshed relationships (see Chapter 11) and codependents engage in dysfunctional relationships in a variety of forms. While it may be somewhat true that ACOAs have boundary issues in their adult relationships, it cannot be seen as being caused by their families of origin. Family therapists see many couples' boundary problems that may be associated with other variables mitigated by a more generalized anxiety in contemporary couples that translates into power and control issues.

Risk Factors

When considering risk factors for children of alcoholics, it is critical to understand that alcoholism is a family disease. As such, alcoholism affects everyone in the family system in some way or another. Alcoholism in families carries a fundamental risk. Adult children are seen as having been raised in families where a parent's drinking is the central factor in the life of a child and has the greatest influence over the child during that time as well as having persisting influence over the child's growth into adulthood. From a family systems perspective, an obvious conclusion would be that ACOAs would experience more risks for the development of problems than would non-ACOAs, and early research confirmed just that (e.g., Ackerman, 1983; Brown, 1988).

More recent research is not as clear. Research is still inconclusive about whether ACOAs are more different than alike when compared to others who have experienced childhood trauma. At the same time, evidence points to the association between substance abuse in one's childhood home and the risk of developing problems later in life. (Braitman et al., 2009; Fischer, Pidcock,

Munsch, & Forthun, 2005; Hall & Webster, 2007). Watt (2002) found that ACOAs are less likely to marry, more likely to be in unhappy marriages, and more likely to divorce. These same researchers report that both males and females whose parents were alcoholic are more likely to marry moderate-to-severe alcoholics. Finally, Olmsted, Crowell, and Waters (2003) report that sons of alcoholics have increased risk for alcoholism. Yet, neither alcoholism nor marriage to an alcoholic is an inevitable outcome for ACOAs.

As illustrated in our case example of Charlene and our previous discussion, some studies suggest that ACOAs do not differ significantly from other adult children who experienced a dysfunctional family home life (Fineran, Laux, Seymour, & Thomas, 2010). Researchers are finding that a number of ACOAs appear stable in spite of their upbringing in alcoholic homes. Moreover, numerous studies on ACOAs and risk factors have been conducted on college students, and research has shown that this population drinks more than the general population. The elevated drinking among the college-age population can confound studies using college students to study ACOAs' risk factors. This leads Fineran et al. (2010) to suggest that ACOAs may not be as homogenous a group as it once was perceived to be. Thus, it is imperative that helpers do not assume that because an individual is raised in a family where alcohol was abused that he or she will categorically have problems. To obtain a clearer picture of college student ACOAs, West and Graham (2006) suggest that this population should be examined for risk over time, and measures of risk should be conducted before, during, and after college.

Few studies have concentrated on ACOAs from diverse backgrounds and their risk factors. However, De La Rosa, Dillon, Ganapati, Rojas, Pinto, and Prado (2010) reviewed the clinical literature for adult Latino ACOA substance use and found that Latina adults who had reported low levels of attachment to their substance-abusing mothers were at heightened risk for substance abuse. Hall (2007a) found that African Americans raised in alcoholic homes had more depression and lower self-esteem, which was similar to the findings for Caucasian samples.

ASSESSMENT AND TREATMENT CONSIDERATIONS

Assessment of ACOAs

Berkowitz and Perkins (1988) reviewed the means by which ACOAs have been identified in the professional literature and found both broad and strict definitions of ACOAs. Clinical diagnosis of parental alcoholism reflects the more strict definition whereas the children's perceptions of parental drinking problems mirror a broader definition. An example of a broad definition is that used in the Russell, Henderson, and Blume (1985) study in which an ACOA is "any person, adult, or child who has a parent identified in any way as having a significant problem related to alcohol use" (p. 1). According to Berkowitz and Perkins, the more strict definition is likely to exclude many individuals whose parents are alcoholic but who have not been formally diagnosed. The more broad definition, based upon the child's perceptions, may also reflect an inaccurate number of ACOAs because the child may see his or her parents only infrequently or may see his or her parent drink only occasionally.

A detailed instrument is the CAST (Jones, A. C., 1985), which stands for Children of Alcoholics Screening Test. It is a simple, 30-item, yes/no instrument, and it takes less than 10 minutes to administer. It takes no special training to administer, which makes it both good and bad. The CAST is designed to measure the chaotic and inconsistent behaviors and experiences of the alcoholic home such as emotional instability, inconsistent child care, family conflict, and lack of close, intimate, and trusting relationships between parents and children (Williams & Collins, 1986).

The CAST6 is a 6-item instrument that is used to assess adult children of alcoholics (over 18 years old) as well as children of alcoholics. The items measure experiences, attitudes, and perceptions about parental drinking in the same yes/no format as the CAST. Two cutoff scores have been used to identify ACOAs. Three or more "yes" responses are used to determine status from conservative perspective, and scores of 2 are more liberal. Thus, if you were to use a cutoff of 2, you would have more people identified as having problems.

Others have used simple, single-item questions as well. For example, DiCicco, Davis, and Orenstein (1984) asked whether one had ever wished that either or both of his or her parents would drink less and found that this single item identified ACOAs reliably over time. In another study, Biek (1981) asked subjects whether their parents' drinking caused problems for them and found this single question accurately selected ACOAs.

Implications for Intervention

Empirical studies on the treatment of ACOAs are significantly lacking (Williams, 1990). Nevertheless, Williams describes two essential goals in intervening with ACOAs. The first goal is to identify and address early symptoms of problem drinking, and the second goal is to identify dysfunctional behaviors and coping skills that may be predisposing risk factors for drinking or other adult problems.

The mixed results of empirical studies do not suggest that specific interventions should be identified for ACOAs, because it is unclear whether such a group exists whose individual members are significantly different from other adults with dysfunctional family backgrounds. Nevertheless, being associated with alcohol or other drug abuse either directly, as in the case of the alcoholic, or indirectly, as in the case of many ACOAs, has been shown to be problematic. In terms of helping clients, mental health professionals may want to provide information regarding AOD use as well as help clients clarify their values about use so that they may make decisions regarding abstention or moderation. Many clients who were raised in homes with alcohol abuse may not identify themselves as ACOAs. So, counselors need to be careful about using jargon that may create client resistance. Mental health professionals who use the label ACOA may leave their clients with the impression that this is a widely accepted clinical syndrome, but such a posture would be misrepresenting the empirical findings about ACOAs.

Adults who were raised in families with substance abuse, physical or sexual abuse, and/or parental death or divorce do seem different from adults with no such history. Moreover, recall from Chapter 11 that a characteristic of families with alcohol or other drug abuse is unresolved grief. This grief, coupled with poor communication skills and a lack of role-modeling on how to express feelings, may leave these clients predisposed to difficulty in trusting the counselor. Because ACOAs may control their emotions and attempt to control others as well, it is advisable that mental health professionals focus on developing a strong and deep rapport with the ACOA client.

The development of strong rapport with ACOA clients is critical in that they seem to have some difficulty in trusting. Given this, you can see how critical it would be for those who are helping diverse ACOAs and their families. Hall (2007a) maintains that the clinical intervention with ACOAs need not necessarily emerge as a special intervention. Although we discuss some concerns with diversity and twelve-step programs below, it seems that ACOAs may benefit from the same support groups that are identified and discussed in Chapter 10, which include Codependents Anonymous (CODA) and Al-Anon. Other self-help groups, such as Sex Addicts Anonymous and Emotions Anonymous, could be used as well, depending upon the identified problem.

CODEPENDENCY

The term *codependency* was introduced in the early 1980s. Originally referring to the co-alcoholic (Whitfield, 1984), this notion was broadened through the writings of Black (1981), Friel (1984), and others who described a variety of compulsive behaviors. With the possible exception of transactional analysis and the famous phrase, "I'm okay–you're okay" (Harris, 1969), few movements in the mental health field have generated so much popular interest and so much professional controversy as has the codependency movement.

The fields of chemical dependency and mental health were beginning to enjoy a healthy, although somewhat acrid at times, relationship once the notion of the dually diagnosed patient came into vogue in professional circles and more routine. However, it was the phenomenon of the patient with a coexisting disorder that sent shudders down the spine of the community mental health system—administrators and clinicians alike, because this dually diagnosed patient suggested the chicken-or-the-egg idea: What caused what? Which was the primary diagnosis? Did the alcohol or other drug problem create the mental disorder or was it the other way around? If patients were active in their addictive behaviors during the time of their entry into the mental health system, what was the proper treatment plan? The very real complications resulting from having a co-existing disorder caused the fear that the financial backbone of community mental health centers would be broken. That a professional could be treating the wrong problem was a good possibility.

One direct result of the numbers of such dual diagnoses was a bringing together of chemical treatment providers and mental health providers under one roof. Although it was not an easy operation in terms of administrative logistics, mental health centers made great strides to do exactly that. Staff meetings, which were once held to discuss mental health cases, now included addictions counselors whose training was quite different from that of their mental health colleagues. The friction that resulted was to be expected, because often mental health professionals had to move their offices or generate other concessions in order to make room for their new colleagues. As each group became more familiar with and received direct benefits from the work of the others, issues of turf and prestige gradually gave way to more amiable working relationships. Patients began to receive improved care, and with this came shared respect for each professional group. It appeared that all was well.

Then the chemical dependency field introduced the concept of codependency, and whatever strides had been made in the salubrious relationship between the mental health field and the addiction field turned sour once again. The definition and characteristics of codependency were seen by many mental health professionals as a new name for an old mental health disorder, which once again brought problems of professional boundaries into sharp focus. However, the problem was not only that the chemical dependency field was seen as trespassing onto the field of mental health nor was it only that those in the addictions field were being trained to treat codependency: The problem was more the issue of whether codependency actually existed. And if it did exist, questions about what constituted codependency would become the next cause of battle.

Some of the fiery debate was fueled by differences over the disease concept inherent in various views of codependency. Recall that, in Chapter 3, one's view of alcoholism as being a disease or nondisease was seen to have profound implications for identification and treatment. Moreover, remember how the discriminating variable casting one into a disease or nondisease orientation essentially revolved around one's view of "loss of control" (with the disease model claiming the centrality of a loss of control). Well, the voracity with which mental health professionals have debated the disease concept has been duplicated in the debate over codependency: Are people responsible for the root of their codependency? In other words, are individuals seen as more responsible for how they manage their impulses rather than being responsible for the impulse itself? Another source of debate centered on the traits of a codependent person. Hoenigmann-Lion and Whitehead (2006) studied whether codependency really exists. For these researchers, codependency is another name for a diagnosis already identified in the *DSM-IV-TR* under Borderline Personality Disorder, Dependent Personality Disorder, Posttraumatic Stress Disorder. Is codependency essentially a thematic variation on one of these disorders? Does it simply extend the boundaries of an already established diagnosis so that codependent characteristics lie more along one pole of a continuum in a given disorder?

Furthermore, some feminists argue that the perennial influence of the *codependency* hypothesis suggests that it is a social construct and is heavily influenced by traditional assumptions of gender. For instance, Dear and Roberts (2002) report that many feminists maintain the view of a society that demands that women be nurturing, caring, and sensitive to others' needs. Yet these are the very characteristics deemed dysfunctional when viewed through a *codependency* paradigm. Perhaps this contentious issue surrounds the notion of whether codependency is a progressive disease.

Definitions of Codependency

Definitions of the term *codependency* are influenced by the degree to which one subscribes to the concept. That is, staunch proponents of the concept may see everyone and almost all of our institutions as codependent. For example, Giermyski and Williams (1986) state that enthusiastic proponents of the concept see codependency

> as a primary disease present in every member of an alcoholic family, which is often worse than alcoholism itself, has its own physical manifestations and is a treatable diagnostic category. Its presence is recognized in individuals, among institutions, in hospitals as well as judicial and legal systems, in schools and even in the Federal Communications Commission (FCC). The last two are viewed as afflicted with codependency because schools expel students for drug-related offenses, and the FCC has not yet banned wine and beer commercials. (p. 7)

Cermak (1986) noted that efforts to define codependency have included metaphoric and interpersonal approaches as well as those approaches based upon ego psychology, behaviorism, and combinations of behaviorism and intrapsychic dynamics. For example, Anderson (1987) uses a metaphor to state that "being codependent is like being a life guard on a crowded beach, knowing that you cannot swim, and not telling anyone for fear of starting a panic" (p. 16). More formalized definitions of codependency are found in the interpersonal approaches of Black (1981) and Wegscheider (1989). Black talks about rules operating in the family structure that prohibit the honest expression of feelings regarding alcoholism and the alcohol-dependent family member. Wegscheider discusses codependency in terms of it being a preoccupation and dependence upon another person or object. Examples of codependency include individuals who are in a significant relationship with an alcoholic, those having one or more alcoholic parents or grandparents, and those who grew up in a family where there was systematic repression of feelings. Schaef (1987) presents a definition that depicts the belief in the progressive nature of codependency. She sees codependency as a disease emanating from an "addictive process" similar to that of alcoholism. This addictive process, unless confronted in much the same manner as alcoholism, can lead to a type of spiritual death—a life aimed at existing rather than thriving—or physical death (Schaef, 1987).

Friel (1984) extended the interpersonal approaches to include codependency and emphasized the impact of such behaviors upon the ego functioning of individuals. These authors maintain that codependency is an emotional and behavioral pattern of interactive coping resulting from one's protracted exposure to a restrictive environment that does not allow the open or direct expression of feelings about oneself or other family members. For example, children who are consistently told that the mother's or father's drinking binges are not problematic, even in the face of drunken rages and subsequent physical abuse, will grow up confused about their reality. Any attempt to talk about the problem when the parents were sober would likely be met with cognitive resistance: "There is no problem." Any attempt to talk about the problem when the parent(s) were drinking is likewise met with physical abuse. Hence, these children often learn to keep their feelings and thoughts about the parents' drinking to themselves. This fear of talking would be introjected and thus carried into one's adult life and relationships.

Whitfield (1984) believes that codependency is a disease of lost selfhood, and that it is the most common type of addiction that people develop. Whitfield states that codependence develops whenever there is "suffering and/or dysfunction that is associated with or results from focusing on the needs and behavior of others" (p. 19). An intrapsychic approach is reflected in Cermak's (1986) definition in which he sees a codependent person as having a personality disorder based upon an excessive need to control self and others. Other symptoms include neglecting one's own needs, boundary distortions centered on approach and avoidance in intimate relationships, attraction to other individuals demonstrating codependent characteristics, denial, a constricted or restricted emotional expression, low-level and persistent depression, and stress-related physical ailments.

As Irvine (1999, p. 29) and others point out (e.g., Krestan & Bepko, 1990), codependency's "definitional ambiguity should not be taken to be 'so vague as to be meaningless.'" Nonetheless, Irvine maintains that one cannot simply ascribe any and all meanings to it. She goes on to say that the constitution of one person's codependency is really defined by what the person sees as troublesome in his or her own history. According to the same researcher, codependency can stand for different issues in an individual's life. For instance, it might mean a series of loveless and oppressive relationships. In another case, codependency might mean distant, aloof, and isolating interpersonal response patterns to others. In yet another instance, codependency might reflect a sense of chronic low self-esteem and boundary problems in relationships (Watt, 2002).

Characteristics of Codependent Individuals

Due to the lack of clear definitions of codependency, it is somewhat difficult to determine characteristics. As a result, several authors have advanced codependent characteristics, and, like the definitions, these characteristics range from less formal to more pedantic (see Kitchens, 1991; Schaef, 1987; Whitfield, 1984).

Dear and Roberts (2002) identified themes of codependency. These include a tendency to put other people's needs before one's own, the tendency to engage in taking responsibility for another person's actions ("caretaking"), and the fixing of the damage cause by another person ("rescuing"). Potter-Efron and Potter-Efron (1989) identified eight characteristics of codependence: (1) Fear is indicated by a preoccupation with the problems of others, an avoidance of interpersonal risk, a general mistrust of others, persistent anxiety, and manipulative attempts to change another's behavior, especially drinking behavior; (2) Shame and guilt are characterized by a persistence of shame and guilt about another's behavior, self-loathing, isolation, and an appearance of superiority that masks low self-worth; (3) Prolonged despair relates to a generalized pessimism toward the world and feelings of hopelessness about changing one's current situation. One may also demonstrate a low sense of self-worth that stands in direct opposition to one's actual accomplishments; (4) Anger is often present but may be expressed in a passive-aggressive manner. One may also fear that becoming angry will mean a loss of control. Another characteristic of anger is that it is persistent; (5) Denial is usually rather consistent, especially when it involves family pain such as drinking behavior. Denial is also demonstrated by a consistent minimization of problems and the use of justifications or rationalizations aimed at protecting the person from perceived or real consequences; (6) Rigidity is identified by cognitive, behavioral, and moral, spiritual, and emotional inflexibility; (7) Identity development is also impaired. This is usually seen as an inability to take care of one's own emotional needs and as having an excessive need for others to validate one's self-worth. Along with this need is an obsessive concern about how one is perceived by others; (8) Confusion about what is normal and what is real is another behavioral pattern. Confusion is also indicated by one's gullibility and indecisiveness.

In examining the definitions and characteristics, Doweiko (2011) states that the core aspect of codependency includes four elements: *overinvolvement, obsessive attempts to control, the extreme tendency to use external sources for self-worth, and the tendency to make personal sacrifices.* In codependency, overinvolvement with the abusing family member is coupled with an obsessive attempt to control the abusing member's behaviors. Using external sources for self-worth is similar to Whitaker's (1991) notion of "looking elsewhere." The issue of personal sacrifices comprises those behaviors aimed at "curing" the abusing family member, in which the helper is seen as "saintly."

According to Kitchens (1991), eight indicators can help to determine the severity of codependence: (1) the extent to which the client equates performance with self-value; (2) the extent to which the client equates self-worth with taking care of others' needs; (3) the extent to which the client believes he or she is helpless to control what happens in life; (4) the extent to which the client attempts to feel more powerful or more in control of life than is actually the case; (5) the extent to which the client ruminates about dysfunctional family of origin behavior; (6) the extent to which the client continues to protect or defend against any criticism of his or her parents in the face of contradictory information; (7) the extent to which the client experiences unexplained or overwhelming anger; and (8) the extent to which the client feels stuck in his or her relationships.

Assessing for Codependency

In its heyday in the 1980s and early 1990s, codependency was not formally recognized in the *DSM-IV*. The fact that codependency does not appear in the *DSM-IV-TR* (American Psychiatric Association, 2000) continues to reflect the lack of formal professional acknowledgment. Nevertheless, mental health professionals should not categorically dismiss the concept. While the lack of formal acknowledgment in the early years hindered the development of sophisticated assessments of codependency, the same cannot be said today. The lack of appearance in the *DSM-IV-TR* has not deterred more recent efforts to legitimize the concept and assessment of codependency.

During the period from the mid-1980s to the mid-1990s, assessing codependency in clients was relatively informal, and professionals and nonprofessionals alike used a few notable nonstandardized instruments. However, the subjectivity and informality in the early years of the codependency movement were not categorical and should not be mistaken for a complete lack of validity. In the early years, the differences in the assessment of codependency were probably attributed to variations in the general assessment skills of practitioners, rather than being attributed to differences over the meaning and definition of codependency. While it is true that clinicians often assessed codependency simply through their subjective clinical impressions of the client, these impressions were partly guided by the professional works of Kitchens (1991), who also cautioned mental health professionals to combine subjective and objective assessment procedures. Interestingly, Harkness and Cotrell (1997) show that the pioneers may have been accurate in their assessments of codependency. These researchers studied more than 2,000 practitioners worldwide and found a remarkable agreement and consistency in the meaning and definition of codependency across practitioner subjects.

Fuller and Warner (2000) reviewed scales that are used to assess codependency. They found the Codependency Assessment Inventory (CAI) (Friel, 1985), the Acquaintance Description Form-C3 (ADF-C3) (Wright & Wright, 1991), Beck Codependence Assessment Scale (Beck, 1991), A Codependence Test (Kitchens, 1991), Co-Dependent Relationship Questionnaire (Kritsberg, 1985), Recovery Potential Survey (Whitfield, 1991), the Spann–Fischer Codependency Scale (Fischer, Spann & Crawford, 1991), and the Potter–Efron Codependency Assessment (Potter–Efron & Potter–Efron, 1989). According to Fuller and Warner, the CAI is lengthy (60 items), and the validity and reliability have not been thoroughly evaluated. Wright and Wright's Acquaintance Description Form-C3 does not have published statistical information.

Fuller and Warner (2000) used the Spann–Fischer and the Potter–Efron Codependency Assessment (Potter-Efron & Potter-Efron, 1989) to study the relationship of these instruments with self-reported chronic family stress. Results of their study showed that women had higher codependency scores on the Spann–Fischer than did the sample of male subjects. This study raises questions about potential gender bias in the instrument, and this issue will be addressed later in the chapter.

Aside from these efforts to update assessments published in the early years of the codependency movement, a review of the current professional literature reveals continued interest in the introduction of new empirically tested psychometric assessments for codependency. For instance, Harkness, Swenson, Madsen-Hampton, and Hale (2001) studied the reliability and validity of a clinical rating scale for codependency. The researchers developed an example-anchored rating scale, based on how clinicians generally construe the term *codependency* in practice. The researchers administered the instrument to a group of practicing counselors. The design controlled for gender and called for counselors to be randomly assigned to one of four groups. The findings suggest that the rating scale yields reliable and valid clinical evaluations of codependency without appreciable gender bias. The Holyoake Codependency Index (HIC) (Dear & Roberts, 2000) is a 13-item scale that measures the extent to which a person endorses or rejects codependent sentiments. It comprises three scales: external focus, self-sacrifice, and reactivity. *External focus* is defined as the tendency to rely on other people in order to obtain approval and a sense of self. *Self-sacrifice* is the tendency to regard others' needs as more important than one's own needs. *Reactivity* is the degree to which one feels overwhelmed by a partner's problematic behavior. According to the authors of the index, these subscales were derived from factor analysis of key themes using a clinical sample of mostly females. Dear (2004) conducted a reliability study for the test and found that over a three-week interval, test-retest reliability was 0.88 and for the full scale test and 0.76–0.82 for the subscales.

As you can see, arguments can be made about the consistency in the validity and reliability of assessment instruments throughout the history of the codependency movement. One current trend in research in assessment is to conduct concurrent validity and reliability studies as ancillary, yet important components, of other research questions. Lindley, Giordano, and Hammer's (1999) study is an example. In this study, the researchers validate the Spann–Fischer scale while primarily looking at the relationship between codependency and age, gender, self-confidence, autonomy, and succorance. These studies, and others like them, provide opportunities for enhancing the clinical assessment of codependency.

Should you, as a mental health professional, choose to administer an instrument, you are advised to use these instruments with extreme caution. Probably the best use of these assessment devices is for the mutual identification of problematic areas occurring in the client's life. Asking the client to share his or her impressions of the assessment results can help focus on areas that might need attention.

IMPLICATIONS FOR MENTAL HEALTH PROFESSIONALS

As far as the controversy is concerned, the mental health profession has the last word for now: The *DSM-IV-TR* does not include codependency in its nomenclature on personality disorders. This may or may not dissuade others from adhering to the concept of codependency, but this omission does make a clear statement that may intensify the chasm that exists over the use of the term between mental health practitioners and those practitioners in the chemical dependency field.

A close examination of the concept of codependency and the criticism surrounding the term and its corollaries will likely indicate that much of the argument involves degrees of acceptance. Even though little empirically based research has been conducted on the subject per se, Giermyski and Williams (1986) maintain that

> It would be a mistake to deny that living or even working side by side with a drug dependent person causes stresses and problems or that wives and children as well as other members of families of drug dependent individuals undergo deprivations and stresses, that they suffer indignities, that such problems deserve help, and that help should be offered. However, the authors wonder if the term "codependency" has not been given connotations far exceeding justification, whether or not the implications (systematic, theoretical, and practical) at the level of the delivery of needed services have been sufficiently examined and the consequences considered. (p. 7)

In this sense, the very least that can be said about the concept of codependency is that it has helped to describe a variety of interpersonal and intrapersonal dynamics in a language that many can understand. In that alcohol and other drugs are rampant in our society across every economic and social line, the concept of codependency may currently be best operating as a paradigm attempting to make sense out of the confusing, paradoxical, and often deleterious effects of one's extended drug involvement and its impact on others. Whether intuitively understood or empirically proved, it is safe to say that the characteristics identified as codependent operate in almost all of us at one time or another. Differences between individuals exist in incidence, degree, and persistence. Our society is based upon competition and achievement. You, as a reader of this book, might be termed an overachiever, but it is often overachievers who are in positions to help others. The need for belonging to powerful groups, identified as indicative of an antisocial and narcissistic personality disorder (Kitchens, 1991), can be functional, and decisions that affect us all are made by groups of powerful people. We all need humor in our lives, so the histrionic personality identified as maladaptive is necessary for us to have perspective on our lives.

Compulsivity is almost a given in undergraduate and graduate school, isn't it? Does that mean you are maladaptive for choosing to go to college or graduate school? The point we are making here is that codependent characteristics, per se, are not inherently good or bad. Sometimes behaving codependently is appropriate, very adaptive, and can lead to satisfaction with oneself and others. Sometimes these same characteristics can lead to problems. An inflexible adherence to codependency as well as an inflexible avoidance of it may become problematic. The advice given here is for you to remain open to the client and to employ an understanding of codependency as it relates to the well-being of that client. Categorically disregarding the presence of codependent behaviors may limit the amount and kind of information being presented by clients and can lead to less than efficacious results in counseling. Moreover, since thousands upon thousands attend CODA meetings and adhere to the principles of codependency as outlined in *The Coda Book,* a limited or myopic understanding of the larger social, political, and economic implications of codependency for women and racioethnic minorities is questionable practice.

Mental Health Professionals' Own Codependency

In a recent study, Martsolf (2002) sampled 149 males and females whose ages ranged from 23 to 73. The sample included nurses, family physicians, psychologists, and social workers. The results of the study indicate a relatively low incidence of codependency in this sample. This stands in contrast to a preliminary study conducted by Fisher and Harrison (1993b), which assessed codependent characteristics of graduate students in a master's degree counseling program. We found that these prospective mental health professionals reported more codependent characteristics than did students in other graduate programs. Moreover, the graduate students in the mental health profession were more likely to have come from an alcoholic home. This preliminary study suggests that mental health professionals' codependency may be a potential problem in a counseling relationship.

Even though these are only two studies (and both are limited in their own ways), some interesting implications are apparent. Given that the pathological discourse of codependency in this culture has been around long enough to be seen and experienced as oppressive by many in the helping professions, one wonders whether clients now show a tendency to be hesitant in identifying themselves as codependent. Fisher and Harrison's earlier study of graduate students occurred when there was widespread interest in the concept, and helping professionals were thought to be potential codependents because of the nature of the work they performed. During the time in which Fisher and Harrison (1993b) conducted their preliminary study, the stigma of codependency was not as harsh as feminists accused it of being in the 1990s. Thus, in the past, a questionnaire measuring codependency in a population that reflected low incidence may well have been due to a lack of subjects' identification with codependent characteristics. Currently, the stigma of being codependent has many pathological connotations. This has created a situation in which both male and female subjects (mental health practitioners included) who are being assessed for codependency may not want to see themselves or be seen by others as codependent.

PROFESSIONAL ENABLING AND TRANSFERENCE/COUNTERTRANSFERENCE   The dynamics that transpire between client and mental health professional in sessions may also reflect transference and counter-transference. Wegscheider (1981) sees attempts to keep an alcoholic from experiencing logical or natural consequences as enabling (see Chapter 11). Thus, your attempts to keep clients from experiencing the natural consequences of their actions can be framed as professional enabling or countertransference and can reinforce maladaptive client behaviors. You might perceive a client's desire to return to a dysfunctional relationship as reflecting your failure to effect client change. By personalizing the client's progress, you might strongly advise the client to avoid returning to the dysfunctional relationship and become angry with the client if the advice is not heeded. You might also overidentify with the experience of the client, resulting in an enmeshed relationship with the client. The loss of these interpersonal boundaries can diminish the effectiveness of the helping process, or at least confound the process. For example, you might identify with the client's feelings of helplessness in changing an alcoholic partner's behaviors. Rather than recognizing and working with the enabling aspects of the client's behaviors, you might prematurely attempt to steer the client into solutions rather than helping him or her gain insight into how his or her behaviors actually enable or reinforce the partner's alcoholism. In this manner, the client is kept from experiencing the consequences of his or her own behaviors.

We could continue with protracted examples of mental health professionals' potential codependent behaviors. Suffice it to say that codependency in the profession can be problematic. Training programs go a long way in helping mental health professionals understand the parameters of interactions with clients. Yet, if you come from a home where there was alcoholism or other family dysfunction, you may be more prone at times to behaving codependently with clients. Personal work can increase awareness of your codependent behaviors and can help you arrive at some strategies and solutions. It may well be that our profession attracts those who have experienced much of the same pain that clients will have experienced. Your experiences with your own pain and codependency can significantly increase the potential for accurate empathy with your clients and, therefore, can be of potential benefit. The extent of the benefit to clients will likely be related directly to the amount of your own work on codependency issues.

RELATIONSHIP OF ACOA, AA, AL-ANON, AND CODEPENDENCY

In her book *Codependent Forevermore*, Irvine (1999) discusses ACOAs and codependency. She states that "codependency and the support group Codependents Anonymous exist today because of the trail blazed by Adult Children of Alcoholics" (p. 19). Thus, for Irvine, the two movements are related. For her, the debate is essentially focused on the extent that the relationship is complementary and/or supplementary.

However, the relationship between ACOA/codependency and AA/Al-Anon is more acrimonious. It goes beyond the fact that AA and Al-Anon were in existence first. According to Irvine, the Adult Child does *not* belong to AA. This is because AA exists for the alcoholic who wishes to become clean and sober and remain so. Second, the ACOA–codependency movement poses a cultural narrative that is in direct opposition to the discourse and tenets of AA and Al-Anon. The ACOA–codependency movement takes the focus off the alcoholic and places the focus on outside factors, specifically on genetic and/or interpersonal factors leading to addictions. In other words, adults who abuse alcohol are seen in the ACOA–codependency movement as doing so because of their childhoods and/or because of some genetic predisposition or proclivity. By locating some, if not all, of the control outside the abuser, a dramatic and deep chasm between ACOA and AA/ Al-Anon is drawn.

Another structural difference is even more pronounced at the macro-level, and Irvine (1999) again provides insight. She says that the AA discourse is a conservative narrative. This means that it conforms more closely to the larger social narrative. If "blame" is to be had at all (remember that in AA, blame is seen as a process to be worked through in order to take responsibility), one could feasibly "blame" it on the bottle—not society. From this perspective, the narrative of ACOA–codependency is anti-AA. This is so because, if "blame" is to be had in codependency, the "blame" is placed on the family. It is imperative for you to understand that we are not saying that "blame" is condoned in any of these venues. We are using "blame" as a means of underscoring a difference between these approaches. While people may enter into these recovery programs blaming, they hopefully learn early-on that blaming is a way of avoiding responsibility. In any case, the difference in worldviews, concomitant with the obvious ensuing implications for treatment and recovery, is hard to understate.

On yet another front, the relationship between ACOA and codependency is an interesting one. According to research results (e.g., Dube, Anda, Felitti, Edwards, & Croft, 2002), it is imperative that mental health therapists not categorically confuse codependency with alcohol use or being an ACOA. As mentioned previously, studies are now showing that the characteristics of ACOAs are not that unique and that these characteristics may also be found in adults who came from homes where there was neglect, abuse, and/or violence.

For instance, Cullen and Carr (1999) studied the differences between young adults on a measure of codependency. Results indicated that those high on codependency scores reported significantly more family-of-origin problems. Yet, the problems were not necessarily alcohol related. The family-of-origin problems included such things as relationships with chemically dependent partners, parental mental health problems, problematic intimate relationships, and personal psychological problems (for example, compulsivity). Moreover, there was no significant difference among those scoring high on codependency levels and the reporting of physical or sexual abuse.

The results of these studies suggest that codependency is one component of a wider multigenerational family systems issue. Thus, it is quite possible that ACOAs may be codependent, yet not all codependents are ACOAs.

Critics of the ACOA–Codependency Movement

POPULAR CRITICISM   The ACOA–codependency movement's narrative was seen (and still is seen by many) as pitting children of any age against parents. The movement is seen as attacking the core structure of family. More significantly, the ACOA–codependency movement has been criticized as blaming *all families and all parents of all children.* Ironically, and to their credit, proponents of the movement adroitly point to the rigidity of the critics' "all or nothing" perspective as demonstrating the very dysfunction of dualistic thinking firsthand. Thus, the separation between AA and Al-Anon is reiterated with the larger social narrative.

Clearly and from a social perspective, any new discourse that runs counter to the larger, prevailing discourse is enough to spawn criticism. It is to be expected, because societies remain stable through the dialectical processes of homeostasis and change. However, at the outset, the ACOA–codependency movement was seen as significantly altering the traditional Euro-Caucasian discourse on families regarding one's position in the family structure. The antifamily nature of the new narrative also had significant structural implications for families themselves.

The movement had its emphasis on confrontation. Rightly or wrongly, it was seen as a movement of "parent bashing." At that time in history, blaming one's (somewhat elderly) parents ran diametrically opposite to the discourse calling for being grateful to one's parents (usually fathers) for fighting World War II and bringing peace and prosperity to the world. The movement was seen by some women and mothers as a movement that discredited their choices, their sacrifices for their family, and, in some cases, their livelihoods. (As you will see, the feminist researchers had critics of their own.) As such, a core basic orientation of the ACOA–codependency movement was seen as crossing the decades-old narrative of "healthy and loving families" (of the 1940s through the 1980s).

PROFESSIONAL CRITICISM As the ACOA–codependency movement grew, professional researchers became interested in studying the concept. After all, from a strict research perspective, the ability to identify, isolate, and profile a (albeit reputed) significantly large segment of society (ACOAs) for study was quite appealing. Yet the enthusiasm in being able to identify and isolate this population waned significantly as researchers designed studies and published results. Enormous methodological challenges in studying ACOA–codependency needed to be overcome. Many of the same problems remain today (Jacobs, Windle, Seilhamer, & Bost, 1999).

In the early 1980s, the definitions of *COA* and *ACOA* were precise and clear: COA meant a child of a parent who abuses alcohol, and ACOA meant an adult child of a parent who drank alcohol excessively. However, such a precise definition would eventually narrow the subject pool and create a diminished ability to generalize results. The problems were numerous. For instance, there would be difficulties attributing length of exposure to alcohol and the subsequent effects that it had. Second, since many alcoholics also used other drugs, this condition limited the population of alcohol-only users. Third was the issue of the validity of self-reports. Were the subjects reporting their patterns accurately? Fourth, even if one could argue in favor of self-reports, self-reports were (and are always) about events in the past. The validity of recollection was significant at the time, and debate continues in the courts. Today, the validity of self-reports is challenged under the rubric *recovered memories*. Fifth, assuming that one could validly recall an event and reliably self-report it, Goodman (1987) and then Williams (1990) argue that such things as parental inconsistencies, double-bind messages, the covert expression of feelings, shame, mistrust, and the existence of childhood roles occur in everyone's life. Therefore, since these experiences are ubiquitous, one should not attribute these characteristics solely to COAs and ACOAs.

From the outset of the movement, researchers were not interested in undertaking studies demonstrating the clinical characteristics of COAs, ACOAs, and codependency (Giermyski & Williams, 1986). Thus, if one were to examine the professional journals in the early 1980s, one would find a dearth of systematic and empirically based studies. Today, this has changed. There is moderate professional research interest in the topic of ACOA–codependency per se.

At the same time, it is important to understand the sequence of the growth and development of the ACOA–codependency movement. Alcoholics Anonymous came first, followed in order by Al-Anon, ACOA, CODA, and Gamblers Anonymous (GA) and other twelve-step recovery programs. This chronology is interesting because it reflects the importance of the ACOA and CODA recovery programs. CODA is the bridge connecting the earlier and more conservative programs of AA and Al-Anon with the other addictions that will be discussed in Chapter 14. As such, the ACOA–codependency narrative has had a significant background effect on the upstream research studies of alcohol, alcoholism, children of alcoholics, fetal alcohol syndrome, and other substance abuse. The downstream effects on research affect studies of gambling and other addictions.

CODEPENDENCY AND DIVERSITY

Feminist Critiques of Codependency

As you would expect, codependency has been thoroughly critiqued from researchers in the fields of sociology and women's studies. Criticism is wide-ranging, and most of it relates to white women. The feminist criticisms of codependency can fall into three broad categories: gender bias, the codependency discourse, and victimization and victimhood.

Most of the vociferous objections have come from those who see codependency as perpetuating a state of victimhood. From the manner in which many of these researchers write, it is easy to generalize many of their findings to racial/ethnic women. However, it is critical to note that, while feminists would readily agree about the presence of the oppression of women on an international scale, they would also agree that the West has tended to dominate both the theoretical and practical aspects of the feminist movement. Hence, the grand narrative of feminism is the story of Western endeavor and relegates the experience of non-Western women to the margins of feminist discourse (Kurian, 1999, p. 66).

In the United States culture, traditional feminism is not necessarily an appropriate voice for some or many racial/ethnic women. This does not mean that the criticisms advanced by feminists about codependency are irrelevant for the minority populations. It means that some of the criticisms discussed by feminists will be relevant and can be loosely generalized to minority populations. Some criticisms will not be able to be appropriately generalized. Perhaps equally important to note is that the codependent discourse affects both males and females. It just affects them differently. To our way of thinking, the impact of the codependent discourse in general is potentially more harmful to the population of women in general than it is to men. This is due to the social, political, and economic barriers that women face in today's culture.

GENDER BIAS   Researchers are in agreement that, given the multiple meanings of codependency, it is largely a social construct, as much perceiver as perceived (Harkness & Cotrell, 1997). Harkness and Cotrell (p. 473) and Rice (1992) believe that the concepts of codependency and enabling reflect a twelve-step culture perspective of the world. With this perspective as a backdrop, feminist critiques of gender bias in codependency argue against its many forms. The crux of their argument is that the concept of codependency is prejudicial toward women on social, political, and economic fronts. It also claims that the issue of gender bias and codependency is critical because the consequences for all women are serious (Hurcom, Copello, & Orford, 2000).

A review of the literature on gender bias and codependency reveals that the very notion of gender is a questionable construct and narrative. For instance, Butler (1990) believes that gender is not represented as "real," but as a boundary that is politically regulated. In agreeing with the principles of Butler's work, Phoca (1999) goes on to say that, since there is no essential masculine or feminine subject, both genders can take up masculine and feminine subject positioning. In essence, this perspective blurs the boundaries surrounding gender in the traditional sense.

Although you may not agree with these researchers, the implications of this blurring of boundaries for the AOD field are important to understand. The blurring of gender boundaries directly affects the definitions of codependency, as well as favorably affecting the ability of codependency research results to be generalized to larger populations. For instance, the AOD field has adopted a gender-neutral definition of codependency, such as the use of "adult," "person," "individual," and "family member." In other words, the definitions of codependency do not include or use the gender-driven terms "women" or "men" or any of their derivatives. Thus, the gender lines do not exist and, theoretically, anyone could be codependent.

Yet, in spite of these gender-neutral definitions, earlier studies conducted by Krestan and Bepko (1990) and Parker (1980) showed that the traditional views of addiction and codependency were rather traditional in that they usually reflected male substance abusers connected with helpful females. These helpful females, who were seen as also depending on addicted men, were labeled as codependent. In more current research, Babcock (1995), Babcock and McKay (1995), and Dear and Roberts (2002) reviewed the definitions and various meanings of codependency and enabling and assert that these concepts continue to be framed by traditional views of male and female. These researchers, along with others (e.g., Hurcom et al., 2000; Krestan & Bepko, 1990), argue that the existing structures of codependency nurture the development of caretaking and self-sacrifice in women while, at the same time, keeping men from developing those same qualities. In reality, men (as illustrated in our case example with Tim), can and do develop these traits. In addition, numerous men attend Codependents Anonymous groups (although figures are kept confidential because of the twelve-step traditions).

Unfortunately, little empirical research on males and codependency exists. One of the main consequences of this misidentification and gender bias is the fact that the use of such words as "(codependent) person" and/or "(codependent) adult" has failed to successfully assign codependency or codependent traits evenly across males and females. For instance, it is a fact that males receive treatment for alcoholism far more often than do women. It is a tragic irony that this treatment differential occurs in spite of the fact that women, who are significantly underrepresented in studies of AOD abuse, may have higher rates of alcoholism or other substance abuse problems than are reported in the professional literature and databases. Hence, from this gender-bias perspective, not only does the concept of codependency propel women into stereotypic roles, but it also is seen as helping to mask their AOD abuse. At the same time, gender bias is hindering the development of nurturing qualities in the male population.

THE CODEPENDENCY DISCOURSE   Several researchers (e.g., Babcock, 1995; Babcock & McKay, 1995; Krestan, 2000; Krestan & Bepko, 1990; Taleff & Babcock, 1998) write about the nature of discourse in our culture as it relates to codependency. Taleff and Babcock (1998) review the literature in the AOD field and identify five dominant discourses that guided the early AOD treatment culture. Two of these dominant narratives relate directly to the concept of codependency. According to Taleff and Babcock (pp. 34–39), the dominant discourses "in AOD work" are these:

- Blame the client for treatment failure
- Blame the victim
- Closeness equals pathology
- Too much knowledge is bad (don't think, it will get you in trouble)
- Never trust the client (all addicts are cons and manipulators)

Blaming the victim and closeness equals pathology related directly to the codependency issue. In examining family systems theory and treatment approaches, Babcock and McKay (1995) believe that the notion of codependency has been the most blatant example of blaming the victim. Hurcom et al. (2000) believe that role-specific behaviors that result from a partner being addicted do more than blame. They pathologize the behavior. This followed the research of Taleff and Babcock (1998), who concluded that the AOD field tends to blame family members for the ongoing addiction (p. 37).

This research stream strongly characterizes an essential concern regarding the codependency discourse and feminism. Through this pathological narrative, helping is not perceived as a well-meaning, misguided, and yet unsuccessful attempt to thwart off the addict's self-destruction. Rather, codependency is an insidious strategy used by the addict's significant other(s) aimed at perpetuating the addiction. The discourse of blame and pathology results in the fact that cultural closeness, love, anxiety, and feminine nurturing are ignored. On a core assumptive level, the argument is that the paradigm reflects that people who are engaging in codependent behaviors are insidious and are not to be trusted. Women engaging in these behaviors are posited as untrustworthy as well as anti-feminine, because their natural tendency to nurture is now seen as unhealthy and is to blame for the addiction.

These researchers, as well as Krestan and Bepko (1990), see the need to understand the phenomenon of *closeness* as a way of overcoming the problems with this perspective. Clinicians need to be able to distinguish between normal, healthy closeness and pathological closeness or dependency. Moreover, clinicians need to assess families with AOD problems in terms of the amount of healthy *interdependence* that exists. If clinicians have a simplistic understanding of the gender-bias issue and codependency, they will miss what is clearly a complex phenomenon.

VICTIMIZATION AND VICTIMHOOD   A related issue is the social discourse of victimization and victimhood. This broad, social narrative is different from the AOD discourses identified by Taleff and Babcock (1998). Nevertheless, the social discourse of victimization clearly has significant implications for the meanings of codependency.

For example, Irvine (1999) presents a subtle and powerful argument regarding the dominant social discourse and victimization as a response. She maintains that the individuals "left or abandoned" are the ones most often claiming the status of victimhood. Moreover, these "victims" are more likely to be unemployed, have fewer commitments to family, and be less committed to service in CODA (p. 148). Through this perspective, victimization and victimhood are structurally tied to the person's position with regard to who "left the relationship first" (p. 148). This same researcher maintains that victims usually have fewer social–structural resources available to them. As a result, the narrative of victimization initially responds to and then, ironically, augments these very social–structural losses. Irvine (1999) sees this as a failure of our larger social structure to protect individuals from these social losses and resulting isolation. Given these insightful assertions, it is appropriate for counselors to assess the extent to which victimization is stated and the extent to which it might be more of a trait in individuals with AOD abuse issues (Irvine, 1999, pp. 156–157).

At the core assumptive level, victimization and victimhood place individuals, mostly women and racial/ethnic minorities, underneath the dominant discourse. This is because this discourse, in which these groups are portrayed as always seeking, presupposes an absence of something. Among other things, this seeking behavior is a "less than" position. The result is a vicious cycle that continues to isolate individuals from the mainstream and into a constant search to balance the scale.

Harkness and Cotrell (1997) also advance a thoughtful critique of codependency from feminist perspectives. These researchers agree with the views of Irvine (1999) and Krestan and Bepko (1990) regarding the issues of pathologizing and blame. Citing the works of Asher (1992), Collins (1993), and others, Harkness and Cotrell discuss the notion that codependency is re-oppressing women through the recapitulation of patriarchal politics of power in recovery. These same researchers also maintain that, from a certain feminist perspective, the cure for codependency is equally as toxic as the disease itself. They agree with Collins in asserting that the recovery is toxic because it is based on the core basic assumption of subordination.

The argument is similar to the argument about powerlessness and recovery for racial/ethnic minorities discussed in Chapter 11. The argument is based on the idea that recovery is toxic because codependent persons must assume a stance of powerlessness in order to become free from addiction. This powerlessness is layered by the experience of powerlessness in the sociopolitical realm. Thus, feminist concerns about codependency and recovery reflect the subtle and powerful social realm impacting the identification and treatment of women in need.

Codependency and Collectivist Cultures

According to many researchers, studies are also needed that examine codependency in women of other cultures. In terms of assessing codependency in women of diverse cultures, Gayol and Lira (2002) conducted a study aimed at validating an instrument for assessing codependency in Mexican women. Gayol and Lira used a sample of 230 Mexican women (aged 18 to 65 years). The Codependency Instrument (ICOD) was designed to assess codependency in this female population. The authors used a sample of 41 women to determine the ability of the instrument to discriminate between codependency and non-codependency. The results demonstrate that the instrument is a valid and reliable method for screening probable cases of codependency in couple relationships in Mexican women. The research results also indicate a higher proportion of codependency women whose relationships included either an alcoholic partner or one who was abusive.

THE SELF AND BOUNDARIES   Central to codependency is the concept of self and the subsequent issue of boundaries (Kelley et al., 2007; Watt, 2002). When codependency first appeared in Western culture and was embraced as a popular movement, it was criticized as being anti-marriage, anti-religion, and antisocial. These same criticisms exist today, although not necessarily in the same vociferous form. Essentially, these arguments center on codependency's overemphasis on the self. Codependency is seen as a relational problem in which a person's self is not complete, not satisfied, and not fulfilled until entering into relation with something or someone. As Whitaker (1991) says, this leads these individuals to constantly be "looking somewhere else" for fulfillment.

Once in relationships, codependent individuals were encouraged to set boundaries and, if the need arose, were encouraged to disassociate from marital partners and organized religion and, instead, focus on one's own needs. The concept of selfishness was reframed into the idea that it is better to be selfish than to be selfless. Codependents were selfless and needed to become more independent. However, Kim (1996) maintains that Americans [*sic*] have created the fantasy that they can live independent lives. For this researcher, Americans believe that being independent is equivalent to being free. In this manner, dependency becomes a negative characteristic and is viewed as a "failure to be autonomous."

Because of the collective nature of many non-Western peoples, it is imperative that mental health professionals understand that the notions of boundaries, such as independence and dependence, are culturally defined. To punctuate the point, Kwon (2001, p. 49) states that codependency theorists have failed to describe the cultural matrix of relationality, since their Western views of selfhood conflict with those of Korean and other Asian philosophies at a core assumptive level. For instance, the self in Asian culture is configured entirely differently from Western notions. In general, Asian peoples have strikingly different construals of such constructs as the self, others, and of the interdependence of the two. In turn, these construals can influence and sometimes determine the nature of individual experience, including motivation and emotion (Kwon, p. 43). The significant impact of these different construals is reflected in the quote by Kim (1996), also cited in Kwon (p. 46). Kim says that if one used the Western notions of codependency to examine Korean or Asian family enmeshment, the resulting blurred ego boundaries and diminished ego strength should be reflected in higher rates of psychopathology in Asia and Korea than in the United States. Kim states that this view is not supported by data. In another illustration, Kwon says that many Americans say to their children who refuse to eat their supper, "Think of all the starving children in Africa and how blessed you are to be *different* from them." In Asia, Kwon says that the same story would go, "Think about the *farmer* who worked so hard to grow this rice for you. Think about how bad the *farmer* will feel if you do not eat your supper.

The farmer's efforts will have been in vain!" Kwon says that both statements seem to involve others (starving kids and farmers). However, the starving kids are only *compared* to American children; they are not *related*.

The notion of relatedness is central in Asian societies. According to Kim, Americans have been cultured into setting boundaries in relation to others. Moreover, this awareness of boundaries has been deeply and inextricably woven into a cultural imperative of *autonomy and self-control*. Relationality becomes odious in that it would force some Americans to surrender this cultural ideal. A final example illustrates Kwon's (2001) views follows:

> When I first came to the United States and was becoming acquainted with American culture, I was bewildered when told by an American friend of mine, "Hey, leave me alone!" At the time, I asked myself a question, "Have I ever told *anyone*, 'please leave me alone'?" In my memory, I had never insisted on setting my boundary by saying, "Leave me alone." (p. 42)

In many collective cultures, the fundamental relatedness of the person is emphasized. In other words, the selfhood of the individual is sought more from a relational than from the internal attributes of rugged individualism. This difference clearly requires a reworking of the notion of blurred boundaries when working with some Korean or Asian individuals and families. Ego boundaries are established to separate or differentiate ourselves from others, and relational boundaries are created when we form our own sense of self in relation to others (Kwon, 2001). Kwon says that Koreans are not used to expressing *themselves*. They are accustomed to engaging in appropriate action that has their self-evaluations focused on normative information such as, "Is it appropriate or does it please others?" Many Asians are taught to feel more comfortable fitting in, rather than being separate or unique.

Therefore, it is not surprising to hear Carr (1997) state that it is more problematic for Koreans to work with self-identity and relatedness than it would be for them to work with identity and autonomy from others. In other words, the problems encountered in that culture move in a different direction than those occurring in America. With respect to mental health, codependent Americans have problems with others and need to be separating from them. Koreans and other Asians have problems because they are alone with the self. (In actuality, it would be more accurate to say that "they are alone and have no self" and need to be joining with others.) For Americans, the difficulty is in the separation. For Koreans, the difficulty is in the joining.

RELATIONSHIP BETWEEN SOCIAL OPPRESSION AND CODEPENDENCY Borovoy (2000, 2005, 2009) and Kwon (2001) are both interested in the impact of the larger social narratives on the meanings of codependency for women in Asian cultures. Borovoy states that since alcoholism in Japan has become more of a social concern the notion of codependency is becoming a more significant issue. Borovoy agrees with many feminist researchers in believing that the codependency narrative pathologized women in the 1980s. Moreover, Borovoy agrees with Kwon in maintaining that the Western meanings of codependency do not transfer well to the Japanese (Asian) culture.

In Japan, the American version of codependency is seen as normal and not viewed as a compromise of the self. Borovoy goes on to state that the codependency discourse in Japan is reminiscent of its postwar national ideologies. These ideologies reflect the value of a family-like (codependent?) intimacy holding together Japanese society. This dominant discourse also implores its social members to develop a highly cultivated sensitivity to social demands.

Kim (2002) is also interested in the impact of a codependent discourse on women of Korea and other Asian cultures. Kim took an accepted feminist perspective in noting the significant influence that social oppression has on codependency. Kim develops a concept of codependency that is derived from the Korean notion of *jong-sok-euee-jon,* known as "subjugated dependency" (p. 2569). In this context, codependency in Korean women is seen as resulting from the oppressive Confucian patriarchy in marriage and family systems. The hypothesis of this qualitative study was that there would be a strong relationship between the persistence of Confucian patriarchal values and practices in the Korean family structure and females' disposition to codependency in their marriages. Results confirmed the hypothesis for this sample: A positive relationship exists between codependency and the practices of Confucian patriarchal values.

The studies underscore the significance of being sensitive to cultural differences when applying the essential concepts of Western codependency to collective cultures, specifically for women in Korea and Japan. Borovoy (2000, 2005) believes that Japanese women who define themselves as codependent need to distinguish between socially valued interdependence and unhealthy or systematically exploitive forms of asymmetrical ties. Borovoy believes that, in this way, these codependent women can reject the exploitive demands of society while continuing to function in familial and neighboring communities (p. 94).

MyCounselingLab™

Go to Topic 8: *Family Treatment* in the MyCounselingLab™ site (www .MyCounselingLab.com) for *Substance Abuse: Information for School Counselors, Social Workers, Therapists, and Counselors,* Fifth Edition, where you can:

- Find learning outcomes for *Family Treatment* along with the national standards that connect to these outcomes.
- Complete Assignments and Activities that can help you more deeply understand the chapter content.
- Apply and practice your understanding of the core skills identified in the chapter with the Building Counseling Skills unit.
- Prepare yourself for professional certification with a Practice for Certification quiz.
- Connect to videos through the Video and Resource Library.

Summary

- The 1980s witnessed a spate of interest in the concept of Adult Children of Alcoholics (ACOAs) and codependency, concepts that, although different, many associate together.
- The clinical characteristics exhibited by ACOAs include low self-esteem, being overly responsible, having depressive symptoms, exhibiting antisocial behavior, anxiety disorders, parentification, and blurred and enmeshed boundaries in relationships.
- Other traits include difficulty with intimacy, discomfort with emotions, indecisiveness, and excessively giving into the needs of others.
- Some evidence exists that ACOAs are at risk for substance abuse.

- Intervening with ACOAs includes the identification and addressing of early symptoms of problematic drinking and dysfunctional behavior and should also include the development of appropriate coping skills to replace those that may predispose clients to relational issues.
- There are many definitions of codependency, and these definitions are influenced by the degree to which one subscribes to the concept; many who do not subscribe believe the characteristics have already been identified in various *DSM-IV-TR* diagnostic classifications.
- Many see codependency as an addiction that is chronic, progressive, and fatal.
- Feminists criticize the concept of codependency asserting that the discourse blames the client for failure, blames the victim, equates closeness with pathology, and advocates for therapists to not totally trust their clients.
- Codependency does not translate well into collective culture narratives because of the emphasis upon "We"; in Asian cultures many see a positive and unhealthy relationship between codependency and Confucian patriarchal values.
- Regarding treatment concerns, the client's use of the label ACOA and/or the term "codependent" can be helpful in that the terms are easy to understand, and many individuals are familiar with the concepts.
- Mental health professionals should remain aware of their own proclivities toward behaving codependently with their clientele.

Internet Resources

Adult Children of Alcoholics
adultchildren.org/

Codependency
mnwelldir.org/docs/mental_health/codependency.htm
mentalhealthamerican.net

Step Families
stepfamilies.info/
stepfamily.org

Further Discussion

1. What are your views of Adult Children of Alcoholics? Is there such a concept?
2. Why is there so much controversy about ACOAs?
3. What is beneficial about labeling oneself as an ACOA and/or codependent?
4. Codependency has been criticized for gender bias. To what extent do you agree or disagree with those claims?
5. In what ways does mental health professionals' codependency help or not help this population?

Chapter *13*

HIV/AIDS

MyCounselingLab™

Visit the MyCounselingLab™ site (www.MyCounselingLab.com) for *Substance Abuse: Information for School Counselors, Social Workers, Therapists, and Counselors,* Fifth Edition to enhance your understanding of chapter concepts. You'll have the opportunity to practice your skills through video- and case-based Assignments and Activities as well as Building Counseling Skills units and to prepare for your certification exam with Practice for Certification quizzes.

CASE EXAMPLES

❶ Ron is HIV-positive and has been on antiretroviral therapy. He has had an undetectable viral load for the past three years. He is applying for a job as a food server and is worried about questions that he may be asked about the lapse of continuous employment that occurred when he first became HIV-infected and depressed. He is afraid that if he is truthful about his chronic illness, he will not be able to get the job.

❷ Emily and Michael have been married for three years. Both have been aware of Michael's HIV status ever since they began dating. Although they have been practicing safe sex, Emily is becoming increasingly concerned about getting infected and has stopped wanting to have sex altogether. Michael understands her concerns, yet he feels helpless, angry, and guilty as a result. He had attended counseling sessions after he first found out that he was infected. However, he stopped going when the counselor pressed him about disclosing his status to potential partners. He did disclose to Emily when they first began to consider sexual relations, but he found himself feeling too vulnerable to want to share more with the counselor whom he perceived as not really understanding.

❸ Charneatha is a 13-year-old middle school student who lives in a low-income urban area. She was sexually abused as a child by one of her parent's friends, which her parents became aware of only after it happened. Recently, Charneatha's parents have been arguing over whether or not to provide birth control pills to their daughter, who has been hinting about sexual activity.

Charneatha's father is against it, but her mother wants Charneatha to take birth control because she is frightened about her daughter being at high risk. During the course of their conversations, they both realized that neither had really come to closure on their daughter's sexual abuse.

❹ Gerardo is a gay male who came out to his friend on his 17th birthday. Neither had been educated about HIV from their families or friends. School policy had precluded any discussion of "safe sex" and both adolescents were raised by heterosexual parents who did not discuss sex at all. He first learned about anal sex from the Internet, where he was watching heterosexual pornography. Still, he did not know about the imperatives of using condoms every time because he did not witness it on the Internet. His first partner was a gay male adolescent of the same age who had only experienced oral sex. Both thought that anal sex was "low risk" if you did not ejaculate. Both also thought that you "make AIDS" rather than contracting it from an infected person.

❺ Jenean, 63, began dating again two years after her husband died. Her first date was with a friend she had known for a long time. After a period of dating, she and George (age 57) decided to have sex. Because she was past the childbearing years, she did not believe she needed him to use a condom. And because of their respective ages, she did not ask him about his sexual background. She was shocked when she tested positive for HIV months later.

In May of 1981, five cases of Pneumocystis carinii pneumonia were reported to the Centers for Disease Control (CDC) in Atlanta, Georgia. In December of the same year, more than 100 gay men were diagnosed with Kaposi's sarcoma (a skin cancer). So much interest was generated that by September 1982, the CDC officially identified and labeled the acquired immunodeficiency syndrome (AIDS) as resulting from HIV infection. To give you some perspective on the disease, consider this: Pretend you were reading this paragraph in 1992, a mere 10 years after the CDC first labeled AIDS. In the time that it would have taken you to read this page in 1992, one American would have been infected with HIV. In the time that it would have taken you to read this chapter in 1992, three more people would have died from AIDS. By the end of one day in 1992, 212 people would have been diagnosed with full-blown AIDS (Primm, 1992). While a new case of HIV infection occurred about every minute or so in 1992, a new HIV diagnosis occurs about every nine minutes in 2011. HIV/AIDS is now considered a chronic disease for those who have both access to and tolerance for the powerful drugs used in treatment (National Institutes of Health, 2011a). There still is no cure.

INCIDENCE AND PREVALENCE

In 2006 in the United States, 1.1 million people were living with HIV infection, and approximately 56,000 of them had been newly diagnosed that year. In 2006, 40 states and five independent areas had confidential name-based reporting of HIV infection. As shown in Figure 13.1, the highest incidence for HIV infection was reported in the 20–24 age group (6,237), followed by the 25–29 age group (5,951), and then by the 40–44 age group (5,519).

Table 13.1 reflects the incidence of HIV infection by race or ethnicity. From these figures, you can see that black/African Americans counted for twice the number of HIV infections (21,652) than the next closest group, whites (11,803).

FIGURE 13.1 Incidence of HIV infection in the United States in 2006. *Source:* Centers for Disease Control and Prevention (2009b).

TABLE 13.1 Diagnoses of HIV Infection by Race/Ethnicity

Race or Ethnicity	Estimated Number of HIV Infections, 2009
American Indian/Alaska Native	189
Asian American	470
Black/African American	21,652
Hispanic/Latino	7,347
Native Hawaiian/other Pacific Islander	34
White	11,803
Multiple	516

Source: Centers for Disease Control and Prevention (2009b).

Although there remains no known vaccine for HIV and no known cure for AIDs, it is clear that we have come a long way in being able to treat and/or manage the disease. According to the National Institute on Drug Abuse (2011), data reflect that the HIV infections and AIDS-related deaths are both declining.

MYTHS AND FACTS ABOUT HIV AND AIDS

Because of the severity of the AIDS epidemic, rumors and misinformation about the disease abound. In general, three areas of interest and of potential misinformation can be identified. One area is information about HIV itself—what it is, what it does, and how an individual infected with HIV will appear to others. Another area of concern relates to how HIV is transmitted, and the third area focuses on the workplace—what employers can and cannot do regarding a worker with HIV or AIDS.

The HIV Virus

Human immunodeficiency virus is known as HIV. The virus attacks a person's immune system, thereby damaging the individual's ability to fight off other opportunistic diseases such as pneumonia or cancers. If left untreated, the majority of persons will develop signs of the illness within five to 10 years after becoming infected. However, it can take 10 to 15 years for AIDS to develop. Individuals infected with HIV develop a characteristic serum antibody response that can usually be detected between two weeks and six months following exposure (Selwyn, 1992). However, as much as six months to two years may pass before one's body begins producing detectable HIV antibodies (Pimentel & Lamendella, 1988). Roughly 5% of all HIV-infected persons remain free from AIDS-related diseases (Hooker, 1996).

TESTING FOR HIV The HIV antibody test reflects only exposure to the AIDS virus, but this exposure does not mean that the person will develop the AIDS disease. It is possible for a person to test positive for HIV antibodies and suffer no detectable immune system damage, feel healthy, and not develop full AIDS disease. The incubation period between HIV infection and AIDS is 10 to 15 years (World Health Organization, 2010). However, once individuals have been infected with HIV, the likelihood that they will develop AIDS is high; the only unknown factor is when this will occur, since the progression of illness is unpredictable. Of the HIV infections diagnosed in 2004, 39% were diagnosed with AIDS within 12 months. The most vulnerable populations for this diagnosis were those older than 35 and intravenous drug users (IDUs). Although early detection of HIV and medical treatment can slow the progression of AIDS significantly, medical treatment cannot stop AIDS from developing.

DIAGNOSIS OF AIDS AND AIDS RELATED COMPLEX AIDS and AIDS Related Complex (ARC) are medical diagnoses indicating a specific set of characteristic symptoms. A diagnosis of AIDS is made when any of 12 opportunistic infections (e.g., Pneumocystis carinii pneumonia) and/or any of three malignancies (e.g., Kaposi's sarcoma) are reliably diagnosed in the absence of any other known cause for immunodeficiency (CDC, 1994). AIDS Related Complex refers to the condition of those individuals who have damaged immune systems and some specific symptoms, which include night sweats, weight loss, and lymphoma, but who do not have any of the opportunistic infections associated with AIDS. An individual may be diagnosed as having AIDS Related Complex and be sick some of the time with less serious opportunistic infections than those found in AIDS cases. Individuals with AIDS or AIDS Related Complex may show signs of a disease, but they will not always be sick. Thus, an individual may test antibody positive but show no signs of opportunistic diseases. On the other hand, an individual may have full-blown AIDS in which any number of opportunistic infections may be present.

To date, no known vaccine is available that can prevent HIV infection, nor does a cure for AIDS exist. Although new information is being discovered every day, as of 2011 no cure for AIDS has been found.

Transmission of HIV

The method by which AIDS is transmitted is undisputed, and no new information regarding this issue is expected. Anyone infected with HIV can infect others. According to World Health

TABLE 13.2 Incidence of HIV in U.S. by Transmission and Gender in 2009

Method of Transmission	Adult/Adolescent Males	Adult/Adolescent Females	Total Estimated Number in 2009
Male-to-male sexual contact	23,846	–	23,846
Injection drug use	2,449	1,483	3,932
Heterosexual contact with known HIV-infected person or one at high risk	4,399	8,461	12,860

Source: Centers for Disease Control and Prevention, 2009b

Communications (1988), "HIV is transmitted primarily during sexual contact through parenteral exposure to blood and blood products, and from mother to child during the perinatal period" (p. 10). Hence, "[t]he virus must be transmitted from the blood stream of a person with AIDS to the blood stream of another person" (Pimentel & Lamendella, 1988, p. 42).

Table 13.2 depicts the types of transmission of HIV, and it is clear that male-to-male contact remains the most common way that HIV is transmitted in 2009. Males continue to outnumber females in contracting HIV from injecting drugs. Yet, the number of females who are diagnosed with HIV from heterosexual contact is almost two times more than males. The probable causes for this will be discussed later in the chapter.

Because of how blood used in hospital settings is now screened, it is rare for someone to become infected through a transfusion or blood clotting factors. Babies born to HIV-infected women may become infected before or during birth or through breast-feeding after birth. Although unusual, health care workers have been infected with HIV after being stuck with needles containing HIV-infected blood or after infected blood gets into a worker's open cut or a mucous membrane, such as the eyes or inside of the nose. Only one instance is known of a patient being infected by a health care worker in the United States, and this involved HIV transmission from one infected dentist to six patients (CDC, 2007b). According to the CDC, research involving more than 22,000 patients of 63 HIV-infected physicians, surgeons, and dentists found no other case of this type of transmission in the United States.

Nevertheless, about 20% of the people infected with HIV do not know they are infected. When this occurs, these individuals often contract AIDS within a year of the diagnosis. What is equally alarming is the fact that someone who is HIV-infected and not cognizant of it can transmit the disease to unsuspecting others. This type of transmission is said to account for roughly one-half of the HIV infections each year. That means that of the 56,000 people infected in 2006, about 28,000 were infected by people unaware of their infection. What is both sad and confusing is that the National Institutes of Health (2011) found that if people would be tested, timely HIV therapy can cut the risk of this transmission by 96%.

LIVING WITH A PERSON WITH HIV/AIDS Many myths surround the fears of living with an HIV-infected individual and becoming infected. An individual living with a person with HIV cannot get HIV through

- Kissing
- Biting
- Saliva, sweat, and tears

- Environmental contact
- Insect bites

With some precautions, living with a person infected with HIV or AIDS is almost completely safe. Only rare occurrences of infection have been identified, and those cases were found to have resulted from contact between skin or mucous membranes and infected blood. The CDC (2007b) provides the following guidelines for prevention of transmission:

- Wear gloves during contact with blood or other body fluids that could possibly contain visible blood, such as urine, feces, or vomit.
- Be sure to cover cuts, sores, or breaks on both the caregiver's and patient's exposed skin with bandages.
- Immediately wash hands and other parts of the body after contact with blood or other body fluids.
- Surfaces soiled with blood should be disinfected immediately and appropriately.
- Avoid sharing razors, toothbrushes, or other objects or engaging in practices that increase the likelihood of blood contact.
- Needles and other sharp instruments should be used only when medically necessary and handled according to recommendations for health care settings. Do not put caps back on needles by hand or remove needles from syringes. Dispose of needles in puncture-proof containers out of the reach of children and visitors.

SEXUAL CONTACT When condoms are used reliably, they have been shown to prevent pregnancy up to 98% of the time among couples using them as their only method of contraception. Similarly, numerous studies among sexually active people have demonstrated that a properly used latex condom provides a high degree of protection against a variety of sexually transmitted diseases, including HIV infection. Condoms are classified as medical devices and are thus regulated by the Food and Drug Administration (FDA). Condom manufacturers in the United States test each latex condom for defects, including holes, before it is packaged. However, only latex or polyurethane condoms provide a highly effective mechanical barrier to HIV. Natural skin condoms may contain natural pores and are not recommended for prevention of HIV. Women should consider using the female condom when a male condom cannot be used.

WORKING OR INTERACTING WITH HIV-INFECTED INDIVIDUALS HIV is not known to be transmitted to coworkers, clients, or consumers from contact in industries such as food-service establishments. In fact, an HIV-infected food-service worker (e.g., cook, waitress, bartender) need not be restricted from work unless he or she has other infections or illnesses (such as diarrhea or hepatitis A) for which any food-service worker, regardless of HIV infection status, should be restricted. This information would be helpful to Ron, the first case example we presented in the chapter opening.

Likewise, no evidence exists of transmission from a personal-service worker to a client or vice versa. This includes hairdressers, barbers, cosmetologists, and massage therapists. No known instance of HIV transmission through tattooing or body piercing has ever been identified. Theoretically, HIV infection could occur from this process, though, if unhealed piercings come into contact with an infected person's blood. Healing from various piercings can take weeks or months. Workers using needles for tattooing, piercing ears or other body parts, or for acupuncture should use them only once. Although the risk of HIV infection is low in these situations, the hepatitis B virus has been transmitted through some of these practices (CDC, 2007b).

Living with an HIV-infected person may also pose a threat in the case of co-occurrence of tuberculosis (Selwyn, 1992). Although prolonged exposure to TB is normally necessary for infection to occur, it is very important that infected individuals cover their mouths and noses when coughing and to take all of the prescribed TB medication (Washington State Department of Health, 1996). Because of the risk of TB infection to household members, it is recommended that all who live with an HIV-infected individual be screened for TB and followed up.

RISK FACTORS AND HIGH-RISK POPULATIONS

General Risk Factors

From the statistics cited at the beginning of this chapter, it seems as though race and gender are risk factors for HIV-infection. The CDC (2008) maintains that black males, Hispanic/Latino males, and black women have the highest rates of new HIV infections. The CDC also reports that 1 in 16 black males and 1 in 32 black women will be diagnosed with HIV at some point in their lives (CDC, 2010f as will 1 in 36 Hispanic/Latino men and 1 in 106 Hispanic/Latina women (CDC, 2008).

The CDC (2006b) has identified the following general risk factors for HIV:

- Sharing needles, syringes, cotton, or water with others while injecting drugs or steroids
- Engaging in unprotected sex, including vaginal, anal, or oral, with men who have sex with other men, with multiple partners, and/or with anonymous partners
- Exchanging sex for drugs or money
- Receiving a blood transfusion or clotting factor between 1978 and 1985
- Receiving diagnosis or being treated for hepatitis, tuberculosis (TB), or a sexually transmitted disease (STD)
- Having unprotected sex with anyone who has any of the risk factors listed above

Co-Infection: HIV Infection and Other Diseases

Since HIV was first diagnosed, an association between HIV infection, drug use, tuberculosis (TB), and sexually transmitted diseases (now more commonly termed *sexually transmitted infections* [STIs]) has been found. Anyone can get TB: people of all races and colors, rich and poor, of any age. Despite a decline in TB nationwide, rates have increased in certain states, and elevated TB rates continue to be reported in certain populations (e.g., foreign-born persons and racial/ethnic minorities). People with HIV also seem to be at higher risk for TB as well as at higher risk for STIs. TB is a lethal disease for those with HIV. It is estimated that more than 11.4 million people worldwide have TB and HIV co-infection (National Institute of Allergy and Infectious Diseases, 2009). Tuberculosis is treatable, and it can usually be cured even in those living with HIV. However, diagnosing TB in individuals with HIV infection is difficult, and some strains of TB are particularly resistant to the common antibodies used to treat them CDC (2005a). Currently, according to the National Institute of Allergy and Infectious Diseases (2009), those individuals with co-occurring HIV and TB primarily die from tuberculosis and not from AIDS.

Sexually transmitted infections (STIs), remain a major public health challenge in the United States. The CDC (2009b) estimates that 19 million new infections occur each year, almost half of them among young people ages 15 to 24. In general, individuals who are infected with STIs are at least two to five times more likely to acquire HIV if they are exposed through sexual contact. However, the risk may be increased up to tenfold, especially where an STI such as syphilis, cancroids, or herpes causes inflammation or open sores on the genital or perineal area of either partner.

Health problems for women with STIs tend to be more severe than those for men. This is due mainly to the fact that many STIs are asymptomatic in the early stages and, therefore, often go undetected and untreated. Most STIs are more easily transmitted to women than to men, and the rate of infection reveals that women are twice as likely to contract gonorrhea, chlamydia, chancroid, or hepatitis B during a single act of unprotected intercourse with an infected partner. Statistics for STIs combined with those for HIV among women and adolescents, highlight the fact that these two populations are at great risk.

The close parallel between HIV infection and AIDS, TB, and sexually transmitted diseases is clearly disturbing. Reasons for such high rates of exposure and infection have been studied by various human interest groups such as the National Institutes of Health, the Centers for Disease Control and Prevention, the World Health Organization, and others. In general, risk for these diseases is correlated with sociopolitical issues. Factors such as immigration (from areas where TB and STIs are prominent), increased poverty, homelessness, IV drug use, limited access to health care, and living in communities with a high prevalence of STIs all have been identified as high-risk factors (CDC, 2006c Hooker, 1996).

Risk Factors for Women

In the United States, the proportion of women among new HIV or AIDS diagnoses has increased sharply from 15% before 1995 to 27% in 2004. According to Mphande-Finn and Sommers-Flanagan (2007) and the CDC (2007a), AIDS among women is on the rise and is partly related to the fact that women are approximately twice as likely as men to contract HIV during vaginal intercourse. Whereas males most often contract HIV through homosexual contact, nearly 80% of new HIV cases in women are caused by heterosexual intercourse. A U.S. Department of Health and Human Services (HHS) Public Health Report (2004, p. 2) found that most women with HIV are racial and ethnic minority women living in urban inner cities who are disproportionately affected by poverty, crime, and social disorganization and represent the most disenfranchised sector of our society. According to the same report, rates of psychiatric disorders among HIV-infected women (53% for any disorder) are higher than for their noninfected counterparts. Of these disorders, a diagnosis of substance abuse disorder occurred in 25% to 66% of these women, 15% had a major depressive disorder, and approximately 35% had posttraumatic stress disorder (PTSD).

The World Health Organization (2007) believes that gender norms impact a women's vulnerability to HIV. The cultural climate allows males to have more sexual partners than women and encourages older males to have sex with younger females, and the statistics showing higher infection rates for younger women than for younger men seem to bear this out. Women may want their partners to use condoms, yet women often lack the power to make them do so. In that one-third of women with HIV report PTSD, it is clear that physical, emotional, and sexual violence also contribute to the vulnerability for women. The impact of such a narrative is seen in several venues. For example, forced sex can contribute to tears and lacerations and thus put women at greater risk for HIV infection. Moreover, violence or the threat of it can prevent the negotiation of safer sex practices and can prevent women from sharing the results of HIV-positive tests.

According to the CDC (2007b) and UNAIDS (2006), approximately 75% of women newly diagnosed with HIV were infected during unprotected sex. More often than not, these women were infected by male partners who had engaged in risky sexual behaviors. Twenty percent of women diagnosed with HIV in 2004 acquired it during unsafe injection drug use.

Although heterosexual women would appear to be more at risk for HIV, lesbian women also have a small risk for becoming infected with HIV. The Centers for Disease Control and Prevention (2010g) maintains that female-to-female transmission of HIV is rare. Nonetheless, lesbian women may be subject to risk factors associated with substance abuse, sex with gay or bisexual men, artificial insemination, and sexually transmitted diseases (CDC, 2006e).

Culturally and Ethnically Diverse Populations

Only seven countries are estimated to have more people living with HIV than the United States (UNAIDS, 2006). According to the CDC (2007a), data from HIV and AIDS prevalence and incidence surveys continue to reflect the disproportionate and differential impact of the HIV epidemic on racial and ethnic minority populations.

According to Shambley-Ebron (2009), African American women are 25 times more likely than their white American counterparts to be HIV-infected. The overwhelmingly high incidence of HIV in minority populations (see Table 13.1) may be partly explained by the concentration of IV drug abuse in those populations. However, because of the paucity of research into minority drug abuse (see Chapter 4), one can really only surmise reasons for this remarkably high incidence. Another factor identified as being associated with a higher incidence of HIV infection among minorities is the general distrust of the health care system by these groups. This is especially true for minority women (O'Leary & Jemmott, 1995; Ullery & Carney, 2000). The CDC (2007a), UNAIDS (2006), and Myers, Javanbakht, Martinez, and Obediah (2003) found African Americans as having the highest overall HIV prevalence, HIV incidence, and HIV mortality. African American youth continue to have disproportionate representation in the incidence and prevalence of HIV (Lightfoot & Milburn, 2009). Moreover, this population "has the greatest number of years of potential life lost to the disease" (Myers et al., 2003, p. 66). These same researchers identify such factors as low socioeconomic status, sexual orientation, HIV serostatus, substance use or abuse, and psychosocial factors such as self-esteem and perceived loss of control as also contributing to the risk.

Adolescents

Adolescents and young adults are significantly overrepresented in the HIV-positive and sexually transmitted infections (STIs) populations (Solórzano & Glassgold, 2010). Teens at increased risk for HIV infection include runaways and homeless youth, gay and bisexual youth, youth in juvenile facilities and adult jails, those in foster care, injecting drug users, crack cocaine users, those who have been sexually assaulted, out-of-school youth, and minority youth (Hooker, 1996). While these risk factors are self-explanatory, one implication of great significance is hidden. Studies have shown that children and adolescents who were sexually abused were more likely to engage in activities that increased their risk for HIV infection (Capuzzi & Gross, 1996; Jones et al., 2010). Specifically, Capuzzi and Gross found that females who were sexually abused were three times more likely to have injected drugs and five times more likely to have had intercourse before the age of 13. The males who reported sexual abuse were nine times more likely to report injecting drugs and nearly four times as likely to have initiated sexual intercourse before the age of 13. This is the information that Charneatha's mother had in Case Example 3. She felt that her daughter was at risk because of her daughter's sexual abuse. Yet, she was unable to convince her husband that providing birth control was not the same as condoning sex.

Another risk factor for adolescents is their age, upbringing, and exposure to information. As shown in Case Example 4, Gerardo and his companion had very little information about

HIV/AIDS and very little information about sex. Instead, they gleaned information off the Internet where they watched heterosexual pornography. This case study reflects the idea of "folk knowledge" about HIV (Kubiceket al., 2008) as opposed to "professional knowledge." Professional knowledge reflects the idea of a "prevention ethic," which revolves around the notion of "a condom every time" (Race, 2003). While adolescents may not be "at risk as an entire group," you can clearly see how younger age, inexperience, and in some cases school policy prohibiting discussions of sex can be critical factors in placing some member of this age group at higher risk.

Race of the adolescent is also a factor. According to Shambley-Ebron (2009), African American female adolescents are at more risk than their Caucasian counterparts. This is likely due to the fact that African American girls generally reach puberty quicker and report sexual initiation at earlier stages. What makes this group at risk, though, is that often the African American female adolescent is involved with an older male who has had more sexual partners. This risk is augmented because age and cognitive development are not always in synch. While they may be physically mature, African American female adolescents are still as undeveloped emotionally and cognitively as their Caucasian counterparts. The lack of cognitive development may place these physically mature girls in situations that are more risky.

Other High-Risk Groups

THOSE IN THE PENAL SYSTEM Adolescents, especially male adolescents who cycle through the juvenile justice system, are at high risk for HIV infection (Lauby et al., 2010). The reason for the higher risk is the fact that juveniles in the justice system often have a history of engaging in higher rates of sexual risk behaviors. This can include initiating sexual activity at younger ages, having multiple sex partners, and inconsistent use of condoms.

Little evidence exists to describe the transmission of HIV in prison. However, tattooing, sex, and injection drug use do occur, and if the safety precautions discussed earlier are not followed, infection can occur. In general, the issues and implications surrounding HIV/AIDS in drug treatment centers are mirrored for adult prisoners and penal institutions. According to Kantor (2006), nearly 7 million people in the United States lived under the jurisdiction of the criminal justice system, and more than 2.2 million were in jail or prison in 2004. Fifty-seven percent of federal prisoners were incarcerated for drug-related offenses in 2001. Because of the association between drug use and HIV, it should be clear that prisoners are at exceptional risk for infection. In fact, it is estimated that one-fourth of all persons with HIV pass through the correctional facilities each year (Braithwaite & Arriola, 2008). According to these same authors, the AIDS case rate among prison inmates is four times higher than the rate in the general United States population. Higher risks for HIV infection are associated with this group due to a number of lifestyle factors such as drug and alcohol abuse, unprotected sex, poverty, homelessness, under-education, and unemployment. As you would expect, female prisoners who have practiced prostitution, which frequently is associated with injection drug use and contact with HIV-infected sex partners, are at additional risk for HIV infection.

Primm (1992) and Kantor (2006) caution that no precise count of HIV cases in prisoners is available. Incarceration numbers usually reflect those currently in prison; criminals who are on probation and parole may go undetected or at least are underrepresented in any reports. Prisoners often enter a high-risk system with little or no knowledge about HIV because many HIV information campaigns "may miss many drug abusers (and their sexual partners) because criminal justice records and arrest or conviction charges are poor indicators of drug abuse" (Primm, 1992, p. 617). Even if individuals do not actually enter jail (many criminals charged and arrested with minor infractions are routinely released back into the community), the problem is that many of these individuals may have drug-abuse problems and may already be infected with HIV.

THE HOMELESS   As you can imagine, drug abuse and HIV statistics for this population are hard to determine. Nonetheless, the population of people who are homeless present another population at high risk for HIV, and they differ from the general population in a number of ways (Friedman et al., 2009; Kerker et al., 2011). Homeless people may be more likely to abuse substances, engage in survival sex and/or high-risk sex, and less likely to adhere to the demands of complex treatment protocols.

Because TB rates are somewhat correlated with HIV rates, it is interesting to note that in 2003, 6.3% of reported TB cases in the United States were among homeless persons (CDC, 2005a). When compared with the general population, people who are homeless have a greater risk for latent TB infection (LTBI) and progression to active disease. These factors, concomitant with the issues of poor hygiene, inadequate nutrition, lack of medical care, crowded shelters, and the unsanitary conditions that prevail among this population all contribute significantly to their high risk.

PEOPLE WITH DISABILITIES AND OLDER ADULTS   In 1998, the United States Supreme Court ruled that asymptomatic HIV infection is constituted as disability (Gagnon & Stuart, 2009). Very few studies have been conducted about persons with disabilities (PWDs) and HIV. However, the international literature suggests that this population is at increased risk. One reason is the lack of sex education. Historically, PWDs have been routinely excluded from sex education because PWDs were seen as either asexual or oversexed and not in need of information (Rohleder, 2010). Moreover, adults with learning disabilities have referred to sexual acts as "rude" and said that sex education was "rude" or "bad" (Heyman & Huckle, 1995). In one study of 99 adolescents of which 56% were males, Maart and Jelsma (2010) found that physically disabled adolescents were engaging in risky sexual behaviors at the same rate as their nondisabled cohorts. Thus, the authors conclude that the population of PWDs should not be overlooked when it comes to being at risk for HIV/AIDS. We are suggesting that you, as mental health professionals, do not fall prey to your own stereotypes about sex and disabilities.

According to the National Institute on Aging (2009), almost one quarter of all people with HIV/AIDS in the United States are over 50 years of age. One reason for this is that the antiretroviral treatments are allowing people to live longer. Recall Jaye in Case Example 5 at the outset of this chapter. She assumed that because of her age and the age of her partner, she did not need to be cautious. She was wrong. Yet she was not alone in her assumptions about age and AIDS. She was equating condoms with birth control and not with HIV.

Doctors do not always test for HIV in older patients. Moreover, the normal "aches and pains" of aging can mask symptoms. Aging and the stigma that accompanies HIV testing can produce shame to the point that this population of older Americans may be afraid of getting tested. Thus, older adults may be less likely to get tested for HIV. When they do get tested, it may be at a late stage and less likely to respond well to treatment (Kearney, Moore, Donegan, & Lambert, 2010). Older Americans often know less about HIV/AIDS than do younger people. Health care professionals, including doctors, nurses, home health care providers, and educators assume this population is either unaffected by the virus or is not at risk. This is coupled with the fact that older adults do not easily communicate about sex as much as younger people do. Therefore, the topic often evades discussion between older adults and health care professionals.

ASSESSMENT OF CLIENTS FOR HIV AND AIDS: SIGNS AND SYMPTOMS

As you saw earlier in this chapter, early detection and medical treatment can forestall the onset of AIDS and ARC, although to date nothing can eliminate the probability of AIDS once a person has been infected with HIV. Although the diagnosis of HIV can be made only by positive tests for the HIV antibody, several indicators might suggest the presence of the infection in clients who have not undergone medical testing for the virus. Therefore, it is important that you, as mental health professionals, be aware of issues that suggest the presence of HIV in order to urge high-risk clients to be tested and, hopefully, to receive appropriate medical intervention if they show early stages of infection. Referral of the client for assessment of HIV infection is crucial when risk factors are coupled with other signs and symptoms. These other signs and symptoms include physical anomalies and neuropsychiatric disturbances, which are discussed next.

Physical Signs and Symptoms

It is customary for mental health professionals to initially elicit a psychosocial, drug, and brief medical history from their clients. In the course of that interview, clients may mention many symptoms that, to them, may seem unrelated to the risk of HIV infection. These signs and symptoms may include complaints of fever, unexplained weight loss or loss of appetite, night sweats, general malaise, coughing and/or shortness of breath, swollen lymph nodes, recurrent or persistent sinusitis, abdominal pain, diarrhea, and visual changes such as visual field defects (Barthwell & Gilbert, 1993). Other symptoms that should alert you to the possibility of HIV may be dermatological conditions such as genital warts, rashes, herpes zoster (shingles), and psoriasis (U.S. Department of Health and Human Services, 2006. Although these symptoms are not diagnostic nor unique to HIV, when coupled with a history of substance abuse they may help guide your efforts in evaluating the possibility of HIV infection.

HELPING HIV-INFECTED CLIENTS

Clients with HIV can manage only the disease process and the disease itself, so once a client is diagnosed with HIV or AIDS, your concern as a mental health professional will be to focus on helping the client attempt to manage and cope with the disease. Remember, the only way to know whether a client is infected is to be tested for HIV. Mental health professionals should not rely on symptoms alone because many people who are infected with HIV do not have symptoms for many years. Someone can look and feel healthy but still be infected.

In all cases, it is critical that clients adhere to the medications prescribed for HIV infection. The virus can replicate and mutate readily, especially if doses are missed. In general, non-HIV cases, individuals can adhere to treatment of chronic diseases about 80% of the time and still be successful. However, with HIV, this level does not work. Patients need to adhere almost 100% of the time in order to keep the virus from replicating. The absence of treatment means that almost all those infected with HIV will eventually get AIDS.

In general, the focus on helping the HIV-infected client is on assisting the client in understanding and accepting the changes that are occurring and will occur in his or her life. Educating the client about the disease and treatment is also important, which includes emphasizing the fact that AIDS is not necessarily fatal. This last statement is critical because general misconceptions about the disease are held by the public and by many HIV-infected individuals. For example, an HIV-infected client of one of the authors stated during the second group therapy session,

"Having HIV is like living with a time bomb. The only thing you know is that the bomb will go off. You never know when or where you'll be in life when it goes off. All you know is just that it will explode someday and you'll die." While this was clearly true at one time, the antiretroviral protocol treatment has shifted the "death sentence" into more of a chronic disease that can be managed as long as treatment starts upon the discovery of HIV infection.

Because practice settings offering HIV care vary according to local resources and needs, mental health professionals need to have some knowledge of the resources that are available for each patient in order to avoid fragmentation of care. Clearly, a single source, capable of providing comprehensive care for all stages of HIV infection, is preferred. However, this is often not possible. In every case involving HIV-infected clients, mental health professionals should make concerted efforts to avoid long delays between diagnosis of HIV infection and access to additional medical and psychosocial services.

The Centers for Disease Control and Prevention (2006b) and the World Health Organization (2007) outline an approach to helping HIV-infected clients. This approach is called palliative care therapy, and it is indicated for clients who are living with an incurable illness. The aim of this approach is to help provide the best quality of life to clients and to offer support and comfort to loved ones. Palliative care is based on work conducted with hospice cancer patients and addresses emotional, psychological, and spiritual needs. Because HIV patients will probably suffer from severe pain at some point, pain control is a central focus of palliative care. Palliative caregivers affirm life and help clients see that dying is a natural process that can neither be hastened nor postponed.

The CDC Treatment Guidelines for HIV (2006b) recommend the following for counseling persons with HIV:

- Counseling should include the behavioral, psychosocial, and medical implications of HIV infection.
- Providers should be acutely aware of medical and psychosocial conditions that may be emergent.
- Providers should address other issues such as psychiatric disorders, emotional distress, or substance abuse.
- Providers should follow up on recommendations given to clients.
- Patients should be educated about what to expect from the medical community.

Regarding the medical community, clients need to know that they will be asked for a detailed medical history that will include sexual and AOD history. They will be given a complete physical examination and blood tests will be conducted. Included will be an assessment for other infectious diseases such as STIs, TB, and HCV. It is also likely that the medical facility will conduct a urinalysis as well as a chest radiograph.

PSYCHOSOCIAL CONCERNS OF HIV-INFECTED CLIENTS Clients with HIV will be distressed when they are first informed of a positive HIV test result. The changes in their lives will likely be all-encompassing and overwhelming. According to the CDC (2006c), changes will include 1) accepting the possibility of a shortened life span, 2) coping with the stigmatization, 3) the need to develop and adopt new strategies for maintaining physical and emotional health, and 4) initiating changes in behavior to prevent HIV transmission to others. In addition, many persons will require assistance with making reproductive choices, gaining access to health services, confronting possible employment or housing discrimination, and coping with changes in personal relationships.

The larger narratives or social discourses shaping the values for males and females in the U.S. culture both create and help to solve issues related to helping clients with HIV/AIDS. This is clearly the situation for women from a feminist perspective. For example, DeMarco, Miller, Patsdaughter, Chisolm, and Grindel (1998) point out that women have learned to use silence as a generalized way to cope when they feel disempowered. Adherence to this discourse can have drastic effects for women with HIV/AIDS, when keeping silent can result in death. Moreover, the social narrative that guides the caregiving values for women in the mainstream culture can be deleterious as well. If a mother who has been socialized to ignore her needs while caring for others ignores her HIV/AIDS issues, she can bring more harm to herself.

In some cases, the social narratives are in conflict with more personal ones and serve to present barriers and challenges to the treatment of infected individuals. This is clearly the case in Walker's (2002) research. The rural women in Walker's study leaned more toward a rugged independence, which runs counter to the larger social discourse for many women. This independence was seen as presenting problems in the identification and treatment of that population.

The issue of stigma and stigmatization is another serious concern. The CDC (2007a), UNAIDS (2006), and Hoffman (1996) state that one of the defining characteristics of the HIV epidemic has been the perpetual association with stigma. One stigma related to the epidemic is homophobia (Trezza, 1994). Hoffman also reports that the disease has always been associated with death and with certain stigmatized groups such as gay men and injecting drug users. However, as the epidemic shifts, HIV is increasingly associated with groups that are more marginalized—economically impoverished people of color, for instance. Hoffman also reports that, aside from the social stigma, the legal aspects of the stigma relating to the protection of the public at large, the interpersonal stigma, and the internalized stigma that diminishes self-esteem are also ever-present.

According to Grov, Golub, Parsons, Brennan, and Karpiak (2010), the AIDS stigma undermines preventive efforts on both public and private levels. These researchers assert that the stigma negatively affects condom use, HIV test-seeking behaviors, care-seeking behavior on diagnosis, quality of care provided to HIV-positive patients, and perception and treatment of persons living with HIV/AIDS by communities, families, and various partners. Nothing is more important to the recovery effort than social support, and nothing so distinctly divides survivors who seem to do well from those who seem to do poorly than the level of social support they receive (Odets, 1995; Springer & Lease, 2000).

Vital in the approach to helping drug-abusing clients with HIV is a coordinated effort among the psychological, medical, social services, legal, pastoral and religious, peer support groups, significant family members, and other community-based service networks (Selwyn, 1992). The plethora of services required by these clients is due to the myriad tasks needing attention once the individual has AIDS. Selwyn (1992) purports that, for the young heterosexual HIV population, there will be issues surrounding childbearing, child support and custody, and orphanhood that will need to be addressed. These family issues will likely require the assistance of social and legal services. Legal services may also be needed in helping to determine a person who will be designated as having power of attorney (POA) for the client; also, this necessity should be addressed before the onset of delirium or AIDS dementia complex, which can leave the client adjudicated as incompetent. The HIV-infected client may be reluctant to ask for help in seemingly unimportant areas of his or her life. This neglect can impact surviving loved ones, so the term *coordinated effort* takes on special significance. Such coordinated effort can also help to identify the services needed to avoid a duplication of services, an issue that might increase client reluctance in asking for assistance.

Another area of concern is the client's sexuality and the risk of HIV transmission. Understanding the sexual aspects of the disease is of paramount importance, and frank communication between you as the mental health professional and your client is essential. Human touch is essential to everyone, and the client should be encouraged to hug his or her loved ones as well as to engage in safe sex. However, if an individual has already been exposed to HIV infection and has unprotected sexual relations with another infected individual, an acceleration of the disease process may be experienced. So it is critical to emphasize the importance of safer sex practices among already infected HIV clients.

Clients tend to do better and remain longer in the home setting when they have a caregiver. Therefore, home health care and other supportive systems should be explored. Often these supportive networks are nontraditional; therefore, some exploration of community resources may be indicated. Identifying individuals and services that the client can access during a time of crisis can help allay fears regarding how he or she will be cared for. One of the goals of this identification is to help the HIV client avoid isolation, and many community, volunteer-based support systems are available for assistance. Ideally, these systems allow the client to live freely within his or her physical limitations.

EMOTIONAL CONCERNS Certainly, client reactions to having a catastrophic illness will be of paramount importance to mental health professionals working with this group of clients. This work may include helping clients prepare for death. It is also important to help clients examine their quality-of-life issues, with a focus on establishing a philosophical understanding about what is acceptable in terms of work and disability status. Regardless of the extent to which one can work, or wants to work, delaying hospitalization as long as possible is recommended.

Clients who have HIV may present a number of emotional reactions that can include anxiety, stress–distress syndrome, panic reactions, suicidal ideation, rumination, depression, and a plethora of defense mechanisms such as denial, anger, guilt, and isolation (Joseph & Bhatti, 2004; Springer & Lease, 2000). These reactions have been gleaned from clinical impressions in working with HIV-infected clients as well as from studies on opiate addicts with AIDS or ARC. For example, Batki, Sorensen, Faltz, and Madover (1988) and Rounsaville, Weissman, Kleber, and Wilbur (1982) have identified that addicts with AIDS or ARC use denial as a defense mechanism and are also angry, isolated, and depressed.

Nord (1997) writes about the initial shock and denial experienced by people with multiple AIDS-related loss. After shock and denial comes overload and confusion, having to face reality, and reinvestment and recovery. This same author goes on to point out various multiple AIDS-related losses, including loss of family and friends, personal history, future, security, emotional range and well-being, hope, interest in life, self-esteem, roles, spirituality and assumptions, community, and celebration and sexual freedom. In Case Example 2, Emily became more and more overwhelmed and scared about Michael's HIV status. Her fears escalated to the point that she did not want him sexually. In this case study, Emily was not as scared of HIV as she was of the communication breakdown that had insidiously crept into their relationship. This situation points out the need for helpers to address more "non-HIV-related" issues than the disease itself. It is critically important to not overlook the "usual" relational issues that can severely impact the mental and emotional health of both.

Denial would certainly be a component of any client's grieving process when confronted with HIV. In HIV-infected, drug-abusing clients, however, denial about drug abuse as well as about having HIV may become more pronounced (Sorensen & Batki, 1992), and, as a result, clients and counselors can face a double-whammy of denial. However, mental health professionals should understand that denial may only be a component of a larger construct of ambivalence: ambivalence about drug abuse and/or ambivalence about having HIV. In Chapter 7, we discussed the motivational interviewing techniques of Miller and Rollnick. One premise used in these techniques is that clients may be more accurately described as being ambivalent rather than being in denial about drug abuse. The client may actually sense that drugs may be a problem but may not be sure of the extent of the problem—or even if a problem truly exists. While this concept was originally intended for application to drug abusers, Miller and Rollnick's (1991) notion of ambivalence can apply as well to both HIV-infected drug-abusing clients and to those infected clients not abusing drugs. So, rather than being in denial about HIV infection per se, clients may be seen as experiencing ambivalence, and the techniques to reduce ambivalence described in Chapter 7 can be helpful and easily adapted to working with HIV-infected individuals. It should be noted, however, that denial and/or ambivalence can also be present in clients who are at high risk for HIV, and, if issues of denial and ambivalence are mishandled, clients might refuse to be tested or refuse medical treatment or counseling interventions.

Anger displayed by people with HIV is to be expected, and in many cases is a sign of healthy adaptation to having been infected. However, it is possible that infected individuals could inappropriately displace their anger onto health care workers, family members, significant others, and their health care management. Covert expression of this anger may be seen in individuals' missing appointments, in their refusal to comply with medical or counseling interventions, in their continued drug abuse, and/or in the selling of their medications. Some of this anger may be due to fear and mistrust of the system and of the care providers. This is exemplified by one of the author's own experiences: When running therapy groups for HIV-infected clients, a few group members attended only sporadically. Attendance became more stable only after the author had been "checked out" (clients' words) by other group members who passed the information along.

Nord (1997) points out that AIDS-related multiple losses create severe trauma and bring up such existential issues as being versus nonbeing, isolation versus a desire for connection, and meaning versus meaninglessness. Concomitantly, mood disturbance such as depression, a phenomenon already common among drug abusers, is exacerbated in HIV-infected individuals (Sorensen & Batki, 1992). Moreover, isolation is characteristic of drug-abusing, HIV-infected individuals. According to Sorensen and Batki (1992), isolation occurs in two ways: First, if the person's drug abuse already places him or her outside of mainstream society, HIV only pushes him or her further away; and, second, if the individual already has difficulty in initiating and maintaining healthy social contacts (as is rather common in drug abusers), then this difficulty may be a significant barrier to treatment. Because of the isolation factor, outreach programs designed to identify high-risk individuals for testing and counseling need to be aggressive and skillfully handled.

While recent advances in medication are slowly changing the status of HIV/AIDS from a terminal illness to a chronic illness, the spiritual issues that HIV-infected persons cope with continue to prevail (Holt, Houg, & Romano, 1999). These researchers identify three broad spiritual themes that may come up in counseling: (1) terminal illness, postdeath existence, and the meaning of life, (2) religious disenfranchisement from God or a higher power ("Why did I get AIDS?"), and (3) cross-cultural spiritual and religious issues in society and families of origin.

In general, these three spiritual themes will be relevant for all individuals. At the same time, the individual's psychosocial development and cultural mores will influence the manner in which these themes are presented and processed. Given the overrepresentation of racioethnic populations with HIV/AIDS, the diverse cultural spiritual beliefs and practices are obviously critical for counselors to consider. For example, mid to late adolescents are already working with issues related to the meaning of life. An aging individual is asking the same questions from the other direction. While both individuals are experiencing questions about the meaning of life, an adolescent's perspective is different from that of an aging person, and the conversations that occur in counseling with the adolescent will be different from the conversations with an older adult.

One difference between the two conversations would relate to the discussion with the older client regarding the client's comorbid health conditions. The multiple losses in physical health experienced by the aging population in general can become overwhelming when HIV/AIDS is present. Because of this situation, Orsulic-Jeras, Shepherd, and Britton (2003) believe that a strengths-based approach can be effectively used with aging HIV-infected individuals. Conversations with adolescents would not normally relate to their physical deterioration.

MEDICAL CONCERNS   We have already discussed the medical concerns related to helping HIV-infected clients and suggested that the medical questions that clients have should be referred to medical personnel. Here, it is important to note that mental health professionals will most likely be confronted with complaints of side effects by their HIV-infected clients who are prescribed any of the anti-HIV agents just discussed. These side effects may increase client resistance to treatment and should be explored with clients who can be reminded that early intervention with these chemotherapies has been shown to slow the disease process (Selwyn, 1992).

Pain management, a focus of palliative therapy, might also be a potential problem because HIV-infected clients will still frequently require analgesia for the pain syndrome that often accompanies the opportunistic infections (Selwyn, 1992). Because drug-abusing HIV-infected clients probably have access to illegal drugs that can be used to numb the pain, this is one issue counselors need to keep in mind when and if their clients talk about pain. With the drug-abusing HIV-infected client, self-medication with AZT and antibiotics may also be a problem, since both can be purchased on the street. Again, clients should be warned of the dangers of self-medicating.

Yoga is gaining interest as a treatment for HIV/AIDS (Foster, 1999; Stukin, 2003). Counselors might encourage clients of any age with HIV/AIDS to inquire about the benefits of yoga. According to both Foster and Stukin , yoga can help with the side effects of the disease as well as of medications. Stukin does not believe that someone with HIV needs to take specially designed classes in yoga, but it might be beneficial. Counselors can suggest that clients utilize the Internet and/or inquire at local community colleges and universities to gather information and resources about yoga.

ISSUES IN THE WORKPLACE   Hergenrather and Rhodes (2008) and Pereira (2010) estimate that approximately 90–97% of people living with HIV are in the economically productive period of their lives, and HIV/AIDS has generated more lawsuits than any disease in the history of the U.S. legal system. These statistics underscore the importance of looking at issues related to HIV/AIDS and the workplace.

The fact that HIV/AIDS is a disability has created a need for more complex systems of delivery that includes vocational services and vocational rehabilitation. Conyers (2004) studied employment and HIV/AIDS and noted various motivations to work among the study participants. Reasons that HIV/AIDS patients gave for wanting to work included 1) the hope of increased mental health, 2) regaining a vocational identity, 3) meeting financial needs, 4) concern about the impact of unemployment on families and loved ones, and 5) decreasing fear related to the loss of needed services. Hergenrather, Rhodes, and Clark (2006) concur with Conyers and add that social skills are increased through employment. Participants in the Hergenrather et al. study identified impediments to employment for persons living with HIV/AIDS (PLWHA). There was the fear that they would not have the ability to adhere to prescribed medical treatment because they might get so involved in work as to forget to medicate. Second was a lack of workplace accommodations. Loss of Medicaid was also identified, as was the lack of HIV/AIDS education in the workplace. However, education in the workplace ". . . can significantly reduce anxiety and discrimination among workers, minimize workplace disruption, and empower employees to protect themselves again HIV infection" (Hergenrather & Rhodes, 2008, p. 38).

According to the American Disabilities Act, private employers with 15 or more employees may not discriminate in any employment practice against qualified individuals with disabilities. This means that, for example, a restaurant may not fire a waitress upon notification that she is HIV positive, nor can a university fire a physical education instructor because her or his boyfriend has AIDS. Although prospective employees with HIV/AIDS have concerns about accommodations, the ADA requires employers to make "reasonable accommodations" to those having a disability. This means that employers are required to modify any aspect of the job so that the PLWHA can perform the essential functions of the job. This would include restructuring the job, modifying work schedules, acquiring or modifying equipment, and reassigning to a vacant position for which the PLWHA is qualified. For example, an HIV-positive individual might be granted longer lunches in order to keep medical appointments and be required to make up the time in flexible ways.

Obviously, the employer would have to know that the employee is disabled in order to make accommodations. This brings up very complex issues. Conyers and Boomer (2005) maintain that research indicates that the vast majority of PLWHA choose not to disclose their status because of fears of discrimination. Research supports this fear (Hergenrather & Rhodes, 2008). Other reasons for not disclosing include a desire for privacy, concerns about the overall work environment, and fear of other repercussions (p. 190). At the same time, PLWHA may choose to disclose in order to access social support, assert personal identity, and accommodate a desire to be open.

HIV-RELATED ISSUES SPECIFIC TO THE HELPING PROFESSIONAL

Confidentiality

From our discussion here (see also Chapter 5), you can readily see that a person with HIV/AIDS has a right to keep his or her HIV status confidential. At the same time, certain issues of HIV testing warrant special consideration. Although some states have resolved the issue of mandatory HIV testing for certain personnel, such testing remains the subject of heated debate in other states (Barthwell & Gibert, 1993). Essentially, the debate centers on mandatory versus voluntary, and anonymous versus confidential, testing for HIV. Anonymous testing assigns a unique identifiable code to each person tested so that the results are not traceable to an individual. Confidential testing links an individual by name to the test result, so that the laws protecting confidentiality protect the test results. According to the Revised Recommendations for HIV testing of Adults, Adolescents, and Pregnant Women in Health-Care Settings (Branson et al., 2006) as well as the Centers for Disease Control and Prevention (Barthwell & Gibert, 1993) and many other professional health care associations that represent the public interest, voluntary and confidential or anonymous testing for individuals at high risk for HIV infection are strongly urged.

The confidentiality of testing is not an issue when it comes to sexually transmitted and other communicable diseases such as TB. However, because of the strong co-occurrence of these diseases among the HIV-infected population (Selwyn, 1992), you should assess for the presence of these diseases during the assessment phase of your work with clients who are at high risk for HIV infection and urge your clients to be tested.

Currently, federal law requires all who enter the military to be tested for HIV as well as requiring testing for HIV of all organ and tissue donors, all blood donors, persons seeking immigration to the United States, and federal prisoners (U.S. Preventive Services Task Force, 1989). Laws that relate to issues such as mandatory testing, confidentiality, reporting of results, and notification vary by state. Because of the statute idiosyncracies concomitant with the catastrophic effects of the disease itself, mental health professionals should take great care in becoming informed of these issues with their clients and learn to handle such clients delicately.

Clearly, health care professionals cannot disclose information without client's approval. At the same time, you as mental health professionals face a quandary regarding "duty of care to the sexual partner(s) of your HIV-infected clients." This is essentially an issue of scope and content of the duty. There have been instances of case law where care providers have been found to have breached the law by failing to take steps available to them to protect an HIV-infected individual's partner from becoming HIV positive (Mair, 2009). Therefore, efforts need to be made to protect HIV-infected client's partners. Even if limited, health care providers can counsel their HIV-positive clients regarding the seriousness of their disease and outline the implications for their partners. Simply referring your clients to an immune clinic for treatment is not sufficient help.

Yet, HIV-infected clients do resist disclosure. Stigma and a perceived lack of support are significant barriers (Emlet, 2008). Serovich (2001) discusses two theories of disclosure: *disease progression theory* and *consequences theory*. In the former, disclosure is made only when the progression of the disease makes it almost impossible to receive care and support without clients disclosing information. *Consequences theory* is a process whereby clients assess the potential cost/rewards of disclosing. This scenariocontains three options: full disclosure, selective disclosure, or remaining secretive. More often than not, you will be working through the *consequence theory paradigm* because the lack of disclosure through *disease progression theory* becomes next to impossible at the late stage of the disease. In the study about disclosure among HIV-infected clients, Emlet found that some most clients utilized "protective silence" to avoid fears of rejection and stigmatization. "Anticipatory disclosure" was the next most often process employed. This process reflected a desire to disclose most often to a particular individual while at the same time continuing to assess potential reactions and consequences.

These models of decision making regarding disclosure or nondisclosure can help guide health care providers' discussions with their clients. You may also be confronted with another situation where the information is divulged either unintentionally or intentionally. A client may have told someone about their HIV status, and that person told others. In this case, you may need to help clients deal with their anger, guilt, remorse, fear, anxiety, and shame at having disclosed and been betrayed. Finally, intentional disclosure is just that: intentional. Health care professionals can help clients process how their disclosure has changed their lives and help clients come to a fuller acceptance of their decision.

Harm Reduction and Needle Exchange

Another issue that can confront you as a mental health professional relates to the controversial issue of needle exchange in which drug-injecting addicts can receive clean needles so as to diminish the risk of sharing needles that might be carrying HIV. Alan Marlatt believes that "we will never get ahead of AIDS and our drug problems. People think that the solution, a softer drug policy or legalization, is worse than the problem. Our ways of handling these problems are not working and they may be making them worse" (Manisses Communication Group, Inc., 1994, p. 1).

The more moderate approach advocated by Marlatt is based on a European approach called harm reduction. Taking a middle-of-the-road approach between prohibition and legalization, the harm reduction approach would include methadone programs for heroin addicts and nicotine replacement therapy for tobacco users, and would attempt to control such addictive or excessive behaviors as binge drinking and overeating. Harm reduction also includes legalized needle-exchange programs as well as including "a more humane approach to drug problems and [would] begin to soften criminal penalties for drug use" (Manisses Communication Group, Inc., 1994, p. 5). The CDC (2005b), Kleinig (2006), Maddow (2002), and Marlatt and Vanden-Bos (1997) believe that a harm reduction approach offers the at-risk populations simple behavioral solutions that can dramatically reduce the danger associated with high-risk activities, and these simple behavioral skills can help prevent the spread of AIDS (through needle-exchange programs and safe-sex and condom-use programs). Safe tattooing information and materials, along with bleach and disinfection materials, would also be included in the harm reduction approach. Currently, 113 needle exchange programs operate in 80 cities across 38 states in the United States.

Needle exchange programs work. These programs are not in the needle distribution business per se. These programs require injecting drug users to return a used syringe in order to obtain a new, sterile one. After 21 years of debate and failure, the U.S. Congress and President Obama repealed the ban on federal funding for local needle exchange programs by passing a bill in 2009. The legislation did not contain any new monies for needle exchanges. However, it allowed programs to use federal funds to provide clean needles, subject to approval by local authorities, including law enforcement and health officials.

MyCounselingLab™

Go to Topic 10: *Working with Selected Populations* in the MyCounselingLab™ site (www.MyCounselingLab.com) for *Substance Abuse: Information for School Counselors, Social Workers, Therapists, and Counselors,* Fifth Edition, where you can:

- Find learning outcomes for *Working with Selected Populations* along with the national standards that connect to these outcomes.
- Complete Assignments and Activities that can help you more deeply understand the chapter content.
- Apply and practice your understanding of the core skills identified in the chapter with the Building Counseling Skills unit.
- Prepare yourself for professional certification with a Practice for Certification quiz.
- Connect to videos through the Video and Resource Library.

Summary

- There is still no cure for HIV/AIDS, and a great number of those with HIV infection do not know they are infected. It is considered a chronic disease.
- Women are approximately twice as likely as men to contract HIV during vaginal intercourse.
- Most women with HIV are racial/ethnic minority women living in urban inner cities and are disproportionately affected by poverty, crime, and social disorganization and represent the most disenfranchised sector of our society.
- Mortality is greatest among those HIV-infected male and female adolescents who were injecting drugs.
- The risk of co-infection, especially with TB, is on the rise.
- By the time that older HIV-infected individuals enter treatment, their HIV-related problems may be already beyond the reach of most human service systems due to a lack of screening.
- An individual living with an HIV-infected person is at minimal to no risk if proper precautions are followed.
- The number of HIV-infected individuals in the workplace has increased and will continue to grow; persons living with HIV/AIDS are protected under the Americans with Disabilities Act, 1990 (ADA), and employers are required to make "reasonable accommodations."
- Reasons that HIV/AIDS patients give for wanting to work include 1) the hope of increased mental health, 2) regaining a vocational identity, 3) meeting financial needs, 4) concern about the impact of unemployment on families and loved ones, and 5) decreasing fear related to the loss of needed services.
- Employers need to know of the disability in order to make workplace accommodations but the vast majority of PLWHA choose not to disclose their status because of fears of discrimination, stigma, a desire for privacy, concerns about the overall work environment, and the fear of other repercussions.
- In treating the HIV/AIDS client, the CDC Treatment Guidelines for HIV recommend that counseling persons with HIV should include the behavioral, psychosocial, and medical implications of HIV infection.
- It is important that mental health professionals have some knowledge of the resources that are available for each patient in order to avoid fragmentation of care; providers should also follow-up on recommendations given to clients, and patients should be educated about what to expect from the medical community.
- Providers should also be acutely aware of medical and psychosocial conditions that may be emergent and should address other issues such as psychiatric disorders, emotional distress, and substance abuse.
- The older adult population is increasing in size and so is the incidence of HIV infection diagnoses.
- The World Health Organization outlines an approach to helping HIV-infected clients called palliative care therapy for clients who are living with an incurable illness in order to help provide the best quality of life to clients and to offer support and comfort to loved ones.
- A federal funding ban on needle exchange programs was lifted in 2009.

Internet Resources

General information: HIV/AIDS
aidsinfo.nih.gov
cdc.gov

Specific populations: Older adults and GLBTQQI
hivoverfifty.org
nia.hin.gov
sageusa.org

HIV/AIDS and disabilities in the workplace
ada.gov/pubs/hivqanda.txt

Women and HIV/AIDS
who.int/gender/hiv_aids/en/

HIV/AIDS
cdc.gov/hiv/resources/factsheets/

Palliative therapy
cdc.gov/std/treatment/2006/hiv.htm

Further Discussion

1. What is your experience with HIV/AIDS? Do you know anyone who is infected?
2. How comfortable would you be interacting with a person living with HIV/AIDS (PLWHA) in a social situation?
3. Would this be different if you were working with a PLWHA?
4. Even though HIV/AIDS is protected under the Americans with Disabilities Act, how far should employers and employees go to accommodate a PLWHA?
5. How does the knowledge of older adults and HIV change or not change your perceptions of that population's sexuality?

Chapter 14

Gambling and Other Addictions

CASE EXAMPLES

❶ Samantha, 33, went to seek counseling because she "just didn't feel right" about the amount of time her husband was spending at home on the Internet. She thought he was hiding things from her. When she asked him about it, he maintained that he was just catching up on work. Yet, whenever she would come into the study unannounced, where they kept their computer, it seemed that he would quickly close out the screen he was on. This raised her suspicions. He would continually deny that anything was going on. She thought that it was just her being insecure and let it go. However, she continued to have feelings of worthlessness and saw herself as sexually undesirable because their sexual relationship was almost nonexistent. When asked, her husband agreed to go in for one counseling session, and during that session, neither of them mentioned their sexual problems. Instead, Samantha spent the time crying about being lonely.

❷ Melanie, 19, was an only child who lived on a several-acre property in the country with her parents. In her younger years, she would run on the dirt road in front of her house for exercise and found that she liked running. In high school, she made the women's track team as a distance runner and won enough races to be offered a scholarship at a large university that was in another state. Melanie was always thin. However, when she came home for the Thanksgiving break during her freshman year, her mother was shocked to see how much weight Melanie had lost. In response, Melanie told her mother that she was just working out to keep up with the competition and left it at that. When she returned for the December holidays, Melanie had lost even more weight. By pleading, Melanie's mother was able to get Melanie to go to the doctor for a check-up. Because Melanie was 19 years old, the doctor was not able to tell her mother that Melanie was suffering from anorexia nervosa. Instead, Melanie and her doctor had discussed ways that Melanie could tell her mother. When she arrived home from the doctor's appointment, though, Melanie told her mother that everything was okay and that she was losing weight because she did not like the cafeteria food at the university. She assured her mother that "it would be fine."

❸ Lynn is a 44-year-old professional woman who has lived in Las Vegas for over 20 years. Lynn started gambling in her mid-20s. For many years, Lynn's gambling could be described as recreational. She would go to casinos with friends, play video poker, and socialize. She never lost more than she could afford. At 32, Lynn married for the second time. She and her husband started using cocaine and gambling more and more frequently. They ran up debt on their credit cards. Lynn's husband developed an addiction to cocaine and Lynn left him. He shot himself to death shortly after they separated. After this traumatic event, Lynn stopped using cocaine and curtailed her gambling. However, in her late 30s, she remarried and started gambling with her third husband. Lynn's gambling started to spiral out of control. She applied for numerous credit cards and took out cash advances on them. To hide her activity, Lynn got a post office box so that her husband wouldn't see the mail. She borrowed money from her parents and friends, making up believable stories to justify the loans. Lynn had a job in which she had a lot of independence, and she spent considerable work time in local bars that had video poker machines. When she finally could not hide her debts any longer, she told her husband. Lynn's husband took care of their debts and made Lynn promise to gamble only with him on weekends. Lynn tearfully agreed and was able to moderate her gambling for a short time. However, within a year, Lynn was gambling out of control and had accumulated over $200,000 in debt. She couldn't sleep and was contemplating suicide.

This case example is a true story, and it does have a happy ending. Lynn has not gambled in many years and regularly attends Gamblers Anonymous. She has cleaned up all her debts, has a demanding professional career, and enjoys an upper-middle-class lifestyle. It's a far cry from the chaos of compulsive gambling, which involved continuous lying, cheating, and stealing. You may be thinking that this kind of problem happens only in places like Las Vegas and Atlantic City. You would be wrong.

PREVALENCE OF GAMBLING AND GAMBLING PROBLEMS

The earliest known six-sided pair of dice dates to about 3000 B.C Some 5,000 years later, in 1997, the U.S. Congress established the National Gambling Impact and Policy Commission. On June 18, 1999, the National Gambling Impact Study Commission's Final Report was released. Prior to the establishment of the commission, the last federal study of gambling had been conducted in 1976. The growth of gambling in the United States since that time has been astounding.

Some form of legal gambling is now available in 48 states (exceptions are Utah and Hawaii) and the District of Columbia. Prior to 1990, the only destination casinos in the United States were in Atlantic City and Nevada. Now more than 100 riverboat and dockside casinos are in operation, and more than 260 casinos operate on Native American reservations. Lotteries operate in 43 states, the District of Columbia, Puerto Rico, and the U.S. Virgin Islands (USA .gov, 2011). According to a Gallup Poll taken in December 2007 that included a national sample of 1,027 adults, aged 18 and older, men are two times more likely than women to gamble on professional sports. Younger Americans are much more likely to gamble on sports than older Americans, and college graduates are significantly more likely to gamble on sports than non-graduates. Of the people who gamble on sports, a direct relationship between money and gambling exists: Only 6% of lower-income households gamble on sports, while 78% of those whose households earn more than $75,000 gamble. Surprisingly, gambling on sports is not the most popular form of gambling. State lotteries are twice as popular. Jones (2008) reports that almost one-half of Americans state that they have purchased at least one lottery ticket in a given year.

We will specify criteria for gambling addiction, as we did for alcohol and other drug problems. However, we will first talk about the scope of the problem as indicated by the number of individuals the commission identified as having gambling problems. According to the National Council on Problem Gambling (2009), about 85% of adults in the United States have gambled at least once in their lives. An estimated 2 million adults in the United States meet the criteria for pathological gambling, with another 4–6 million adults considered problem gamblers (those not meeting the full diagnostic criteria for pathological gambling). This means that approximately 6–9 million adults (3%–4%) have problems with gambling. Statistics on youth and gambling are equally astounding. For example, the National Council on Problem Gambling (2009) says that a vast majority of children in the United States have gambled by the time they are 18, and that children are more likely to develop gambling problems than are adults.

Social and Economic Costs

The social cost to families and communities include bankruptcies, divorce, crime, and loss of jobs. Both the National Council on Problem Gambling (2009) and Quirk, Hodgen, Springborn, Howell, and Daus (2010) have estimated the loss of money due to gambling to be about $7 billion dollars each year.

In some geographic areas, casino gambling has resulted in increased employment and income; increased tax revenues; enhanced tourism and recreational opportunities; and rising property values in some economically depressed communities. In other areas, casino gambling has had the opposite effect. For instance, the lack of a broad-based tax structure and almost total reliance on gaming revenues left Nevada with severe economic problems in 2011. Some Native American tribes have used casinos to rebuild infrastructure, diversify holdings, and reduce unemployment. However, most of the major economic benefits of gambling seem to be limited to casino gambling and parimutuel wagering, because these forms of gambling employ the most people and often attract tourists. Other forms of gambling (e.g., lotteries) simply redistribute income among state or local residents. In many cases, lotteries have been shown to be a form of regressive taxation. In other words, those people least able to afford to play lotteries spend proportionately more than those who can afford it.

CRIME   The relationship between crime and gambling has been difficult to establish because of methodological problems in studies designed to examine this relationship. In testimony before the commission, anecdotal incidents related pathological gambling and crime. The National Gambling Impact and Policy Study Commission's Final Report (1999) shows that they heard repeated testimony of desperate gamblers committing illegal acts to finance their problem and pathological gambling, including a Detroit man who faked his own son's kidnapping to pay back a $50,000 gambling debt, a 14-year hospital employee who embezzled $151,000 from her employer for gambling, and the wife of a Louisiana police officer who faced 24 counts of felony theft for stealing to fund her pathological gambling" (pp. 7–13).

FINANCIAL AND OTHER ECONOMIC IMPACT   According to the commission, nearly one-fifth of pathological gamblers have filed for bankruptcy compared to 4.2% of nongamblers. In Iowa, 19% of Chapter 13 bankruptcies involved gambling debt. Three-quarters of the Iowa counties with the highest bankruptcy rates had gambling facilities in or near them. In a study involving Southern Nevada (Las Vegas), the commission estimated the amount of bankruptcy debt losses and civil court costs at $10,000 per pathological gambler. In addition, these researchers estimated the cost of missed work, productivity losses, forced terminations, and unemployment compensation at $6,000 per pathological gambler. With 20,000 to 40,000 pathological gamblers in Southern Nevada, the financial and other economic impact was estimated to be between $320 million and $640 million.

SUICIDE   Pathological gambling is associated with suicidal ideation and attempts (Wong, Chan, Conwell, Conner, & Yip, 2010). According to the National Council on Problem Gambling (1997), nearly 20% of pathological gamblers have attempted suicide, and Zangeneh and Hason (2006) give similar figures of 18% to 20% of gamblers reporting suicide attempts. This is higher than the suicide rate for any other addictive disorder. The commission heard testimony that a survey of Gambler's Anonymous members showed that two-thirds had contemplated suicide, 47% had a firm plan, and 77% stated that they have wanted to die. It should also be noted that Nevada regularly has the highest suicide rate in the nation. While gambling problems cannot be clearly established as a primary cause, they would certainly be suspected.

HOMELESSNESS   The National Gambling Impact and Policy Study Commision (1999) heard testimony associating gambling problems and homelessness. In interviews with 7,000 homeless persons in Las Vegas, 20% reported gambling problems. In a survey of Chicago homeless providers, 33% reported that gambling was a contributing factor to homelessness of people in their program. Finally, the Atlantic City Rescue Mission told the commission that 22% of its residents were homeless due to gambling (National Gambling Impact and Policy Study Commission 1999).

ABUSE AND NEGLECT   The news stories on the more dramatic cases of abuse and neglect related to gambling are depressing. Recently, in Las Vegas, a 3-year-old was stabbed to death in her home while her mother and stepfather were gambling. Several years ago, a young girl was sexually assaulted and killed in a Southern Nevada casino bathroom in the early morning hours. Her father had left her in the video game section of the casino while he gambled. The commission reviewed two studies that showed that between 25% and 50% of pathological gamblers had abused their spouses. Increases in domestic violence were noted in communities after the advent of casinos. Finally, the commission report stated:

> Children of compulsive gamblers are often prone to suffer abuse, as well as neglect, as a result of parental problems or pathological gambling. The Commission heard testimony of numerous cases in which parents or a caretaker locked children in cars for an extended period of time while they gambled. In at least two cases, the children died. (pp. 7–28)

INTERNET GAMBLING   Ciaccio (2010) asks, "Have you ever wondered whether Internet gambling is legal in the United States?" (p. 529). He answers the question by saying, "The answer seems to depend on the source." This researcher claims that while a federal law was enacted in 2006 and new regulations in 2009, the laws related to Internet gambling are "frustratingly murky." Laws say nothing about "unlawful Internet gambling" or define what that would be. No federal or state government regulates online sites.

Ciaccio maintains that the stakes are high because, in 2008, Americans gambled $6 billion online, and the federal government may lose up to $62.7 billion in taxes between 2008 and 2018 by not legalizing and regulating online gaming.

In addressing the U.S. House of Representatives in 2006, the executive director of the National Council on Problem Gambling, Keith White, stated that between January and March of 2006 the National Problem Gambling Helpline received over 30,000 calls, of which 8% were for problematic Internet gambling. The predominant age range was 18 to 25. He also cited statistics from the Annenberg Foundation reflecting 600,000 youths (age 14 to 22) gambling online on a weekly basis. In the National Gambling Impact and Policy Study Commissions's Final Report (1999), White estimated the social cost of problem gambling from bankruptcy, divorce, job loss, and criminal justice costs at $6.7 billion in 2005. We will discuss Internet addiction later in this chapter. However, suffice it to say here that the Internet makes gambling more available than ever before. Wood, Williams, and Lawton (2007) cite four main reasons why gamblers prefer online to land-based gambling: (1) convenience; (2) an aversion to land-based atmospheres; (3) preference for the pace of online gambling; and (4) the potential for higher wins.

As mentioned earlier, Internet gambling is regulated to some extent through the Unlawful Internet Gambling Enforcement Act passed into law in October 2006. This law prohibits financial transactions from banks and credit card companies to the Internet casinos, poker rooms, and sports betting sites. Gamblers addicted to the Internet may have more serious gambling problems than other gamblers (British Broadcasting Company [BBC], 2002). According to the BBC report, the reason is that, since Internet addiction can occur in private, these gamblers may go deeper into their addiction and be able to hide their addiction longer. Although Internet gambling addiction has not been widely researched, the data available suggest that those with Internet gambling problems may be more likely to be unmarried and have lower socioeconomic and education levels (Ladd & Petry, 2002).

DEFINITIONS OF GAMBLERS AND PROBLEM GAMBLING

Perhaps the most well-known model for conceptualizing gamblers was developed by Robert Custer (Custer & Milt, 1985). Custer described the following six types of gamblers:

1. *Professional gambler*   This relatively rare type of gambler is not usually considered one who has a gambling problem. However, many people with gambling problems may have a fantasy about becoming, or the illusion of being, a professional gambler. The true professional gambler controls the amount of time spent gambling and the amount of money wagered.

2. *Antisocial gambler*   The antisocial gambler is also relatively rare. This is the individual who is involved with cheating to win at gambling. This may involve the popular shell game that you have most likely seen on television or at the movies, marking cards, or rigging slot machines. This type of gambler may develop a gambling problem but, obviously, has antisocial personality issues as well.

3. *Casual social gambler*   As the label implies, this type of gambler is one who does not experience problems from gambling. Gambling may be a regular activity (e.g., buying a weekly lottery ticket) or part of the person's recreation (e.g., periodic trips to Las Vegas). The casual social gambler would not lose more than intended or find it difficult to stop gambling.

4. *Heavy social gambler*   For this type of gambler, recreation involves gambling. While the heavy social gambler may rarely lose more money than intended, he or she spends a great deal of time in gambling or gambling-related activities. For example, someone involved with sports betting may spend hours going over point spreads, injury reports, scouting reports, and trades in order to make "educated" bets. The gambling and associated behavior of this type of gambler can affect vocational functioning and family relationships because of the amount of time spent on preparing for gambling and following bets (i.e., watching games).

5. *Relief-and-escape gambler*   Custer describes this type of gambler as the one who gambles to escape life problems or life situations. Problem gamblers may be lonely, anxious, or depressed and use gambling as a method to numb themselves against negative feelings. This is similar to the way some people use alcohol and other drugs to temporarily dull unpleasant emotions.

6. *Compulsive gambler*   The compulsive gambler is preoccupied with gambling and with getting money to gamble. He or she cannot control the amount of time spent gambling or the amount of money lost gambling. According to Custer, gambling becomes the most important aspect of the person's life. The compulsive gambler may engage in illegal activity to get the money to gamble.

There are several different models for defining gambling problems. Shaffer, (1999) described three levels of gambling. Level 1 gamblers experience few or no adverse consequences as a result of gambling. Level 2 gamblers experience negative consequences related to gambling, but do not meet *DSM-IV-TR* criteria for pathological gambling (see the next section). Level 2 gamblers may either progress to level 3, remain at level 2 indefinitely, or become level 1 gamblers or abstainers. Level 3 gamblers do meet *DSM-IV-TR* criteria for pathological gambling. The following section gives a more thorough description of these criteria.

ASSESSMENT AND DIAGNOSIS

Much of what you read in Chapter 6 about the screening and assessment of alcohol and other drug problems is applicable to gambling. Most importantly, if a person has experienced problems in school or job, family, and other relationships, with finances or the law or in other areas as a result of gambling, then that person has a gambling problem to some degree. Helping professionals should consider gambling as a possible causal factor for the presenting problems of clients and should ask about gambling in the psychosocial history. This is especially true when clients present with depression. The Statistics Canada researchers and others (e.g., Zimmerman, Chelminski, and Young, 2006) conclude that the comorbidities of substance abuse and/or mood/anxiety disorders reflect higher risk for gambling problems.

As with alcohol and other drug problems, screening and assessment instruments have been developed for gambling problems. For a thorough discussion of these instruments, we suggest you read the chapter on this topic in *Best Possible Odds: Contemporary Strategies for Gambling Disorders* by William McCown and Linda Chamberlain (2000).

The best known and most commonly used screening instrument is the South Oaks Gambling Screen (SOGS) (Lesieur & Blume, 1987). According to McCown and Chamberlain (2000) and Miller, Meier, and Weatherly (2009), the SOGS is highly correlated to the *DSM-IV-TR* diagnosis of pathological gambling, is easily scored, can be used by helping professionals in generalist settings, and can be used with older adolescents and college students. However, Weibe and Cox (2005) caution against using the SOGS with the older adult population until it can be further refined for this at-risk population. Dixon and Johnson (2007) have developed the Gambling Functional Assessment (GFA), which is a 20-item self-report measure that isolates the consequences that may be maintaining the person's gambling behavior. Miller et al. (2009) state that this assessment has promise, the GFA needs further evaluation in terms of validity and reliability.

In our own clinical work, we have found that the Twenty Questions used by Gamblers Anonymous are very useful for screening and client self-awareness. As with the SOGS and other self-report inventories, clients can easily lie to either minimize or exaggerate their symptoms in response to these questions. However, for clients and family members with genuine questions or concerns about gambling, we believe that the Twenty Questions are helpful. According to Gambler's Anonymous, most compulsive gamblers answer yes to at least seven questions.

1. Did you ever lose time from work or school due to gambling?
2. Has gambling ever made your home life unhappy?
3. Did gambling affect your reputation?
4. Have you ever felt remorse after gambling?
5. Did you ever gamble to get money with which to pay debts or otherwise solve financial difficulties?
6. Did gambling cause a decrease in your ambition or efficiency?
7. After losing, did you feel you must return as soon as possible and win back your losses?
8. After a win, did you have a strong urge to return and win more?
9. Did you often gamble until your last dollar was gone?
10. Did you ever borrow to finance your gambling?
11. Have you ever sold anything to finance gambling?
12. Were you reluctant to use gambling money for normal expenditures?
13. Did gambling make you careless of the welfare of yourself and your family?
14. Did you ever gamble longer than you had planned?
15. Have you ever gambled to escape worry or trouble?
16. Have you ever committed or considered committing an illegal act to finance gambling?
17. Did gambling cause you to have difficulty sleeping?
18. Do arguments, disappointments, or frustrations create within you an urge to gamble?
19. Did you ever have an urge to celebrate any good fortune by a few hours of gambling?
20. Have you ever considered self-destruction as a result of your gambling?

The term *pathological gambling* is used in the *DSM-IV-TR* to describe a severe gambling problem. As we have seen, Shaffer et al. use *level 3* to define the most serious type of gambling problem; Custer and Gamblers Anonymous use *compulsive gambling*. While there might be some academic debate about the most appropriate terminology or subtle differences between terms, we think these three terms are essentially equivalent. The *DSM-IV-TR* does not have the equivalent diagnosis of *abuse,* as is the case with alcohol and other drugs. Terms like *level 2 gambler* or *problem gambler* are the closest descriptors.

The *DSM-IV-TR* describes pathological gambling as follows:

Diagnostic criteria for 312.31 Pathological Gambling

A. Persistent and recurrent maladaptive gambling behavior as indicated by five (or more) of the following:

  (1) is preoccupied with gambling (e.g., preoccupied with reliving past gambling experiences, handicapping or planning the next venture, or thinking of ways to get money with which to gamble)

  (2) needs to gamble with increasing amounts of money in order to achieve the desired excitement

  (3) has repeated unsuccessful efforts to control, cut back, or stop gambling

  (4) is restless or irritable when attempting to cut down or stop gambling

  (5) gambles as a way of escaping from problems or of relieving a dysphoric mood (e.g., feelings of helplessness, guilt, anxiety, depression)

  (6) after losing money gambling, often returns another day to get even ("chasing" one's losses)

  (7) lies to family members, therapist, or others to conceal the extent of involvement with gambling

  (8) has committed illegal acts such as forgery, fraud, theft, or embezzlement to finance gambling

  (9) has jeopardized or lost a significant relationship, job, or educational or career opportunity because of gambling

  (10) relies on others to provide money to relieve a desperate financial situation caused by gambling

B. The gambling behavior is not better accounted for by a Manic Episode.

You can clearly see the relationship between these criteria and the criteria for substance use disorders. The first criterion involves preoccupation, the next two are equivalent to increasing tolerance and lack of control, and the final three involve trouble as a result of gambling. The similarities between pathological gambling and substance use disorders raise this question: Is pathological gambling really an addiction?

Pathological Gambling: Addiction or Behavioral Disorder?

Many people have difficulty seeing pathological or compulsive gambling as an addiction, similar to alcoholism or drug addiction. It is easy to see why. With alcohol or other drugs, *substances* are introduced into the body and changes in neurotransmitters result. In other words, there are observable biological and chemical changes in the body. Drug dependence can be observed in the laboratory in nonhuman animals. Tolerance and withdrawal can be observed in humans.

With gambling, no substance enters the body. However, researchers have been able to demonstrate that changes in the brain occur during gambling, and these changes are similar to what occurs when drugs are ingested (e.g., Breiter, Aharon, Kahneman, & Shizgal, 2001). As we noted in Chapter 6, tolerance and withdrawal are not necessary conditions to define addiction. However, compulsion to engage in the activity, inability to predict when control will be lost, and continued involvement in the activity regardless of negative consequences are the necessary and sufficient conditions to define addiction to alcohol or other drugs. Compulsive or pathological gambling certainly is defined by these conditions. Clinically, we have seen individuals whose lives have been just as devastated as for the most serious alcoholic or drug addict. We have known cases of people committing suicide due to the problems resulting from compulsive gambling. We know people who lost every material possession they ever had and became homeless as a result of their gambling. We interviewed a famous compulsive gambler who lost more than $40 million in the Atlantic City casinos and lived on the charity of family and friends. In spite of the enormity of these losses and the condition of his life, this man continued to spend his Social Security money on lottery tickets.

The point is that the question of whether compulsive gambling is a "real" addiction is academic. For clinicians, it doesn't make any difference. If someone meets the criteria for pathological gambling, that person needs help. From our point of view, the etiology of the condition and neurochemical correlates are irrelevant. However, theoretically, if pathological gambling is viewed as a behavioral disorder, it has treatment implications. One could conceivably use techniques of behavior modification and contingency management to moderate gambling behavior. Our argument would be, Why do this? Gambling is not necessary. Other forms of recreation abound. It is not too challenging to avoid gambling establishments and opportunities. You don't show up at a party and have someone offer you a video poker machine. As with alcohol and other drugs, you can be absolutely sure that a person will not have problems if he or she simply abstains. With any process that involves moderate or controlled use, the probability for problems is considerable. Why risk it? And, if abstinence is the most logical course, it doesn't matter if compulsive or pathological gambling is a true addiction or a behavioral disorder.

TREATMENT, RESOURCES, AND SUPPORT

Treatment

Although similarities exist between treatment for substance use disorders and treatment for pathological or compulsive gambling, so do significant differences. One practical difference is that health insurance rarely covers treatment for gambling problems. Furthermore, federal support is not available for compulsive gambling treatment as it is for alcohol and other drug treatment. Since problem gamblers almost always seek help only when the problem has become severe, they generally have accumulated large debts and cannot afford to pay for treatment. Therefore, unless a family member or friend has the financial resources to pay for treatment (which is usually expensive), the cost of treatment may be prohibitive.

In some states, a portion of the taxes levied on casinos, race tracks, lotteries, or gambling devices is used to provide treatment for compulsive gamblers. For example, Oregon allocates a portion of its lottery proceeds to publicly support compulsive gambling treatment. Nevada, unquestionably the state with the highest proportion of problem gamblers, had also allocated funds for treatment, but economic conditions forced that allocation to be cut in half in order to balance the state budget.

As with treatment for substance use disorders, compulsive gambling treatment can take place in inpatient or outpatient settings and usually includes a component for family members and/or significant others. According to McCown and Chamberlain (2000), inpatient treatment, often in a hospital setting,

> may be medically necessary for a client who has experienced a major life disruption— a vocational, financial, or marital disaster associated with either excessive gambling or suicidal attempts. Inpatient treatment probably is also indicated if the patient is experiencing insomnia, anxiety attacks, depression, mania, tangential thinking, extreme grandiosity, suicidal thinking, or frequent dissociative experiences. (p. 115)

Additionally, McCown and Chamberlain (2000) point out that inpatient treatment may also be necessary for many compulsive gamblers because they tend to be more impulsive and give in to cravings more frequently than alcoholics and drug addicts. Furthermore, a period of isolation may provide relief from the pressure of creditors, loan sharks, and gambling associates.

Outpatient treatment for compulsive gamblers is also available and has the obvious advantages of less expense than inpatient treatment and more convenience for those who continue to work and have families. However, as McCown and Chamberlain (2000) point out, there are no biological tests for gambling equivalent to drug testing for substance abusers. Therefore, the compulsive gambler could, theoretically, continue to gamble undetected while in treatment.

According to de Lisle, Dowling, and Allen (2011), although evaluations of the interventions for gambling problems are still in their infancy, analyses of the problem-gambling treatment literature suggests that gambling is amenable to intervention. For instance, Westphal (2006) studied attrition rates and found attrition rates of 23.5% for short-term pharmacological treatment; 42% for psychosocial interventions, 50.4% for long-term pharmacological treatment, 67.5% for Gamblers Anonymous, and 75% for community multimodal approaches. Nevertheless, Nower and Blaszcynski (2008) maintain that recovery is a diffuse concept that makes evaluation of interventions complex and difficult. These researchers suggest that future investigations should examine gambling recovery along a continuum. This spectrum should include (1) decrease in time and frequency spent on gambling; (2) abstinence or controlled gambling that meets financial obligations; (3) the absence of symptoms reflecting impaired control; and (4) the absence of negative consequences and improved quality of life over time (p. 1844).

Resources

The National Council on Problem Gambling (www.ncpgambling.org) is a nonprofit organization whose mission is "to increase public awareness of pathological gambling, ensure the widespread availability of treatment for problem gamblers and their families, and to encourage research and programs for prevention and education." The council administers programs and services, including a 24-hour confidential hotline (800-522-4700), a gambling-specific certification program for treatment professionals, an academic journal (*Journal of Gambling Studies*), literature distribution, and sponsorship of research and conferences. The National Council on Problem Gambling has 34 state affiliates. On their website, you can link to a state affiliate. It should be noted that the council maintains a neutral stance on gambling and receives financial support from the gambling industry.

Support

Gambler's Anonymous (GA) is the best known and most widely utilized source of support for compulsive gamblers. GA was established in 1957 and is based on the Twelve Steps and Twelve Traditions of Alcoholics Anonymous (discussed in Chapter 10). One difference between GA and AA is that more members of AA have been involved in a formal treatment program than those in GA. The reason is simple: There simply aren't as many treatment options for compulsive gamblers. Therefore, for many people with gambling problems, GA may be the *only* form of assistance they receive.

While some differences in format and language are apparent, open GA and open AA meetings have many similarities. The Twelve Steps and Twelve Traditions are read, people introduce themselves by saying, "Hi, my name is _____ and I am a compulsive gambler," and members share their experience, strength, and hope with each other. Cross talking is not allowed and participants have sponsors. McCown and Chamberlain (2000) argue that GA is less spiritual and more pragmatic than AA and that GA meetings (particularly closed meetings) are more confrontational than AA. We have not found this to be true, but our experience with GA is less extensive than with AA.

A unique part of the GA program is the *pressure relief* group. After about 30 days of continuous abstinence, a member can request a pressure relief group meeting. The meeting usually includes the GA member, the spouse or significant other, the sponsor, and other GA members with long-term recovery. The group helps the new member develop a budget and a plan for repayment of debts. Members of the group may contact creditors and assist in debt negotiation. The spouse or significant other (assuming that he or she doesn't have a gambling problem) is encouraged to take control of the household finances. The new member is given an allowance and removed from credit card and bank accounts. There are also Gam-Anon meetings, the equivalent of AlAnon, for the family and significant others.

OTHER ADDICTIONS

While the purpose of various support groups and twelve-step programs is to help gamblers abstain, there are other compulsive problems for which abstention is not an option or would be very difficult. These problems include compulsive behaviors around eating, sex and love, the Internet, and work. To some researchers, the fact that the latter behaviors cannot be dealt with through abstention is reason enough to eliminate them from the field of addictions and addictive behaviors. Moreover, many researchers have argued that the term *addiction* should be applied only to issues related to the ingestion of AOD (Young, 2004). In any case, the extension of a model of addiction from substances to behaviors remains controversial (Morahan-Martin, 2005; Yellowlees & Marks, 2005).

Mental health professionals are strongly encouraged to formulate an opinion about whether behaviors other than AOD use can be classified as addictions. Because of the content in many popular magazines, books, and television talk shows, you will quite likely encounter clients who believe they are addicted to gambling, food, work, the Internet, sex, or relationships. While professionals generally agree that excessive engagement in these and other behaviors can result in a variety of problems, they don't necessarily agree about whether these behaviors can be classified as addictions. We believe that you should be informed about the different arguments in this controversy so that you can develop your own view. After outlining the arguments pro and con regarding the existence of other addictions, we will describe pathological eating, sex and love, Internet use, and work behaviors. Finally, we will present information on assessment and treatment issues.

Two Points of View About Other Addictions

In preparing to write this book, we submitted a prospectus that included a proposed table of contents. One reviewer was particularly impressed with the fact that we had included a chapter on other addictions. This reviewer commented that this area was usually neglected in books in the AOD field. Another reviewer was quite critical of our inclusion of this topic and chastised us for creating the impression that behaviors such as overeating, excessive gambling, and other behaviors were addictions. This was a clear demonstration to us that there are different points of view on the topic of other addictions and that these perspectives are expressed with considerable fervor.

Critics of Other Addictions

There are three main groups who discount the notion that behaviors related to eating, excessive work or Internet use, and sexual compulsions can be addictions. One group claims that classifying compulsive behaviors as *addictions* is inappropriate because these behaviors are already well defined in the mental health field. The debate is similar to the one regarding codependency that was discussed in Chapter 12. It can be argued that compulsions involving sex are already identified in the *DSM-IV-TR*. For example, the sexual disorders called *paraphilias* include many of the sexual behaviors often referred to as *addictive* (e.g., exhibitionism, fetishism, voyeurism). Furthermore, the criteria for Histrionic Personality Disorder include "interaction with others [that] is often characterized by inappropriate sexually seductive or provocative behavior" (APA, 2000, p. 657), suggesting that those who are "addicted" to sex may have a personality disorder. Therefore, no new diagnostic category of sex addiction is necessary. For other interpersonal relationship problems, such as the compulsive need for love and attention, critics of other addictions point out that these symptoms may also be characteristic of a personality disorder, such as Dependent Personality Disorder, Narcissistic Personality Disorder, or Histrionic Personality Disorder, or may be classified as an Other Condition That May Be a Focus of Clinical Attention (e.g., Partner Relational Problem). Similarly, Pathological Gambling is already classified as an Impulse-Control Disorder Not Elsewhere Classified, and the *DSM-IV-TR* has an Eating Disorders category.

A second group of critics of "other addictions" are the same people who view alcohol and other drug problems as bad habits, willful misconduct, or irresponsible and irrational behavior (Drewnowski & Bellisle, 2007). These conceptualizations have been described in Chapter 3 and may be held by professionals promoting a certain theoretical model of addiction or by lay people who see addictive behaviors from a moral model. For example, Alan Marlatt has written extensively regarding a social learning model of addictive behaviors (see Chapters 3 and 9). In his words, "addictive behaviors represent a category of 'bad habits' including such behaviors as problem drinking, smoking, substance abuse, overeating, compulsive gambling, and so forth" (Marlatt, 1985, p. 9).

Finally, there are also "purists" who see addiction from a medical model and restrict this label to those who are dependent on alcohol or other drugs. From this point of view, the demonstration of tolerance and withdrawal (see Chapter 2) in an individual who uses alcohol and/or other drugs is indicative of addiction. Since physiological tolerance and withdrawal cannot be shown in regard to behaviors such as overeating, gambling, and sex, these behaviors cannot be thought of as "addictions." Purists see the use of the term *addiction* when applied to behaviors different from alcohol and other drug use as diminishing the disease model of addiction.

Somewhere in between these groups of critics are Stanton Peele and Archie Brodsky who, in their book on love addiction (1991), claim that love addiction—and any other addiction—is not a disease. These authors maintain that while putting love addiction in a disease model gave it a broad, popular appeal that was helpful in the 1980s, now a need exists to redefine what is meant by the addictive process.

Peele and Brodsky (1991) maintain that an addiction is an experience that takes on significant meaning and power with respect to an individual's needs, desires, beliefs, expectations, and fears. Further, these authors maintain that compulsive, dependent attachments arise from the punctuated contrast between the void and anxiety that people experience in the totality of their lives and the immediate fulfillment they expect will occur when engaged with the addictive object or sensation.

Proponents of Other Addictions

The proponents of other addictions point out the similarities between alcoholics and drug addicts and those who engage in excessive behaviors other than AOD use (Grant, Potenza, Weinstein, & Gorelick, 2010). For example, Yellowlees and Marks (2005) and Young (2004) associate problematic Internet use and Internet addiction. Carnes (2001), and Tripodi (2006) present research linking compulsive sexual practices with sexual addiction. According to Sussman, Lisha, & Griffiths (2011), the range of addictive behaviors is broad, and includes tobacco, alcohol, illicit drugs, eating, gambling, Internet, love, sex, exercise, shopping, and work. Given this range, these researchers suggest that approximately 47% of the U.S. adult population suffers from maladaptive signs of an addictive disorder over a 12-month period (pp. 3–4).

If you go back to Chapter 6 and review the criteria for Substance Dependence from *DSM-IV-TR,* you will see that only three of the criteria are necessary for the diagnosis. Even if we ignore the first two criteria, since they involve the controversial topics of tolerance and withdrawal, it is still easy to see that a client who overeats, gambles too much, is constantly changing sex partners, or uses the Internet excessively would meet the criteria for dependence if that behavior were substituted for the word *substance*. For example, Steve, a compulsive gambler with whom we worked, often gambled more money than he intended and tried to cut down on his gambling on many occasions. His marriage and job were adversely affected by his gambling. With these symptoms, it could be argued that Steve was dependent on gambling.

A less scientific argument to support the similarity of behavioral addictions to alcohol and other drug addictions is the development of twelve-step support groups for overeaters, gamblers, and "sex addicts" (see Chapter 10). Because twelve-step groups are based on the principles of Alcoholics Anonymous, and because these groups have helped many people with problem behaviors in many areas other than alcohol and other drugs, it is argued that these "other" behaviors should be seen as addictions. It is clear that someone can feel powerlessness over eating, gambling, or sex, which is consistent with the first of the twelve steps.

Finally, proponents of other addictions contend that adoption of this concept has resulted in organized efforts to help people with these problems. Popular books and talk shows, the heightening awareness of mental health professionals, and the development of support groups have all helped people label their problems. While some people believe that the labeling process is used as an excuse for problematic behavior, the opposite may be true. For example, if you have some troubling physical symptoms that you cannot explain, it is often comforting to receive a diagnosis of the condition, even if no cure exists. Perhaps you find out that you are hypoglycemic. You will always have the condition, but you can modify dietary habits to reduce the unpleasant symptoms. Similarly, if Steve identifies himself as a gambling addict, he may believe that he will always be a gambling addict but that he also has some resources for help (e.g., Gamblers Anonymous). Therefore, the open discussion about problems involving eating, gambling, and sex has resulted in many people acknowledging that they have one of these problems, that many people share their problem, and that they can seek help for these problems.

FOOD ADDICTION: THE EATING DISORDERS

We eat to survive. We eat for a variety of other reasons as well, such as in celebration, for enjoyment, for social acceptance, or to relieve boredom. We also eat to win affection, as reflected in the often-heard phrase "The way to a man's heart is through his stomach." Our eating is often ritualized: hot dogs at a sporting event, popcorn at the movies, snacking in front of the television, or setting aside meals as the time when the family can meet to discuss family issues or the day's events. Ritualistic eating can likewise be reflected in a tradition of overeating at Thanksgiving or other holidays. Eating patterns also vary: Some may eat when they feel stress or to avoid painful feelings, while others may restrict their intake under the same circumstances. It can safely be said that most of us, at one time or another, eat for reasons other than to survive.

You are probably most familiar with the eating disorder anorexia nervosa, described by Bruch (1986) as the relentless pursuit of thinness, and bulimia nervosa, described as chronic episodes of binge eating followed by purging. These two disorders are cited in the *DSM-IV-TR* under the section Eating Disorders (p. 539). Our cultural preoccupation with food, thinness, and its relationship with success has been cited as a cause of the increase in the incidence of eating disorders—especially among women (Schwartz, Thompson, & Johnson, 1983). However, there are other disordered eating patterns such as chronic obesity, binge eating, and chronic overeating that are not yet cited in the *DSM-IV-TR*. These eating behaviors can eventually become problematic as well. Over recent decades, eating disorders have become the most widespread mental health concern in young women (Newton & Ciliska, 2006). Recent estimates suggest that clinically diagnosable eating disorders such as anorexia nervosa and bulimia nervosa, affect from 0.5% to 2.8% of the U.S. population (Hudsen, Hiripi, Pope, & Kessler, 2007). These same researchers maintain that eating disorders are among the most lethal psychiatric illnesses and kill up to 20% of those afflicted.

In U.S. culture, being overweight is a symbol of illness and ugliness, and being slim represents health, beauty, and success. The pressures to be thin have resulted in a substantial proportion of adolescents from a variety of ethnic backgrounds, regardless of gender (although females make up a disproportionate number of those with an eating disorder), to engage in excessive weight control behaviors (Lynch, Heil, Wagner, & Havens, 2007). Dissatisfaction with one's body in terms of size, shape, and form can lead to personal distress and/or psychosocial impairment about one's body image. In some cases, this leads to body image disturbances (BID). It is this disturbance that is seen as a significant causative factor in the development of disordered eating and eating disorders.

Body Image

According to Cash (1997, p. 2) and Vocks, Legenbaurer, Rüddel, and Troje (2007), body image does not refer to what you actually look like. Body image is a phrase that refers to an individual's *personal relationship* with his or her body. This relationship is formed around beliefs, perceptions, thoughts, feelings, and actions that are associated with physical appearance.

Body image is affected by strong sociocultural factors, including peer and media (Ferguson, Munoz, Contreras, & Velasquez, 2011). Levine and Smolak (2001) state that body image is a complex synthesis of psychophysical elements that are perceptual, emotional, cognitive, and kinesthetic in nature. Body image is seen as integral to gender identity, and disturbances in it can cause interpersonal anxiety and self-consciousness.

According to Cash (1997), one's attitude toward one's body and the emotional and cognitive elements are more amenable to change than is one's perception. In fact, the perception of one's body size and shape is considered difficult, if not impossible, to change. This same researcher sees a disturbed body image as lowering one's self-esteem. In addition, Cash asserts that roughly one-third to one-fourth of one's self-esteem is related to appearance.

Cash sees that body image disturbances can also influence body dysmorphic disorder and clinical depression. While you are probably somewhat familiar with major depressive states, body dysmorphic disorder may be unfamiliar. Essentially, it is the disorder of *imagined ugliness* at the same time when others look at these individuals and see them as okay or even beautiful or handsome. Researchers have demonstrated the association between disturbances in body image and eating disorders, including anorexia nervosa, bulimia nervosa, and binge-eating disorder (e.g., Cummins & Lehman, 2007; Dounchis, Hayden, & Wilfley 2001; Levine & Smolak, 2001; Lynch et al., 2007; Wolfe, Faan, Baker, Smith, & Kelly-Weeder, 2009).

While men's body image has not received the attention in the professional literature that women's body image has, Levesque and Vichesky (2006) report that males experience body image dissatisfaction as well. In particular, gay males, as opposed to heterosexual males, may have pronounced concerns with body image and can be at high risk for eating disorders. In a different stream of research, Lynch et al. (2007) maintain that in spite of the lack of agreement on the source of racial/ethnic and cultural differences related to eating problems, a link is clearly apparent between body mass index, body concerns, and risk of eating disorders among these various groups. However, the strength of that association varies from one ethnic group to another. It stands to reason that as we are able to prevent body image disturbance we will also witness a diminishing number of eating disorders.

Chronic Obesity

Chronic obesity is a worldwide epidemic (Coutinho, Moreira, Spagnol, & Appolinario, 2007). *Obesity* occurs when one is 20% over the desirable weight for one's height (Burrows, 1992), and *chronic obesity* occurs when individuals are at least 20% overweight for protracted periods of time. In general, there are mild, moderate, and severe degrees of obesity. However, sensitivity to diversity issues regarding obesity is important in that different cultures value different body types. For example, Becker (2007) cites the fat phobia among Hong Kong Chinese who appear to meet the qualifications for anorexia, and Lynch et al. (2007) cite studies demonstrating variations in attitudes toward eating, the meaning of food and meals, culturally related eating behaviors, as well as cultural influences on individuation, maintenance of control, and emotional expression.

According to the Centers for Disease Control and Prevention (CDC, 2007c), the prevalence of being overweight or obese has increased sharply for both adults and children in the United States. These increasing rates are concerning in that being overweight or obese increases the risk for many diseases and health conditions, such as hypertension, type 2 diabetes, coronary heart disease, stroke, gallbladder disease, osteoarthritis, sleep apnea, respiratory problems, and some cancers (endometrial, breast, and colon) (CDC, 2007c; Dounchis et al., 2001; Levine & Smolak, 2001). Because of this, Jarosz, Dobal, Wilson, and Schram (2007) state that the reduction of obesity is one of the most important public health objectives for the 21st century.

Some research suggests that obesity has a genetic component and that obesity in childhood has a strong positive correlation with weight status in adulthood (Brownell & Stunkard, 1978; Robinson & Killen, 2001). However, Burrows qualifies this assertion by stating that a high fat cell count in infancy and childhood is predictive of adult obesity only when other factors such as overeating and inactivity persist. In addition to the genetic component and ensuing environmental factors leading to obesity in adulthood, two other avenues lead to this condition: a pattern of chronic binge eating or chronic overeating. Chronic overeating occurs when individuals routinely eat more than they need to eat in order to be healthy. Whenever you sit at a dinner table and say to yourself or to others, "I am so full, but I don't want that last piece of chicken to go to waste," you are engaging in overeating. Imagine if you were to repeat this at every meal—that is the experience of the chronic overeater. In contrast to chronic overeating, binge eating involves consumption of large and unnecessary quantities of food in one sitting and in a relatively short amount of time. Movies that depict first-century Romans lying on their couches and engaged in an eating orgy show a good example of binge eating. Although binge eating and obesity commonly co-occur, the relationship of one to the other is not always causal. For example, Gormally, Black, Dastrom, and Rardin (1982) estimated that only 50% of those seeking treatment for obesity indicated a pattern of binge eating at least once per week.

CHRONIC BINGE EATING Binge-eating disorder (BED) is a newly recognized entity that is characterized by uncontrollable consumption of food without any inappropriate compensatory behaviors (Coutinho et al., 2007). While some debate surrounds the definition of binge eating, there is little disagreement that binge eating is a cardinal symptom for the diagnosis of bulimia nervosa (discussed later in this chapter) (Wolfe et al., 2009).

Bennett and Dodge (2007) cite mounting evidence that warrants including chronic binge eating as a third type of eating disorder. Estimates of the prevalence of binge eating suggest that it affects between 2% and 5% of Americans in any six-month period. BED mostly affects women ages 46 to 55 and affects African Americans at the same rate as Euro-Americans. There are no reliable statistics related to other ethnic groups (National Institutes of Health, 2007).

Symptoms include eating an excessive amount of food within a discrete period of time, usually defined as 2 days per week for 6 months, with a sense of lack of control over eating during the episode (Wilson & Sysko, 2009). Generally, the binge-eating episodes include eating much more rapidly than normal; eating until feeling uncomfortably full; eating large amounts of food when not feeling physically hungry; eating alone because of being embarrassed by how much one is eating; and feeling disgusted with oneself, depressed, and/or feeling guilty after overeating. Individuals with BED are distressed about the binge-eating behavior. Binge-eating disorder is not associated with regular use of inappropriate compensatory behaviors such as purging or fasting. Although similar to bulimia, the main difference between them is that individuals with binge-eating disorder do not purge their bodies of excess calories. Hence, it would be expected that individuals with this disorder would be overweight for their age and height.

Bennett and Dodge (2007) claim that even though BED is most common in people who are overweight, it can affect people with appropriate weight as well. Adult females comprise about two-thirds of those with BED, and it is on the rise among teenagers, too. According to Robinson and Killen (2001) and Striegel-Moore et al., (2007), binge eating episodes can be triggered by feelings of anger, sadness, boredom, or anxiety. In addition, Bennett and Dodge have demonstrated that feeling embarrassed and feeling out of control are two distinguishing features delineating binge eating and BED from chronic overeating. Recently, evidence has emerged that stress associated with sexual assault is related to an increase in binge eating (Cameron, Maguire, & McCormack, 2011). Symptoms can include a child eating a lot of food very quickly, feelings of shame and disgust about the amount of food ingested, a pattern of eating in response to emotional stress, eating late at night in secret, and hiding food containers in one's room. In addition, depression often accompanies BED (National Institutes of Health, 2007). A vicious cycle can occur where one becomes depressed and binges, which then creates more depression and more binging.

Bulimia Nervosa and Anorexia Nervosa

Anorexia nervosa (AN) is often a persistent and severe mental illness that has the highest mortality rate among all psychiatric disorders. Research suggests that puberty is the most common period for the onset of eating disorders, with the onset of bingeing peaking at 16 years and the onset of purging peaking at 18 years (Day et al., 2011). Prepubertal onset of bulimia nervosa (BN) is extremely rare, and the highest incidence of bulimia nervosa occurs during adult life. However, given the increase in childhood obesity and the prevalence of dieting among female adolescents, it can be expected that the incidence of bulimia nervosa will increase.

Anorexia nervosa (AN) and bulimia nervosa (BN) are estimated to occur in about 0.5%–1% and 1%–4% of the U.S. adult population respectively (Herzog & Eddy, 2009). Reports show the incidence of anorexia in adolescent women to be between 5% and 7% of the population, and the incidence of bulimia to be about 1%–2% of the population (Bravender et al., 2010). Males, especially gay men, represent approximately 5%–20% of people with eating disorders (Feldman & Meyer, 2007). Although research is lacking on eating disorders and gender and ethnicity, it is believed that the incidence is underreported for these populations (Wingfield, Kelly, Serdar, Shivy, & Mazzeo, 2011).

Traditionally, eating disorders have been seen as a disorder of adolescents and young women. However, recent research suggests that eating disorders can often occur across the life span (Brandsma, 2007). Exact figures are difficult to determine in that many older women will not seek treatment. In some cases, these individuals are treated for depression and/or anxiety, while the eating disorder goes undiagnosed. The opposite can be true in other cases where the rise in incidence is due to better recognition among diagnosticians. Morley and Castele (1985) believe that a diminished sense of smell and taste concomitant with appetite disorders contribute to the incidence among female elderly. Goodman, Blinder, Chaitin, and Hagman (1988) assert that anorexia in older adults can be present in the absence of depression. Bereavement can influence appetite or eating altogether in this population.

Cause for alarm is signaled by studies that have demonstrated that only a minority of college women have normal eating habits (Hesse-Biber, 1989; Mintz & Betz, 1988). Kashubeck, Walsh, and Crowl (1994) believe that many college campuses may promote disordered eating behaviors by emphasizing perfection, competition, and physical attractiveness. The presence of such sociocultural pressures is at least partially responsible in the development of eating disorders during adolescence. Researchers in the field generally agree. However, early childhood trauma, unmerciful teasing about body size and shape, and other factors also influence the pressures leading to the final development of the illness (Kitsantas, Gilligan, & Komata, 2003; Robinson & Killen, 2001).

Research suggests that risk of serious comorbidity is higher with other disorders as well, such as depressive and anxiety disorders, substance abuse, suicide attempts, general psychological distress, impaired social (interpersonal) functioning, and a reduced quality of life (Jappe et al., 2011; Newton & Ciliska, 2006). Humphreys, Clopton, and Reich (2007) maintain that a link exists between eating disorders and obsessive-compulsive disorder (OCD). They estimate that between 15% and 41% of those with eating disorders also suffer from OCD. It is clear that serious health consequences result from prolonged bulimia nervosa and anorexia nervosa.

BULIMIA NERVOSA Bulimia nervosa (BN) emerged as a new disorder in the 1970s, and incidence rates rose from the 1980s to early 1990s, with concerns being expressed that this disorder might be affecting increasingly larger numbers of adolescents.

In general, bulimia nervosa is characterized by recurrent episodes of binge eating where the person experiences a lack of a sense of control and eats an excessive amount of food within a discrete period of time. People with bulimia also practice recurrent inappropriate compensatory behavior in order to prevent weight gain, such as self-induced vomiting or misuse of laxatives, diuretics, enemas, fasting, or excessive exercise. The fact that people with bulimia nervosa usually weigh within the normal range for their age and height is interesting. This is due to the compensatory behaviors that keep weight down. Individuals with this disorder can fear gaining weight and can feel intensely dissatisfied with their bodies to the point of having BID. Often, compensatory behaviors occur in secrecy. During the episode, individuals report feeling disgusted and ashamed when they binge, yet relieved once they purge. According to the *DSM-IV-TR,* specific diagnostic criteria for bulimia nervosa include recurrent episodes of binge eating, recurrent inappropriate compensatory behavior aimed at preventing weight gain, binge eating and inappropriate compensatory behaviors occurring on the average two times per week for three months, the overinfluence of body shape and weight upon one's self-evaluations, and that the disturbance does not occur exclusively during periods of anorexia nervosa.

Rogers and Petrie (2001) found that women with bulimia generally have a diminished ability to regulate tension, have lowered impulse control, have a need for immediate gratification, and have a lowered sense of worth. Forbush, Heatherton, and Keel (2007); Brouwers and Wiggum (1993); and others report an association with perfectionism and an array of eating disorders in women. Forbush et al. found that the associations were strongest for fasting and purging and, for males, perfectionism was associated more with fasting than for other disordered eating.

Brouwers and Wiggum (1993) see internal conflict as abounding within the bulimic population. An individual with bulimia often gets caught up in a psychic no-win situation, in which one side of her insists that she must eat only the right foods and the other side begs for spontaneity with food and a natural acceptance of herself. The classic case of this conflict is the binge–purge cycle, in which the person eats a large quantity of food spontaneously (the "all") followed by purging ("the nothing"), or when she tells herself that she can eat anything and everything since she can always purge (Neuman & Halvorson, 1983).

In most cases, bulimia will result after a period of anorexia. Again, it is an "all or nothing" thought process. In other words, these individuals say to themselves, "I won't eat anything today (nothing)." Eventually, the body must receive nourishment, and the bulimic person, after a period of starvation, will gorge with food (all).

ANOREXIA NERVOSA   Garfinkel and Kaplan (1986) state,

> Anorexia is an increasingly common complex order . . . that overrides the patient's physical and psychological well-being. . . . Pursuing a thin body becomes an isolated area of control in a world in which the individual feels ineffective; the dieting provides an artificially dangerous sense of mastery and control. As the weight loss progresses, a starvation state ensues, which eventually develops a life of its own, leading to features of anorexia nervosa. (p. 266)

According to the U.S. Department of Health and Human Services (2007), approximately 0.5% to 3.7% of females suffer from anorexia nervosa in their lifetime. In general, individuals with anorexia nervosa are characterized by intense fear of gaining weight or becoming fat, food restriction and weight loss, body image distortions, amenorrhea, and disturbances in the way in which one's body weight or shape is experienced (Jappe et al., 2011). There may also be negative self-evaluations related to one's body weight as well as a denial of the acute crisis resulting from severe underweight.

The two types of anorexia nervosa are restrictive anorexia and bulimic anorexia. As you would expect, bulimic anorexia is characterized by the use of compensatory measures such as purging. However, the main difference between bulimic anorexia and bulimia nervosa is that the former does not binge before purging. Individuals with the restrictive type of anorexia nervosa can restrict the amount of food intake and/or can engage in excessive exercise.

It is interesting to note that individuals with restrictive anorexia do not suffer from a loss of appetite. Rather, they are "frantically preoccupied with food and eating . . . [they] deliberately, seemingly willfully, restrict their food intake and overexercise. These girls are panicky with the fear that they might lose control over their eating" (Bruch, 1986, p. 331). As a result, the actual process of eating can become obsessive, and unusual eating habits will develop. These habits can include such things as assessing or weighing the portion of food, restricting the foods that one eats to only a few, and/or avoiding food and even missing meals.

Even though anorexia nervosa is not usually found in women over the age of 25, the same can be said for the incidence of anorexia nervosa in African Americans and Latino/Hispanic populations. For example, Goodman et al. (1988) found that only 5% of the reported cases of anorexia nervosa were reflected in these ethnically diverse populations. Regarding anorexia in women over the age of 25, Dally (1984) maintains that these anorexics tend to come from upper-middle-class families. Other researchers found anorexic women over the age of 25 to have had stress secondary to childbirth or marriage (Kellett, Trimble, & Thorley, 1976) or death of a spouse (Price, Giannini, & Colella, 1985).

The course and outcome of anorexia nervosa vary across individuals. Some will recover after a single episode. Others can have a fluctuating pattern of gaining weight and relapsing. Still others can experience this chronically with a concomitant deterioration of their body. Males can experience anorexia. However, the proportion of females to males with anorexia is approximately 10 to 1 (Lindblad, Lindberg, & Hjern, 2006). Males with anorexia often display perfectionism, obsessions, passive dependencies, and antisocial characteristics (Anderson & Michalide, 1983).

According to the DHHS (2007), the mortality rate for individuals with anorexia has been estimated at 0.56% per year, or approximately 5.6% per decade. This means that death due to anorexia is about 12 times higher than the annual death rate due to all causes of death among females ages 15 to 24 in the general population. The most common causes of death among persons who are anorexic are suicide, cardiac arrest, and electrolyte imbalance.

ADDICTION TO SEX AND LOVE

In the 1800s, sexual addiction was referred to as moral insanity, satyriasis, and nymphomania (Levine, 2010). However, at least 18 other labels are now used to describe ways that individuals express sexual excess, including hypersexuality and sexual obsession. Levine maintains that sexual addiction is a confusing topic because the stigma often conjures up visions of individuals who betray, illuminate previously hidden sexual behaviors, expose unsuspecting partners to disease risk, and continually present a proclivity to abandon their partners. The scientific literature seems to favor the term *Hypersexual Disorder*, for many reasons. Mainly, this term neutralizes the stigma as much as possible (Samenow, 2010).

Sex and love addiction is seen by many as comprising three addictions: love passion, love addiction, and sex addiction (Reynaud, Karila, Blecha, & Benyamina, 2010). Popular tabloids and even mainstream "news" outlets teem with examples. An incident of Brittany Spears and her cohorts being photographed exiting from automobiles in revealing clothing and compromised positions brought to mind questions about whether it is the stars or the paparazzi who are addicted to sex. Even those who stalk the stars could be considered, among other things, to be addicted to love. Members of the U.S. Congress and celebrity athletes have posted inappropriate pictures of themselves to their followers, and a sensational case in New York involved a French politician (the charges were later dropped). The media is replete with stories of one spouse attempting to kill the other in order to be able to carry on with a lover.

Griffin-Shelley (1991) writes that our physical and psychological identity is made up in part by sex and love, and "Letting go of sex and love, even for a short amount of time, seems [to addicts] like giving up [their] whole identity" (p. 19). According to Forward (1986) and Norwood (1985), sex addictions are gender-free and cut across all socioeconomic lines, racial/ethnic groupings, and sexual orientations. The compulsive behavioral problems of sex addiction can include excessive masturbation, preoccupation with pornography, excessive sexual relations, and engaging in prostitution.

Sex and love addiction combines sex and love and can reflect individuals who involve themselves in numerous affairs in spite of promises to the contrary. More often than not, these individuals may use sex in attempting to get the love they feel they need. In many of these cases, sex is only the enticer, or the avenue through which other emotional, intellectual, or spiritual needs are met. But the act of sex does not characterize all individuals addicted to sex and love. Being in a primary relationship and compulsively fantasizing about others is also characteristic of those addicted to sex and love. Constantly fantasizing about someone other than the one to whom a person is making love also reflects a sex and love addiction.

Even without sexualizing the relationship, many sex and love addicts maintain that they compulsively engage in emotional affairs. For example, one of our clients told us of a time when she was paralyzed at a traffic light on a busy street trying to decide whether she should drive by her fantasy lover's office "just to see him, not to talk to him." She remained immobilized for an entire light cycle, with cars honking on both sides of her while she engaged in an internal debate about whether to drive straight ahead or whether to turn and drive by his office. (She drove straight ahead.)

Regarding sex and love addiction, Griffin-Shelley (1991) writes,

> The habit of thinking or fantasizing and then having to compulsively act out is like the binge/purge cycle of the bulimic. As thoughts fill the addict with excitement, anticipation, and energy, he or she feels closer and closer to losing control. When the rush into action takes place, it consumes the person with the passion of the moment, and all reason and rationality are lost in the explosion. What a "rush." What a release. What an orgasm. The guilt, shame, remorse come later. For the time being, the addict feels fulfilled. The pattern of riding the wave of sexual and romantic excitement to the crash on the beach is worth the ride and is difficult to give up. Ordinary life pales in comparison to the highs and lows of the obsession/compulsion routine. (p. 80)

For sex and love addicts, the consequences can be profound. Losses can include serious financial problems, being fired from a job for sexual harassment, overwhelming feelings of shame, personal distress, guilt, and relationship breakups (Garcia & Thibaut, 2010). Kasl (2002) includes other consequences such as issues related to health (e.g., STIs), as well as educational, parental, safety, and spiritual issues. Emotional consequences can revolve around guilt, resentment, suicidal ideation, depression, fear, self-loathing, and a diminished sense of self-worth.

Even in the face of such catastrophic consequences, individuals with sexual addiction persist. For instance, a national network broadcasts a syndicated television show *To Catch a Predator* that (while controversial) demonstrates the power of sexual addiction (among other disorders). In this series, a house in an everyday neighborhood in a variety of cities is set up for the purpose of catching predators who have made contact with "minors" online. (The "minors" are actually actors and actresses). The show airs weekly, and in spite of its being on primetime national television, there are numerous males who visit the various houses and are confronted by a news anchor while a crew films the interactions. Then the perpetrators are usually arrested. What is amazing and what supports the gravity of the sexual addiction is that some men are arrested more than once. So, even after getting caught on national television, some continue and get caught again in the same trap on the same show!

Clearly, the rise of the Internet in the early 1980s has completely altered the landscape for sexual and love addiction. MySpace and Facebook are used not only socially for relationships and for sharing information, but by sexual predators to lure minors into meetings. YouTube gets sexual postings daily. There are disgruntled ex-lovers who post nude pictures of themselves or their former lovers as a way of getting even. A related issue is the use of the Internet for pornography or cybersex and online affairs (cyberaffairs) increasing at an alarming rate (Beard, 2005; Young, 2004).

INTERNET ADDICTION

It is clear that cybersex and cyberaffairs, while reflecting a high incidence rate, represent only one dimension of compulsive Internet use. When was the last time you checked your Facebook page? The Facebook webpage (Facebook, 2011) claims more than 750 million users, and more than 50% of users log on to Facebook in any given day. The average user has 130 friends, and people spend over 700 billion minutes per month on Facebook. Although it is very likely that a certain number of Facebook users are compulsive, it is clear that the culture is changing as to what would be considered "normal use."

These two issues are really symptoms of what might be considered a comorbidity of sexual addiction and Internet addiction disorder (IAD). That means that addiction to the Internet is primary, and the particular use of the Internet, such as use for cybersex and/or cyberaffairs are only manifestations of a deeper issue. Problematic use of the Internet is found in every age, social, educational, and economic bracket. The hackneyed view that Internet addiction was relegated to young, introverted, computer-oriented males is no longer valid (Beard, 2005). Block (2008) maintains that IAD includes four components: 1) excessive use associated with loss of sense of time or neglect of basic drives; 2) withdrawal that leads to feelings of anger, tension, and/or depression when access is denied; 3) tolerance that lends itself to increased purchasing or accumulation of software or advanced computer equipment; and, 4) negative social consequences.

A review of the research on Internet sexuality reveals several types of activities (Döring, 2009). *Pornography on the Internet* gives users access to commercial and noncommercial online pornography as well as allows them to produce, distribute, and discuss material. *Sex shops* on the Internet offer a second activity. Here users may purchase sexual aids and toys such as vibrators, condoms, sexy lingerie, and erotic magazines. The sex shops can be commercial and represent offline shops, or they can be independent online sex shops. *Sex work* on the Internet is a third activity in which users can offer services or obtain sexual services. Often these activities are in real time. Broadcasts of sex shows, advertising for brothels, and information about escort services fall under the heading of sex work on the Internet. The fourth type of activity is *sexual education*. This can include traditional sex education material as well as more discrete information related to coming out, sexual awareness, attitudes, and behaviors. *Sex contacts* on the Internet is the fifth type of activity. This is typically referred to as online sex or cybersex. Contacts are initiated exclusively for computer-mediated sexual exchanges that can lead to real world sexual encounters (offline sex). In this venue, there is no monetary exchange as there might be in the sex work discussed above. Finally, the sixth activity relates to *sexual subcultures* in which nonmainstream sexual orientations or preferences can be addressed. Usually, these Internet platforms involve the exchange of information such as political activism, social support, and groups that exist offline and online.

According to Suhail and Bargees (2006) and Young (2004), Internet use in the United States has grown from less than 50% of Americans in 2000 to about 68% by 2004. Morahan-Martin (2005) maintains that there are 700 million users worldwide, with 103 million people from China alone going online (Cao & Su, 2006). There are estimates that between 1% and 13% of these users exhibit disturbed behavior on the Internet (Morahan- Martin, 2005; Tao et al., 2010). Chou, Condron and Belland (2005) conducted a review of the literature on Internet addiction and identified the nature of these Internet users. These researchers found that the Internet was used for 1) sex, 2) an altered state of consciousness, 3) achievement and mastery, 4) belonging, 5) relationships, and 6) self-actualization and transcendence of self. Adult users of Internet pornography are likely to be male, younger, homosexual or bisexual, sexually active, nonreligious, unmarried, and having higher levels of education (Stack, Wasserman, & Kern, 2004; Træen, Nilsen, & Stigum, 2006). Adolescent users of Internet pornography tend to be African American who are in their late teens and come from families with less education and lower socioeconomic status (Brown & L'Engle, 2009).

Rather than taking a pathological approach toward Internet addiction, Hall and Parsons (2001) and Beard (2005) lean more toward a mental health model approach. These researchers see these issues of Internet addiction as problems affecting the lives of otherwise healthy people and state that "excessive Internet use is a benign problem in living" (p. 314). Hall and Parsons see their definition as reflecting a more "holistic framework that complements our understanding of the client's world" (p. 314).

Hall and Parson have a good point. Yet it may be that the client's addiction to the Internet also includes being addicted to gambling on the Internet: the double-whammy. In this case, where does the gambling addiction end and the addiction to the Internet begin, and vice versa? This co-occurring addiction may only get worse as increasing numbers of individuals log onto the Internet.

There is an increase in research efforts focused on specific symptoms of *cybersex compulsion* (Waskul, 2004). Research reveals 6.5% of male Internet users spend at least six hours per week engaging in cybersex. Orzach (2004) identifies specific psychological and psychical symptoms that include the following: a) euphoria and sense of well-being while online; b) feeling unable or unwilling to stop; c) an increasing desire to stay online or to go online; d) experiencing feelings of emptiness, distress, or irritability when prevented from going online; e) lying to others about extent of use; f) carpal tunnel syndrome; g) dry eyes; h) neglect of personal hygiene; i) migraines; j) sleep disturbances; k) experiencing more general problems related to work and/ or school; and l) neglecting interpersonal relationships.

Impact of Internet Abuse on Relationships, Students, and Workers

Cyberaffairs are defined as a romantic and/or sexual relationship that are initiated and maintained online (Young, 1999). According to this researcher, online affairs differ dramatically from in vivo affairs in several ways. In cyberaffairs, individuals can be more honest, open, forthright, less inhibited, and can be more culturally diverse (which augments the perceived glamour). The impact of cyberaffairs on existing real-life relationships can be dramatic and can include the following: a change in sleep patterns, a new demand for privacy, ignoring other responsibilities, lying, personality changes, loss of interest in sex, and a declined investment in the real-life relationship. The declined interest in one's real-life relationship is often reflected by no longer valuing rituals, no longer taking vacations together, an avoidance of making long-range plans together, and a general distancing between partners with the concomitant loss of intimacy. A profound effect is found in the works of Carnes (2001) and Cooper, Delmonico, and Burg (2000), who maintain that cybersex may actually speed up the process of addiction in individuals who otherwise would not have addictive disorders.

Ceyhan, Ceyhan, and Gürcan (2007) assert that university students were one of the first groups identified as having problems with Internet addiction. Research conducted internationally also reveals that teachers, librarians, computer coordinators, and college administrators are now recognizing that all of the money put into technological endeavors for education can be abused by students (Cao & Su, 2006; Young, 2010; 2004). College counselors have argued that college students have become the most vulnerable population due to these increases in technological resources. Velezmoro, Lacefield, and Roberti (2010) and Young (2010; 2004) see several factors that influence the rise in Internet addiction among college students. These include having free and unlimited use; huge blocks of unstructured time with no or very little monitoring; institutional values that encourage the use of technology for readings, assignments, viewing syllabi online, and taking online courses; higher drinking ages that restrict locations to meet others; and the social intimidation that some students can feel when they arrive on large campuses. Studies have shown that 58% of students who use the Internet excessively suffer from poor study habits or late-night logins (Young, 2004, 1998). Velezmoro et al. found that perceived stress was predictive of Internet usage for sexual purposes among college students. When college students get bored or perceive hopelessness, they tend to use the Internet for nonsexual purposes.

Employee abuse of the Internet is also of concern to researchers and employers alike, and there is some evidence that the phenomenon is of epidemic proportions. Young (2010) states that nearly 64% of employees use the Internet for personal interest during office hours. Queen's University in Belfast conducted a survey of 350 companies from the United States, Australia, and the United Kingdom and found that 28% percent of those surveyed admitted downloading sexually explicit content while on the job (Sullivan, 2004).

The impact of Internet abuse on the workplace is multifaceted. For example, the loss of productivity is staggering. Stewart (2001) sees the loss to revenues in the billions. The losses stem from employees who are slow to respond to customers' needs, from employees unable to meet deadlines consistently, and often fail to complete tasks because they are preoccupied with surfing the Internet. There is also negative publicity associated with class action suits or individual lawsuits that claim sexual harassment in the workplace as a result of pornography or other content being passed around. Legal liabilities are also involved. This means that as Internet abuse is increasingly being touted as an addiction, it makes those abusing the Internet at work "disabled." With protection under the American Disabilities Act, an employee may in turn sue his or her former employer for wrongful termination.

Due to the increasing demand and availability of computers and the Internet in the workplace, the problems associated with abuse will continue to rise (Nie & Erbing, 2000; Young, 2010). To combat this, a new industry that focuses on spy software and the development of Internet policies in the workplace has been spawned and is flourishing. It seems as though the Internet has not only changed the landscape of sex and love addiction, it has changed and complicated the construct of workaholism as well. Workaholics, especially those who bring work home, may actually be bringing Internet-based addictive behaviors home instead of the work. Nonetheless, there still remains a discrete issue related to the traditional notions of workaholism.

ADDICTION TO WORK: WORKAHOLISM

Because the Internet provides opportunities for individuals to work more at home, it also provides opportunities for excessive work. Aziz and Tronzo (2011) maintain that today's workers put in more time than they did in 1990. Robinson (2000, p. 29) sees work as possibly being the "great unexamined therapy issue of our time." This researcher says that, for some, work is the venue in which real life takes place. It can become the secret repository where an individual's life drama and primary emotional experiences take place.

As a student, you probably have engaged in compulsive work behaviors. These behaviors will most often occur around exam time or when assignments are due. Remember the phrase "The early bird catches the worm"? Many of us have subscribed to the tenets of this phrase. However, some believe this phrase and others like "Idle hands are the devil's workshop" to be rules to follow and believe these dictums to be essential to one's very own sense of well-being or survival.

According to Oates (1971), a workaholic is

a person whose need for work has become so excessive that it creates noticeable disturbance or interference with his [*sic*] bodily health, personal happiness, and interpersonal relations, and with his [*sic*] smooth social functioning. (p. 4)

Since Oates's definition was first published, the term *workaholism* has infused itself into the mainstream U.S. cultural narrative. One would think that because of this infusion, our scientific understanding of the concept would have increased. According to McMillan, O'Driscoll, and Burke (2003) and Taris, Schaufeli, and Verhoeven (2005), the professional field is only slowly coming into its own. Although workaholics are seen as people who work excessively hard, the motivation for such hard work varies across individuals. A strong inner drive, considered by many as the root cause of this affliction (Burke, 2000; Liang & Chu, 2009), may also be mediated by other factors. These include external factors, contextual issues that impact one's finances, poor relationships, the organizational culture itself, and the pursuit of promotion.

Taris et al. (2005) reviewed the literature and organized their findings along four dimensions: workaholism and the nonwork domain, workaholism at work, workaholism and health, and workaholism as a type-A behavior and commitment. Their findings reveal that while the effects of workaholism appear to have a negative impact on the person's nonwork domain, there is no evidence that this leads to higher rates of divorce (p. 40). Early research demonstrated that workaholics spend more time on their work than others (e.g., McMillan et al., 2002). Nonetheless, Taris et al. and Liang and Chu (2009) claim that current research is rather inconclusive. Workaholics might actually work harder than their counterparts. Yet, they work harder without the concomitant rewards for their efforts. The same researchers maintain that this reflects the strong inner drive that characterizes workaholics. Health is the one dimension where research is consistent: Workaholics do report higher levels of stress and health complaints. It is interesting to note that the professional literature on the relationship between type-A behavior and workaholism shows only modest correlations. This suggests that type-A and workaholism are not that closely associated. Still, it can be hard to work with a person who is a workaholic (Liang & Chu, 2009).

Styles of Workaholism

Robinson (2000) identifies four predominant styles of workaholism. These four styles help therapists to organize their thoughts about a given client's symptoms. At the same time, the clients themselves will likely present with a combination of styles or with alternating styles.

The *bulimic workaholic style* reflects a perfectionistic orientation toward work. Individuals who use this style often cycle through procrastination, work binges, and exhaustion. It is hard for these individuals to get started. However, once a deadline approaches, they can work excessively to the point of staying up nights to finish before falling into bed from exhaustion.

A second style is the *relentless workaholic style*. This style mirrors the dictum "It has to be finished yesterday" (Robinson, 2000, p. 37). While the bulimic style reflects procrastination, the relentless style reflects just the opposite. These individuals start early. One reason for this might be the fact that the relentless style of workaholism is also characterized by taking on too much work. Saying no is as difficult as prioritizing. Moreover, these individuals can complete projects long before deadlines without much input from coworkers.

Those who invoke an *attention-deficit workaholic style* are seen as using the adrenaline of overwhelming work pressure as a focusing device (Robinson, 2000, p. 37). Living on the brink of chaos and destruction, persons use this style to get high from the rush of new ideas. Whereas projects are completed early by those using the relentless style, the attention-deficit style reflects a plethora of unfinished projects.

Finally, in the *savoring workaholic style* individuals move slowly, methodically, and in an overly scrupulous manner. Projects are savored in and of themselves. When projects are close to completion, additional work is generated because these individuals have difficulty distinguishing when a job is good enough.

If you are a student, the bulimic style probably sounds familiar. This is especially true for those times when you are watching television, playing video games, or otherwise occupied while feeling excessive guilt over not doing what should be done. Remember, this experience does not mean that you are a workaholic. Workaholism and maladaptive styles of workaholics lie on a continuum.

ASSESSMENT AND TREATMENT ISSUES

Assessment

As we stated in Chapter 6, assessment is crucial in planning for treatment. Individuals with other addictions will probably reflect problems in a variety of areas such as physical health, psychological and social functioning, reproduction and sexuality, cross-addictions, and family relationships. However these same problems may also exist in individuals whose behaviors are not addictive. For example, the client who comes in to work on grieving the intense feelings of a lost relationship may or may not be a sex and love addict. Such a determination will result from exploring thematic patterns in the client's various relationships. Clearly, questions addressing an individual's eating, gambling, sex and love issues, and work habits should be included in your routine psychosocial history. The nature and extent of information gathering in these areas will, of course, depend on the presenting problem. However, as you gather such data, facts disclosed about a client's family of origin or a client's current behavioral patterns may suggest areas for further exploration. For example, in listening to a bright, thin, college-aged woman with a family history of perfectionism and conflict, you might want to ask her about her eating patterns or about her attitudes regarding eating.

EATING DISORDERS   Cummins, Simmons, and Zane (2005) reviewed the literature in their study of eating disorders in Asians and maintain that the multitude of ways to define eating disorders raises questions about the relevancy of diagnostic criteria for all groups. These researchers maintain that assessments used to measure eating disorders must be culturally sensitive. Western-based criteria might not be germane or even relevant to Asian and other diverse populations. These same researchers emphasize the importance of studying *symptom patterns* rather than diagnostic criteria. This is because that even when differences among groups are found, researchers are left to surmise as to the actual patterns of differences in the presentation of an eating disorder.

Fairburn, Cooper, and Shafran (2003) go further and state that the classifications of Anorexia Nervosa, Bulimia Nervosa, and Eating Disorder Not Otherwise Classified share similar psychopathological mechanisms to a degree that a transdiagnostic approach to assessment and treatment is more appropriate. Even though the professional literature addressing the impact of sociocultural factors on eating disorders is cloudy, little doubt exists as to the importance of a culture-centered understanding of eating disorders for accurate assessment. The Eating Disorder Inventory (EDI-3) (Garner, 2005) is a popular 91-item standardized test that is easy to administer in order to assess and treat eating disorders in white women ages 13 to 53. The test consists of three eating disorder specific scales and nine general psychological scales that are highly relevant to eating disorders, which yield six composites. One is eating disorder specific, while the remaining five reflect ineffectiveness, interpersonal problems, affective problems, overcontrol, and general psychological maladjustment.

In general, Hill and Pomeroy (2001) believe that those with anorexia nervosa tend to minimize their symptoms and the medical complications, and primary care physicians may find it difficult to detect eating disorders in the early stages of the disorder (Sim et al. 2010). Quite often, seeking professional help comes only after the individual has experienced pressure from family members and cohorts at work or school. In Case Example 2 at the beginning of the chapter, Melanie felt the pressure to go to the doctor only after her mother had pleaded with her. Melanie had downplayed her symptoms for quite some time, and it was only after her weight had dropped so much that she listened to her mother. However, as is often the case, Melanie kept her eating disorder a secret.

Behavioral and attitude changes often accompany anorexia nervosa and bulimia nervosa and include an increased interest in cooking, nutrition, and concomitant increase in exercise. Mental health professionals will want to examine the client's family for evidence of enmeshment, overprotectiveness, rigidity, lack of conflict resolution, and the involvement of the client in unresolved marital and family conflicts. In addition, information about weight loss is critical in assessing the severity of anorexia nervosa and bulimia nervosa.

Ferguson et al. (2011), Levesque and Vichesky (2006), and others have demonstrated the impact of body image on eating disorders. Hence, clinicians need to be aware of the need to assess body image as it relates to the client's eating patterns. In doing so, clinicians need to keep in mind that ethnicity and sexual orientation play a significant part in body image. This is especially true when considering that Dounchis et al. (2001) and Lynch et al. (2007) report that body dissatisfaction is more pervasive in nonwhite females within the United States than originally thought. For instance, Allison (2002) found that binge eating, age, and black racial status are *positively correlated* with heightened scores in body mass index (BMI). For Asian subjects, racial status is *negatively correlated* with BMI. At the same time, other research suggests that binge eating may not be the significant and sole variable accounting for being overweight in the African American community (Dounchis et al., 2001). Patterson et al. (1997) point to the differences in physical maturation and sexual development as a significant factor influencing research results. In general, clinicians should contextualize treatment approaches so that they reflect the larger issues influencing diverse clients with body image disturbance and eating disorders.

ADDICTION TO SEX AND LOVE, THE INTERNET, AND WORK   We stated in Chapter 6 that a simple rule for determining whether a behavior is problematic is to ask yourself the question, "Does a normal drinker drink like this client?" For sex and love addiction, the mental health counselor can assess the normality of the client's relationship with a spouse or companion, the client's past and present extended family environment, other intimate relationships both present and past, and the client's relationships with strangers (Logan, 1992).

Clinicians will also want to examine the client's history of sexual abuse and its relationship to current acting out behaviors. Southern (2002) found that a relationship exists between chemically dependent women who have no prior memory of sexual abuse and who have a pattern of sexual acting out. Southern found that the women in his study reported their mothers as being unsafe, that tension and stress were present in the family of origin, and that clients experienced isolation. Optiz, Tsytsarev, and Froh (2009) and Valenti (2002) concur with Southern's findings and report that sexually addicted women are significantly more likely to come from families of origin where they experienced abandonment, abuse, physical punishment, crisis, chaos, and depression. These issues clearly could be significant areas for mental health clinicians to explore with clients.

Regarding Internet addiction, Hall and Parsons (2001) outline four key areas in need of assessment: Internet usage, usage content, environmental distress, and comorbidity. Regarding Internet usage, these researchers say that it is difficult to determine because of the tendency to underreport the hours spent on the Internet. It is suggested that the assessment might include other significant social contacts, such as friends and family members, in order to get a more accurate picture of usage. Individuals who are Internet dependent spend an inordinate amount of time online engaged in social activities such as participating in chat rooms, newsgroups, and various bulletin boards. Nondependent individuals spend more time on email and web browsing.

Beard (2005) presents a model to conceptualize problematic Internet use. It is based upon the biopsychosocial model of addiction that we discussed in Chapter 3. Beard's model integrates genetic, psychological, biochemical, familial, cultural, and environmental dynamics. This same researcher presents 72 questions that can be used for assessment. These questions address the following: presenting problem (21 questions), biological areas (17), psychological areas (12), social areas (16), and relapse prevention (6). Thatcher and Goolam (2005) developed the Problematic Internet Use Questionnaire (PIUQ). These researchers conducted an exploratory factor analysis study and identified three subscales: online preoccupation, adverse effects, and social interactions. The instrument should not be used for clinical screening because the predictive validity of the instrument has yet to be established. The reason we mention it is because this seems to be a promising measure for future use and because of its alignment with Young's (2004) eight criteria for Internet addiction, discussed next.

Young (2010; 2004) believes that since there is no formal disorder of Internet Addiction, clinicians and researchers should use the criteria for pathological gambling as a frame. Young cites the following criteria in the form of eight questions (p. 404):

1. Do you feel preoccupied with the Internet in terms of thinking about previous online activity or anticipating the next online session?
2. Do you feel the need to use the Internet for increasing amounts of time to achieve satisfaction?
3. Have you repeatedly made unsuccessful attempt to control, cut back, or stop Internet use?
4. Do you feel restless, moody, depressed, or irritable when attempting to cut down or stop Internet use?

5. Do you stay online longer than originally intended?
6. Have you jeopardized or risked the loss of a significant relationship, job, or educational or career opportunity because of the Internet?
7. Have you lied to family members, therapists, or others to conceal the extent of involvement with the Internet?
8. Do you use the Internet as a way of escaping from problems or relieving a dysphoric mood (e.g., feelings of helplessness, guilt, anxiety, depression)?

A few measures are used to assess workaholism. The early works of Spence and Robbins (1992) diverges from the later work of Robinson (1999). Referred to as the Workaholism Battery, Spence and Robbins postulate that a workaholic triad consists of work involvement, drive, and work enjoyment. Toward that end, they identify *true workaholics* (high on involvement and drive, low on enjoyment), *work enthusiasts* (high on enjoyment and involvement, low on drive), and *enthusiastic workaholics* (high on enjoyment, involvement, and drive). Workaholism can also be assessed using the Work-Addiction Risk Test (WART) (Robinson, 1999). It is a 25-item, self-administered test that assesses work habits. The higher the score, the more likely one is a workaholic. Flowers and Robinson (2002) conducted a discriminate analysis on the WART and found that it has five dimensions: (a) compulsive tendencies, (b) control, (c) impaired communication/self-absorption, (d) inability to delegate, and (e) self-worth.

Treatment

EATING DISORDERS In that various types of eating disorders exist, with only anorexia nervosa and bulimia nervosa appearing in the *DSM-IV-TR,* you can understand the difficulty in treating this disorder from a structural sense. Insurance companies do not readily pay for in-patient treatment of eating disorders. Perhaps, the reason for this is the lack of agreement on what constitutes recovery from an eating disorder. Noordenbos and Seubring (2006) maintain that due to the various definitions of "recovery" related to eating disorders, therapists and other mental health professionals should understand that prioritizing the criteria for recovery may vary among clients. Weight is clearly an issue. However, how much weight needs to be regained in order to be "recovered" is questionable. A pound of weight versus a half-pound of weight is significant for an eating disorder client. In any case, Noordenbos and Seubring state that weight needs to be taken into account with other factors such as age, gender, racioethnicity, height, bone structure, as well as one's physical constitution.

Nevertheless, eating disorders can be treated and a healthy weight restored. From your reading, it is clear that eating disorders require a comprehensive treatment plan that addresses medical and psychological issues. This often includes medical monitoring (including medical management), psychosocial and psychological interventions, and some nutritional counseling. With anorexia nervosa, there are three main phases of treatment: a) cessation of weight loss and the restoration of weight; b) addressing the psychological issues related to body image, depression, anxiety, and compulsive behaviors; and c) achievement of long-term remission and rehabilitation. Medications should be administered after the client has experienced some weight gain.

Vocks et al. (2010) conducted a meta-analysis of the effectiveness of treatments and found that psychotherapy and cognitive–behavioral interventions should be the first form of treatment. The primary goal is to reduce or eliminate the cycle of binging and purging (for bulimia) and the bingeing (for binge-eating disorder). While in-patient treatment is often recommended for anorexia, bulimia nervosa and binge-eating disorder can be treated through individual psychotherapy. Other treatments include using early memories that focus on the client's current issues (Strauch & Strauch, 2010), group psychotherapy that uses a cognitive-behavioral approach, and family or marital therapy. The goals include attempts to establish a pattern of regular, nonbinge meals. Therapy also aims to improve clients' attitudes about their eating disorder as well as addressing the often co-occurring mood disorder.

As we pointed out in Chapter 8, it is critically important for mental health professionals to determine the client's learning style or learning capacity before initiating psychoeducational approaches. In addition to individual, family, and group psychotherapy, twelve-step support groups, such as Overeaters Anonymous (OA), may be of some help to clients whose problems include binge eating and overeating. These support groups can be especially helpful with relapse prevention, since clients with full-blown anorexia nervosa and bulimia nervosa will probably have problems in other areas of functioning. Specifically, support groups may help with important issues related to the initiation of pathological eating behaviors. For example, clients with eating disorders may demonstrate codependent behaviors or complain of other family dysfunction, factors that trigger compulsive eating behavior. Learning how to identify these triggers concomitant with hearing about how others deal with them may help to prevent a relapse.

ADDICTION TO SEX AND LOVE   Sex addiction can be difficult to detect in the treatment of couples. Usually, there are other problems that present such as discord, communication issues, infidelity, and/or generic sexual dissatisfaction. Turner (2009) says that couples are often reluctant to talk about sex addiction because the effects of lying, secrets, and emotional distance can create so much distance as to cause suspiciousness or ambivalence about the relationship. This was illustrated in Case Example 1, where Samantha sensed something was wrong in her relationship. Yet, when it came time to discuss the issues in counseling, both were hesitant to do so.

When examined, counselors are likely to see that the sex addiction started in adolescence and reflects some intergenerational family history where children are neglected, mistreated, or exploited. Being vulnerable, these children often inadvertently find addiction as a means to cope with their wounds. Reynaud et al. (2010) and Katehakis (2009) have found that recent neuroscience can accentuate the treatment impact of traumatic early childhood attachment patterns on the affective, cognitive, and behavioral dimensions of sex addicts.

There are other issues that influence the treatment of compulsive behaviors around sex and love. For instance, imagine a lesbian woman being treated for sexual addiction, compulsivity, and codependency. While knowledge and interpersonal skills are needed to counsel lesbian women, numerous dynamics need further understanding. According to Manley and Feree (2002), these include understanding patterns of sexual addiction in lesbian relationships and basic knowledge of the issues, such as personal homophobia and feelings of oppression, experienced daily by lesbian women. In addition, awareness of the level of internalized oppression in the lesbian client is essential. From our perspective, the social discourse regarding individuals with gay and lesbian orientations presents a difficult challenge for many. It is important to have dialogue with clients about these issues in order to more fully understand their experience of the coming-out process, along with the subculture dynamics. Manley and Feree also suggest that the need for a broad understanding of the dynamics of oppression can be helpful in facilitating the client's integration (p. 191).

McCarthy (2002) sees the opportunity to include women in the disclosure, assessment, treatment, recovery, and relapse prevention process for men addicted to sex. Women are viewed as vital in rebuilding couple trust, intimacy, and sexuality. Milrad (1999) believes that couples can benefit in couples therapy for the treatment of codependence and sex addiction. She urges mental health clinicians to understand the beginning recovery stages of codependency, because the stages relate to the dynamics that couples often experience in dealing with a sex-addicted spouse. Feree (2002) believes that more and more women within Christian circles will seek treatment for sexual compulsions. Clinicians need to understand ways to help this special population.

ADDICTION TO THE INTERNET As mentioned, sex and love addiction has been greatly influenced by the Internet, and Young (2008) sees that our technologically advanced culture makes it very difficult for Internet sex addicts to go "cold turkey" (p. 33). This is because individuals use the Internet, or at least the computer, almost every day. Thus, self-control is usually not effective. As you would expect, discovering that a partner is heavily involved in Internet pornography creates conditions for substantial reappraisal of the relationship. Feelings of worthlessness, of being weak and stupid, sexually undesirable, and of living a lie are common reactions of their partners. While the nonaddicted partner's focus would likely be on changing the addictive behaviors of the partner, it is more effective if therapists help reframe the situation and provide a clearer understanding of the issue, help the partner become more objective, and help the person be less devastated about it. Young (2008) and Delmonico, Griffin, and Carnes (2002) both see that immediate "first order" interventions should be used to diminish the behavior, and concrete steps include moving the computer to a public area in the house, installing filtering software such as Cyber Patrol, Surfwatch, or Net Nanny, and disclosing the nature of the problem to at least one other individual. "Second order" or more long-term changes must also be utilized, and these suggestions are congruent with what Freeman (1992) and Hall and Parsons (2001) advocate: cognitive–behavioral interventions. Young believes that insight-oriented therapies are also important. These efforts can be supplemented with the development of a concise sexual recovery plan that acts to remind the addict of the issue and challenges. This plan has addicts assessing their current use in order to become clear about the high-risk situations, feelings, and events that trigger the behavior. The plan also identifies target behaviors that increases accountability and responsibility. The treatment of sexual addicts is seen as ". . . an ongoing self-exploration that must separate the behavior from the person, relieve shame about the behavior, correct maladaptive behavior, and promote opportunities to learn from mistakes" (p. 35). Finally, group therapy can be effective because it can help addicts manage their behavior, explore the dynamics of their addictive processes, and help develop bonds with others, thereby diminishing the sense of isolation and loneliness (Hook, Hook, & Hines, 2008).

ADDICTION TO WORK Workaholism is a major source of marital problems as well as psychological and physical health problems. At the same time, marital strife can influence a person's approach to work, thereby "creating" workaholism. Interestingly, addiction to work and its implications require that treatment include both the organization as well as the individual. This is true because workaholic behaviors are often rewarded by the organizations and because entire organizations can exhibit a workaholic environment.

Short of treating the entire organization, specific treatment approaches can be used for individuals. For example, cognitive approaches can be effective. For instance, Robinson (2000, p. 37) sees the bulimic workaholic style benefiting from the disputation of irrational beliefs about needing to be perfect. Those with a more relentless work style may benefit by focusing on impulse control, forethought, and attention to detail. Deliberately slowing down, such as slowing one's walking or driving speed, is also an effective treatment approach. Sometimes a medical evaluation might be needed for individuals who work compulsively. This is especially important if the person has trouble focusing on finishing or becomes easily bored with projects at work. It is important to remember that some workaholics make it difficult for other workers in the workplace. So, with the savoring workaholic person, helping him or her to learn the advantages of teamwork, cohesion, and trusting fellow workers will probably be important.

Counselors can also examine the marital relationship of individuals complaining of excessive work patterns. As mentioned, marital discord can pose problems in such a fashion as to help create the conditions of workaholism. Thus, counselors need to assess the extent to which these compulsive patterns are intertwined with marital problems. Obviously, the identification of which comes first is necessary. Because of this, family therapists can use the concept of "equifinality" in their treatment approach. This means that as long as counselors are aware of the possible connections between marital strife and workaholism, counselors can help couples explore their issues from a variety of perspectives and conceptualizations because all of these are connected and lead to the same treatment outcome.

MyCounselingLab™

Go to Topic 10: *Working with Selected Populations* in the MyCounselingLab™ site (www.MyCounselingLab.com) for *Substance Abuse: Information for School Counselors, Social Workers, Therapists, and Counselors,* Fifth Edition, where you can:

- Find learning outcomes for *Working with Selected Populations* along with the national standards that connect to these outcomes.
- Complete Assignments and Activities that can help you more deeply understand the chapter content.
- Apply and practice your understanding of the core skills identified in the chapter with the Building Counseling Skills unit.
- Prepare yourself for professional certification with a Practice for Certification quiz.
- Connect to videos through the Video and Resource Library.

Summary

- Pathological gambling lifetime prevalence rates are between 3% and 4% of the general population.
- Sixty-six percent of underage youth have gambled, and rates of gambling problems are two to four times greater than for adults.
- Eight percent of college students have gambling problems, and college graduates are significantly more likely than nongraduates to gamble on sports.
- Younger Americans are much more likely to gamble on sports than older Americans.
- The cost of problem gambling is approximately $6.7 billion per year.
- From 25% to 50% of pathological gamblers have abused their spouses.

- The rise of Internet use has created a new gambling industry, and Internet gamblers prefer this venue because of convenience, aversion to land-based gambling, the pace of online gambling, and the potential for higher wins.
- There is a significant increase for gambling problems among those with a co-occurring psychiatric disorder, and higher rates of suicide are reported for pathological gamblers.
- Types of gamblers include professional, antisocial, casual social, heavy social, relief-and-escape, and compulsive gamblers.
- The South Oaks Gambling Screen is the best-known assessment of pathological gambling.
- While treatment of gambling problems approximates the approaches for other addictions, most insurance does not cover gambling treatment.
- In treatment, gamblers have very high attrition rates.
- Pathological gamblers can benefit from twelve-step groups for gamblers, such as Gamblers Anonymous and Gam-Anon (similar to Al-Anon).
- "Other Addictions" include eating disorders, compulsive work, Internet abuse, and sex and love addiction, although not all professionals agree that these are addictions because the symptoms are already covered under various Axis II diagnoses in the *DSM-IV-TR.*
- Proponents of other addictions see the benefits as calling attention to a variety of problems associated with work, the Internet, and sex and love.
- Eating disorders include chronic binge eating, anorexia nervosa, bulimia nervosa, chronic overeating, and binge eating.

- Only anorexia nervosa and bulimia nervosa are formal diagnoses in the *DSM-IV-TR,* but some researchers are calling for a Binge-Eating Disorder (BED) diagnosis.
- Eating disorders are prevalent in women across their life spans, most often diagnosed in younger females; males have lower rates.
- Body Image Disturbance (BID) is strongly associated with all of the eating disorders, including chronic overeating and binge eating.
- Eating disorders are often medical emergencies, and mental health professionals need to refer clients for medical workups when they suspect these problems.
- Internet addiction creates problems at the workplace and at home.
- Cybersex and cyberaffairs are results of Internet addiction and are considered double addictions in that there can be an addiction to the Internet without addiction to cybersex or cyberaffairs.
- There are four types of workaholics: bulimic workaholic (characterized by perfectionistic and work bingeing), relentless workaholic (starting early and finishing up late), attention-deficit workaholic (living on the brink of chaos with a lot of adrenaline), and savoring workaholic (loves the work).
- Workaholics may not always be type-A personalities.
- Workaholics tend to have strong internal drives that are more related to their behaviors than to the pursuit of accomplishment and praise.
- Cognitive–behavioral treatments and the utilization of in-patient treatment facilities are effective in working with those afflicted with other addictions.

Internet Resources

Gambling addiction
ncpgambling.org
MyAddiction.com

Assessment for Internet addiction
netaddiction.com

Eating disorders
edap.org

Workaholism
workaholics-anonymous.org

Further Discussion

1. How often have you gambled? Discuss ways in which a person could become addicted to it.
2. What is your experience with disordered eating?
3. Discuss the ways in which the cultural narrative play in the initiation and maintenance of disordered eating and eating disorders.
4. Do you know anyone who leaves the table immediately after eating? If so, what do you think is going on?
5. When you are on the Internet, what are the alluring features of the interaction between you and the computer? Discuss the ways in which the Internet could become addictive.
6. Discuss the various ways that Internet use should be monitored in the workplace.
7. In what ways has cyberporn and cyberaffairs affected people or couples that you know?
8. Now that you know that type-A personalities and workaholism are not necessarily correlated, can you distinguish between the two in your own experience?

Chapter *15*

Prevention

CASE EXAMPLES

❶ Montel is a 12-year-old who has just started middle school. He is caught smoking before school with a group of other students.

❷ Sarah is a fifth-grader who is doing poorly academically. At a conference with her mother, the school counselor learns that her biological father (who is no longer involved with the family) is an active alcoholic.

❸ Manuel is in the fourth grade. He is a good student and is well-behaved in class.

If you have read this text in sequence, you can see that most of the book involves topics related to the abuse of AOD. This reflects our view regarding the need for mental health professionals to acquire this information, given the frequency of AOD abuse in our society. However, this frequency is related to the effectiveness of efforts to prevent AOD abuse. Therefore, do not conclude that because there is only a single chapter devoted to this topic, that prevention is less important than the other topics in this book. On the contrary, we believe that prevention is critically important from both policy and program standpoints. In particular, those of you who are planning to work in public schools as counselors or social workers should go beyond the information in this chapter. Also, a growing number of prevention specialists who work for public and private organizations are involved with substance abuse prevention. These professionals also need a more thorough understanding of this field than is found in this chapter. The section "Prevention Resources" is a good place to start.

WHY ARE PREVENTION EFFORTS NEEDED?

Why are prevention efforts needed? It is not a difficult question to answer. As you have read this text, you have received information on the problems caused by the abuse of AOD. So, if you take some action or actions that decrease the frequency of abuse, logically, the associated problems should also be reduced. For example, if there is a reduction in the number of people who chronically abuse alcohol, there should be a concomitant reduction in the number of people with medical problems resulting from chronic alcohol abuse. Therefore, prevention efforts designed to reduce the number of people who will end up abusing alcohol for many years are important and beneficial.

Most prevention efforts are directed toward young people. Again, this is logical because people generally make decisions about their use of tobacco, alcohol, and other drugs before they reach adulthood. As you know, it is illegal for people under 18 to use tobacco, for those under 21 to use alcohol, and for any age to use "street" drugs. Therefore, an examination of survey data on the use of tobacco, alcohol, and other drugs by young people can provide information on the need for substance abuse prevention. Although several prominent surveys are conducted annually on the use of tobacco, alcohol, and other drugs by young people, the information in Table 15.1 is from the Monitoring the Future (MTF) study (Johnston, O'Malley, Bachman, & Schulenberg, 2011). MTF is a survey conducted by the University of Michigan and is funded by the National Institute on Drug Abuse. In 2010, 46,500 8th, 10th, and 12th graders were surveyed. MTF has been conducted for the past 36 years, which makes trends easy to identify.

Although one may look at the data generated by these surveys in numerous ways, we find it helpful to compare 30-day prevalence rates, which mean that a respondent has said that the substance in question has been used in the past 30 days. The following table is a report of 30-day prevalence data on 8th, 10th, and 12th graders from 2010, as well as changes since last year and over the last 10 years.

TABLE 15.1 30-Day Prevalence and Change-Use-Patterns

	Year	8th graders	10th graders	12th graders
Cigarettes	2010	7.1	13.6	19.2
	2009–2010	0.7	0.5	−0.9
	2000–2010	−7.5	−10.3	−12.2
Alcohol	2010	13.8	28.9	41.2
	2009–2010	−1.2	−1.5	−2.3
	2000–2010	−7.7	−12.1	−8.8
Marijuana	2010	8.0	16.7	21.4
	2009–2010	1.5	0.7	0.8
	2000–2010	−1.1	−3.0	−0.2
Other illicit drugs	2010	3.5	5.8	8.6
	2009–2010	0.1	0.1	−0.1
	2000–2010	−2.1	−2.7	−1.8

The MTF survey generates much more data than are reported here. However, even this small amount contains interesting information on substance use by young people and has implications for the prevention field. Clearly, tobacco and alcohol use are far more frequent than illicit drug use. While that is not surprising, it certainly indicates that prevention efforts must involve the legal drugs in our society. The trend over 10 years has been large decreases in tobacco and alcohol use and smaller decreases in marijuana and other illicit drugs. Finally, young people frequently believe that "everybody" is using. However, most young people report that they do *not* use tobacco, alcohol, or illicit drugs.

POLICY ISSUES IN PREVENTION

Drug Free?

On a surface level, it might seem that prevention scarcely needs a policy discussion. After all, most people would agree that preventing AOD misuse, especially by young people, is positive and that that's the only policy necessary. Clearly, the issues are more complicated. For example, when federal agencies set "drug-free" goals, *drug-free* does not include tobacco or alcohol. The MTF survey identified that tobacco and alcohol are by far the most widely used drugs by young people. In addition, these legal substances (for adults) cause more harm to society than all illegal drugs combined. Unfortunately, the illogical dichotomy of legal/illegal drugs persists. So, while *drug-free* may be politically popular, this concept may divert attention and resources from efforts to prevent the use of tobacco and alcohol by young people.

An alternative conceptualization to drug-free is the harm reduction model. This model is based on the premises that drug use (including tobacco and alcohol) cannot be eliminated from our society, that the misuse or abuse of any drug can cause harm, and that strategies can be implemented to reduce the harm caused by misuse or abuse. A widely publicized example of a harm reduction strategy is needle exchange. This example reflects acknowledgment that some people are intravenous drug users who will not discontinue their use. By sharing needles with others, these hardcore drug users spread diseases such as hepatitis and HIV. The distribution of clean needles should reduce needle-sharing as a cause of infection. In fact, these programs have been successful in reducing the spread of AIDS (see literature review in Clark & Fadus, 2010). However, in spite of the evidence supporting needle exchange programs, the federal government, until recently, has fought efforts to fund these programs.

Harm reduction efforts are also directed at the legal drugs in our society. Sobriety checkpoints and designated driver publicity campaigns are intended to reduce the harm caused by alcohol-impaired drivers. Sting operations to identify and penalize retailers who sell tobacco to minors are designed to reduce the access of tobacco to young people. If a minor has trouble purchasing cigarettes, he or she will smoke less or not at all.

Some harm reduction processes involving alcohol use by minors are quite controversial. For example, some parents of teenagers may allow alcohol use at parties to discourage drinking and driving. Parents who allow this are engaging in a dangerous activity since it is a crime to contribute to the delinquency of a minor. In addition, in many cases they are enabling alcohol abuse. On prom and graduation nights, organizations such as Mothers Against Drunk Driving (MADD) may organize volunteers to drive for impaired students. This is certainly a difficult issue since no one wants a situation in which an impaired minor is involved in an accident, and responsible adults do not want minors to drink. Reconciling these issues is a dilemma for parents.

Gateway Drugs

Related to these issues is the fact that federal prevention efforts have not focused on gateway drugs as much as they should. Gateway drugs are those that precede the use of other drugs and are usually considered to be alcohol, tobacco, and marijuana[1] (Kandel, 1989). In fairness, more recent publications from the Center for Substance Abuse Prevention now refer to "alcohol, tobacco, and other drug problems," and underage drinking initiatives have been developed. But, this has not always been the case. As we will discuss, the reasons for the lack of focus on tobacco and alcohol probably are related to political pressure as opposed to best practice. It makes sense to focus on gateway drugs in prevention programs because drug users rarely begin with drugs such as cocaine or heroin (New York State Division of Alcoholism and Alcohol Abuse, 1989). A young person usually begins drug use with tobacco or alcohol, since these drugs are readily available and their use is perceived as dangerous, exciting, and adultlike. Once a young person "takes the plunge" (begins use), it is much easier to go on to the next class of drugs. Furthermore, Hawkins, Catalano, and Miller (1992) have shown that the age of first use of any drug is related to later drug abuse by adolescents. Finally, alcohol and tobacco cause more health-related problems than other drugs. For example more than 500,000 deaths annually are associated with tobacco and alcohol, as opposed to 23,500 deaths annually from all of the currently illegal drugs combined (Fisher, 2006).

For all these reasons, it makes sense to focus on preventing the initiation of use of gateway drugs. However, the alcohol and tobacco industries have powerful lobbies that present constant barriers to prevention efforts. To give you one simple example, the tobacco industry is allowed to market a product that has no medically useful purpose, is highly addicting, and kills 400,000 people a year. A product with these characteristics would never be allowed to be introduced today, and the failure to ban the promotion of tobacco is unconscionable. Since the tobacco master settlement agreement in 1998, cigarette advertisements in youth magazines increased by $54 million (Turner-Bowker & Hamilton, 2000). Obviously, alcohol is also marketed widely. In 2007, the alcohol industry spent over $1.6 billion on advertising, including nearly $900 million on television advertising. The beer industry alone spent over $700 million on television ads (Alcohol Policies Project, 2008). In comparison, the federal government's National Youth Anti-Drug Media Campaign, designed to convince young people to avoid illicit drugs, was budgeted at $45 million in fiscal year 2010 (Office of National Drug Control Policy, 2011a). That is about 3% of what the alcohol industry spent to convince young people to drink. According to the Center on Alcohol Marketing and Youth (2010) at the Johns Hopkins Bloomberg School of Public Health, exposure to alcohol advertising and alcohol marketing increases the probability that young people will start drinking and that they will drink more if they are already using alcohol. Of course, the alcohol industry claims that it does not target underage drinkers. However, youth exposure to alcohol advertising on television increased 71% between 2001 and 2009 which was more than the exposure of alcohol to adults over 21. Furthermore, most of the increase was on cable shows more likely to be watched by minors (Center on Alcohol Marketing and Youth, 2010). The alcohol industry does place "responsibility" advertising on television. However, between 2001 and 2009, the alcohol industry spent 44 times more on advertising their products than on ads regarding responsible alcohol use (Center on Alcohol Marketing and Youth, 2010). Therefore, any efforts designed to prevent young people from initiating alcohol or tobacco use

---

[1]Recent research (e.g., RAND Drug Policy Research Center, 2002) has raised questions about whether marijuana is a gateway to other illicit drug use.

are directly countered by the marketing of these products. Legislators are heavily lobbied and receive campaign contributions from the alcohol and tobacco industries and have little motivation to pass laws that restrict or prohibit advertising. The attempt by the 1998 Congress to pass a comprehensive tobacco bill is an excellent example. The tobacco companies launched a successful effort to defeat this bill. So research indicates that we need prevention efforts that focus on the gateway drugs, but federal and state government officials do not want to upset the tobacco and alcohol industries. Furthermore, prevention efforts are sabotaged by the sophisticated marketing of tobacco and alcohol. Can you see how policy affects prevention?

Supply versus Demand

The White House Office of National Drug Control Policy (ONDCP) is responsible for the development, management, and implementation of all federal programs involving illicit drugs. These programs are broadly classified as being "supply reduction," including domestic law enforcement, interdiction, and international efforts, or "demand reduction," including treatment and prevention. Our federal public policies regarding illicit drugs are demonstrated by how monetary resources are distributed between supply reduction and demand reduction. Domestic law enforcement includes agencies such as the Drug Enforcement Administration. Interdiction involves efforts by the Coast Guard and Customs and Border Protection to stop illegal drugs from entering the United States. International efforts include the initiatives in Colombia to destroy coca plants and in Afghanistan to stop the growing of poppies. Most treatment and prevention dollars are distributed to states by block grants administered by the Center for Substance Abuse Treatment and the Center for Substance Abuse Prevention, both in the Substance Abuse and Mental Health Services Administration in the U.S. Department of Health and Human Services.

In the fiscal year 2011 budget proposal, ONDCP allocated 64% of the budget to supply reduction and 36% to demand reduction (Office of National Drug Control Policy, 2011b). This proportion of allocation between supply and demand reduction has been consistent for many years.

With this large proportion of financial resources allocated to law enforcement and military initiatives, it would be expected that the supply of illicit drugs in this country would be significantly disrupted. However, that is not the case. Since 2001, the Department of Justice has issued an annual report called the "National Drug Threat Assessment" on the availability of illicit drugs in this country. According to the 2010 report, the availability of heroin, methamphetamine, and ecstasy was widespread and increasing (United States Department of Justice, 2010). Cocaine shortages have been seen since 2007 because of reduced production in Colombia, high demand outside of the United States, and increased seizures and efforts to stop smuggling in Mexico.

With all the competing interests for federal funds, reprioritizing the proportion of money allocated to supply reduction and demand reduction would certainly make sense. We now have ample evidence to conclude that the amount of money devoted to supply reduction is not justified. This money would be better spent on prevention and treatment.

Legalization

Legalization is an extremely controversial policy issue and one that generates highly emotional arguments from both sides. Proponents of legalization argue that crime, violence, and diseases would be reduced. If all drugs were legal, the argument goes, the profitability of black-market distribution would be reduced and those who inject drugs could always use clean needles. The quality of currently illegal substances could be controlled to prevent contamination. The number of people incarcerated for possession or for crimes related to the need to buy drugs would be reduced. More money would be available for prevention and treatment due to reduced prison populations and the decreased need to interrupt drug supplies.

Opponents of legalization counter by saying that the use of currently illegal drugs would increase, especially among youth. More social problems would result from drug use because of the increased access. They doubt that black-market distribution would decrease because buying drugs on the street would still be easier than buying them from the government. Therefore, violence and crime would still characterize drug distribution. Both sides use the experience of history (e.g., prohibition) and policies from European countries to support their arguments.

As with many controversial issues, legalization is not as simple as either side would have you believe. First, drugs are legal. Alcohol and nicotine are drugs. Many other drugs with addictive potential are distributed with a physician's prescription. The legalization issue usually involves marijuana, cocaine, methamphetamine, and heroin. Second, many proponents of legalization are actually supporting *decriminalization*. Decriminalization involves allowing individuals to possess small amounts of currently illegal drugs for personal consumption. Distribution would remain illegal. This would prevent the arrest, prosecution, and incarceration of individuals who use drugs but do not commit other crimes. Third, the concept of legalization can have numerous operational definitions from unlimited and uncontrolled access and distribution to highly controlled access and distribution. Clearly, the consequences of legalization would be dependent on these processes. Finally, discussing the legalization of marijuana, cocaine, methamphetamine, and heroin together makes little sense. As we discussed in Chapter 2, the acute and chronic effects of these drugs are quite diverse, and the concept of dangerousness is vastly different.

We believe that it makes more sense to advocate for a logical and comprehensive discussion of our policies regarding alcohol, tobacco, and illicit drugs than to discuss the legalization of illegal drugs in isolation from other substances. For example, if marijuana were legal and marketed and distributed as alcohol and tobacco are, we have little doubt that use would dramatically increase. We believe that the legalization issue, although fun to discuss, is a diversion from a focus on all the drugs (legal and illegal) we abuse.

PREVENTION CLASSIFICATION SYSTEMS

The Institute of Medicine Classification System

This classification system is based on the target population of prevention activities. Universal prevention strategies are directed toward the entire population of a country, state, community, school, or neighborhood. The goal is to deter the onset of substance abuse by providing all individuals in the population with the information and skills perceived as necessary to prevent substance abuse. Screening to assess the risk of substance abuse is not targeted to subsets of the population because everyone is assumed to be at risk for substance abuse and capable of benefiting from the prevention activities. For example, a national media campaign is part of the federal government's prevention efforts. The television advertisements created as a part of this campaign are directed at all people who view them. School-based prevention programs that are implemented in the classroom are considered universal prevention.

Selective prevention strategies are targeted at subsets of a population who are considered at risk for substance abuse. For example, children of alcoholics or addicts, students who are failing academically, and abused children are considered "high risk" because research has shown that these children have a higher probability of later substance abuse than other children (Hawkins et al., 1992). The risk factors may be biological, psychological, social, or environmental, and the targeted subgroups may be determined by age, gender, family history, or place of residence (e.g., high-drug-use neighborhoods). The only criterion for inclusion is membership in the selected subgroup. Therefore, some individuals may be at low personal risk for substance abuse while others may already be involved with alcohol or other drug use or abuse. A mentoring program for children from a low-income, high-drug-use neighborhood is an example of a selective prevention strategy. Another example of a selective prevention strategy would be a support group for children of alcoholics and addicts.

Indicated prevention strategies are directed toward individuals who have demonstrated the potential for substance abuse based on their behavior. For example, a minor in possession of tobacco, alcohol, or other drugs would fit this criterion. It is important to determine if the individual is a substance abuser or substance dependent because the latter would indicate the need for treatment (see Chapter 6). Other indicated behaviors include involvement with the juvenile justice system for nonalcohol or other drug-related offenses, dropping out of school or excessive truancy, and conduct disorders. Examples of indicated prevention strategies include social skills classes for juvenile offenders, drug education for minors in possession, and family counseling.

Classification by Prevention Strategy

The Center for Substance Abuse Prevention (CSAP), the federal agency that coordinates prevention efforts throughout the country, has utilized a prevention classification system based on six strategies. This system is not in conflict with the Institute of Medicine system since a strategy may be targeted to universal, selective, or indicated populations. The six strategies are as follows:

INFORMATION DISSEMINATION This involves communication of the nature, extent, and effect of substance use, abuse, and addiction on individuals, families, and communities. In addition, these strategies may involve information on prevention programs and services. One-way communication between a source and an audience, with limited or no contact between the two, characterizes information dissemination. Public service announcements, didactic instruction, audiovisual materials, displays of drugs, and publications are examples of information dissemination.

EDUCATION These activities are designed to build or change life and social skills—such as decision making, refusal skills, assertiveness, and making friends—that are usually thought to be associated with substance abuse prevention. Education is differentiated from information dissemination in that education encourages interaction between the facilitator or instructor and the participants. Education strategies also imply an expectation that participants will develop skills as a result of the education. Most school-based prevention programs are considered to be education, although they may include an information dissemination component. Programs designed to improve parenting skills are also examples of education strategies.

ALTERNATIVES These strategies involve the development of activities that are incompatible with substance use. This is based on the assumption that young people may use AOD because of boredom or lack of access to other activities. Therefore, if healthy, productive, and fun activities are available, young people will participate in these activities rather than in AOD use. In addition, this participation may expose high-risk youth to positive role models and provide an expanded view of the possibilities for the future. Midnight basketball is often used as an example of an alternative strategy. Another common alternative strategy is the development of after-school programs, designed to provide a supervised, productive program for young people at a time when much of the youth crime is committed (3 to 7 P.M.).

PROBLEM IDENTIFICATION AND REFERRAL This strategy is generally targeted to indicated populations who have been identified as using tobacco, alcohol, or other drugs or who have engaged in other inappropriate behaviors. Depending on the nature and severity of the problem, referrals may be made to educational programs, family therapy, or other forms of treatment. For young people who are caught in possession of tobacco, alcohol, or other drugs, consequences may be combined with mandatory education.

COMMUNITY-BASED PROCESSES These strategies involve the mobilization of communities to more effectively provide prevention services. Interagency collaborations, coalition building, and networking are considered community-based strategies. For example, representatives from county government, social services, juvenile justice, education, the faith community, and the business community may join together to develop seamless (i.e., no barriers to access services from different agencies) services for youth.

ENVIRONMENTAL APPROACHES Within this strategy are the written and unwritten standards, codes, laws, and attitudes that impact substance use and abuse in a community. The clearest examples are laws regarding tobacco and alcohol. States and counties have very different laws relating to the taxation and distribution of tobacco and alcohol.

A social service organization that relies on alcohol-related events (e.g., wine tasting) to raise funds is communicating a value that is counterproductive for prevention. An environmental strategy would be to lobby this organization to change its fund-raising activities. Another example would be efforts to prohibit university campus newspapers from accepting advertisements that promote excessive alcohol use.

Classification by Risk and Protective Factors

David Hawkins and his colleagues at the University of Washington have done a considerable amount of work on the identification of factors that are associated with an increased probability of AOD abuse (risk factors) or with a decreased probability of AOD abuse (protective factors) (e.g., Hawkins et al., 1992). This conceptualization has become so popular that many states build their prevention systems by assessing the extent of each risk factor in their communities and then by designing prevention strategies to reduce these risk factors (Wong, Catalano, Hawkins, & Chappell, 1996).

Risk factors have been organized by community, family, school, and individual or peer categories. Community risk factors include the availability of tobacco, alcohol, and other drugs; community laws and norms favorable toward substances; community mobility (i.e., frequent movement of people in and out of the community); low neighborhood attachment and community disorganization; and extreme economic deprivation. Family risk factors include a family history of problem behaviors, family management problems, family conflict, and parental attitudes toward and involvement with substance use. In the school area, the risk factors are early and persistent antisocial behavior, academic failure beginning in elementary school, and lack of commitment to school. Finally, individual or peer risk factors include alienation and rebelliousness, association with peers who engage in problem behaviors, favorable attitudes toward problem behaviors, early initiation of problem behaviors; and constitutional factors (i.e., genetic predisposition to addiction or sensation seeking).

In spite of being exposed to multiple risk factors, some young people do not develop problems with alcohol or other drugs. Certain protective factors seem to buffer youngsters by reducing the impact of the risk factors or by changing the way in which the individual responds to the risks. These protective factors have been categorized as individual characteristics, bonding, and healthy beliefs and clear standards. The individual characteristics include gender (females are more protected than males), a resilient temperament, a positive social orientation, and intelligence. Obviously, these individual characteristics are difficult or impossible to change. Bonding involves the attachment to positive families, friends, school, and community. The beneficial aspects of bonding cannot be overemphasized. A child who develops a bond to positive role models or healthy systems can overcome the disadvantages of exposure to risk factors. To facilitate the development of bonding, children need the opportunity to bond, the skills to take advantage of the opportunity, and recognition for making efforts to bond. For those of you who wonder if you can make a difference in a young person's life, this information on bonding should be a strong affirmation that you can have a major impact. Healthy beliefs and clear standards go hand-in-hand with bonding. The people and systems to which young people bond must communicate positive values and hold young people accountable for their behavior. Protection is enhanced when clear standards of behavior are expressed and consequences are applied for violations of these standards.

Although the risk and protective factor model is logical, a caution is necessary. Much of this research is correlational rather than causal. To illustrate, let's look at one family risk factor: family conflict. Family conflict has been identified as a risk factor because of evidence that children from families in which excessive family conflict is present have a higher probability of developing substance abuse problems (and other problems as well) than children who come from families in which minimal family conflict is present. However, this does not mean that family conflict causes substance abuse problems or that reducing family conflict will prevent a child from developing a substance abuse problem. Perhaps the family conflict is due to the substance abuse of one or more of the caretakers in the family. As a result of some type of intervention, perhaps the family learns to resolve its problems in a more reasonable manner. However, the caretaker continues to abuse substances. In this instance, family conflict is just one symptom of dysfunction in the family system as a result of substance abuse. Therefore, treating one symptom is not likely to affect the development of substance abuse (or other problems) in the children.

It should be noted that a causal relationship between risk and protective factors and substance abuse is not proposed in the model developed by Hawkins and his colleagues. However, many intervention programs designed to reduce risk factors and increase protective factors have been based on an assumption that such a causal relationship exists. In our view, these factors interact in a complex fashion. As we will discuss in the next section, the development of prevention strategies and programs should be based on research on what works.

AT A GLANCE

Institute of Medicine Classification System

- Universal (everyone regardless of risk factors)
- Selective (those with some risk factors)
- Indicated (those who have begun to demonstrate high-risk behaviors)

Prevention Strategies

- Information dissemination (no interaction)
- Education (information and skill building with interaction)
- Alternative activities (non-AOD activities for youth)
- Problem identification and referral (usually for indicated populations)
- Community-based processes (mobilization, interagency cooperation, coalition building)
- Environmental approaches (standards, codes, laws, regulations)

Risk and Protective Factors

- Community (availability of AOD, laws and norms, mobility, neighborhood attachment, economic deprivation)
- Family (history of problem behavior, management problems, conflict, involvement with AOD)
- School (antisocial behavior, academic failure, lack of commitment)
- Individual (alienation and rebelliousness, peers who use AOD, favorable attitudes toward AOD, early problem behaviors)
- Protective: Bonding and healthy beliefs and clear standards

---

WHAT WORKS IN PREVENTION

Evaluation of Prevention Programs

Several issues need to be considered in evaluating prevention programs. Clearly, local, state, and federal government entities are interested in evaluating the success of prevention programs because of the money spent on the programs. As you might imagine, the typical method for evaluating success is the implementation of a prevention program in classrooms or schools and to later see whether the individuals who were involved in the program use AOD to a lesser extent than individuals who were not involved in the program. One problem is that the initiation of use by young people depends on a complex interaction of personal, familial, cultural, and societal variables. To expect a school-based prevention program to singularly impact a behavior influenced by so many variables is unrealistic. Second, we know that attitudes and behavior can be influenced by a consistent, long-term, and comprehensive effort. For example, when many of us were young, cars did not have seat belts. Seat belts were then made optional, but we still never used them. Today, they are standard features in all cars, and many states have legislation requiring their use. So, our children don't even think about it. When they get in the car, they put on their seat belts. We do, too. However, this change in attitude and behavior in adults who grew up with seat-belt-free cars was accomplished through a long-term process involving public policy (legislation) and public awareness. Similarly, school- and community-based prevention programs should be viewed as a part of long-term, consistent, comprehensive prevention efforts and not as isolated "cures" for the problem of tobacco, alcohol, and other drug use by young people.

However, we believe that the effectiveness of prevention efforts would be enhanced if the contradictory messages were less pervasive. Marketing of tobacco and alcohol products, positive depictions of tobacco, alcohol, and drug use in the media, and modeling by adults and peers are powerful influences on young people. It is not currently possible, given financial and practical constraints, for the prevention community to counteract creative and funny beer commercials, cigarette smoking in youth-oriented movies, and mom and dad smoking a joint with their friends in the living room. Society's prevention message is not consistent or comprehensive. Finally, school-based prevention programs are often viewed in a similar manner to other programs in a school. If you want to evaluate a new reading program, you compare the reading performance of children in the new program with the performance of children in another program. However, we would argue that prevention programs are different. For example, imagine that you begin a prevention program that costs $10,000 in materials and training. In the entire school, only one student who would have become dependent on tobacco, alcohol, or other drugs is impacted and avoids use. You will have more than made up for the money invested in the program by preventing the financial and societal impact on health care, work productivity, the legal system, and family members that this person would have caused. We are not arguing that prevention programs should be purchased and implemented without careful evaluation. We are arguing that prevention programs should not be blamed for failing to solve a complex and multifaceted problem.

Because of the importance of the problem and the money spent on prevention, the federal government has become very interested in determining which prevention strategies and programs are the most effective. For example, the National Institute on Drug Abuse has a publication on principles of effective prevention (National Institute on Drug Abuse, 2003). In addition, Paglia and Room (1998) presented an excellent review of the prevention literature, and Tobler (1992) and Tobler and Stratton (1997) conducted meta-analyses of school-based prevention programs. From these sources, conclusions regarding effective (and ineffective) prevention strategies can be reached. We will present these conclusions for each of the six CSAP strategies.

INFORMATION DISSEMINATION School-based information dissemination methods have been unsuccessful in impacting tobacco, alcohol, and other drug use. As Botvin and Botvin (1992) stated,

> studies have rather consistently indicated that informational approaches do *not* reduce or prevent tobacco, alcohol, or drug use; they indicate quite clearly that increased knowledge has virtually no impact on substance use or on intentions to engage in tobacco, alcohol, or drug use in the near future. (p. 914, italics in original)

Similarly, Tobler (1992) found that prevention programs that only presented information did increase knowledge of participants but had no effect on attitudes and drug use. This is not surprising when you consider the analogy of the prevention of heart disease. Most Americans know that quitting smoking, regular aerobic exercise, eating fresh fruit and vegetables, and so forth will reduce the risk of heart disease. However, this information alone is usually insufficient to result in a significant behavior change for most people. Similarly, simply learning about the negative consequences of using tobacco, alcohol, and other drugs does not affect the reasons for use by most young people.

Although information dissemination alone is not sufficient, providing accurate information is an important component for school-based prevention programs. Paglia and Room (1998) recommend an emphasis on the short-term adverse effects of use, rather than on the long-term effects. The reasoning is that, from a developmental standpoint, short-term adverse effects have more impact on young people, particularly the effects that involve social attractiveness. Additionally, information on health risks and consequences of use should be based on research and should be delivered in a nonjudgmental manner (Bachman, Johnston, & O'Malley, 1991). Scare tactics and moral lecturing have not been shown to be effective and may actually have a detrimental effect if the information is in conflict with the personal experience of students.

As might be expected, information dissemination via the mass media should be aired at times when young people are likely to be listening or watching. The use of authority figures and exhortations has not been shown to be effective. As with school-based information dissemination, short-term risks involved in substance use should be emphasized (Brounstein, Zweig, & Gardner, 1998).

EDUCATION In contrast to previously discussed school-based prevention programs that are "information only," Tobler (1992) has categorized some school-based programs as affective. This model is based on the assumption that young people use AOD because of low self-esteem, inadequate social skills, and ambiguous values. Through discussion and activities involving feelings, values, and self-awareness, an attempt is made to improve self-concept and social skills and to clarify the students' values.

The results from Tobler's (1992) meta-analysis show that prevention programs that used only affective education were ineffective in impacting knowledge, attitudes and values, self-reported drug use, or decision-making, assertive, and refusal skills. Furthermore, drug incident reports, school grades and attendance, and achievement test scores also were unaffected. Approaches that combine cognitive (information dissemination) and affective approaches did have a positive effect on knowledge of participants but a negligible effect on the other outcomes. Part of the problem with this approach to prevention may be the consistent finding that very little relationship has been established between self-esteem and drug use (Clayton, Leukefeld, Grant-Harrington, & Cattarello, 1996; Coggans & McKellar, 1994; Schroeder, Laflin, & Weis, 1993).

Another educational approach to prevention is based on the influences on young people that result in the initiation of tobacco, alcohol, and other drug use. Family use patterns (including parents and siblings), peer pressure, and media all may influence young people to use (or not to use). Social resistance skills approaches (also called *social influence* or *refusal skills* approaches) have been developed to counteract environmental influences. According to Botvin and Botvin (1992),

> these interventions were designed to increase students' awareness of the various social influences to engage in substance use. A distinctive feature of these prevention models is that they place more emphasis on teaching students specific skills for effectively resisting both peer and media pressures to smoke, drink, or use drugs. (p. 916)

According to Botvin and Botvin (1992), social resistance skills approaches generally contain the following components: recognizing situations in which a high probability exists that a young person will experience peer pressure to use, formulating strategies to avoid these high-risk situations, teaching students what to say and how to say it when confronted with peer pressure, and developing awareness of techniques used by the media to encourage use by young people.

Peers are frequently used in implementing these programs, since peers, particularly older adolescents with perceived status, may be more influential than teachers or other adults. Information dissemination, with a focus on prevalence of use by young people, is used to counter the argument that "everyone is doing it."

In evaluating social resistance skills approaches, Botvin and Botvin (1992) report that these programs have been associated with reductions in tobacco, alcohol, and marijuana use for up to three years. However, long-term follow-up studies have shown that these reductions are not maintained over time. Tobler (1992) found that programs using peers as implementors had a positive impact on knowledge, attitudes, self-reported drug use, and skills. However, no beneficial effect was noted on drug incident reports or on indirect measures of use such as school grades and attendance. The age group of the students, number of training sessions, use of booster sessions, instructional materials, and characteristics of the students may all impact evaluation of these programs, and Botvin and Botvin suggest that additional research is necessary to clarify the variables that are important for success.

Competency enhancement approaches are more comprehensive than the other approaches, and focus on the interaction between the individual and environment in the prevention of substance use by young people. Competency enhancement approaches emphasize the development and use of personal and social skills that are directly related to substance use but that are also applicable to many other adolescent problems. According to Botvin and Botvin (1992), competency enhancement approaches typically teach two or more of the following:

1. General problem-solving and decision-making skills
2. General cognitive skills for resisting interpersonal or media influences
3. Skills for increasing self-control and self-esteem
4. Adaptive coping strategies for relieving stress and anxiety through the use of cognitive coping skills or behavioral relaxation techniques
5. General social skills
6. General assertive skills

These skills are taught using a combination of instruction, demonstration, feedback, reinforcement, behavioral rehearsal (practice during class), and extended practice through behavioral homework assignments. (p. 320)

Evaluation studies of competency enhancement approaches seem generally positive. In a summary of these studies, Botvin and Botvin (1992) report reductions in initiating use of tobacco, alcohol, and marijuana. Effectiveness has been demonstrated using many types of trainers (e.g., peers, teachers, project staff) as well as with ethnically diverse groups. With booster sessions, the effects have been maintained for up to six years (Botvin, Baker, Dusenbury, Botvin, & Diaz, 1995). However, this long-term follow-up study has been criticized for failing to report negative results and for issues regarding sample selection (Brown & Kreft, 1998; Gorman, 1998).

In reviewing the literature on school-based prevention, Paglia and Room (1998) and Brounstein et al. (1998) have presented some general guidelines in the structure, content, and delivery of prevention education. The recommendations include prevention programming throughout the grades, with the greatest emphasis on the median ages of first use (late elementary school and middle school). While long-term programs are superior to short-term programs, periodic booster sessions following the completion of programs are necessary to maintain benefits. Information presented should be factual. If the instructor does not know an answer, this should be admitted to students. Students should have the opportunity to discuss the reasons why people use AOD, alternatives to meeting these needs, and the dangers and benefits to using and not using. While both short-term and long-term effects should be presented, the short-term effects should be emphasized. Perceptions regarding "everybody does it" should be challenged with data. An interactive style of presentation is most beneficial, including cooperative learning, role-plays, and group exercises. Peer facilitators can be effective if they are trained and are perceived as credible. The instructional atmosphere should be tolerant and free from moralizing and scare tactics. Finally, as Paglia and Room (1998) state, "*most importantly, anything taught in the school must be reinforced in the community by parents, media, and health policies*" (p. 16, italics in original).

While many commercially prepared school-based prevention programs are available, the Drug Abuse Resistance Education (DARE) program should be specifically mentioned. The DARE program is unique among school-based prevention programs with its use of police officers as instructors. The program was developed by Daryl Gates, former Los Angeles chief of police. DARE officers are trained in child development, classroom management, teaching techniques, and communication skills prior to classroom instruction. Due to the fact that evaluation studies showed that DARE did not produce the desired outcomes (e.g., Ennett, Tobler, Ringwalt, & Flewelling, 1994), the elementary curriculum is being revised and expected to be implemented in 2011. A middle school curriculum, Keepin' It Real, has been included in the National Registry of Evidence-Based Programs and Practices (see Chapter 8) but that curriculum is taught by teachers rather than by police officers.

A variety of education programs focused on the family have also been hypothesized to prevent substance use among youth. These programs can involve parent education, parenting skills training, parent support groups, and family therapy. It is particularly useful to combine school-based prevention programs with family-based programs. Most studies of family-based prevention have focused on "high-risk" families. An example of such a program is the Strengthening Families program (Kumpfer, Williams, & Baxley, 1997). Parent, child, and family skills training was targeted to substance abusing families with children in the 6- to 10-year range. Improvements were found in the problem behaviors of the children, in intentions to use AOD, in parenting skills, in family communication, and in family conflict.

A major research problem with high-risk family-focused programs is the recruitment and retention of families. In spite of this problem, programs "that include parenting skills and children's skills training and structured family sessions, may be effective in reducing risk factors and strengthening protective factors which etiological models link to drug use. However, whether these types of effects actually become translated into the prevention of substance use or abuse among youth has yet to be confirmed by long-term empirical evaluations" (Paglia and Room, 1998, p. 22).

ALTERNATIVES The research evidence regarding the effectiveness of alternative activities is mixed.

Botvin and Botvin (1992) indicate that entertainment, vocational, and social alternatives programs have been associated with more rather than less substance use, although academic, religious, and sports activities are associated with less use. They report that evaluations of alternatives programs have failed to demonstrate an impact on adolescent use. In contrast, Tobler's (1992) meta-analysis of alternatives programs for high-risk youth showed positive effects on skills and behavior, including school grades, school attendance, and independent reports of observed drug use.

According to the review of literature conducted by Brounstein et al. (1998), alternatives should be part of a comprehensive prevention plan that includes other activities with proven effectiveness. However, when alternative activities are being developed, they must be attractive to the target group or participation will not occur. Therefore, young people must be involved in the planning process. Not surprisingly, the more intensive the activity (in terms of both hours required and length), the more effective it is.

Carmona and Stewart (1996) and Tobler (1986) point out that alternative activities serve a more general purpose than just providing something else to do besides using substances. For some high-risk youth, alternative activities are an opportunity for personal development and positive bonding to adults and the community. The development of these protective factors may be beneficial in a variety of ways. One type of alternative activity that is popular is mentoring. Mentoring programs provide young people, particularly high-risk youth, with structured time with positive adult role models. Mentoring programs have been associated with reductions in substance use; increases in positive attitudes toward others, the future, and school; and increased school attendance. As would be expected, the more highly involved the mentor, the greater the impact. It is particularly important to screen and train potential mentors. Clearly, mentors must be positive role models and must complete their commitment to the young people in the program. Many of the high-risk youth in these programs have been disappointed by adults in the past and should be protected from having similar experiences with mentors.

PROBLEM IDENTIFICATION AND REFERRAL   Certain factors are important to consider in the development of any problem identification and referral system. First, experimental users should be differentiated from problematic users. Although any use of tobacco, alcohol, or other drugs by a minor is a problem, experimentation is not uncommon and does not require intensive intervention. A significant consequence combined with education is usually the appropriate level of intervention for experimental use. In addition, if experimental users are placed in more intensive programs, they will be grouped with problematic users. This could have the unintended consequence of enabling further use. Because of these issues, problem identification and referral programs must have valid procedures and trained personnel to determine where the individual is on the use continuum (see Chapter 6).

Substance use among young people is often associated with other problems, including family dysfunction, school failure, sexual activity, and violence. Therefore, a problem identification and referral program must be prepared to screen for other problems in addition to substance use and must have adequate referral resources to assist the targeted individuals. This may include very concrete issues such as transportation. For example, a 15-year-old female was referred to a guidance team at her high school after she was found in possession of marijuana. She admitted to frequent, unprotected sex with a variety of partners. The young woman was receptive to a referral to the local health department for contraception and testing for sexually transmitted diseases, but she had no way to get there. Fortunately, school personnel were able to arrange public transportation.

COMMUNITY-BASED PROCESSES   Community-based coalitions are formed to improve the nature and delivery of services to the community (comprehensive service coordination), generate community activism to address substance-related problems (community mobilization), or to perform both functions (community linkage). Comprehensive service coordination requires the involvement of the leaders of the organizations in the coalition, whereas community mobilization is dependent on grassroots activists and community citizens. In order to elicit change at a systems or individual-behavior level, community partnerships must have a clear and shared vision of their objectives, commitments to participate from all partnership members, participation from diverse community groups, and comprehensive prevention activities directed at a large number of individuals.

Appropriate organization, leadership, and evaluation have been shown to be important components in successful community partnerships. While committees are usually necessary, those with specific purposes sustain higher levels of involvement than those with elaborate structures. A dynamic leader may be effective but this type of individual cannot normally be replaced. Therefore, opportunities for leadership roles from a variety of participants are helpful. Community coalitions are also advised to implement evidenced-based prevention strategies and to incorporate procedures for measuring the effectiveness of their strategies.

ENVIRONMENTAL APPROACHES   The approaches in this category generate a great deal of discussion in the prevention community and in state and federal governments. Environmental approaches have demonstrated a direct impact on the use of tobacco and alcohol and on the problems associated with the use of these substances. However, environmental strategies have not been as effective with regard to illicit drugs, as we saw in the earlier discussion in this chapter on supply reduction efforts.

Increasing the taxes on tobacco and alcohol is one type of environmental strategy. Tax increases have resulted in reductions in the use of both tobacco and alcohol as well as reductions in associated problems, such as alcohol-related traffic accidents. The tobacco legislation considered by the 1998 Congress included a significant tax increase on tobacco and was bitterly fought (and defeated) by the tobacco industry. Moreover, efforts to increase the price of illicit drugs through law enforcement efforts generally have not been successful.

Laws regarding the purchase of tobacco and alcohol by minors have also been effective. When the minimum purchase age for alcohol was raised to 21 in all states, alcohol consumption among minors decreased, as did alcohol-related problems. Sting operations, using underage individuals who attempt to purchase tobacco or alcohol, are effective in increasing retailer compliance with restricting sales to minors. In addition, "use and lose" laws that result in driver's license suspension for minors convicted of an alcohol or drug violation have also been shown to increase compliance with minimum-purchase-age laws.

Deterrence laws and policies have also been shown to be effective in reducing alcohol-related accidents and underage drinking and driving. These include lowering the blood-alcohol level from 0.10 to 0.08 or lower, enforcement of drinking and driving laws, sobriety checkpoints, and zero tolerance for alcohol use by underage drivers. While sobriety checkpoints do not result in high levels of detection, publicizing that they will occur seems to have a deterrent effect.

Local communities can also implement proven environmental strategies by placing restrictions on the location and number of retail outlets authorized to sell tobacco and/or alcohol. Neighborhoods have been able to disrupt illicit drug sales through citizen surveillance and through pressure on landlords who own property where drug sales occur.

Training for individuals who serve alcohol (i.e., bartenders) and clerks who sell tobacco and alcohol is an effective strategy when it is combined with law enforcement efforts. Training is intended to educate servers and clerks about the laws, as well as teach them to identify intoxication and false identification and to provide skills in refusing to serve or sell.

Although environmental strategies are clearly effective in reducing the use of tobacco and alcohol, the involvement of community coalitions is usually essential to implement these strategies. Since many require action by policy makers and since many policy makers receive campaign contributions from the tobacco and alcohol industries, pressure from community groups is often necessary.

CASE EXAMPLE APPLICATIONS

Our three cases at the beginning of the chapter illustrate the three possibilities in the Institute of Medicine classification system. Montel would be included in an indicated population. He has already begun to demonstrate the problem behavior by smoking cigarettes at a very young age. It would be important to assess how frequently Montel smokes and whether he has begun to experiment with AOD. This assessment would determine what type of intervention would be the most appropriate. In this case, Montel was not smoking regularly and had not really begun to use AOD. It was determined that he was smoking to "fit in" with a peer group in middle school. Therefore, for breaking a school rule, Montel did receive a consequence that included staying after school for an educational group on AOD (including tobacco) and cleaning up the school grounds. In addition, he was provided a peer mentor (a ninth grader) and had some visits with the school counselor.

Sarah would be part of a selective population because she has risk factors for substance abuse. Her poor academic performance and family history of alcoholism are both risk factors. Sarah was placed in a tutoring program to improve her academic skills and a support group at the school for children from substance abusing homes.

Manuel is in the universal population. No risk factors are present and he has not engaged in any high-risk behaviors. Manuel participates in an evidence-based school prevention program for his grade level.

EVIDENCE-BASED PREVENTION

In Chapter 8, we discussed evidence-based treatment and the National Registry of Evidence-Based Programs and Practices (NREPP). While this registry currently contains prevention, intervention, and treatment programs, it was initially started as a process to determine which prevention programs could be called "model programs" and, as of 2011, contains 77 programs in substance abuse prevention. Because so many evidence-based programs are available, states can ensure that the prevention programs they fund have evidence to support their effectiveness. In Chapter 8, we reviewed the process that NREPP follows to determine if a program should be included as evidence-based.

So you can get a sense of the variety of prevention programs on NREPP, the following are some of the programs and a brief description: (1) Across Ages, a school- and community-based substance abuse prevention program for youth ages 9 to 13. The unique feature of Across Ages is the pairing of older adult mentors (55 years and older) with young adolescents, specifically those making the transition to middle school. (2) The Border Binge-Drinking Reduction Program provides a process for changing the social and community norms associated with underage and binge drinking that has proven effective at reducing alcohol-related trauma caused by young American's binge drinking across the U.S.–Mexican border. (3) Building Assets—Reducing Risks (BARR) is a multifaceted school-based prevention program designed to decrease the incidence of substance abuse (tobacco, alcohol, and other drugs), academic failure, truancy, and disciplinary incidents among ninth-grade youth. (4) Celebrating Families! is a parenting skills training program designed for families in which one or both parents are in early stages of recovery from substance addiction and in which a high risk for domestic violence and/or child abuse exists. (5) Familias Unidas is a family-based intervention for Hispanic families with children ages 12–17. The program is designed to prevent conduct disorders; use of illicit drugs, alcohol, and cigarettes; and risky sexual behaviors by improving family functioning. (6) LifeSkills Training (LST) is a school-based program that aims to prevent alcohol, tobacco, and marijuana use and violence by targeting the major social and psychological factors that promote the initiation of substance use and other risky behaviors. (7) Start Taking Alcohol Risks Seriously (STARS) for Families is a health promotion program that aims to prevent or reduce alcohol use among middle school youth ages 11–14. The program is founded on the Multi-Component Motivational Stages prevention model, which is based on the stages of behavioral change found within the Transtheoretical Model of Change (Substance Abuse and Mental Health Services Administration, 2011).

PREVENTION RESOURCES

The federal Substance Abuse and Mental Health Services Administration (SAMHSA) includes the National Clearinghouse for Alcohol and Drug Information (NCADI). NCADI has federal prevention (and treatment) publications available, generally at no cost. The website is included in "Internet Resources."

In addition, the federal Center for Substance Abuse Prevention (in SAMHSA) has a program called the Center for the Application of Prevention Technologies (CAPT). The purpose of the CAPT is to help states and community-based organizations apply evidence-based prevention strategies. The CAPT includes regionally-based staff members and consultants to cover different areas of the country. The website is included in Internet Resources. In addition, each state has a single state agency for treatment and prevention coordination. Some staff in this agency will be involved with prevention efforts.

Finally, for those of you who are interested in exploring the prevention field in more depth, we recommend a textbook by Hogan, Reed-Gabrielsen, Luna, and Grothaus (2003), *Substance Abuse Prevention: The Intersection of Science and Practice.*

PREVENTION SPECIALISTS

Many institutions of higher education, community-based organizations, and school districts hire professional staff members to coordinate prevention programs. In many cases, the prevention specialist has responsibility for the prevention of suicide, violence, teen pregnancy, and other public health issues in addition to substance abuse. Prevention specialists are involved in developing and implementing programs, providing training and technical assistance, writing grants, evaluating programs, and preparing policies and procedures.

Because of an increase in the number of prevention specialists, many states have adopted certification standards and have recognized prevention specialists as a distinct professional group. While you must consult your particular state for requirements, many states have adopted the certification standards and examination process developed by the International Certification and Reciprocity Consortium (IC&RC). We have included the certification standards for the IC&RC prevention specialist in Internet Resources.

MyCounselingLab™

Go to Topic 12: *Prevention* in the MyCounselingLab™ site (MyCounselingLab .com) for *Substance Abuse: Information for School Counselors, Social Workers, Therapists, and Counselors,* Fifth Edition, where you can:

- Find learning outcomes for *Prevention* along with the national standards that connect to these outcomes.
- Complete Assignments and Activities that can help you more deeply understand the chapter content.
- Apply and practice your understanding of the core skills identified in the chapter with the Building Counseling Skills unit.
- Prepare yourself for professional certification with a Practice for Certification quiz.
- Connect to videos through the Video and Resource Library.

Summary

- Public policies regarding tobacco, alcohol, and other drugs have an impact on prevention efforts.
- Prevention activities are classified by the target audience (universal, selective, indicated) or the type of prevention strategy (information dissemination, education, alternative activities, problem identification and referral, community-based processes, environmental).
- The Risk and Protective Factor theory is widely used to identify variables associated with the increased or decreased probability of AOD abuse.
- Evidence-based prevention programs have been identified through a federal review process.

Internet Resources

National Registry of Evidence-Based Programs and Practices
nrepp.samhsa.gov

Center for the Application of Prevention Technologies
captus.samhsa.gov

Prevention principles
drugabuse.gov/pdf/prevention/RedBook.pdf

National Clearinghouse for Alcohol and Drug Information (NCADI)
store.samhsa.gov/home

Prevention specialist certification
internationalcredentialing.org/PSStandards.asp

Further Discussion

1. What would be the advantages and disadvantages of parents teaching their children to drink responsibly?
2. After reading the risk factors for adolescent substance abuse, do you think it is possible to significantly reduce these risk factors? How would you design a prevention program to accomplish this?
3. Is the goal of "drug-free" schools realistic? If so, how would you go about accomplishing this? If not, how would you minimize the harm from adolescent drug use? Do you include tobacco and alcohol in your definition of "drug-free"? Why or why not?

REFERENCES

AA Grapevine. (1985). New York: Alcoholics Anonymous Grapevine.

Abadinsky, H. (2007). *Drug abuse: An introduction* (6th ed.). Chicago: Nelson-Hall.

Abney, P. C., & Harrison, T. C. (June 19, 2003). *RESOURCERY counseling: A model for the 21st century.* Paper presented at the annual convention of the International Association of Phenomenology, Constructivism, and Psychotherapy. Bari, Italy.

Ackerman, R. J. (1983). *Children of alcoholics. A guidebook for educators, therapists, and parents.* New York: Simon & Schuster.

Ackerman, R. J. (1987). *Same house, different homes: Why adult children of alcoholics are not all the same.* Deerfield Beach, FL: Health Communications.

Al-Anon Family Group. (1973). *Alateen: Hope for children of alcoholics.* New York: Al-Anon Family Group Headquarters.

Alcohol (in Korean). *Fifty-nine authors, fifty-nine essays.* (1978). Gi So Rhim Publishing.

Alcohol Policies Project, Center for Science in the Public Interest. (2008). *Alcoholic-beverage advertising expenditures. Fact sheet.* Retrieved May 23, 2011, from http://www.cspinet.org/booze/FactSheets/AlcAdExp.pdf

Alcoholics Anonymous General Services Office. (2010). Estimates of A.A. groups and members as of January 1, 2010. Retrieved May 20, 2011, from http://www.aa.org/en_pdfs/smf-53_en.pdf

Alcoholics Anonymous World Services. (2001). *Alcoholics Anonymous* (4th ed.). New York: Alcoholics Anonymous World Services.

Alcoholics Anonymous World Services. (2008). Alcoholics Anonymous 2007 membership survey. Retrieved May 20, 2011, from http://www.aa.org/pdf/products/p-48_07survey.pdf

Alcoholics Anonymous World Services. (2009). *Alcoholics Anonymous: Twelve steps and twelve traditions.* New York: Alcoholics Anonymous World Services.

Alegria, M., Carson, N. J., Goncalves, M., & Keefe, K. (2011). Disparities in treatment of substance use disorders and co-occurring disorders for ethnic/racial minority youth. *Journal of the American Academy of Child and Adolescent Psychiatry, 50*(1), 22–31.

Allison, S. K. (2002). A path model using codependency and binge eating as mediating variables with selected biographic correlates to explain body mass index in a nursing sample. *Dissertation Abstracts International, 63*(2-B), Section B, 757. (Order Number AAI3042860).

Ambrogne, J. A. (2007). Managing depressive symptoms in the context of abstinence: Findings from a qualitative study of women. *Perspectives in Psychiatric Care, 43*(2), 84–92.

American Heart Association. (1999). *Cigarette and tobacco smoke: Biostatistical fact sheets* [Online]. Retrieved October 11, 2007, from www.amhrt.org/statistics.

American Psychiatric Association. (2000). *Diagnostic and statistical manual of mental disorders- IV-Text Revised.* Washington, DC: American Psychiatric Association.

American Temperance Union. (n.d.). *Temperance tract for the freedman.* New York: Author.

Andersen, A. E., & Michalide, A. D. (1983). Anorexia nervosa in the male: An underdiagnosed disorder. *Psychosomatics, 24,* 1066–1069, 1072–1075.

Anderson, G. L. (1987). *When chemicals come to school.* Greenfield, WI: Community Recovery Press.

Anderson, J. Z. (1992). Stepfamilies and substance abuse: Unique treatment considerations. In E. Kaufman & P. Kaufman (Eds.), *Family therapy of drug and alcohol abuse* (2nd ed., pp. 172–189). Boston: Allyn & Bacon.

Andre, J. M. (1979). *The epidemiology of alcoholism among American Indians and Alaska Natives.* Albuquerque, NM: U.S. Indian Health Services.

Andrews, C. (2008). An exploratory study of substance abuse among Latino older adults. *Journal of Gerontological Social Work, 51*(1), 87–108.

Annis, H. M. (1982). *Inventory of drinking situations.* Toronto: Addiction Research Foundation of Ontario.

Annis, H. M. (1986). A relapse prevention model for treatment of alcoholics. In W. R. Miller & W. Heather (Eds.), *Treating addictive behaviors: Process of change* (pp. 407–433). New York: Plenum.

Annis, H. M. (1990). Relapse to substance abuse: Empirical findings within a cognitive-social learning approach. *Journal of Psychoactive Drugs, 22,* 117–124.

Annis, H. M., & Davis, C. S. (1989). Relapse prevention. In R. K. Hester & W. R. Miller (Eds.), *Handbook of alcoholism treatment approaches: Effective alternatives* (pp. 171–182). New York: Pergamon.

Archambault, D. L. (1992). Adolescence: A physiological, cultural, and psychological no man's land. In G. W. Lawson & A. W. Lawson (Eds.). *Adolescent substance abuse: Etiology, treatment, and prevention* (pp. 11–28). Gaithersburg, MD: Aspen Publications.

Arcidiancono, C., Velleman, R., Procentese, F., Berti, P., Albanesi, C., Sommantico, M., & Copello, A. (2010). Italian families living with relatives with alcohol or drug problems. *Drugs: Education, Prevention, and Policy, 17*(6), 659–680.

Armor, D. J., Polich, J. M., & Stambul, H. B. (1978). *Alcoholism and treatment.* New York: Wiley.

Aronson, K. (2003). Alcohol: A recently identified risk factor for breast cancer. *Canadian Medical Association Journal, 168,* 1147–1148.

Asher, R. (1992). *Women with alcoholic husbands: Ambivalence and the trap of codependency.* Chapel Hill, NC: University of North Carolina Press.

Attneave, C. (1982). American Indians and Alaska Natives families: Emigrants in their own homeland. In M. McGoldrick, J. K. Pierce, & J. Giordano (Eds.), *Ethnicity and family therapy* (pp. 55–83). New York: Guilford Press.

Austin, A., Hospital, M., Wagner, E. F., & Morris, S. L. (2010). Motivation for reducing substance use among minority adolescents: Targets for intervention. *Journal of Substance Abuse Treatment, 39*(4), 399–407.

Austin, A., & Wagner, E. F. (2010). Treatment attrition among racial and ethnic minority youth. *Journal of Social Work Practice in the Addictions, 10*(1), 63–80.

Austin, A. A. (2004). Alcohol, tobacco, other drug use, and violent behavior among Native Hawaiians: Ethnic pride and resilience. *Substance Use and Misuse, 39*(5), 721–746.

Aziz, S., & Tronzo, C. L. (2011). Exploring the relationship between workaholism facets and personality traits: A replication in American workers. *Psychological Record, 61*(2), 269–285.

Babcock, M. (1995). Critiques of codependency: History and background issues. In M. Babcock & C. McKay (Eds.), *Challenging codependency: Feminist critiques* (pp. 3–27). Toronto: University of Toronto Press.

Babcock, M., & McKay, C. (1995). *Challenging codependency: Feminist critiques.* Toronto: University of Toronto Press.

Babor, T. F., de la Fuente, J. R., Saunders, J., & Grant, M. (1992). *AUDIT: The alcohol use disorders identification test: Guidelines for use in primary health care.* Geneva, Switzerland: World Health Organization.

Babor, T. F., Higgins-Briddle, J. C., Saunders, J. B., & Monterio, M. G. (2001). *The alcohol use disorders identification test: Guidelines for use in primary care* (2nd ed.). New York: World Health Organization.

Bachman, J. G., Johnston, L. D., & O'Malley, P. O. (1991). How changes in drug use are linked to perceived risks and disapproval: Evidence from national studies that youth and young adults respond to information about the consequences of drug use. In L. Donohew, H. E. Sypher, & W. J. Bukoski (Eds), *Persuasive communication and drug abuse prevention* (pp. 133–155). Hillsdale, NJ: Erlbaum.

Back, S. E., Contini, R., & Brady, K. T. (2007). Substance abuse in women: Does gender matter? *Psychiatric Times, 24*(1), 48–58.

Ball, J. C., Corty, E., Petroski, S. P., & Bond, H. (1987). Treatment effectiveness: Medical staff and services provided to 2,394 patients at methadone programs in three states. *National Institute on Drug Abuse: Research Monograph Series #76,* 175–181.

Ball, J. C., & Ross, A. R. (1991). The effectiveness of methadone maintenance treatment: Patients, programs, services and outcomes. New York: Springer-Verlag.

Bamatter, W., Carroll, K. M., Añez, M. P., Ball, S. A., Charla, N., Franforter, T. L., . . . Martino, S. (2010). Informal discussions in substance abuse treatment sessions with Spanish-speaking clients. *Journal of Substance Abuse Treatment, 39*(4), 353–363.

Barón, M. (2000). Addiction treatment for Mexican-American families. In J. Krestan (Ed.), *Bridges to recovery. Addiction, family therapy, and multicultural treatment* (pp. 219–252). New York: Free Press.

Barrett, A. E., & Turner, R. J. (2006). Family structure and substance use problems in adolescence and early adulthood: Examining explanations for the relationship. *Addiction, 101,* 109–120.

Bartholomew, N. G., Courtney, K., Rowan-Szal, G. A., & Simpson, D. D. (2005). Sexual abuse history and treatment outcomes among women undergoing methadone treatment. *Journal of Substance Abuse Treatment, 29,* 231–235.

Barthwell, A. G., & Gilbert, C. L. (1993). Screening for infectious diseases among substance abusers. Treatment improvement protocol (TIP) series, No. 6. Rockville, MD: U.S. Department of Health and Human Services.

Batki, S. L., Sorensen, J. L., Faltz, B., & Madover, S. (1988). Psychiatric aspects of treatment of intravenous drug abusers with AIDS. *Hospital and Community Psychiatry, 39,* 439–441.

Beard, K. W. (2005). Internet addiction: A review of current assessment techniques and potential assessment questions. *CyberPsychology & Behavior, 8*(1), 7–14.

Beattie, M. (1987). Codependent no more: How to stop controlling others and start caring for yourself. Center City, MN: Hazelden.

Beck, W. H. (1991). *Codependence assessment manual.* Chicago: Administrative Services.

Becker, A. E. (2007). Culture and eating disorders classification. *International Journal of Eating Disorders.* Retrieved July 24, 2007, from http://0-www3 .interscience.wiley.com.innopac.library.unr.edu/cgi-bin/ fulltext/114295153/PDFSTART

Beckman, L. J. (1994). Treatment needs of women with alcohol problems. *Alcohol Health & Research World, 18,* 206–211.

Bell, T. L. (1990). Preventing adolescent relapse: A guide for parents, teachers, and counselors. Independence, MO: Independence Press.

Bennett, L. A., Wolin, S. J., & Reiss, D. (1988a). Deliberate family process: A strategy for protecting children of alcoholics. *British Journal of Addiction, 83,* 821–829.

Bennett, L. A., Wolin, S. J., & Reiss, D. (1988b). Cognitive, behavioral, and emotional problems among school-age children of alcoholic parents. *American Journal of Psychiatry, 145,* 185–190.

Bennett, S., & Dodge, T. (2007). Ethnic-racial in feelings of embarrassment associated with binge eating and fear of losing control. *International Journal of Eating Disorders, 40*(1), 454–459.

Berkowitz, A., & Perkins, H. W. (1988). Personality characteristics of children of alcoholics. *Journal of Consulting and Clinical Psychology, 56,* 206–209.

Biek, J. D. (1981). Screening test for identifying adolescents adversely affected by a parental drinking problem. *Journal of Adolescent Health Care, 2,* 107–113.

Black, C. (1981). *It will never happen to me.* Denver: MAC.

Black, L., & Jackson, V. (2005). Families of African origin: An overview. In M. McGoldrick, J. Giordano, & N. Garcie-Preto (Eds.), *Ethnicity and family therapy* (3rd ed., pp. 77–86). New York: Guilford Press.

Blau, M. (1990). Adult children: Tied to the past. *American Health, 9,* 56–65.

Block, J. J. (2008). Issues for DSM-V: Internet addiction. *American Journal of Psychiatry, 165,* 360–370.

Blume, S. A. (1997). Women and alcohol: Issues in social policy. In S. Wilsnack & R. Wilsnack (Eds.), *Gender and alcohol* (pp. 462–477). New Brunswick, NJ: Rutgers Center for Alcohol Studies.

Borovoy, A. (2000). Recovering from codependence in Japan. *American Ethnologist, 28*(1), 94–118.

Borovoy, A. (2005). *"The too-good wife": Alcohol, codependency, and the politics of nurturance in postwar Japan.* Berkeley: University of California Press.

Borovoy, A. B. (2009). "The too-good wife": Alcohol, codependency, and the politics of nurturance in postwar Japan. *The Journal of Japanese Studies, 35*(2), 460–464.

Botvin, G. J., Baker, E., Dusenbury, L., Botvin, E. M., & Diaz, T. (1995). Long-term follow-up results of a randomized drug abuse prevention trial in a White middle-class population. *Journal of the American Medical Association, 273,* 1106–1112.

Botvin, G. J., & Botvin, E. M. (1992). School-based and community-based prevention approaches. In J. H Lowinson, P. Ruiz, R. B. Millman, & J. G. Langrod (Eds.), *Substance abuse: A comprehensive textbook* (2nd ed., pp. 910–927). Baltimore: Williams & Wilkins.

Bourne, P. G. (1973). Alcoholism in the urban Negro population. In P. G. Bourne & R. Fox (Eds.), *Alcoholism: Progress in research and treatment* (pp. 211–226). New York: Academic Press.

Bowen, M. (1978). *Family therapy in clinical practice.* New York: Jason Aronson.

Boyd, M. B., Mackey, M. C., Phillips, K. D., & Travakoli, A. (2006). Alcohol and other drug disorders, comorbidity and violence in rural African American women. *Issues in Mental Health Nursing, 27,* 1017–1036.

Bradley, K. A., Boyd-Wickizer, J., Powell, S. H., & Burman, B. L. (1998). Alcohol screening questionnaires for women: A critical review. *Journal of the American Medical Association, 280,* 166–171.

Bradley, K. A., Bush, K. R., Epler, A. J., Dobie, D. J., Davis, T. M., Sporleder, J. L., . . . Kivlahan, D. R. (2003). Two brief alcohol screening tests from the Alcohol Use Disorders Identification Test (AUDIT): Validation in a female veterans affairs patient population. *Archives of Internal Medicine, 163*, 821–829.

Braithwaite, R. L., & Arriola, K. R. J. (2008). Male prisoners and HIV prevention: A call for action ignored. American Journal of Public Health, Supplement, Vol. 98. Retrieved June 10, 2011, from http://web.ebscohost.com/ehost/detail?vid=55&hid=126&sid=c46adbdd-a498-4ecc-a752-84a09c0abea1%40sessionmgr114&bdata=JnNpdGU9ZWhvc3QtbGl2ZQ%3d%3d#db=aph&AN=34060861

Braitman, A. L., Kelley, M. L., Ladage, J., Schroeder, V., Gumienny, L. A., Morrow, J. A., & Klostermann, K. (2009). Alcohol and drug use among college student adult children of alchoholics. *Journal of Alcohol and Drug Education, 53*(1), 69–88.

Brandsma, L. (2007). Eating disorders across the lifespan. *Journal of Women and Aging, 19*(1–2), 155–172.

Branson, B. M., Handsfield, H. H., Lampe, M. A., Jassen, R. S., Taylor, A. W., Lyss, S. B., & Clark, J. E. (2006). *Revised recommendations for HIV testing of adults, adolescents, and pregnant women in health-care settings.* Retrieved July 24, 2007, from www.cdc.gov/mmwr/preview/mmwrhtml/rr5514a1.htm

Bravender, T., Bryant-Waugh, R., Herzog, D., Katzman, D., Kriepe, R. D., Lask, B. . . . Zucker, N. (2010). Classification of eating disturbance in children and adolescents: Proposed changes for the DSM-V. *European Eating Disorders Review, 18*, 79–89.

Breiter, H. C., Aharon, I., Kahneman, A. D., & Shizgal, P. (2001). Functional imagery of neural responses to expectancy and experience of monetary gains and losses. *Neuron, 30*, 619–639.

British Broadcasting Company. (2002, March 17). *Internet gambling TA breeds addiction.* Retrieved August 2, 2003, from http://news.bbc. co.uk/1/hi/health/1872731.stm

Brooks, M. K. (1992). Ethical and legal issues of confidentiality. In J. H. Lowinson, P. Ruiz, R. B. Millman, & J. G. Langrod (Eds.), *Substance abuse: A comprehensive textbook* (pp. 1049–1066). Baltimore: Williams & Wilkins.

Brounstein, P. J., Zweig, J. M., & Gardner, S. E. (1998). *Science-based practices in substance abuse prevention: A guide.* Rockville, MD: Center for Substance Abuse Prevention.

Brouwers, M., & Wiggum, C. D. (1993). Bulimia and perfectionism: Developing the courage to be imperfect. *Journal of Mental Health Counseling, 15,* 141–149.

Brown, J. H., & Kreft, I. G. (1998). Zero effects of drug prevention programs: Issues and solutions. *Evaluation Review, 22,* 3–14.

Brown, J., & L'Engle, K. (2009). X-rated: Sexual attitudes and behaviors associated with U.S. early adolescents' exposure to sexually explicit media. *Communication Research 36*(1), 129–151.

Brown, L. (1993). *New Shorter Oxford English Dictionary.* Oxford, UK: Clarendon Press.

Brown, R. (2010). Systematic review of the impact of adult day-treatment courts. *Translational Research, 155,* 263–274.

Brown, S. (1988). Treating children of alcoholics: A developmental perspective. New York: Wiley.

Brown, S. L., & Rinelli, L. N. (2010). Family structure, family processes, and adolescent smoking and drinking. *Journal of Research on Adolescents, 20*(2), 259–273.

Brownell, K. D., & Stunkard, A. J. (1978). Behavioral treatment of obesity in children. *American Journal of Diseases in Children, 132,* 403–412.

Bruch, H. (1986). Anorexia nervosa: The therapeutic task. In K. D. Brownell & J. P. Foreyt (Eds.), *Handbook of eating disorders* (pp. 328–332). New York: Basic Books.

Brucker, D. L. (2008). Prescription drug abuse among persons with disabilities. *Journal of Vocational Rehabilitation 29,* 105–115

Burk, J. P., & Sher, K. J. (1988). The "forgotten children" revisited: Neglected areas of COA research. *Clinical Psychology Review, 8,* 285–302.

Burke, B. L., Arkowitz, H., & Dunn, C. (2002). The efficacy of motivational interviewing and its adaptations: What we know so far. In W. R. Miller & S. Rollnick (Eds.), *Motivational interviewing: Preparing people for change* (2nd ed., pp. 217–250). New York: Guilford Press.

Burke, R. J. (2000). Workaholism and divorce. *Psychological Reports, 86,* 219–220.

Burlew, A., Johnson, C., Flowers, A., Peteet, B., Griffith-Henry, K., & Buchanan, N. (2009). Neighborhood risk, parental supervision and the onset of substance use among African American adolescents. *Journal of Child and Family Studies, 18*(6), 680–689.

Burns, C. M., & D'Avanzo, C. E. (1993). Alcohol and other drug abuse in culturally diverse populations: Hispanics and Southeast Asians. Faculty resource. Washington, DC: Cosmos Corporation.

Burns, E., Gray, R., & Smith, L. A. (2010). Brief screening questionnaires to identify problem drinking during pregnancy: A systematic review. *Addiction, 105*(4), 601–614.

Burrows, B. A. (1992). Research on the etiology and maintenance of eating disorders. In E. M. Freeman (Ed.), *The addiction process: Effective social work approaches* (pp. 149–160). White Plains, NY: Longman.

Butler, J. (1990). Gender trouble: Feminism and the subversion of identity. London: Routledge.

Button, D. M., & Gealt, R. (2010). High risk behaviors among victims of sibling violence. *Journal of Family Violence, 25*(2), 131–140.

Cadiz, S., Savage, A., Bonavota, D., Hollywood, J., Butters, E., Neary, M., & Quiros, L. (2004). *The portal project: A layered approach to integrating trauma into alcohol and other drug treatment for women.* Retrieved August 3, 2007, from www.haworthpress.com/web/ATQ

Cameron, M. J., Maguire, R. W., & McCormack, J. (2011). Stress-induced binge eating: A behavior analytic approach to assessment and intervention. *Journal of Adult Development, 18,* 81–84.

Campbell, J. M., & Oei, T. P. (2010). A cognitive model for the intergenerational transference of alcohol use behavior. *Addictive Behaviors, 35*(2), 73–83.

Cao, F., & Su, L. (2006). Internet addiction among Chinese adolescents: Prevalence and psychological features. *Child: Care, Health and Development, 33*(3), 275–281.

Capuzzi, D., & Gross, D. R. (Eds.). (1996). *Youth at risk.* Alexandria, VA: American Counseling Association.

Carmona, M., & Stewart, K. (1996). A review of alternative activities and alternatives programs in youth-oriented prevention. (CSAP Technical Report No. 13). Rockville, MD: Center for Substance Abuse Prevention.

Carnes, P. J. (2001). Cybersex, courtship, and escalating arousal: Factors in addictive sexual desire. *Sexual Addiction and Compulsivity, 8,* 45–78.

Carr, A. (1997). *Family therapy and systemic consultation.* Lanham, MD: University Press of America.

Cartwright, B. Y., & D'Andrea, M. (2005). A personal journey toward culture-centered Counseling. *Journal of Counseling and Development, 83,* 214–221.

Cash, T. F. (1997). The body image workbook. An 8-step program for learning to like your looks. Oakland, CA: New Harbinger.

Center for Substance Abuse Treatment. (1995). *Planning for alcohol and other drug abuse treatment for adults in the Criminal Justice System* (Treatment Improvement Protocol #17). Rockville, MD: Center for Substance Abuse Treatment.

Center for Substance Abuse Treatment. (1998). *Naltrexone and alcoholism treatment (Treatment Improvement Protocol #28).* Rockville, MD: Center for Substance Abuse Treatment.

Center for Substance Abuse Treatment. (1999a). *Brief interventions and brief therapies for substance abuse (Treatment Improvement Protocol #34).* Rockville, MD: Center for Substance Abuse Treatment.

Center for Substance Abuse Treatment. (1999b). National evaluation data services (NEDS). The costs and benefits of substance abuse treatment. Findings from the National Treatment Improvement Evaluation Study (NTIES). Retrieved June 8, 2003, from http://neds.calib.con/products/pdfs/cost-ben.pdf

Center for Substance Abuse Treatment (2005). *Substance Abuse Treatment for Persons With Co-Occurring Disorders.* Treatment Improvement Protocol (TIP) Series 42. DHHS Publication No. (SMA) 05-3922. Rockville, MD: Substance Abuse and Mental Health Services Administration. Retrieved May 18, 2011, from http://www.ncbi.nlm.nih.gov/books/NBK14528/

Center on Addiction and Substance Abuse. (2010). *Behind bars II: Substance abuse and America's prison population.* Retrieved May 16, 2011, from http://www.casacolumbia.org/templates/publications_reports.aspx.

Center on Alcohol Marketing and Youth. (2010). Youth exposure to all alcohol advertising on television, 2001–2009. Retrieved May 23, 2011, from http://www.camy.org/bin/u/r/CAMYReport2001_2009.pdf

Centers for Disease Control. (1994, May). *HIV/AIDS prevention: Facts about the human immunodeficiency virus and its transmission.* Atlanta, GA: U.S. Department of Health and Human Services/Public Health Service.

Centers for Disease Control and Prevention. (2005a). *Tuberculosis transmission in a homeless shelter population, 2000–2003.* Retrieved August 8, 2007, from www.cdc.gov/mmwr/preview/mmwrhtml/mm5406a4.htm

Centers for Disease Control and Prevention. (2005b). *Access to sterile syringes.* Retrieved August 8, 2007, from www.cdc.gov/idu/facts/aed_idu_acc.htm

Centers for Disease Control and Prevention. (2006a). *Fetal alcohol spectrum disorders.* Retrieved August 4, 2007, from www.cdc.gov/nvbddd/fas/fasask.htm

Centers for Disease Control and Prevention. (2006b). *Sexually transmitted diseases treatment guidelines 2006.* Retrieved August 8, 2007, from www.cdc.gov/std/treatment/2006/hiv.htm#hiv1#hiv1

Centers for Disease Control and Prevention. (2006c). *Trends in reportable sexually transmitted diseases in the United States, 2005: National surveillance data for chlamydia, gonorrhea, and syphilis.* Retrieved August 7, 2007, from www.cdc.gov/std/hiv/STDFact-STD&HIV.htm#WhatIs

Centers for Disease Control and Prevention. (2006d). *Minorities and drugs: Facts and figures.* Retrieved May 16, 2011, from http://www.whitehousedrugpolicy.gov/drugfact/minorities/minorities_ff.html

Centers for Disease Control and Prevention, (2006e). *HIV among women who have sex with women.* Retrieved November 23, 2011, from http://www.cdc.gov/hiv/topics/women/resources/factsheets/wsw.htm

Centers for Disease Control and Prevention. (2007a). *Revision of the 2005 HIV/AIDS surveillance report.* Retrieved August 5, 2007, from www.cdc.gov/hiv/topics/surveillance/resources/reports/2005report/default.htm

Centers for Disease Control and Prevention. (2007b). *HIV and its transmission.* Retrieved August 7, 2007, from www.cdc.gov/hiv/resources/factsheets/transmission.htm

Centers for Disease Control and Prevention. (2007c). *Preventing obesity and chronic diseases.* Retrieved August 1, 2007, from www.cdc.gov/search.do?queryText=chronic+obesity&action=search&searchButton.x=22&searchButton.y=8

Centers for Disease Control and Prevention. (2008). Subpopulation estimates from the HIV Incidence Surveillance System—United States, 2006. *Morbidity and Mortality Weekly Report, 57*(36), 985–989.

Centers for Disease Control and Prevention. (2009a). National Vital Statistics System, National Marriage and Divorce Rate Trends. Retrieved May 18, 2011, from http://cdc.gov/nchs/nvss/marriage_divorce_tables.htm

Centers for Disease Control and Prevention. (2009b). HIV prevalence estimates—United States, 2006. *Morbidity and Mortality Weekly Report, 57*(39), 1073–1076.

Centers for Disease Control and Prevention. (2010a). *Alcohol and public health.* Retrieved December 22, 2010, from http://www.cdc.gov/alcohol/

Centers for Disease Control and Prevention. (2010b). *Tobacco use: Targeting the Nation's leading killer: At a glance 2010.* Retrieved December 22, 2010, from http://www.cdc.gov/chronicdisease/resources/publications/aag/osh.htm

Centers for Disease Control and Prevention. (2010c). *Injuries among American Indians/Alaska Natives (AI/AN): Fact sheet.* Retrieved May 6, 2011, from http://www.cdc.gov/motorvehiclessafety/native/factsheet.html

Centers for Disease Control and Prevention. (2010d). *Alcohol & public health.* Retrieved December 16, 2010, from http://www.cdc.gov/alcohol/

Centers for Disease Control and Prevention. (2010e). Healthy Youth! Alcohol and drug use. Retrieved November 15, 2010, from http://www.cdc.gov/ViolencePrevention/childmaltreatment/riskprotectivefactors.html

Centers for Disease Control and Prevention. (2010f). *HIV among African Americans.* Retrieved June 7, 2011, from http://www.cdc.gov/hiv/topics/aa/

Centers for Disease Control and Prevention. (2010g). *HIV transmission.* Retrieved June 7, 2011, from http://www.cdc.gov/hiv/resources/qa/transmission.htm

Centers for Disease Control and Prevention. (2011). *HIV surveillance report: Diagnosis of HIV infection and AIDS in the United States and Dependent Areas, 2009.* Volume 21. Retrieved May 25, 2011, from http://www.cdc.gov/hiv/topics/surveillance/basic.htm#hivest

Cermak, T. L. (1986). *Diagnosing and treating codependence: A guide for professionals who work with chemical dependents, their spouses, and children.* Minneapolis: Johnson Institute.

Ceyhan, E., Ceyhan, A. A., & Gürcan, A. (2007). The validity and reliability of the Problematic Internet Usage Scale. *Educational Sciences: Theory and Practice, 7*(1), 411–416.

Chafetz, M. E. (1964). Consumption of alcohol in the Far and Middle East. *New England Journal of Medicine, 271,* 297–301.

Chan, J. G. (2003). An examination of family-involved approaches to alcoholism treatment. *Family Journal, 11,* 129–138.

Chaney, M. P., Filmore, J. M., & Goodrich, K. M. (2011). No more sitting on the sidelines. *Counseling Today, 53*(11), 34–37.

Chang, G. (2002). Brief interventions for problem drinking and women. *Journal of Substance Abuse Treatment, 23,* 1–7.

Chang, P. (2000). Treating Asian/Pacific American addicts and their families. In J. Krestan (Ed.), *Bridges to recovery. Addiction, family therapy, and multicultural treatment* (pp. 192–219). New York: Free Press.

Chartier, K. G., Hesselbrock, M. N., & Hesselbrock, V. M. (2011). *Addictive Behaviors, 36,* 167–174.

Chi, I., Lubben, J. E., & Kitano, H. H. (1989). Differences in drinking behavior among three Asian-American groups. *Journal of Studies on Alcohol, 50,* 15–23.

Chittenden, H. (1935). *American fur trade of the Far West: A history of pioneer trading posts and early fur companies of the Missouri Valley and Rocky Mountains and of the overland commerce with Santa Fe (Vol. 1).* New York: Barnes & Noble.

Cho, Y. I., & Crittenden, K. S. (2006). The impact of adult roles on drinking among women in the United States. *Substance Use and Misuse, 41,* 17–34.

Chong, J., Fortier, Y., & Morris, T. L. (2009). Cultural practices and spiritual development for women in a Native American alcohol and drug treatment program. *Journal of Ethnicity in Substance Abuse, 8*(3), 261–182.

Chou, C., Condron, L, & Belland, J. C. (2005). A review of the research on Internet addiction. *Educational Psychology Review, 17*(4), 363–388.

Christopher, J. (1988). *How to stay sober: Recovery without religion.* Buffalo, NY: Prometheus Books.

Ciaccio, C. P. (2010). IV. Cyber Law: A. Notes: Internet gambling: Recent developments and state of the law. *Berkeley Technology Law Journal Annual Review.* Berkeley: Regents of the University of California.

Clark, P. A. & Fadus, M. (2010). Federal funding for needle exchange programs. *Medical Science Monitor, 16,* PH1-13.

Clark, T. T., Belgrave, F. Z., & Nasim, A. (2008). Risk and protective factors for substance use among urban African American adolescents considered high risk. *Journal of Ethnicity in Substance Abuse, 7*(3), 292–303.

Clayton, R. R., Leukefeld, C. G., Grant-Harrington, N., & Cattarello, A. (1996). DARE (Drug Abuse Resistance Education): Very popular but not very effective. In C. B. McCoy, L. R. Metsch, & J. A. Inciardi (Eds.), *Intervening with drug-involved youth* (pp. 101–109). Thousand Oaks, CA: Sage.

Cleveland, M. J., Collins, L. M., Lanza, S. T., Greenberg, M. T., & Feinberg, M. E. (2010). Does individual risk moderate the effects of contextual-level protective factors? A latent class analysis of substance use. *Journal of Prevention & Intervention in the Community, 38*(3), 213–228.

Cochran, B. N., Peavy, K., M., & Cauce, A. M. (2007). Substance abuse treatment providers' explicit and implicit attitudes regarding sexual minorities. *Journal of Homosexuality, 53*(3), 187–207.

Cochran, S. D., Ackerman, D., Mays, V. M., & Ross, M. W. (2004). Prevalence of non-medical drug use and dependence among homosexually active men and women in the US population. *Addiction, 99,* 989–998.

Codependents Anonymous. (1995). *The CODA book.* Phoenix, AZ: Coda Service Office.

Coggans, N., & McKellar, S. (1994). Drug use amongst peers: Peer pressure or peer preference. *Drugs: Education, Prevention, and Policy, 1,* 15–24.

Collins, B. (1993). Reconstructing codependency using self-in-relation theory: A feminist perspective. *Social Work, 38,* 470–476.

Collins, R. L., & McNair, L. D. (2002). Minority women and alcohol use. *Alcohol Research and Health, 26*(4), 251.

Colliver, J. D., Compton, W. M., Gfroerer, J. C., & Condon, T. (2006). Projecting drug use among aging baby boomers in 2020. *Annals of Epidemiology, 16*(4), 27–265.

Conner, L. C., LeFauve, C. E., & Wallace, B. C. (2009). Ethnic and cultural correlates of addiction among diverse women. In K. T. Brady, S. E. Back, & S. F. Greenfield (Eds.) *Women and addiction* (Chapter 27, pp. 453–470). New York: Guilford Press.

Conyers, L., & Boomer, K. B. (2005). Factors associated with disclosure of HIV/AIDS to employers among individuals who use job accommodations and those who do not. *Journal of Vocational Rehabilitation, 22,* 189–198.

Conyers, L. M. (2004). Expanding understanding of HIV/AIDS and employment: Perspectives of a focus group. *Rehabilitation Counseling Bulletin, 48*(1), 5–18.

Cook, C. C. (1988). The Minnesota model in the management of drug and alcohol dependency: Miracle, method, or myth? (Part I: The philosophy of the programme). *British Journal of Addiction, 83,* 625–634.

Cook-Daniels, L. (2008). Transforming mental health services for older people: Gay, lesbian, bisexual, and transgender (GLBT) challenges and opportunities, *Journal of GLBT Family Studies, 4*(4), 469–483.

Cooney, N. L., Kadden, R. M., & Steinberg, H. R. (2005). Assessment of alcohol problems. In D. M. Donovan & G. A. Marlatt (Eds.), *Assessment of addictive behaviors* (2nd ed.). New York: Guilford Press.

Cooper, A., Delmonica, D., & Burg, R. (2000). Cybersex users, abusers, and compulsives: New findings and implications. *Sexual Addiction and Compulsivity: The Journal of Treatment and Prevention, 7*(1–2), 5–30.

Cooper, S. E., & Robinson, D. A. G. (1987). Use of the Substance Abuse Subtle Screening Inventory with a college population. *Journal of American College Health, 36,* 180–184.

Copello, A. G., Templeton, L., & Powell, J. (2010). The impact of addiction on the family: Estimates of prevalence and costs. *Drugs: Education, Prevention, and Policy, 17*(1), 63–74.

Copello, A. G., Velleman, R. D. B., & Templeton, L. J. (2005). Family interventions in the treatment of alcohol and drug problems. *Drug and Alcohol Review, 24,* 369–385.

Corey, G. (2008). *Theory and practice of group counseling* (7th ed.). Belmont, CA: Brooks/Cole.

Cork, M. (1969). The forgotten children: A study of children with alcoholic parents. Toronto: Addiction Research Foundation.

Cornish, E., Schreier, B. A., Nadkarni, L. I., & Metzger, L. H. (2010). *Handbook of multicultural counseling competencies.* Hoboken, NJ: Wiley.

Corrigan, P. W., & Miller, F. E., & Watson, P. J. (2006). Blame, shame, and contamination: The impact of mental illness and drug dependence stigma on family members. *Journal of Family Psychology, 20*(2), 239–246.

Coutinho, W. F., Moreira, R. O., Spagnol, C., & Appolinario, J. C. (2007). Does binge eating disorder alter cortisol secretion in obese women? *Eating Behaviors, 8*(1), 59–64.

Coyhis, D. (2000). Culturally specific addiction recovery for Native Americans. In J. Krestan (Ed.), *Bridges to recovery: Addiction, family therapy, and multicultural treatment* (pp. 77–114). New York: Free Press.

Coyhis, D., & Simonelli, R. (2008). The Native American healing experience. *Substance Use and Misuse, 43*(12/13), 1927–1949.

Coyhis, D., & White, W. L. (2002a). Alcohol problems in Native America: Changing paradigms and clinical practices. *Alcoholism Treatment Quarterly, 20,* 157–165.

Coyhis, D., & White, W. (2002b). *Addiction and recovery in Native America: Lost history, enduring lessons.* Retrieved May 12, 2011, from http://www.quantumunitsed.com/materials/1540_addictionrecoveryinnativeamericans.pdf

Crome, I. B. (1999). Substance misuse and psychiatric comorbidity: Towards *improved service provision. Drugs: Education, Prevention & Policy, 6,* 151–174.

Cullen, J., & Carr, A. (1999). Codependency: An empirical study from a systemic perspective. *Contemporary Family Therapy, 21,* 505–526.

Cummings, C., Gordon, J. R., & Marlatt, G. A. (1980). Relapse: Strategies of prevention and prediction. In W. R. Miller (Ed.), *The addictive behaviors: Treatment of alcoholism, drug abuse, smoking and obesity* (pp. 291–321). New York: Pergamon Press.

Cummins, L. H., & Lehman, J. (2007). Eating disorders and body image concerns in Asian American women: Assessment and treatment from a multicultural and feminist perspective. *Eating Disorders, 15,* 217–230.

Cummins, L. H., Simmons, A. M., & Zane, N. (2005). Eating Disorders in Asian Populations: A critique of current approaches to the study of culture, ethnicity, and eating disorders. *American Journal of Orthopsychiatry, 75*(4), 443–453.

Cunningham, J. A., Sobell, L. C., Sobell, M. B., & Kapur, G. (1995). Resolution from alcohol problems with and without treatment: Reasons for change. *Journal of Substance Abuse, 7,* 365–372.

Cunningham, P. B., Foster, S. L., & Warner, S. E. (2010). Culturally relevant family-based treatment for adolescents' delinquency and substance abuse: Understanding within-session processes. *Journal of Clinical Psychology, 66*(8), 830–846.

Custer, R., & Milt, H. (1985). *When luck runs out: Help for compulsive gamblers and their families.* New York: Facts on File.

Cyr, M. G., & McGarry, K. A. (2002). Alcohol use disorder among women. *Postgraduate Medicine, 112,* 31–40.

Daley, D. C., & Marlatt, G. A. (2005). Relapse prevention. In J. H. Lowinson, P. Ruiz, & R. B. Millman (Eds.),

Substance abuse: A comprehensive textbook (4th ed., pp. 772–785). Baltimore: Williams & Wilkins.

Dally, P. (1984). Anorexia tardive—Late onset marital anorexia nervosa. *Journal of Psychosomatic Research, 28,* 423–428.

Day, J., Schmidt, U., Collier, D., Perkins, S., Van den Eynde, F., Treasure, J., . . . Eisler, I. (2011). Risk factors, correlates, and markers in early-onset bulimia nervosa and EDNOS. *International Journal of Eating Disorders, 44*(4), 287–294.

De La Rosa, M., Dillon, F. R., Ganapati, E., Rojas, P., Pinto, E., & Prado, G. (2010). Mother-daughter attachment and drug abuse among Latinas in the United States. *Journal of Drug Issues, 40,* 379–404.

De La Rosa, M., Rice, C., & Rugh, D. (2007). Understanding Latino family attitudes in relation to Latino gang members' substance abuse: A content analysis. *Journal of Human Behavior in the Social Environment, 16*(4), 1–18.

De la Rosa, M., Rugh, D., & Rice, C. (2006). An analysis of risk domains associated with drug transitions of active Latino gang members. *Journal of Addictive Diseases, 25*(4), 81–90.

de Lisle, S. M., Dowling, N. A., & Allen, J. S. (2011). Mindfulness-based cognitive therapy for problem gambling. *Journal of Clinical Case Studies, 10*(3), 210–228.

Dear, G. E. (2004). Test-retest reliability of the Holyoake Codependency Index with Australian students. *Psychological Reports, 94*(2), 482–484.

Dear, G. E., & Roberts, C. M. (2000). The Holyoake Codependency Index: Investigation of the factor structure and psychodynamic properties. *Psychological Reports, 87,* 991–1002.

Dear, G. E., & Roberts, C. M. (2002). The relationship between codependency and femininity and masculinity. *Sex Roles, 46,* 159–165.

Delgado, M. (2002). Latinos and alcohol: Treatment considerations. *Alcoholism Treatment Quarterly, 20,* 187–192.

Delmonico, D. L., Griffin, E., & Carnes, P. J. (2002). Treating online compulsive sexual behavior: When cybersex is the drug of choice. In A. Cooper (Ed.), *Sex and the Internet: A guidebook for clinicians* (pp. 147–167). New York: Routledge.

Delva, J., Wallace, J. M., O'Malley, P., Bachman, J. G., Johnston, L. D., & Schulenberg, J. E. (2005). The epidemiology of alcohol, marijuana, and cocaine use among Mexican American, Puerto Rican, Cuban American, and other Latin American eighth grade students in the United States: 1991–2002. *American Journal of Public Health, 95*(4), 696–702.

DeMarco, R. F., Miller, K. H., Patsdaughter, C. A., Chisolm, M., & Grindel, C. G. (1998). From silencing the self to action: Experiences of women living with HIV/AIDS. *Health Care for Women International, 19,* 539–552.

Dennis, M. L., Foss, M. A., & Scott, C. K. (2007). An eight-year perspective on the relationship between the duration of abstinence and other aspects of recovery. *Evaluation Review, 31,* 585–612.

Desire for drugs fuels crime. (1991, August 26). Associated Press.

Dethier, M., Counerotte, C., & Blairy, S. (2011). Marital satisfaction in couples with an alcoholic husband. *Journal of Family Violence, 26,* 151–162.

DeWit, D. J., Adlaf, E. M., Offord, D. R., & Ogborne, A. C. (2000). Age at first alcohol use: A risk factor for the development of alcohol disorders. *American Journal of Psychiatry, 157*(5), 745–750.

Dhalla, S., & Kopec, J. A. (2007). The CAGE Questionnaire for alcohol misuse: A review of reliability and validity studies. *Clinical & Investigative Medicine, 30*(1), 33–41.

Diamond, G. S., & Liddle, H. A. (1996). Resolving a therapeutic impasse between parents and adolescents in Multidimensional Family Therapy. *Journal of Consulting and Clinical Psychology, 64,* 481–488.

DiCicco, L., Davis, R., & Orenstein, A. (1984). Identifying the children of alcoholics from survey responses. *Journal of Alcohol and Drug Education, 30,* 1–17.

Didenko, E., & Pankratz, N. (2007). "Substance Use: Pathways to homelessness? Or a way of adapting to street life?" *Visions: BC's Mental Health and Addictions Journal, 4*(1), 9–10. Retrieved April 25, 2011, from http://www.heretohelp.bc.ca/

Dixon, M. R., & Johnson, T. E. (2007). The gambling functional assessment (GFA): An assessment device for identification of the maintaining variables of pathological gambling. *Analysis of Gambling Behavior, 1,* 44–49.

Donohue, B., Allen, D. A., & Lapota, H. (2009). Family Behavior Therapy. In D. Springer & A. Rubin (Eds.), *Substance abuse treatment for youth and adults* (pp. 205–255). New York: Wiley.

Donovan, D. M. (2005). Assessment of addictive behaviors for relapse prevention. In D. M. Donovan & G. A. Marlatt (Eds.), *Assessment of addictive behaviors* (2nd. ed.). New York: Guilford Press.

Donovan, D. M., & Marlatt, G. A. (Eds.) (2008). *Assessment of addictive behaviors.* New York: Guilford Press.

Döring, N. M. (2009). The Internet's impact on sexuality: A critical review of 15 years of research. *Computers in Human Behavior, 25*(5), 1089–1101.

Douglass, F. (1855). *My bondage, my freedom.* New York: Ortin and Mulligan.

Dounchis, J. Z., Hayden, H. A., & Wilfley, D. E. (2001). Obesity, body image, and eating disorders in ethnically diverse children and adolescents. In J. K. Thompson & L. Smolak (Eds.), *Body image, eating disorders, and obesity in youth* (pp. 67–98). Washington, DC: American Psychological Association.

Doweiko, H. E. (2011). *Concepts of chemical dependency* (5th ed.). Pacific Grove, CA: Brooks/Cole.

Drake, R. E., O'Neal, E. L., & Wallach, M. A. (2008). A systematic review of psychosocial research on psychosocial interventions for people with co-occurring severe mental and substance use disorders. *Journal of Substance Abuse Treatment, 34*, 123–138.

Drew, S. M., Wilkins, K. M., & Trevisan, L. A. (2010). Managing medication and alcohol misuse by your older patients. *Current Psychiatry*, 9, 21–24, 27–28, 41.

Drewnowski, A., & Bellisle, F. (2007). Is sweetness addictive? *Nutrition Bulletin, 32* (Suppl. 1), 52–60.

Du Bois, W. E. B. (1928). Drunkenness. *The Crisis, 35,* 348.

Dube, S. R., Anda, R. F., Felitti, V. J., Edwards, V. J., & Croft, J. B. (2002). Adverse childhood experiences and personal alcohol abuse as an adult. *Addictive Behaviors, 27,* 713–725.

Duncan, D. F., Nicholson, T., White, J. B., Bradley, D. B., & Bonaguro, J. (2010). The baby boomer effect: Changing patterns of substance abuse among adults ages 55 and older. *Journal of Aging & Social Policy, 22*(3), 237–248.

Dunn, M. G., Tartar, R. E., Mezzich, A. C., Vanyukov, M., Kirisci, M., & Kirillova, G. (2002). Origins and consequences of child neglect on substance abusing families. *Clinical Psychology Review, 22,* 1063–1090.

Ebberhart, N. C., Luczak, S. E., Avanecy, N., & Wall, T. L. (2003). Family history of alcohol dependence in Asian Americans. *Journal of Psychoactive Drugs, 35*(3), 375–377.

Eiden, R. D., Molnar, D. S., Colder, C. Edwards, E. P., & Leonard, K. E. (2009). A conceptual model predicting internalizing problems in middle childhood among children of alcoholic and nonalcoholic fathers: The role of marital aggression. *Journal of Studies on Alcoholism and Drugs, 70*(5), 741–750.

El-Guebaly, N., & Offord, D. R. (1977). The offspring of alcoholics: A critical review. *American Journal of Psychiatry, 134*(4), 357–365.

El-Guebaly, N., & Offord, D. R. (1979). On being the offspring of an alcoholic: An update. *Alcoholism: Clinical & Experimental Research, 3*(2), 148–157.

Emlet, C. A. (2008). Truth and consequences: A qualitative exploration of HIV disclosures in older adults. *AIDS Care, 20*(6), 710–717.

Ennett, S. T., Tobler, N. S., Ringwalt, C. L., & Flewelling, R. L. (1994). How effective is drug abuse resistance education? A meta-analysis of project DARE outcome evaluations. *American Journal of Public Health, 84,* 1394–1401.

Ewing, J. A. (1984). Detecting alcoholism: The CAGE questionnaire. *Journal of the American Medical Association, 252,* 1905–1907.

Ewing, J. A., & Fox, R. E. (1968). Family therapy of alcoholism. In F. Messerman (Ed.), *Current psychiatric therapies* (pp. 86–91). New York: Grune & Stratton.

Facebook, (2011). Facebook statistics. Retrieved July 13, 2011, from http://www.facebook.com/press/info.php? statistics

Fairburn, C. G., Cooper, Z., & Shafran, R. (2003). Cognitive behavior therapy for eating disorders: A "transdiagnostic" theory and treatment. *Behavior Research and Therapy, 41*(5), 509–528.

Falicov, C. J. (2002). Ambiguous loss: Risk and resilience in Latino immigrant families. In M. Suarez Orozco & M. Paez (Eds.), *Latinos: Remaking America* (pp. 274–288). Berkeley: University of California Press.

Falicov, C. J. (2005). Mexican families. In M. McGoldrick, J. Giordano, & N. Garcie-Preto (Eds.), *Ethnicity and family therapy* (3rd ed., pp. 134–163). New York: Guilford Press.

Fals-Stewart, W. (2003). The occurrence of partner physical aggression on days of alcohol consumption: A longitudinal diary study. *Journal of Consulting and Clinical Psychology, 71,* 41–52.

Fals-Stewart, W., & Kenndy, C. (2005). Addressing intimate partner violence in substance-abuse treatment. *Journal of Substance Abuse, 29*, 5–17.

Feldman, M. B., & Meyer, I. H. (2007). Eating disorders in diverse lesbian, gay, and bisexual populations. *International Journal of Eating Disorders, 40*, 218–226.

Feree, M. C. (2002). Sexual addiction and co-addiction: Experiences among women of faith. *Sexual Addiction and Recovery, 9*(4), 285–293.

Ferguson, C. J., Munoz, M. E., Contreras, S., & Velasquez, K. (2011). Mirror, mirror on the wall: Peer competition, television influences, and body image dissatisfaction. *Journal of Social and Clinical Psychology, 30*(5), 458–483.

Fineran, K., Laux, J. M., Seymour, J., & Thomas, T. (2010). The Barnum Effect and chaos theory: Exploring college student ACOA traits. *Journal of College Student Psychotherapy, 24*(1), 17–31.

Fingarette, H. (1988). *Heavy drinking: The myth of alcoholism as a disease.* Berkeley: University of California.

Fiorentine, R., & Hillhouse, M. P. (2000). Drug treatment and 12-step program participation: The addictive effects of integrated recovery activities. *Journal of Substance Abuse Treatment, 18*, 65–74.

Fischer, J. L., Pidcock, B. W., Munsch, J., & Forthun, L. (2005). Parental abusive drinking and sibling role difference. *Alcoholism Treatment Quarterly, 23*(1), 79–97.

Fischer, J. L., Spann, L., & Crawford, D. W. (1991). Measuring co-dependency. *Alcoholism Treatment Quarterly, 8*(1), 87–100.

Fisher, G. L. (2006). Rethinking our war on drugs: Candid talk about controversial issues. Westport, CN: Praeger.

Fisher, G. L. (2011). *Understanding why addicts are not all alike: Recognizing the types and how the differences affect intervention and treatment.* Westport, CN: Praeger.

Fisher, G. L., & Harrison, T. C. (1992). Assessment of alcohol and other drug abuse with referred adolescents. *Psychology in the Schools, 29*, 172–178.

Fisher, G. L., & Harrison, T. C. (1993a). The school counselor's role in relapse prevention. *School Counselor, 41*, 120–125.

Fisher, G. L., & Harrison, T. C. (1993b). *Codependent characteristics of prospective counselors as compared to other graduate students.* Paper presented at American Counseling Association National Conference, Atlanta, GA, March.

Flaskerud, J. H. (2008). Cultural context and treatment of substance related disorders: An invitation. *Issues in Mental Health Nursing, 29*(4), 427–431.

Flowers, C. P., & Robinson, B. (2002). A structural and discriminant analysis of the Work Addiction Risk Test. *Educational and Psychological Measurement, 62*(3), 517–526.

Forbush, K., Heatherton, T. F., & Keel, P. K. (2007). Relationships between perfectionism and specific disordered eating behaviors. *International Journal of Eating Disorders, 40*(1), 37–41.

Forward, S. (1986). *Men who hate women and women who love them.* New York: Basic Books.

Foster, B. (1999). The mind-body connection. *Body Positive, 12*(9), 1–5. Retrieved April 4, 2003, from www.thebody.com/bp/sept99/yoga.html

Franklin, A. J. (2004). *From brotherhood to manhood: How Black men rescue their dreams and relationships from the invisibility syndrome.* Hoboken, NJ: Wiley.

Fraser, J. J., McAbee, G. N., & Committee on Medical Liability (2004). Dealing with the parent whose judgment is impaired by alcohol or drugs: Legal and ethical considerations. *Pediatrics, 114*(3), 869–873.

Fredrickson, G. M. (1971). The Black image in the White mind: The debate on Afro-American character and destiny, 1817–1914. New York: Harper & Row.

Freehling, W. W. (1968). *Prelude to civil war: The nullification controversy in South Carolina, 1818–1836.* New York: Harper & Row.

Freeman, E. M. (Ed.). (1992). *The addiction process: Effective social work approaches.* White Plains, NY: Longman.

Fried, P. A. (2011). Cannabis use during pregnancy: Its effects on offspring from birth to young adulthood. In *Alcohol, drugs and medication in pregnancy: The long-term outcome for the child.* London: Mac Keith Press.

Friedman, M. S., Marshal, M. P., Stall, R., Kidder, D. P., Henny, K. D., & Courtenay-Quirk, C. (2009). Associations between substance use, sexual risk taking and HIV treatment adherence among homeless people living with HIV. *AIDS Care, 21*(6), 692–700.

Friel, J. C. (1984). *Co-dependency and the search for identity: A paradoxical crisis.* Pompano Beach, FL: Health Communications.

Friel, J. C. (1985). Co-dependency assessment inventory: A preliminary research tool. *Focus on Family, 20–21*, 98–111.

Friese, B., Grube, J. W., Seninger, S., Paschall, M. J., & Moore, R. S. (2011). Drinking behavior and sources of alcohol: Differences between Native American and White youths. *Journal of Studies on Alcohol and Drugs, 72*(1), 53–60.

Fukuyama, M., & Inoue-Cox, C. (1992). Cultural perspectives in communicating with Asian/Pacific Islanders. In J. Wittmer (Ed.), *Valuing diversity and similarly: Bridging the gap through interpersonal skills* (pp. 93–112). Minneapolis: Educational Media Corporation.

Fuller, J. A., & Warner, R. M. (2000). Family stressors as predictors of codependency. *Genetic, Social and General Psychology Monographs, 126*(1), 5–23.

Fuller, R. K., & Gordis, E. (2001). Naltrexone treatment for alcohol dependence. *New England Journal of Medicine, 345,* 1770–1771.

Gagnon, M., & Stuart, M. (2009). Manufacturing disability: HIV, women and the construction of difference. *Nursing Philosophy, 10*(1), 42–52.

Gallardo, M. E., & Curry, S. J. (2009). Shifting perspectives: Culturally responsive interventions with Latino substance abusers. *Journal of Ethnicity in Substance Abuse, 8*(3), 314–329.

Galvan, F. H., & Caetano, R. (2003). Alcohol use and related problems among ethnic minorities in the United States. *Alcohol Research and Health, 27,* 332–337.

Garcia, F. D., & Thibaut, F. (2010). Sexual addictions. *American Journal of Drug and Alcohol Abuse, 36,* 254–260.

Garcia-Preto, N. (2005). Latino families: An overview. In M. McGoldrick, J. Giordano, & N. Garcia-Preto (Eds.), *Ethnicity and family therapy* (pp. 153–165). New York: Guilford Press.

Garfinkel, P. E., & Kaplan, A. S. (1986). Anorexia nervosa: Diagnostic conceptualizations. In K. D. Brownell & J. P. Foreyt (Eds.), *Handbook of eating disorders* (pp. 266–282). New York: Basic Books.

Garmezy, N. (1991). Resilience and vulnerability to adverse developmental outcomes associated with poverty. *American Journal of Behavioral Science, 34,* 416–430.

Garner, D. M. (2005). *Eating Disorder Inventory-3. Professional manual.* Odessa, FL: Psychological Assessment Resources.

Gayol, G. N., & Lira, L. R. (2002). Construction and validity of the codependency instrument (ICOD) for Mexican women. *Salud Mental, 25*(2), 38–48.

George, W. H., La Marr, J., Barrett, K., & McKinnon, T. (1999). Alcoholic parentage, self-labeling, and endorsement of ACOA-codependent traits. *Psychology of Addictive Behaviors, 13*(1), 39–48.

Gerstein, D. R. (1997). *Final report: The National Treatment Improvement Evaluation Study.* Rockville, MD: Center for Substance Abuse Treatment.

Giermyski, T., & Williams, T. (1986). Codependency. *Journal of Psychoactive Drugs, 18,* 7–13.

Gilley, B. J., & Co-Cké, J. H. (2005). Cultural investment: Providing opportunities to reduce risky behavior among gay American Indian males. *Journal of Psychoactive Drugs, 37*(3), 293–298.

Giordano, J., & McGoldrick, M. (2005). Euro-American families. In M. McGoldrick, J. Giordano, & N. Garcia-Preto (Eds.), *Ethnicity and family therapy.* New York: Guilford Press.

Gladding, S. T. (2011). *Family therapy: History, theory, and practice.* Boston: Pearson.

Goodman, R. W. (1987). Adult children of alcoholics. *Journal of Counseling and Development, 66,* 162–163.

Goodman, S., Blinder, B. J., Chaitin, B. F., & Hagman, J. (1988). Atypical eating disorders. In B. J. Blinder, B. F. Chaitin, & R. S. Goldstein (Eds.), *The eating disorders: Medical and psychological bases of diagnosis and treatment* (pp. 393–404). New York: PMA.

Gordon, J. U. (Ed.). (1994). Managing multiculturalism in substance abuse services. Thousand Oaks, CA: Sage.

Gormally, J., Black, S., Dastrom, S., & Rardin, D. (1982). The assessment of binge-eating severity among obese persons. *Addictive Behaviors, 7,* 47–55.

Gorman, D. M. (1998). The irrelevance of evidence in the development of school-based drug prevention policy, 1986–1996. *Evaluation Review, 22,* 118–146.

Gorski, T. T. (1988). *The staying sober workbook: A serious solution for the problem of relapse.* Independence, MO: Independence Press.

Gorski, T. T. (1989). *Passages through recovery: An action plan for preventing relapse.* Center City, MN: Hazelden.

Gorski, T. T. (1990). The Cenaps model of relapse prevention: Basic principles and procedures. *Journal of Psychoactive Drugs, 22,* 125–133.

Gorski, T. T. (1992). Creating a relapse prevention program in your treatment center. *Addiction & Recovery,* July/August, 16–17.

Gorski, T. T. (1993). Relapse prevention: A state of the art overview. *Addiction & Recovery,* March/April, 25–27.

Gorski, T. T., & Miller, M. M. (1986). *Staying sober: Guide to relapse prevention.* Independence, MO: Herald House.

Grafsky, E. L., Letcher, A., Slesnick, N., & Serovich, J. M. (2011). Comparison of treatment response among GLB and non-GLB street-living youth. *Children & Youth Services Review, 33*(5), 569–574.

Gragon, M., & Stuart, M. (2009). Manufacturing disability: HIV, women, and the construction of difference. *Nursing Philosophy, 10*(1), 42–52.

Granfield, R., & Cloud, W. (2001). Social context and "natural recovery": The role of social capital in the resolution of drug-associated problems. *Substance Use and Misuse, 36,* 1543–1570.

Grant, J. E., Potenza, M. N., Weinstein, A., & Gorelick, D. A. (2010). Introduction to behavioral addictions. *American Journal of Drug and Alcohol Abuse, 36,* 233–241.

Greeff, A. P., & Du Toit, C. (2009). Resilience in remarried families. *American Journal of Family Therapy, 37*(2), 114–126.

Greenfield, S. F., & Grella, C. E. (2009). Alcohol and drug abuse: What is "women-focused" treatment for substance abuse disorders? *Psychiatric Services, 60,* 880–882.

Greenfield, S. F., Brooks, A. J., Gordon, S. M., Green, C. A., Kropp, F., McHugh, R. K., . . . Miele, G. M. (2007a). Substance abuse treatment entry, retention, and outcome in women: A review of the literature. *Drug and Alcohol Dependence, 86*(1), 1–21.

Greenfield, S. F., Trucco, E. M., McHugh, R. K., Lincoln, M., & Gallop, R. J. (2007b). The women's recovery group study: A stage 1 trial of women-focused group therapy for substance use disorders verses mixed-gender group drug counseling. *Drug and Alcohol Dependence, 90*(1), 39–47.

Gresham, S. L. (2009). Negotiating cultural contexts: An exploratory investigation of Black gay male strategy employment. *Journal of GLBT Family Studies, 5*(3), 247–267.

Griffing, S., Fish-Ragin, D., Sage, R. E., Madry, L., Bingham, L. E., & Primm, B. J. (2002). Domestic violence survivors' self-identified reasons for returning to abusive relationships. *Journal of Interpersonal Violence, 17,* 306–319.

Griffin-Shelley, E. (1991). *Sex and love.* New York: Praeger.

Griffith, J. D., Rowan-Szal, G. A., Roark, R. R., & Simpson, D. D. (2000). Contingency management in outpatient methadone treatment: A meta-analysis. *Drug and Alcohol Dependence, 58,* 55–66.

Grov, C., Golub, S. A., Parsons, J. T., Brennan, M., & Karpiak, S. E. (2010). Loneliness and HIV-related stigma explain depression among older HIV-positive adults. *AIDS Care, 22*(5), 630–639.

Guerrero, E. G. (2009). Managerial capacity and adopton of culturally competent practices in outpatient substance abuse treatment organizations. *Journal of Substance Abuse Treatment, 39*(4), 329–339.

Hahm, H. C., & Adkins, C. (2009). A model of Asian and Pacific Islander sexual minority acculturation. *Journal of LGBT Youth, 6*(2), 155–173.

Haley, J. (1973). *Uncommon therapy: The psychiatric techniques of Milton H. Erickson, M.D.* New York: Ballantine Books.

Hall, A. S., & Parsons, J. (2001). Internet addiction: College student case study using best practices in cognitive behavior therapy. *Journal of Mental Health Counseling, 23,* 312–327.

Hall, C. W., & Webster, R. E. (2002). Traumatic symptomatology characteristics of adult children of alcoholics. *Journal of Drug Education, 32*(3), 195–211.

Hall, C. W., & Webster, R. E. (2007). Multiple stressors and adjustment among adult children of alcoholics. *Addiction Research and Theory, 15*(4), 425–434.

Hall, C. W., Webster, R. E., & Powell, E. J. (2003). Personal alcohol use in adult children of alcoholics. *Alcohol Research, 8*(4), 157–162.

Hall, J. C. (2007a). An exploratory study of differences in self-esteem, kinship social support, and coping responses among African American ACOAs and non-ACOAs. *Journal of American College Health, 56*(1), 49–54.

Hall, J. C. (2007b). An exploratory study of the role of kinship ties in promoting resilience among African American adult children of alcoholics. Journal of *Human Behavior in the Social Environment, 15*(2), 61–78.

Hall, W., & Pacula, R. L. (2003). *Cannabis use and dependence: Public health and public policy.* Cambridge, UK: Cambridge University Press.

Hammad, T. A., Laughren, T., & Racoosin, J. (2006). Suicidality in pediatric patients treated with antidepressant drugs. *Archives of General Psychiatry, 63,* 332–339.

Hanson, G., Venturelli, P. J., & Fleckenstein, A. E. (2006). *Drugs and society* (9th ed.). Boston: Jones and Bartlett.

Harkness, D., & Cotrell, G. (1997). The social construction of codependency in the treatment of substance abuse. *Journal of Substance Abuse Treatment, 14,* 473–479.

Harkness, D., Manhire, S., Blanchard, J., & Darling, J. (2011). Codependent attitude and behavior: Moderators of psychological distress in adult offspring of families with alcohol and other drug (AOD) problems. *Alcoholism Treatment Quarterly, 25*(3), 39–52.

Harkness, D., Swenson, M., Madsen-Hampton, K., & Hale, R. (2001). The development, reliability, and validity of a clinical rating scale for codependency. *Journal of Psychoactive Drugs, 33,* 159–171.

Harper, F. D. (Ed.). (1976). *Alcohol abuse and Black America.* Alexandria, VA: Douglass.

Harper, F. D. (1978). Alcohol use among North American Blacks. In Y. Israel, F. B. Glaser, H. Kalant, R. E. Popham, W. Schmidt, & R. G. Smart (Eds.), *Research advances in alcohol and drug problems* (Vol. 4, pp. 349–364). New York: Plenum Press.

Harper, M. (2006). Ethical multiculturalism: An evolutionary concept analysis. *Advances in Nursing Science, 29*(2), 110–124.

Harris, T. A. (1969). *I'm okay–you're okay.* New York: Avon Books.

Harrison, T. C. (2004). *Consultation for contemporary helping professionals.* Boston: Allyn & Bacon.

Harter, S. L. (2000). Psychosocial adjustment of adult children of alcoholics: A review of the recent empirical literature. *Clinical Psychology Review, 20,* 311–337.

Harter, S. L. (2000). Psychosocial adjustment of adult children of alcoholics: A review of the recent empirical literature. *Clinical Psychology Review, 20,* 311–337.

Harwood, H. (2000). *Updating estimates of the economic costs of alcohol abuse in the United States: Estimates, update methods, and data.* Report prepared by the Lewin Group for the National Institute on Alcohol Abuse and Alcoholism. Rockville, MD: National Institutes of Health. Based on Harwood, H., Fountain, D., & Livermore, G. (1998). *The economic costs of alcohol and drug abuse in the United States 1992.* Report prepared for the National Institute on Drug Abuse and the National Institute on Alcohol Abuse and Alcoholism, National Institutes of Health, Department of Health and Human Services. NIH Publication No. 98–4327. Rockville, MD: National Institutes of Health.

Hawkins, D. M. (1986). Understanding reactions to group instability in psychotherapy groups. *International Journal of Group Psychotherapy, 36,* 241–260.

Hawkins, J. D., Catalano, R. E., & Miller, J. Y. (1992). Risk and protective factors for alcohol and other drug problems in adolescence and early adulthood: Implications for substance abuse prevention. *Psychological Bulletin, 112,* 64–105.

Hawkins, J. D., Lishner, D. M., & Catalano, R. E. (1985, April). *Childhood predictors and the prevention of adolescent substance abuse.* Presented at the National Institute on Drug Abuse research analysis and utilization system meeting, etiology of drug abuse: Implications for prevention.

Heather, N. (1995). Interpreting the evidence on brief interventions for excessive drinkers: The need for caution. *Alcohol and Alcoholism, 30,* 287–296.

Henderson, C. E., Dakof, G. A., Greenbaum, P. E., & Liddle, H. A. (2010). Effectiveness of multidimensional family therapy with higher severity substance-abusing adolescents: Report from two randomized controlled trials. *Journal of Consulting and Clinical Psychology, 78*(6), 885–897.

Herd, D. (1991). The paradox of temperance: Blacks and the alcohol question in nineteenth-century America. In S. Barrows & R. Room (Eds.), *Drinking: behavior and belief in modern history* (pp. 354–375). Berkeley: University of California Press.

Hergenrather, K. C., & Rhodes, S. D. (2008). Consumers with HIV/AIDS: Application of theory to explore beliefs impacting employment. *Journal of Rehabilitation, 74*(1), 32–42.

Hergenrather, K. C., Rhodes, S. D., & Clark, G. (2006). Windows to work: Exploring employment seeking behaviors of persons with HIV/AIDS through PhotoVoice. *AIDS Education and Prevention, 18*(3), 243–258.

Herzog, D. B., & Eddy, K. T. (2009). Eating disorders: What are the risks? *Journal of the American Academy of Child and Adolescent Psychiatry, 48*(8), 782–783.

Hesse-Biber, S. (1989). Eating patterns and disorders in a college population: Are college women's eating problems a new phenomenon. *Sex Roles, 20,* 71–89.

Hester, R. K. (2003). Behavioral self-control training. In R. K. Hester & W. R. Miller (Eds.), *Handbook of* alcoholism treatment approaches: Effective alternatives (3rd ed., pp. 152–164). Boston: Allyn & Bacon.

Hettema, J. Steele, J., & Miller, W. R. (2005). Motivational interviewing. *Annual Review of Clinical Psychology, 1,* 91–111.

Heyman, B., & Huckle, S. (1995). Sexuality as a perceived hazard in the lives of adults with learning disabilities. *Disability and Society, 10,* 139–155.

Higgins, S. T., Budney, A. J., Bickel, H. K., Badger, G., Foerg, F., & Ogden, D. (1995). Outpatient behavioral treatment for cocaine dependence: One-year outcome. *Experimental & Clinical Psychopharmacology, 3,* 205–212.

Hill, K., & Pomeroy, C. (2001). Assessment of physical status of children and adolescents with eating disorders and obesity. In J. K. Thompson & L. Smolak (Eds.), *Body image, eating disorders, and obesity in youth* (pp. 171–192). Washington, DC: American Psychological Association.

Hines, P. M., & Boyd-Franklin, N. (1982). Black families. In M. McGoldrick, J. Pierce, & J. Giordano (Eds.), *Ethnicity and family therapy* (pp. 84–107). New York: Guilford Press.

Hines, P. M., & Boyd-Franklin, N. (2005). African American families. In McGoldrick, M., Giordano, J., & Garcia-Preto, N. (Eds.), *Ethnicity and family therapy* (3rd ed., pp. 87–100). Guilford Press: New York.

Hispanic Health Council. (1987). Conference proceedings: Alcohol use and abuse among Hispanic adolescents. Hartford, CT: Hispanic Health Council.

Ho, M. K. (1992). *Minority children and adolescents in therapy.* London: Sage.

Hoenigmann-Lion, N. M., & Whitehead, G. I. (2006). The relationship between codependency and borderline and dependent personality traits. *Alcoholism Treatment Quarterly, 24*(4), 55–77.

Hoffman, M. A. (1996). *Counseling clients with HIV disease.* New York: Guilford Press.

Hogan, J. A., Reed-Gabrielsen, K., Luna, N., & Grothaus, D. (2003). *Substance abuse prevention: The intersection of science and practice.* Boston: Allyn & Bacon.

Holt, J. L., Houg, B. L., & Romano, J. L. (1999). HIV/AIDS can clearly punctuate the spiritual concerns of individuals. *Journal of Counseling and Development, 77,* 160–170.

Hong, J. S., Hui, H., Sabir, B., & Kim, J. S. (2011). Substance abuse among Asian American youth: An ecological review of the literature. *Children and Youth Services Review, 33*(5), 669–677.

Hood, C. H. (2003). Women in recovery from alcoholism: The place of leisure. *Leisure Sciences, 25,* 51–80.

Hook, J. N., Hook, J. P., & Hines, S. (2008). Reach out or act out: Long-term group therapy for sexual addiction. *Sexual Addiction and Compulsivity, 15*(3), 217–232.

Hooker, T. (1996). *HIV/AIDS, facts to consider: 1996.* Denver, CO: National Conference of State Legislatures.

Howard, K. N., Heston, J., Key, C. M., McCrory, E., Serna-McDonald, C., Smith, R. K., & Hendrick, S. S. (2010). Addiction, the sibling, and the self. *Journal of Loss and Trauma, 15*(5), 465–479.

Hser, Y., Grella, C. E., Hubbard, R. L., Hsieh, S. C., Fletcher, B. W., Brown, B. S., Anglin, M. D. (2001). An evaluation of drug treatment for adolescents in four U.S. cities. *Archives of General Psychiatry, 58,* 689–695.

Hubbard, R. L., & French, M. T. (1991). New perspectives on the benefit-cost and cost-effectiveness of drug abuse treatment. In W. S. Cartwright & J. M. Kaple (Eds.), *Economic costs, cost-effectiveness, financing and community-based drug treatment* (NIDA Research Monograph #113, pp. 94–113). Rockville, MD: National Institute on Drug Abuse.

Hudsen, J., Hiripi, E., Pope, H., & Kessler, R. (2007). The prevalence and correlates of eating disorders in the national comorbidity survey replication. *Biological Psychiatry, 61,* 348–358.

Hughes, T. L., Wilsnack, S. C., Szalacha, L. A., Johnson, T., Bostwick, W. B., Seymour, R., . . . Aranda, F. (2006). Age and racial/ethnic differences in drinking and drinking-related problems in a community sample of lesbians. *Journal of Studies on Alcohol, 67,* 579–590.

Humphreys, J. D., Clopton, J. R., & Reich, D. A. (2007). Disordered eating behavior and obsessive-compulsive symptoms in college students: Cognitive and affective similarities. *Eating Disorders, 15,* 247–259.

Hurcom, C., Copello, A., & Orford, J. (2000). The family and alcohol: Effects of excessive drinking and conceptualizations of spouses over recent decades. *Substance Use & Misuse, 35,* 473–502.

Hussong, B. M., Huang, W., Curran, P. J., Chassin, L., & Zucker, R. A. (2010). Parent alcoholism impacts the severity and timing of children's externalizing symptoms. *Journal of Abnormal Child Psychology, 38*(3), 3677–380.

Iron Eye Dudley, J. (1992). *Choteau Creek: A Sioux reminiscence*. Lincoln: University of Nebraska Press.

Irvine, L. (1999). *Codependent forevermore*. Chicago: University of Chicago Press.

Ivey, A. E., Bradford-Ivey, M., & Simek-Morgan, L. (1996). *Counseling and psychotherapy: A multicultural perspective* (4th ed.). Boston, MA: Allyn & Bacon.

Ivey, A. E., D'Andrea, L., Bradford-Ivey, M., & Simek-Morgan, L. (2007). *Counseling and psychotherapy: A multicultural perspective* (6th ed.). Boston: Allyn & Bacon.

Jackson, D. D. (1957). The question of family homeostasis. *Psychiatric Quarterly Supplement, 31,* 79–90.

Jacobs, T., Windle, M., Seilhamer, R. A., & Bost, J. (1999). Adult children of alcoholics: Drinking, psychiatric, and psychosocial status. *Psychology of Addictive Behaviors, 13*(1), 3–21.

Jappe, L. M., Frank, G. K. W., Shott, M. E., Rollin., M. D. H., Pryor, T., Hagman, J. O., . . . Davis, E. (2011). Heightened sensitivity to reward and punishment in anorexia nervosa. *International Journal of Eating Disorders, 44*(4), 317–324.

Jarosz, P. A., Dobal, M. J., Wilson, F. L., & Schram, C. A. (2007). Food cravings and disordered eating among urban obese African American women. *Eating Behaviors, 8*(3), 374–381.

Jay, S., Freisthler, B., & Svare, G. M. (2004). Drinking in young adulthood: Is the stepparent a risk factor? *Journal of Divorce and Remarriage, 41*(2/3), 99–114.

Jellinek, E. M. (1952). Phases of alcohol addiction. *Quarterly Journal of Studies on Alcohol, 13,* 673–684.

Jellinek, E. M. (1960). *The disease concept of alcoholism*. New Haven, CT: Hillhouse Press.

Jennison, K. M., & Johnson, K. A. (2001). Parental alcoholism as a risk factor for DSM-IV-Defined alcohol abuse and dependence in American women: The protective benefits of dyadic cohesion in marital communication. *American Journal of Drug and Alcohol Abuse, 27*(2), 349–374.

Johnson, G. M., Shontz, F. C., & Locke, T. P. (1984). Relationships between adolescent drug use and parental drug behavior. *Adolescence, 19,* 295–298.

Johnson, J. L., & Rolf, S. (1988). Cognitive functioning in children from alcoholic and nonalcoholic families. *British Journal of Addiction, 83,* 849–857.

Johnson, V. E. (1973). *I'll quit tomorrow*. Toronto, Canada: Harper & Row.

Johnston, L. D., O'Malley, P. M., Bachman, J. G., & Schulenberg, J. E. (2010). *Trends in 30-day prevalence of use of various drugs for eighth, tenth, and twelfth graders*. Retrieved January 11, 2011, from http://monitoring thefuture.org/data/10data/pr10t3.pdf

Johnston, L. D., O'Malley, P. M., Bachman, J. G., & Schulenberg, J. E. (2011). *Monitoring the future: National results on adolescent drug use. Overview of key findings, 2010*. Retrieved May 23, 2010, from http://monitoringthefuture.org/pubs/monographs/mtf-overview2010.pdf

Jones, A. C. (1985). Psychological functioning in black Americans: A conceptual guide for use in psychotherapy. *Psychotherapy, 22,* 363–369.

Jones, A. S. (2007). Maternal alcohol abuse/dependence, children's behavior problems, and home environment: Estimates from the national longitudinal survey of youth using propensity score matching. *Journal of Studies on Alcohol and Drugs, 68*(2), 266–275.

Jones, D. J., Runyan, D. K., Lewis, T., Litrownik, A. J., Black, M. M., Wiley, T., . . . Nagin, D. S. (2010). Trajectories of childhood sexual abuse and early adolescent HIV/AIDS risk behaviors: The role of other maltreatment, witnessed violence, and child gender. *Journal of Child and Adolescent Psychology, 39*(5), 667–680.

Jones, J. M. (2008). One in six Americans gamble on sports: Gallup Poll, December 6–9, 2007. Retrieved June 20, 2011, from http://www.gallup.com/poll/104086/One%E2%80%90Six%E2%80%90Americans%E2%80%90Gamble%E2%80%90Sports.aspx

Jones, J. W. (1985). *Children of alcoholics screening test*. Chicago: Camelot Unlimited.

Joseph, E. B., & Bhatti, R. S. (2004). Psychosocial problems and coping patterns of HIV seropositive wives of men with HIV/AIDS. Retrieved July 24, 2007, from www.haworthpress.com/web/SWHC

Juliana, P., & Goodman, C. (1997). Children of substance abusing parents. In J. H. Lowinson, P. Ruiz, R. B. Millman, & J. G. Langrod (Eds.), *Substance abuse: A comprehensive textbook* (2nd ed., pp. 808–815). Baltimore: Williams & Wilkins.

Jung, J. (1994). *Under the influence: Alcohol and human behavior.* Pacific Grove, CA: Brooks/Cole.

Kam, J. A., & Cleveland, M. J. (2011). Perceived discrimination as a risk factor for Latina/o youth's substance use: D parent-and peer-based communication and relationship resources act as protective factors? *Health Communication, 26*(2), 111–124.

Kaminer, W. (1990). Chances are you're codependent too (p. 16). *New York Times Book Review, February 1.*

Kandel, D. B. (1989). Issues of sequencing of adolescent drug use and other problem behaviors. *Journal of Drug Issues, 3,* 55–76.

Kantor, E. (2006). *HIV transmission and prevention in prisons.* Retrieved August 5, 2007, from http:/vinsite.ucsf.edu/InSite?page=kb-07-04-3#S2X

Kanuha, V. K. (2005). Nāóhaha: Native Hawaiian families. In M. McGoldrick, J. Giordano, & N. Garcia-Preto (Eds.), *Ethnicity and family therapy* (pp. 64–76). New York: Guilford Press.

Kaplan, L. (2008). *The role of recovery support services in recovery-oriented systems of care.* DHHS Publication No. (SMA) 08-4315. Rockville, MD: Center for Substance Abuse Treatment, Substance Abuse and Mental Health Services Administration.

Karacostas, D. D., & Fisher, G. L. (1993). Chemical dependency in students with and without learning disabilities. *Journal of Learning Disabilities, 26,* 491–495.

Kashubeck, S., Walsh, B., & Crowl, A. (1994). College atmosphere and eating disorders. *Journal of Counseling and Development, 72,* 640–645.

Kaskutas, L. E. (2009). Alcoholics Anonymous effectiveness: Faith meets science. *Journal of Addictive Disease, 28,* 145–157.

Kasl, C. D. (2002). *Many roads, one journey: Moving beyond the 12 steps.* New York: HarperCollins.

Kasl, C. S. (2002). Special issues in counseling lesbian women for sexual addiction, compulsivity, and sexual codependency. *Sexual Addiction and Compulsivity, Special Issue: Women and Sexual Addiction, 9*(4), 191–208.

Katehakis, A. (2009). Affective neuroscience and the treatment of sexual addiction. *Sexual Addiction and Compulsivity, 16,* 1–31.

Kaufman, E., & Kaufman, P. (1992). From psychodynamic to structural to integrated family treatment of chemical dependency. In E. Kaufman & P. Kaufman (Eds.),

Family therapy of drug and alcohol abuse (2nd ed., pp. 34–45). Boston: Allyn & Bacon.

Kearney, F., Moore, A. R., Donegan, C. F., & Lambert, J. (2010). The ageing of HIV: Implications for geriatric medicine. *Age and Ageing, 39,* 536–541.

Kearns-Bodkin, J. N., & Leonard, K. E. (2008). Relationship functioning among adult children of alcoholics. *Journal of Studies on Addiction and Drugs, 69*(6), 941–950.

Kellett, J., Trimble, M., & Thorley, A. (1976). Anorexia nervosa after the menopause. *British Journal of Psychiatry, 128,* 555–558.

Kelley, M. L., Cash, T. F., Grant, A. R., Miles, D. L., & Santos, M. T. (2004). Parental alcoholism: Relationships to adult attachment in college women and men. *Addictive Behaviors, 29*(8), 1633–1636.

Kelley, M. L., French, A., Bountress, K., Keefe, H. A., Schroeder, V., Steer, K., . . . Gumienny, L. (2007). Parentification and family responsibility in the family of origin of adult children of alcoholics. *Addictive Behaviors, 32,* 675–685.

Kelley, M. L., French, A., Schroeder, V., Bountress, K., Fals-Steward, W., Steer, K., & Cooke, C. G. (2008). Mother-daughter and father-daughter attachment of college student ACOAs. *Substance Use and Misuse, 43*(11), 1562–1573.

Kerker, B. D., Bainbridge, J., Kennedy, J., Bennani, Y. Agerton, T., Marder, D., . . . Thorpe, L. E. (2011). A population-based assessment of the health of homeless families in New York City, 2001–2003. *American Journal of Public Health, 101*(3), 546–553.

Keyes, K. M., Hatzenbuehler, M. L., McLaughlin, K. A., Link, B., Olfson, M., Grant, B. F., & Hasin, D. (2010). Stigma and treatment for alcohol disorders in the United States. *American Journal of Epidemiology, 172*(12), 1364–1372.

Kidney, C. A., Alvarez, J., Jason, L. A., Ferrari, J. R., & Minich, L. (2011). Residents of mutual help recovery homes, characteristics and outcomes: Comparison of four US ethnic subgroups. *Drugs: Education, Prevention & Policy, 18*(1), 32–39.

Kim, H. J. (2002). Codependency: The impact of Confucian marriage and family structure on women in Korea. *Dissertation Abstracts International: Section B: The Sciences and Engineering, 63*(5-b), 2569.

Kim, J., Xiang, H., Yang, Y., & Lewis, M. W. (2010). Disparities in alcohol treatment utilization by race and type of insurance. *Alcohol Treatment Quarterly, 28*(1), 2–16.

Kim, L. I. (1996). Korean ethos. *Journal of Korean American Medical Association, 2,* 13–23.

King, L. M. (1982). Alcoholism: Studies regarding Black Americans: 1977–1980. In *Alcohol and health monograph No. 4: Special Populations Issue* (pp. 385–410). Rockville, MD: National Institute on Alcohol Abuse and Alcoholism.

Kingree, J. B., & Sullivan, B. F. (2002). Participation in Alcoholics Anonymous among African Americans. *Alcoholism Treatment Quarterly, 20*(3–4), 175–186.

Kinney, J. (2012). *Loosening the grip: A handbook of alcohol information* (10th ed). New York: McGraw-Hill.

Kirkpatrick, J. (1986). *Goodbye hangover, hello life: Self-help for women.* Canada: Collier Macmillan Canada.

Kirkpatrick, J. (1990). *Turnabout: New help for the woman alcoholic.* New York: Bantam Books.

Kitano, H. H. L. (1982). Alcohol drinking patterns: The Asian Americans. In *U.S. Department of Health and Human Services, Alcohol and Health, Monograph 4, Special Populations Issue* (pp. 411–430). Rockville, MD: National Institute on Alcohol Abuse and Alcoholism.

Kitchens, J. A. (1991). *Understanding and treating codependence.* Upper Saddle River, NJ: Prentice Hall.

Kitsantas, A., Gilligan, T. D., & Komata, A. (2003). College women with eating disorders: Self-regulation, life satisfaction, and positive/negative effect. *Journal of Psychology, 137*(4), 381–395.

Klar, H. (1987). The setting for psychiatric treatment. In A. J. Frances & R. E. Hales (Eds.), *American Psychiatric Association Annual Review* (Vol. 6, pp. 336–352). Washington, DC: American Psychiatric Association Press.

Kleinig, J., & Einstein, S. (Eds.) (2006). *Ethical challenges for intervening in drug use: Policy, research and treatment issues.* Huntsville, TX: Office of International Criminal Justice.

Krejci, J., Margolin, J., Rowland, M., & Wetzell, C. (2008). Integrated group treatment of women's substance abuse and trauma. *Journal of Groups in Addiction & Recovery, 3*(3/4), 263–283.

Krestan, J. (2000). Addiction, power, and powerlessness. In J. Krestan (Ed.), *Bridges to recovery. Addiction, family therapy, and multicultural treatment* (pp. 15–44). New York: Free Press.

Krestan, J., & Bepko, C. (1990). Codependency: The social reconstruction of the female experience. *Smith College Studies in Social Work, 60,* 216–232. Also reprinted in Babcock and McKay, 1995.

Kritsberg, W. (1985). *The adult children of alcoholics syndrome: From discovery to recovery.* Pompano Beach, FL: Health Communications.

Kroll, B. (2004). Living with the elephant: Growing up with parental substance misuse. *Child and Family Social Work, 9,* 129–140.

Kubicek, K., Carpineto, J., McDavitt, B., Weiss, G., Iverson, E. F., Au, C., . . . Kipke, M. D. (2008). Integrating professional and folk models of HIV risk: YMSM's perceptions of high-risk sex. *AIDS Education and Prevention, 20*(3), 220–238.

Kumpfer, K. L., Williams, M. K., & Baxley, G. B. (1997). *Drug abuse prevention for at-risk groups.* Rockville, MD: National Institute on Drug Abuse.

Kurian, A. (1999). Feminism and the developing world. In S. Gamble (Ed.), *Feminism and postfeminism* (pp. 66–79). New York: Routledge.

Kurtz, E. (1979). *Not-God: A history of Alcoholics Anonymous.* Center City, MN: Hazelden.

Kwate, N. O., & Meyer, I. H. (2009). Association between residential exposure to outdoor alcohol advertising and problem drinking among African American women in New York City. *American Journal of Public Health, 99*(2), 228–230.

Kwon, S. Y. (2001). Codependence and interdependence: Cross-cultural reappraisal of boundaries and relationality. *Pastoral Counseling, 50*(1), 39–52.

Ladd, G. T., & Petry, N. M. (2002). Disordered gambling among university-based medical and dental patients: A focus on Internet gambling. *Psychology of Addictive Behaviors, 16*(1), 76–79.

Larkin, J. R. (1965). *Alcohol and the Negro: Explosive issues.* Zebulon, NC: Record.

Lauby, J. L., LaPollo, A. B., Herbst, J. H., Painter, T. M., Batson, H., Pierre, A., & Milnamow, M. (2010). Preventing AIDS through live movement and sound: Efficacy of a theater-based HIV prevention intervention delivered to high-risk male adolescents in juvenile justice settings. *AIDS Education and Prevention, 22*(5), 402–416.

Laudet, A. B., Savage, R., & Mahmood, D. (2002). Pathways to long-term recovery: A preliminary investigation. *Journal of Psychoactive Drugs, 34,* 305–311.

Laudet, A. B., & White, W. (2004). *An exploration of relapse patterns among former poly substance users.* Retrieved May 19, 2011, from http://www.ndri.org/ctrs/cstar/apha.pdf

LaVeist, T. A., & Wallace, J. M. (2000). Health risk and inequitable distribution of liquor stores in African American neighborhoods. *Social Science & Medicine, 51*(4), 613–617.

Lawson, A., & Lawson, G. (1998). *Alcoholism and the family.* Gaithersburg, MD: Aspen.

Lawson, G. W., Lawson, A. W., & Rivers, P. C. (2001). *Essentials of chemical dependency counseling* (3rd ed.). Gaithersburg, MD: Aspen.

Lay, K., King, L. J., & Rangel, J. (2008). Changing characteristics of drug use between two older adult cohorts: Small sample speculations on baby boomer trends to come. *Journal of Social Work Practice in the Addictions, 8*(1), 116–126.

Ledoux, S., Miller, P., Choquet, M., & Plant, M. (2002). Family structure, parent-child relationships, and alcohol and other drug use among teenagers in France and the United Kingdom. *Alcohol and Alcoholism, 37,* 52–60.

Lee, E., Esaki, N., & Greene, R. (2009). Collocation: Integrating child welfare and substance abuse services. *Journal of Social Work Practice in the Addictions, 9,* 55–70.

Lee, E., & Mock, M. R. (2005). Asian Families: An overview. In M. McGoldrick, J. Giordano, & N. Garcia-Preto (Eds.), *Ethnicity and family therapy* (pp. 269–289). New York: Guilford Press.

Lemert, E. M. (1964). Forms and pathology of drinking in three Polynesian societies. *American Anthropology, 66,* 361–374.

Leshner, A. I. (2000). Treating the brain in drug abuse. *NIDA Notes, 15,* 1.

Lesieur, H. R., & Blume, S. B. (1987). The South Oaks Gambling Screen (SOGS): A new instrument for the identification of pathological gamblers. *American Journal of Psychiatry, 144,* 1184–1188.

Lester, B. M., Andreozzi, L., & Appiah, L. (2004). Substance use during pregnancy: Time for policy to catch up with research. *Harm Reduction Journal, 1*(5), 28–37.

Levesque, M. J., Vichesky, D. R. (2006). Raising the bar on the body beautiful: An analysis of the body image concerns of homosexual men. *Body Image, 3*(2), 45–55.

Levine, M. P., & Smolak, L. (2001). Primary prevention of body image disturbances and disordered eating in childhood and early adolescence. In J. K. Thompson & L. Smolak (Eds.), *Body image, eating disorders, and obesity in youth* (pp. 237–260). Washington, DC: American Psychological Association.

Levine, S. B. (2010). What is sexual addiction? *Journal of Sex and Marital Therapy, 36,* 261–275.

Levinson, D. J. (1978). *The seasons of a man's life.* New York: Knopf.

Li, L., & Moore, D. (2001). Disability and illicit drug use: an application of labeling theory. *Deviant Behavior, 22*(1), 1–21.

Liang, Y., & Chu, C. (2009). Personality traits and personal and organizational inducements: Antecedents of workaholism. *Social Behavior and Personality, 37*(5), 645–660.

Liddle, H. A. (2010). Multidimensional family therapy: A science-based treatment system. *Australian & New Zealand Journal of Family Therapy, 31*(2), 133–148.

Lightfoot, M. A., & Milburn, N. G. (2009). HIV prevention and African American youth: Examination of individual-level behavior is not the only answer. *Culture, Health, & Sexuality, 11*(7), 731–742.

Lindblad, F., Lindberg, L., & Hjern, A. (2006). Anorexia nervosa in young men. *International Journal of Eating Disorders, 39*(8), 662–666.

Lindley, N. R., Giordano, P. J., & Hammer, E. D. (1999*).* Codependency: Predictors and psychometric issues. *Journal of Clinical Psychology, 55*(1), 59–64.

Lipsky, S., & Caetano, R. (2009). Epidemiology of substance abuse among Latinos. *Journal of Ethnicity in Substance Abuse, 8*(3), 242–260.

Logan, S. M. L. (1992). Overcoming sex and love addiction: An expanded perspective. In E. M. Freeman (Ed.), *The addictive process: Effective social work approaches* (pp. 207–222). White Plains, NY: Longman.

Longabaugh, R. (2001). How does treatment work? *Brown University Digest of Addiction Theory and Application, 20,* 8.

Lopez, F. (1994). *Confidentiality of patient records for alcohol and other drug treatment* (Technical Assistance Publication, #13). Rockville, MD: Center for Substance Abuse Treatment.

Lundahl, B. W., Kunz, C., Brownell, C., Tollefson, D., & Burke, B. L. (2010). A meta-analysis of motivational interviewing: Twenty-five years of empirical studies. *Research of Social Work Practice, 20,* 137–160.

Lurie, N. O. (1971). The world's oldest on-going protest demonstration: North American Indian drinking patterns. *Pacific Historical Review, 40,* 311–332.

Lussier, J. P., Heil, S. H., Mongeon, J. A., Badger, G. J., & Higgins, S. T. (2006). A meta-analysis of voucher-based reinforcement therapy for substance abuse disorders. *Addiction, 101,* 192–203.

Lynch, W. C., Heil, D. P., Wagner, E., & Havens, M. D. (2007). Ethnic differences in BMI, weight concerns, and eating behaviors: Comparison of Native American, White, and Hispanic adolescents. *Body Image, 4*(2), 179–190.

Maart, S., & Jelsma, J. (2010). The sexual behavior of physically disabled adolescents. *Disability and Rehabilitation, 32*(6), 438–443.

Macrory, F., & Murphy, M. (2011). Management of the effects of prenatal drugs on children of drug-abusing parents. In *Alcohol, drugs and medication in pregnancy: the long-term outcome for the child.* London: Mac Keith Press.

Maddow, R. (2002). *Pushing for progress. HIV/AIDS in prisons.* Washington, DC: National Minority AIDS Council.

Madras, B. K., Compton, W. M, Avula, D., Stegbauer, T., Stein, J. B., & Clark, H. W. (2009). Screening, brief interventions, referral to treatment (SBIRT) for illicit drug and alcohol use at multiple healthcare sites: Comparison at intake and 6 months later. *Drug and Alcohol Dependence, 99,* 280–295.

Mair, J. (2009). Duty of confidentiality and HIV/AIDS: PD v Harvey. *Health Information Management Journal, 38*(2), 49–54.

Manisses Communication Group (1994). *Alcoholism and Drug Abuse Weekly.* Retrieved September, 22, 2003, from manissess.com/2newsletters/newsletters/adaw/adaw.htm

Manley, G., & Feree, M. C. (2002). Special issues in counseling lesbian women for sexual addiction, compulsivity, and sexual codependency. *Sexual Addiction & Compulsivity, 9*(4), 191–209.

Marino, T. M. (1995). Writing your way out of trouble. *Counseling Today,* February 8, 10.

Marlatt, G. A. (1985). Relapse prevention: Theoretical rationale and overview of the model. In G. A. Marlatt & J. R. Gordon (Eds.), *Relapse prevention: Maintenance strategies in the treatment of addictive behaviors* (pp. 3–70). New York: Guilford Press.

Marlatt, G. A., & Gordon, J. R. (Eds.). (1985). *Relapse prevention: Maintenance strategies in the treatment of addictive behaviors.* New York: Guilford Press.

Marlatt, G. A., & VandenBos, G. R. (Eds.). (1997). *Addictive behaviors.* Washington, DC: American Psychological Association.

Marlatt, G. A., Demming, B., & Reid, J. B. (1973). Loss of control drinking in alcoholics: An experimental analogue. *Journal of Abnormal Psychology, 81,* 223–241.

Martin, J. K., Tuch, S. A., & Roman, P. M. (2003). Problem drinking patterns among African Americans: The impacts of reports of discrimination, perceptions of prejudice, and "risky" coping strategies. *Journal of Health and Social Behavior, 44,* 408–425.

Martsolf, D. S. (2002). Codependency, boundaries, and professionalism. *Orthopaedic Nursing, 21*(6), 61–68.

May, P. A., & Gossage, J. P. (2001). Estimating the prevalence of fetal alcohol syndrome: A summary. *Alcohol Research & Health, 25,* 159–167.

McCarthy, B. W. (2002). The wife's role in facilitating recovery from male compulsive sexual behavior. *Sexual Addiction and Recovery, 9*(4), 275–285.

McCarthy, J. C. (1988). The concept of addictive disease. In D. E. Smith & D. R. Wesson (Eds.), *Treating cocaine dependency* (pp. 21–30). Minneapolis: Hazelden.

McCarty, C. A., Zimmerman, F. J., DiGuiseppe, D. L., & Christakis, D. A. (2005). Parental emotional support and subsequent internalizing and externalizing problems among children. *Journal of Developmental and Behavioral Pediatrics, 26,* 267–275.

McCown, W. G., & Chamberlain, L. L. (2000). Best possible odds: Contemporary treatment strategies for gambling disorders. New York: Wiley.

McCrady, B. S. (2009). Couple behavioral alcohol treatment appears efficacious for women with AUDs. *The Brown University Digest of Addiction Theory and Application, 28*(9), 1–6.

McCrady, B. S., Horvath, A. T. & Delaney, S. I. (2003). Self-help groups. In R. K. Hester & W. R. Miller (Eds.), *Handbook of alcoholism treatment approaches: Effective alternatives* (3rd ed. pp. 165–187). Elmsford, NY: Pergamon Press.

McGoldrick, M. (1998). *Re-visioning family therapy: Race, culture, and gender in clinical practice.* New York: Guilford Press.

McGoldrick, M., Giordano, J. & Garcia-Preto, N. (2005). *Ethnicity and family therapy* (3rd ed.). New York: Guilford Press.

McKinney, C. M., Caetano, R., Rodriguez, L. A., & OKoro, N. (2010). Does alcohol involvement increase the severity of intimate partner violence? *Alcoholism: Clinical & Experimental Research, 34*(4), 655–658.

McLellan, A. T., Lewis, D. C., O'Brien, C. P., & Kleber, H. D. (2000). Drug dependence, a chronic medical illness: Implications for treatment, insurance, and outcome evaluation. *Journal of the American Medical Association, 284,* 1689–1695.

McLellan, A. T., Luborsky, L., O'Brien, C. P., & Woody, G. E. (1980). An improved diagnostic instrument for substance abuse patients: The Addiction Severity Index. *Journal of Nervous and Mental Disorders, 168,* 26–33.

McMillan, L. H. W., Brady, E. C., O'Driscoll, M. P., & Marsh, N. (2002). A multifaceted validation study of Spence and Robbins' (1992) Workaholism Battery. *Journal of Occupational and Organizational Psychology, 75,* 357–368.

McMillan, L. H. W., O'Driscoll, M. P., & Burke, R. J. (2003). Workaholism: A review of theory, research, and future directions. In C. L. Cooper & I. T. Robertson (Eds.), *International Review of Industrial and Organizational Psychology, 18,* 167–189.

Mee-Lee, D. (2005). *Overview of the ASAM Patient Placement Criteria Second Edition Revised (ASAM PPC-2R).* Retrieved May 10, 2011, from http://coce.samhsa.gov/cod_resources/PDF/ASAMPatientPlacementCriteria Overview5-05.pdf

Meness, M. M. (2000). The specificity of disrupted processes in families of adult children of alcoholics. *Alcohol and Alcoholism, 35,* 361–367.

Menezes, P. R., Johnson, S., Thornicroft, G., Marshall, J., Prosser, D., Bebbington, P., Kuipers, E. (1996). Drug and alcohol problems among individuals with severe mental illness in south London. *British Journal of Psychiatry, 168,* 612–619.

Metlife Mature Market Institute®2 and The Lesbian and Gay Aging Issues Network of the American Society on Aging, (2010). 'Out and aging: The MetLife study of lesbian and gay baby boomers. *Journal of GLBT Family Studies, 6*(1), 40–57.

Miller, J. C., Meier, E., & Weatherly, J. N. (2009). Assessing the reliability of the gambling functional assessment. *Journal of Gambling Studies, 25,* 121–129.

Miller, W. R. (1998). Researching the spiritual dimensions of alcohol and other drug problems. *Addiction, 93,* 979–990.

Miller, W. R. (2003). Enhancing motivation for change. In R. K. Hester & W. R. Miller (Eds.), *Handbook of alcoholism treatment approaches: Effective alternatives* (3rd ed., pp. 131–151). Boston: Allyn & Bacon.

Miller, W. R., & Hester, R. K. (2003). Treating alcohol problems: Toward an informed eclecticism. In R. K. Hester & W. R. Miller (Eds.), *Handbook of alcoholism treatment approaches: Effective alternatives* (2nd ed., pp. 1–12). Boston: Allyn & Bacon.

Miller, W. R., & Kurtz, E. (1994). Models of alcoholism used in treatment: Contrasting AA and other perspectives with which it is often confused. *Journal of Studies on Alcohol, 55,* 159–166.

Miller, W. R., & Rollnick, S. (2002). Motivational interviewing: Preparing people for change (3rd ed.). New York: Guilford Press.

Miller, W. R., Westerberg, V. S., & Waldron, H. B. (1995). Evaluating alcohol problems in adults and adolescents. In R. K. Hester & W. R. Miller (Eds.), *Handbook of alcoholism treatment approaches: Effective approaches* (3rd ed., pp. 61–88). Boston: Allyn & Bacon.

Miller, W. R., Wilbourne, P. L., & Hettema, J. E. (2003). What works?: A summary of alcohol treatment outcome research. In R. K. Hester & W. R. Miller (Eds.), *Handbook of alcoholism treatment approaches: Effective approaches* (3rd ed., pp. 13–63). Boston: Allyn & Bacon.

Milrad, R. (1999). Coaddictive recovery: Early recovery issues for spouse of sex addicts. *Sexual Addiction and Recovery, 6,* 125–136.

Minino, A. M., Xu, J. Q., & Kochanek, K. D. (2010). *Deaths: Preliminary data for 2008.* Retrieved December 22, 2010, from http://www.cdc.gov/nchs/data/nvsr/nvsr59/nvsr59_02.pdf

Mintz, L. B., & Betz, N. E. (1988). Prevalence and correlates of eating disordered behaviors among undergraduate women. *Journal of Counseling Psychology, 35,* 463–471.

Minuchin, S. (1974). *Families and family therapy.* Cambridge, MA: Harvard University Press.

Mojtabai, R. (2005). Use of specialty substance abuse and mental health services in adults with substance abuse use disorder in the community. *Drug and Alcohol Dependence, 78,* 345–354.

Moore, D. G., Turner, J. J. D., Goodwin, J. E., Fulton, S. E., Singer, L. T., & Parrott, A. C. (2011). In utero exposure to the popular "recreational" drugs MDMA (ecstasy) and methamphetamine (ice, crystal): Preliminary findings. In *Alcohol, drugs and medication in pregnancy: the long-term outcome for the child.* London: Mac Keith Press.

Moos, R. H., Brennan, P. L., Schutte, K. K., & Moos, B. S. (2010). Spouses of older adults with late-life drinking problems: Health, family, and social functioning. *Journal of Studies on Alcohol & Drugs, 71*(4), 506–514.

Morahan-Martin, J. (2005). Internet abuse: Addiction? Disorder? Symptom? Alternative explanations? *Social Science Computer Review, 23*(1), 29–48.

Morley, J. E., & Castele, S. C. (1985). Death by starvation: The Sepulveda Grecc Method No. 6. *Geriatric Medicine Today, 4,* 76–78, 83.

Mphande-Finn, J. T., & Sommers-Flanagan, J. S. (2007). The experience of HIV/AIDS among rural women in the northwestern United States: A qualitative analysis. *Journal of Community Psychology, 35*(1), 3–11.

Mueller, M. D., & Wyman, J. R. (1997). Study sheds new light on the state of drug abuse treatment nationwide. *NIDA Notes, 12,* 1, 4–8.

Myers, H. F., Javanbakht, M., Martinez, M., & Obediah, S. (2003). Psychosocial predictors of risky sexual behaviors in African American men: Implications for prevention. *AIDS Education and Prevention, 15* (Supplement A), 66–79.

NA World Services (2010). Narcotics Anonymous membership survey. Retrieved May 20, 2010, from http://www.na.org/admin/include/spaw2/uploads/pdf/NA_membership_survey.pdf

Nace, E. P. (1987). *The treatment of alcoholism.* New York: Brunner/Mazel.

Nace, E. P. (2005). Alcoholics Anonymous. In J. H. Lowinson, P. Ruiz, R. B. Millman, & J. G. Langrod (Eds.), *Substance abuse: A comprehensive textbook* (4th ed., pp. 587–599). Baltimore: Williams & Wilkins.

Najavits, L. M., Weiss, R. D., & Shaw, S. R. (1997). The link between substance abuse and posttraumatic stress disorder in women. *American Journal on Addictions, 6,* 273–283.

Napoli, M., Marsiglia, F. F., & Kullis, S. (2003). Sense of belonging in school as a protective factors against drug abuse among Native American urban adolescents. *Journal of Social Work Practice in the Addictions, 3*(2), 25–41.

National Center on Addiction and Substance Abuse at Columbia University. (2010). *Behind bars II: Substance abuse and America's prison population.* Retrieved January 5, 2011, from http://www.casacolumbia.org/templates/PressReleases.aspx?articleid=556&zoneid=85

National Center on Addiction and Substance Abuse at Columbia University. (2009). *Shoveling up II: The impact of substance abuse on federal, state, and local budgets.* Retrieved January 5, 2011, from http://www.casacolumbia.org/articlefiles/380-ShovelingUpII.pdf

National Coalition for the Homeless. (2011). Homepage. Retrieved April 25, 2011, from http://www.nationalhomeless.org/

National Council on Problem Gambling. (1997). *Problem and pathological gambling in America: The national picture.* Washington, DC: The Council.

National Council on Problem Gambling. (2009). *About problem gambling.* Retrieved June 17, 2011, from http://www.ncpgambling.org/i4a/pages/Index.cfm?pageID=3315

National Gambling Impact and Policy Study Commission. (1999). *National Gambling Impact Study Commission's final report, June 18, 1999.* Retrieved March 11, 2003, from http://govinfo. library.unt.edu/ngisc/reports/fullrpt.html

National Institute of Allergy and Infectious Diseases. (2009). *Tuberculosis and HIV infection.* Retrieved June 7, 2011, from http://www.niaid.nih.gov/topics/tuberculosis/understanding/pages/tbhiv.aspx

National Institute on Aging. (2009). *AgePage: HIV, AIDS, and older people.* Retrieved June 10, 2011, from http://www.nia.nih.gov/HealthInformation/Publications/hiv-aids.htm

National Institute on Alcohol Abuse and Alcoholism. (2007). *Helping patients who drink too much: A clinician's guide* (updated edition). Retrieved May 4, 2011, from http://pubs.niaaa.nih.gov/publications/practitioner/cliniciansguide2005/guide.pdf

National Institute on Alcohol Abuse and Alcoholism. *Helping patients who drink too much: A clinician's guide*. Updated 2005 Edition, NIM Publication No. 07-3769. Bethesda, MD: National Institute on Alcohol Abuse and Alcoholism; 2007. Retrieved June 13, 2011, from http://pubs.niaaa.nih.gov/publications/Practitioner/CliniciansGuide2005/guide.pdf

National Institute on Drug Abuse. (2003). *Preventing drug abuse among children and adolescents: A research-based guide* (2nd ed.). Retrieved May 23, 2011, from http://www.drugabuse.gov/pdf/prevention/RedBook.pdf

National Institute on Drug Abuse. (2006). National Institute on Drug Abuse Conference: Children of Parents in the Criminal Justice System: Children at risk. Bethesda, Nov. 6, 2006. Retrieved August 9, 2007, from www.drugabuse.gov/whatsnew/meetings/children_at_risk/powerpoint/Mullen.ppt+

National Institute on Drug Abuse. (2011). *New report on the global AIDS epidemic*. Retrieved June 7, 2011. from http://international.drugabuse.gov/about-us/news/2011/01/new-report-global-aids-epidemic

National Institutes of Health. (2007). *Binge eating disorder*. Retrieved July 5, 2007, from http://win.niddk.nih.gov/publications/PDFs/bingedis10.04.pdf

National Institutes of Health. (2011a). *HIV/AIDS: Turning discovery into health*. Retrieved June 7, 2011, from http://www.nih.gov/about/discovery/infectiousdiseases/hiv.htm

National Institutes of Health. (2011b). *NIH study examines best time for healthy HIV-infected people to begin antiretrovirals*. Retrieved June 7, 2011, from http://www.niaid.nih.gov/news/newsreleases/2011/Pages/START.aspx

National Institutes of Health. (2011c). *Neonatal abstinence syndrome*. Retrieved June 30, 2011, from www.nlm.nih.gov/medlineplus/ency/article/007313.htm

Neff, J. A. (2008). A new multidimensional measure of spirituality-religiosity for use in diverse substance abuse treatment populations. *Journal for the Scientific Study of Religion, 47*(3), 393–409.

Neuman, P. A., & Halvorson, P. A. (1983). *Anorexia nervosa and bulimia: A handbook for counselors and therapists*. New York: Van Nostrand Reinhold.

New York State Division of Alcoholism and Alcohol Abuse. (1989). *The gateway to other drug use*. Buffalo, NY: Research Institute on Alcoholism.

Newton, M. S., & Ciliska, D. (2006). Internet-based innovations for the prevention of eating disorders: A systematic review. *Eating Disorders, 14*(5), 365–385.

Nie, N. H., & Erbing, L. (2000). *Internet and society: A preliminary report*. Palo Alto, CA: Stanford Institute for Quantitative Study of Society.

Noone, R., & Reddig, R. (1976). Case studies in the family treatment of drug abuse. *Family Process, 15,* 325–332.

Noordenbos, G., & Seubring, A. (2006). Criteria for recovery from eating disorders according to patients and therapists. *Eating Disorders, 14,* 41–54.

Nord, D. (1997). *Multiple AIDS-related loss*. Washington, DC: Taylor & Francis.

Norwood, R. (1985). *Women who love too much: When you keep wishing and hoping he'll change*. New York: Pocket Books.

Nower, N., & Blaszcyznski, A. (2008). Recovery in pathological gambling: An imprecise concept. *Substance Use and Misuse, 43,* 1844–1864.

O'Farrell, T. J., & Fals-Stewart, W. (2003). Marital and family therapy. In R. K. Hester & W. R. Miller (Eds.), *Handbook of alcoholism treatment approaches: Effective alternatives* (3rd ed., pp. 188–212). Boston: Allyn & Bacon.

O'Leary, A., & Jemmott, L. S. (1995). General issues in the prevention of AIDS in women. In A. O'Leary & L.S.D. Jemmott (Eds.), *Women at risk: Issues in the primary prevention of AIDS* (pp. 1 – 12). New York: Plenum Press.

O'Malley, S. S., & Kosten, T. R. (2006). Pharmcotherapy of addictive disorders. In W. R. Miller & K. M. Carroll (Eds.), *Rethinking substance abuse: What the science shows, and what we should do about it* (pp. 240–256). New York: Guilford Press.

Oashi, K., & Nishimura, H. (1978). *Alcoholic problems in Japan*. Paper presented at the 9th World Congress of Sociology, Uppsala University, Sweden.

Oates, W. (1971). *Confessions of a workaholic*. New York: World.

Odets, W. (1995). *In the shadow of the epidemic: Being HIV-negative in the age of AIDS*. Durham, NC: Duke University Press.

O'Farrell, T. J., & Fals-Stewart, W. (2006). *Behavioral couples therapy for alcoholism and drug abuse*. New York: Guilford Press.

Office of Applied Studies. (2002). *National and state estimates of the drug abuse treatment gap: 2000 National Household Survey on Drug Abuse* (NHSDA Series H-14, DHHS Publication No. SMA 02-3640).

Rockville, MD: Substance Abuse and Mental Health Services Administration.

Office of Applied Studies, Substance Abuse and Mental Health Services Administration. (2010). *Results from the 2009 National Survey on Drug Use & Health: Detailed Tables.* Retrieved December 16, 2010, from http://oas.samhsa.gov/NSDUH/2k9NSDUH/tabs/Sect1peTabs24to28.pdf

Office of National Drug Control Policy. (2011a). No title. Retrieved May 23, 2011, from http://www.whitehousedrugpolicy.gov/publications/policy/11budget/ondcp.pdf

Office of National Drug Control Policy. (2011b). Table 1: Federal drug control spending by function. Retrieved May 23, 2011, from http://www.whitehousedrugpolicy.gov/publications/policy/11budget/table1.pdf

O'Hannessian, C. M., & Kesselbrock, V. M. (2009). A finer examination of the role that negative affect plays in the relationship between parental alcoholism and the onset of alcohol and marijuana use. *Journal of Studies on Alcoholism and Drugs, 70*(3), 400–408.

Ohlms, D. L. (1995). *The disease concept of alcoholism.* Cahokia, IL: GWC.

Olmsted, M. E., Crowell, J. A., & Waters, E. (2003). Assortive mating among adult children of alcoholics and alcoholics. *Family Relations, 32,* 64–71.

Opitz, D. M., Tsytsarev, S. V., & Froh, J. (2009). Women's sexual addiction and family dynamics, depression and substance abuse. *Sexual Addiction & Compulsivity, 16*(4), 324–340.

Orsulic-Jeras, S., Shepherd, J. B., & Britton, P. J. (2003). Counseling older adults with HIV/AIDS: A strength-based model of treatment. *Journal of Counseling and Development, 25,* 233–244.

Orzack, M. H. (2004). *Computer compulsion services.* Retrieved July 24, 2007, from www.computercompulsion.com

Ostermann, J., Sloan, F. A., & Taylor, D. H. (2005). Heavy alcohol use and marital dissolution in the USA. *Social Sciences and Medicine, 61*(11), 2304–2316.

Otten, R., van der Zwaluw, C. S., van der Vorst, H., & Engels, R. C. M. E. (2008). Partner effects and bidirectional parent-child effects in family alcohol use. *European Addiction Research, 14*(2), 106–112.

Owen, B. (2004). Women and imprisonment in the United States: The gendered consequences of the U.S. imprisonment binge. In B. Price & N. Sokoloff (Eds.), *The*

criminal justice system and women (2nd ed., pp. 195–206). New York: McGraw-Hill.

Paglia, A., & Room, R. (1998). *Preventing substance use problems among youth: A literature review and recommendations.* Paper presented at the Alcohol Policy XI Conference, May 10–13, 1998, Chicago.

Palfai, T., & Jankiewicz, H. (1997). *Drugs and human behavior* (2nd ed.). Dubuque, IA: W. C. Brown.

Paltrow, L. M. (2004). The war on drugs and the war on abortion. In B. Price & N. Sokoloff (Eds.), *The criminal justice system and women* (2nd ed., pp. 165–194). New York: McGraw-Hill.

Pargament, K. I. (2006). The meaning of spiritual transformation. In J. D. Koss-Chioino & P. Hefner (Eds.), *Spiritual transformation and healing: Anthropoligical, theological, neuroscientific, and clinical perspectives* (pp. 10–24). Lanham, MD: AltaMira.

Parker, F. (1980). Sex-role adjustment in women alcoholics. In C. Eddy & J. Ford (Eds.), *Alcoholism in women* (pp. 6–15). Dubuque, IA: Kendall/Hunt.

Parrino, M. W. (2002). Methadone maintenance and other pharmacotherapeutic interventions in the treatment of opioid dependence. *Drug Court Practitioner Fact Sheet, III,* 3.

Parsai, M., Marsiglia, F. F., & Kulis, S. (2010). Parental monitoring, religious involvement and drug abuse among Latino and non-Latino youth in the Southwestern United States. *British Journal of Social Work, 40*(1), 100–114.

Parsai, M. N., Voisine, S., Marsiglia, F. F., Kulis, S., & Nieri, T. (2009). The protective and risk effects of parents and peers on substance use, attitudes, and behaviors of Mexican and Mexican American female and male adolescents. *Youth Society, 40*(3), 353–376.

Patock-Peckham, J. A., & Morgan-Lopez, A. A. (2009). Mediational links among parenting styles, perceptions of parental confidence, self-esteem, and depression on alcohol-related problems in emerging adulthood. *Journal of Studies on Alcohol and Drugs, 70*(2), 215–226.

Patterson, M., Stern, S., Crawford, P., McMahon, R., Similo, S., & Schreiber, G. (1997). Sociodemographic factors and obesity in preadolescent black and white girls: NJLBI's growth and health study. *Journal of the National Medical Association, 89,* 594–600.

Patterson, T. L., & Jeste, D. V. (1999). The potential impact of the baby boom generation on substance abuse among elderly persons. *Psychiatric Services, 50,* 1184–1188.

Pattison, E. M., & Kaufman, E. (1982). The alcoholism syndrome: Definitions and models. In E. M. Pattison & E. Kaufman (Eds.), *Encyclopedic handbook of alcoholism* (pp. 3– 30). New York: Gardner Press.

Paul, N. (1967). The use of empathy in the resolution of grief. *Perspectives in Biology and Medicine, 2,* 153–169.

Pedersen, P. B. (2002). Ethics, competence, and other professional issues in culture-centered counseling. In P. B. Pedersen, J. Draguns, W. Lonner, & J. Trimble (Eds.), *Counseling across cultures* (5th ed., pp. 3–28). Thousand Oaks, CA: Sage.

Peele, S. (1984). The cultural context of psychological approaches to alcoholism: Can we control the effects of alcohol? *American Psychologist, 39,* 1337–1351.

Peele, S. (1988). On the diseasing of America. *Utne Reader, 30,* 67.

Peele, S. (1989). *Diseasing of America: Addiction treatment out of control.* Lexington, MA: Lexington Books.

Peele, S., & Brodsky, A. (1991). *Love and addiction* (2nd ed.). New York: Signet.

Pereira, A. (2010). HIV/AIDS and discrimination in the workplace: The cook and the surgeon living with HIV. *European Journal of Health Law, 17,* 139–147.

Peteet, J. R. (1993). A closer look at the role of a spiritual approach in addictions treatment. *Journal of Substance Abuse Treatment, 10,* 263–267.

Petry, N. M., & Martin, B. (2002). Low-cost contingency management for treating cocaine- and opioid-abusing methadone patients. *Journal of Consulting and Clinical Psychology, 70,* 398–405.

Phoca, S. (1999). Feminism and gender. In S. Gamble (Ed.), *Feminism and postfeminism, 1999* (pp. 55–65). New York: Routledge.

Pickett, K. E., & Wakschlag, L. S. (2011).The short-term and long-term developmental consequences of maternal smoking during pregnancy. In *Alcohol, drugs and medication in pregnancy: The long-term outcome for the child.* London: Mac Keith Press.

Pimentel, R., & Lamendella, J. (1988). *Perspectives: AIDS in the workplace.* Northridge, CA: Milt Wright & Associates.

Polich, J. M., Armor, D. M., & Braiker, H. B. (1981). *The course of alcoholism: Four years after treatment.* New York: Wiley.

Pope, R. C., Wallhagen, M., & Davis, H. (2010). The social determinants of substance abuse in African American baby boomers: Effects of family, media images, and environment. *Journal of Transcultural Nursing, 21*(3), 246–256.

Potter-Efron, R. T., & Potter-Efron, P. S. (1989). Assessment of codependency with individuals from alcoholic and chemically dependent families. *Alcohol Treatment Quarterly, 6,* 37–57.

Prendergast, M., Podus, D., Finney, J., Greenwell, L., & Roll, J. (2006). Contingency management for treatment of substance use disorders: A meta-analysis. *Addiction, 101,* 1546–1560.

Price, W. A., Giannini, A. J., & Colella, J. (1985). Anorexia nervosa in the elderly. *Journal of the American Geriatric Society, 33,* 213–215.

Primm, B. J. (1992). Future outlook: Treatment improvement. In J. H. Lowinson, P. Ruiz, R. B. Millman, & J. C. Langrod (Eds.), *Substance abuse: A comprehensive textbook* (2nd ed., pp. 612–627). Baltimore: Williams & Wilkins.

Prochaska, J. O., & DiClemente, C. C. (1982). Transtheoretical therapy: Toward a more integrative model of change. *Psychotherapy: Theory, Research, and Practice, 19,* 276–288.

Proehl, R. A. (2007). Social justice, respect, and meaning-making: Keys to working with the homeless elderly population. *Health & Social Work, 32*(4), 304–307.

Project MATCH Research Group (1997). Matching alcoholism treatments to client heterogeneity: Project MATCH posttreatment drinking outcomes. *Journal of Studies on Alcohol, 58,* 7–29.

Quirk, D. E., Hodgen, C., Springborn, D., Howell, G. E., & Daus, L. J. (2010). *Gambling patient placement criteria (GPPC): A guide to placing problem gamblers at the optimum level of care.* Reno: Institute for the Study of Gambling & Commercial Gaming, College of Business, University of Nevada, Reno.

Race, K. D. (2003). Revalutaion of risk among gay men. *AIDS Education and Prevention, 15*(4), 369–381.

Rangarajan, S., & Kelly, L. (2006). Family communication patterns, family environment, and the impact of parental alcoholism on offspring self-esteem. *Journal of Social and Personal Relationships, 23,* 655–671.

Rawson, R., Shoptaw, S., Obert, J. L., McCann, M., Hasson, A., Marinelli-Casey, P., . . . Brethen, P. R. (1995). An intensive outpatient approach for cocaine abuse: The

Matrix Model. *Journal of Substance Abuse Treatment, 12,* 117–127.

Reilly, D. M. (1992). Drug-abusing families: Intrafamilial dynamics and brief triphasic treatment. In E. Kaufman & P. Kaufman (Eds.), *Family theory of drug and alcohol abuse* (pp. 105– 119). Boston: Allyn & Bacon.

Reynaud, M., Karila, L., Blecha, L., & Benyamina, A. (2010). Is love passion an addictive disorder? *American Journal of Drug and Alcohol Abuse, 36*(5), 261–267.

Rhodes, T., Bernays, S., & Houmoller, K. (2010). Parents who use drugs: Accounting for damage and its limitation. *Social Science & Medicine, 71*(8), 1489–1497.

Rice, J. (1992). Discursive formation, life stories, and the emergence of codependency: Power/knowledge and the search for identity. *Sociological Quarterly, 33,* 337–364.

Ringwald, C. D. (2003). Spirituality: An evidence-based practice for treatment and recovery. *Counselor, The Magazine for Addiction Professionals, 4,* 32–37.

Roberts, L. J., & McCrady, B. S. (2003). Alcohol problems in intimate relationships: Identification and intervention. A guide for marriage and family therapists. Washington, DC: National Institute of Health (Publication No. 03-5284).

Robins, L. N., & Guze, S. B. (1971). Drinking practices and problems in urban ghetto populations. In N. K. Mello & J. H. Mendelson (Eds.), *Recent advances in studies of alcoholism* (pp. 825–842). Rockville, MD: National Institute on Alcohol Abuse and Alcoholism.

Robinson, B. (2000). Chained to the desk. *Family Therapy Networker, 24*(4), 26–33.

Robinson, B. E. (1999). The Work Addiction Risk Test: Development of a tentative measure of workaholism. *Perceptual and Motor Skills, 88,* 199–210.

Robinson, T. N., & Killen, J. D. (2001). Obesity prevention for children. In J. K. Thompson & L. Smolak (Eds.), *Body image, eating disorders, and obesity in youth* (pp. 237–260). Washington, DC: American Psychological Association.

Rogers, R. L., & Petrie, T. A. (2001). Psychological correlates of anorexic and bulimic symptomatology. *Journal of Counseling and Development, 79,* 178–187.

Roget, N., & Johnson, M. (1995). Pre and post treatment planning in the substance abuse treatment case management process. Carson City, NV: Bureau of Alcohol and Drug Abuse.

Rohleder, P. (2010). Educators' ambivalence and managing anxiety in providing sex education for people with learning disabilities. *Psychodynamic Practice, 16*(2), 165–182.

Room, R. (2005). Multicultural contexts and alcohol and drug use as symbolic behavior. *Addiction Research and Theory, 13*(4), 321–331.

Room, R., & Mäkelä, K. (2000). Typologies of the cultural position of drinking. *Journal of Studies on Alcohol, 61,* 475–483.

Roozen, H. G., Boulogne, J. J., van Tulder, M. W., van den Brink, W., De Jong, C. A. J., & Kerkhof, A. J. F. M. (2004). A systematic review of the effectiveness of the community reinforcement approach in alcohol, cocaine and opioid addiction. *Drug and Alcohol Dependence, 74,* 1–13.

Ross, L. (2004). Native women, mean-spirited drugs, and punishing policies. *Social Justice, 31*(4), 54–63.

Rounsaville, B. J., Weissman, M. M., Kleber, H. D., & Wilbur, C. (1982). Heterogeneity of psychiatric diagnosis in treated opiate addicts. *Archives of General Psychiatry, 39,* 161–166.

Rowan, N. L., & Faul, A. C. (2011). Gay, lesbian, bisexual, and transgendered people and chemical dependency: Exploring successful treatment. *Journal of Gay & Lesbian Social Services, 23*(1), 107–130.

Rowe, C. L., La Greca, A. M., & Alexandersson, A. (2010). Family and individual factors associated with substance abuse involvement and PTS symptoms among adolescents in Greater New Orleans after Hurricane Katrina. *Journal of Consulting and Clinical Psychology, 78*(6), 806–817.

Royce, J. E. (1989). *Alcohol problems and alcoholism: A comprehensive survey* (Rev. ed.). New York: Free Press.

Russell, M., Henderson, C., & Blume, S. (1985). *Children of alcoholics: A review of the literature.* New York: Children of Alcoholics Foundation.

Ryan, S. M., Jorm, A. F., & Lubman, D. I. (2010). Parenting factors associated with reduced adolescent alcohol use: A systematic review of the longitudinal studies. *Australian and New Zealand Journal of Psychiatry, 44*(9), 774–783.

Sager, C., Brown, H., Crohn, H., & Walker, L. (1983). *Treating the remarried family.* New York: Brunner-Mazel.

Saint-Jean, G., Martinez, C., & Crandall, L. (2008). Psychosocial mediators of impact of acculturation on adolescent substance abuse. *Journal of Immigrant & Minority Health, 10*(2), 187–195.

Samenow, C. P. (2010). Classifying problematic sexual behaviors—It's all in the name. *Sexual Addiction & Compulsivity, 17,* 3–6.

Sanders, M. (2002). The response of African American communities to alcohol and other drug problems: An opportunity for treatment providers. *Alcoholism Treatment Quarterly, 20*(3–4), 167–173.

Satir, V. M. (1964). *Conjoint family therapy: A guide to theory and technique.* Palo Alto, CA: Science and Behavioral Books.

Schaef, A. W. (1987). *When society becomes addict.* San Francisco: Harper & Row.

Schroeder, D. S., Laflin, M. T., & Weis, D. L. (1993). Is there a relationship between self-esteem and drug use? Methodological and statistical limitations of the research. *Journal of Drug Issues, 23,* 645–665.

Schuck, A. M., & Spatz, W. C. (2003). Childhood victimization and alcohol symptoms in women: An examination of protective factors. *Journal of Studies on Alcohol, 64,* 247–257.

Schultz, E. (1994). If you use firm's counselors, remember your secrets could be used against you. *Wall Street Journal,* May 26, C2.

Schwartz, D. M., Thompson, M. G., & Johnson, C. (1983). Anorexia and bulimia: The sociocultural context. *International Journal of Eating Disorders, 1,* 20–36.

Secular Organizations for Sobriety (SOS) (n.d.). Brief history of the SOS movement. Retrieved May 20, 2011, from http://www.cfiwest.org/sos/find.htm#Brief%20History

Selwyn, P. A. (1992). Medical aspects of human immunodeficiency virus infection and its treatment in injecting drug users. In J. H. Lowinson, P. Ruiz, R. B. Millman, & J. G. Langrod (Eds.), *Substance abuse: A comprehensive textbook* (2nd ed., pp. 744–774). Baltimore: Williams & Wilkins.

Selwyn, P. A., Feingold, A. R., & Iezza, A. (1989). Primary care for patients with human immunodeficiency virus (HIV) infection in a methadone treatment program. *Annals of Internal Medicine, 111,* 761–763.

Selzer, M. L. (1971). The Michigan Alcohol Screening Test: The quest for a new diagnostic instrument. *American Journal of Psychiatry, 127,* 1653–1658.

Senreich, E. (2009). A comparison of perceptions, reported abstinence, and completion rates of gay, lesbian, and heterosexual clients in substance abuse treatment. *Journal of Gay & Lesbian Mental Health, 13,* 145–169.

Senreich, E. (2010). Are specialized LGBT program components helpful for gay and bisexual men in substance abuse treatment? *Journal of Gay and Lesbian Social Services, 45,* 1077–1096.

Senreich, E. (2011). Differences in outcomes, completion rates, and perceptions of treatment between White, Black, and Hispanic GLBT clients in substance abuse programs. *Journal on Studies of Alcohol, 78*(2), 687–694.

Serovich, J. (2001). A test of two disclosure theories. *AIDS Education and Prevention, 13,* 355–364.

Shaffer, H. J. (1999). Gambling, drinking, smoking and other health risk activities among casino employees. *American Journal of Industrial Medicine, 36*(3), 365–372.

Shambley-Ebron, D. Z. (2009). My sister, myself: A culture- and gender-based approach to HIV/AIDS prevention. *Journal of Transcultural Nursing, 20*(28), 28–36.

Sher, K. (1991). *Children of alcoholics: A critical appraisal of theory and research.* Chicago: University of Chicago Press.

Shon, S. P., & Ja, D. Y. (1982). Asian families. In M. McGoldrick, J. Pierce, & J. Giordano (Eds.), *Ethnicity and family therapy* (pp. 208–228). New York: Guilford Press.

Sideman, L. M., & Kirschbaum, E. (2002). The road to recovery: A gender-responsive program for convicted DUI females. *Corrections Today, 64,* 84–89.

Simpson, D. D., Joe, G. W., & Broome, K. M. (2002). A national 5-year follow-up of treatment outcomes for cocaine dependence. *Archives of General Psychiatry, 59,* 538–544.

Sim, L. A., McAlpine, D. W., Grothe, K. B., Himes, S. M., Cockerill, R. G., & Clark, M. M. (2010). Identification and treatment of eating disorders in the primary care setting. *Mayo Clinic Proceedings, 85*(8), 746–751.

Singer, L. T., & Minnes, S., (2011). Effect of drugs of abuse on the fetus: cocaine and opiates including heroin. In *Alcohol, drugs and medication in pregnancy: the long-term outcome for the child.* London: Mac Keith Press.

Skinner, H. A. (1982). The drug abuse screening test. *Addictive Behaviors, 7,* 363–371.

Slomkowski, C., Conger, K. J., Rende, R., Heylen, E., Little, W. M., Shebloski . . . Conger, R. D. (2009). Sibling contagion for drinking in adolescence: A micro process framework. *European Journal of Developmental Science, 3*(2), 161–173.

Small, J., Curran, G. M., & Booth, B. (2010). Barriers and facilitators for alcohol treatment for women: Are there more or less for rural women? *Journal of Substance Abuse Treatment, 39*(1), 1–13.

SMART Recovery (2011). Frequently asked questions about SMART Recovery. Retrieved May 20, 2011, from http://www.smartrecovery.org/resources/faq.htm#Q.%20What%20is%20SMART%20Recovery%C2%AE

Sobell, L. C., Cunningham, J. A., & Sobell, M. B. (1996). Recovery from alcohol problems with and without treatment: Prevalence in two population surveys. *American Journal of Public Health, 86,* 966–972.

Sobell, L. C., & Sobell, M. B. (1973). A self-feedback technique to monitor drinking behavior in alcoholics. *Behavior Research and Therapy, 11,* 237–238.

Sobell, L. C., Sobell, M. B., & Toneatto, T. (1991). Recovery from alcohol problems without treatment. In N. Heather, W. R., Miller, & J. Greeley (Eds.), *Self-control and addictive behaviors* (pp. 198–242). New York: Pergamon Press.

Solórzano, L., & Glassgold, S. (2010). Powerful youth: Determining successful participation in an HIV support group for youth. *Social Work with Groups, 33*(4), 288–303.

Sorensen, J. L., & Batki, S. L. (1992). Management of the psychosocial sequelae of HIV infection among drug abusers. In J. H. Lowinson, P. Ruiz, R. B. Millman, & J. G. Langrod (Eds.), *Substance abuse: A comprehensive textbook* (2nd ed., pp. 788–793). Baltimore: Williams & Wilkins.

Southern, S. (2002). A qualitative case study of two chemically dependent women with compulsive sexual behaviors. *Sexual Addiction and Recovery, 9,* 231–249.

Spence, J. T., & Robbins, A. (1992). Workaholism: Definition, measurement, and preliminary results. *Journal of Personality Assessment, 58*(1), 160–179.

Springer, C. A., & Lease, S. H. (2000). The impact of multiple-AIDS related bereavement in the gay male population. *Journal of Counseling and Development, 78*(3), 297–305.

Stack, S., Wasserman, I., & Kern, R. (2004). Adult social bonds and use of Internet pornography. *Social Science Quarterly, 85*(1), 75–88.

Stampp, K. (1956). *The peculiar institution: Slavery in the ante-bellum South.* New York: Knopf.

Steer, R. A., Shaw, B. F., Beck, A. T., & Fine, E. W. (1977). Structure and depression in Black alcoholics. *Psychological Reports,* 1235–1241.

Steinglass, P., Bennett, L. A., Wolin, S. J., & Reiss, D. 1987). *The alcoholic family.* New York: Basic Books.

Sterne, M., & Pittman, D. J. (1972). *Drinking practices in the ghetto.* St. Louis, MO: Washington University, Social Science Institute.

Sterne, M. W. (1967). Drinking patterns and alcoholism among American Negroes. In D. J. Pittman (Ed.), *Alcoholism* (pp. 66–98). New York: Harper & Row.

Stevens, E. P. (1973). Marianismo: The other face of machismo in Latin America. In A. Pescatello (Ed.), *Female and male in Latin America: Essays* (pp. 89–102). Pittsburgh, PA: University of Pittsburgh Press.

Stewart, S. (2001). Internet acceptable use policies: Navigating the management, legal, and technical issues. *Information Systems Security, 9*(3), 46–53.

Stewart, S. D. (2010). The characteristics and well-being of adopted stepchildren. *Family Relations, 59*(5), 558–571.

Stitzer, M. (2006). Contingency management and the addictions. *Addiction, 101,* 1536–1537.

Stivers, R. (2000). *Hair of the dog: Irish drinking and its American stereotype* (Rev. ed.). New York: Continuum.

Stoltzfus, K. M. (2007). Spiritual interventions in substance abuse treatment and prevention: A review of the literature. *Journal of Religion & Spirituality in Social Work, 26*(4), 49–69.

Strauch, M., & Strauch, I. (2010). Using current-day reconstructions in the treatment of eating disorder. *Journal of Individual Psychology, 66*(4), 356–365.

Striegel-Moore, R. H., Dohm, F., Kraemer, H. C., Schreiber, G. B., Taylor, C. B., & Daniels, S. R. (2007). Risk factors for binge eating disorder. *International Journal of Eating Disorders, 40*(1), 481–487.

Streissguth, A. P., Barr, H. M., Kogan, J., & Bookstein, F. L. (1996). *Understanding the occurrence of secondary disabilities in clients with fetal alcohol syndrome*

(FAS) and fetal alcohol effects (FAE). Seattle: University of Washington, Fetal Alcohol & Drug Unit.

Stuart, G. L., O'Farrell, T. J., & Temple, J. R. (2009). Violence, intimate partner and substance abuse treatment. In G. L. Fisher & N. A. Roget (Eds.), *Encyclopedia of substance abuse prevention, treatment, and recovery* (pp. 990–993). Los Angeles: Sage.

Stukin, S. (2003). Health, hope and HIV. *Yoga Journal.* Retrieved April 4, 2003, from www.yogajournal.com/health/581.cfm

Substance Abuse and Mental Health Services Administration. (2001). National household survey on drug abuse. Retrieved July 6, 2003, from www.samhsa.gov.oas/nhsda 2k1nhsda/vol1/chapter7.htm

Substance Abuse and Mental Health Services Administration and Department of Veterans Affairs. (2003). Self-help organizations for alcohol and drug problems: Towards evidence-based practice and policy. Workgroup on substance abuse self-help organizations. Retrieved August 16, 2003, from www.chce.research.med .va.gov/chce/pdfs/Vasma_feb1103.pdf

Substance Abuse and Mental Health Services Administration. (2005). *Substance use during pregnancy: 2002–2003 update.* Rockville, MD: SAMSHA.

Substance Abuse and Mental Health Services Administration, Office of Applied Studies. (2008). *National survey of substance abuse treatment services (N-SSATS):Data on substance abuse treatment facilities.* Retrieved May 6, 2011, from http://wwwdasis.samhsa.gov/07nssats/ nssats2k7web.pdf.

Substance Abuse and Mental Health Services Administration. (2009a). *Guiding principles and elements of recovery-oriented systems of care: What do we know from research?* Retrieved May 12, 2011, from http://www.pfr .samhsa.gov/docs/Guiding_Principles_Whitepaper.pdf

Substance Abuse and Mental Health Services Administration, Office of Applied Studies (2009b). *Treatment Episode Data Set (TEDS) Highlights—2007 National Admissions to Substance Abuse Treatment Services.* OAS Series #S-45, HHS Publication No. (SMA) 09-4360, Rockville, MD: Substance Abuse and Mental Health Services Administration. Retrieved May 6, 2011, from http://oas.samhsa.gov/TEDS2k7highlights/toc .cfm

Substance Abuse and Mental Health Services Administration, Office of Applied Studies. (2009c). *Substance abuse treatment admissions by primary substance of abuse, according to sex, age group, race, and ethnicity, year—2008, United States.* Retrieved May 13, 2011, from http://wwwdasis.samhsa.gov/webt/quicklink/ US08.htm

Substance Abuse and Mental Health Services Administration. (2010). *National survey on drug use and health.* Retrieved December 22, 2010, from http://oas.samhsa .gov/NSDUH/2k9NSDUH/2k9ResultsP.pdf

Substance Abuse and Mental Health Services Administration. (2011). *NREPP: SAMHSA's national registry of evidence-based programs and practices.* Retrieved May 23, 2011, from http://nrepp.samhsa.gov/ViewAll.aspx.

Suhail, K., & Bargees, Z. (2006). Effects of excessive Internet use on undergraduate students in Pakistan. *Cyber-Psychology and Behavior, 9*(3), 297–307.

Sullivan, B. (2004). *Porn at work problem persists.* Retrieved August 3, 2007, from www.msnbc.msn.com/ id/5899345

Sunshine, R. M., & Starks, B. M. (2010). Racial/ethnic differences in religiosity and drug use. *Journal of Drug Issues, 40*(2), 729–753.

Sussman, S., Lisha, N., & Griffiths, M. (2011). Prevalence of the addictions: A problem of the majority or the minority? *Evaluation & the Health Professions, 34*(1), 3–56.

Sutton, C. T., & Broken Nose, M. A. (2005). American Indian families. In M. McGoldrick, J. Giodano, & N. Garcia-Preto (Eds.), *Ethnicity and family fherapy* (pp. 43–54), New York: Guilford Press.

Szapocznik, J., & Kurtines, W. M. (1989). *Breakthroughs in family therapy with drug-abusing and problem youth.* New York: Springer.

Taggart, L., McLaughlin, D., Quinn, B., & McFarlane, C. (2007). Listening to people with intellectual disabilities who misuse alcohol and drugs. *Health and Social Care in the Community, 15*(4), 360–368.

Taleff, M. J., & Babcock, M. (1998). Hidden themes: Dominant discourse in the alcohol and other field. *International Journal of Drug Policy, 9,* 33–41.

Talley, A. E., & Sher, K. J., (2010). Sexual orientation and substance abuse trajectories in emerging adulthood. *Addiction, 105.* 1235–1245.

Tani, N., Haga, H., & Kato, N. (1975). A survey of concern for drinking and alcoholics. First report: Students of junior high school. *Japan Journal of Alcohol Studies, 10,* 35–40.

Tao, R., Huang, X., Wang, J., Zhang, H., Zhang, Y., & Mengchen, L. (2010). Proposed diagnostic criteria for Internet addiction. *Addiction, 105*(3), 556–564.

Taris, T. W., Schaufeli, W. B., & Verhoeven, L. C. (2005). Workaholism in the Netherlands: Measurement and implications for job strain and work-nonwork conflict. *Applied Psychology: An International Review, 54*(1), 37–60.

Taylor, O. D. (2010). Barriers to treatment for women with substance abuse disorders. *Journal of Human Behavior in the Social Environment, 20*(3), 393–409.

Teen Challenge (2009). *Teen Challenge USA*. Retrieved May 10, 2011, from http://teenchallengeusa.com/program/

Templeton, L., Velleman, R., & Russel, C. (2010). Psychological interventions with families of alcohol misusers: A systematic review. *Addiction Research and Theory, 18*(6), 616–648.

Thai, N. D., Connell, C. M., & Tebes, J. K. (2010). Substance use among Asian American adolescents: Influence of race, ethnicity, and acculturation in the context of key risk and protective factors. *Asian American Journal of Psychology, 1*(4), 261–274.

Thatcher, A., & Goolam, S. (2005). Development and psychometric properties of the Problematic Internet Use Questionnaire. *South African Journal of Psychology, 35*(4), 793–809.

Tobler, N. S. (1986). Meta-analysis of 143 adolescent drug prevention programs: Quantitative outcome results of program participants compared to a control or comparison group. *Journal of Drug Issues, 16,* 537–567.

Tobler, N. S. (1992). Drug prevention programs can work: Research findings. *Journal of Addictive Diseases, 11,* 1–28.

Tobler, N. S., & Stratton, H. H. (1997). Effectiveness of school-based drug prevention programs: A meta-analysis of the research. *Journal of Primary Prevention, 18,* 71–128.

Todorova, I. L. G., Falcon, L. M., Lincoln, A. K., & Price, L. L. (2010). Perceived discrimination, psychological distress and health. *Sociology of Health and Illness, 32*(6), 843–861.

Torres, S. (1993). Cultural sensitivity: A must for today's primary care provider. *Advance for Nurse Practitioners, 1,* 16–18.

Towers, R. L. (1989). *Children of alcoholics/addicts.* Washington, DC: National Education Association.

Traeen, B., Nilsen, T. S., & Stigum, H. (2006). Use of pornography in traditional media and on the Internet in Norway. *Journal of Sex Research, 43*(3), 245–254.

Treatment Communities of America (2008). What is a therapeutic community (TC)? Retrieved May 10, 2011, from http://www.therapeuticcommunitiesofamerica.org/main/

Trezza, G. R. (1994). HIV knowledge and stigmatization of persons with AIDS: Implications for the development of HIV education for young adults. *Professional Psychology, 25,* 141–148.

Tripodi, C. (2006). Long term treatment of partners of sex addicts: A multi-phase approach. *Sexual Addiction and Compulsivity, 13*(2/3), 269–288.

Trocki, K. F., Drabble, L. A., & Midanik, L. T. (2009). Tobacco, marijuana, and sensation seeking: Comparisons across gay, lesbian, bisexual, and heterosexual groups. *Psychology of Addictive Behaviors, 23,* 620–631.

Tuchfield, B. S. (1981). Spontaneous remission in alcoholics: Empirical observations and theoretical implications. *Journal of Studies on Alcohol, 42,* 626–640.

Tuchman, E. (2010). Women and addiction: The importance of gender issues in substance abuse research. *Journal of Addictive Diseases, 29*(2), 127–138.

Tucker, R. (2006). Review of ethnicity and family therapy. *Psychology and Psychotherapy: Theory, Research, and Practice, 79*(2), 306–307.

Turner, M. (2009). Uncovering and treating sex addiction in couples therapy. *Journal of Family Psychotherapy, 20,* 283–302.

Turner-Bowker, D., & Hamilton, W. L. (2000). *Cigarette advertising expenditures before and after the master settlement agreement: Preliminary findings.* Massachusetts Department of Public Health and Abt Associates, Inc. Available from Cesar Fax, Volume 9, Issue 26.

Ullery, E. K., & Carney, J. S. (2000). Mental health counselors' training to work with persons with HIV disease. *Journal of Mental Health Counseling, 22,* 334–342.

UNAIDS. (2006). *Global summary of the AIDS epidemic.* Retrieved August 7, 2007, from http://data.unaids.org/pub/EpiReport/2006/006_EpiUpdate_en.pdf

UNAIDS. (2007). *Joining forces to tackle TB and HIV.* Retrieved August 7, 2007, from www.unaids.org/en/MediaCentre/PressMaterials/FeatureStory/061124_TB+and+HIV_en.asp

U.S. Census Bureau (2011). State and Country Quickfacts .Retrieved February 14, 2011, from http://quickfacts.census.gov/qfd/states/00000.html

U.S. Census Bureau. (2010). State and County Quickfacts. Retrieved February 14, 2011, from http://quickfacts.census.gov/qfd/states/00000.html

U.S. Department of Health and Human Services, (2010). Retrieved February 14, 2011, from http://www.oas.samhsa.gov/2k10/182/AmericanIndian.htm

U.S. Department of Health and Human Services, Office of Minority Health, (2008). American Indian/Alaska Native profile. Retrieved May 16, 2011, from http://www.minorityhealth.hhs.gov/templates/browse.aspx?lvl=2&lvlID=52

U.S. Department of Health and Human Services. (2003). *2001 National Household Survey on Drug Abuse* (NHSDA). Washington, DC: Author. http://www.cdc.gov/hiv/resources/qa/definitions.htm

U.S. Department of Health and Human Services. (2004). Integrating mental health services into primary HIV care for women: The whole life project. *Public Health Report, 119,* 48–59.

U.S. Department of Health and Human Services. (2006). HIV/AIDS Basics. Retrieved November 23, 2011, from http://www.hhs.gov/ocr/civilrights/resources/special-topics/hiv/CDCHIVFactsheet2010.pdf

U. S. Department of Health and Human Services. (2007). Eating away at health. Retrieved on July 5, 2007 from www.nimh.nih.gov/publicat/eatingdisorders.cfm?textSize=L

U.S. Department of Health and Human Services. (2010, June 24). National Survey on Drug Use and Health. Retrieved June 7, 2011, from http://www.oas.samhsa.gov/2k10/182/AmericanIndian.htm

U.S. Preventive Services Task Force. (1989). *Screening for infection with human immunodeficiency virus. Guide to clinical preventive services.* Baltimore: Williams & Wilkins, Eds.

United States Department of Justice, National Intelligence Center. (2010). National drug threat assessment 2010. Retrieved May 23, 2010, from http://www.justice.gov/ndic/pubs38/38661/execSum.htm#Top

United States Department of Labor, Office of Disability Employment Policy. (2011). Frequently asked questions. Retrieved March 18, 2011, from http://www.dol.gov/odep/faqs/people.htm

USA.gov. (2011). Lottery results. Retrieved June 17, 2011, from http://www.usa.gov/Topics/Lottery_Results.shtml

Usher, K., Jackson, D., & O'Brien, L. (2005). Adolescent drug abuse: Helping families survive. *International Journal of Mental Health Nursing, 14*(3), 209–214.

Vaillant, G. E. (1983). *The natural history of alcoholism.* Cambridge, MA: Harvard University Press.

Valencia, E. Y., & Johnson, V. (2008). Acculturation among Latino youth and the risk for substance use: Issues of definition and measurement. *Journal of Drug Issues, 38*(1), 37–68.

Valenti, S. A. M. (2002). Family-of-origin characteristics among women married to sexually addicted men. *Sexual Addiction and Recovery, 9,* 263–274.

van der Walde, H., Urgensen, F. T., Weltz, S. H., & Hanna, F. J. (2002). Women and alcoholism: A biosocial perspective and treatment approaches. *Journal of Counseling and Development, 80,* 145–153.

Vanable, P. A., King, A. C., & deWit, H. (2000). Psychometric screening instruments. In G. Zernig, A. Saria, M. Kurz, & S.S. O'Malley (Eds.), *Handbook of alcoholism.* New York: CRC Press.

Vandermause, R., & Wood, M. (2009). See my suffering: Women with alcohol use disorders and their primary care experiences. *Issues in Mental Health Nursing, 30*(12), 728–735.

Vasilaki, E. I., Hosier, S. G., & Cox, W. M. (2006). The efficacy of motivational interviewing as a brief intervention for excessive drinking: A meta-analytic review. *Alcohol and Alcoholism, 41.* 328–335.

Vasquez, M. J. T. (2009). Latino/a culture and substance abuse. *Journal of Ethnicity in Substance Abuse, 8*(3), 301–313.

Vazsonyi, A. T., Trejos-Castillo, E., & Young, M. A. (2008). Rural and non-rural African American youth: Does context matter in the etiology of problem behaviors? *Journal of Youth Adolescence, 37,* 798–811.

Vega, W. A., Canino, G., Cao, Z., & Alegria, M. (2009). Prevalence and correlates of dual diagnoses in U. S. Latinos. *Drug and Alcohol Dependence, 100*(1–2), 32–38.

Velezmoro, R., Lacefield, K., & Roberti, J. W. (2010). Perceived stress, sensation seeking, and college students' abuse of the Internet. *Computers in Human Behavior, 26*(6), 1526–1530.

Vernig, P. M. (2011). Family roles in homes with alcohol-dependent parents: An evidence-based review. *Substance Use and Misuse, 46*(4), 535–542.

Vocks, S., Legenbaurer, T., Rüddel, H., & Troje, N. (2007). Eating to live. *International Journal of Eating Disorders, 40*(1), 59–66.

Vocks, S., Tuschen-Caffier, B., Pietrowsky, R., Rustenbach, S. J., Kersting, A., & Herpertz, S. (2010). Meta-analysis of the effectiveness of psychological and pharmacological treatments for binge-eating disorder. *International Journal of Eating Disorders, 43*(3), 205–217.

Wagner, T. H., Harris, K. M., Federman, B., Dai, L., Luna, Y., & Humphreys, K. (2007). Prevalence of substance use disorders among veterans and comparable nonveterans from the National Survey on Drug Use and Health. *Psychological Services, 4*, 149–157.

Wahl, A. G., & Eitle, T. M. (2010). Gender, acculturation, and alcohol use among Latina/o adolescents: A multi-ethnic comparison. *Journal of Immigrant Minority Health, 12*, 153–165.

Waldron, H. B., & Turner, C. W. (2008). Evidence-based psychosocial treatments for adolescent substance abuse. *Journal of Clinical Child & Adolescent Psychology, 37*, 238–261.

Walker, J. (2002). Rural women with HIV and AIDS: Perceptions of service accessibility, psychosocial, and mental health counseling needs. *Journal of Mental Health Counseling, 24*, 299–316.

Walters, K., & Simoni, J. (2002). Reconceptualizing Native women's health: An "indigenist" stress-coping model. *American Journal of Public Health, 92*(4), 520–524.

Washington State Department of Health. (1996). *Tuberculosis fact sheet* [On-line]. Retrieved August 8, 2004, from www.doh.wa.gov/Topics/TB.html

Waskul, D. D. (2004). *Net.seXXX: Readings on sex, pornography, and the Internet.* New York: Peter Lang.

Watt, T. T. (2002). Marital cohabiting relationships of adult children of alcoholics. *Journal of Family Issues, 23*(2), 246–265.

Wegscheider, S. (1989). *Another chance: Hope and health for the alcoholic family* (2nd Ed.) Palo Alto, CA: Science and Behavior Books.

Weibe, J. M. D., & Cox, B. J. (2005). Problem and probable pathological gambling in older adults assessed by the SOGS-R. *Journal of Gambling Studies, 21*(1), 205–221.

West, S. L., & Graham, C. W. (2006). Assessing parental alcoholism. *Alcoholism Treatment Quarterly, 24*(3), 93–107.

West, S. L., Graham, C. W., Cifu, D. X., (2009). Rates of alcohol/other drug treatment denials to persons with physical disabilities: Accessibility concerns. *Alcoholism Treatment Quarterly, 27*, 305–316.

Westermeyer, J. (1999). The role of cultural and social factors in the cause of addictive disorders. *Psychiatric Clinics of North America, 22*, 253–271.

Westermeyer, J. O. (1991). Cultural perspectives: Native Americans, Asians and new immigrants. In J. H. Lowinson, P. Ruiz, R. B. Millman, & J. G. Langrod (Eds.), *Substance abuse: A comprehensive textbook* (2nd ed., pp. 890–896.) Baltimore: Williams & Wilkins.

Westermeyer, J., & Baker, J. M. (1986). Alcoholism and the American Indian. In N. J. Estes and M. E. Heinemann (Eds.), *Alcoholism: Development, consequences, and interventions* (pp. 273–282). St. Louis, MO: Mosby.

Westermeyer, J., Bennett, L., Thuras, P., & Yoon, G., (2007). Substance use disorder among adoptees: A Clinical comparative study. *American Journal of Drug and Alcohol Abuse, 33*, 455–466.

Westermeyer, J., Yargic, I., & Thuras, P. (2004). Michigan Assessment-Screening Test for Alcohol and Drugs (MAST/AD): Evaluation in a clinical sample. *American Journal on Addictions, 13*, 151–162.

Westphal, J. R. (2006). The evidence base supporting the subtyping of gamblers in treatment. *International Journal of Mental Health and Addiction, 5*(2), 127–140.

Whitaker, C. L. (1991). *Co-dependence: Healing the human condition: The new paradigm for helping professionals and people in recovery.* Deerfield Beach, FL: Health Communications.

White Bison Inc. (2002). *The red road to wellbriety in the Native American way.* Colorado Springs, CO: White Bison Inc.

White, W. L. (2001). *The rhetoric of recovery advocacy: An essay of the power of language.* Retrieved January 25, 2011, from http://www.williamwhitepapers.com/pr/2001RhetoricofRecoveryAdvocacy.pdf

White, W. L. (1998). *Slaying the dragon: The history of addiction treatment and recovery in America.* Section 5: A.A. and the modern alcoholism movement (pp 127–198). Bloomington, IL: Chestnut Health Systems/Lighthouse Institute.

White, W. L. (n.d). *Recovery as a heroic journey.* Retrieved June 21, 2003, from www.efavor.org/ADVOCACY .HTM

Whitfield, C. L. (1984). *Alcoholism, other drug problems and spirituality: A transpersonal approach.* Baltimore: Resource Group.

Whitfield, C. L. (1991). *Codependence: Healing the human condition.* Deerfield Beach, FL: Health Communications.

Wilens, T. E., Faraone, S. V., Biederman, J., & Gunawardene, S. (2003). Does stimulant therapy of attention-deficit/hyperactivity disorder beget later substance abuse? A meta-analytic review of the literature. *Pediatrics, 111,* 179–185.

Wilk, A. I., Jensen, N. M., & Havighurst, T. C. (1997). Meta-analysis of randomized control trials addressing brief interventions in heavy alcohol drinkers. *Journal of General Internal Medicine, 12,* 274–283.

Williams, C. N. (1990). Prevention and treatment approaches for children of alcoholics. In M. Windle & J. S. Searles (Eds.), *Children of alcoholics. Critical perspectives* (pp. 187–216). New York: Guilford Press.

Williams, C. N., & Collins, E. W. (1986). The connection between alcoholism, child maltreatment, and family disruption. In S. H. Lease & B. J. Yanico (1995), Evidence of validity for the children of alcoholics screening test. *Measurement and evaluation in counseling and development, 27*(4), 200–210.

Williams, M. (1986). Alcohol and ethnic minorities: Native Americans: An update. *Alcohol Health and Research World, 11,* 5–6.

Wilson, G. T., & Sysko, R. (2009). Frequency of binge eating episodes in bulimia nervosa and binge eating disorder: Diagnostic considerations. *International Journal of Eating Disorders, 42,* 603–610.

Wingfield, N., Kelly, N., Serdar, K., Shivy, V. A., & Mazzeo, S. E. (2011). College students' perceptions of individuals with anorexia and bulimia nervosa. *International Journal of Eating Disorders, 44*(4), 369–375.

Woititz, J. G. (1983). *Adult children of alcoholics.* Pompano Beach, FL: Health Communications.

Wolfe, B. E., Faan, A., Baker, C. W., Smith, A. T., & Kelly-Weeder, S. (2009). Validity and utility of current definition of binge eating. *International Journal of Eating Disorders, 42,* 674–686.

Wong, M. M., Klingle, R. S., & Price, R. K. (2004). Alcohol, tobacco, and other drug use among Asian American and Pacific Islander adolescents in California and Hawaii. *Addictive Behaviors, 29*(1), 127–141.

Wong, P. W. C., Chan, W. S. C., Conwell, Y., Conner, K. R., & Yip, P. S. F. (2010). A psychological autopsy study of pathological gamblers who died by suicide. *Journal of Affective Disorder, 120*(1–3), 213–216.

Wong, S. C., Catalano, R. F., Hawkins, J. D., & Chappell, P. J. (1996). *Communities that care prevention strategies: A research guide to what works.* Seattle, WA: Developmental Research and Programs.

Wood, R. T., Williams, R. J., and Lawton, P. K. (2007). Why do Internet gamblers prefer online versus land-based venues? *Journal of Gambling Issues.* Retrieved August 5, 2007, from www.camh.net/egambling/issue20/07wood.htm

Woolfall, K., & Sumnall, H. (2010). Evaluating interventions for children of substance using parents: A review of outcome measures. *Addiction Research and Theory, 18*(3), 326–343.

World Health Communications. (1988). *Management of HIV disease. Treatment team workshop handbook.* New York: World Health Communications.

World Health Organization. (2007). *Women and HIV/AIDS.* Retrieved August 7, 2007 from www.who.int/gender/hiv_aids/en

World Health Organization, (2010). *HIV/AIDS: Online Questions and Answers.* Retrieved June 7, 2011, from http://www.who.int/features/qa/71/en/index.html

World Health Organization, (2011). *Global health observatory: HIV/AIDS in 2009.* Retrieved June 7, 2011, from http://www.who.int/gho/hiv/en/

Wright, P. H., & Wright, K. D. (1991). Codependency: Addictive love, adjusting relating, or both? *Contemporary Family Therapy, 13,* 435–454.

Wu, P., Bird, H. R., Liu, X., Duarte, C. S., Fuller, C., Fan, B., ... Canini, G. J. (2010). Trauma, Posttraumatic Stress Symptoms, and Alcohol-Use Initiation in Children. *Journal of Studies on Alcohol and Drugs, 71*(3), 326–334.

Yamaguchi, R., Johnston, L. D., & O'Malley, P. M. (2003). The relationship between student illicit drug use and school drug-testing policies. *Journal of School Health, 73,* 159–164.

Yellowlees, P. M., & Marks, S. (2005). Problematic Internet use or Internet addiction? *Computers in Human Behavior, 23,* 1447–1453.

Young, K. (2010). Killer surf issues: Crafting an organizational model to combat employee Internet abuse. *Information Management, 44*(1), 34–38.

Young, K. S. (1998). *Caught in the act: How to recognize the signs of Internet addiction and a winning strategy for recovery.* New York: Wiley.

Young, K. S. (1999). The evaluation and treatment of Internet addiction. In L. VandeCreek & T. Jackson (Eds.), *Innovations in clinical practice: A source book* (pp. 17, 19–31). Sarasota, FL: Professional Resource Press.

Young, K. S. (2004). Internet addiction. *American Behavioral Scientist, 48*(4), 402–415.

Young, K. S. (2008). Internet addiction: Risk factors, stages of development, and treatment. *American Behavioral Scientist, 52*(21), 21–37.

Young, T. J. (1991). Native American drinking: A neglected subject of study and research. *Journal of Drug Education, 21,* 65–72.

Young, T. J. (1992). Substance abuse among Native American youth. In G. W. Lawson & A. W. Lawson (Eds.), *Adolescent substance abuse: Etiology, treatment and prevention* (pp. 381–390). Gaithersburg, MD: Aspen.

Yu, J., Clark, L. P., Chandra, L., Dias, A., & Lai, T. M. (2009). Reducing cultural barriers to substance abuse treatment among Asian Americans: A case study in New York City. *Journal of Substance Abuse Treatment, 37*(4), 398–406.

Zangeneh, M., & Hason, T. (2006). Suicide and gambling. *International Journal of Mental Health and Addiction, 4*(3), 191–193.

Zimmerman, M., Chelminski, I., & Young, D. (2006). Prevalence and diagnostic correlates of DSM_IV pathological gambling in psychiatric outpatients. *Journal of Gambling Studies, 22*(2), 255–262.

Zucker, R. A., Donovan, J. E., Masten, A. S., Mattson, M. E., & Moss, H. B. (2009). Developmental process and mechanisms. *Alcohol Research & Health, 32*(1), 16–29.

INDEX

A

ABCT. *See* Alcohol behavioral couple therapy (ABCT)
Abstinence, 139, 154, 161
Abstinence violation effect (AVE), 174, 182
Abuse
  alcohol, 2
  of Alcohol and other drugs (AODs), 2–3, 52
  child, 2, 3, 4
  definitions of, 104
  drug, 2, 13
  gambling and, 281
  Internet, 299–300
  substance .*See* Substance abuse.
Acamprosate, for treatment of alcoholism, 142
Acculturation
  adolescent substance abuse and, 62
  African Americans and, 67
  Asian and Pacific Islander Americans and, 59
  influence of, 63
  Latino and Hispanic populations and, 72, 82
  Native Americans and, 54
  process of, 62
ACEs. *See* Adverse childhood experiences (ACEs)
Acetone, 29
Acid, 26
ACOA (Twelve-step support for children of alcoholics), 145
A Codependence Test, 243
Acquaintance Description Form-C3 (ADF-C3), 243
Acquired immunodeficiency syndrome (AIDS). *See* HIV/AIDS
Action stage, in motivational interviewing, 129, 130, 131
Adderall, 33, 34
Addiction, 139. *See also* Addiction models; Addiction to sex and love; Alcoholics; Alcoholism; Disease concept of addiction; Other addictions
  adolescents and, 39–40
  critics of, 289
  definition of, 14
  disease of, 42
  food, 290–291

Internet, 298–300, 304–405, 307
  neurobiology of, 16
  neuroscience of, 44–45
  points of view about, 288
  proponents of, 290
  relapse in, 44, 47
  relapse in *vs.* other conditions, 170–171
  to work, 301–302, 304–305, 307–308
Addiction models
  biopsychosocial model, 38, 48–49
  case examples, 36–37
  disease concept of addiction, 38, 42–48
  Internet resources, 50
  moral model, 38, 39
  psychological models, 38, 40–41
  sociocultural model, 38, 39–40
Addiction or dependence, definitions of, 104
Addiction Severity Index (ASI), 114
Addiction to sex and love, 296–298
  assessment of, 306–307
  treatment of, 304–305
Addictive behavior, 41, 42
Addictive disorders, 77
Addictive personality, 40–41
ADF-C3. *See* Acquaintance Description Form-C3 (ADF-C3)
"Adolescent Community Reinforcement Approach", 153
Adolescents
  addiction and, 39–40
  African Americans, 70, 74
  alcoholism and, 43
  eating disorders and, 294
  female Native American, 56–57
  HIV in, 264–265
  Latino, 74
  Problem-Oriented Screening Instrument for Teenagers (POSIT), 114
  sibling influence of drug use, 220
  signs of substance abuse in, 109, 111–112
  treatment of, 155
Adoptee group, 77
Adult children of alcoholics (ACOAs)
  African Americans and, 237
  assessment of, 237–238
  case examples, 233
  clinical characteristics and empirical research, 235–236

codependency and, 221, 246–248
  implications for intervention, 238
  labeling, 234–235
  relationship of Alcoholics Anonymous (AA), Al-Anon, codependency and, 246–247
  research on, 235
  risk factors, 236–237
Adult children of Alcoholics (ACOAs)-codependency movement
  critics of, 247–248
  relationship of AA, Al-ANON, codependency and, 246
Adult Children of Alcoholics (Woititz), 234
Adult Offspring of Families with Alcohol and Other Drug Problems (AODF), 234
Adults, use of Internet pornography, 299
Adverse childhood experiences (ACEs), 220
Aerosol sprays, 19t, 29
Affective disorders, drugs for, 33
Affective roles, 212–213
African American Cubans, 71
African Americans
  Adult Children of Alcoholics (ACOAs) and, 237
  alcohol and, 64–67
  background of, 65–67
  children of, 71, 213
  disengagement and, 219, 220
  family subsystem in, 218
  female adolescents, HIV and, 265
  gay men, 76
  at a glance, 70–71
  HIV and, 262, 264
  HIV infection and, 257
  sibling subsystems, 218
  traditional, 204
  values of, 67–70
  women, anorexia nervosa and, 296
  working with, 81–82
African American Survivors Organization, 82
Aftercare, 147
Age
  HIV infection and, 258f
  as risk factor for adolescents, HIV and, 264
Agonist Therapy, 117
AIDS Related Complex (ARC), diagnosis of, 259